50 GREAT
MODERN LIVES

50
Great Modern
Lives

INSPIRING BIOGRAPHIES OF
MEN AND WOMEN WHO HAVE GUIDED
MANKIND TO A BETTER WORLD

By
HENRY THOMAS
and
DANA LEE THOMAS

HANOVER HOUSE
Garden City, N.Y.

LIBRARY OF CONGRESS CATALOG CARD NUMBER 56–7089

Contents

Introduction   vii
Christopher Columbus   1
Leonardo da Vinci   10
Michelangelo Buonarroti   21
Martin Luther   32
Saint Ignatius of Loyola   42
Benvenuto Cellini   51
Francis Bacon   59
William Shakespeare   72
Galileo Galilei   81
Isaac Newton   91
Thomas Jefferson   102
Johann Wolfgang von Goethe   111
Ludwig van Beethoven   121
Simon Bolivar   131
John Henry Newman   141
Abraham Lincoln   150
Charles Robert Darwin   160
Pope Leo XIII   171
Wilhelm Richard Wagner   180
Giuseppe Verdi   189
Queen Victoria   200
Florence Nightingale   210
Gregor Johann Mendel   219
Louis Pasteur   227
Leo Tolstoy   238
Paul Cézanne   246
William James   256
Thomas Alva Edison   264
Mother Cabrini   274

Woodrow Wilson   283
Sigmund Freud   292
George Bernard Shaw   302
Henry Ford   310
George Washington Carver   319
Marie Curie   329
The Wright Brothers   341
Mohandas K. Gandhi   349
Guglielmo Marconi   359
Winston Churchill   366
Albert Schweitzer   377
Albert Einstein   387
Helen Keller   399
Franklin Delano Roosevelt   407
Samuel Goldwyn   417
Sister Elizabeth Kenny   430
Dwight David Eisenhower   439
Helen Hayes   451
William Samuel Paley   467
Marian Anderson   479
Ralph Johnson Bunche   489

Introduction

THE PURPOSE OF THIS BOOK is to ennoble our own lives through contact with the noble lives of the great. For, in the words of Carlyle, "we cannot look upon a great man without gaining something by him." And thus, as you will note, these biographies will enrich your own experiences by adding to them the experiences of your "loftier brothers, but of the same blood." It will help you to see the world, so to speak, through many pairs of eyes, and to deal with your neighbors through many new chords of sympathetic understanding.

And so we have selected fifty great men and women—the physical, mental and spiritual road-makers of modern history—to serve you as guides along the difficult course of your own journey. In the making of our selections, we have tried to get together a group as varied as the diversified spectacle of human endeavor. This book is intended to be a panorama of modern history at its bravest and best. For, to quote Carlyle again, "history is nothing but the biography of great men and women."

As examples of the diversity of human greatness, you will find here inventors like Thomas Edison, the Wright Brothers and Henry Ford; painters like Leonardo, Michelangelo and Cézanne; composers like Beethoven and Wagner; scientists like Newton, Darwin, Einstein and Marie Curie; dramatists like Shakespeare and Goethe and Bernard Shaw; philosophers like Francis Bacon and William James; emancipators like Bolivar and Lincoln; statesmen like Jefferson and Churchill and Franklin D. Roosevelt; physical explorers like Columbus and spiritual adventurers like Mother Cabrini, Schweitzer and Gandhi; and religious leaders like Luther, Loyola and Pope Leo XIII.

And you will find that all the great characters in this book, despite their different talents and careers, have had one thing in common—that eager essence of personality generally known as devotion. Unswerving devotion to art, literature, science, heroism, loyalty, freedom, philosophy, or the betterment of mankind. Nothing great was ever achieved without devotion. Translated into the everyday language of our own lives, these great men and women teach us the simple lesson of faith—in ourselves, our fellow men, and the possibility of making the world nobler by our presence.

> "Lives of great men all remind us
> We can make *our* lives sublime."

This is the one important lesson of all good biography.

H.T.
D.L.T.

50 GREAT
MODERN LIVES

Christopher Columbus

1451–1506

Young christopher—he had been named after the patron saint of travelers—was serving wine to the customers in his father's tavern. A motley crowd of sailors and adventurers. French traders in silks and satins; Irish rovers with daggers in their eyes and laughter on their lips; Muscovite merchants, their unkempt beards agitated in lively conversation; Spanish cavaliers with long lean bodies and long lean swords; Moorish seamen, ebony statues of volcanic lava; Palestinian jobbers with hooked noses and shrewd kindly eyes; Greek courtesans, disturbing creatures with soft voices, soft skins, and hair the flame of the sunrise. The babel of sounds and sights and passions that were Genoa in the Year of Our Lord 1470.

And the arguments that they had, and the stories that they told! About the Green Island of Barbary, whose oysters contained a fluid that cured lepers. About the cliffs of basalt in Madeira, a strange land that produced reeds of sugar. And beyond these, and past the Pillars of Hercules—said these outlandish adventurers—lay the island of Atlantis, wider than Europe and Africa combined—a kingdom of fabulous cities and fabulous riches and the most ravishing women in the world. And beyond Atlantis lay still other islands that contained still greater wonders.

And there were tales about a region beyond all these—the Enchanted Isles. "Nobody within our generation"—it was a Spanish sailor who was telling the story—"has ever seen these Islands, for a spell has been cast upon them. Long years ago, when the Moors were laying waste to Europe, a Spanish bishop sailed to these islands for refuge. And there he lived for a time; and when he departed, he cast an enchantment upon the islands, so that never again shall they be visible to mortal eye until all kingdoms of Europe have been embraced within the Catholic fold."

How, if no one had ever seen these islands, could anyone know of their existence? Simply enough, answered the sailor. "I myself, and many others, have seen flocks of land-birds flying over the sea from the Enchanted Isles. And I have seen fragments of sweet-scented forests floating against our ship. And this, let me tell you, is no fairy tale. Why, King Charles of France has had his reading room at the Louvre paneled with this fragrant wood of the Enchanted Isles."

And more strange stories about the lands that lay even beyond the Enchanted Isles. The Land of Cypango, for instance. "In this land, they say, gold is so plentiful that the people use the grains for scouring their cooking pots . . ."

Young Christopher listened to these stories and thought about them as he lay in bed after the customers had left the tavern. At such moments a deep yearning filled his soul. How grand it would be if some day he could sail beyond the Pillars of Hercules and go off adventuring after the secrets of those enchanted lands!

II

Twenty years old, and Christopher was now a partner in his father's business. Every few months he boarded a sloop and went coasting down to the vineyards along the shore in quest of shipments of wine. He loved the song of the surf and the singing of the wind and the salt sea tang of the air. It was no great tragedy to him, therefore, when his father went bankrupt and left his children—there were four of them besides Christopher—to shift for themselves.

Christopher left Genoa—and drifted away into several years of obscurity. It was the fault of Columbus himself that so little is known of those years. For later on, when he wrote the story of his early life, he was more anxious to be impressive than to be factual. Columbus was not only a sailor but a poet; and his poetical dreams often steered him into the uncharted seas of the imagination. Thus he informs us, probably without foundation, that for a time he served as commander of a pirate crew. In the course of this career, he wrote to King Ferdinand, "the good king Reinel . . . sent me to Tunisia, to capture the galley *La Fernandina*." But—Columbus went on to relate—"on arriving at the harbor of San Pedro, in Sardinia, I learned that the galley was being protected by two ships and a carraca, which so alarmed the crew that they resolved to proceed no farther, but to return to Marseilles . . . Upon which"—and here Columbus describes a trick which he was to employ years later, on his first voyage to America—"I pretended to give in to their wish and to turn about for home—*first, however, having changed the points of the compass,* so that, while all believed that they were sailing for Marseilles, they were really sailing for Tunisia."

Shortly after his career as a pirate—he tells us—he took part in a "bloody naval engagement" out of which he barely escaped with his life. His vessel, hit by "a ball of fire," had burst into flames. "But, being a good swimmer, and finding myself two leagues from the land, I seized an oar, and by its aid succeeded in reaching the coast."

His next venture—he tells us, still spinning a good part of the story out of his imagination—was a voyage to Iceland. This island was then called *Ultima Thule*, the final shore on the edge of the world. "Yet I, in the year 1477, sailed one hundred leagues beyond the island of Thule."

All these stories, whether truthful or fanciful, combine to give us a vivid picture of the dreamer-pioneer ever on the alert, forever poised to reach out from the security of the known into the dangers of the unknown.

III

TWENTY-EIGHT YEARS OLD, and for a spell the adventurousness of Columbus seemed threatened to be submerged under the domesticity of marriage. His restless footsteps had taken him to Lisbon. Here, while kneeling one day at the Convent of Santos, the tall, suntanned, and yellow-haired young rover with the dream in his eyes and the dimple in his chin, noticed a young woman who was kneeling at his side. A dark-eyed, dark-haired, and dark-skinned little creature with a voluptuous smile. Even in repose she seemed a vision of graceful animation. Their eyes met.

After the services, mutual interrogations about each other from their various friends. This young man? Oh, he's a sailor from Genoa with strange ideas in his head. And this young woman? The daughter of a courtier—half Italian, half Portuguese. Donna Filepa Perestrello. A very pretty name.

They were introduced to each other. Her father too, before he had become a courtier, had sailed the seas with a strange quest in his heart. He had sought, like so many others, to fathom the mystery of the ocean which tumbled, as most people believed, over the edge of the world. But Perestrello, Filepa told Columbus, believed otherwise. He had collected quite a large library of books and manuscripts and maps that dealt with the possibility of unknown lands beyond the lands that were known. And with a new and startling theory. The world, in accordance with this theory, was not flat, but round.

Columbus thought a great deal about this matter. If the world really was round, then by sailing to the west you would come to the east. To the kingdoms described in the *Travels of Marco Polo*. To the jewels and the gold of the Great Khan of Cathay . . .

An impossible dream? To the foster-child of St. Christopher, the spirit of derring-do, nothing was impossible.

But for the present he was wrapped up in another dream. Donna Filepa. They were married, and the young Ligurian closed his eyes and sipped the fragrance of his love and rested from his adventures.

And in his spare moments he read the books in his father-in-law's library. And thought.

Before long his thoughts began once more to travel far away from home—all the way around the world. A rival had arisen to tear him away from the arms of Filepa. The lure of the unknown.

And—let it be admitted—the thirst for gold. Columbus was consumed by two passions: the love of adventure, and the yearning for wealth. And, in addition to these, by a third passion—an eagerness, like Marco Polo, to make Christian converts.

These three passions would be fulfilled, Columbus believed, by a single stroke. If only he could get a few ships to sail across the sea—it was a very narrow sea, Columbus thought—he would reach new lands and bring back new wealth and open the way for new souls into the Kingdom of Heaven.

At this time Columbus met an odd sort of fellow—a Galician pilot who had lost an eye in a shipwreck. This man had sailed on a Portuguese vessel with a cargo of merchandise for Flanders. The ship had been driven from its course. Day after day it had scudded before the tempest—westward, ever westward. Finally they had come to a land "far beyond the knowledge of any man."

The return voyage of the ship was even more terrible than the voyage out. "Without provisions, without water, without strength, one by one my comrades died. At last the ship went down, and I alone am left alive to tell the tale."

As Columbus kept questioning the sailor, he became more and more convinced that this "new and unknown land" was the eastern coast of Cathay—the land of spices and gold. And he was more eager than ever to seek out this land for himself.

But before he translated his eagerness into a final determination, he wrote for advice to Pagolo Toscanelli, the leading geographer of the day. And Maestro Pagolo sent in reply a warm letter of encouragement and Godspeed. "I learn of your great and magnificent desire to discover the way to the land of spices . . . I send you a marine chart which I have made and which will satisfy your needs . . . Although I know that this chart could best be made, like the world, in the form of a sphere, I have nevertheless decided, for greater clearness and ease, to draw it up in the way used to make marine charts . . .

"Upon the chart I have pointed out the best way *westward* . . . to reach the *eastward* regions that are richest in spices and precious stones . . .

"And be not surprised that I say these regions lie to the *westward*, although commonly they are called *oriental*. For to those who go by sea, these lands will lie always to the West; while he who goes by land will have them always to the East . . .

"This land to which you will come is populous and rich . . . the whole under the rule of one sovereign, called the Great Khan, which means the King of Kings . . .

"It is very fitting that we Latins should search out this land . . . of gold and silver and precious stones and aromatic plants and learned men . . . men who show a disposition to come to terms with the Christians . . .

"My best wishes to you, my dear friend."

A very encouraging letter from a very learned man. And now the time was past for further learning and further letters. The moment for action had arrived.

Columbus was ready for the Great Adventure.

IV

BUT nobody else was ready. To the rest of the world his project was still an impossible dream. He went with it to King John of Portugal, who turned him flatly down. He went to King Ferdinand and Queen Isabella of Spain. "Give me a few ships and a handful of men, and I will bring back to you innumerable coffers of gold." The queen hesitated, but the king put an end to her hesitation with a definite *no*.

In the meantime Donna Filepa had died. After a due period of mourning, Columbus went on with his quest for men, money, and ships. He journeyed to England, to France, and then back again to Spain. Everywhere the same answer—No!

"I will bring you gold enough to launch a new crusade against the Saracens."

"No!"

An endless series of wanderings from court to court. Eloquent pleas. Despair.

A brief passionate romance with Beatriz de Arana, "a woman without friend or fortune." They met at Cordova, whirlpool of passion and sunlight and sand. He left her with an infant in her arms, and went on.

He made and sold maps for a living, but his earnings were not enough for the nourishment of his body and his dreams. "At this period," writes a contemporary historian, "deprived of all human support, betrayed by his friends, besieged by poverty, Columbus had fallen into such a state that he was forced to go to a Franciscan monastery near the city of Marchena, as a humble suppliant begging food to sustain his very life."

But he had made friends—a Portuguese shipbuilder, a Jewish financier, a Spanish courtesan who had the ear of the king. These friends spoke up boldly in his behalf. When these had shown the way, a number of his other supporters plucked up the courage to speak. And on a midwinter day, as Columbus was dejectedly dragging his footsteps two leagues out of Granada, an alguazil on the gallop overtook him. "The King and the Queen have commanded you to come to them at once!"

Three months later (April 17, 1492) the contracts were signed for the beginning of the Adventure. Columbus was to retain all the glory of whatever conversions he might make, and one-tenth of the profits from whatever business he might transact—"leaving the other nine parts to the profit of Your Majesties."

There is an Oriental proverb: "The devil laughs at the credulity of the subject and the cruelty of the king." Their majesties, as Columbus was to learn later on, were to defraud him both of his profit and of his glory. The entire investment of the Spanish crown in the discovery of America was $6000. The profits on this investment within a century, in gold alone, amounted to $1,750,000. And all the reward that Columbus was to get was a prisoner's chains.

But on the day that his ships floated out toward the unknown land (August 3, 1492), his heart was afloat somewhere among the stars.

V

From the Journal of Columbus on the first "voyage of his dreams":

Monday, August 6—"The helm of the *Pinta* broke . . . Suspect two mariners, Gomez Rascon and Cristobal Quintero, of conspiracy to turn back . . ."

Thursday, August 9—"The *Pinta* developed a leak. Stopped at Teneriffe for repairs . . ."

Sunday, September 9—"Went nineteen leagues and resolved to reckon less than he had gone"—Columbus, in his Journal, always referred to himself in the third person—"so that if the voyage be a long one, his people would not be frightened and discouraged . . ."

Monday, September 10—"Went sixty leagues . . . but computed only forty-eight leagues . . ."

Saturday, September 15—"At the beginning of this night . . . saw a marvelous branch of fire fall from the heavens into the sea . . . Mariners greatly disturbed thereat . . ."

Sunday, September 16—"Saw many tufts of very green grass . . . Land apparently not far away . . ."

Monday, September 17—"Sea water less salty than before . . . Mariners all expectant and joyful . . . Fastest vessels hurried onward . . . Everybody eager to be the first to land . . ."

Sunday, September 23—"Still sailing on the westward course . . . No land in sight . . . Mariners disturbed, saying that . . . the wind would never blow for the return to Spain . . . Always the wind blew westward . . . Mariners muttered they would soon be blown over the rim of the world . . ."

Tuesday, September 25—"Land sighted from the stern of the ship . . . Proved to be only a mirage . . . Sailed on . . ."

Wednesday, October 3—Rebellion among the mariners . . . Calmed them down . . . Sailed on . . ."

Saturday, October 6—"No land . . . Sailed on . . ."

Thursday, October 11—"Signs of land again . . . petrels . . . a green branch . . . a little twig of dog-roses . . . At these signs everybody breathed and rejoiced . . ."

Another mirage perhaps? Another disappointment, another mutiny? But look at the entry in the Journal made several hours later:

"A sailor by the name of Roderigo de Traina reported that he definitely sighted land . . . At ten o'clock that night the Admiral (Columbus), standing in the forecastle, saw a light, but it was so concealed that he could not declare it to be land . . . Two or three others remarked that they, too, saw this light, and it was like a small wax candle, which rose and fell . . . The Admiral was now certain that they were near land . . . The sailors sang the *Salve* . . . At two hours after midnight the land stood clearly out of the sea . . ."

And thus, simply, Columbus announced the greatest discovery of the ages.

VI

COLUMBUS landed on an island which, in his opinion, was on the outskirts of Cypango (Japan). In reality it was one of the West Indies, just south of Florida. He had been right in his conjecture about the roundness of the earth, but he had underestimated its size. He thought that the Orient lay just about where America is situated. To his dying day he felt certain that he had reached Asia instead of a new continent.

In the certainty of his belief, he set about searching for the riches that had been reported to exist so plentifully in Asia. "These islands which I have reached," he wrote to the king and the queen, "contain an infinite number of precious stones and gold incalculable . . . Their Highnesses can see that I will give them as much gold as they may need . . ."

And also, he reminded his sovereigns, he would enrich the Church with "an incalculable wealth" of converted souls. "For the which, all Christendom ought to feel delight and make great feasts and give solemn thanks to the Holy Trinity."

Columbus was to be disappointed in both of these hopes. It was not until thirty years later that the Spanish conquistadors discovered—and plundered—the gold of Montezuma. As for the conversion of the Indians, they would have nothing of the new faith. For they soon learned to distrust the visitors from over the sea. At first they had looked upon them as strange white gods who brought them beautiful gifts—pitchers and caps and sashes and slippers, and little glass beads that you strung around your neck and that held in them the colors of the rainbow. But before long they noticed that these newcomers were not white gods but white devils. They had come to these shores not to befriend them but to cheat them. ("Our men," wrote Columbus, "are defrauding the natives of their most valuable possessions in exchange for bits of broken pitchers.") And these white devils were kidnaping their strongest and their handsomest people and sending them off to hard labor across the sea. ("His Highnesses," wrote Columbus, "shall have as many Indian slaves as they shall order to be shipped.")

The Indians resented this treatment they received from the "white devils," who carried a crucifix in the one hand and a whip in the other. And when Columbus, after a short visit to Spain, returned to the West Indies, he found not a living trace of the garrison he had left behind him.

He paid, in all, four visits to America; and on each of these occasions he searched diligently for the gold and the jewels which he believed to be scattered throughout the islands. But his searching was all in vain.

King Ferdinand, in the meantime, had become impatient. He had expected gold from Columbus, and he received nothing but words. He determined to show this "wild and worthless dreamer" an example of his royal temper. First of all he deprived Columbus of his promised share in the profits that might accrue from his discovery. "A king's promises," Machiavelli had written, "are made only to be broken." And then Ferdinand sent one of his courtiers, Bobadilla, to the West Indies in order to spy upon the movements of Columbus. "I dare say this Genoese adventurer has found plenty of gold, but is keeping it all for himself."

Bobadilla, after a careful investigation, found Columbus innocent of the charge of dishonesty. But he found him guilty of another charge—stupidity. "This man has been stupid enough to discover a poor instead of a rich country." He therefore arrested Columbus and sent him back a chained prisoner to King Ferdinand.

This was quite in keeping with Spanish justice in the latter part of the fifteenth century. "I have done for my King," wrote Columbus, "more than any other prince has ever had from a subject . . . Now I am in such condition that even the vilest may affront me."

Yet even in his despair, he ends upon a note of hope. "God willing, the day will come when none can hear of my suffering without regret . . . and without some admiration for what I have done."

VII

THE hoped-for day did not come within the lifetime of Columbus. He died in obscure poverty.

The irony of the gods, with their lopsided and incomprehensible scales of justice. The strange and fragmentary gifts that they bestow upon the stepchildren of the earth. Talent without power, power without talent; beauty without goodness, goodness without beauty; success without merit, merit without success. Columbus discovered a continent; an impostor gave it his name. In 1503 an Italian adventurer, Amerigo Vespucci, published an account of a "new world" which he claimed to have discovered in 1497. The whole story was a fabrication. But a young German professor, who was publishing a geography at the time, named the new continent *America*, after the dishonest author of the fictitious discovery.

IMPORTANT DATES IN THE LIFE OF CHRISTOPHER COLUMBUS

1451—Born at Genoa.

1470–72—Engaged in trade at Genoa.

1476—Went to England.

1478—Married Filepa Perestrello.

1479—Corresponded with Toscanelli about the possible roundness of the earth.

1482—Tried to interest King John II of Portugal in voyage of discovery.

1492—April 17, signed agreement with Ferdinand and Isabella for voyage of discovery.
August 3, set sail into the Unknown.
October 12, discovered the New World.

1493—March 15, returned to Spain. September 24, started on second voyage across the Atlantic.

1496—June 11, returned again to Spain.

1498—May 30, started once more for New World.

1499—Sent as prisoner in chains by Bobadilla back to Spain.

1502—Restored to royal favor, started on fourth and last great voyage.

1504—Returned to Spain.

1506—May 20, died.

Leonardo da Vinci

1452–1519

Leonardo da Vinci represents the most perfect type of manhood in the modern world. That was his great glory—and his great tragedy. He had the unlimited dreams of a god but the limited powers of a man. His ambition was to do all things and to do them flawlessly. He conceived a thousand and one projects, and he completed only a handful. For he left his works undone the moment he discovered that the execution fell short of his vision. His life was an unfinished roadway, littered with the debris of sublime fragments. "I have never," he wrote bitterly toward the end of his life, "achieved a single work."

II

This man who "never achieved a single work" dreamed a greater number of dreams, in a vaster variety of fields, than any other man of the Renaissance. And the men of the Renaissance were noted for the universality of their intellect.

The universality of Leonardo was the astonishment of his generation. "And still they gazed, and still their wonder grew, that one small head could carry all he knew." The scope of his artistic, mental, and moral activities embraced the entire world. He tried to re-create its beauty, to measure its immensity and to interpret its mystery. He was a painter, a sculptor, an architect, an engineer, a musician, an anatomist, a mathematician, a naturalist, an inventor, an astronomer, a stage designer and a philosopher all rolled into one. At his death he left about five thousand pages of unpublished manuscript. A brief glance at only fifty of those five thousand pages will perhaps serve as the best introduction to the versatility of his mind.

Here, then, is a partial list of the subjects which Leonardo included in those fifty pages: ancient fables and medieval philosophy; the causes of the tides in the sea and the movement of the air in the lungs; the measurements of the earth and the distance between the earth and the sun; the nocturnal habits of the owl and the physical laws of human vision; the nature of flame and the formula for squaring a circle; the law of gravitation and the rhythmical swaying of trees in the wind; the sketch of a flying machine and a medical prescription for a stone in the bladder; a device for swimming with an inflated leather jacket and an essay on light and shade; a design for a pleasure garden and a new set of war engines; a recipe for making perfume and a list of original geometrical theorems; a series of hydraulic studies on the pressure of water in a fountain; a host of observations on the habits of birds and beasts; an article on vacuum; a device for using steam as a motive power; a chapter of original maxims; and a disquisition on the nature of the moon.

This comprises about one fifth of the subjects treated in only fifty out of the five thousand pages of Leonardo's notes. Add to this the fact that Leonardo painted probably the most perfect portrait of the ages (*Mona Lisa*), created perhaps the most beautiful fresco known to man (*The Last Supper*) and modeled an equestrian statue (of Sforza) which was in its day regarded as the eighth wonder of the world, and then try, if you can, to measure the boundaries of Leonardo da Vinci's genius.

Every once in a while the Great Sculptor designs a model of the super-man He is to create in the future. Leonardo was one of the most perfect of these divine experiments in human clay.

III

HE WAS the illegitimate son of Ser Piero Antonio, a Florentine lawyer who lived among the Tuscan foothills in the Castle of Vinci. The rocky paths of the countryside exercised the boy's body, and the lights and shadows that played over the hilltops gave nourishment to his soul. Even as a child he dazzled everyone with his beauty. With his rose-colored cloak and golden hair he looked like an angel of Botticelli descended from the clouds. He could sing divinely. At an early age he learned to accompany himself on the lute, and he improvised both the words and the music as he sang, to the astonishment of his father's guests.

But not satisfied with his musical genius, Leonardo tried to master every phase of human thought. He had an observant eye, a firm hand, and an artistic soul. Once as a young boy he lost his way in the mountains. He came upon the entrance of a dark and yawning cave. Writing of this experience in his later years, he said, "Suddenly two emotions arose in me, fear and desire: fear of the dark cavern, desire to see whether there were any marvelous things within." Throughout his days he was to be mastered by these two emotions—fear of the dark mystery of life, or rather of his own inability to penetrate it, and desire to bring the wonder of this mystery into the light, to study it, to explain its meaning and to paint its glory. He decided early in life to be an investigator, a teacher, and, above all, an artist.

He begged his father to apprentice him to a painter. But his father objected. Painters in those days were looked down upon as inferior creatures. Ser Piero wanted his son to be a lawyer like himself. One day Leonardo, without his father's knowledge, painted upon a wooden panel the blackness of the cave in which he had been lost and, leaping out of it, a frightful dragon with fiery eyes, wide-open jaws, and distended nostrils that spurted flames and poisonous vapors.

When the work was finished Leonardo asked his father to come into his room. With true dramatic instinct he had half covered the window and had placed the easel in such a position that the light fell upon the fiery dragon. Ser Piero stepped into the room, and the first thing he saw was this horrible monster ready to spring upon him. With a cry he leaped back toward the door. "Don't be afraid, Father," smiled Leonardo. "It's only a painted dragon." And then, with a wisdom beyond his years, he added, "I see I've done an adequate job."

Ser Piero, too, admitted that his son could do an adequate job in painting. Accordingly he apprenticed him (in 1470) to the famous Florentine painter, sculptor, and architect, Andrea del Verrocchio.

When he entered upon his apprenticeship Leonardo was eighteen years old. Verrocchio, his master, was his senior by seventeen years. Like Leonardo, he was interested in the sciences as well as in the arts. Painting, to him, was a mathematical demonstration of three-dimensional beauty. All art must be based upon a geometric design. It must be concrete and solid; it must have not only length and width but depth. Verrocchio was one of the first Italian artists to realize the importance of perspective in painting. His scientific attitude toward art exerted a powerful influence, as we shall see, upon the developing genius of Leonardo.

A hard worker himself, Verrocchio kept all his apprentices constantly at work. Yet Leonardo managed somehow to find time for his scientific and his philosophic studies. As a young boy he had fallen under the influence of Toscanelli, the naturalist, philosopher, and mathematician whose daring pronouncements were the amazement of Florence and whose theory about the roundness of the earth was destined a few years later to launch Columbus upon his dream of discovery. Leonardo, too, as a result of his conversations with Toscanelli, began to dream great dreams of discovery. But he confined his adventures to the mental instead of the physical world. He began to busy himself with the problems of geography, astronomy, physics, natural history, and engineering. He invented labor-saving tools, he drew maps, he observed the flights of birds, he designed machines for turning and grinding and transportation, and he began to fill his notebooks with scientific and artistic sketches. Dozens of them. And again and again, at the bottom of a sketch, he would write: "This is simple and good. But try to do better."

This was to be his motto throughout his life—*good, but try to do better.*

IV

HIS WORK at Verrocchio's studio brought him into contact with the fashionable world of Florence. His eyes were dazzled by the gold and the silver, the pearls and the diamonds and the rubies, the silks and the brocades and the satins and the velvets, the waving plumes and the prancing horses—all the extravagant splendor which the Medicis, headed by Lorenzo the Magnificent, displayed with such proud abandon. Accumulated wealth meant power, and wealth displayed meant the respect and the admiration of your fellows. Young Leonardo's heart was filled with a hunger for luxury. His fine figure must be set off by equally fine garments. Let the Florentines recognize him for what he was—a young god living for a while among mortals.

Yet this young Florentine god had the most abstemious of appetites. He spent nearly all his earnings on his clothes, leaving very little for his food. His own tastes were simple, but he must cater to the tastes of the mighty. To make an impression. To curry their favor. To win their patronage. To bring his artistic and his intellectual visions into the concrete world of reality.

And so, in spite of his private modesty and his innate simplicity, he presented himself in public as a dashing cavalier and incomparable master of all knowledge. His business was to dazzle. At thirty-one he applied to Ludovico Sforza, the Duke of Milan, for a position as general director of Milan in the arts of peace and the arms of war. The letter which he addressed to Sforza, and in which he enumerated his talents, could have been written, as Jean Paul Richter points out, "only by a genius or by a fool." In a tone that seemed cold and businesslike and matter-of-fact this amazing young artist informed Ludovico that he could build portable bridges for the pursuit of the enemy and that he knew how to destroy the enemy's bridges; that he was able to drain ditches and rivers; that he possessed a secret whereby he could ruin any fortress that was not built on a stone foundation; that he could build a new and destructive type of cannon; that he had discovered a noiseless method for constructing tunnels under rivers; that he knew how to build covered tanks for attacking the enemy; that he possessed plans for the making of strange submarine weapons of defense and attack; that, furthermore, in times of peace he could equal anyone in architecture, and in painting he could "do as much as any other, be he who he may"; and that, finally, he would engage to execute an equestrian statue of Sforza's illustrious father, a colossal sculpture the like of which the world had never seen!

Instead of committing the young Leonardo to the nearest insane asy-

lum, the count invited him to come to the palace. Leonardo impressed the
gentlemen and charmed the ladies of the court of Milan. He remained in
the service of Ludovico Sforza for twenty years.

At Milan he became the official engineer and the unofficial master of
gaiety. He planned the entertainments, he wrote the music, he painted
the scenery, he designed the costumes, and he took the leading role in
the pageants of the court. He was, in short, the most active participant
in the frenzied life of his day.

Active, yet aloof. Like the cynical court jesters of old, he despised the
men and the women whom he flattered. And he despised himself for the
part he was obliged to play in this stupid and artificial life of the court.
He was compelled to stoop in order to conquer, to turn himself into a
buffoon in order to secure his commissions as an artist. But he had his
revenge. In a series of bitterly brilliant fables which he wrote at this
time he lashed out savagely against that most shameful and most pitiable
of living creatures—Man. "Men," he confided to the pages of his notebook at this time, "are nothing else than passages for food, augmenters of
filth, and fillers of privies. . . . Nothing else in the world is effected
through them, and they are without any virtue. . . . There can surely be
no question that Nature must desire to extinguish the human race as a
useless thing."

He despised the miserable human race and yet he was anxious to help it
out of its misery. While he was at Milan he tried to build and to beautify
and to ennoble the City of the Renaissance. He planned roads with two
levels for safer travel. He advocated wider streets for safer sanitation. He
dreamed of transforming the landscapes of Italy with a network of temples
and cataracts and canals and lakes and gardens. He designed a system of
small cities, each of them to consist of five thousand houses with no more
than six inhabitants to a house. For he believed that humanity was too
congested to be happy. "We must separate this great congregation of people who live crowded together like herds of goats, filling the air with stench
and spreading the seeds of pestilence and death."

The cities that he planned were to be built along riverbanks. For in
this way he could introduce into each city a sanitary sewage system—
something undreamt of in his day—nothing less than a series of under-
ground canals that would carry all the refuse of the city into the river.

His model cities were to have no ugly sights or evil smells. They were
to be full of space and air and beauty and cleanliness and freedom and
culture and joy. The great dream cities of a healthier, happier race of
men.

But they remained dreams. For Sforza was not interested in advancing
money for so utopian a project. Instead he gave Leonardo an assignment
of another sort. He commissioned him to model an equestrian statue of
his illustrious father, Francesco Sforza. This equestrian statue, or, as it was
popularly called, "the horse," was as colossal in size as it was magnificent

in conception. In 1493 the clay model was unveiled for exhibition. Displayed under an improvised triumphal arch, it became a thing of wonder to all Milan. Here, on the verge of realization, stood one of the most stupendous and one of the most beautiful dreams in the entire history of sculpture. All that was necessary to fulfill the dream was to cast the statue in bronze. But the casting was never done. It required too much bronze for so tremendous a job. Milan was at war with France, and all the spare metal within the city had to be melted into arms and ammunition. Destruction won a victory over creation. Leonardo's statue remained unfinished. In 1499 the French troops occupied Milan, and Leonardo's noble and masterly work became a target for the Gascon bowmen. Today, thanks to the war, not a trace is left of this "eighth wonder of the world."

V

LEONARDO was now a man of great fame and meager purse. Ludovico Sforza was the sort of patron who paid his artists with golden phrases rather than with gold coin. And of late even his admiration for Leonardo's genius had cooled. Too close proximity had bred contempt. He began to neglect Leonardo and to give out his best commissions to other and inferior artists. And so Leonardo, with a heavy heart, sat down to write a letter to Sforza. "Your Excellency," he began, "it vexes me deeply that you are giving me no further commissions . . . I know that your thoughts are turned in other directions . . . I should like to recall to Your Magnificence my poor services . . ." And then he went on, hesitantly, to remind Sforza that there were payments still due him for three years' work and that he was at present in "great financial difficulties . . . And may I conclude, Your Lordship, that my life is at your service. I hold myself in readiness to obey you . . ."

This letter shamed Sforza into giving Leonardo a new commission. This commission was to make the name of Leonardo immortal. He finished this "most sublime of all human paintings" in 1498. It was *The Last Supper*, depicted upon the front wall of the dining room in the Church of Santa Maria delle Grazie. This fresco has become blurred and cracked with the passage of time. Leonardo mixed his colors with oil, a fatal innovation for a fresco painting. The paint has peeled off in many places, and the faces of Jesus and his disciples have been retouched by less skillful hands. Yet the soul of beauty still shines through the crumbling paint of *The Last Supper*. Like most of the other paintings of Leonardo, it is geometric in design. For Leonardo's art, like Plato's philosophy, is based upon the symmetry of mathematics. A long narrow table, with its white cover embroidered in blue like a Jewish prayer shawl, stands in front of three windows. Through the center window the light streams in upon Jesus, who sits with his back to the window, with six disciples on either side of him. Jesus has just spoken the bitter words, "One of you shall betray me." The twelve disciples, each group of six further subdivided into groups of three, show their reaction to the words of Jesus by the expression of their faces and the motions of their bodies. James the elder, his mouth open in amazement, seems to be repeating the words of Jesus. Thomas, the everlasting doubter, is raising his index finger, as if about to ask a question. Philip, his arms crossed over his breast and his eyes dimmed with tears, is protesting his innocence. John, his hands clasped together, looks on with a helpless despair. Peter, the man of action, has sprung from his seat, with a knife clasped in his hand. Judas, immersed in shadow, shows his guilt in his almost imperceptible recoil and in his shifty eyes. Matthew, his arms outstretched, seems to be appealing to the others: "No, we must not let this happen!" And so on, down to the last psychological and geometrical detail of the painting—one of the supreme achievements of the human mind. In this painting, as one of Leonardo's biographers has remarked, "science is wedded to art, and philosophy imprints a kiss upon the perfect union."

It took Leonardo a long time to paint *The Last Supper*. Aiming at perfection, he did his work slowly and meticulously, always revising what he had done the day before and never quite satisfied with the results. "When setting to work to paint," writes his biographer, Lomazzo, "it was as if he were mastered by fear. . . . His soul being full of the sublimity of Art, he was enabled to see in his own pictures faults which others hailed as miraculous creations." Another of his biographers, Signor Bandello, tells us that "he would often come to the church at early dawn . . . Hastily mounting the scaffolding, he worked diligently until the shades of evening compelled him to cease, never thinking to take food at all, so absorbed was he in his work. At other times, however, he would remain there three or four days without touching his picture . . . standing with folded arms, gazing at his figures as if to criticize them himself."

It was this perpetual self-criticism that prevented him from completing another masterpiece, *The Battle of Anghiari*. In spite of his scientific interest in military engines he was one of the few men of the Renaissance who saw war in all its realistic ugliness. Writing about it in his notebook, he called it "that insanity most bestial." When, therefore, he received a commission from his native city to celebrate the Florentine victory at the Battle of Anghiari he proceeded to paint not the glory but the fury of war. He drew sketches of the battle such as Tolstoy might have painted had he been an artist. And as an accompaniment to the sketches he wrote a word picture of the battle which is worthy of the great Russian novelist at his best. The dust and the smoke of the conflict, the reddish glare of the sun upon the agonized faces of the combatants, the tangled heaps of wounded men and horses, the thick rain of arrows falling in every direction, the backward-flying hair of the pursuers, the furrows made by the horses as they drag their riders through the slippery and bloodstained mud, the broken shields and spears and swords and helmets scattered on the ground between the legs of the dead and the dying, the winding trickle of blood from the gaping wounds, the staring eyes, the clenched fists and the grotesque poses of the slain soldiers, the dirt and the sweat and the blood upon the faces of the exhausted soldiers—all these are but a handful of the thousand and one details which Leonardo introduces into his description of the battle. It is a pity that he did not match his verbal pictures and his sketchy outlines with a completed painting. This painting, like so many other of his grandiose conceptions, remained an unfulfilled dream. He felt that it was a job beyond the power of a genius even like himself. The *art* of man, he believed, was not quite equal to the task of painting the *cruelty* of man.

VI

BEHOLD HIM NOW at fifty: tall, noble, erect, dressed in a scarlet velvet cloak, his mustache carefully waxed, his long hair and beard gleaming like threads of finespun copper embroidered here and there with a touch of gray, his hands white, slender, aristocratic, yet strong enough to bend a horseshoe or break a sword, his eye bright and his step elastic and firm— a poet in quest of beauty, a philosopher in search of truth. From now to the end of his life he will be a restless wanderer, going from Milan to Florence, from Florence to Venice, from Venice to Rome, from Rome to Amboise, seeking everywhere for new patrons, new ideas, new dreams, new ways to make men less stupid, less cruel, less sad. And wherever he goes, there plays about his mouth a strange smile. There is wisdom in that smile, and sorrow and cynicism and contempt. But, over and above all, there is pity in it. And frequently he transfers this smile of his to the faces of the portraits that he paints—St. Anne, Leda, the Virgin Mary, John the Baptist, Bacchus, and Mona Lisa. They call him "Leonardo, the painter of the smiling faces."

And so he wandered about the world, this painter of the smiling faces, dreaming, inventing, sketching, modeling, building, philosophizing, and amusing the lords and ladies of the court with his caustic wit, his worldly wisdom—and his magical tricks. For this Dr. Faustus of the Renaissance had acquired a reputation as a great magician. He would put a saucer of boiling oil on the table, pour red wine on top and "set the wine on fire," to the amazement of his audience. On festive occasions he made mechanical lions that walked and glared and roared like living creatures. Once, having procured the entrails of a sheep, he showed them to his guests on the palm of his hand. Then, after the manner of a professional juggler, he asked them to come into his workshop. Here he began to inflate the entrails with a pair of bellows. Gradually the handful of intestines blew up into transparent balloons, pushing through the door, filling the entire room and compelling the astonished guests to flatten themselves against the walls. When the trick was over he smilingly explained to his visitors that he had merely shown them a symbol of human virtue, which at first may seem insignificant but which by careful tending may be capable of infinite growth.

Always, even in his playful moments, he was the philosopher. His notebooks are full of profound observations about life and death. Much of his writing is hard to decipher. For he was left-handed and wrote his Italian, as if it were Hebrew or Arabic, from right to left. No attempt has been made as yet to systematize his philosophical aphorisms. Even in their fragmentary state, however, we can see in them the courage of a Stoic tempered with the gentleness of a Christian. Leonardo was not a member of the Church. But he was a follower of Jesus. He showed this not only in his exquisitely sympathetic drawing of Christ's face but in his equally sympathetic understanding of Christ's thought. Like Christ himself, or like the Stoics of Rome, he took his own sorrows lightly and sympathized with the sorrows of others. He suffered much from the malice of his enemies and the envy of his friends. But he bore his sufferings and his insults with a patient dignity. "Patience," he wrote in one of his manuscripts, "serves as a protection against wrongs as clothes do against cold. For if you put on more clothes as the cold increases, it will have no power to hurt you. So in like manner you must grow in patience when you meet with great wrongs and they will then be powerless to vex your mind."

He was willing to endure the foolishness of the individual. But he had a great contempt for the follies of mankind. "What do you think, Man, of your own species?" he asks. "Are you not ashamed of your stupidity?"

He was frequently amused by the struggles of the princes for empty honors. While his patrons tried to perfect themselves in the art of royalty, Leonardo devoted himself to the royalty of art. In beauty alone he found the solid satisfaction of life. All else he regarded, with the wisdom of a Koheleth, as the baseless hungering for nonexistent fruits. Ambition is vain, and hope leads only to disappointment. "Desire," he wrote, "is sweeter than fulfillment." It is ridiculous to break your neck, and other people's necks, in your scramble for fame. "The fruit that seems sweet on the tree often turns bitter in the mouth." We must learn the limitations of our strength. To aim too high is not only foolish but dangerous. Let us measure our ambition by our talents, and let not our desires outstrip our ability to fulfill these desires. "Since we cannot attain what we wish, let us wish only what we can attain."

Desire is sweet, but fulfillment is bitter. "There is no perfect gift without great suffering." Especially is this true in the case of an artist like Leonardo. The greater the capacity for beauty, the greater the sensitivity to pain. The artist achieves more because he suffers more. The Greek poets had a theory, based upon their profound understanding of life, that knowledge comes through sorrow. *Pathei Mathos*. We are able to learn because we are ready to suffer.

Leonardo's learning and Leonardo's art and Leonardo's gentleness were the result of his suffering. He showed pity toward all because very few showed pity toward him. Having suffered humiliation all his life at the hands of his patrons, he refrained from hurting or humiliating anyone else. The very thought of inflicting pain upon any living creature was abhorrent to him. His biographer Vasari tells us that "when he passed the market place where birds were sold, he would frequently take them from the cages with his own hands; and having paid the sellers the price that was asked, he would let them fly away in the air, thus giving them back their liberty."

His pity for all living things led him to be a vegetarian. Life to him was sacred. As we have no power to create life, we have no right to destroy it. "It is an infinitely atrocious act," he wrote, "to take away the life of any creature. . . . The soul wills not that rage or malice should destroy life. . . . He who values not life does not deserve to have it."

Leonardo knew whereof he spoke. For he had observed the pity and the irony and the cruelty of life at first hand. At the court of Ludovico Sforza, at the castle of Cesare Borgia, at the palace of King Francis I, in the cities, the towns, the villages, the military camps—everywhere he had seen men imprison and slaughter their fellow men for the pettiest of ambitions and the flimsiest of prizes. His contemplation of the beauty of man had made him an artist. His observation of man's barbarity turned him into a philosopher.

VII

AND A PHILOSOPHER he remained to the end of his days. He had good need of his philosophy, for he possessed very little else. He offered to the world his superb statues and paintings, and he was repaid with empty praise. He tried to build great buildings, to design beautiful cities and to conquer the sea and the earth and the air with his inventions of the submarine, the steam carriage and the airship, and he received no encouragement from his patrons. At last, toward the end of his life, he did receive some encouragement and a chance to make a good living. Doing what? Making mirrors and building stables! Pearls to the swine, luxurious stables for the horses. Such are the tasks to which humanity reduces the most precious of its souls.

His life, as he saw it, ended in failure. "He was passed over not only for great commissions but for high offices." His dreams, his ambitions, his plans, his inventions, his hopes, all lay about him in ruins. "We always hope for the future," he wrote in his last years, "but the future has only one certainty in store for us—the death of all hope." His whole existence, he observed, had been nothing but a preparation for death. "When I thought I was learning to live, I was but learning to die."

Yet he accepted the necessity of death, as he had accepted the uncertainties of life, with the resignation of the Stoic. When the final summons came he was ready, like a tired child, to go to his rest. "As a well-spent day brings happy sleep," he wrote just before the end, "so does a well-used life bring happy death."

He died in France on May 2, 1519, at the age of sixty-seven. The only mourners who followed his coffin were a handful of faithful servants who had lost a gentle master, and the paid poor of the village who raised their professional lament for a stranger they knew nothing about. There was only one man at that time who was able to measure Leonardo's greatness. This man was Leonardo's pupil and friend, Francesco Melzi. "The death of Leonardo," wrote Melzi, "is a loss to everyone. . . . It is not in the power of nature to reproduce such another man."

IMPORTANT DATES IN THE LIFE OF LEONARDO DA VINCI

1452—Born, April 15, near Florence.

1470—Apprenticed to Andrea Verrocchio.

1482—Entered service of Duke of Milan, Ludovico Sforza.

1493—Finished clay model of Francesco Sforza's equestrian statue, later destroyed by French invasion of 1499.

1498—Finished *The Last Supper*.

1502—Became military engineer for Cesare Borgia.

1504—Painted *Mona Lisa*.

1513—Went to Rome, but was rejected by the Pope.

1516—First engineer and painter to the French King, Francis I.

1519—Died, May 2, Cloux.

Michelangelo Buonarroti

1475–1564

ONE DAY LEONARDO, elegant, smiling, trim, was walking down the Piazza della Trinita in Florence. A number of prominent citizens were sitting on a bench discussing a passage in Dante. One of the citizens looked up and saw Leonardo. "Gentlemen," he said, "here is the man who can settle our argument."

Just at this moment a young man appeared on the other side of the square. His face, with its flattened, broken nose, seemed to hold a perpetual grudge against the world. His short tumbled hair fell untidily over his forehead. His clothes were crumpled, his boots were covered with marble dust, and his hands were rough, with bits of clay clinging to the nails. Leonardo pointed to him. "There comes Michelangelo, gentlemen. You had better ask *him* to explain Dante."

Michelangelo, always on the watch for insults, took Leonardo's words as a direct challenge. "Explain it yourself!" he shouted in derision. "You can do everything, you know. Didn't you make a model of a horse and then quit the job because you couldn't cast it in bronze?"

Michelangelo passed on but turned back for a final fling: "And those fat geese of Milan entrusted *you*, of all people, with that job!"

This explosion of ill will was the outlet for Michelangelo's resentment against his fate. For he was still young and comparatively unknown, whereas Leonardo, who was his senior by twenty-three years, was already acclaimed as one of the leading artists of the day. Later on Michelangelo was to outstrip his older rival both in fortune and in fame. But at this moment he was as yet unaware of his great destiny.

II

His FATHER, Ludovico di Lionardo Buonarroti, was the mayor of Caprese. The little boy grew up in a family of men, for he had four brothers and no sisters, and his mother died with he was six years old. The elder Buonarroti, of noble birth but poor and often out of a job, was ill-tempered and violent and hard on his children. He was especially irritated at Michelangelo's repeated declaration that he wanted to be an artist. No Buonarroti, he was determined, should be allowed to waste his time with the plebeian instruments of the chisel and the brush. His five sons must go into business. They must become bankers, like the famous families of the Pitti, the Sforzi, the Medici! And so he took his young dreamer of a son and tried to whip some sense into him.

But in vain. In spite of all his beatings and his scoldings, Michelangelo still insisted that he wanted to be an artist. And so, reluctantly, he apprenticed the thirteen-year-old boy to Messer Ghirlandajo and washed his hands of him.

Ghirlandajo was at that time painting the walls of Santa Maria Novella. He set his apprentices to the task of grinding the colors and copying bits of drapery from his carefully prepared sketches. But the copies of Michelangelo were better than the originals, and this made Ghirlandajo extremely jealous. He showed his jealousy in a hundred and one petty annoyances; and the sensitive young boy, having endured the misunderstanding of his father, now suffered from the envy of his teacher. He therefore conceived a mistrust of his fellow men, and this mistrust was to remain with him to the end of his days.

It was a fortunate thing, however, that Ghirlandajo disliked Michelangelo. For, in his determination to get rid of him, he palmed him off upon Bertoldo, the old man who was teaching youngsters the sculptor's art from the recently excavated antiques in the Garden of the Medici. This place was a veritable Garden of Eden to Michelangelo. For here he learned the work for which God had shaped his hands, and here he met the man who introduced him to the world of learning, of art, of music, of poetry, of beauty, of wit—everything for which his eager young soul so passionately thirsted. One day, as Michelangelo was chiseling out the face of an old man in the garden of Lorenzo de' Medici, Lorenzo the Magnificent himself happened to be strolling through the garden. He stopped when he came to Michelangelo's bit of statuary. He examined it and then turned to the young sculptor. "My boy," he said, "don't you know that an old man must have lost some of his teeth?"

Michelangelo was all excitement at the thought that Lorenzo had spoken to him. Seizing his tools, he knocked out one of the teeth and then turned to Lorenzo. "Is this better?"

"Yes," laughed Lorenzo. "Very much better!"

Lorenzo became interested in this quick-witted and talented youngster of fourteen. He took him into the Palazzo Medici, he allowed him to sit at his table, he encouraged him to play with his children, he presented him with a violet cloak, he offered him five ducats (equivalent in purchasing power to about fifty dollars) a month, and he opened his eyes to the glories of the pagan world. Here Michelangelo drank beauty and wisdom from the lips of the mystic Ficino, the philosopher Pico Mirandola, the poet Poliziano, and the numerous scholars and writers and artists who came to the Medici palace from all the corners of the earth. At the Medici table, the center of the civilization of the day, Apollo was the Lord of Light and Plato his leading prophet and saint.

It was under this pagan influence that Michelangelo was encouraged to produce his first original work—the *Battle of the Centaurs*, modeled in relief—a living, fighting entanglement of half men, half horses, full of the symmetrical beauty of Greek nakedness, a myth of the dead past reborn into the world of the Renaissance.

It was a world in which Michelangelo felt perfectly at home. For at this period of his life he was supremely happy. But then there came a tragedy, and he was to bear the physical and mental scars of this tragedy throughout the rest of his days. One of his talented fellow apprentices was the quick-tempered and strong-fisted Torrigiano. This fellow could fight even better than he could paint, and it was an evil hour that prompted Michelangelo to criticize his painting. What happened after that is best told in Torrigiano's own words: "On that day I was more than usually annoyed by his criticism. I clenched my fist and gave him such a whack on his nose that the bones and cartilage felt as soft as a wafer. So he bore my mark as long as he lived."

Michelangelo was carried home for dead. When the wound was healed he saw his disfigured face in the mirror. From that time on he withdrew into himself. He never fully recovered from this tragic disfigurement of his body and the equally tragic distortion of his soul.

III

AT ABOUT THIS TIME Michelangelo heard the preaching of Savonarola, the apostle-politician who inveighed against the pagan immorality and the unrepentant savagery of the secret rulers of the city. This preaching exerted a tremendous influence upon the sensitive young artist. One of his brothers, under this influence, entered a Dominican monastery. Michelangelo, too, was tempted for a time to renounce his art and to shut himself away from the world. There began in his soul a violent struggle between skepticism and religion, between beauty and duty, between the ideas of the old world and the ideals of the new. But after a time the struggle ceased and, fortunately for his art, Michelangelo was able to reconcile the two apparently irreconcilable elements. After all, he concluded, there is no good reason why an artist cannot subscribe to the best features of paganism *and* of Christianity. Perhaps the highest kind of art lay precisely in the *marriage* of the two, in the ultimate union of the holiness of beauty and the beauty of holiness. This reconciliation between paganism and Christianity brought peace to Michelangelo's spirit and proved to be the harmonizing principle of all his future masterpieces.

While this struggle was going on in Michelangelo's soul his patron died. The passing of Lorenzo the Magnificent precipitated an age of political turmoil. Savonarola had aroused the populace against the wanton frivolity of Piero de' Medici, the son of Lorenzo. King Charles of France was marching against the city. A mob of penitent fanatics was tearing down the pictures and the statues of Florence. The treasures of the centuries lay about the streets in heaps of ruins. Michelangelo, his young dream of art temporarily shattered, fled from the city.

He went to Bologna, where he received a commission to make a statue for the parish church. It was a light-bearing angel, a sort of baptized Apollo, a symbol of the reunion between the old world and the new.

But again Michelangelo was pursued by the resentment of his fellow artists, who were jealous of the fact that this young upstart was already surpassing their own best achievements. Literally hounded out of Bologna, he went back to Florence; and after a brief but not altogether welcome sojourn in his native town he went on to seek his fortune in Rome. When he arrived in the City of the Vatican he had just turned twenty-one.

IV

ROME, the eternal city of faith. But the guardians of the faith had betrayed their trust. What Michelangelo found on his arrival in 1496 was a city of music and murder, of culture and beauty and debauchery, of dancing and feasting and poetry and poison, of beautiful temples and ugly prison cells, of piety in the homes of the humble and lust in the palaces of the rich. And for two years he found himself a stranger there, out of tune with the world. "I have no friends," he said, "I need none, and I will have none."

At twenty-three, however, he found recognition even in this city of savage self-interest and merciless rivalry. He applied for a commission to model a statue of Christ and the Mother for the Church of St. Peter. "The work," he wrote in his application, "will be such that no living master could do it better." He won the competition and made the statue. All the artistic people in Rome flocked to see the work. The dead Christ, his arms emaciated (they had actually been modeled from a corpse), was lying across the lap of a very beautiful woman much younger than himself. The spectators admired and were amazed. They asked the sculptor why he had made the Mother so much younger than the Son. "Don't you know," retorted Michelangelo, "that any woman who is pure preserves her youth for many years? How much more true is this of the Madonna, who has never yielded to human desire and whose features, moreover, have been transfigured by divine love!"

Throughout his life Michelangelo was to paint and to model figures, not in accordance with the conventions of the day but rather in accordance with the promptings of his own philosophy. He was one of the first of the moderns to apply psychology to art.

When this statue was finished Michelangelo yielded for the first and the last time in his life to the weakness of vanity. He had himself locked into the church at night; and there, under the light of a candle, he chiseled his name and his native town upon the statue. Thereafter he never signed any of his other completed works. Like the trees and the mountains of nature, the masterpieces of Michelangelo have no need to bear the signature of their creator.

V

MICHELANGELO returned to Florence at the age of twenty-six. Passing one day through the courtyard of the Cathedral, he stopped to examine a magnificent block of marble that had been lying there idly for forty-six years. He offered to do something with this marble if given the chance. The offer was accepted. Michelangelo began the work on August 2, 1502. On January 25, 1504, the colossal statue of David was completed.

This Giant, as it was called, became so epoch-making that for decades the people of Italy reckoned their time by it. "The year the Giant was set up" came to be known as the first year of the New Era. For the statue of David is indeed the introduction to a new era in sculpture. The statue now stands in the Florentine Academy of Arts—a naked athletic figure with a small head, huge body, slender waist, thin arms and strong hands whose veins stand out like whipcords. With his left hand he takes the sling from his shoulder, and in his right hand he holds the stone ready for its flight against the foe. But the most arresting part of the statue is the face. It is the face of a virile, determined, scornful and at the same time compassionate young man—the idealized face of Michelangelo himself. Like David, he too was ready to challenge the Goliaths of the day. The singer of Judea and the sculptor of Florence, two men with resolute, sensitive souls, two artists who knew how to fight!

The fame of the Giant brought Michelangelo back to Rome. The new Pope, Julius II, was anxious to perpetuate his memory with a tomb such as the world had never seen. And the one man to do the job was Michelangelo. For Michelangelo, like himself, was a dreamer of stupendous dreams. Together they planned this magnificent tomb. It was to consist of forty figures, larger than life, who were to stand guard around the body of the Pope. Two of the figures were to portray Moses and Paul; two others were to be allegorical symbols of heaven and earth; the rest were to represent the greatest saints and heroes of the past. "How much," asked the Pope, "will this monument cost?"

Michelangelo thought it better to aim too high than too low. Accordingly he replied: "One hundred thousand scudi."

"Suppose we make it two hundred thousand." And before Michelangelo could recover from his astonishment the Pope waved him away. "Don't stand there gaping, young man. Get to work!"

Elated with his commission, Michelangelo betook himself to Carrara, where he selected a thousand ducats' worth of marble. When these "mountains of stone" arrived at St. Peter's Michelangelo began to hew them into life. But the progress was slow, and the payments from the Pope were too irregular for steady work. Once more the genius of Michelangelo was being hampered by the jealousy of his rivals. One of these rivals was Bramante, an artist with a great talent and a puny soul. Anxious to win for himself the favor and the ducats of the Pope, he told him that to dig a man's grave in his own lifetime would be an evil omen. Why not, he suggested, build a church instead of a tomb? He, Bramante, would be the architect. He would rebuild St. Peter's and make it a landmark for the ages!

The Pope listened to Bramante. Michelangelo, in conversation with one of the Pope's jewelers, heard that he was to receive not another penny from the Vatican. "This news," he wrote to a friend, "alarmed me very much. I came to beg for the money that was due me, so that I might go on with the work. His Holiness told me to come again on Monday. I went on Monday and on Wednesday and on Thursday and on Friday. Finally a groom of the chambers said to me, 'I have orders not to admit you.' At these words my anger flared up, and I shouted: 'Then tell the Pope that in the future, if he wants me, he will have to look for me himself!' "

And so, snubbed by the Pope, he fled from Rome and went back to Florence. His distrust of humanity was now more intense than ever. The whole world, he felt, was against him. In all his business deals he was convinced that the other fellow was trying to rob him. If his tailor made his vest a little too tight, he believed that it was done deliberately, in order to vex him. He refused to receive presents from anybody. "Beware," he said, "of the Greeks—or of the Italians—bearing gifts." He always locked his workshop, for fear that his fellow artists might steal his ideas. As for ideas of their own, he believed they had none. All of them, he remarked caustically, were imitators. Once he was called upon to criticize a portrait painted by another artist. "Very nice," he said, "but everything in this picture is borrowed." And then, with a sarcastic smile, he continued: "I'm just wondering what will happen to this picture on the Day of Judgment, when all the bodies will want their limbs back again."

Whenever he was hurt he withdrew into the shell of his pride and would let no one come near him. The Pope ordered him again and again to come back, but Michelangelo refused. He would brook no commands from anyone. "He who begins by being a prince's pack mule," he said, "will have the load on his back till he dies." Finally the Pope *entreated* him to return, for an artist of Michelangelo's genius was an asset to the Vatican. Michelangelo yielded to the entreaty and went to meet the Pope. Not, however, at Rome, but halfway, at Bologna.

"You are a strange man," said the Pope. "Instead of coming to us, you have waited until we came to you."

"Your Holiness has done me a great hurt."

"But I shall heal it, I promise you." Laying his hand on the kneeling artist's head, he blessed him.

And thus their quarrel was patched up. "Michelangelo," wrote Soderini, the ruler of Florence, "is one of those men from whom you can get anything by kind words. . . . You must show him affection, assure him of your esteem—and then he will produce such works as will amaze the world."

VI

As a result of the Pope's kindness Michelangelo now produced one of those works that amazed the world. The project of the tomb had been abandoned, at least for the present. For the Pope was still superstitious about the matter of planning for his death during his lifetime. Instead he asked Michelangelo to paint the ceiling of the Sistine Chapel—the twelve figures of the apostles, conceived in such dimensions as no painter before him had even dared to imagine.

Here, then, was another undertaking worthy of Michelangelo's genius. For four years he literally locked himself into the chapel, admitting no one except the color grinder and, occasionally, the Pope. He painted most of the work with his head thrown back and his eyes looking upward. Long after the painting was finished he was obliged to hold every letter and every book that he wanted to read high above his head. For the muscles of his eyes had become accustomed to this peculiarly abnormal point of view.

When the Pope beheld the completed work he was enchanted with it—except for one detail. Most of the saints and apostles in the earlier pictures had been painted with gilded embroidery lavishly displayed over their garments. "Why," asked the Pope of Michelangelo, "have you omitted the gold trimmings?"

"Holy Father," replied Michelangelo, "in those days the men and the women were poor and honest. They had faith, but they had no gold."

In one of his sonnets George Santayana writes that God doubled creation when he created Shakespeare. The same may be said of Michelangelo. For the painting of the Sistine Chapel is creation created anew. The Pope's original plan of the twelve apostles had now grown into a complete vision of heaven and earth. At first there is darkness and divine loneliness—the expectant moment before the birth of the world. And then —the Eternal, borne aloft by clouds of angels. He divides the light from the darkness; He fashions the sun and the moon; He separates the water from the land; He stirs Adam into life with the touch of His finger (to Michelangelo God is the Divine Sculptor); He shapes Eve out of the flesh of Adam; He displays before her the trees of the garden and the tempting fruit; He dispatches the angel to drive Adam and Eve out of Paradise with his flaming sword; and He sends down the waters of His wrath upon the sinful race of men. And round about this central picture of creation and destruction sit the sibyls and the prophets, looking on, reflecting, hoping, exhorting, praying—the eternal intermediaries between God and Man.

VII

POPE JULIUS DIED, and his heirs requested Michelangelo to complete the tomb which he had begun during the Pope's lifetime. The times were tragic. War and pestilence ravaged the land. Buildings were torn down, paintings were demolished, and bronze statues, including some of Michelangelo's best works, were melted into cannon. But Michelangelo, in spite of all these discouragements, went on. New Popes were elected, ruled, and died; new wars came and devastated the country; new promises were made and broken; and throughout it all Michelangelo continued with his work on the monument. Illness came and still further ravaged his none-too-prepossessing features. Disappointments seared more and more deeply into his ravaged soul. But his fingers, fashioned by God for the creation of beauty, went on with their inspired labor. He was accused of laziness, self-interest, dishonesty. His rivals insinuated that he was being bribed by the owners of the Carrara quarries to purchase their marble for his commissions. The accusation was, of course, baseless. But Michelangelo's patrons listened to the evil tongues and compelled him to get the inferior marble of Saravezza. Michelangelo, "a lowly, impoverished, crazy human being," as he described himself at this time, went on with his monument and confided his bitterness and his vision to the silent marble figures that he was bringing into life. He has given us a vivid portrait of himself at the age of forty-seven—short curly hair, a forehead wrinkled with the furrows of suffering, thoughtful, penetrating, yet haunted eyes, narrow lips compressed into a defiant firmness, a short straggly black beard, and the entire face dominated by the broad, flat, broken nose—the features of a man who has known cynicism and sorrow, rebellion and beauty, stubbornness and resignation, the face of a satyr and a saint.

For twenty-three years he went on with his work on the monument, this lonely god lost in the world of men. The plague carried off his

favorite brother and came near to costing him his own life. It was almost
impossible, as he tells us in one of his sonnets, to struggle on:

> In thraldom such as this, in such disgust,
> With plans miscarried, spirit tossed and torn—
> And then strike fire from marble, if you can!

But even under these circumstances he succeeded in striking fire from
the marble. At last, at the age of seventy, he finished the monument of
Pope Julius II. The central figure of the monument is the statue of Moses
—"the supreme achievement," as it has been called, "of modern sculpture." This statue is half god, half man, a perfect blending of Christianity
and paganism. Two horns protrude from the narrow skull. He is seated,
and his beard descends like a tangled vine from his face to his knees. His
huge knotted arms are bare, and one of his hands, strong, vibrant, sensitive, rests upon the tablet of the law. His right foot is planted firmly
upon the pedestal, and his left foot is thrown back as if he is ready to
rise and to thunder forth his commandments to a disobedient people.
And there is thunder, too, in the fierceness of his eye and the angry
projection of his lower lip. It is passion held back but ready, upon the
least provocation, to burst into fury. The terrible prophet of an angry
God, the judgment of the superman upon the folly and the savagery of
mankind.

And at this time Michelangelo himself, like Moses, pronounced judgment upon the folly and the savagery of mankind. He painted the *Last
Judgment* upon the walls of the Sistine Chapel. This painting is a companion piece to the *Creation* which, a quarter of a century earlier, he had
painted upon the ceiling of that chapel. Again, as of old, he painted most
of his figures naked. "This work," said one of the cardinals, "is fit for a
tavern, not for a chapel." And when the Pope suggested that Michelangelo
cover those figures with draperies the artist replied bluntly: "Let His
Holiness attend to the souls of the people and let *me* attend to the bodies."

The *Last Judgment* is the painting of an innumerable swarm of human
beings—the world—whirled along in a dizzy maelstrom around the figure
of Christ. And Christ in this painting is not the God of Love but the
God of Vengeance. He had come once to redeem the world, and the
world had rejected Him. He now comes again, but this time to *judge*
the world. There is now no pity in His judgment. There is only implacable justice, tempestuous grandeur, majestic force. The Virgin stands
sorrowfully and helplessly by, with her eyes averted, as her Son waves
the trembling multitude to their last place of retribution—a handful of
them upward to their heavenly reward, the vast majority of them downward, to their eternal damnation. The everlasting struggle between
Heaven and Hell. The history of the Human Race. The symbolical repre-
sentation of the inexorable destiny of Man.

One day, as he was working on the *Last Judgment*, he fell from the scaffolding and severely hurt his leg. Discouraged over the accident, he crawled home and shut himself up to die. But a doctor climbed in through the window and nursed him back to health. He returned to his enormous task and completed it on Christmas Eve, 1541.

VIII

MICHELANGELO FINISHED the *Last Judgment* at the ripe old age of sixty-six. He was rich now and famous and the envy of all the artists of the world. Yet he was more unhappy than ever. For he had to pay the penalty of a long life—the loss of his dearest friends, one by one. Within a very short time three of them died. The first was a boy of fifteen, a young artist whom the childless Michelangelo had loved with the tenderness of a father. The second was the boy's uncle, Riccio, Michelangelo's financial adviser and most ardent admirer. "This man," he said, "was to me more than a brother." But the greatest of all was the third blow—the death of Vittoria Colonna. This brilliant and beautiful mystic was the only woman who had shown more than mere admiration for Michelangelo. For years they had interwoven their sentiments toward each other into a garland of letters and sonnets which are among the treasures of Italian literature. And then, suddenly, his belated dream of love came to an abrupt end. As he stood by the body of the woman he had idolized but had never embraced he took her cold hand and kissed it. "Nothing," he later confided to one of his intimate apprentices, "grieves me more than the fact that, even on her deathbed, I dared to kiss only her hand and not her lips."

And thus was the lonely old artist deprived of his last chance at mortal happiness. The death of Vittoria Colonna brought about a breakdown in his health. For weeks he lay critically ill. His great life was apparently nearing its end.

But he recovered. For his labor was not yet completed. He was to give the world one more masterpiece—considered by many the greatest of all his masterpieces—before the final summons came. He was seventy-three years old when the Pope asked him to design the new dome for St. Peter's. He refused. For he felt too old to undertake so tremendous a task. But the Pope insisted, and finally Michelangelo consented—on one condition. He would receive no pay for this work. At most he would be able to give only a few months to this task, perhaps a year or two if the fates would be unusually kind to him. How much longer could a man of seventy-three be expected to summon the physical and the mental vigor necessary for so tremendous an undertaking?

And so, with this reservation, he undertook the job. The Pope died and four other Popes after him—and Michelangelo was still busy at the task. For sixteen years he kept at it, the power of his body and his mind undiminished to the end. Finally, at the age of eighty-nine, he rested from his labor.

But not altogether. He spent the last months of his life designing and hewing out the statues for his own monument. There were to be four statues in all—Christ taken down from the cross, supported by the Madonna, who in turn is sustained by the helping hands of Mary Magdalen and Nicodemus. The face of Nicodemus is covered by a heavy cowl. But the features showing through the cowl are the grief-stricken features of Michelangelo. Years ago, at the beginning of his career, he had represented himself as a fellow conqueror of David. Now, at the end, he depicted himself as a fellow sufferer of Jesus.

On February 12, 1564, he stood all day working on the figure of Christ. On the fourteenth he went out on horseback in a pelting rain. Four days later, still in his full consciousness, he died.

On his deathbed he regretted, not the cessation of his life, but the end of his labors. "I am dying," he said to Cardinal Salviati, who was ministering to him, "when I have scarcely got through learning the A B C of art. I was just getting ready for my real work!"

IMPORTANT DATES IN THE LIFE OF
MICHELANGELO BUONARROTI

1475—March 6, born at Caprese.

1488—Apprenticed to Domenico Ghirlandajo.

1489—Came under influence of Lorenzo de' Medici.

1504—Completed statue of *David*.

1505—Called to Rome by Julius II.

1508-14—Decorated the Sistine Chapel.

1528—Helped in the fortification of Florence.

1529—Enlisted in the defence of Florence.

1537—Began painting of the *Last Judgment*.

1538—Friendship began with Vittoria Colonna.

1541—Finished painting of the *Last Judgment*.

1547—Appointed architect of St. Peter's.

1564—February 18, died at Rome.

Martin Luther

1483–1546

PEASANTS in those days had coats of arms like kings. Family arms, a poor man's fleur-de-lys. Old Luther, a miner in Thuringia, had his hovel-heraldry. It was a hammer on a block of granite, the symbol of a medieval Thor in the German forest. The god of lightning and thunder hovered over Old Luther's forest hut. And here a new Siegfried was born. His name was Martin.

Martin Luther lived through a boyhood "without joy or beauty or love." His father had no time for soft affection. He grappled all day long with metals in the earth. His mother hardly saw the sunlight, for her face was in the cupboard and the pots. When Martin stole a hazelnut, she beat him till the blood flowed.

He could not find his way out of the forest. No one had found the way out for fifteen hundred years. A forest full of darkness and superstitions and fears. Martin carried his fears like welts across his back. He could not strike out against them, for nobody showed him anything tangible to strike. There was just enough light to see the shadows of things; and Martin looked upon the shadows as the things themselves. When he asked for information, the old wives shrieked horribly into their cooking pots about the devil. "Every tree is a devil," ready to seize the first poor soul who wanders too far from his hut. His mother terrified him with her superstitious stories until his heart quaked. And then she sent him out to sing among the neighbors for his supper.

A rude, aching life! The entire world of the Middle Ages was imprisoned in a forest hut, waiting for the day when someone would arise to overthrow the demons who lurked among the shadows of the trees.

Martin sang and earned a little money for his folks. He acquired a smattering of Latin at the local seminary and then he entered the University at Eisenach. He studied law and seemed a little happier. For now he was receiving an answer to some of his questions. He was arriving at a just balance in the relationship between man and man.

But what about the relationship between man and God? One day he was walking in the forest with a friend. Suddenly a bolt of lightning laid his companion dead at his feet—in the middle of a sentence! It was destiny flashing her teeth in a savage laugh of thunder at the huge cosmic joke of justice. Martin Luther was terrified. The old wives' tales of his childhood came rushing back at him. Instinctively he took shelter in his studies. New lessons must be learned. New secrets must be probed. From the practice of law to the problems of religion. He took holy orders and entered the Augustinian monastery at Erfurt.

II

FOR TWENTY YEARS his ruddy honest face was like a beacon light in the gloom of the monastery. He was a man of all work. He swept out the cells, opened the church doors for morning and evening prayers, wound up the clock, washed the windows and begged alms for the Order. Yet throughout this period he remained unhappy. For his spirit had found no peace.

One morning he failed to emerge from his cell. The brothers came and knocked, but heard no stirring within. They broke open the door and found Fra Martin stretched out on the ground. He seemed near death. And one of the brothers saw, lying near him, a flute upon which Fra Martin was always fond of playing. With tears in his eyes the brother picked up the flute and piped a favorite melody of Luther's. And gradually Martin came back to life.

But not to happiness. Once in the silent watches of the night he went to the kindly Dr. Staupitz, Vicar-General of the monastery, and confessed to him that he was a monk without faith in the love of God. He knew only a God of anger and revenge. "The Lord acts in a frightful manner toward us! Who can serve Him if He strikes terror all around Him?"

And the Vicar-General replied patiently: "My son, learn to form a better judgment of God." A *Christian* judgment. "If He were not to act thus, how should He overcome the headstrong and the willful? He must guard against the tall trees, lest they pierce through the heavens."

Martin feared he was not a Christian. For he had no faith in his superior's words. The mystery was not so simple as all that.

In the year 1510 he was sent to Rome on a mission for the Order. And here the iconoclast came face to face with the idols of the Church. Rome—he declared—was a painted harlot, selling her charms to the highest bidder. The Holy See was "the center of fasts but not the center of faith." Martin Luther was stunned by the revelation. He had come into the stronghold of Christianity, and he had found no Christians there.

He returned to Germany and received an appointment to a professorship at the University of Wittenberg. And now, released from the extreme rigors of the monastic life, he had more time to think. The content of his thought, he confessed, was purely selfish. He did not care about reforming the world. He was merely uneasy in his own mind and wanted to save his own soul. He was an intelligent and honest student of life who had come to the conclusion that a man was a Christian not by birth but by conversion. And he wished to be converted to Christianity—that is, quite literally he wished to be converted to the religion of Christ. It is the genius of the prophets to be quite literal and quite personal in their religion. That is why they are so devastating. Here in Wittenberg stood a prophet squarely on his own feet. And a peddler came to challenge him until the whole world shook.

Here is how it happened: A number of agents, in the name of the Pope, were traveling over Christendom to collect funds for the repairing of the Church of St. Peter. By their contributions to the "holy treasury," explained these agents, the people could buy "indulgences"—that is, promissory notes upon God's mercy. An indulgence, said the papal agents, possessed the power to release a man's soul from purgatory into heaven.

Now one of these peddlers of indulgences came into the office of the Wittenberg professor and tried to explain to him the "principles" of this heavenly traffic in human salvation. Luther felt it only his duty to warn the people against this "fatuity . . . I began to preach mildly that all the indulgences in the world will not save a soul that is not repentant . . . I declared that the perfectly contrite soul is saved without indulgences. I told them that there is no episcopal power in the world which can insure to man his salvation."

And then he nailed to the door of the church at Wittenberg—a building similar to the American meetinghouse—ninety-five theses stating his conclusions about the matter. For now he knew the answer to his perplexity. Christianity must be justified by a new kind of faith—a faith engendered by the promptings of the heart and not by the prescriptions of the Church.

With the announcement of this credo the professor in the little town of Wittenberg started a world revolution.

III

THE CHRISTIAN WORLD was aghast. What right had this Augustinian upstart to tell an establishment of fifteen centuries' duration how to run its business? What Saxon effrontery! His head must have been turned with the drinking of too much beer!

The authorities wrote letters to the Holy Roman Emperor, Charles, to look into this matter of ecclesiastical insubordination. The verdict was decisive. A dangerous young radical with an unruly temper. Ordinarily the Inquisition could silence him quietly or chastise him publicly and be done with it. But too many "stupid people" were siding with him. It appeared that he had given vent to an idea which flourished like a hydra with a thousand heads. "No sooner do we destroy one thesis than two theses spring up in its place." What was to be done with this "Saxon sired by the devil"?

They sent word to him that he was not considered kindly at Rome. If he felt himself out of step with the world, let him at least keep his silence. Had he any right to force the world into tune with his own crazy harmony? Surely there were corrupt practices around him. But in what society had there been absolute honesty? Because certain churchmen were imperfect, was that any reason for overthrowing an institution that had saved Europe and had held it together for fifteen hundred years? "There are some foolish people who think that they alone know what is good for humanity. They alone propose to shoulder the responsibility for the entire human race—until they turn fifty. And then they feel only too thankful if they have succeeded in managing their own affairs."

Such was the spirit in which they tried to approach him. They pointed out the folly of his idea. And its futility. "Come, come, Martin, do you think that any prince will raise an army to defend you? Of course not! If you persist in your agitation, where will you remain in safety?"

"Under Heaven," replied Luther, and proceeded with the publishing of his theses and his tracts.

And the people all over Germany were convulsed with excitement and rushed for the polemics that streamed defiantly from his pen. Vicariously they suffered the danger of the outlaw. They thrilled to his forbidden words. Here was a man staking his life in the greatest gamble ever. But more: here was a German standing up to Rome. Princes, nobles, burghers —all alike were swept along in a wave of national feeling. "At Nuremberg, at Strasbourg, at Mayence, there is a constant struggle for his least pamphlets." And although the writings are banned, "the wet sheets are brought from the press under someone's cloak, and are passed along from shop to shop . . ."

He is in vast demand as a lecturer throughout the German provinces. Armed students guard his carriage as he travels from city to city.

And then the Pope pronounces the fatal sentence against him. "Martin Luther—excommunicated from the Church."

He feels no hatred against anybody—only a great emptiness. The fallen archangel felt no more keenly the emptiness of space through which he descended from the grace of his high estate. How fearless is the man who calls himself alone and mighty in the world—until the world takes up his challenge and compels him to live truly alone!

Doubt! "How much pain it has cost me, though I had the Scripture on my side . . . that I should dare to make a stand against the Pope . . . How many times do I not ask myself with bitterness the same question . . . Are you alone wise? Can everybody else be so mistaken? Can so many ages have been mistaken? How will it be if after all you are wrong?" On the side of those who excommunicated him—"learning, genius, numbers, grandeur, rank, power, sanctity, miracles! . . . On that side the sanction of so many centuries, noble martyrs, academies, councils, bishops, pontiffs . . . On my side—Wycliffe and Lorenzo Valla—and Luther, a poor creature, a man of yesterday, standing well-nigh solitary with a few friends . . ."

Excommunicated. Well, he came from a tough people who had toiled for centuries in the darkness of the mines. They too had been excommunicated from the sun. Yet they lived to work on. "Let the notice of excommunication go into the fire!" He burns it. He feels strong again. He grins defiantly with lips full of soot and ashes. Here in the burning fire was light for him. Vulcan, too, had forged his finest weapons by this light and had found his place by the other gods. Is Martin Luther no longer a priest? A battlecry is stirred by the bellows of his heart into a flame on his lips. "We are all priests, each man with his own Bible, ordained by the grace of God alone, in the great crucible of His suffering . . ."

IV

THE EMPEROR summoned Luther to Worms, where he was to be tried on the charge of heresy. "I promise that no violence will be done to your person while you remain there." But of what value was the promise of an emperor?

However, Luther called for his carriage, took his flute, and played constantly to assuage the pains in his stomach—for he was now suffering from chronic ulcers. "Music is the art of the prophets."

From town to town he rode like a conquering hero. He sang hymns with the peasants, drank beer with the burghers, received honors from the princes. All the solid people saluted this solid man with good cheer on the way. One morning he preached at Erfurt, and the little church was overcrowded long before the hour of his arrival. The pains in his stomach were severe. At Eisenach he was tempted to turn back and to get into bed. But for the time being the pains diminished. A few days later they attacked him again. But he went on. He received from his admirers a picture of the martyr Savonarola and kissed it fervently. At Plifflingheim, on the outskirts of Worms, he blessed a peasant who was planting an elm by the wayside. And then his eyes caught sight of the hills and the turrets of the fatal city just beyond. What a mighty fortress! And then an inspiration came to him and he burst out into song—a defiant hymn that was to become the battlecry of the Reformation, *Eine feste Burg ist unser Gott*. Our Lord, too, is a mighty fortress.

He entered Worms. The heralds conducted him along the byways in order to avoid the throngs that had assembled in the leading streets. Notwithstanding this precaution, there were numbers who had collected at the doors of the town hall. The surrounding housetops, too, were crowded with people who had come to see this "Doctor Martin who defied the Pope."

And now he was face to face with the Emperor Charles. He refused to kneel down as was expected of a monk, even of an excommunicated monk. He stood unperturbed, as the courtroom was hushed.

Around him were thronged the mightiest princes of Christendom. They grasped the massive handles of their swords as they waited for a word of heresy from his lips. They ordered him to recant. He asked them for a few hours to think over the order, to prepare his statement. And then he stood once more facing the emperor. "One rebuke from him, and it might just as well be all over." Yet Luther did not flinch as he spoke:

"Since his Imperial Majesty requires a simple and straightforward answer, here it is . . . Unless I am overcome with the testimony of the Scripture or with clear and transparent reasons, I will and shall not recant a single word, for it is wicked and dangerous to act contrary to conscience."

The emperor was taken aback. He had expected something different. Apologetic words. Not this quiet and honest avowal of a personal belief. "Here I am . . . I cannot do otherwise. God help me. Amen."

The emperor had promised him a temporary safe conduct. Relying upon this promise, Luther ordered his carriage and started back for Wittenberg. Whereupon Charles issued an imperial decree. "Death to anyone who offers asylum to Martin Luther from the day on which his safe conduct expires . . . From that day, let all persons be enjoined to watch for him and to seize him and to place him in safe custody until justice shall decide what must be done with him."

In the thickest part of the Thuringian forest a number of horsemen intercepted the outlaw. These men were not the agents of the emperor. They were the friends of Martin Luther. They had come to abduct him and to place him in safe keeping. The Elector of Saxony had been won over to the cause of a Saxon heart.

V

LUTHER SPENT a whole summer and autumn and winter in the castle of Wartburg as guest of the Elector. But so far as the world and the Roman party knew, he might have been swallowed up in the darkness.

Secure in the fortress of Wartburg, he played his flute and sang his German psalms. Daily his table was provided with game and with plenty of Rhenish wine of which he was very fond. And with bags of sweetmeats and nuts. "One evening when I had retired to my chamber, extinguished the light and got into bed, it seemed to me all at once that the nuts had come to life, jumping about in the sack, knocking violently against each other. They came to the side of my bed to make noises at me! . . ."

Everything here was fantastic. He wrote letters to his friends and addressed them "from the region of the air"—"from amidst the singing birds." Here was a world of Merlin's enchantment. And it was a magic that threatened to destroy the entire world.

In the meantime he had started upon a daring work—he took the Holy Bible which only the learned doctors could read and translated it into the German vernacular. "Let the common people read the Word of God for themselves," in order that they may learn to *think* for themselves. "No tariff on our brains." *Gedanken sind zollfrei.* Thought must be free! A born writer and orator, Martin Luther had developed a genius for "possessing the public." Calling to the common man in the national language, he addressed his pamphlets to *Herr Everybody.* Every man is a prince, an elected Son of God.

And then word reached him at Wartburg as to what *Herr Everybody* had been doing in his absence. Smashing the windows and the images in the Catholic churches, clubbing the priests, indulging in orgies of anarchy and riot, celebrating a Saturnalian carnival of bloodshed and murder in the name of liberty. He despatched letters to Wittenberg, pleading with his followers to desist from their violence. And finally, when he realized that only his personal presence might avail to check them, he left Wartburg in secret without asking the permission of his protector. He laid aside his pilgrim's staff for a rider's whip. For he was returning to a world of violence, to chastise a race of men who had never understood the battles of the spirit.

But he had unwittingly started an avalanche of discontent. The forces which his philosophy had liberated were entirely out of the hands of any one man. The revolt against the Pope had spread from Germany to the lowlands and through most of the countries of the North. Burghers and nobles alike had taken up arms against the Church. "What are Zwingli, Melanchthon, Erasmus to these legions of warriors, madmen, and saints?"

The entire world seemed headed toward civil war. But how could a hymn by Luther on his flute lead the armies who looked for a Caesar? "What sprang from the soul of this religious lyricist was a poem. It was not a plan of action."

His followers came to him and demanded that he organize a new Church. And he smiled at them—or frowned—depending on his mood. What had been his doctrine in its crudest form? "God wills that we eat, drink, and be merry. . . . He asks only that we acknowledge Him for our Lord, and thank Him for His gifts."

Rauch und Dampf! All this idol-smashing and hair-splitting—nothing but smoke and vapor. These people pushed and hauled and challenged him—for what? To build a new world institution? But he was interested only in the world of the spirit.

Nonetheless he draws up the platform for a Protestant Church. He does not desire to establish a uniform church with an official dogma. He is not interested in the external ritual of the Mass. "Let German hymns be sung . . . Let the priests be elected by the suffrage of the people . . . All the people may teach the Word of God, may administer baptism, may consecrate the bread and the wine."

And the battlecry spread among the Lutherans—"Masses in German. Sausages on Friday." But soon there were matters of a more revolutionary nature. The Protestant princes began to confiscate the property of the Catholic orders. Monks were marrying nuns turned loose from the convents. And the nuns who still remained within the walls were encouraged to escape and to take husbands. They flocked by the hundreds to Wittenberg to seek the protection of Martin Luther. "I yesterday received nine nuns who had emancipated themselves from their captivity in the monastery of Nimpschen." "The Duchess of Montsberg has escaped, almost by a miracle, from the convent of Freyburg. She is now in my house, with two other girls." "The unfortunate Elizabeth von Reinsberg, who was expelled from the Seminary of Altenberg, having now nothing to live on, has addressed herself to me." "I am head over ears in business."

The "Reformation" was no longer simply a reform in religion. It had become nothing less than a social revolution. The German peasants, having slumbered for ages under the weight of feudal oppression, "had heard the learned men and the princes speak of liberty, and now they applied to themselves that which was not designed to extend to them." The tyranny of the feudal seigneurs was "based upon the authority of the Roman Church." Waving a boot over their heads—the emblem of their revolt—the peasants raised their rallying cry, *Bundschuh, Bundschuh,* and called for a war against the nobility. Down with the tithes and the taxes and the game laws! Up with the new order! "Every laborer is entitled to the wages of his labor." Crush all authority! "Jesus Christ by His precious blood redeemed all men without exception, the herdsman equally with the emperor."

The leaders of the peasants came to Martin Luther and asked him to support their cause. And Luther warned them to negotiate their dispute peacefully. To the nobles he addressed a letter: "It is your crimes that God is about to punish." To the peasants—"No violence!" He pleaded with all his eloquence. "How, my friends, I ask you, has it happened that neither the Emperor nor the Pope has been able to effect anything against me? I have never drawn the sword." But his words were lost in the tumult. This was no time to listen to a professor. "Impractical fellows, these teachers who seek to build a world with love. Can't be done." The nobles, on their part, took a terrible revenge. They smashed the peasants with an iron fist.

But it was not the nobles against whom Martin Luther's anger had been aroused. It was the peasants, the toilers of the Black Forest, the common folk in whom he had placed his trust. In them he had planted the birth and the death, the flesh and the blood, of an ideal. But now his love had turned to the cold implacable hatred of a lover who had been betrayed. Martin Luther could never forget or forgive the uprising of this lower stratum of *Herr Everybody*. The mind of the lover was fanatical, unbalanced. The aching of the heart had thumped away all reason. Madness seized him. He had leveled the Saxon forest. But where was the sun?

VII

THERE ARE two kinds of suns. The one is a star that shines over great worlds and events. The other is a radiance whose area of influence is undimensional. It pours into a private world of two people in love. It brightens the inside of a hut when the whole out-of-doors is raining. Martin Luther in the last flight of his years received a goodly portion of the second sun. His hut had become bright within; for—sublime blasphemy! —he had torn off his monk's robes and had taken the holiest of sacraments, a wife. He, an excommunicated monk; she, a runaway nun! Together they had left God's monastery to build a family of love.

Now he lived at last the "normal life which God had given to man." He learned the mechanic's trade, made watches, cultivated a garden. He became very poor; oftentimes his children were sick. He sat at the head of the table and carved the meat and bantered his friends and blessed his wife and took the good and the evil without a shrug. Many of his friends, especially those who were ambitious for him, grieved over the feebleness of his declining years. "Fatness had invaded the lower part of his face." His more timid acquaintances shuddered at the coarse jokes with which he was wont to spice his conversation. He had become a very common fellow, they complained. He was no longer formidable to his enemies. Yet his enemies knew better. Here was a sinner crossing swords with the saints to determine which of them in the future would control the human race.

There were times when he had not as much as eight florins in his pocket. But he had an infinity of love in his heart. When the plague broke out in Wittenberg, his house became a regular hospital for all the homeless sufferers. His little daughter, Elizabeth, was too ill to speak. For the last twelve days she had not tasted a morsel. "This is no time for me to read or to write or to do anything at all." God help the enemies of the Reformation! For here was an Augustinian monk who knelt weeping by the dying body of his little daughter, reaping tears and suffering out of the creation of his own flesh and blood. This is the very triumph of the human spirit—the martyrdom out of which new great ideas are born.

Luther had retired from the field. He declared that he was "no longer a man of action." But was that an anticlimax, a cause for disappointment? When the princes banded themselves together into a Protestant

League and prepared to wage war against the Catholics, he had but one word for them—"Assassins." But they could not possibly understand him. "Assassins" did not ring so very harshly in their ears. For they had never created an ideal of their own, and so they had no scruples about assassinating the ideal of their neighbors. They were ready to strike down the divine right of popes and to institute in its place the divine right of kings. They were prepared to torment the world with a half century of religious wars and murders.

No wonder Martin Luther kept much sharp wine in his cellar. For wine makes a jest out of sadness. And he was privy to the great cosmic paradox at last.

IMPORTANT EVENTS IN THE LIFE OF MARTIN LUTHER

1483—November 10, born at Eisleben, Saxony.

1501—Entered University of Erfurt.

1505—Received degree of M.A.

1505—Entered Augustinian monastery at Erfurt.

1507—Ordained priest.

1508—Appointed professor of philosophy at University of Wittenberg.

1511—Made journey to Rome.

1512—Returned to Wittenberg. Made doctor of theology.

1517—Issued his 95 theses against the orthodox creed.

1519—Held famous debate with Eck.

1520—Excommunicated from Church.

1520—His writings burned.

1521—Went on trial at Diet of Worms.

1521—Escaped to Wartburg; translated *New Testament* into German.

1525—Married Katharina von Bora.

1529—Prepared new church service.

1532—Translated *Old Testament* into German.

1534—Publication of Lutheran translation of Bible.

1546—February 18, died at Eisleben.

Saint Ignatius of Loyola

1491–1556

IN THE YEAR 1553, August 4, the eve of the feast of Our Lady of the Snows, while Saint Ignatius was in the garden," wrote Father Gonzalez, "I began to give him an account of my soul . . . An hour or two later we went to dinner, and while Master Polancus and I were dining with him, Saint Ignatius said that Master Natalis and others of the Society had often asked him to give a narrative of his life, but he had never as yet decided to do so."

Gradually, however, "God had enlightened" the Founder of the Society of Jesus. He became inclined at last to dictate his autobiography. "In the following September he called me, and began to relate his whole life clearly and distinctly with all the accompanying circumstances . . . Father Natalis was overjoyed that a beginning had been made, and told me to urge Saint Ignatius to complete it, often saying to me, 'In no other way can you do more good to the Society.' . . . Afterward in the same month, he called me three or four times, and told me the history of his life up to the time of his dwelling at Manresa . . .'"

For two years Ignatius dictated his life to Gonzalez. There were numerous interruptions. Again and again, "after saying Mass I went to ask him if it were the time." The Pope became ill and the narrative was postponed until the election of a new Pope, "who died after the election." In the summer time, Gonzalez remarks ruefully, "the biography did not make much progress on account of the heat." In the winter time, "colleges for the Society must be established, and ambassadors must be received."

But when the disciple caught from his master a few precious moments of leisurely dictation he was duly rewarded, indeed overwhelmed. "The method followed by Saint Ignatius is so clear that he places vividly before our eyes the events of the past . . . It was not necessary to ask him anything, as nothing important was omitted . . . While taking these notes I tried to see the expression on his face, and kept drawing near to him . . ."

II

IT IS the reign of Ferdinand and Isabella. The Spanish nobility is a flashing blade in the scabbard of international knighthood. Do not let them deceive you with their thin faces white as the winding-sheet. Their veins boil blood. Their hearts are seething crucibles in which the flesh of all they touch is transmuted into the spirit of all they worship. They are violently in love with love, and they are unafraid of death. From the pleasures of a romance under the stars they go without a shrug to a duel of vengeance in the courtyard. For one moment of ecstasy before the lady of the crucifix they will carry the sword over the world and die anyhow and anywhere in her service.

Let us therefore not be amazed at the story of a soldier turned into a saint. The pendulum of the Spaniard's temperament swings easily from the spirited to the spiritual.

Ignatius of Loyola is home from the wars a casualty. A French bullet has lodged in his thigh. Not a shudder, not a sound from his lips as they reset his shattered leg. He is a nobleman. The military tradition runs strong in his family and disinfects all pain. He looks impassively on and dreams of better days when he will limp his way back to the king's court, carrying a love sonnet at the point of his sword and a kiss for a cheek behind a fan. His ancestors have fought the Moors and his own brothers have fallen in battle for no more than this.

Ignatius had followed these warriors in the courtly tradition. As a boy he had been taken away from his parents, to be educated under the guidance of the Secretary of the King's Treasury. He had been baptized in the fires of knighthood. And now he had injured a leg in the knight's routine. Limb by limb, he would offer himself through battle to the Goddess of Love. And when his heart grew weary of her blandishments, he would commit it with a prayer to a soldier's grave.

They repair his wounded leg. As he lies convalescing in his castle, he asks for a book to read—*Amadis of Gaul*—the exciting story of a knight. But the book is not at hand. Instead, his attendants bring him a book of a far different content—*The Flower of the Saints*. He opens the pages of the book. Saints? There is a sneer on his lips. Why waste his time upon those who beat their flesh in prayer, instead of risking it in a fight?

But he reads the book through to the end. And slowly he shares the battles of religion with these strange warriors of Christ. When he turned the final page, he lay back and pondered. These saints were *knights like himself!* They, too, had fought against whole armies—not of Frenchmen, but of the aggressive spirits of temptation and evil. They, too, had thrilled to the sights and the sounds that raised a soldier's blood! The flashing of

heavenly visitations, the cannon roar of God's voice in the conscience.
The artillery skirmishes of the awakened soul.

He closed his eyes and dreamed. He found himself on a barren and
wind-blasted wasteland where—holy miracle!—a crucifix of roses grew.
And now he realized that his love was for one woman only. For in his
dream, tending the crucifix of roses, was Mother Mary.

He got up from his bed hearty and well. With the ardor of a Spanish
lover he pressed his courtship.

III

HIS FAMILY sensed, when he left his bed, that a strange change had taken
place in him. When he told them that he was not taking the road back
to the king's court, they were uneasy. "Don't do anything unworthy of
your ancestors," they begged. And he nodded his head. He would do
nothing unworthy of his ancestors of the Gospel—the men who dated far
beyond the history of Loyola. First of all, like Saint Francis before him, he
gave his rich clothing to a beggar. And then he started on his adventure
of religious knight-errantry.

To Manresa, a little town on the way to Barcelona, he came. And he
entered a hospital to tend the sick and the dying. In a cave he prayed
and saw deeply into himself. He fasted and flagellated himself and tried
hard to wear his body down to the point where it might reveal his soul.
He was a little man in stature, only five feet two. His girth grew more
scanty and his frame more spare until the good fathers of the hospital
begged him to desist from his ascetic practices and to leave a little of
himself for the service of the world. And so he took to food and drink
and put on health again.

He had entered a darkened cave on the hillside of Manresa, a hermit
seeking God in his loneliness. He emerged "filled with the presence of
God" and with the conviction that he must teach his fellow men. With
the energy of the soldier he had drilled himself into a saint. And now
that he was a saint, he found that he had surrendered none of the im-
petuosity of the soldier. The life of his spirit was but the consummation
of the life of his body. It was the properly organized body fighting and
dying under the generalship of the will.

And now he wrote out his first teaching—the explanation of the steps
whereby all novices-at-arms and sinners and kitchen cooks and vagabonds
might find their way to God. He called his book a *Manual of Exercise.*
"As walking, marching and running are bodily exercise, so the different
methods of preparing and disposing the soul . . . with the object of se-
curing its salvation, are spiritual exercise." He prescribed not only the
attitudes of the mind but the positions of the body for prayer. He enumerated the subjects of speculation to joust with, the vices to hurdle, the
virtues to pursue, before the final laurel wreath for the spirit is won.

Here was no corpulent and stationary friar with the "frosty stars" in his eyes—the church was filled to overflowing with these obese consciences. Ignatius was a lean-limbed, active knight-at-arms riding like the wind; and on his crest the strenuous motto, *Gymnasticize thyself unto Godliness!*

IV

BUT he did not go tilting at windmills. He was a realistic knight. He decided to educate himself, to make himself learned in Greek and Latin, to become perhaps a doctor. Then to preach. But first he made the holy pilgrimage to Jerusalem. Then he returned to Spain and entered a college to commence his education.

But he could not stay silent in a cell of learning! His blood was hot under the Barcelona skies. The cross must have a voice. He burst the bounds of the classroom and went begging of each person he met in the market place for the alms of a few precious moments of his time. He found his way into houses where citizens were not behaving just right, and pricked them like a gadfly into better ways. He spoke of how he felt about Jesus, poked around "mending like an old wife," drawing little knots of exalted listeners to him, walking in and out of masses, asking questions, bringing comfort.

The professors were annoyed. A fledgling student, disgracing the dignity and the aristocracy of the University. He was not yet a priest. What right had he to preach and to *reform* people? On whose authority? A dangerous radical.

Well, in cases such as this the Church had a "board of inquiry" to protect itself . . . The Inquisition. An instrument that probed deep and discovered any poison lurking in the religious body of the day.

They summoned Ignatius and put him into prison. A professor of the University paid a visit to the young student who had so boldly "discoursed about spiritual matters." And he came away strangely moved. Drawing close to a friend of his, he whispered—so low that no one in authority could overhear him—"Have you seen Ignatius of Loyola?" And then he continued, "I have just seen—Paul, in chains."

Finally they released this little "trouble-maker, no taller than a child," and sent him on his way. And this way led to Paris and the famous University where he hoped to do his work in peace. He collected a few of his books with the care of a peddler whose wares might buy him his final meal. He slung all his education on his back and walked barefoot and bowed. It was a long walk, right into the "heart of the enemy country"; for Spain had entered upon another of her interminable wars with France. Yet the agile little salesman of God's mercy no longer bothered about the mighty military passions of men. He took his food and his drink in the poorest quarters and gossiped about the quiet humble things. And finally, after dawdling and dreaming and consorting with the quiet humble people and counting his rosary a thousand times, he arrived at his destination.

But no sooner has he sat down to listen to the learned Parisian professors than he feels the impulse to jump up and to *act*. It is apparent he will never become "the greatest of scholars." His mind stutters over abstract theory. He has too much influence over people to bind himself to the companionship of books. Once again his soldier's blood is up. He has outraged the dignity of the University. He leaves the halls of the learned and becomes a sort of mendicant friar, a street-beggar with his name enrolled in the most efficient of all educational institutions—God's world. He begs indeed—for another sentence in prison!

Men are fascinated by his voice, even though it is not dressed up in the most precise grammar. Men are held by an eye that flashes the command of a warrior mind. Women are melted at the touch of his ideas. Not a thousand books written by his learned colleagues, who have washed their hands of him, can produce the number of converts made by a single one of his sermons. His is truly a *creative* art.

Young men of fortune, family, and ideals draw near him. Like himself, they are active and restless and ready for a crusade. They feel uneasy without being able to define the source of their disease. There is an odor of deadly putrefaction in the air. The smell of disintegrating hearts.

Instinctively they gather around Ignatius to form a little society. They hearken back to the spirit of the first chivalric orders—to the times when members of the same blood formed a clan against the common foe. They behold a great schism in the soul of things. They know that they are a green island of faith in a great dead sea. They take their vows of loyalty together at Notre Dame de Montmartre in the middle of August, 1534. And then they step outside. What are they going to do with their mighty numbers, seven in all! They cannot change the world. Yet they feel sanctified. They have pooled all their resources for a common adventure. But where?

One day Ignatius knelt in prayer in a little chapel and a vision of Christ came to him. The voice of the Saviour said, "In Rome I will be favorable to you." And so Ignatius called together his little company and set foot for the Eternal City. Their way was clear.

V

THE LIFE OF IGNATIUS met history with a mighty impact at the intersection of the Eternal City. The meaning of his own destiny in the universal pattern came upon his mind in a flash from the Mind of the Weaver. Always he had been meant to be a *battler* for religion. And at this moment a mighty battle was raging. The sacred institution of the papacy had been rocked to its foundations by the revolt of Martin Luther. The Holy Father needed help if he were going to survive—help not from his *meek* but from his *militant* children. This was an age of armed camps and of mobile armies. The old orders—Franciscans, Augustinians, and Carthusians—were the noncombatant organizers of morale on the home front. But Ignatius conceived the plan for a new order of monks to serve in the front line of the Pope's command. They would be the skirmish troops in the vast war area of the spirit.

He petitioned Pope Paul III to endorse his volunteers of Montmartre under the name of the *Society of Jesus*. This new company would not settle down to lead a sedentary life in a monastery, devoting itself to meditation and prayer; it would "stand with one foot poised ready for instant action." It would rove all over the world at the orders of Paul III, responsible to him alone—his special guard, spreading the Catholic banners wherever the heathen lived, restoring the faith wherever it had receded or wasted away.

Gradually in the mind of Ignatius, out of the ruins of old Rome, this idea of a new Rome took living shape. His troops would enlist in a new crusade. Scouts of the flaming word! "In war, scouts do not serve less than the soldiers who fight, nor do the engineers who make subterranean mines do less to undermine the strength of the enemy than those who, when the walls are down, make the assault . . . I see our men, a light cavalry who hold themselves ready to resist the enemy, to attack them and to retire, and to go skirmishing now in one place and now in another," with the mightiest weapons in the arsenal—teaching, preaching, proselytizing . . . The first mobile company in the service of Christ. Wherever there are heathen, there Ignatius will send his legion of priests. A legion free from all ties of place and country, taking the vows of poverty and chastity, sworn to "forlorn, solitary, unnamed" adventure. A fighting, suffering, international legion of faith.

The Pope and his counselors listened politely. But they were frankly skeptical and weary of a new monkhood. Several of the old orders had changed from their original purity of ideals, "giving way to new formulae for loose-living." The scandals of many of these friars of the Church had been explosive material for Martin Luther's propaganda. Yes, the blueprint of a new order always measured strictly up to the ideal. But how about the material and the structure of the finished building? How much rotten wood and rough edges, how many faulty foundations? The authorities knew practically nothing about the qualifications of this architect. What schooling had he in building? Had he ever reared grand cathedrals, or even a peasant's hut to withstand the first onslaught of the weather?

The Pope looked dubious; but Ignatius soon melted away all the perplexities of his mind. And cautiously he permitted the "madcap of Loyola" to clear the ground and to try his hand. "Nothing grandiose, you understand." The building must be a modest one-story model. The enrollment of the Order must be restricted to sixty members and no more. On September 27, 1540, Paul III took his pen and signed his consent to the petition. And the Society of Jesus was born.

VI

FOR SIXTEEN YEARS another Caesar sat in Rome directing his legions. But he was a new kind of Caesar—a man who "consolidated an empire without territory." He did not receive twenty-three dagger wounds. He did not even ask for a crown. When his army of priests made him their general, he accepted the distinction with a quite un-Roman humility. He performed the duties of a kitchen boy.

Yet the Roman state had never stood more firmly behind a Caesar than did this Society of Jesus. The Jesuit priests—as their enemies had dubbed them—marched forward under the motto: *It is necessary to obey but not to live.* Loyola inculcated in each one of his cohorts the soldier's ideal of obedience as a "science and an art to be excelled in."

At first he had prepared his followers for a pilgrimage to Jerusalem. But later he realized that there was a far greater crusade for him to fight. "Heaven closed the door of Palestine to open up the Universe."

The Pope had canceled all restrictions as to the size of the Society, and its numbers had multiplied by leaps and bounds. Forward rolled the great wave of "the counter-revolution against the Lutherans." To Switzerland and Poland and Ireland and Germany Loyola sent his fighters—and everywhere the two hosts ranged themselves under the Bible and the Ikon, and stood ready for combat. The Pope and the Catholic princes had large armies to end the matter—if need be—with the sword. But in many cases the word was stronger. Into the fortresses of the enemy went the Jesuits preaching, and by their propaganda they paved the way for the final attack. A word might stagger an army and win the battle. Psychological warfare can take a continent.

Loyola became a master of this psychological warfare. It was the vow of obedience taken by each priest that served as the very root and fiber of Loyola's plan of conquest. This plan was one and indivisible and not the product of many minds. The "united mind" was Rome. "I am not my own," each Jesuit vowed. "I am His who created me, and His who stands in His place, to manage and govern me as soft wax is moulded. In the first place, I must make myself like a dead body which has neither will nor sense. In the second place, like a little crucifix, which can be turned from one side to the other. In the third place, I must make myself like a staff in the hand of an old man, so that he can place it where he pleases, and so that it can best aid him."

And yet the government of the Jesuits was not a despotism. The obedience of its members was not the passive obedience given to the ancient Caesar. On the contrary, it was an active, aggressive, and willing obedience, entered into freely and proudly, with a modern saint. Not the subservient fidelity of the slave to the master, but the equal fidelity of all to all in a common cause.

Ignatius drew up for the society a constitution which limited his own power and in certain matters gave the widest discretion to the power of his followers. In general, there were two classes of membership—the clerics and the regulars. And, among the clerics, only a chosen few of the so-called *Professed* took a special vow to the Pope and dedicated themselves to the more hazardous tasks of conversion. The other members devoted themselves to the less dangerous work of education. But all were prepared to follow a single aim. "In this school we are taught to acquire a rich poverty, a free slavery, a glorious humility." Within the ranks there was a strict sense of democracy. No man was less great than another.

They took the vows of chastity and of poverty and held no benefices. They expected no reward for their services and refused to accept anything from the world. Unlike the other orders, they wore no uniform dress to distinguish themselves. For by remaining outwardly anonymous they could the better carry out their secret errands. No outward physical emblem, but an inward moral badge. *Ad Majorem Dei Gloriam—To the Greater Glory of God.*

And there was need at that time for the Jesuits to re-establish the glory of God. Piety for too many of their Catholic brethren had lost its original meaning. Virtue had come to be identified with virtuosity, prayer with pretentiousness, welfare with wealth. "What, is Paradise shut off from those who have no money?" taunted Martin Luther and his followers who had broken away from the Church.

And the Jesuits gave answer—not only in word but in action—bringing everywhere the mercy of God, toiling over difficult terrain, dying under a portion of the sky they had never seen before, restoring lost faiths, reviving dead hopes—"a spectacle to angels and men."

And the general of it all sat with his staff of assistants building in his garden. Around him were the colors of the Italian landscape whose glory Raphael was at that very moment painting for eternity.

Ignatius felt that his was only a layman's eye. No artist he, but a mere artisan of faith. Could he too, like that painter of the divine in human form, establish a masterpiece that would last across the years? Could he foresee the words that would be spoken of his order three centuries later by the Protestant historian, Macaulay? "In spite of oceans and deserts . . . of spies and penal laws, of dungeons and rocks . . . the Jesuits will be found under every disguise, in every country; scholars, physicians, merchants, servingmen, in the hostile court of Sweden, in the old manor houses of Cheshire, among the hovels of Connaught. Arguing, instructing, consoling, animating the courage of the timid, holding up the crucifix before the eyes of the dying."

But Ignatius was not concerned about the praise he might receive. He was interested only in the service he could give.

VII

To THE FOUR CORNERS of the earth came the mission from the little garden in Italy where Ignatius sat drawing the plans for his battle of mercy. To the cities of China and the islands of Japan. To the Spanish provinces in North America, the Negro colonies in Cartagena, the Indian settlements in Paraguay, Mexico, Brazil. To the jungles of Africa, the plains of Hindustan, across the ranges of the Himalayas and into the frozen heights of Tibet.

And throughout the length and breadth of Europe. "We have come to fight the battle of faith against faithlessness." Relying upon the weapon of the mind in the arsenal of the spirit, they dotted Europe with "Roman camps of learning"—universities for Catholic education. They initiated thousands upon thousands into "all the secrets of knowledge," from the simplest grammar to the highest theology. Their Jesuit schools were the training ground of cardinals, emperors, popes. And of some of the world's greatest playwrights, philosophers, scientists, and soldiers—Molière, Descartes, Bossuet, Montesquieu, Galileo, Buffon, Wallenstein, to mention just a few.

And all these fruits of scholarship had been planted by a man whose own mistakes in grammar were such "as only a saint can expect to see forgiven, either in this world or in the next."

This unlearned "father of learning" had come to the rescue of his Church in her hour of decline. He put new breath into an institution that was threatened by "too much casuistry from without and too much complacency from within." For he inspired his followers with a saving idea: "Ambition, hope for preferment, is the mother of all evils." And his followers had the daring not only to *believe* but to *live* this idea.

IMPORTANT DATES IN THE LIFE OF
SAINT IGNATIUS OF LOYOLA

1491—December 24, born in Guipúzcoa, Spain.
1521—Wounded at siege of Pampeluna.
1522—Made religious pilgrimage to Montserrat.
1523—Made pilgrimage to Holy Land.
1524—Began to study Latin.
1528—Entered University of Paris.
1534—Received degree in theology.
1534—Founded Society of Jesus.
1537—Ordained as priest in Vienna.
1540—Society received approval of Pope Paul III.
1541—Elected first general of Society.
1548—Completed famous book of *Spiritual Exercises.*
1551—Founded Roman College.
1552—Founded German College.
1556—July 31, died in Rome.

Benvenuto Cellini

1500–1571

THE NAME *Benvenuto* means *Welcome*. For twenty years his parents had prayed for a manchild; but thus far, Heaven had answered their prayers with one daughter. Finally, on All Saints' Day in 1500, the midwife came out of the delivery room with a new child for Giovanni Cellini. "I bring you a fine gift," she said, "a blessing such as you do not expect." Giovanni looked at the infant, raised his eyes to Heaven, and exclaimed: "I thank Thee, my Lord, for this welcome surprise!" And right then and there he decided to name the child *Benvenuto*.

II

BENVENUTO had been slow in coming, but he was very fast in getting ahead. "The child is a hurricane of capability and contentiousness." His father wanted him to be a flute-player, but the boy insisted on becoming a goldsmith. "I hate the tinkle of music, but I love the glitter of precious stones." At fifteen he apprenticed himself, against the wish of his father, to a jeweler by the name of Antonio di Sandro; and before long, he tells us unblushingly, "I overtook even the ablest of the young goldsmiths of Florence."

His apprenticeship at Florence, however, was short-lived. At sixteen he got into a scrap—it was always the other fellow, he assures us, who started the fighting—and was banished from Florence. Within a few months he was recalled to his native city, only to leave it again as the result of a quarrel he had with his father. He went to Pisa, secured a job with a goldsmith "who adored me for my honesty and my talent," and left his "adoring" master for further adventures in Florence. Another quarrel with his father—"he still persisted in making a musician out of

me"—and again he ran away from Florence. This time, a roughneck young
genius of nineteen, he went to seek new fights and new fortunes in Rome.

For two years he fashioned his trinkets, reveled in his duels and his
ducats and his glory, and finally attacked singlehanded an "entire tribe-
ful" of his detractors. "Like a maddened bull I came among them, I
threw four or five of them to the ground, and I fell on top of them,
plying my dagger now on this one, now on that." For this escapade he
was put under the ban, and for a while the firebrand of his temper
burned low.

But the flames of his passion began to burn high. He collected and
cast away his mistresses as recklessly as he collected and cast away his
money. On one occasion, when the mother of his favorite courtesan took
her away from Cellini and left for parts unknown, the distracted young
lover traveled all over Italy to find her again. And when, to his delight,
he did find her, he abruptly abandoned her because the mother had set
too high a price upon her.

And yet, although he had no compunction about *throwing* away his
mistresses, woe unto those who dared to *take* them away! One day he
surprised his colleague, a goldsmith by the name of Pagolo Miccieri, in
the arms of his mistress, Caterina. "When I beheld this stealing of my
love," writes Cellini, "I felt a fever leap upon me." His first impulse was
to kill Miccieri. But then he hit upon a far more subtle revenge. He
compelled his rival to *marry* Caterina, and then he in turn stole her love
from her husband.

Yet his dallyings and his duels were but of secondary importance to
Cellini. Always foremost in his mind was the development of his genius.
It was his ambition to perfect himself in "every phase of jewel-sculpture,"
from the carving of a tiny medallion to the modeling of a colossal statue.
"In all these different branches I set myself to learn with very great attention." He realized that he had undertaken an almost superhuman task,
but he believed that he was endowed with an almost superhuman talent.
"No man before me has excelled in all these branches, because no man
before me has received from Heaven a temperament of such diversified
richness."

He believed so profoundly in his own genius that he inspired everybody
else to believe in it. Bishops, cardinals, emperors and popes were ready
to pay homage to him. And he, so proud was he of his achievements, was
ready to pay homage to none. On one occasion, Pope Clement VII commissioned Cellini to model for him a chalice representing the nativity
of Christ. For this work, His Holiness undertook to pay him in regular
installments. But when the installments were slow in reaching him,
Cellini was equally slow in completing the work. Finally Pope Clement
decided to call him to task. "I command you to attend to my chalice!"

"And I," replied Cellini, "request you to attend to my gold."

Unable to do anything himself with this young "upstart of a goldsmith," Pope Clement ordered his legate, Cardinal Salviati, to apply the necessary spur. "This beast of a Cardinal"—writes Cellini in his *Autobiography*—"sent for me at the end of eight days, telling me to bring along the chalice; to whom I went without it. When I arrived, the Cardinal said to me insolently: 'Where is that hodgepodge of yours? Have you finished it?'

"To which I replied with equal insolence: 'I shall not finish my hodgepodge until you give me the onions with which to season it.'

"At these words"—continues Cellini—"the Cardinal flew into a rage, and cried: 'I will send you to the galleys, and then you will have the grace to finish the job!'

"'My Lord,' I rejoined, 'you cannot send me to the galleys unless I commit a crime. Until then, I am a free man and I refuse to bow to an uncivil tongue . . . A pleasant good day to you, sir!'"

And Cellini went home and sulked "like Achilles in his tent" until both the Cardinal and the Pope yielded to his demands. "They couldn't help it," concludes Cellini in his usual tone of arrogant naïveté. "For they knew that I was the greatest man that ever was born in my profession."

III

ONE DAY, as he was walking through the streets of Rome, Cellini met a group of "ruffians who disliked my work." When they arrived at about "the length of two Ave Marias" from Cellini, they stopped and "laughed with derision" in his direction. This act of disrespect so infuriated Cellini that he drew his dagger and rushed upon them. "As I aimed to strike their leader (Pompeo) in the face, the fear that he experienced made him turn his countenance away"—note how Cellini always puts the blame upon his adversary—"so that I caught him exactly under the ear." The man died of the blow, "a thing I had never intended—why *did* he turn his face away?"

Cellini was lucky enough to escape the consequences of this crime. The new Pope—Clement VII was now dead—granted him a pardon on the ground that the murder was an act of self-defense. "And it was a fortunate thing that they saved me. For I proceeded to astonish the world with the marvels of my creative genius." More adventures, more loves, more crimes. His superabundant energy was forever boiling over into new quarrels, and his exuberant imagination was forever exaggerating small insults into great injuries. Once, as he was traveling toward Florence, he stopped at an inn where the landlord insisted upon being paid "before I went to sleep" instead of receiving his pay, "as was customary, in the morning." Fuming with rage, Cellini paid the inn-keeper "according to his evil method" and went to bed. "I had a very fine bed, entirely new, and very clean. For all this, I couldn't fall asleep, meditating all that night how I must act to avenge myself. Once it came into my thoughts to set

fire to the house; at another moment, to cut the throats of four fine horses
that he had in his stable . . ." Finally, in the morning, he hit upon the
following revenge: "I took out of my pocket a small knife that cut like a
razor, and with that knife I whittled four of his new beds into splinters."
By the time the inn-keeper was up, Cellini was already too far away to
be overtaken.

His fiery temper and his consuming energy resulted again and again
in a physical breakdown. But out of every illness—once he was taken for
dead and prepared for burial—he came out with greater vitality than
before. "The reason why I always recovered was that I followed my own
prescriptions rather than those of the doctor." Whatever Cellini did was
—he was convinced—for Cellini's best.

And Cellini—he was equally convinced—was the greatest of artists
and the noblest of men. "In art," he quotes from a sonnet written about
himself, "he is superior to all men; in character, equal to all the angels."
Whenever he undertook a job, he not only came up to everybody's expectations—he tells us—but he greatly surpassed them. In every new undertaking he tried not only to outdo his rivals, but to outdo himself.
"Benvenuto," declares Cellini with the complacency of Little Jack
Horner, "is the glory of the world."

Yet, on one occasion, his glory received the tarnish of a prison sentence.
He was charged with having stolen a number of precious stones from the
Pope's tiara. He defended himself vigorously against this charge and—he
declares—completely established his innocence. "Yet so powerful were
my enemies that I remained in prison as though I were guilty."

His active body was confined, but not his active brain. He set to work
devising a plan of escape; and, having devised it, he at once put it into
execution. He secured from one of the jailers a pair of pincers, wrested
away the nails which held together the iron bands of his cell-door, slipped
out at night through the loosened door, and then let himself down from
the tower by a rope made out of a sheet which he had cut into strips. "In
my descent from the tower, I had scraped the skin off the palms of my
hands, which were bleeding . . ."

This, however, was not the end of his troubles. When he tried to rise,
he found that his leg had been broken in the escape. "Yet this did not
dismay me . . . Binding the leg together with a strip of the cloth which
I had used for my rope, I crawled towards the city gate"—only to find it
closed . . . "Nor did even this dismay me . . . Seeing a certain stone
exactly beneath the gate, I laid hold of it and tore it loose . . . And by
this means I entered the city of Rome."

Whereupon a pack of dogs "threw themselves upon me"—it is hard
to tell where reality leaves off and Cellini's imagination begins—"and bit
me severely." He fought the dogs off with his dagger, and dragged himself laboriously to the house of a friend.

But he was discovered and taken back to prison—this time, as he thought, for life.

His sufferings in prison were almost unendurable. "I was carried into a dark chamber . . . where there was much water, full of tarantulas and many noxious worms . . . I remained continuously on a pallet of coarse hemp without being able to move, since I had a broken leg . . . For one hour and a half of the day I had a little reflection of light, which entered that miserable cavern by a very tiny aperture; and, during that short space of time only could I read, and the rest of the day and of the night I remained always in the dark." His nails grew so long that he "couldn't touch himself without wounding himself," and his teeth "died in their sockets," so that their roots lacerated his gums. Again and again he tried to do away with himself; "but some heavenly power always held me back." The world, he felt, still needed his genius, which somehow, some time, would be able to reassert itself. With a little charcoal that he had found imbedded in the earthen floor, he drew upon the wall of his cell a picture of Jesus surrounded by His angels. To this picture he prayed daily for his final deliverance.

And deliverance finally came. One day, just as he had concluded his prayer, his guardian angel lifted him up "after the manner of a whirlwind" and—he tells us—carried him to Heaven. Here he spoke "face to face with the Father, the Son, and the Holy Virgin." And they promised him to soften the hearts of his jailers so that they would set him free. "And that very day I was set free."

As a proof of the divine grace that had enveloped him in Heaven, Cellini pointed out to his friends—"and every one of them can see it"— a halo that hovered around his head. "This halo may be observed above my shadow in the morning from sunrise until two hours after sunrise . . . It may be observed also in the evening at sunset . . ."

Cellini had now arrived at the very apex of self-adoration.

IV

To CELEBRATE his deliverance from prison, Cellini got into another quarrel and committed another murder—a rather strange business for a man with a halo. And then, to escape further trouble, he went to Paris and entered the service of King Francis I. At the king's request, he undertook a group of three silver statues—"a work of genius such as even the ancients had never seen."

The king was delighted with Cellini's art. But Cellini was not at all pleased with the king's avarice. "When we talked about my salary, the prince tried to beat me down as if I were a load of wood." However, they finally compromised upon a payment of 750 gold ducats a year—"the same allowance that King Francis had given to Leonardo da Vinci. This sum, though far from sufficient, was at least respectable."

There now began a period of comparative quiet for "the greatest man that ever was born"—we are quoting Cellini's own words about himself. Under the cooler rays of the Parisian sun he was able—as a general rule —to restrain his temper and to channel his superabundant energy into creative work. Among the many things that he made for King Francis was a saltcellar of ivory and gold. Cellini gives us a vivid description of its exquisite design. "This saltcellar was oval in shape . . . and fashioned into the (figured) likeness of the Sea and Earth, both seated. And they intertwined their legs, just as . . . the Sea runs into the Earth and the Earth juts into the Sea . . . And in the right hand of the Sea I had fixed a trident, and in his left hand I had placed a boat . . . which was to receive the salt. There were beneath this said figure his four animals of the Sea, each of them represented with the head of a horse and the tail of a fish . . . The water was enameled in the various colors of the waves . . . For the Earth I had fashioned a very beauteous woman—with the Horn of Plenty in one hand, and in the other a small Ionian temple which was to receive the pepper. Beneath this female figure I had placed the handsomest animals that the Earth produces. And the rocks of the Earth I depicted partly in enamel and partly in gold . . . I had then placed this work upon a pedestal of black ebony carved into the four figures of the Night, the Day, the Twilight, and the Dawn . . . Interspersed among these were the figures of the four winds—the East, the North, the South and the West . . . a work to arouse the astonishment and the admiration of all men everywhere . . ."

Eloquent as he was in extolling the virtues of his own work, he was equally eloquent in disparaging the defects of his rivals' works. Asked to explain why he disliked the Hercules of Bandinello, he said: "Because it is bad, from top to toe . . . If you were to shave the hair off the skull, there wouldn't be left enough of a head to house his brain . . . As regards the face, there's no telling whether it represents the features of a man or of an ox . . . The shoulders resemble the two pommels of an ass's saddle . . . His breasts and the rest of his muscles are not copied from those of a man, but are drawn from an old sack full of melons . . . And now look at the legs; they seem to have no connection with that ugly body. You can't tell upon which of his legs he is resting his weight . . . The calves have neither muscles nor sinews nor blood . . . And his feet are so utterly devoid of life that one of them seems to be buried in the earth and the other shriveled in a flame . . ."

His caustic tongue finally resulted in a quarrel between Cellini and the king. Disappointed at the royal neglect of an artist "greater even than Michelangelo," Cellini returned to the hot sun and the fiery adventures of his native Florence. Added to his "natural" vices, he was now accused of an "unnatural" vice and was compelled to flee from the city until the storm blew over. And then came a pardon from the duke, and Cellini returned to his aberrations under serene skies again. Serene, but for one dark cloud that tempted him—to quote his picturesque expression—"to throw myself into despair." Among his illegitimate children there was a two-year-old son whom he loved better than his own life. One day he went to visit this child whom he had placed with a wet-nurse. "When I reached him, I found him in good health, and I so unhappy kissed him." But when Cellini rose to depart, the child clung to him with his little hands, and "with a passion of tears and screams" begged his father not to go. "It seemed as if he had a presentiment of some great tragedy." And sure enough, three days after his return to Florence, Cellini heard that the wet-nurse had accidentally smothered his little son. "And this news," writes Cellini, "gave me so great a sorrow as I have never felt a greater."

V

THE FIRES and the desires of his youth had now almost completely subsided. When his enemies insulted him, he no longer rushed upon them with his sword. Instead, he transfixed them with his pen. But his lampoons were no less keen than his sword thrusts.

And equally keen was the ever-shining instrument of his genius. Like Michelangelo, he had that rare faculty of improving with age. "My last works"—and he spoke the simple truth—"were the best." When he unveiled his statue of *Perseus*, hundreds of sonnets in praise of the work were nailed to the posts of his door. "For, since it was the vacation at the University of Pisa, all those most excellently learned scholars vied with one another upon that subject."

This unveiling of the *Perseus* was the culmination of Cellini's triumph. He was now universally recognized as one of the greatest artists of all time.

And now, having tasted all the exciting pleasures of life, he settled down to the more quiet contentments of old age. He bought a farm, entered the primary grade of the Holy Orders, and—at the age of sixty —married for the first time. He ushered into the world—with or without benefit of clergy—five daughters and three sons, the last of whom was born when Cellini was sixty-nine years old.

The following year the young-old artist laid down the burden of a too impetuous life. And the world was so much the emptier for the passing of one who had proved himself "a master of the greatest as well as of the smallest things."

IMPORTANT DATES IN THE LIFE OF
BENVENUTO CELLINI

1500—Born in Florence on November 1.

1515—Apprenticed to a goldsmith.

1519—Went to Rome.

1527—Took part in defense of Rome.

1537—Arrested on (apparently false) charge of embezzlement.

1540–45—Worked for King Francis I in Paris.

1545—Returned to Florence.

1558—Received the tonsure of the first ecclesiastical orders.

1560—Renounced orders and married.

1560–70—Wrote Autobiography.

1571—Died in Florence on February 14.

Francis Bacon

1561–1626

ENGLAND under good Queen Bess was a land of merry mortals and easy morals. The court and the aristocracy lived through a brilliant midsummer's night. A thousand aspiring politicians wore asses' heads for power and played Bottom to the Fairy Queen. Never did literary men write more slavishly for court advancement. In every cowslip lurked a poet to toss a fragrant rhyme. It was the age of Puck, a buoyant, mischief-making elf age that courted wickedness with malicious grace, practiced deceit in the midst of beauty, concealed poison in the scent of the musk rose, talked treachery in a refined whisper, and girdled the world with a belt of pirate ships. It was an age of vicious intrigue that lay like a roast crab in the gossip bowl of history.

Into this world, this age, this forest of exquisite dreams and evil enchantments, a man of science was born.

II

FRANCIS BACON'S FATHER was a politician—the Keeper of the Great Seal; and his mother was a scholar—the preserver of the Greek and Latin tradition. While Sir Nicholas upheld the laws of the modern world Lady Anne translated the manuscripts of the ancient world. Under the influence of such parents it is no wonder that young Francis developed into a politician and a scholar—and a snob. At the age of twelve he entered Trinity College, Cambridge, where he immediately tilted the nose of his intelligence at the established scholarship of fifteen hundred years. At sixteen he declared openly that the Cambridge professors who based their teaching on Aristotle were in error. They suffered, he said, from a naïve science that was grounded on a crude and scanty observation of nature.

Francis Bacon felt that he had a "mission" in life. He would free the world from that "Aristotelian theology" which everybody regarded as an authoritative science. But more immediately he was concerned with another mission—to free Francis Bacon from debt. For Sir Nicholas, who had apportioned his estate among all his sons with the exception of Francis, died just as he was preparing to make provision for his sixth son. And thus Francis found himself almost penniless at the age of nineteen.

This was a hard blow for a young man who had emptied wine bottles with princes and who had played with the hearts of the great court ladies. He petitioned for a post in the royal palace. And he chose his uncle, Sir William Cecil, prime minister of England, to plead his cause. But Cecil had a son of his own whom he wished to advance. He did nothing for his nephew.

Francis was faced with a practical problem, and he was not the young man to avoid it. He could choose philosophy and face destitution or he could take up law and carve out a career for himself. He decided upon a combination of the two. He would depend upon law to fill his purse and upon philosophy to feed his soul.

He entered Gray's Inn and graduated to the bar. He was blessed with a forceful voice and a brilliant forensic style, and it was not long before he gained a seat in Parliament. Yet rapid as was his progress, his imagination was always several laps ahead of his achievement. Already he saw himself swept into the woolsack of the chancellery and beyond it into the council chamber of the queen.

To be sure, he was the son of his scholarly mother as well as of his political father. The problems of theoretical knowledge continued to bother him. Did he not see the light in the realm of science? Could he not bring humanity back to truth? Ah, but the light from the palace chandeliers and from the eye of a dainty duchess were far more pleasing to him! "Whereas I believe myself born for the service of mankind and could bring the truth to shine upon every nook and cranny of nature," nevertheless, as he confessed, "political power is what I want, power over men and affairs," with the Great Seal of England in his hand and a hundred servants. Away with the contemplative life! "Men ought to know that in the theater of human affairs it is only for gods and angels to be spectators."

III

FOR TWELVE LONG YEARS he sought a foothold at court—unsuccessfully. Time and again he threatened his uncle—who at a word could have secured him the coveted position—that he would leave his legal profession and retire to the scholarly seclusion of Cambridge University. Such threats failed to put Cecil out of countenance. He answered his nephew coldly and turned to other affairs.

But there was at court a faction whose power rivaled that of his uncle. It was headed by the dashing Lord Essex, the queen's favorite. To this powerful and affable nobleman Bacon addressed himself. And with his elaborate manners and his gift of eloquence he won the heart of Essex.

Bacon looked upon his friendship with Essex, as he looked upon everything else, with a practical eye. "There is little friendship in the world," he reasoned, "and least of all between equals. . . ." But there is a *kind* of friendship to an end, "between a superior and his inferior, for mutual advantage." The wise master had thus obtained a faithful servant, and the crafty servant had found a master who could be used as a steppingstone to higher things.

Bacon had great need of a steppingstone just then. He was constantly falling into debt. He loved to dine well and to put on a fine appearance. Lord Essex made him frequent gifts of money, and this lessened the dunning of his creditors. Philosophy had earldom enthralled. But as yet no political office for Francis Bacon. He wrote speeches flattering the vanity of the queen. He published political treatises glorifying her reign. "Mr. Bacon is beginning to frame well up to our desires," remarked Her Majesty. But when the office of Master of the Rolls became vacant she passed Bacon over for someone else in spite of the remonstrances of Essex. A grave disappointment. "I must bear the yoke," sighed the philosopher. Essex lessened the burden of the yoke. He presented Bacon with a large estate.

One good turn deserves another, thought Bacon. Now that Essex had given him a rich house, someone ought to give him a rich wife. A judicious marriage might present him with a fine opportunity to reimburse himself. His eye had chanced upon a widow of ample means and noble blood. Instantly he presented himself as a suitor and enlisted Essex in the cause. But in spite of Essex's recommendation the lady refused him. She accepted instead Sir Edward Coke, a rival lawyer who had been appointed over him to the office of Queen's Attorney. Bacon shrugged his shoulders philosophically, though he could not understand how the affluent widow could prefer the elderly gentleman against whom, as the gossip went, there were seven objections—"his six children and himself."

To unburden himself of his bitterness Bacon wrote an essay on injustice, plunged into an orgy of spending, and landed in a debtors' prison. As usual, Essex came to the rescue.

And still he sought to free the human spirit from the prison of its Aristotelian scholasticism. The whole system of theological metaphysics must be torn down. There must be a new liberal education for the sons of a new dawn. The horizons of knowledge must be widened. The medical sciences must be reconstructed; disease must be tracked down. "The betterment of man is my province; the foundation of a new civilization of the intellect is my duty. . . . This is what I ought to do if only I had the time, the leisure, the financial security." He must teach man to become *the architect of his own success.*

IV

SLOWLY Essex was losing favor with his queen. There had been violent quarrels between them. Essex had been sent against his wishes to command the army in Ireland. He feared that in his absence his rivals might supplant him in the queen's graces. The smile of the court was as unsubstantial as it was dazzling. The fortunes of Essex hung on the dizzy pinnacle of the royal caprice, ready to fall at the slightest contrary wind. The earl rushed home from Ireland without the queen's leave. Elizabeth had him imprisoned. Although she released him before long, she never took him back into her favor. Clearly the nobleman was no longer the architect of his own success. Powerful enemies were plotting against him. He began to lose his reason, and there was imminent danger that he would shortly lose his head.

Where was his friend Bacon? What counsel did Bacon give him? What consolation? The queen's heart had been set relentlessly against Essex, and it was whispered in the court circles that "Mr. Bacon is thought to be the man who moves Her Majesty thus. . . ."

For he found it a good policy to side with the queen now that Essex could no longer be of any use to him. Francis Bacon had wrung Essex dry, and it was time for him to look elsewhere for new revenue. Few people at first believed these rumors. Even Lord Robert Cecil, the son of the former prime minister and the foremost political enemy of Essex, was shocked at the story. He wrote a letter to Bacon, "Cousin, I hear it, but I believe it not, that you should do some ill service to my Lord of Essex!" But it was true. It was all so scientifically sound.

As the state prepared to try Essex on a charge of disloyalty to the queen, Bacon pleaded to be allowed a part in the prosecution. For this would greatly enhance his legal career. But common decency forbade Elizabeth from granting this heartless request.

It seemed evident that the only crime of which Essex was guilty was a hot temper. He had gathered his kinsmen around him to "teach a lesson" to those men who had banished him from the "sunlight of Her Majesty's smile." Knowledge of the gatherings at his house had come to the ears of the government. His plot was thwarted. He was arrested and confined to the Tower. The question immediately resolved itself as to whether Essex was guilty of a rash impulse against his political opponents or of a much more serious attempt against the life of his sovereign queen. There was little doubt in anyone's mind that the former was the case. He had lost his head. No charge of deliberate treason was thought likely to be entered against him.

Essex was brought before the bar. And Francis Bacon rose to his feet.

The court looked at him inquiringly. He was not officially a member of the prosecution. What was he going to say, and in what capacity? The court soon discovered that he would speak as a voluntary witness for the state, especially as a man who had been an intimate friend of the accused and who therefore possessed a thorough knowledge of his ambitions and his motives. Here would be weighty testimony indeed. The court was hushed. A brilliant orator, a suave advocate this. What a charming manner he had!

Brushing aside the theory that Essex was responsible for nothing more than a rash impulse, Francis Bacon charged the earl with the deliberate conspiracy to usurp the throne—a crime punishable by death. With great and learned oratory, with all the resources of his mind at his command, Bacon stated the case. He spoke, he said, not before a provincial jury of ignorant men who could be swayed by emotion, but before a bench of learned and impartial judges, and he begged them to look at the facts with the utmost objectivity. Could Essex deny that he had intended treachery to the person of the queen? "My lords, even Cain, our first murderer, feigned impudency to outshame the facts of his crime." And then Bacon brought forth an imposing array of parallel cases from his great wealth of historical knowledge. Had not the traitor Pisistratus lanced himself and rushed into the city bleeding with wounds and calling on the people for pity at the very moment when his kinsmen were seizing the power of the state at his command? "I speak not as learned counsel of the prosecution but as friend of the accused," he said in a voice that sounded husky with emotion. And it was as a friend, he insisted, that he was obliged to confess—although against his will: Essex had planned to murder the queen and to seize her throne. He could therefore be subject to no extenuating circumstances. Bacon scoffed at the idea that the earl had temporarily lost his sanity and that he could not have known what he was doing. Essex was a traitor, he concluded, and he must pay for his treachery with his life.

This testimony, given against Essex by the man to whom Essex had given an estate, convinced the judges. They condemned the unfortunate nobleman to the block.

What had been Bacon's motive in sending his best friend to his death? In return for "services rendered" he received twelve hundred pounds from the state. "Ah well," he remarked sadly as he pocketed the money, "the queen has done something for me, but not so much as I had hoped for."

Then he sat down to write a medical treatise on the methods for the prolongation of human life.

V

BACON had a fertile, versatile intelligence. He could employ it for good as well as for evil. If he found it expedient to resort to treachery in order to make his way in the world, he found it fascinating to plunge more deeply into philosophy than anyone before him when the mood seized him. "I possess a passion for research unequaled by any man. . . . I know more legal precedent than any Englishman. Can anyone compete with me in my knowledge of Latin and Greek? . . . I am an encyclopedia of learning. . . . I have understood what is wrong with all the science of man since Aristotle." The trouble with the Greeks was that they confused moral ends and purposes with purely mechanical functions. Thus they described a rainstorm not only in terms of atmospheric conditions but also in terms of theology. Water evaporates into air and falls on the earth, they said, because God wishes to feed the crops and to make the world fruitful for man. This sort of naïve and unscientific reasoning, declared Bacon, has got to stop. We must separate our ideas about God from the physical universe and we must judge things in terms of their natural functions. We must become modest in our aims and specialized in our investigations. We must begin not with certainties but with doubts. We must organize large armies of men from all the leading universities of the world, each of them to investigate thoroughly his own special field of learning. And thus only, through the common coöperation of countless nameless workers, will the sum total of truth be attained. "Already I have drawn up the plans for this great Restoration of Knowledge. I shall classify the different branches of natural science, allocating to my workers the investigation of the unsolved problems in each field. We shall put Nature on the rack and compel her to bear witness. The very thought makes me dizzy. But when shall I find the time to organize all this?"

Once more he was thrust into prison for debt, and once more he was released through the intercession of the royal court. But within two years after the death of the Earl of Essex Queen Elizabeth passed away and the Scottish King James ascended the English throne. James had been very friendly to Essex. What an embarrassment to those who had condemned the unfortunate earl to death! But Bacon was unperturbed. Time to change face! He was a master analyst of the human heart. Having ascertained that the new king prided himself on being a classical scholar, Bacon sent him a message of greeting commencing with a line from the Vulgate and closing with a line from Ovid. And in the body of the message he declared, "There is no subject of Your Majesty's who could more desire to sacrifice himself as a burnt offering to Your Majesty's service." He had his eye on the office of the King's Attorney.

When the king ignored his petition Bacon turned to Robert Cecil, his wealthy cousin. He informed him that he was in debt again and he begged him for a little credit. He assured him that he had bidden farewell to politics for good, that his thirst for office had been entirely quenched, and that he now intended to devote his energy to a search for an "affluent bride" so that he might settle down to a life of comfortable tranquillity. Parenthetically he suggested that as a means to assuage his disappointment at his failure in his petition for a court office he could bring himself to accept the "almost prostituted" title of knighthood, provided Robert Cecil interceded in his behalf. But he added that he deprecated the vulgar custom of conferring the title on large groups of people assembled at the same time. He would prefer to be knighted all by himself, as befitted his dignity. A week later, at the coronation of King James I, Sir Francis Bacon rose to his feet a knight—together with three hundred other people.

But he intended at all costs to win personal recognition at the court. King James was extremely vulnerable to flattery. Bacon showered him with letters in which he compared this rather ordinary mortal "to the Lord God, the Prime Mover of the Universe." Moreover, as a member of Parliament, he took every occasion to defend the king's illiberal policies, his arbitrary dispensation of justice without regard for the advocates of the people or for the common law, and his illegal taxes which bulged his revenue and made him independent of the people's representatives. Bacon was lavish with his advice for "better scientific methods" of suppressing popular government. And in the meantime he married the daughter of an alderman. Upon being congratulated on the happy occasion, he replied dryly that his "finances had been somewhat improved by this match." As for love, this sort of emotion never entered his mind. "Great men," he wrote in one of his *Essays*, "always keep away from this weak passion."

At last his practical and opportunist mind brought him recognition from the king. He was appointed solicitor general of England. What especially recommended him in the eyes of King James was his ingenious suggestion that a foreign war could always serve to kill off the excess population of a country. Bacon was a man after the king's own heart.

Bacon's split personality was an amazing manifestation of that greatest of all mysteries—the human mind. He increased the number of scholarships at Oxford and Cambridge, so as to give the masses of England a greater opportunity for education, and he presided at the king's Star Chamber of torture. He wrote a glowing essay on charity, he published a magnificent work *On the Advancement of Learning*, and he pointed out to his public in a little essay how a man might "work" his friend by discovering his "weaknesses and disadvantages." And then without a blush he penned a treatise on the virtue of goodness and truth. "There is no vice that so covers a man with shame as to be found false and perfidious," he said.

He always found an excuse for his unscrupulous ambition. He depended upon it, he said, to provide him with material security so that he might be free to offer his gift of philosophy to mankind. "I will liberate my fellows from false thinking," he reasoned. "I will show men the true nature of heat, the laws of motion, the principles of diet. But first I must gather wealth so that I may have leisure for my experiments. You will suspend judgment on me until you see the results. Let me reach the height of power; and then, when I retire, I shall found new universities and endow new chairs. I shall write and search and benefit mankind. Are my ends unworthy? He who would reach these ends must not shudder at the means."

VI

As HE GREW OLDER his mind became more powerful. He wrote the most famous prose work of the age, *Novum Organum (The New Organon)*. Philosophy had long been in need of a new method of scientific inquiry. And here it was.

Before we can investigate the truth—said Bacon—we must destroy a number of fallacies, or *Idols*, that have hampered the human mind. First there are the *Idols of the Tribe*. This class of idols represents the tribal or universal fallacy that man is the measure of all things. Man analyzes the universe as if it had been created and ordered for *his* convenience. "The human understanding, from its peculiar nature, easily supposes a greater degree of order and regularity in things than it really finds . . . although most cogent and abundant instances may exist to the contrary. . . ."

A second class of idols consists of the *Idols of the Cave*. "For everyone . . . has a cave or den of his own, which refracts and discolors the light of nature." Some minds are analytical—they tend to divide the world into its differences; other minds are synthetic—they try to organize the world into a coherent structure. To the first group belongs the scientist, to the second the artist. But all of us must realize that the truth lies independently of them both.

Third there are the *Idols of the Market Place*, emanating "from the commerce and association of men with one another." "There arises, from a bad and inept formation of words, a wonderful obstruction to the mind." Scholars as well as laymen talk about the universe in glib generalities of which we should beware. We must expurgate from the language of science such vague and misleading expressions as *first cause, uncaused, the absolute, prime substance, infinity*. We must be merciless with our definitions. We must make a fresh start with rigorous exactitude.

The fourth and last class comprises the *Idols of the Theater*. These spring from the dogmas of the philosophers. All our accepted systems of philosophy "are but so many stage plays, representing worlds of their own creation after an unreal and scenic fashion." The worlds constructed in the fancies of the thinkers are "more as we should wish them to be than true stories . . . out of history."

Now that we have cleared a path through the forest of ignorance, we are ready to build our new highway to knowledge. What is the new method? It is the method of doubt, of trial and error, of classification and reclassification. It is the method of *simple experiment*. "The true method of experience first lights the candle and then, by means of the candle, shows the way." First we must collect by diligent research the available data; then we must arrange these data of our experience into a well-digested order from which we may formulate axioms. From these axioms we may then proceed to new experiments, and from these new experiments we may finally deduce facts. This method is therefore one of hypothesis, experiment, and deduction.

The process of deduction from hypothesis through experimentation to fact is not easy. And in order to facilitate this process Bacon proposed a convenient *modus operandi*. He constructed a "table of more or less." By means of this table all data could be classified and eliminated one by one until the essential facts pertaining to the case stood out in the clear. Bacon illustrated his method by examining the nature of heat. He looked for some phenomenon that invariably increased with the increase of heat and invariably decreased with the decrease of heat. One by one he examined the various physical phenomena that react to heat until he chanced upon the one factor which is so correlated to the expansion of heat that it eliminates heat itself upon its own elimination. This factor is motion. Whereupon Bacon concluded that heat is a form of motion.

Unfortunately his ingenious table proved in the end impracticable, owing to unforeseen difficulties. And yet *Novum Organum* is the scientific Declaration of Independence. For its general method of elimination through experimentation has become the common usage of science to the present day. The "laboratory plan" has opened a new path to knowledge. "No man has better known than Bacon the cause (and the cure) of human error."

VII

In the meantime the king was not advancing him rapidly enough to suit his political ambitions. Other people were being promoted. Why not he? "My love must creep where it cannot go," he reflected unblushingly. Few men had ever descended to such lengths to obtain office. He fairly groveled at His Majesty's feet.

"If it please Your Majesty to perceive how some people are being favored above me and some below me . . ." "God preserve Your Majesty. . . ." "Accept my sacrifice of thanksgiving for your gracious favor. . . ." "Ah, sire, do not my words require a place very near you from which to praise you everlastingly?" "My sovereign, do not permit me to waste to nothingness for want of your favor. . . ." "I crave leave to make at this time a humble offering of myself. . . ." "I shall be a ready chessman to be wherever Your Majesty's royal hand shall set me. . . ." These and many similar petitions.

Finally His Majesty raised Sir Francis from his knees and made him attorney general at a goodly salary. More servants, more comfort, more power—and more ambition. When the Lord Chancellor, the highest political officer in the kingdom, fell ill Bacon rushed to his bedside with a silent prayer that the obsequies might be soon forthcoming. He watched over the sick man with a great display of solicitude and sent to the king daily reports of the dying man's condition. Finally he wrote with assumed sadness, "Your worthy Chancellor, I fear, goes his last day. . . . Now I beseech Your Majesty, let me put the present case truly. . . . If you appoint my Lord Coke (his great rival) to the Lord Chancellery, nothing but misfortune will follow you. . . . If you take my Lord Hubbard, your royal prerogative shall be broken. . . . But if *I* were the man . . . it would be the *least* of my duties to act as an impartial judge in equity between parties. I would be a faithful overseer for you, a zealous disciple among your peoples, the machinery through which you may ever advance your divine right."

But the Lord Chancellor refused to die. "I was with him yesterday," Bacon wrote, "almost half an hour. He used me with wonderful tokens of kindness. I wept, which I do not often." The Lord Chancellor resumed his position, and Bacon looked around for another office.

But at last death took the Chancellor, and Francis Bacon received his reward. He was made the new Lord Chancellor of England.

He was inducted into the office with great pomp. He was given the titles of Baron Verulam and Viscount St. Albans. "Crafty men *condemn* studies," he had written in one of his essays; "wise men *use* them." Knowledge put to the right use meant power. "Happy the man who has learned the causes of things. . . ." He had learned the causes of fame, the mainsprings of political influence. He had reached the very pinnacle of fortune. And he was about to learn the effects.

For tragedy struck quickly. Within three years after his installation into the chancellery the House of Commons brought sensational charges against him. Francis Bacon was accused of taking bribes in court! The country was stunned. His past political record was well known. So, too, were his philosophical achievements. Who was this man of dual personality—the devil incarnate?

A large number of witnesses came forward and testified to the chancellor's habit of "gift taking." The Commons drew up a formal indictment. When the messengers brought the indictment to Bacon they found him sick in bed. How did he answer to the charges? "My lords," he said, casting his eyes to heaven, "I have withdrawn my mind from worldly matters. I am thinking of my account and my answers in a higher court. . . ."

The whole country is aroused. Speeches everywhere, from the pulpits, in the streets, demanding the punishment of the Lord Chancellor. Can he deny the accusation? What is his defense? All his philosophy is now unavailable to save him.

The "sick" man takes up his learned pen. "There are three degrees of bribery. First, the least degree: bribery to pervert justice while the case is still pending; second, when the judge conceives the case to be at an end; third . . ." Stop this verbal hairsplitting, this crass hypocrisy! You are not analyzing chemical elements. Answer the question, "Were you bribed?" . . . "Of the first type of bribery I have mentioned," he goes on, "I am as innocent in my heart as any babe born upon St. Innocent's day. Of the second . . ." Loudly they demand a categorical answer. Whereupon he replies with much erudition, "I do ingeniously confess and acknowledge that, having understood the particulars of the charge, not formally from the House but enough to inform my conscience and memory, I find the matter sufficient and full, both to move me to desert the defense and to move your lordships to condemn and censure me." But he adds slyly that a moderate rebuke will be just as effectual to deter him from taking further bribes as a severe punishment. He reminds his judges that the times are generally immoral and that someday perchance any one of them may be brought before the bar on the same charge—in which event they will have reason not to regret their former leniency. Finally he writes jestingly to the king that a "man who has taken bribes is apt to give bribes" and that therefore he will present His Majesty with a history glorifying his reign for all future time.

By his refusal to reply to the specific counts in the indictment Francis Bacon had confessed nothing in particular. The judges, however, were not to be put off by his bland acknowledgment of his general guilt. They demanded his signature to a full and specific confession. And Francis Bacon was finally compelled to submit.

Twelve lords of the realm visited him and received the confession from him. "Is this your handwriting?" they asked.

"My lords, it is my act, my hand, my heart. . . ."

"Then return to us the Great Seal of your office."

He bowed his head. "By the king's great favor I have received the Seal; by my own great fault I have lost it."

As he sat in the Tower, a humble, broken prisoner, the scholar in him asserted that at least he had never handed down a wrong decision through ignorance of the law. And in the light of his own strange reason he was absolved. "I was the justest judge that was in England these fifty years. But," he added wryly, "it was the justest sentence in Parliament these two hundred years."

VIII

FIVE YEARS PASSED. He had been released from prison almost immediately upon his confinement, with the injunction that he must forever stay away from Parliament and the courts of England and that in the future he would be debarred from any office in the land. But the incorrigible optimist did not renounce his political ambitions even then! He sent a flood of letters to the king—flattering him, wheedling him and beseeching him with every argument at his command. But to no avail. His day was done. He could not flatter his old age into a second youth and vigor. He could not wheedle the burden of a disgraceful reputation away from his shoulders.

And one day, as he rode on horseback, he pondered the problem of preserving the human body after death. He dismounted and killed a fowl. Then he stuffed it with snow and was about to bring it home for observation when a sudden chill seized him. He stopped at a house near by and sent a note to one of his friends. "I am likely to have the fortune of Caius Plinius the elder, who lost his life by trying an experiment. . . ." Then he took to his bed and looked forward to the last great experiment of them all.

He was confident and calm. He knew that when he put to sea there would await him, undisturbed by the tides of time, a great Island of Utopia, his own *New Atlantis*—one of the dreams of his philosophical system—glittering in the sunlight of Eternity. Here was a promised land with a happy and flourishing population under a government of wise and enlightened men. Here were no politicians, no office seekers, no king's favorites harassed by ambition, but an administration of scientists, chemists and biologists, physicians and architects, sociologists and philosophers and astronomers. They were not engaged in campaign speeches or in gathering factions of followers by political promises, but rather they observed the stars and harnessed the water power for industry and studied anatomy and developed healing balms to combat disease. They constructed ships to fly in the air and vessels to speed underneath the waves. They traded not for gold and silver or silk and spices, "but only for God's first creature"—light!

And death approached so humbly it brought a tear to his eye.

IMPORTANT DATES IN THE LIFE OF
FRANCIS BACON

1561—January 22, born in London.
1573—Entered Trinity College, Cambridge.
1576—Began legal studies at Gray's Inn.
1582—Admitted to bar.
1584—Entered Parliament.
1601—Helped in the prosecution of Essex.
1603—Knighted by King James I.
1604—Received pension from king.
1605—Finished *Advancement of Learning*.
1607—Became solicitor general.

1608—Became Secretary to the Council of the Star Chamber.
1612—Became Judge of the Court of the Verge.
1613—Appointed attorney general.
1617—Made Lord Keeper.
1618—Made Lord Chancellor.
Made Baron Verulam of Verulam.
1620—Published *Novum Organum*.
1621—Created Viscount St. Albans. Imprisoned for taking bribes. Later released.
1626—April 9, died.

William Shakespeare

1564–1616

O_F ALL_ the mysteries in the world, the genius of Shakespeare is the most difficult to explain. His parents were rather less than ordinary. His father, a glover and wool-stapler, was not able even to sign his name. Shakespeare came of an obscure line, blazed across the skies, and then left an equally obscure line after him. Of his three daughters, two were of average intelligence and the third was downright stupid.

Much ink has been spilled in the battle of scholars who have tried to prove that the plays of Shakespeare were written by a man with another name. What a useless thing to waste our time in such empty pedantries! The work that goes under the name of Shakespeare seems as infinitely beyond the ability of a professor as it is above the capacity of a butcher. Whatever may have been the training or the social standing of the author, it is amazing that anyone bearing a mere human name should have produced a rose of such divine sweetness.

Shakespeare was a freak of nature—a demigod born out of the race of men. No critic as yet, not even Carlyle or Emerson or Brandes or Kittredge or Taine, has been able to probe to the depths of Shakespeare's mind. And the chances are that no critic ever will. To understand Shakespeare is to understand the complex mystery of creation. For his plays are a reproduction, in miniature, of the whole stupendous drama of life.

Shakespeare was a man gifted with the thoughts and the language of a god. Yet, externally, his life was anything but godlike. The career of this greatest of poets was quite unpoetical. At fourteen he was apprenticed to a butcher. At seventeen he was looked upon as one of the most reckless tipplers and wildest roisterers in the town of Stratford. At eighteen he seduced—or perhaps was seduced by—Ann Hathaway, a woman of twenty-six. He married her in the nick of time, as she was about to become a mother. Shortly after his marriage to her, he fled from Stratford in order to avoid arrest for deer-stealing. Coming up to London, he drifted into the theatrical channels and started out as a low comedian—one of "His Majesty's poor players." For the next seventeen years he devoted himself to the writing of sublime dramas and to the acting of motley parts in them. He was an indifferent actor; and as for his plays, he never thought enough of them to get them published during his lifetime.

He made money in his profession, lent out some of it on interest, invested the profits in real estate, knew how to drive a hard bargain, had his debtors imprisoned when they were delinquent in their payments, visited his family once a year, and finally bought an estate in Stratford and settled down to a life of commonplace respectability as a gentleman farmer.

His conduct during his stage career, however, was anything but respectable. On one occasion he drank himself into such a stupor that he was found the next morning under a tree by the roadside. He had his share of unsuccessful love affairs. "When my love swears that she is made of truth," he complains (Sonnet 138), "I do believe her, though I know she lies." Apparently he was not much of a ladies' man. The gentlewomen of London preferred the young lords, with their yellow curls and courtly manners, to the somewhat uncouth country bumpkin who wrote poetry and played the clown. Yet within his own little circle of actors and playwrights he was able now and then to outwit his rivals. An anecdote, written in 1602 on the authority of Tooley, relates how "his comrade Burbadge, who played Richard III, having a rendezvous with the wife of a citizen, Shakespeare went before, was well received, and was pleasantly occupied when Burbadge arrived, to whom he sent the message that William the Conqueror came before Richard III."

His family life seems to have been rather stormy. Whatever his success with other people's wives, he enjoyed very little success with his own. To Ann Hathaway, he was anything but William the Conqueror. She nagged him to the very end of his life, and he retaliated by leaving her in his will his "second-best" bed—nothing more.

This, in brief, is the story of Shakespeare's life. But it gives us not the slightest insight into the story of Shakespeare's mind. As a man he was, like most of us, just a little higher than Caliban—one of the earthiest of his creations. But as a teacher of mankind, he seems to belong to another planet, born as if by accident into this puny-minded race of ours.

The foremost intellects in the world have tried to grapple with the intellect of Shakespeare and to reduce his ideas to a logical sequence. But in vain. The critics have made him out to be, in turn, a patriot and a pacifist, a Catholic and an infidel, a sermonizer and a cynic, a humanitarian and a misanthrope, a democratic utopian and a royalist snob. He was none of these; or rather—amazing paradox!—all of these in one. His genius transcended the ideas and the beliefs of any one man, or of any group of men. He entered with an equal degree of sympathy and affection into the mind of every character that he created. Caliban was as intimate a part of Shakespeare as Prospero. The mind of Shakespeare was coextensive with the mind of the human race.

We shall make no effort to analyze Shakespeare or to delve extensively into the "antres vast and magical groves" of his unfathomable genius. It would be useless to try it. For greater minds have made the attempt and failed. The art of literary criticism has not as yet invented the yardstick that can gauge the dimensions of Shakespeare's intellect. All we shall try to do here is to explore a little way into one of the many corners of Shakespeare's mind—to dip up, as it were, a mere thimbleful of wisdom out of the inexhaustible ocean of his genius.

With this object in view, let us glance at three of his plays which represent him in three of his distinct attitudes toward life—first as a satirist, then as a man of the world, and finally as a philosopher. These three plays are—*Timon of Athens*, *Hamlet*, and *The Tempest*.

II

In *Timon of Athens* Shakespeare cries out against the injustice of the world with the bitterness of an Isaiah. In his other plays he simply mirrors life, but he rarely moralizes about it. When, occasionally, he does stop in his dramatic action to offer a hasty comment on life, he dismisses it, like some superior visitor from another planet, as an insubstantial and worthless dream—"a tale told by an idiot, full of sound and fury, signifying nothing." But in *Timon of Athens* his contempt flares up into indignation. Life here is a tale told, not by an idiot, but by a crafty devil. And far from signifying nothing, it signifies treachery, meanness, hatred, hypocrisy, and fraud. Timon was a wealthy citizen of Athens who generously gave all his money away to his friends. When they were troubled by their creditors, he paid their debts. When they were married, he gave them dowries and set them up in their new lives. When he invited them to a banquet, he sent them home with presents of money and of precious stones. His steward, Flavius, warned him time and again that his generosity would bring about his ruin. But Timon, overestimating both the extent of his resources and the gratitude of his friends, paid no attention to Flavius. He kept spending all his money on other people until he had nothing left for himself.

When his own creditors began to bother him, he felt certain that his friends, to whom he had given away everything, would come to his rescue. But one by one they refused to help him, each of them offering a different excuse for his refusal.

Whereupon Timon invited them once more to a banquet—and this time he served them nothing but dishes of warm water. Then, before the "affable wolves"—miscalled in the past his friends—were able to recover from their surprise, he dashed the water in their faces and ended by throwing the dishes at them and driving them out of the house.

And thus, having learned the bitter lesson that unselfishness is dangerous in a selfish world, Timon left the city of Athens and went to live in a cave in the woods. Here he found "the unkindest beast more kinder than mankind." While digging in front of his cave for roots to eat, he discovered hidden gold—the "yellow slave and tyrant" of the human race. But its glitter had lost its power. It aroused now within him nothing but contempt. He threw it back into the earth and kept only a few pieces to be used as stones against unwelcome strangers.

When the Athenians learn of this discovery, they come one by one to his cave. Poets, painters, warriors, prostitutes, statesmen, beggarmen, thieves—all of them are eager once more to become the friends of Timon. To each of them in turn he gives a handful of gold, and then like a scornful god he sends them scurrying back to hoard it or spend it in the pigsty of their city. "Go," he cries to several of the thieves as he hands them the gold. "Rob one another. There's more gold. Cut throats. All that you meet are thieves. To Athens go, break open shops; nothing can you steal but thieves do lose it."

All the world, to Timon, is a den of thieves. That is, all the world with the exception of one man. When Timon's old steward, Flavius, arrives to commiserate with his master in the hour of bitterness, Timon feels persuaded that there is, after all, some decency left in the world. "I do proclaim one honest man—mistake me not—but one; no more, I pray—and he's a steward." But he warns Flavius against his own goodness. "Methinks thou art more honest now than wise; for, by oppressing and betraying me, thou mightst have sooner got another service. For many so arrive at second masters upon their first lord's neck."

Shakespeare has been accused of despising the so-called lower classes. His critics tell us that he never showed any sympathy for them, that he always spoke of them with an aristocratic sneer, and that he looked upon them as mere "sticks and stones and worse than senseless things." Such critics do not understand the universality of Shakespeare's genius. The only lovable character in the entire human race, as represented in *Timon of Athens*, is a Roman slave. There are more sympathies in the mind of Shakespeare than are dreamt of in the philosophy of his critics.

Shakespeare was perhaps the only man in the world who could see life from every angle. He could be, on occasion, as revolutionary as Shelley, as bitter as Heine, as pessimistic as Euripides, as cynical as Byron, as disillusioned as Swinburne, as philosophical as Goethe, and as hopefully resigned as Tennyson. He was a poet who consecutively looked upon life through spectacles of different colors. In *Timon of Athens* he sees life through the dark glass of despair. Nothing in the world seems worthwhile. The erstwhile friend of Timon, Alcibiades, has tried to help his native city of Athens in a crisis. His city repays him with exile for his trouble.

He raises an army and marches against the city in retaliation for his unjust banishment. The senators, alarmed over the approaching danger, visit Timon in his cavern and implore him to return to Athens in the hour of their need. But Timon pays no attention to their entreaties. He invokes upon them all the noxious pestilences he can think of. And then, as if on second thought, he informs them that there is something he *will* do for them to save them from death at the hands of Alcibiades:

> I have a tree, which grows here in my close,
> That mine own use invites me to cut down,
> And shortly must I fell it; tell my friends,
> Tell Athens, in the sequence of degree
> From high to low throughout, that whoso please
> To stop affliction, let him take his haste,
> Come hither ere my tree have felt the axe,
> And hang himself.

And then, having sent the final shaft of venomous cynicism after his retreating countrymen, Timon digs his grave on the "verge of the salt flood" and puts an end to the evil nightmare of his life. Better to feast the grateful worms underneath, than the two-legged beasts who grovel thanklessly above.

Timon is not the only cynic in the play. The churlish philosopher, Apemantus, is also contemptuous of the stupidity of mankind. But there is a vast difference between the mournful bitterness of Timon and the sarcastic vulgarity of Apemantus. Timon kills himself because he cannot endure the spectacle of man's inhumanity to man. Apemantus, on the other hand, derives the keenest joy out of the selfsame spectacle. Timon would like to destroy the world and to build in its place a world of true friends. But Apemantus would rather find fault with the world than improve it. When one of the noblemen of Athens asks him what time it is, he replies, "Time to be honest." Yet if he ever found himself in an honest world, he would set about immediately to corrupt it, in order that he might be able once more to snarl about its dishonesty. The ingratitude of friends is to Timon no less than a mortal blow. To Apemantus, it is merely an occasion for laughter. It required the most subtle shading of character to draw both Timon and Apemantus in the same play. Yet each without the other would be incomplete. The two men together are the complete answer of Shakespeare, the satirist, to the injustice of the world.

III

In *Hamlet*, we get the answer of Shakespeare, the man of the world, to the same problem. Confronted with the baseness of humanity, Timon kills himself and Apemantus is merely amused. But Hamlet, less sensitive than Timon but more noble than Apemantus, tries to meet injustice with punishment and murder with revenge. He believes in the Old Testament doctrine of an eye for an eye, a tooth for a tooth, a life for a life. His reaction toward evil is the reaction of the average man. He does not run away from it like Timon, or mock at it like Apemantus. Instead, he broods over it and philosophizes about the meaning of it all; and finally, when his courage and his frenzy have been nursed to the highest pitch, he strikes —not against the evil deed but against the evil doer. And in so striking, he destroys himself as well as the object of his wrath.

Revenge, to Hamlet, was a noble mission. Nothing else, not even his love for Ophelia, must stand in the way. The world of *Hamlet*, in spite of its beautiful maxims and philosophical meditations, is a world of barbarians in which the highest ethical principle is the spirit of vengeance. Strip it of its poetry, and *Hamlet* is an ugly play. A young prince of fairly average intelligence loses his reason through his belief in spirits. Thinking that his father's ghost has urged him to avenge his murder, he goes crazy, reviles his mother, spurns and drives to suicide the girl he is about to marry, kills her father and her brother, and then brings about his mother's death and his own—all because he has promised a ghost that he will punish the king for having committed a murder. It is a rather high and stupid price to pay for a single act of vengeance. This play would indeed seem to be, as Voltaire called it, "the work of a drunken savage." The whole drama of our human existence, for that matter, often appears like the work of a drunken savage. But that is because we regard life, as some of the critics regard Shakespeare, from too narrow a point of view. *Hamlet* represents but a single aspect of Shakespeare's genius, just as vengeance represents but a single aspect of human life. Shakespeare, the magician who could imitate Nature so perfectly, knew better than to let Hamlet stand for his entire philosophy. He had other, and higher, ideas in his dramatic bag of tricks. Nature could produce a Confucius as well as an Orestes, and Shakespeare was able to create a Prospero as well as a Hamlet. In their final analysis, both Nature and Shakespeare have something finer to show to the world than the spirit of mere revenge. Just what this "something finer" is, we shall see in *The Tempest*.

IV

In *Timon of Athens*, Shakespeare repays injustice with bitterness; in *Hamlet*, with revenge; in *The Tempest*, with forgiveness. Like Timon and Hamlet, Prospero has been tried by suffering. But his sadness makes him all the more compassionate even toward those who have brought the suffering upon him. He does not storm against the world, he does not even laugh at its foolishness, but he smiles with the indulgence of a man who looks upon the follies of children. In *The Tempest*, Shakespeare has risen above the spirit of satire. He has entered into the world of true philosophy. In many of his other dramas he makes merry, like a heartless god, over the pettiness of humanity. He loves to drag the king down from the throne and to point out to him how with all his pomp he will some day be eaten by a worm, which in turn will be swallowed by a fish, which then in *its* turn will go into the guts of a beggar. But in *The Tempest*, even when he scolds, he scolds in a gentle voice. The tone of bitter scorn which he often employed in his earlier dramas has been transformed, in this play, into a tender note of pity.

And now—the story of *The Tempest*.

Prospero, the exiled Duke of Milan, lives with his daughter, Miranda, upon an enchanted island. Twelve years before, his brother Antonio, with the aid of Alonso, King of Naples, had treacherously driven him out of Milan and set him afloat, with his three-year-old daughter, in a leaky ship upon the open sea. Having fortunately drifted to this enchanted island, Prospero has spent his time in the education of his daughter and in the study of magic. He has enlisted in his service the faithful spirit, Ariel, and the treacherous savage, Caliban.

One day a ship passes by the island. There is a wedding party on board, returning from Tunis to Italy. Among others in this wedding party are King Alonso and Antonio, who have brought about the banishment of Prospero; and with them are the King's brother, Sebastian, and the King's son, Ferdinand.

Prospero, by means of his magic art, unleashes a tempest over the ocean and drives the vessel upon the enchanted island. He orders Ariel to rescue all the passengers, but to scatter them, in various groups, over the seashore. Ferdinand, thus separated from his father and believing him lost, wanders as it seems to him aimlessly over the island. In reality, however, he is being guided by Prospero's magic to the old enchanter's cell. Here the prince and Miranda, seeing each other for the first time, transact a mutual exchange of hearts even before they have had the opportunity to exchange a single word.

Meanwhile, in one part of the island, Sebastian and Antonio are plotting the murder of the King; and in another part, Caliban and a couple of drunken sailors from the shipwrecked crew are plotting to murder Prospero. Unaware of the fact that this island is enchanted, the newcomers are already trying to establish upon it the immoralities and the stupidities of the world from which they have come. But Prospero, all-knowing and all-powerful, frustrates their savage plans.

At first he is inclined to punish the King and his company for the injuries that they have inflicted upon him. But Ariel, with his more than human wisdom, converts him to a saner point of view. "The King, his brother, and yours," Ariel points out to him, "are all distracted, and . . . brimful of sorrow and dismay . . . Your (magic) charm so strongly works 'em, that if you now beheld them, your affections would become tender."

> *Prospero:* Dost thou think so, spirit?
> *Ariel:* Mine would, sir, were I human.
> *Prospero:* Hast thou, which art but air, a touch, a feeling
> Of their afflictions? and shall not myself,
> One of their kind, that relish all as sharply,
> Passion as they, be kindlier moved than thou art?
> Though with their high wrongs I am struck to the quick,
> Yet, with my nobler reason, 'gainst my fury
> Do I take part . . . Go, release them, Ariel . . .

Compare the words that Timon spoke to the senators with these words that Prospero speaks to Ariel, and you have the difference between the reaction of the man and that of the superman toward the injustice of the world.

For Prospero is a superman—the most sublime type of human character that either Shakespeare or Nature has been able to create. He is the Confucius of the Shakespearean world. He forgives—not so much because of his superior sympathy, but because of his superior wisdom. His mind works upon a plane which is far removed from the quarrels and the hatreds, the ambitions and the passions, the betrayals and the jealousies, and the oppressions and the retributions of the world into which he has been sent down to live. He is not a "stern censurer" of life, but an amused, though somewhat sorrowful, onlooker. When Miranda for the first time sees human beings other than her father on the enchanted island, she rapturously exclaims, "O wonder . . . How beauteous mankind is! O brave new world, that has such people in't!" But Prospero, smiling at her enthusiasm, replies, " 'Tis new to thee." He knows from experience that every human creature is "a devil, a born devil," on whom his teachings are "all, all lost, quite lost." He believes no man, and yet he loves all mankind.

Prospero is not only the best of Shakespeare's creations, but he is Shakespeare himself at his best. Like Prospero, Shakespeare too is an enchanter whose magic art has peopled the earth with elves and puppets and sprites and men, who has "bedimm'd the noontide sun, call'd forth the mutinous winds, and 'twixt the green sea and the azured vault set roaring war." Graves at his command "have waked their sleepers, oped, and let 'em forth" by his so potent art.

V

AND NOW, having reached the height of creation by creating *The Tempest*, Shakespeare, like Prospero, abjured his magic, broke his staff, and, folding up the bag of his enchantments, retired from the stage. He was through with teaching and amusing and scolding this dull-witted race of ours. From now on, he preferred to be an interested spectator.

He died in obscurity. The world knew nothing about the genius of Shakespeare. But then, Shakespeare cared nothing about the plaudits of the world.

IMPORTANT DATES IN THE LIFE OF
WILLIAM SHAKESPEARE

1564—April, born at Stratford-on-Avon.

1582—Married Ann Hathaway.

1584—Compelled to leave Stratford for poaching.

1592—Attained success as actor and playwright.

1593—Published *Venus and Adonis*.

1594-1610—Acted and wrote plays, at the rate of two a year.

1597—Bought a house at Stratford.

1602—Bought a large estate at Stratford.

1609—Published collection of his sonnets.

1610—Retired to Stratford.

1616—March 25, wrote his will. April 23, died in Stratford-on-Avon.

Galileo Galilei

1564–1642

A YOUNG MEDICAL STUDENT at Pisa was kneeling in the Cathedral. There was silence over the vast auditory save for the annoying rattle of a chain. A sacristan had just filled a hanging oil lamp and had carelessly left it swinging in the air. The tick-tack of the swinging chain interrupted the student's prayer and started him upon a train of thought that was far removed from his devotions.

Suddenly he jumped to his feet, to the amazement of the other worshipers. A flash of light had descended upon him in the rhythm of the swinging lamp. It seemed to him that this rhythm was regular, and that the pendulum of the rattling chain was taking exactly the same time in each of its oscillations although the distance of these oscillations was constantly becoming less and less.

Was this evidence of his senses correct? If so, he had hit upon a miracle. He must rush home and find out immediately whether he had suffered an illusion or discovered one of the great truths of nature.

When he arrived home, he hunted up two threads of the same length and attached them to two pieces of lead of the same weight. He then tied the other ends of the threads to separate nails and was ready for his experiment. He asked his godfather, Muzio Tedaldi, to help him in this experiment. "I want you to count the motions of one of the threads while I count the motions of the other."

The old man shrugged his shoulders. "Another of Galileo's crazy ideas," he mumbled to himself. But he agreed to help.

Galileo took the two pendulums, drew one of them to a distance of four hands' breadths and the other to a distance of two hands' breadths from the perpendicular, and then let them go simultaneously. The two men counted the oscillations of the two threads, and then compared notes. The total was exactly the same—one hundred counts in each case. The two threads, in spite of the great difference in their starting points, had arrived at the same point at the same time.

And thus, in the swinging motion of a cathedral oil lamp, Galileo had discovered the rhythmic principle of nature which today is applied in the counting of the human pulse, the measurement of time on the clock, the eclipses of the sun, and the movement of the stars.

II

GALILEO was always experimenting. Even as a child he refused to rely upon the authority of others. He submitted everything to the scrutiny of his own senses and his own mind. The son of a music master, he showed almost from infancy an interest in "the music of the spheres." His father referred to him as an absent-minded little stargazer who saw strange visions and heard uncanny sounds. At school, when the teacher was trying to explain the importance of the Latin preposition or of the Italian verb, young Galileo's mind was floating among the clouds in the wake of the toy balloon which his father had bought him as a birthday present. In his playtime he constructed all sorts of crude little instruments resembling carts and mills and boats—anything that his unusually keen senses had observed in his daily walks.

At the age of twelve he was sent to the monastery school at Vallombrosa, that "shady vale where pilgrims leave their soul in a kiss." Here, under the influence of the Benedictine monks, Galileo flirted for a time with the thought of entering the religious order. But his father discouraged him from this thought and removed him from Vallombrosa. He had other designs for Galileo—he wanted him to be a cloth merchant.

Galileo, however, had ideas of his own. He now insisted upon a scientific career for himself. He was eager to specialize in mathematics—a field which in those unscientific days meant a lifetime of obscure poverty. Finally the father and the son came to a compromise. Galileo entered the University of Pisa to study medicine.

And to plunge, secretly and heartily, into the study of mathematics. Under his medical textbooks of Hippocrates and Galen he concealed the works of Euclid and of Archimedes. And in his spare moments he conducted experiments with instruments of his own construction.

His professors soon got wind of his studies and his experiments. And they disapproved of them. For it was nothing short of heresy for a student to think for himself. All the scientific problems, the professors declared, had been finally and conclusively settled by Aristotle. Whenever a student dared to raise an objection to a dogmatic pronouncement, the professor would settle the argument with a citation from Aristotle: *Magister dixit*, the Master has spoken. And that was that. But here was a young student foolhardy enough to check the dogmas of his professors with his own observations. His recklessness must be curbed—for the good name of the university, for the good of his own soul. They wrote to Galileo's father about it, and the old musician warned his son to mind his professors and to stop meddling with the unknown.

But Galileo disregarded the warning. He had made a profound discovery—the fact that "the science of mathematics is the language of nature." And to the study of this language he was now ready to dedicate his life.

III

GALILEO'S PROFESSORS refused to give him his doctor's diploma. And so he left the University of Pisa—a reputed failure in medicine and a "crack-brained juggler of useless figures." But his skill in the juggling of figures had won for him a brilliant reputation among some of the leading mathematicians of Italy—Giuseppe Moletti, Father Cristoforo Clavio, and Guidubaldo del Monte—men to whom he communicated some of his scientific observations and who honored him with the title of "the Archimedes of his day."

But the Archimedes of his day found mathematics a poor substitute for medicine. For at that period many were sick, but few were curious. Galileo tried to get a number of pupils among the nobility, only to discover that hardly anybody cared to exchange abstract figures for concrete loaves of bread and butter. Fortunately, however, the chair of mathematics had become vacant at the University of Pisa and Galileo was able to secure the position—largely because of the fact that nobody else cared for it. For the salary was only 60 scudi (about $65) a year.

In order to increase his income beyond the starvation point, he began to practice medicine in his leisure moments. But his leisure moments were few. For he was now busier than ever with his experiments. It was his purpose, he said, to re-examine the scientific doctrines of Aristotle instead of accepting them as gospel truth. The way to arrive at a scientific truth, he maintained, was not to memorize the books of Aristotle, but to study the Book of Nature.

The students listened to his lectures with ill-concealed smiles, and the professors hurled anathemas upon his head. What did this insolent young upstart mean by removing from their shelves the sacred tomes of Aristotle and by replacing them with those ridiculous contraptions of pieces of string and lumps of lead and levers and circles and angles and planes? Why, these were toys for children and not tools for the serious study of the mysteries of the world. "Let him stop this nonsense," they threatened, or they would teach him a lesson he would never forget.

But he refused to stop his experiments, and therefore they decided to put their threat into execution. Contrary to the teachings of Aristotle, Galileo had asserted that two different weights released simultaneously from the same height would fall to the ground at the same time. This assertion, insisted the professors, was sheer nonsense. "Nobody but a fool can believe that a feather and a cannon ball will travel downward through space at the same speed." Now was the time to expose this absurdity, to the eternal disgrace of Galileo. They would compel him, in the presence of the entire faculty and student body of the university, to make a public exhibition of himself and his stupid theories.

Galileo was only too happy to accept the challenge. The place chosen for the "exhibition" was the Leaning Tower of Pisa. On the appointed day the professors dressed themselves in their long velvet robes and marched to the Tower. The students and many of the townspeople had preceded them. It was a noisy and hilarious crowd of merrymakers, prepared to see the execution of a man's character. Curiously enough, it had never entered anybody's head to verify for himself the simple fact about falling bodies. *Magister dixit.* Aristotle had spoken, so why bother to exercise your own brain?

And so the audience jeered on as Galileo climbed the steps of the Leaning Tower. In one hand he carried a ten-pound shot and in the other a one-pound shot. The moment came. Galileo released the two balls from the top of the tower. A shout of derision—and then a murmur of amazement. The unbelievable had actually happened! The two balls of iron had started together from the top of the tower, had dropped through the air together, and together had reached the ground.

Galileo had proved his theory. But some of the professors still maintained that he was wrong. In spite of the evidence of their eyes, they continued to advance the doctrines of Aristotle. And to persecute Galileo.

III

UNDISMAYED by his persecution, Galileo went on with his unconventional teaching—and his unconventional living. It was an academic rule at Pisa for professors to wear their robes not only in the classroom but on the streets as well. Galileo disobeyed this rule, since he looked upon it as utterly ridiculous. The robes, he insisted, interfered with his movements. Physically as well as mentally he wanted to be at all times free. "Conventional clothes, like conventional ideas, are the invention of the devil." Time and again he was compelled to pay a fine out of his meager salary for his persistent infraction of the rule. Finally the authorities of the university became impatient with this young rebel who dared to defy the established thoughts and customs of the day. He was not, they concluded, the right sort of man to guide the young. They must find some sort of pretext to dismiss him from the university.

And this pretext was not long in forthcoming. Prince Don Giovanni de Medici, the bastard son of Cosimo I, had invented a dredging machine with which he proposed to clean the harbor of Leghorn. A model of this machine was sent to Galileo for his examination and report. Galileo's report—which subsequently proved to be correct—was unfavorable. The machine, he said, was extremely ingenious with the exception of one item —it could not work. Incensed at this "affront" to his dignity, Don Giovanni demanded the dismissal of Galileo from the university on the ground of incompetence. The authorities of the university were only too ready to accede to his demand. The students, egged on by their Aristotelian professors, joined in the general chorus of yelping, and Galileo was hounded out of the University of Pisa.

But he had his friends—Moletti, Clavio, Guidubaldo, other mathematicians and physicists who had followed his brilliant experiments and appraised them at their proper value. With the help of some of these friends he was able to secure another, and better, position at the University of Padua. His salary was now almost $200 a year—a fabulous sum to Galileo.

But even more gratifying than the increase in his pay was the advance in his freedom. At Padua he was allowed to have his say without the interruption of catcalls and hisses. When he stepped upon the platform to deliver his first lecture (December 7, 1592) he was greeted with an ovation. Pupils and professors alike predicted a great future for him at this seat of learning where men were free to think. For Padua, together with the entire Venetian Republic, had been banned by the Church and was therefore exempt from the restrictions of the Inquisition. The Venetian scholars—and this included the faculty at Padua—were true to their faith, but they insisted upon the principle of the separation of their scientific studies from their religious devotions.

It was therefore with a clear conscience and an unfettered mind that Galileo was now able to continue with his experiments. And these experiments covered a wide range of theoretical and practical knowledge—from the courses of the stars to the maneuvers of the battlefield. Although he had never served in the army, he had acquired a thorough knowledge of military architecture. And this knowledge enabled him to secure a number of private pupils—princes, nobles, soldiers—men who aspired to devote their lives either to ruling or to fighting. These private pupils, in accordance with the custom of the day, came to live with Galileo. Some of them brought their servants along with them. It was a merry and stimulating group that gathered around the table of this young professor of twenty-eight.

But it was also a noisy group. And at times Galileo was glad to escape from it—into the arms of the Venetian courtesans. These "honored ladies," like the famous courtesans of ancient Greece, were regarded not as a vulgar class of "gold-diggers" but as a charming group of female companions trained especially for the purpose of supplying mental as well as physical diversion to their distinguished clientele. They could discourse intelligently on music, literature, and art. They were invited to the banquets and introduced to the wives of the nobles. Their clothes and their manners were "modest yet seductive." They taught many a great lady of Venice how to take better care of her body and her mind. In their bath water they used aromatic plants. They anointed their hair, polished their nails and their speech, and devoted themselves exclusively to the fine art of stimulating the senses of their lovers.

And Galileo was a man of susceptible senses as well as of good sense. He found great pleasure in the company of the courtesans. Especially of one of them—Marina Gamba. He never married—like Cicero he believed that a man cannot be both a good philosopher and a good husband—but he took Marina into his house as his mistress and he became the father of three of her children.

His paternal obligations, added to the costs of his social diversions and to the expenses of his scientific instruments, proved to be a bottomless sieve to his inadequate earnings. Although his salary kept constantly increasing, he was never out of debt. At one time he was obliged to ask the treasurer of the university for a two years' advance in his pay. The treasurer granted his request, though not without displeasure.

And his obligations kept mounting up. The harassed young teacher of Padua had now another source of worry to contend with. His relatives in Pisa, having heard of his academic success, had come to look upon him as the financial pillar of the family. Their demands upon his purse were inexhaustible. His brother, anxious to enter the service of a Polish nobleman, insisted that Galileo advance him the money for his trip to Poland. This requisite sum was greater than Galileo's earnings for an entire year. Galileo borrowed the money and sent it to his brother. And then his sister, having fallen in love with a worthless young scamp, demanded that Galileo supply her with her dowry. Galileo borrowed one-third of the amount asked for, and promised to pay the balance at a later date. But right after the marriage his brother-in-law sued him for the unpaid balance. Another debt, another burden—and the demands from his family kept coming on and on.

Yet in spite of his burdens and his worries, Galileo found time for his amusements—dinners and dances in Venice; private musicales which he attended frequently as an auditor and occasionally as a performer, for he was an expert player on the lute; popular recitations and serenades and carnivals and burlesques. He even composed several of the burlesques and probably acted in some of them—broad suggestive farces written with little delicacy and much wit. For Venice at that period was a city of free thinking, frank living, and boisterous laughter.

But these were merely the surface activities of Galileo's life. From first to last, his mind was dedicated to the pursuit of science. He organized, in a palace situated near the bridge of Santa Sophia, an *Academy of Refugees* —a scientific and philosophical club consisting of men who had "escaped" to Venice from various parts of Italy in order that they might be free to continue their studies and express their thoughts. It was at this club that

Galileo first disclosed the results of many of his observations and experiments. He acquainted the members with the mysteries of the *magnet* and the magnetic forces of the earth; he explained to them the intricacies of the *compass*, a new instrument he had just invented; he demonstrated to them another of his inventions, a machine designed to raise water and to irrigate the soil; he showed them how to measure the temperature of the air by still another of his invented instruments, the *thermometer*. And finally he aroused their admiration with the most amazing invention of them all—the *telescope*, "a gazer into the distant stars."

For the invention of the telescope Galileo neither deserved nor claimed the full credit. On one of his visits to Venice he had heard that a Dutch optician by the name of Hans Lipperhey had accidentally chanced upon a strange discovery. As he was working on his spectacle lenses in his shop, this man had noticed that by placing a convex and a concave glass together he could make distant objects near. This accidental discovery interested Galileo. With his usual thoroughness he began to study the subject, to examine the curvatures and the groupings of various types of glasses and to calculate, by means of precise mathematical formulas, the visual results of these different curvatures and groupings.

Finally (on August 21, 1609) he was ready to make a public demonstration of the first scientifically constructed telescope in history. Followed by a crowd of his friends and admirers, he climbed to the top of the Campanile in Venice. And then one by one he allowed them to look through his "magic magnifying glass." To their astonishment they beheld "sails and shipping . . . so far off that it was two hours before they could be seen with the naked eye." They beheld "the traffic in a dozen harbors, the cattle grazing on the distant hillsides and the worshipers going in and out of their churches in the faraway towns and villages." And then at night, turning their gaze to the heavens, they beheld "the nearness of the distant stars."

Galileo was overwhelmed with orders for his telescope. But he presented it, without compensation, to the Duke of Venice. Whereupon the Duke, not to be outdone in generosity, ordered Galileo's election to a professorship for life at the University of Padua—at a salary equal in purchasing power to about $5000 a year.

Galileo had reached the height of his prosperity and his fame. Yet he was unhappy. "The wings of Fortune," he wrote in one of his letters, "are swift. But the wings of Hope are drooping." Ever since his arrival in Padua he had entertained the hope of returning in triumph to Pisa, the city out of which he had been hounded in disgrace. Again and again he had petitioned Cosimo de Medici, the Grand Duke of Florence (and of Pisa), to hire him as his court mathematician. He had even dedicated one of his books, *Operations of the Compass*, to Cosimo. But the Grand Duke had remained deaf to his petitions. And now that he had accepted his lifelong professorship at Padua, Galileo resigned himself to perpetual exile, the venerated prisoner of his fame.

And then Cosimo died, and his son Cosimo II, a former pupil of Galileo's, came to the throne. He offered Galileo the position which the famous scientist had so vainly and so ardently sought. Galileo broke his contract with the University of Padua and eagerly made his way to the court of Cosimo II.

And to the great tragedy of his life.

IV

THE CAUSE of Galileo's tragedy—and of his everlasting glory—was his epoch-making book, *Sidereus Nuncius* (*The Messenger of the Stars*). Galileo had written this book in the free atmosphere of Padua. And he was now confronted with it in the inquisitorial environment of Florence.

Galileo had printed his *Sidereus Nuncius*, as he wrote to his friend, Belisario Vinta, in order to "acquaint all the philosophers and mathematicians with some observations which I have made on the celestial bodies by means of my spy-glass (*mio occhiale*) and which infinitely amaze me . . . I give thanks to God, who has been pleased to make me the first observer of marvellous things unrevealed to bygone ages . . . I have ascertained that the moon is a body similar to the earth . . . I have beheld a multitude of fixed stars never before seen . . . Moreover, I have ascertained . . . the nature of the Milky Way . . . But the greatest marvel of all is the discovery of four new planets . . . I have observed that they move around the sun."

And, he might have added, "I have observed that the earth, too, moves around the sun." But he failed to make this assertion, either in his letter or in his book. He merely mentioned it orally to some of his more liberal friends. To blazon it forth in writing would be tantamount to delivering himself into the torture chamber of the Inquisition. He remembered the fate of Giordano Bruno, who had been burned at the stake (in 1610) for his scientific declarations. Galileo felt that it would be safer for himself, and healthier for science, if he could continue to live and to conduct his experiments without the interference of the Inquisition. Together with the Koran he believed that "the ink of the scholar and the blood of the martyr are of equal value in the eye of Heaven."

But Galileo, in spite of his precaution, was destined to be a martyr as well as a scholar. For throughout the Florentine territory the Inquisition ruled with unlimited power and unflagging watchfulness. The Grand Inquisitor, Cardinal Bellarmine, had noted the fact that Galileo, while ignoring the question of the earth's movement around the sun, had nevertheless declared himself as a follower of Copernicus. Accordingly, on March 26, 1616, Galileo was ordered to present himself before the Inquisition.

When Galileo arrived at the Holy Office, Cardinal Bellarmine "advised" him to "abandon his heretical opinions about the earth and the sun and the stars." He was not to think such thoughts, nor to teach them, nor to defend them either orally or in writing, "under the threat of persecution."

Galileo, "with death in his soul," signed his renunciation and promised to obey. And the Cardinal released him with a triumphant smile. With a single stern decree he had stopped the planets from moving around the sun.

As for Galileo, he returned to Florence disheartened and ashamed. For a time he continued with his experiments in the quiet of his laboratory—and dared not disclose his discoveries to the world. But genius is born to be expressed just as the seed is planted to grow. In the long run, Galileo was unable to stifle his thoughts. He published another book on astronomy, and again he fell afoul of the dogmatic beliefs of the orthodox. Once more he was summoned to appear before the Inquisition—and this time on a far more serious charge. For he was now accused of "recidivism"—that is, the second commission of a crime after punishment for the first commission. The penalty for this "double crime" was death.

When he received the second summons to the Inquisition, Galileo was ill. The doctors issued an affidavit to that effect. "Galileo is in bed, and he runs the risk of going to another world rather than to Rome." But the Inquisitors were relentless. "If he is in any condition to come, let him be seized, bound in chains and transported to Rome."

He left for Rome in the frost of winter (January, 1633), and arrived there more dead than alive. When he presented himself before his judges he was in no condition, either physically or mentally, to defend himself.

His trial lasted six months. In the course of this trial he received the support not only of free thinkers but of many Catholic scholars and churchmen as well. For the Inquisition was as unpopular as it was powerful.

But the Inquisition had its way. On June 22, 1633, he was compelled to abjure his belief in the movement of the earth. "Before the Holy Sainted Gospels which I touch with my hands, I swear that . . . I reject and detest my former heresies . . . I confess that my error has been one of vain ambition and pure ignorance . . . I now declare and swear that the earth does not move around the sun . . ."

As his friends led him, trembling and exhausted, away from the tribunal, Galileo is said to have remarked under his breath, *"Eppur si muove"* —But the earth does move!

V

"IN THE MOST HOLY NAME of our Lord Jesus Christ, and of His Most Glorious Virgin Mother, Mary," wrote the cardinals of the Inquisition, "we decree that Galileo's books be prohibited by a public edict, and we condemn their writer to the formal prison of this Holy Office for a period determinable at our pleasure."

"Yet in spite of everything," exclaimed Galileo, "I shall remain a Christian!"

And a scientist. Although he had received strict orders to refrain from his scientific pursuits, he wrote another—and his greatest—book while he was in prison at Arcetri. This book, *The Laws of Motion*, was a summary of all the basic principles of mechanics. He wrote this work in secret, and had it smuggled out for publication in Holland.

Galileo never saw a printed copy of the book. For he had grown blind in his prison. But he enjoyed the comfort of holding the book in his arms as he lay on his deathbed (January 8, 1642). "I esteem this the most of all my works," he murmured. "It is the outcome of my extreme agony."

IMPORTANT DATES IN THE LIFE OF
GALILEO GALILEI

1564—Born, February, at Pisa.

1581—Entered University of Pisa.

1583—Discovered "rhythm of Nature."

1586—Invented hydrostatic balance.

1592—Appointed professor at University of Padua.

1592–1610—Absorbed in study of Astronomy.

1597—Invented first thermometer.

1609—Credited with invention of telescope.

1610—Discovered four satellites of Jupiter.
Appointed philosopher to Cosimo, the Grand Duke of Tuscany.

1613—Wrote *Dissertation on the Solar Spots*.

1616—Arrested by the Inquisition. Released.

1633—Arrested for the second time and imprisoned.

1642—His greatest book, *The Laws of Motion*, published.
Died, January 8, Arcetri.

Isaac Newton

1642–1727

He WAS BORN shortly after his father's death—a puny, premature and sickly caricature of a child. The midwife who attended at his birth did not expect him to live. "Why, he was so small I could have put him into a quart mug!" Such was destiny's whimsical way of introducing a prodigious mind to the world.

Newton's early years were spent with his mother. Then, by reason of her remarriage, he was transferred to the care of his grandmother. At twelve he entered public school and boarded with a druggist. But he was a "poor boarder and mischievous knave." He was always up to tricks that kept the poor apothecary's wits in a panic. It was difficult to cope with a boy of such an unruly temperament and such unpredictable habits. He would collect small hatchets, saws, and hammers of all sizes and build curious devices. He had become thoroughly acquainted with the mechanism of a windmill that was being constructed near the apothecary's house and he decided to build a windmill of his own. And it would be an improvement on all the others, he declared. He would run his machine with animal power! He would place a mouse on a treadwheel and deposit a morsel of corn above the wheel just beyond the desperate reach of this hungry miller. "Trust nature to set the mechanism in motion!"

He was always up to some trick of this sort. "Please, sir," he said one day to the druggist's brother-in-law. "May I have that box in the cellar to turn into a clock? I am certain you will never again be late through ignorance of the correct time." He built a clock whose hands were regulated by the action of dripping water that he poured into a pan every morning in the proper quantity. Next he built a "mechanical carriage" that was regulated by the hands and the feet of the rider. "Unfortunately, it could move only on a smooth level. It just obstinately refused to travel over the rough surfaces and ditches of the road." He took to flying kites and became interested in the "magic of sailing through the atmosphere." And one night he called his playmates together and told them with a devilish gleam in his eye: "I'm going to give the country folk the scare of their lives. I've just made some lanterns which I shall attach to the tails of my kites and fly them over the rooftops. People will think they are falling comets!"

Such were the amusements of the boy. In his more quiet moments he wrote poetry and drew charcoal sketches on the walls of his bedroom. But his relatives expected him to be neither a poet nor an artist. They wanted him to till the soil for his living. He had gained a great deal of weight and stature, and he looked like a promising farmer. And so his mother took him away from his studies and sent him to work in the fields. Once every week she made him go to market with her servant in order that he might become acquainted with the "gentle art" of haggling. But whenever he approached the town, Newton begged the servant to go to the market and to transact the business himself. "You'll find me here on the way back," he said. "I shall be studying my books behind the hedge."

One day Newton's uncle became suspicious and trailed him on his way to market. He came upon his nephew stretched out in the grass, hard at work on the solution of a problem in mathematics. The old man shook his head with grave and majestic resignation. "Go back to your studies, Isaac," he said. "Either you're a great loafer or a great genius—the Lord alone knows which."

II

As THE LAD PURSUED his studies through Trinity College, Cambridge, he found himself possessed of a great handicap—mathematical knowledge came too easily to him. What comes easily, is easily despised. During his graduate work at Cambridge he not only anticipated the academic solutions of the problems but he frequently suggested to his professors newer and simpler methods of solution.

But the study of mathematics was of no special interest to Newton. He regarded this science merely as a rather indistinct pathway into the mysteries of nature. He was concerned with far greater mental conquests. For he was not only a thinker but a dreamer, not only a mathematician but a poet. His was the method not of the stodgy observer, but of the imaginative creator. It was his purpose to plunge boldly rather than to grope timidly into the unexplored forests of human speculation.

As a boy he had written verses expressive of a fundamental attitude that the years could never extinguish. One of his poems was entitled *The Three Crowns*:

> *Earth's crown, thus at my feet I can disdain,*
> *Which heavy is, and at the best but vain.*

But now a crown of thorns I gladly greet;
Sharp is this crown, but not so sharp as sweet;
The crown of glory that I yonder see
Is full of bliss and of eternity.

Thus spoke the poet who was willing to suffer in the fulfillment of his vision—to accept the crown of thorns as a prelude to the greater crown of glory. Every great scientist is a poet with a vision. But he is a special type of poet who seeks to interpret his vision in the scientific light of the spectrum. In his university lodgings Newton had constructed a chemical laboratory, and on the ground by his window he had planted a garden. The poet paced among the chemicals and the man of science walked among the flowers. Before he had reached the age of thirty his hair had turned gray—as if paling before the immensity of thought confined within his head.

And he gave full sway to his thought, taking the entire universe for his domain. First he peered into the heavens as his great dreamer-predecessors had done. He discovered the curious fact that there are different degrees of refraction among the different rays of light, and upon this principle he constructed a reflector telescope which was designed to bring the heavenly bodies to a brighter focus. He next investigated the nature of white light, since he suspected that it was merely a composite of all the colors in the spectrum. And finally he turned to his own little corner of the earth and studied the plants in his garden—the shapes of the stems, the texture of the leaves and the hues of the flowers—the magic raiment of the growing things that "outrivalled Solomon in all his glory."

As a reward for his efforts, Newton was elected to membership in the British Royal Academy of Science. And he was appointed—at the age of twenty-seven—to a full professorship in mathematics at Cambridge University. This appointment, to a mind of inferior caliber, would have meant a lifelong banishment into the nebulous dreams of academic hairsplitting. Cambridge was full of these men who called themselves professors and research fellows and who were nothing but "perpetual undergraduates." They were a queer lot, these research scholars. One of them, a "youngster" of three score and ten, had shut himself completely up with his books and vowed that he would never see the sunlight again. But at night he tottered down the stairs, leaning feebly on his cane, and made the rounds of the campus for exercise. He stared at the ground through dim-sighted eyes, and whenever he caught sight of a worm he jabbed at it with his stick and exclaimed viciously, "Damn you, you haven't got me yet!"

And even Newton, though he escaped the intellectual sterility of many of his colleagues, was not quite able to escape their eccentricities. Busy with his cosmic dreams, he had little time to look after his personal appearance. Often he entered the university dining hall with his neckband loose, his hose ungartered and his breeches unbuttoned at the knee.

Yet with all his untidiness, Newton was a young man with a romantic heart. On one occasion "the flame of a breathless passion" prompted him to propose to a young lady of his acquaintance. Tenderly he held her hand and looked into her eyes. But at the critical moment his mind wandered into other fields of thought. He had become absorbed in the binomial theorem for infinite quantities. Dreamily he grasped his sweetheart's finger—in his fit of abstraction he took it for his pipe-cleaner—and tried to ram it up the stem of his pipe. Awakened by her cry of pain he apologized sheepishly. "Ah, my dear, I beg your pardon! I see it will not do! I am afraid I am doomed to remain a bachelor."

He had few students in his classes. When he tried to teach his latest discovery, the infinitesimal calculus, his class shuddered at the novelty and the complexity of the subject and stayed away from the formidable individual who had "foisted it upon the world." His fellow teachers were amazed at the facility of his computations. He had discovered a method—and that as a mere student—for the evaluation of infinity. By means of this "secret method" he had computed the area of a hyperbola to "two hundred and fifty figures." But he had not bothered to make his formula public. Living as he did in the subjective realm of his fancy, he never dreamed of the sensation his discovery might produce upon other people. Mathematics was but a game for his personal amusement, and not an instrument for practical use. For Newton had a queer sense of practical values. Once a visitor asked him to appraise the worth of a prism. Fascinated with the prism as an object of scientific research, he replied unhesitatingly: "The value is so great I can not even ascertain it." Whereupon the visitor offered to sell the prism to him—at an exorbitant price. Newton accepted the offer. "Why, you silly man," exclaimed his housekeeper when she saw the purchase. "You need only have paid a price according to the weight of the glass!"

The weight of the glass! He was baffled at the weights and the values set upon things by other people. On what principles of logic did they measure, buy and sell? Often on his vacations he would return to his mother's home and sit for many hours in her garden meditating upon the strangeness of the world. And once, as had happened so often before, an apple fell accidentally from a nearby tree. It marked one of the turning points in the history of human thought, this casual fall of an apple to the ground. For it set the mind of the man seated in the garden spinning as dizzily as the earth. Here was the true value of things—a value that the appraisers of gems and the merchants of gold had never even dreamed of! It took the moonstruck poets, the only sane among the insane, to interpret aright the riddle of the universe.

And this is how Newton interpreted the riddle of the falling apple: *The law of the universe is the attraction of mass to mass.* In a crude and fragmentary form this law had been recognized for some time. People knew that weights fall to the earth because of the gravity at the center.

But they did not know that this principle of gravity applies not only to the earth but to the entire universe. From planet to planet and star to star, throughout the incalculable terrain of space, this interplay of mutual attraction keeps every particle of the universe rolling over its appointed orbit in its appointed time to its appointed place—a complicated system of motion obeying the simple law of gravity under the watchful eye of the Eternal.

Newton returned to Cambridge in order to formulate this simple key to the riddle of the universe. As a result of his leisurely observation of the unimportant little things of his daily life, he had made one of the most important discoveries of history. He had raised the province of the physicist to the comprehensive plane of the astronomer and he had directed the imagination of man from the fall of an apple to the movement of the stars.

III

AT FIRST Newton was reluctant to publish the results of his observations. For he was a shy and retiring philosopher. "I'll print nothing," he had declared to his friends. "For that would only result in attracting acquaintances. And that is what I seek to avoid." His discoveries were a private pastime designed to amuse him in his solitary study. He was not bothered by a sense of obligation toward society. He was alone in a fanciful superworld of his own creation, trying to track down the footprints of the Eternal. It was a fascinating game—an excitement he wished to share with no one.

Finally, however, his friends convinced him that he owed a duty to his fellow men. And so reluctantly he began to prepare his manuscript for publication. He kept awake nights pacing back and forth in his study and refreshed himself for the long days ahead by a few hours' nap at dawn. "The meals that were carried to him warm for supper he would often eat cold for breakfast." A turn around his garden and then a sudden cry, "I have found it!" A mad scramble up the stairs into his room to make a few hasty notations while standing at his desk. An absent-minded saunter through the streets when he was invited to dinner and a sudden realization that he would be too late for his appointment. And then with a sigh he would go dinnerless back to his lodgings and resume the work on his theory. For hours on end he would stare trancelike into a telescope which he had mounted at the head of his garden. Sometimes he would turn with a puzzled look to the gardener whom he had overheard muttering, "This man knows more than the whole human race combined." The college librarian at Cambridge would refer to him with a significant motion of his finger toward his head. "A queer chap." He had few intimates, but rumor had it that he kept a cat. "Disturbed by her comings and goings," gossiped the librarian, "Mr. Newton had a hole cut in the wall for her convenience. And one day, when the cat came down with kittens, he resigned himself like a philosopher to the situation and cut a smaller hole for them beside the first one . . . But this," added the librarian, "is only a story. I don't know about it for sure."

Nobody knew much about Newton "for sure." Throughout his life his personality had been a problem too difficult to unravel. And finally, when the *Principia Mathematica* came off the press, the public found the book as difficult as the author. Even the scholars were nonplussed. A philosopher of the first rank called upon Newton and asked the scientist to suggest a course of study that might prepare him to understand the complex mathematics of the *Principia*. Newton graciously drew up a list of "necessary books"—an array so formidable that the philosopher in despair decided to give up his examination of the *Principia*. "The reading of the preliminary list alone," he explained, "would consume the greater part of my life."

Yet in reality, argued Newton, his book was not hard to understand. "The principles of my theory are within the intellectual grasp even of those who are unacquainted with the higher mathematics. For the book deals merely with the simple laws of matter." Every particle of matter in the universe gravitates toward every other particle of matter with a force inversely proportional to the square of their distances. "Do not be disturbed by my three volumes of geometric analysis." The essential attribute of matter is force—the innate power of resistance by which every body "endeavors to persevere in its present state . . . unless acted upon by some external force." This element of force—the tendency of the smaller body to resist and of the larger body to pull, the reaction and the attraction of matter—has transformed the static universe of the ancients into the dynamic universe of modern science. "Just give me the mass, the position and the motion of a system of heavenly bodies at any given moment and I will calculate their future positions and motions by a set of rigid and unerring mathematical calculations . . . I will calculate the tides and the motions of the waters and the earth. For the earth attracts the moon and the moon attracts the earth . . . and the force of each in turn tends to keep them both in a state of perpetual resistance. Attraction and reaction —reaction and attraction . . . The great masses of the planets and the stars remain suspended in space and retain their orbits only through this mysterious law of universal gravitation."

The leading scholars and scientists hastened to challenge this "outlandish" theory that the heavenly bodies moved in accordance with mechanistic laws. What a strange new divinity he had created with this mathematical theory of his—a machine-god without a will! And what a soulless sort of universe he had concocted in his "deranged poetical fancy"—a conglomeration of bodies whose only attributes are mass, position, and extension! "This crazy mathematician," declared one of his critics, "will not have twenty followers in his lifetime."

And the prediction of this critic proved to be correct. Isaac Newton lived forty years after the publication of his book and his converts at the end of that period "numbered less than a dozen." But he remained unperturbed. It was with the utmost indifference that he had published his book in the first place. He cared little about the prospects of a general reading public and he made no concessions to the reader. At no point did he offer any clarification of his intricate text. Indeed he seemed to write the book with only two or three of his scientific friends in mind. It was to them alone that he addressed his arguments. "As for the rest of the world, it can go hang for all I care." To the criticism that the universe as envisaged in his theory was "the lifeless story of a planless mind" he replied: "The fact that the universe is so beautifully designed in accordance with such harmonious laws . . . must presuppose the existence of a Divine Wisdom, the hand of a Divine Creator." But he refused to be drawn into any controversy as to the nature of God. "I can frame no hypothesis about Him. I am a scientist and I do not speculate about theological matters. I deal not with God, but with His observable laws."

Few of his contemporaries understood Newton. But that was hardly surprising; the complex and paradoxical mathematician scarcely understood himself. At the very hour of his triumph—the completion of a cosmic theory that was to become the basis of all future science—he was a dreadfully unhappy man. For, ironically enough, he was anxious to be recognized as a second-rate gentleman rather than as a first-rate genius. It was not enough that he possessed a noble mind; he must try to acquire a noble rank. Again and again during the writing of the *Principia Mathematica* he begged his influential friends to secure him a political position with the royal court. It bothered him not in the least that the world did not appreciate him as the supreme philosopher since Aristotle so long as his countrymen would recognize him as a paid political retainer of the British king.

IV

IT WAS IMMEDIATELY after the publication of his *Principia* that Newton went into politics. At first he had shown himself a fearless opponent of James II when that stubborn monarch had attempted to stifle the freedom of the universities. At the overthrow of the Stuarts and the accession of William and Mary, he sat as a member of the Convention that debated the new constitutional order. By nature, however, Newton was not an orator. He spoke only once at the Convention during the great debates— and that was to request an usher to close the window. The new king was not impressed with Newton's parliamentary ability. On one occasion, when asked to consult Newton on a political matter, William replied: "Oh, no. Newton is only a philosopher."

Yet the philosopher never relaxed his effort to become a courtier. And at last, when the office of warden of the mint fell open, Newton secured the appointment through the solicitation of his influential friends. His great mathematical mind was turned to the problems of coinage. The irony did not escape his countrymen. A character in a play remarked: "Newton? Oh ay—I have heard of Mr. Isaac—everybody has heard of Mr. Isaac—great man—master of the Mint." The name of Newton had become an object of ridicule from the lowest to the highest. "Some of my enemies," wrote Swift in exquisite burlesque, "have industriously spread the rumor that one Isaac Newton, an instrument-maker living near Leicester Fields, and afterwards a workman at the Mint in the Tower, might possibly pretend to vie with me for fame in future time."

This descent of Newton's from genius to mediocrity, remarked his more relentless critics, was only to be expected. To write the *Principia* had been merely a hobby with him. To become assistant master of the king's Mint had been his life's ambition. Newton had lost his sense of perspective, they said. His mind had broken down under the strain of writing the *Principia* and never again would he be "fit for mental service." Indeed, it was whispered that during the writing of the book "which neither he nor anyone else understood" he had suffered for a time a stroke of insanity. One windy morning, so the story went, he had returned from chapel and found that his cat had overturned a lighted candle on the table and set fire to many of his important papers. "Oh, Diamond," he had cried, "little do you realize the mischief you have done me!" And—continued the gossips—it was the grief at the loss of those papers, the result of many years of investigation, that had finally overturned his mind. "Perhaps too," observed some of the London wags, "he had caught a little touch of madness looking at the moon." And, indeed, some of his caprices were hardly those of a normal mind. "I must withdraw from your acquaintance," he wrote suddenly to a friend, "and see neither you nor the rest of my acquaintances any more." To another of his friends he wrote an apology for a letter he had sent him during a period when "I sat too often by the fire and was seized with a distemper." On one occasion he had severely criticized the work of his friend, the philosopher Locke. Upon receiving from Locke a letter of grieved expostulation, Newton replied: "I remember that I wrote to you, but what I said of your book I remember not. If you please to send me a transcript of that passage, I will give you an account of it if I can." Fits of temper, loss of memory, sudden outbreaks of suspicion and equally sudden outbursts of compunction—were not these the symptoms of a disordered mind? "No doubt all these rumors are exaggerated. But on the other hand, what else can you expect of a man who keeps constantly gazing at the moon?"

V

Now that he was drawing an adequate income as the king's servant, Newton felt that he must live in the proper style. He installed himself in the fashionable neighborhood of Jermyn Street, near Westminster, and took with him a favorite niece to become mistress of his household. His next job was to establish himself, if possible, as a "gentleman." Pretty embarrassing that his estate was so pitifully small. Yes, but he was the lord of his little manor, and he would testify on oath at the Herald's College that he was descended from the famous Newton family of Lincolnshire. "Can you trace the connection?" he was asked. "Why, no." Actually he could trace a connection only as far back as his grandfather, an honest but obscure farmer. But why despair? He would bolster up his shaky pedigree by attaching himself to an impecunious Scotch laird. After all, it was not impossible to *buy* a noble pedigree. "Do you know," he remarked casually to a Scotch nobleman, "that I too am a Scotchman? My grandfather was a gentleman of East Lothian—or was it West Lothian? Perhaps it was my great-grandfather . . ." "Never heard of him," replied the laird bluntly.

Ah, well, if he could not be a nobleman he could at least be a *rich* man. In addition to his city home he bought a country estate. Admiring scholars who came to visit him there discovered the "father of higher mathematics" engaged in the quite lower mathematics of disputing with his neighbors as to the number of cattle and sheep that he was entitled to feed on the village grazing grounds. Far from being immersed in planetary laws he was absorbed in haggling with his tenants over the price of repairing their barns and in threatening them with law suits if they failed to pay. The man who had discovered "the language of the solar system" was busily perfecting a language of violent invective against his ne'er-do-well nephew.

But he never quarreled with his niece, a woman of extraordinary wit and beauty. Indeed, there were rumors that he found in her a convenient advocate for the furtherance of his ambition. "When I was a young man," remarked Voltaire, "I used to imagine that the Court and the City of London had named Isaac Newton Master of the Mint by acclamation. But I was wrong. He had a most charming niece . . . She greatly pleased the Chancellor of the Exchequer . . . The infinitesimal calculus and gravitation would have been of no assistance to Newton without a pretty niece."

And at last—thanks again to the charms of his niece, it was whispered—Newton was knighted and introduced into the company of the Prince Consort, that "kindly, negligible mortal who drank like a fish." The now contented scientist settled down to a quiet old age of backgammon in the evening afterglow of a belated fame. But once more he was drawn into a stormy controversy. It had come to the ears of the Royal Academy, the

learned society of which Newton was now president, that the aggressive
German philosopher, Leibnitz, was claiming the sole credit for the invention of calculus. Newton's colleagues at the Royal Academy were outraged at the thought that a "foreigner" was trying to appropriate the
discovery of a British mind. For it was Newton, they believed, who had
first acquainted Leibnitz with the possibilities of calculus—"a method
which Leibnitz had later perfected, to be sure, but had never invented."

The members of the Royal Academy took up the cudgels in behalf of
Newton and England. The German savants, on the other hand, were
equally vehement in their defense of Leibnitz and Germany. They lam-
pooned the British as no scientists at all but as mere pseudoscientists.
"The British proclaim their discovery of an elephant on the moon when all
they see is a fly on the end of their telescope."

Back and forth raged the international quarrel as to the priority of the
invention of calculus. At first Newton tried to keep out of this quarrel.
But finally, when even the British king had been drawn into it, Newton
undertook to prepare a defense of his scientific reputation with something
of the vigor he had employed in his effort to establish a family tree. But
the controversy was as inconclusive as it was violent. Leibnitz went to his
eternal rest, Newton returned to his backgammon, and the world accepted
its calculus with a gratitude directed not so much to the ingenuity of an
Englishman or of a German as to the genius of the human mind.

VI

As the years progressed, Newton lost his interest in the foolishness of
controversy and the vanity of politics. His fame and his fortune were
secure. Time now to look for the security of his soul—the final evaluation
of his life not in the way of worldly success but in the measure of human
achievement. He was finally convinced that he had been first and foremost a scientist. He had foolishly regarded his mathematical investigations as a pastime and his pursuit of success as the primary business of his
life. He knew better now. "The value of life is not measured by the
weight of its accumulated baubles of glass." The prism of the human
mind is not to be exchanged for minted coin. At seventy-five he had
learned to look through his telescope with a brighter eye. "Knowledge
is an accumulation of vision"—the vision of the present superadded to
that of the past. "If I have seen farther," he said with a humility he had
not shown in his earlier days, "it is by standing on the shoulders of
giants."

From this lofty eminence he was able to look fearlessly toward his
own approaching end. Men die, as the stars and the planets die, in order
to give birth to new energy, new planets and stars, new life.

And he listened to the music of the spheres as they whirled incessantly
over their eternal course from life to death to renewed life. It was in this

music that he finally lulled himself to sleep. Music, sleep, death, life—light. Aye, that was it! In his mathematical formulas Newton had somewhere caught and imprisoned this secret of the universe.

Nature and Nature's laws lay hid in night.
God said, "Let Newton be!"—and all was light.

IMPORTANT DATES IN THE LIFE OF ISAAC NEWTON

1642—December 25, born at Woolsthorpe.
1661—Matriculated at Cambridge (Trinity College).
1665—Graduated from Cambridge.
1665—Began his studies on gravitation.
1668—Became major fellow of Trinity.
1668—Became a master of arts.
1669—Made a Lucasian Professor at Cambridge.

1671—Elected a member of the Royal Society.
1687—Published his famous *Mathematical Principles of Natural Philosophy.*
1689—Sat in Parliament for Cambridge.
1699—Became Master of the Mint.
1703—Elected President of the Royal Society.
1705—Knighted by Queen Anne.
1727—March 20, died at Kensington.

Thomas Jefferson

1743–1826

WHEN JEFFERSON ran for the presidency (1800), the following "intimate portrait of his character came from the lips of an opposition stump orator:"

"Tom Jefferson . . . is nothing but a mean-spirited, low-lived fellow, the son of a half-breed Indian squaw, sired by a Virginia mulatto father, as is well known in the neighbourhood where he has been raised wholly on hoe-cake . . . bacon and hominy, with an occasional change of fricasseed bullfrog, for which abominable reptiles he has acquired a taste during his residence among the French at Paris, to whom there can be no question he will sell his country at the first offer made to him cash down, should he be elected to fill the Presidency . . ."

Jefferson, continued his opponents, was not only a half-breed but a scoundrel. "He has defrauded the widows and the fatherless children!" And—they added—he was not only a scoundrel but an atheist. "If Jefferson is elected, the ties of marriage will be dissolved, our wives and daughters will be thrown into the stews, our children will be cast into the world and forgotten. Can the imagination paint anything more dreadful this side of hell?" The women of America were warned, in the event of his election, to bury their Bibles in their gardens, or he would confiscate and burn them "in a general holocaust of infidelity."

And what was Jefferson doing all this time? Quietly sitting at home and compiling the *Morals of Jesus*. He made no effort to reply to the avalanche of accusations that had been let loose against him. "While I should be answering one, twenty new ones would be invented." It is a common human failing, he observed, "to transfer to the person the hatred they bear to his political opinions."

And they hated his political opinions for but a single reason. He believed in the protection of the weak against the strong.

II

ON HIS MOTHER'S SIDE he was descended from the aristocracy; on his father's, from farmer and pioneer stock. His heritage therefore was two-fold. He possessed a genteel love for beauty and a rugged respect for work. His father, a giant of a man morally as well as physically, had expressed three wishes for his son. He wanted Tom to have a strong body, a classical education, and a gentle heart. Although he died when Tom was only fourteen, his three wishes were granted. For he had taken care to give the boy a proper start in life. He had taught him to ride hard, to study diligently, and to put himself whenever possible "in the other fellow's place."

At seventeen he entered William and Mary College at Williamsburg —Jefferson referred to it as "Devilsburg." Here, at the "headquarters of the aristocracy," he lived a studious, observant, and somewhat aloof life. He took frequent rides into the countryside, in order to escape from the "drinking and the gambling and the fox-hunting gentry" into the homes of the farmers and the trappers dressed in their coonskin caps, moccasins, and buckskin breeches. Much of his time he whiled away playing on his fiddle. He was very fond of his music. In one of his early letters he complained that while he slept at a friend's house during the Christmas holidays, "the cursed rats" had eaten up his pocketbook, his "jemmy-worked silk garters and half-a-dozen new minuets I had just got." But then he added good-naturedly, "Oh well, rats will be rats."

Good-natured, tall, rangy, soft-spoken, shy, freckled, and blue-eyed and redheaded, young Tom Jefferson made a favorable impression on Dr. William Small, professor of mathematics at William and Mary. And Dr. Small, in turn, made a favorable impression on Tom Jefferson. "From his conversation," wrote Jefferson many years later, "I got my first views . . . of the system of things in which we are placed." Thanks to Dr. Small, Jefferson became acquainted with a "young lawyer named George Wythe" (who was later to be one of the signers of the Declaration of Independence). This man of inflexible integrity, wrote Jefferson, inspired within him a feeling of "warm patriotism" and a respect for "the natural and equal rights of man."

Such were some of the influences that went into the growth of the character that was Thomas Jefferson. Yet when he left college his character was still in the formative stage. He could not make up his mind as to his future career—whether to become "a lawyer, a farmer, or a lover." He settled his perplexity by becoming all three—he passed the bar, he enlarged his inherited farm, and he began to pay court to Rebecca Burwell. In the first two ventures he was fairly successful, but in the third he failed. Rebecca married his rival, and for a time he plunged into the "dissipation of dancing and flirting" with the pretty girls at "Devilsburg." Jefferson, however, was not cast in the character of a devil's disciple. He enjoyed neither smoking nor drinking nor gambling. Before long he found himself out of step with the light-footed denizens of the primrose path. He returned to his studies and his hard work. "His working day," we are told, "averaged fifteen hours." Although he had a great many servants, as became a landed aristocrat at that period, he always rose early to build his own fire in his bedroom. "For what purpose have our hands been given us if not for labor?"

Man is made for labor—and for love. At thirty Jefferson once more began to pay court to a young woman. And this time he was successful. On New Year's Day, 1772, he married the twenty-three-year-old Martha Skelton, and carried his "personable little bride" over the threshold of his newly built home on the hilltop of Monticello.

It was a journey of a hundred frosty miles from her home in Charles City to Monticello. They had started in a phaeton, but they had been obliged to abandon it and to go forward on horseback. The last stage of the journey was over a footpath two feet deep in snow. When they arrived at Monticello late at night, there were no servants, no fire, no food to greet them. But the bride and the bridegroom were happy in the warmth of a mutual affection.

This wedding journey to Monticello was symbolical of their wedding journey through life—sad and bleak and affectionate. And tragically short. Within ten years they lost three of their children. And then the mother followed them. Jefferson never married again.

III

SHORTLY after his marriage Jefferson gave up his law and went into politics. "The lawyer tries to take advantage of *bad* laws. The politician—or rather the statesman—tries to bring about the adoption of *good* laws." He regarded his politics as an adjunct to his farming. It is the business of the farmer to produce the proper food for the nation. It is the business of the politician to see that the nation is properly fed. The immortal Declaration of Independence, which Jefferson wrote, was but a step in this direction. This Gospel of Justice, based upon the philosophy of Plato, Locke, Montesquieu, Rousseau, and Voltaire, "will enable the citizenry . . . to understand their rights, to maintain them, and to exercise with intelligence their parts in self-government." And in self-sustenance. His objective was not only political and social independence, but economic independence as well. He was anxious to "prevent the accumulation and perpetuation of wealth in select families."

It was this spirit that animated his entire political life. He endeavored to transform America from an *aristocracy* to a *democracy*—from the arbitrary rule of *private wealth* to the equitable rule of the *commonwealth*.

Jefferson entered upon his political career with no personal hope of gain. Statesmanship in those days was not an attractive profession. It meant hard work, inadequate pay, and neglect of one's private affairs at a time when such neglect might prove very costly. Many a well-to-do statesman found himself, at the end of his official career, financially ruined. This was to prove true in the case of Jefferson, and he probably knew it from the very start. It was with reluctance, therefore, that he accepted his political jobs. He would have preferred the uninterrupted enjoyment of "my family, my friends, my farm, and my books." Nature, he observed in one of his letters, had intended him "for the tranquil pursuits of science." But the nation demanded his services, and Jefferson accepted his job as a public duty.

He first served his nation as the governor of Virginia (1779). Plunged into his gubernatorial duties in the middle of the Revolution, he had little opportunity to display his constructive statesmanship. But even at this early period of his career he distinctly showed the democratic trend of his philosophy. He stood for free education, free libraries, religious tolerance, the emancipation of the Negroes, and the abolition of primogeniture—that is, the custom of handing down the entire inheritance of an estate to the first-born. Through the abolition of primogeniture he hoped to keep the land of the nation divided into small parcels among a large number of people, instead of allowing it to pass into the hands of a few owners of enormous estates. "Ill fares the land, to hastening ills a prey, where wealth accumulates and men decay." Like the English poet, Jefferson wanted to see a land of distributed blessings rather than one of concentrated glory. And that was why the Tories—the men who held the reins of concentration in their hands—so heartily detested Jefferson. "He was the first American," as Claude G. Bowers points out in his *Jefferson and Hamilton*, "to invite the hate of a class."

It was as an enemy of the exploiting class that he was hailed in Paris when he arrived there as ambassador in 1784. He came there both as a student and as a teacher of revolution. He traveled over the countryside, observed the life of the peasants, sat with them at table to see what they ate, rested on their beds to note whether they were comfortable, and inquired into their ideas and their hopes and their fears. As a result of his study he came to the conclusion that "every man here is either the hammer or the anvil." And he threw himself heartily into the cause of the "ever-beaten, ever-resisting" anvils. The government of France, the governments of all the other European countries, he observed, are "mere devices for taking money out of one man's pocket and putting it into another's." They are "governments of wolves over sheep." He returned from France more firmly convinced than ever that "the republican is the only form of government which is not eternally at open or secret war with the rights of mankind."

IV

ON HIS RETURN to America he was invited to enter George Washington's cabinet as Secretary of State. He arrived in New York, the temporary capital, in the winter of 1790. And immediately he found himself with a first-class fight on his hands. America had won the war, but it had not attained its independence. The country was now threatened by a new tyranny—the absolute power of wealth. The people who had shed their blood in the Revolution now discovered, to their dismay, that they had exchanged an English *autocracy* for an American *aurocracy*—a government of gold. There was an open struggle between the *producers* of wealth on the one hand and the *exploiters* of wealth on the other. Jefferson aligned himself on the side of the producers—the manufacturers, the farmers, and the laborers—all those who used either their money or their hands to make goods. The other side had found their leader in Alexander Hamilton, who represented the interests of the exploiters—the monopolists, the bankers, and the speculators—all those who used either their capital or their ingenuity to make money. Jefferson was an idealist, a dreamer ahead of his day. Hamilton was a realist, a perfect product of his day.

And, strangely enough, the idealist was triumphant over the realist. When the smoke of the battle had lifted, America was seen heading diffidently but definitely in the direction of democracy. And out of the fight emerged two opponents worthy of one another's respect. For both of them were sincere, and each of them respected the sincerity of the other. "Alexander Hamilton," wrote Jefferson of him some years later, "was disinterested, honest, and honorable in all private transactions." As for his public acts, "Mr. Hamilton formed his conclusions after the most mature consideration . . . His principles were conscientiously adopted." And Hamilton, though given to invective in the heat of battle, retired after his defeat with the acknowledgment that America might have been put into less trustworthy hands than Jefferson's. "After all, Jefferson has . . . character."

V

JEFFERSON had character. This was clearly shown in his relations toward his servants. And in the relations of his servants toward their master. He is on his way to Monticello, returning home for a spell after a term of public service. The slaves, "all adorned in their Sunday splendor," are waiting for him at the foot of the hill. The carriage appears around a bend in the road. The slaves, singing, laughing, shouting, weeping for joy, rush forward to greet "Marse Jeff'son." Unhitching the horses, they pull and push the carriage up the hill. "Glory be you'se back home safe!" They kiss his hands, his feet, the hem of his cloak. And now they have arrived at the summit. Lifting their beloved master on their shoulders, they carry him in to a banquet fit for a king. "Only you'se no king, praise de Lawd, you'se a republican."

And it was as a republican—a believer in the public administration of the public affairs—that Jefferson was elected to the presidency. Almost the entire press had fought against him. "With Jefferson holding the reins our civilization will be wrecked . . . It is dreadful to contemplate the results of his election."

But there was nothing dreadful either in the ideas or in the acts of President Jefferson. His first inaugural may be not inaccurately described as a political Sermon on the Mount. In this inaugural he outlines his policy as the servant of a free and democratic country. "I approach my task," he begins, with those anxious and awful presentiments which the greatness of the charge and the weakness of my powers so justly inspire." For he realizes that his country, young and inexperienced and none too vigorous, is entering upon a career among nations "who feel power and forget right." Yet this country, he goes on, "is the world's best hope." The republican government is "the strongest government on earth."

And what is this republican government that he envisions in this inaugural? It is a government in which the will of the majority shall rule, the rights of the minority shall be protected, religious intolerance shall be abolished, labor shall not be exploited, justice shall be dispensed equally to all men, peace and honest friendship shall be maintained with all nations, and entangling alliances shall be made with none. And then he ends his inaugural with a simple and sincere prayer to the Infinite Power "to lead our councils to what is best, and to give them a favorable issue for our peace and prosperity."

In Washington—which had now become the seat of the government— Jefferson lived as peacefully and as simply as he had lived at Monticello. The British minister to the United States, a sullen individual by the name of Merry, was scandalized one day when, calling on business at the White House, he was received by Mr. Jefferson in slippers and a dressing gown.

"I want to be known as plain Mr. Jefferson . . . I hope that the terms of Excellency, Worship, and Esquire have disappeared from among us forever." He disliked official kowtowing and ceremonial formality. "We have suppressed," he wrote to Kosciusko, "those public forms and ceremonies which tended to familiarize the public eye to the . . . less democratic forms of government."

He was a plain man administering justice from a plain city. "Washington," wrote Gouverneur Morris sarcastically, "is the best city in the world to live in—in the future." One could travel through the city for miles, remarked Abigail Adams, without seeing a human being. Washington was indeed a capital of "magnificent distances." The streets were "unlighted swamps and forests." A party of Federalist leaders, returning home from a friend who lived only two miles away, lost their bearings in the "impenetrable blackness" and wandered all night over the waste-lands. The inhabitants of the city were few and widely scattered. "From the steps of the Capitol one could count seven or eight boardinghouses, one tailor's shop, one shoemaker's, one printing establishment, the home of a washerwoman, a grocery shop, a stationery store, a drygoods house, and an oyster market." A symbol of American democracy at that period. And of Jefferson's character. Wide horizons, and an all-inclusive sympathy from printer to President.

Jefferson's two terms in Washington were on the whole uneventful. His great liberalizing work had been completed before his election to the presidency. One of the events of his administration, however, was of the greatest importance. This was the purchase of Louisiana (1803) from Napoleon, who had previously acquired it from the Spanish king. The territory which then became a part of the United States is not to be confused with the present state of Louisiana. The land which Jefferson's envoys purchased from Napoleon, and which at that period went under the name of Louisiana, comprised an enormous territory reaching all the way from the Mississippi to the Rockies and from Canada to the Gulf of Mexico. It more than doubled the size of the United States, and it opened up the West to the flood of pioneers who poured in from the East. And all this territory Jefferson was able to get for only fifteen million dollars. It was "the most stupendous bargain in history."

VI

JEFFERSON retired from political life "with hands as clean as they are empty." He had always as a public servant refused presents, however small. For he was anxious, as he wrote to Samuel Hawkins, "to retain that consciousness of a disinterested administration of the public trusts which is essential to perfect tranquillity of mind."

And so it was with perfect tranquillity of mind that he departed from his public duties. "Nothing is more incumbent on the old," he observed, "than to know when they should get out of the way, and relinquish to younger successors . . . the duties they can no longer perform."

He returned to Monticello—and to financial ruin. Far from enriching himself at the expense of the government, he had paid out of his own pocket for the many social functions necessitated by his official duties. And his plantation, under the inefficient management of his overseers during his absence, had sunk into a deep morass of red ink. He now found himself burdened with a debt from which he was unable to emerge to the end of his days. In order to pay off a part of this debt, he was obliged to sell his entire library—a collection of books he had accumulated during a lifetime of diversified interests.

Yet in spite of his poverty he retained the catholic scope of his interests. Echoing the ancient Latin poet, he said, "I am a man, and therefore everything human is within my horizon." He devoted his declining years to farming, philosophy, science, art, music, literature, religion—and, above all, education. For "education, the ploughing and the planting of human thought, produces the universal food of human progress."

With this object in mind, he not only conceived the idea, but drew up the architectural plans, for the University of Virginia. His chief interests, he said, were intellectual and ethical rather than political. He requested that his tombstone should proclaim nothing of his career as governor and ambassador and President. He wanted the inscription to mention only three things by which he hoped to be remembered: his writing of the Declaration of Independence, his fighting for religious freedom, and his founding of the University of Virginia.

And now, in his eighty-fourth year, he found himself face to face with the prospect of being turned out-of-doors. He was obliged to sell his estate in a lottery in order to save his "home in Monticello to lay my head in, and a plot of land for my burial."

Assured at last of his home and his grave, he was ready for the end—"that great adventure, untried by the living, unreported by the dead." He was tired, he said, of "pulling off my shoes and stockings at night, and putting them on again in the morning." He prayed for only one thing—that "the Benevolent Being who presides over the world" might spare his life until the next Independence Day.

And God heard his prayer. Thomas Jefferson died on the Fourth of July, 1826.

IMPORTANT DATES IN THE LIFE OF
THOMAS JEFFERSON

1743—April 2/13, born, Albemarle County, Virginia.

1760–62—Student at William and Mary College, Williamsburg, Virginia.

1762–67—Studied law.

1769–75—Member of the Virginia House of Burgesses.

1775–76—Delegate to the Second Continental Congress at Philadelphia.

1776—Wrote the Declaration of Independence.

1779–81—Governor of Virginia.

1785—Succeeded Benjamin Franklin as Minister to France.

1790—Appointed Secretary of State in the first administration of President Washington.

1793—Resigned from cabinet in protest against Hamilton's financial policy.

Founded party of "Democratic-Republicans."

1796—Elected Vice-President in administration of John Adams.

1800—Elected third President of the United States.

1801–02—Successful war against Barbary pirates.

1803—Purchased Louisiana Territory from France.

1807—Declared embargo against French and British to retaliate against their impressment of American sailors.

1809—Retired to private life after two terms in the White House.

1819—Established the University of Virginia.

1826—July 4, died, Monticello, on the same day as John Adams.

Johann Wolfgang von Goethe

1749–1832

THE YOUNG MEN and young women of the eighteenth century were Modernists. Like the young men and women of today, they were dissatisfied with the world in which they found themselves and tried to create in its place a world that would be nearer to their heart's desire. In France and in America the rebellion took a political turn. In other countries, however, and especially in Germany, the revolt against tradition was purely intellectual. The soldiers of the German revolution discarded the antiquated ideas of their nation, but they left the antiquated government alone. Theirs was a revolution of the pen, and not of the sword. They liberated the minds of their countrymen, but they were not much concerned about their bodies. They believed in free thought, but not in free action. They were the conservative radicals of the eighteenth century.

The leader of these intellectual revolutionists was Johann Wolfgang von Goethe. At the age of six he rebelled against God. At seven he expressed his doubts about the justice of men. At eight he composed a Latin essay in which he compared the wisdom of the pagans with that of the Christians. At eleven he wrote a cosmopolitan novel in seven languages. At twelve he fought a duel. At fourteen he fell violently in love for the first time. At seventy-four he fell violently in love for the last time. And at eighty-two he completed his greatest poem, the second part of *Faust*.

II

GOETHE was born in 1749. His great-grandfather had been a blacksmith and his grandfather was a tailor. But the tailor made a man out of his son, Johann Caspar, who became the Imperial Councilor of Frankfurt and promptly forgot about his humble origin.

Goethe, the son of Johann Caspar, never mentioned the blacksmith and the tailor among his ancestors.

Like the great French philosopher, Voltaire, he was born half-dead. But unlike Voltaire, he enjoyed good health for the greater part of his life. In all his eighty-three years he suffered only three serious illnesses. He was one of those few fortunate mortals endowed with a perfect mind in a perfect body.

He was educated at home. His father, somewhat of a classical scholar and a strict disciplinarian, put him through a course of study which trained the intellect rather than the imagination. His mother, on the other hand, a simple, hearty, joyous, and well-read *Jungfrau*—she was only eighteen at the time of Goethe's birth—stimulated his poetic faculty by telling him stories of her own making and by encouraging him to help her in the weaving of the plots and in the creation of the characters. "To my father," he said, "I owe my serious outlook on life; to my little mother, my love for telling tales."

His father wanted him to study law and to become a college professor. But Goethe was interested neither in law nor in teaching. To please his father, he entered the University of Leipzig (1765); but to please himself, he became a student of life rather than of books.

Plentifully supplied with money, for his father was well-to-do, he proceeded to break through the conventional shell of his home environment and to experiment recklessly with the ways of the world. For his teachers he had not the slightest respect. "I fancied I knew as much about God and the world as the professors themselves." He felt that he could learn much more about life if he neglected the classroom and went into the haunts of the people. "In society, concerts, theater, feastings, promenades, the time flies. Ha, it goes gloriously! But also expensively. The devil knows how my purse feels it!"

One of his fellow students, writing about the unrestrained conduct of Goethe at this time, remarked that it would be easier to "influence the trees and the rocks than to bring Goethe to his senses."

But he came to his senses of his own accord. Throughout his life he experimented with wine and women, and then he transmuted his experience into song. Having learned all he needed to know about the society of Leipzig, he left it for the solitude of the country, where he took long rambles, reading his Shakespeare and his Homer and dreaming his poetical dreams.

For he lived in order to sing. He had begun his literary career as a mere child. And now, at the age of seventeen, he dashed off his first important drama, dealing—of all the subjects in the world—with the rascalities and the adulteries of married people! *Die Mitschuldigen* (*The Fellow Sinners*) is written with a sophistication that is astonishing in a youngster of seventeen. Like most of the adolescent dramas, it is a story with a moral; but the moral has within it the concentrated wisdom of all the sad old men who have sinned and suffered for their sins. "Inasmuch as the majority of us are guilty," concludes the indulgent young philosopher of Leipzig, "the wisest thing for all of us to do is to forgive and forget."

III

THE dissipation of his Leipzig days—and nights—came near to putting an end to his life. In the summer of 1768 he was seized with a violent hemorrhage, and for a time it was doubtful whether he would recover. When at last he was able to leave his bed, he returned home—to an adoring mother and a disappointed father. Herr Johann Caspar Goethe had tried to make a lawyer out of his son, and the boy had turned out to be nothing but a poet!

The Councilor made another attempt to put Wolfgang on what he considered to be the right road. This time he sent him to Strassburg, to complete his studies "without any further nonsense" and to get his doctor's degree in Jurisprudence.

But here too, as in Leipzig, Goethe neglected his law and resumed his study of life. He dabbled in art, he learned to play the cello, he took up medicine, he philosophized, he flirted, and he became the leader of the Strassburg intelligentsia. His health was completely restored now. He walked through the streets of the city like a Greek god. On one occasion, when he entered a restaurant, the diners laid down their knives and their forks to stare at the magnificent young stranger.

He was, to use his own expression, "intoxicated with youth," and all those who came into contact with him were infected with something of his own spirit.

An excellent swordsman and rider, and a singer of magical phrases such as Germany had never heard before, he turned the heads of all the Strassburg *Fräuleins*. And his own head was almost always in a whirl.

But if he loved easily, he easily forgot. Whether jilting or jilted, he translated his experience into a poem and then turned to his next adventure.

In his eagerness to study life from every possible angle, he fell in with all sorts of people—inn-keepers, inn-keepers' daughters, evangelists, dancing masters, merchants, manufacturers, workers, rabbis and priests. And, like Spinoza, he found something lovable and divine in everyone that he met.

He was especially fond of the stage. A passionate admirer of Shakespeare, he tried to transfuse some of the rich blood of the Elizabethan drama into the anemic productions of the German theater. With the exuberant optimism of youth, he set out to revolutionize not only the *art* but the very *thought* of his nation. He examined the history of Germany for dramatic material that would give full scope to his lawless genius. He found it in the life of Götz von Berlichingen, the Robin Hood of Germany. This man's exploits against the bishops and the barons in behalf of the peasants inflamed Goethe's imagination into producing one of the wildest, yet one of the most magnificent, of German dramas. It became for a time the Bible of the younger generation, and Goethe was worshiped as the prophet of the new religion of unrestraint.

Yet, much to his father's gratification, he was able to spare enough time from his "lawless activities" to obtain a degree as doctor of law. His father sent him, for further training, to the Supreme Court of Wetzlar. But Goethe noticed on his arrival that there were twenty thousand cases awaiting the Imperial Judges' decision, and that it would take them no less than three hundred and thirty-three years to get through with all these cases. This settled his own case. He lost all respect for the law and definitely turned to literature as his life's work.

During his short stay at Wetzlar he fell, as usual, desperately in love. This time the situation was complicated by the fact that Lottchen, the young lady of his choice, was already engaged. For a time he thought of committing suicide. He kept a dagger under his pillow, and every night he tried to muster up sufficient courage to plunge it into his heart. Finally, however, he decided to write a novel about his unfortunate love affair, and to kill the hero in the novel instead of killing himself. The result was *The Sorrows of Werther*, a book of romantic nonsense and sublime beauty. It is the autobiography of a misfit—a sensitive artist who does not feel at home among his fellows and who finds companionship only in the solitude of the fields. It is an elegy on the sadness of life, a hymn to the joyousness of death.

The Sorrows of Werther produced a tremendous effect upon the German public. All the young men imitated Werther's blue coat and yellow waistcoat, and the girls adopted Lottchen's white dress with the pink bows. In Germany the book was sold like a newspaper on the street corners; and even in China, Werther and Lottchen were modeled in porcelain. In some places the more sentimental admirers of the book went so far as to organize "Werther societies for the suppression of life." An epidemic of suicides swept over Europe as a tribute to the genius of Goethe.

But Goethe himself had no desire to put an end to his life now. Leaving his love and his book and his admirers behind, he pressed on to new fields and new adventures.

IV

ALTHOUGH he flouted the conventions, Goethe had a deep-seated reverence for authority. "I cannot blame you," he writes to one of his friends, "for living in the world and making acquaintances amongst men of power and influence. Intercourse with the great is always advantageous to him who knows properly how to use it." And so, when Prince Karl August asked him to come to his court at Weimar, Goethe accepted the invitation with alacrity.

He reached Weimar (in 1775) at the age of twenty-six. He stayed there for the rest of his life. Taking up his residence in a "garden-house" near the palace, he divided his time between poetry and politics. He became not only the devoted priest of Apollo, but the equally devoted servant of Karl August. He was the German Confucius who tried to teach his prince how to rule; and in so doing, he gave up his own independence. Confining his rebellious spirit to his books, he became in his private life one of the most submissive of courtiers. On one occasion, when he was walking with Beethoven, the prince's retinue happened to pass by. The composer, who respected nothing but his art, threw out his chest and walked defiantly through the pompous crowd. Goethe, however, who worshiped royalty even more than his art, stepped aside, took off his hat, and bowed in deepest reverence. For he was a true son of Germany. He was proud of his distinction as the poet-laureate of the world; but he was even more proud of his dignity as the private secretary of one of the least important of German princes.

Saxe-Weimar, the little province over which Karl August ruled, boasted an army of only 600 men. But it was an army of little tin gods adored by the military idolatry of the Germans. Every German prince, even though his domain consisted of only a few acres, was constrained to support an army for the worship of his subjects. One of Karl August's fellow princes, for example, boasted a "superb military force" of seven officers and two men in the ranks!

Such was the childish pretentiousness of official Germany in the eighteenth century. And Goethe, in spite of his great genius, was not altogether free from it. Yet life at the court of Weimar was gay, and his duties sat lightly upon his shoulders. He made hunting and skating popular, and he turned flirting into one of the most fashionable amusements of the day. "We are somewhat mad here," he writes in one of his letters, "and play the devil's own game." If he sacrificed his independence to Karl August, he got from him in return "what the great seldom bestow—affection, leisure, confidence, garden and house." He loved his art, but he was equally fond of his comfort. He was not a prophet who was willing to die for Truth, but a poet who was anxious to live for Beauty.

V

FOR FIFTY YEARS he made Weimar the literary center of the world. He gathered about him a group of brilliant men and women who, under his leadership, discussed philosophy, devoted themselves to poetry, and played at love. He organized and became the director of a Little Theater, and he wrote for it some of the greatest dramas of the century. As long as his youth lasted, the tone of his writing remained wild, and at times flippant. In *Stella*, for example, he allowed the hero to live with his wife and his mistress at the same time—to the mutual satisfaction of all three. This "plea in favor of bigamy" aroused violent opposition on the part of the public. And so, with his tongue in his cheek, Goethe rewrote the end of the play. He got his hero, who was unable to quit either his wife or his mistress, to solve the difficulty by blowing out his brains.

Gradually, however, we find this note of exuberant irregularity less and less dominant in Goethe's works. Finally it disappeared altogether. The intoxication of his youth had subsided. From now on, he was no longer a rebel who wanted to destroy the world, but a philosopher who tried to understand it.

His lifelong quest was now for more light—more beauty. He sought for beauty even in ugliness, and for dignity in the midst of humility. Like Walt Whitman, he was passionately fond of human beings, however lowly their station. If he bowed to princes, he did not shun the society of paupers. Throughout his life he was on the most intimate terms with "the butchers and the bakers and the candlestick makers" of the world. "How strong my love has returned upon me for these lower classes!" he wrote after visiting a group of miners. "These so-called lower classes are, in God's eyes, assuredly the highest!"

His expressions of sympathy for the underdog were not mere rhetoric. Out of the meager salary of $1000 a year which he received as the Councilor of Karl August, he supported two strangers who had appealed to him for aid. Though spared from suffering for the greater part of his life, he could yet sympathize with the sufferings of others. For he possessed the imaginative faculty to see beyond the horizon of his own existence.

His was perhaps the most versatile mind of the eighteenth century. He was not only a poet and a painter and a musician, but a scientist of no mean achievement. As a poet, he recognized the absolute unity under the apparent diversity of things. And as a scientist, he tried to demonstrate this unity. He made a thorough study of botany and anatomy and the theory of colors. He wrote a book on the metamorphoses (the structural changes) of plants in which he showed that flowers are nothing but glorified leaves—leaves turned into poems, so to speak. He examined the human skull and he discovered in it a bone—the intermaxillary—which established the relationship between man and the lower animals.

Like Terence, he was interested in everything pertaining to the human race—in everything, except war. For Goethe was essentially a man of peace. There was nothing in him of the Prussian lust for conquest. When Karl August was fighting against the French, he invited Goethe to come to his camp and to watch the maneuvers of his troops. Goethe accepted the invitation; but instead of interesting himself in the battles, he made a study of the stones and the flowers in the neighborhood of the camp. He had a deep and passionate love for his country, but he refused to be a chauvinist. Charged with being a slacker because he would not write inflammatory war songs, he replied: "I have never uttered anything which I have not experienced . . . I have composed love songs only when I have loved. How, then, can I write songs of hatred without having hated?"

VI

THE middle period of his life was blessed with three of the greatest of human blessings: a loving wife, a son, and a devoted friend. In 1788, at the age of thirty-nine, he met Christiane Vulpius. At first they indulged in a free relationship; but after several years of this freedom they yielded to the "greater freedom of marriage." In 1789 his son was born; and in 1794 he became intimately acquainted with Schiller. Goethe was forty-five at the time, and Schiller was thirty-five.

The friendship between Goethe and Schiller was a more radiant poem than any which either Goethe or Schiller ever wrote. It was a friendship between a demigod and a dying man (for Schiller had already lost one of his lungs). Goethe was a pagan, with a reverence for beauty. Schiller was a Christian, with a passion for justice. Both had started out as rebels, but both had surrendered at last. Goethe had been tamed by his good fortune, and Schiller by his poverty. But the two poets still believed in the rebelliousness of Art. Poetry, to them, was the sacred medium which would transform men into supermen. And so they worked together, these two apostles of salvation through the religion of the Word, and each of them supplemented and encouraged the genius of the other. When Schiller died, after their all-too-brief comradeship of eleven years, Goethe shut himself up into his room and wept like a child. "The half of my existence," he wrote to an acquaintance, "is gone from me . . . My diary is a blank at this period. The white pages intimate the blank in my life."

Goethe lived to an old age, but he had to pay the price of loneliness in return for the gift of a long life. One by one he lost all those whom he loved—his dearest friends, his sister, his wife, and finally his only son. But he went bravely ahead, turning his sorrows as well as his joys into immortal song. "I have never uttered anything which I have not experienced." He wrote sixty books of his spiritual and his mental experiences —lyrics, elegies, satires, epics, dramas, essays, and novels—fantastic fables about elves and ghosts and goblins, and philosophical stories about myths

and mortals and devils and gods. Finally he gathered all his genius into
one masterpiece and created *Faust*. It took him thirty years to write the
first half, and twenty-five years longer to complete the second half.

VII

THE purpose of Goethe in writing this drama was to understand Humanity—to measure its powers and to define its duties. The keynote of the
drama is struck in the Prologue. God and the Devil make a wager about
the soul of Man. The Devil has no respect for mortals. He is the everlasting skeptic, the spirit of denial. He believes that *not to be* is better than
to be. He sees no sense in "destiny's ceaseless play" which creates men
only to destroy them. He would prefer the "eternal emptiness" out of
which the universe started upon its "needless journey" through time and
space. His business, therefore, is to thwart the creation of God and to
deny the goodness of men. "Even the old Doctor Faust, the most learned
and the most upright of mortals," maintains the Devil, "can easily fall a
prey to my wiles if only I should take the trouble to tempt him."

But God knows better. It is true, he admits, that the vision of Man is
imperfect, so that he struggles forever through a haze of semidarkness.
"He strives and sins throughout his life." And yet, through his very sin-
ning, "he struggles instinctively toward the light."

And so it is agreed that the Devil is to tempt Faust and to see whether
he can destroy the immortal part of his soul. In accordance with the
wager, the Devil is to be declared the winner if Faust ever finds the passing moment (of mortal existence) so beautiful that he is loath to move
on from that moment to the next.

In the first half of the story, which is familiar to most readers, Goethe
relates how the Devil restores the youth of Faust and tempts him with
many of the selfish joys of life—beauty, wealth, sensuality, recklessness,
and the pleasures without the responsibilities of love. Guided by the
Devil, Faust seduces Marguerite and then abandons her to her sins and
her sorrows. Throughout this first part of the story, Faust is possessed by
"a passion for error." But in all his erring ways he finds not a moment of
happiness, not a single incident to which he is able to say, "Verweile
doch, du bist so schön." (Linger awhile, thou art so beautiful.)

After the death of Marguerite, the Devil tries to win him with tempta-
tions of a different sort. Faust, who is the symbol of Universal Man, is
eager to try every experience of life, "to bare his breast to every pang, to
know all human joy and sorrow," to live and work with men, "and to
share with them the shipwreck of mankind."

Accordingly the Devil enables Faust to become (like Goethe) a councilor at the royal court. Here, by his able service, Faust wins gratitude
and honors—but no happiness. Dissatisfied with his present life, he con-
jures up for himself the life of the past. He brings out of antiquity the

spirit of Helen of Troy, restores her to life, and tries to become wedded to her (just as Goethe tried to become wedded to the classical thought of the Greek poets). But when Faust embraces Helen, she vanishes, leaving only her cloak behind. It is useless even for a Faust, or a Goethe, to try to understand the glory that was Greece. In spite of all their endeavors, the beautiful soul of antiquity escapes them, and they are left with nothing but the outward garment in their hands.

And thus Faust moves on from one experience to another, and finds satisfaction in none. "His very walk is a series of falls." Whatever he undertakes to do, whether of good or of evil, ends in failure, or in an empty triumph which is even worse than failure. He wins an important battle for his emperor, and he finds that his victory in war means death and devastation for both sides. The Devil offers him cities, kingdoms, castles, beautiful women, glorious achievements, and eternal fame. But Faust is sick of it all. The arc of his life has begun to turn downward. The pleasures of youth and the achievements of middle age have brought him nothing but disillusion. Care has taken possession of his house, and the fires and desires of his youth have all turned to ashes. He is stricken with blindness, and he is ready at last to give up his lifelong quest for happiness.

But—strangely enough—at the very moment that he renounces happiness, he finds it. He starts upon a vast project to reclaim the swamps near the sea and to make them fit for human habitation. Here he plans to build homes, upon free soil, for millions of people who will best enjoy their freedom by conquering it anew with their labor every day. This thought fills him with a great joy. This is the self-forgetful goal toward which he has subconsciously struggled all his life. This at last is the golden moment to which he can say, "Linger awhile, thou art so beautiful!"

And now that he has arrived at the supreme moment of his life, his life comes to an end. Apparently the Devil has won the bet. He claims the soul of Faust as the price of his victory. But the angels descend amidst a shower of roses and carry his soul to heaven. Faust has erred grievously, to be sure, but through all his erring he has struggled instinctively toward the light.

The first to greet him in heaven is Marguerite. She has sinned and died through the sins of Faust. But all this is forgiven and forgotten. It is her mission now to show him the way. *Das ewig Weibliche zieht uns hinan.* Woman is the eternal savior of Man.

VIII

AND NOW, having completed the supreme work of his life, Goethe—like Faust—was ready to sleep. His numerous admirers were preparing a royal celebration in honor of his eighty-second birthday. In order to escape from the festivities, he went to the mountains of Ilmenau. There, in a hut where he and Karl August had often stayed together, he saw the lines which he had penciled on the wall a number of years ago.

"Over all the hilltops, there is quiet peace; in the treetops, thou canst scarce perceive the slightest breath; the little birds in the forest have stilled their voices. Be patient now—soon thou too wilt be at rest."

Brushing away the tears from his eyes, he reëchoed the last words— "Soon thou too wilt be at rest."

He returned home. For a little while longer he sang those magical songs in which—as Heine observes—"the word embraces you while the thought imprints a kiss." At last, on the 16th of March in 1832, he was unable to get up from his bed. Six days later, amidst the hushed whispers of his household, he closed his eyes—and the song of his life trailed off into eternal silence.

His last audible words were—"*More light!*"

IMPORTANT DATES IN THE LIFE OF
JOHANN WOLFGANG VON GOETHE

1749—August 28, born at Frankfort-on-Main.
1765—Entered Leipzig University.
1770—Began legal studies at Strassburg.
1771—Licensed to practice law.
1773—Wrote first important drama, *Götz von Berlichingen.*
1774—Wrote *The Sorrows of Werther.*
1774—Met Karl August, Prince of Weimar.
1775—Settled down at Weimar.
1777—Began *Wilhelm Meister.*
1786—Went to Italy.

1789—Had son by Christiane Vulpius.
1791—Appointed director of ducal theater.
1794—Started friendship with Schiller.
1800—Completed *Wilhelm Meister.*
Completed first part of *Faust.*
1805—Schiller died.
1832—Completed second part of *Faust.*
March 22, died at Weimar.

Ludwig van Beethoven

1770–1827

Bᴀᴄʜ was the mathematician of music; Mozart, the poet; Beethoven, the philosopher. In the garden of the human mind the seed of philosophy is the last to come to full flower.

Beethoven was no child prodigy. Nor was he precocious even as a young man. He made little impression upon his teachers. "Beethoven," said Albrechtsberger, who was trying to teach him composition, "never has learned anything and never will learn anything. As a composer he is hopeless." Even Haydn, who taught Beethoven harmony for a time, was unable to recognize the latent genius of this young Philistine who refused to clip his wings to his master's dainty little flights of lyrical sweetness. Beethoven's imagination dwelt in heights above the vision of his masters. But as yet it had not found a familiar home there. It was not until his thirtieth year (in 1800) that he composed his *First Symphony*.

Yet as a pianist he showed early promise. His short, stubby fingers were able to play magic with the keyboard. His father, the Kapellmeister at the court of the Elector at Bonn, began to teach him both clavier and violin in his fourth year. Shiftless, improvident, and poor, Johann van Beethoven was anxious to raise his talented child as an assistant bread-winner. And Ludwig was expert enough to play in public at seven. At thirteen he began to contribute to the family income through his appointment as the assistant court organist. Four years later he spent a short time in Vienna, where he took a few lessons under Mozart. His mother's illness, however, recalled him to Bonn. Shortly after his return his mother died of tuberculosis, and for a time he feared that he, too, was threatened with this disease.

His father in the meantime had given way to drink, and Ludwig was obliged to take upon his shoulders the entire support of the family. In

addition to the father there were two younger brothers—Caspar Anton
Carl and Nikolaus Johann. It was no easy task for Ludwig to attend to
the petty details of the household. For great thoughts were beginning to
stir within him. Disgusted with his lot and anxious about his health, he
became bitter, sarcastic, morose. He acted toward his friends like a caged
young lion—hair disheveled, eyes scowling, lips tightly pressed together,
conversation reduced to a growl. Hardly a pleasant companion for the
members of the theater orchestra at Bonn, where Beethoven played viola.
They called him "the mad Spaniard," because of his swarthy complexion
and his black temper. (There may possibly have been a strain of Spanish
blood in him, since the Beethovens on the male side were Belgians and
the Spaniards had occupied Belgium in the seventeenth century.)

He was subject to wild fits of rage and equally wild outbursts of re-
morse. "Dearest! Best!" he wrote to his friend Dr. Wegeler, after one of
his volcanic eruptions. "In what an odious light you have exhibited me
to myself! I acknowledge it, I do not deserve your friendship . . . but,
thank heaven, it was no intentional or deliberate malice which induced
me to act as I did towards you. It was my inexcusable thoughtlessness
which prevented me from seeing the matter in its true light. . . . Ah,
Wegeler, do not reject this hand of reconciliation . . . I am coming to
throw myself into your arms. . . . Pray give yourself back to me, your
penitent, loving, never-forgetting friend."

He had a knack of making friends in spite of his fiery temper and his
caustic tongue. People admired his genuine, untamed, rebellious spirit,
his utter disregard of the niceties in the presence of the realities of life.
He was strangely out of place in the drawing room, yet he completely
dominated it. There was a powerful fascination in his stumpy, uncouth,
athletic figure and his stubborn, assertive, uncompromising mind. "I am
glad," said a friend after Beethoven's visit to the court, "that you knew
the proper etiquette in the presence of the nobility." Whereupon Beethoven retorted, "You ought to be glad that the nobility knew the proper
etiquette in the presence of genius."

II

AT THE AGE OF TWENTY-TWO he settled permanently in Vienna. He was
now able to stand on his own feet—or, to use a more appropriate metaphor,
to lean on his own hands. For those hands of his were blessed with a
power and technique possessed by few of his contemporary rivals. His
skill at the piano attracted to him the friendship of Prince Carl
Lichnowsky, a member of the Austrian aristocracy and a passionate devotee of music. The prince and his wife took Beethoven into their home,
they gave him a pension of six hundred florins (about three hundred
dollars) a year, and they introduced him to the most exclusive social circles
of Vienna.

For a time Beethoven tried to assume the role of the gay cavalier. He even permitted himself the luxury of a horse and a carriage. He dressed himself in rich colors, he took dancing lessons, and he set out to conquer the fickle hearts of the ladies who showered him with their homage. He became the hub of the social whirl of Vienna. He was invited everywhere. "Come next Wednesday if you can," wrote the Baron von Swieten. "We shall expect you at half-past eight—with your nightcap in your pocket."

But the rapid turning of the wheel of admiration made Beethoven dizzy. His was not a spirit born for play. "Happiness," he said, "is not intended for me; or rather, I am not intended for happiness." His genius needed solitude for its development. Solitude and suffering. "I have been put into the world not to enjoy a pleasant life, but to accomplish a great work." He withdrew from society into the hermit shell of his rebelliousness and his gruffness. His manners often tried the patience of the Prince and the Princess Lichnowsky. But they bore with his caprices. The prince even went so far as to tell his servant that if Beethoven's bell and his own were to ring at the same time he was to attend to Beethoven first. "Art before everything."

Beethoven's temperament was explosive and arrogant—and sad. For he who feels intensely suffers intensely. An instrument attuned to beauty is sensitive to pain. Beethoven was a hypochondriac. The same nervous responsiveness which gave him his genius gave him also his unhappiness. All his life he complained of real or imaginary illness. And the pain is real even when the illness is imaginary.

Added to his physical suffering was his mental distress. Everybody praised him as a player, and nobody recognized him as a composer. His early compositions were regarded as the clever exercises of a musician who could play but who could not create. Yet creation was the absorbing passion of his life. Even at Bonn he had made it the sole end of his ambition to become a great composer. But here he was, in his late twenties, and the dreams that kept crowding so powerfully into his mind became dissolved, when he tried to put them on paper, into the tenuous mists of unimportant little trills and trifles.

He longed to be himself. A lady once asked him if he went to see Mozart's operas. "No," he replied, "I do not care to hear the music of others lest I forfeit some of my own originality." Someday, he told his friends, he would show them. They would hear his music and marvel at the new creative giant that had stalked over the horizon. But his friends looked at his pock-marked face and his stumpy little peasant figure and laughed. This man a creative giant? Preposterous!

Yet Beethoven, in spite of the inability of his friends to recognize the fact, was moving in the right direction. His "unimportant little trills and trifles" were the first auroral flushes of a new sunrise. He took the gay and rollicking minuets of Haydn and transformed them into satirical scherzos of irony and pity—the laughter of the gods at the stupidities of mankind. His *First Symphony*, though still reminiscent of the music of the past, was an instinctive groping toward a different kind of music. It was an old language with a new idiom. A few of his friends understood and waited breathlessly for the further development of this strange and enchanting idiom. Most of the critics, however, merely nodded their heads and snickered at this "bumpkin who called himself a genius." They advised him to stick to the old forms and not to plunge recklessly into waters that were beyond his depth.

Yet plunge he did, and soon he learned to swim about familiarly in these strange waters. His *Second Symphony* was a still further departure from the musical conventions and the advice of his critics. In the second movement of this symphony, the *Larghetto*, he introduced an innovation that almost threw his critics into a fit. This innovation was a musical tête-à-tête between the various instruments of the orchestra—an animated interchange of song gossip in which one group broke in upon another group, only to be interrupted in turn by a third group, so that the audience got the effect of listening to a brilliant and stimulating human conversation. "If Beethoven continues this sort of trash," said one of the scandalized critics, "our orchestras will degenerate into instrumental debating societies."

But Beethoven merely growled at his critics and went right ahead with his experimentations. "A few fly bites," he said, "can not stop a spirited horse." Whereupon his critics insisted that his music was not only conversational but ungrammatical. It was the speech of an uneducated man. "Ah yes," retorted Beethoven, "they are amazed and they put their heads together because they have never found it in any book on thorough bass."

He was impatient of any spur upon his genius. When his critics observed—and this time justly—that some of his musical passages were beyond the capacity of the instruments for which he wrote them, he made the utterly illogical but adequately artistic reply, "Do they believe that I think of a wretched fiddle when the spirit speaks to me?" As well expect a volcano to pour its lava into artificial molds prepared by human hands.

III

In keeping with his ardent temperament, Beethoven was always falling in love with some woman or other. He strictly refrained, however, from poaching upon the preserves of married folk. "It is one of my foremost principles," he said, "never to occupy any other relations than those of friendship with the wife of another man." Perhaps it is true, as some cynics would have us believe, that chastity is largely a question of physical appearance rather than one of spiritual restraint. It is easy for a homely person to remain morally pure. Certainly Beethoven was not the type of man to conquer the female heart. In his youth he made a proposal of marriage to the beautiful opera singer, Magdalena Willmann, but nothing came of the proposal. In later years, when asked why she had refused Beethoven, she laughingly replied, "Because he was so ugly, and half crazy!"

Added to his other physical defects was his increasing deafness, which had begun to press down upon him shortly before the completion of his *First Symphony*. Deafness and romance have never yet been on speaking terms. Tender words of affection are meant to be whispered, not shouted. The women of Beethoven's circle admired him, pitied him, at times even adored him; but they never loved him. They showered him with invitations to give concerts at their homes. So busy was he at times with these concerts that he was obliged to begin some of them as early as six o'clock in the morning. And he always drew audiences to fill "the capacity of the house." It was an age of musical virtuosity. "In Vienna," remarked the famous pianist Hümmel, "there are a hundred ladies who can play the piano better than I." And these ladies were anxious to hear and to applaud Beethoven. But not to flirt with him. One does not flirt with a god—especially when he is homely and deaf.

Beethoven's deafness was almost more than he could bear. For it not only isolated him from society but it removed him from the sound of his own music. "This affliction," he wrote, "is more difficult for the artist than for any other man . . . It was impossible for me to say to my friends, 'Speak louder, shout, for I am deaf.' Ah, was it possible for me to proclaim a deficiency in that one sense which in my case ought to have been more perfect than in all others? . . . For me there can be no recreation in human society, refined conversation, mutual exchange of thoughts and feelings . . . I must live like an exile . . . A little more and I should have put an end to my life."

But he soon gave up the thought of death. He had something to live for—his art. "Art alone has detained me . . . I have emptied the cup of bitter suffering . . . It shall be transformed into beauty in my soul . . ." Suffering, and patience, and work. "I owe it to myself, to mankind and to the Almighty . . . I must write my music . . . to the eternal glory of God."

To sing to the eternal glory of God and to the brotherhood of man —*this*, henceforth, was to be the chief purpose of Beethoven's life. He renounced the world in order to attain salvation—salvation through music. And on the battlefields of Europe at that moment there was another man who, like Beethoven, seemed to be aiming at salvation—salvation through conquest. Beethoven had a great admiration for Napoleon, whom he regarded as the archenemy of imperialism and the savior of mankind. He dedicated his *Third Symphony* to him. But just as he was preparing to send the work to Paris he received the news that Napoleon had betrayed his principles and declared himself emperor. In a rage he tore off the title page bearing the dedication. "So Napoleon is nothing

but an ordinary man!" he cried. "Like all the other tyrants he is tram-
pling on the human heart!" He renamed the symphony the *Eroica,* "in
memory of a great man"—a man whose body was still alive but whose
soul was dead.

IV

BEETHOVEN'S CYNICISM grew with the years. To many of his contemporaries he was not a genius but a crank. He fumed at his friends and threw
books at his servants and insulted his patrons even to their face. One evening, as he arrived at the Silesian castle of Prince Lichnowsky, he found
there a number of French officers who had been quartered at that estate.
For Napoleon had overrun Silesia, and his soldiers were living off the
land that they had conquered. When Beethoven saw Napoleon's officers
at his patron's house he scowled, and when they asked him to play for
them, he flatly refused. He knew that he was regarded merely as a curiosity, like a juggler or dancer or sleight-of-hand magician. But the prince,
who was playing host to the Frenchmen, insisted that Beethoven should
accede to the officers' request. "Either you play for us," he said by way
of a jest, "or you will be confined in the castle as a prisoner of war."
Whereupon Beethoven, without another word, stormed out of the castle
and walked three miles to the next village through a pelting rain. Here,
while waiting for the post chaise, he wrote the following letter to Prince
Lichnowsky:

"Prince! What you are you owe to chance and birth. What I am, I am
through myself. There have been and there will be thousands of princes.
But there is only one Beethoven."

His biting sarcasm extended to his pupils. "You will have to practice
long and faithfully," he said to one of them, "before you realize that you
cannot play." Not even in the presence of his female students was he
able to curb his temper. "Wild? Impetuous? Ah yes," writes his famous
pupil, the Baroness Ertmann. "But it was the wildness and fire of a volcano, the great forces of Nature herself, for in him a Titan sat. At my lessons he would tear the music into bits and stamp on it on the floor."

Yet his outward bluster concealed a gentle heart. "When my child
died," continues the Baroness Ertmann, "it was Beethoven's gentleness
and tenderness that consoled me most." In his more serene moments he
was the very spirit of generosity. He had no conception of the value of
money save as a convenient thing to give to a friend in distress. And when
a friend asked him for money and he had none he would give him one of
his compositions and tell him to turn it into cash.

His friendships, however, were but an incident in his life. His one passion was music. Creation in solitude. "The artist," he said, "carries his
happiness within him . . . I live alone, but I do not regret it. For I know
that God is nearer to me than to the others."

Beethoven calling to God—and a new music is born. With the *Third Symphony* he had finished his apprenticeship. From now on he was his own master. The years following the first approach of his deafness were years of prolific creation. A Niagara of music poured forth from his heart —dramatic music in *Fidelio*, tragic music in the *Appassionata Sonata*, tranquil music in the *Fourth Symphony*—and in every case music with a unique, original and divine stamp, minted out of the pure metal of Beethoven's fantasy. The music of Beethoven, interpreting the ideas of God.

And then came the *Fifth Symphony*. It is useless to add any further words to the library of praise that has already been written about this work. Suffice it to say that the *Fifth Symphony* is the first full utterance of Beethoven's mature genius, the New Testament in the religion of music —the story of the struggle of Man against Fate and the victory of Man under the guidance of Heaven. It is the epic of Man's pilgrimage from suffering to wisdom, from wisdom to courage, from courage to hope, and from hope to eternal life.

V

ONE OF THE GREAT EVENTS in Beethoven's life was his meeting with Goethe. He had suffered a nervous breakdown and had gone for a cure, upon the advice of his physician, to the Bohemian baths of Teplitz. It was here that the tone-poet made the acquaintance of the word-poet. Goethe, who was already advanced in years, made a profound impression upon his younger fellow artist. "He is the most precious jewel of our nation," observed Beethoven. "The appearance of such a man is, in my opinion, the greatest thing that can happen in any epoch." As for Goethe's attitude toward Beethoven, he regarded this "young man"—although Beethoven was forty-two at the time—as an "entirely untamed personality, but the sincerest artist I ever saw."

The two men saw a good deal of each other during their summer vacation at Teplitz. They entered into few discussions, for conversation was difficult owing to Beethoven's deafness. But they took long walks together, each absorbed in his own ideas—two supreme artists translating the mystery of the world into diverse languages. At times their ideas of the world came to a violent clash—as, for example, on the following occasion: Goethe and Beethoven were walking through the streets of Teplitz when they met the entire royal family, including the Empress of Austria and the various archdukes. Goethe stepped aside, removed his hat and bowed low. Beethoven, however, walked straight through the party with his arms folded and his hat firmly planted on his head. Goethe was scandalized at this "ill-mannered rudeness" of Beethoven, and not a few of Beethoven's biographers are in agreement with Goethe on this point. Yet is not this a one-sided view of the matter? Was it more rude of genius to show its contempt for kings than of kings to show their contempt for genius? Was it a sign of good breeding for a nobleman to kick a musician downstairs and ill breeding for a musician to stand up proudly before a nobleman? It would seem rather that the philosophy of Goethe was that of the slave and the philosophy of Beethoven that of a free man. And the submission of slavery is no better sign of good breeding than the assertion of freedom. The difference between the attitude of Goethe and that of Beethoven lay far beneath the mere surface artificialities of good or ill breeding. It was a difference in principles, a profound disagreement as to the real values of life. To Goethe royalty was more important than genius. To Beethoven genius was more important than royalty.

And before we dismiss this incident let us not forget the courage of Beethoven. His livelihood depended almost entirely upon the good will of his royal and his other aristocratic patrons. Indeed, three of his patrons, the Archduke Rudolph, Prince Lobkowitz, and Prince Ferdinand Kinsky, had agreed to provide him with a yearly pension of four thousand florins (about two thousand dollars). But for one reason or another this pension was hardly ever paid in full. Financially Beethoven was compelled to struggle for the greater part of his life. Goethe's submissiveness, if not the more ideal, was certainly the more practical philosophy. He took care never to offend his royal patrons at Weimar. And he always received his pensions promptly.

VI

TOWARD HIS RELATIVES Beethoven presented the same personality that he did toward the rest of the world—a surly demeanor and a tender heart. One of his younger brothers, Johann, had prospered in the drug business; but Beethoven showed him none the greater respect for all his prosperity. Naïvely proud of his success, Johann boasted about it on every occasion. He was especially anxious to advertise the fact that he had bought a sumptuous country estate at Gneixendorf. One New Year's Day, as Beethoven was sitting down to dinner, a card was brought in:

Johann van Beethoven
Gutsbesitzer (Landowner)

Beethoven took the card and wrote on the back of it:

Ludwig van Beethoven
Hirnsbesitzer (Brainowner)

To his brother Caspar, however, Beethoven showed an entirely different disposition. For a time he employed him as his secretary, and when Caspar died Beethoven undertook the guardianship of his little son Carl, who was nine years old at the time.

When he offered to take care of his little nephew, Beethoven brought upon himself a burden that was to plague him for the rest of his days. Carl's mother, who was the daughter of a rich upholsterer, contested Beethoven's right to the possession of her child and instituted legal proceedings against her brother-in-law. The litigation lasted for several years, the courts ruling now in favor of the one and now in favor of the other. The responsibility of the boy's care, and the lawsuits attendant upon it, proved to be a drain upon Beethoven's purse as well as upon his health. Yet he managed to lay aside a sum of money for Carl's future, frequently undergoing privation himself as a result.

Beethoven had laid ambitious plans for his nephew, hoping that the child might grow up into a great musician or scholar. But in this hope he was doomed to disappointment. Carl was an unmanageable child whose tastes ran to the billiard room rather than the classroom. As he grew older he got into undesirable company and ran up debts that were far beyond his weekly allowance. And once, when Beethoven refused to pay these debts, the boy made an attempt at suicide. The attempt was frustrated, but it left Beethoven a broken man.

It is interesting to note, in passing, that Carl grew up to be a respectable citizen, fond of his music, and devoted to the memory of his uncle. But Beethoven did not live to see this transformation in Carl's character. He knew his adopted child only in the turmoil of his adolescence but not in the placidity of his manhood.

And it was through those years of turmoil that Beethoven was obliged to steer the final course of his own destiny. His productiveness had slowed down considerably under the burden of his worries and his ill health. He had written his first eight symphonies before 1815, the year in which he adopted Carl. His *Ninth Symphony* was not completed until 1824. Nine years of sorrow, resulting in a final outburst of joy. Professor Santayana once remarked that God created the world in order that the *Ninth Symphony* might be written. And Wagner had this to say of the *Ninth Symphony*: "We stand today before it as before the landmark of an entirely new period in the history of universal art, for through it there came into the world a phenomenon not even remotely approached by anything the art of any age or any people has to show us." It has been suggested that Beethoven wrote this symphony as a musical counterpart to Goethe's *Faust*—the poem of the soul's adventure from Earth through Hell to Heaven. This is to an extent true of all his other *Symphonies*, especially the *Fifth*. Yet nowhere is Beethoven's philosophy of life so completely and so satisfactorily summarized as in the five instrumental and seven vocal movements of the *Ninth Symphony*. Let the critics quarrel about the propriety or the impropriety of introducing choral passages into symphonic structures. All such discussions are petty and irrelevant in the presence of this music. In the Song of Creation the Lord united a multitude of sounds into a single harmony—man and beast, wind and wave, ripple and roar, the crash of the thunder and the still small voice of the growing plant; all these are blended into one concordant hymn to the glory of life. And in the *Ninth Symphony* Beethoven has caught an authentic echo of this hymn. Beethoven's deafness was no accident and it was no tragedy. It was the preparation of the soil for the flowering of his genius. The sounds of the earth were stilled for him, that in the silence he might catch the harmonies of heaven.

And what is the secret and the meaning of these harmonies? The oneness of all, the unity of mankind into a brotherhood of love. "Universal love alone can transform and redeem the world." It is the teaching of all the great poets, all the great artists, all the great saviors of mankind. It is the doctrine of Jesus, of Buddha, of Zoroaster, of Plato, of Spinoza —the dreamers of the East, the thinkers of the West. And it is the doctrine, expressed in music instead of words, that Beethoven sings to us triumphantly in his *Ninth Symphony*. The Testament of Love. *Seid umschlungen, Millionen! Diesen Kuss der ganzen Welt.* "Be embraced in love, ye millions! Here's a kiss for all the world."

This, then, is the substance of Beethoven's *Ninth Symphony*. In spite of our defeats and our doubts the heart of the world is sound, the plan of God is good, and the destiny of Man is joy.

For the keynote of life is Love.

VII

BEETHOVEN lay on his deathbed. He had been ill for several months. The final death struggle had lasted forty-eight hours. He was unconscious now. Outdoors a terrific storm was raging. A sudden flash of lightning. The dying musician opened his eyes and raised his clenched fist into the air. Then he fell back dead.

The spirit of Man, unconquerable to the end!

IMPORTANT DATES IN THE LIFE OF
LUDWIG VAN BEETHOVEN

1770—December 16, born at Bonn.

1787—Met Mozart in Vienna.

1792—Became court organist at Cologne.

1792—Studied under Haydn in Vienna.

1795—Began public career as composer and pianist.

1800—Gave the first concert of his own compositions.

1795–1802—Wrote his first series of masterpieces (Opus numbers 1–50).

1802—Deafness began to be serious.

1803–15—Wrote his second series (51–100), beginning with the *Eroica*.

1816–27—Wrote his last and greatest series, ending with the *Ninth Symphony*.

1827—March 26, died in Vienna.

Simon Bolivar

1783–1830

It was a dangerous thing to rebel against the Spanish rule in South America. In 1781, when Tupac-Amaru attempted to liberate Peru, the Spanish governor tore out his tongue and then compelled him to look on while his wife and his son were being pulled apart by four horses driven in different directions. At the end of the spectacle, he himself was accorded the same treatment.

The story of this atrocity was still fresh upon everybody's lips when Bolivar was born (July 24, 1783). His father wanted to call him Santiago. But the priest who baptized the infant gave him the name of Simon. "I have a presentiment that this child will some day become the Simon Maccabeus (the old Judean liberator) of the New World."

Dedicated from his infancy to rebellion, this child of a noble family in Venezuela grew up into a reckless, restless, and audacious youngster. Having lost his father at the age of three, he was put into the care of the distinguished Caracas jurist, Miguel José Sanz. His escapades were at once the admiration and the terror of Don José. "My child," he once remarked, "you are a regular *polvorin* (horn of gunpowder)." Whereupon the child retorted, "Then you had better keep away from me—I'm liable to explode."

Slight, wiry, effervescent, he captivated everybody with his impudent dark eyes and his ingratiating bright smile. He lived like a prince in an enchanted tale. At the death of his mother—he was nine years old at the time—he came into a considerable estate. Mines of valuable mineral deposits, spacious *haciendas,* vast acres of sugar cane, mills, ranches, distilleries, fruit orchards, and thousands upon thousands of animals and slaves—all these were his to share with his brother and his two sisters.

But Simon cared next to nothing for his wealth. He was interested only

in his adventures. Gathering around him a group of mischievous youngsters, he became a "constant pain and irritation" to the conventional old
magistrates and merchants of Caracas. He accepted as his tutor in all his
escapades a vagabond philosopher by the name of Rodriguez—a half-
cracked utopian who walked around with a copy of Rousseau's *Émile* in
his pocket and with all sorts of social and political panaceas in his head.
"In this crazy world of ours," he remarked to Bolivar, "there are two
outstanding facts—the sacredness of the human body and the stupidity of
the human mind." And to demonstrate the "sacredness" of his own body
to the "stupid" minds of his contemporaries, he occasionally appeared in
public *au naturel*. He was among the first of the nudists.

But the crazy doctrines of Rodriguez had their serious as well as their
frivolous side. This "Socrates of South America" taught Bolivar the importance of a healthy body for the spiritual tussle in the arena of life.
He took his young pupil on long and dangerous hikes through the forests
and over the mountains of Venezuela. Together they traveled on mule-
back to the Bolivar ranches where Simon learned from the *vaqueros* (cowboys) the art of taming wild horses, of wielding the lasso and the lance,
and of galloping full tilt to the side of a bull, seizing his tail with one
hand and hurling him to the ground with a sudden snap of the wrist.

Rodriguez looked on with admiration as his young protégé became
the most iron-muscled expert among the *vaqueros*. "You will need this
iron constitution in the great battles that await you." Venezuela, South
America, the entire world needed to be reshaped. The priest had named
him Simon because he was destined to be a liberator. Eagerly he absorbed his tutor's ideas about a new age of freedom. There were great
events stirring in South America—rebellions, suppressions, executions,
new rebellions. Bolivar and his tutor were among those who witnessed the
decapitation of the revolutionist, José Chirinos, in the public square of
Caracas. In one of the numerous uprisings Rodriguez himself was involved. Thanks to the influence of Bolivar's family, he managed to escape
the death penalty. But he was compelled to leave the country.

Bolivar missed his tutor. But he found consolation in the arms of his
beautiful cousins, the Aristiguietas—a couple of warm-blooded young ladies with receptive ears and prodigal hearts. "When I die," he observed
to a friend, "I hope to go to Purgatory; for there I shall be able to continue
my flirtations with the Aristiguietas."

His flirtations, however, formed but an episode in his restless life. He
enlisted in the militia, and the impetuous lover proved himself an equally
impetuous soldier. At the end of two years of maneuvering over the *llanos*,
he was commissioned *alferez* (sub-lieutenant).

And then he directed his adventures toward the Old World. On January 19, 1799, he set sail for Madrid where his uncle, Esteban Palacio,
enjoyed a favored position in the palace of the king and—it was whispered—in the boudoir of the queen.

Bolivar came to Madrid highly recommended as a loyal subject of King Carlos and Queen Maria Luisa. Yet within a few months an order was issued for his arrest. He was suspected of having joined a conspiracy, together with his uncle Esteban, against the royal couple. He fled to Paris where he paid homage to Napoleon, the "savior of the French Republic," and made love to another member of the far-flung and fascinating Aristiguieta family. In the midst of his flirtation he learned that the king's charges against him had been dropped. Whereupon he promptly left his French girl, returned to Madrid, and married a Spanish girl. Bolivar was only nineteen at the time.

The young couple set sail for Caracas. Here they enjoyed a honeymoon of uninterrupted fiestas given by their friends in their honor. And after their honeymoon they settled down to a life of idyllic happiness in one of Bolivar's *haciendas* at San Mateo.

Their idyl continued for eight months and then ended abruptly when his wife died of a sudden malignant fever. "This tragedy," he observed, "marked the end of my playtime, and the beginning of my work."

II

To FORGET his grief, he returned to Madrid. Here he fell in with a group of South American intellectuals who, like himself, were dreaming dreams of freedom. They organized themselves into a secret society and accepted Bolivar as one of their leaders. Though of medium height, he produced the impression of commanding stature because of his well-proportioned muscles and his supple slenderness. His deep-set, dark and thoughtful eyes, his high, broad forehead, his long, thin, aristocratic face and his fiery voice demanded—and received—the respect of his fellows.

And aroused once more the suspicion of the Spanish court. A royal edict ordered him out of Madrid.

Again, as before, he went to Paris where he became the life of the fashionable *salons*. With his ingratiating smile he won the affection of practically all the French men and women of any importance—Talleyrand, General Duroc, Marshal Oudinot, Napoleon's young stepson Beauharnais, the great French actor François Talma, Madame Recamier, and Madame de Staël. He became especially intimate with Alexander von Humboldt, the great German naturalist who was then visiting Paris. Humboldt had just returned from his scientific expedition to South America. "Do you think," Bolivar asked him one day, "that South America is ready for independence?"

"Yes," replied Humboldt, "I think it is. All that your country needs is a great leader."

Bolivar's heart leaped up when he heard these words. "A great leader." Perhaps he himself might prove to be the man. His old tutor, Rodriguez, had finally drifted to Paris with his *Émile* and his utopian dreams. "Of

course you are to be the man!" But, first of all, Bolivar must complete
his education. Rodriguez supplied him with those books that had served
as a bugle call to freedom—Plato, Voltaire, Rousseau, Montesquieu,
Helvetius, Hobbes, Hume, Spinoza. And then, after the strengthening
of Bolivar's mind, must come a further toughening of his body. "An end
to your luxurious living!" A modest house. A hard mattress. A strict diet.
A rigorous course in fencing until Bolivar became equally adept with either hand. And finally, Bolivar and Rodriguez started off on a walking
tour over southern Europe. Down the valley of the Saône, across the Alps,
and into the plains of Italy. Milan, Venice, Verona, Padua, Ferrara. At
Naples, Bolivar was the guest of Humboldt's brother. At Alessandria, he
saw Napoleon reviewing his army on the battlefield of Marengo. The
"savior of the French Republic" was on his way to crown himself king of
Italy. "What a mighty fall is this!" exclaimed Bolivar. Napoleon had de-
generated from a demigod into a dictator.

Rome, and a visit to the Vatican. Here, to the amazement of the onlookers, Bolivar refused to kneel and to kiss the Pontiff's slipper. "I
respect His Holiness, but I bow to no man."

One day the two pilgrims climbed the hill of Monte Sacro. The city
below them was golden-red under the light of the setting sun. Rodriguez
was delivering a stirring dissertation on the glory that was Rome. For a
long time Bolivar was silent. And then, "his eyes moist, his breast pal-
pitating, his face flushed with a feverish animation," he spoke:

"Rodriguez, I swear by the God of my forefathers that my hands shall
never rest until they have delivered my country from the shackles of
Spain!"

III

BOLIVAR returned to his country by way of the United States where he
saw the spirit of independence in its practical application. When he arrived at his native city of Caracas, he found it in an uproar. A liberator
had appeared in Venezuela—a strange fighter-prophet by the name of
Miranda. This "soldier of misfortune," like Bolivar a native of Venezuela,
had fought in the American Revolution and in the French Revolution.
He had distinguished himself under Napoleon and had attained the rank
of general. And now he was back in South America in an effort to inspire
a rebellion against the Spanish king. In the summer of 1811 he gathered
together a number of Venezuelan patriots at Caracas, and on July 5 he
issued a South American Declaration of Independence.

His next step was to establish this independence by force of arms. He
took to the field and examined the troops. His heart sank. A rabble of
undisciplined and barefoot peasants who could neither shoot nor drill.
But he did not give up. They were brave men, and with hard work they
might be transformed into good soldiers.

Incessant drill under exacting taskmasters, the foremost of whom was Colonel Simon Bolivar. Irregular meals, irregular pay, and nondescript rags in place of uniforms. But finally they were whipped into a fighting army. With this army of amateur soldiers Miranda twice defeated the troops of the Spanish king.

And then, treachery. A Venezuelan sentinel had delivered to the enemy the stronghold of Puerto Cabello. Miranda was giving a victory dinner to a hundred officers when he received the news of the betrayal. "Gentlemen," he said, "Venezuela is wounded to the heart."

The Spaniards were victorious. Miranda was captured and imprisoned at Cadiz where he died of a broken heart. The Venezuelan rebellion was at an end.

One of the leaders of the rebellion, however, had managed to make his escape from the Spaniards. Under cover of the night Bolivar had boarded a ship that sailed safely away from the fortress of Puerto Cabello. He returned to Caracas where, concealing himself in the hut of a friendly Indian, he laid the plans for another and more successful revolution.

IV

MIRANDA had failed because he could not perform the impossible. Bolivar succeeded because he could. His property had been confiscated, his army had melted away, and twenty thousand Venezuelans had been swallowed up in an earthquake. "Nature herself is fighting against us!" wailed the survivors. "Very well," shouted Bolivar into the clamor. "Then we shall compel Nature, too, to give in to us!"

And he did compel Nature to give in to his indomitable will. Captured and exiled to the Island of Curaçao, he escaped and set sail westward and southward to New Granada—a country across the Andes from Venezuela. Here, in a land which he had never seen and in which his name had never been heard, he issued a manifesto of liberation and a call to arms. And the people, captivated by the magnetism of his personality, listened and obeyed. An army sprang up as if by magic. "Let us free Granada—and then, on to Venezuela!" With a company of two hundred men loaded upon ten rafts he poled up the Magdalena River to Teneriffe, a stronghold occupied by a sizable Spanish force. He reached the stronghold in the dead of the night. Out of the darkness came the sentinel's call, "*Quién vive?*"

Bolivar fell upon the sentinel and cut his throat. Then, concealing his handful of soldiers behind the rocks and the trees, he ordered them to make a terrific clatter so as to convey an exaggerated impression of their numbers. The Spaniards thought that an entire army had descended upon them. Bolivar called upon their commander to give himself up. "If you refuse, I shall blow the fortress to smithereens with my cannons!" The commander fled precipitately with his entire force, and Bolivar entered the town without the loss of a single man.

The townspeople looked with amazement at the soldier who had "routed an army by the mere sound of his voice." But where were his cannon? they wanted to know. "My cannon?" laughed Bolivar. "I didn't have any." And then, as he surveyed the arsenal that he had just captured, "But I see that we shall have plenty of arms for our future campaigns."

His next objective after Teneriffe was the fortress of Mompox, further up the river. Here, too, he was able to enter without a fight, for the Spaniards had fled at the word of his approach.

Higher and higher toward the source of the river he advanced, up amongst the cliffs of the Andes; and wherever his army encamped, hundreds of recruits rallied to his standard. The Spanish army "melted like the sands" before his onslaught. Within six days he fought six battles and won them all.

And then, an eastward and upward ascent into the peaks of the Andes toward his native Venezuela. "It is a feat beyond human endurance," his lieutenants warned him. "Then our endurance," he retorted, "must be *more* than human."

He started the crossing of the Andes in the middle of the winter. His soldiers, brought up in the tropical valleys of New Granada, were unaccustomed to the snowdrifts and the sleetstorms of the upper ranges. But into the teeth of the tempest they marched, scrambled up the faces of slippery rocks, held on precariously with their knees and their fingers, crawled in single file across ledges so narrow that two mules could not pass each other, and groped their way through the blinding mists that swirled around the mountaintops. Again and again, after an exhausting climb, they found it necessary to retrace their steps in order to avoid gorges too deep to cross. Hardly a day passed without the loss of men and animals who missed their footing and crashed down over the precipices as the mountains reëchoed their cries amidst the howling of the wind. "We shall never get across," moaned the living. But a fiery spirit drove them on. Bolivar seemed to be everywhere—smiling, tireless, undismayed, impervious to the cold, unconcerned about his life. "We have a mission to fulfill, and nothing shall stop us!"

And nothing *did* stop them. With five hundred crusaders he charged down from the Andes into Venezuela. The Spanish royalists looked upon them with superstitious amazement. "These soldiers are veritable devils!" To which Bolivar retorted—"Not devils, but avenging spirits!" He addressed his men as they reached the boundaries of his native land: "Soldiers, your arms have brought freedom to the gates of Venezuela . . . As the darkness scatters before the light of the dawn, the Spaniards will disappear at the mere sound of your guns . . . Brave soldiers, it is to your hands that America looks for salvation . . . You have conquered the Andes. It is now your proud task to conquer the Spanish king!"

V

THROUGH scenes of indescribable enthusiasm he marched across Venezuela toward his native city of Caracas. In every town and village he found eager volunteers for his army—not only South Americans but native Spaniards as well. For the resentment against the Spanish misrule was intense. One of Bolivar's Spanish volunteers, Major Vicente Elias, was so fanatical in his hatred of his countrymen that he vowed destruction to every last one of them. "When I have killed all the Spaniards I will do away with my own family and then with myself, so that none of that race will be left alive."

Major Elias had brought along with him an entire company of volunteers. Bolivar was now the commander of a considerable force, an army of inspired men determined to see but a single end to their crusade—victory. Reckless of their lives and regardless of the odds, they kept charging again and again at the enemy until they put them to flight. In one of their stubborn battles they renewed the charge twenty times, with Bolivar always galloping at their head. He seemed to lead a charmed life. "God is preserving him for America's sake." His followers had become imbued with a religious conviction of their invincibility. "America is destined to be free!"

On August 6, 1813, they entered Caracas in triumph. The city lay in the hollow of the mountains like a huge bowl filled with flowers. Bolivar, in full dress uniform, marched at the head of the column amidst the garlands and the banners and the happy throngs that lined the streets. Shouts of acclamation on every side. The soldiers, ragged, barefoot, covered with wounds but with faces aglow, displayed the flags they had captured from the enemy.

They marched into the public square. Here, upon a raised platform, the notables of the city bestowed upon Bolivar the title by which he was henceforth to be known to his countrymen—*Libertador*—the Liberator of Venezuela.

VI

BOLIVAR had conquered his enemies. But he was unable to conquer his friends. Many of them had become envious of his success. They accused him of dictatorial ambitions. Several of his former lieutenants had set themselves up as dictators on their own account. They refused to acknowledge the authority of their Commander-in-Chief. Venezuela had become entangled in a confusion of civil wars. Street broils, mutinies, desertions. Bolivar tried to keep his people united by every psychological weapon at his command—flattery, persuasion, encouragement, reprehension, rewards, promises, threats, appeals to their self-interest, their patriotism, their common sense. Sometimes, when the occasion demanded, he resorted to *physical* weapons in order to rid his country of its malcontents. One day he ordered the execution of five hundred men. "If I am forced to retaliate by terrible means, which are repugnant to me, it is solely to deliver my country from its enemies."

Bolivar was not a cruel man. But he was obliged to fight fire with fire. His enemies, both Spanish and American, were the type that would stop at nothing. One of them, Morales, was always followed by a gigantic slave known as "the Executioner," a monster whose chief amusement was to clear his master's path of its "human vermin." Another of Bolivar's enemies, Zuazola, had adorned his hat with the ear of a slain rebel. Still another, Antonanzas, was in the habit of presenting his friends with boxes full of hands and feet and noses—the trophies of his battles. Such was the character of some of the men against whom Bolivar was obliged to fight.

But he fought against them and overthrew them, one by one. Time and again he came near to losing his life, either in open combat or as the result of treachery. One night he left his house to meet an Englishman sympathetic to the Venezuelan cause. During his absence an intimate friend came to visit him. Finding the house empty, the visitor lay down in Bolivar's hammock to await his return. When Bolivar came home, he saw his friend lying in a pool of blood, stabbed to the heart. Some enemy had mistaken this man for the Liberator.

This was but one of many seemingly miraculous escapes. The assassins never knew where or when to find him. "It's hard to shoot the shadow of an eagle on the wing," remarked his admiring friends.

And the "eagle on the wing" covered an amazing range of territory in his crusade to disemburden his country of its tyrants and its traitors. North, east, south, west—across unfordable rivers, insurmountable mountains and impenetrable forests he struck at the enemy with the swiftness of lightning. And with the tantalizing *irregularity* of lightning. His blows invariably descended upon the places where they were least expected. Everywhere he was hailed as a savior. The Liberator of Venezuela, New Granada, Colombia, Ecuador, Bolivia, Chile, Peru. "The Spanish domination in South America is now nothing but a memory."

VII

By SEPTEMBER 4, 1826, Bolivar had completed his work of liberation. "Whatever remains of his life after that date," writes his great biographer, Rodo, "is tragedy." His campaigns had broken down his health. He suffered from recurrent attacks of fever. He saw the disintegration of the countries he had tried to unite. He tried to convene a Pan-American

Congress in Panama, but failed in his attempt. "I am like the crazy Greek who stood on a rocky headland and tried to direct the vessels that sailed around it." The cross currents of personal envy and national intrigue were everywhere threatening to whirl his beloved countries into anarchy. He started on a personal tour of these countries. "Let there be no more regionalism—no more Venezuela, no more Ecuador or Bolivia or Chile or Peru. Let us all be united into a single family of Americans." Everywhere the people cheered these words and promised to heed them—and promptly forgot them the moment Bolivar was out of sight.

Rivalries, conspiracies, assassinations. In Bolivia there were three presidents, two of whom were killed, within a single week. Revolts in Ecuador, New Granada, Venezuela. Bolivar, too ill to take an active part in the suppression of the revolts, implored his countrymen to come to their senses. They voted him a pension of 30,000 pesos—to keep him quiet—and went on with their fighting. He refused the pension although he was now penniless, having sacrificed his entire fortune to the cause.

He was left virtually alone. Nearly all his friends had either died or deserted. Only a handful had remained loyal to him—his lieutenant Sucre, his old tutor Rodriguez, his Irish aide-de-camp O'Leary, his mistress Mansuela. He had met Mansuela in Quito, when he rode triumphantly into the city after his victorious Battle of Pichincha. She tossed him a flower from a balcony and a few days later she tossed him her heart. The wife of an English doctor in Quito, she left her husband to follow Bolivar in his adventures. And she remained with him in his sorrow. Time and again her husband had begged her to return. But she always refused. "I am more honored by being the mistress of General Bolivar than the wife of any other living man."

Bolivar was her god, and she stood by him even after his crucifixion.

But Bolivar wanted to be alone in his sorrow. He had determined to exile himself from the painful scene of his military victories and his political defeats. Where would he go? It did not matter. Anywhere away from the hatreds, the jealousies, and the squabbles of his countrymen. He had brought freedom to a people who did not know how to use it. The Americans had won their war, and they had lost their peace. So much toil, so little gain! "Those of us who have served the Revolution have ploughed the sea."

Quietly he boarded a frigate and sailed away to his lonely death. The ship was bound for Jamaica; but when Bolivar's illness took a turn for the worse, the captain decided to sail for Santa Marta on the Colombian coast. They carried him to the shore on a litter—a shivering bundle of bones that had been the Liberator of South America.

He lingered on for a few days. "My last wish, as I die, is to see my countrymen united."

Twelve years after his death his wish came partially true. On a December day in 1842, a united fleet of all the nations he had liberated escorted

his body home to his native city. Now at last they knew him for the great
man that he was.

IMPORTANT DATES IN THE LIFE OF
SIMON BOLIVAR

1783—July 24, born in Caracas.
1801—Married Maria Teresa Toro.
1803—Wife died.
1805—Traveled in Europe.
1806—Returned to Caracas, "a
  rebel dedicated to freedom."
1811—Declared Venezuelan independence from Spain.
1813—Started war for liberation of
  Venezuela.
1815—Defeated, exiled to Jamaica.
1817—Returned to Venezuela.

1819—Crossed Andes with "Army
  of Liberation."
  Defeated the Spanish army
  at Boyaca (August 7).
  Became president of liberated Venezuela (December
  17).
1820-26—Fought for liberation of
  other South American countries.
1828—Escaped attempt to assassinate him.
1830—December 17, died at San
  Pedro.

John Henry Newman

1801–1890

THE FALL of 1845 was a season of unprecedented storms. And not the least of these were the tempests of the spirit that rocked the religious world. Within a single week in October, two great churchmen underwent a conversion in opposite directions. Ernest Renan, the Catholic, became a Rationalist; and John Henry Newman, the Protestant, became a Catholic.

Both conversions were the result of considerable soul-searching on the part of the leading actors. Renan was determined to seek the truth through the path of trial and error. And Newman was convinced that, after his years of trial and error, he had at last discovered the truth.

Two fascinating examples of the human quest for certainty in this world of shadows and doubts. And of the two examples, the story of Cardinal Newman is perhaps closer to the meaning of life. For it leaves us at the end upon solid ground, while the story of Renan plunges us into quicksands from which there seems to be no safe exit in sight.

So let us retrace the journey of John Henry Newman as he tried, "amid the encircling gloom," to follow the vision of the kindly light.

II

FROM early childhood, he was a dreamer who "mistrusted the reality of material things." But he loved to write and to make speeches. For words, he said, are the bridges that convey our thoughts from heart to heart. Educated at the Ealing Academy for Young Gentlemen, he was one day selected to deliver an oration before the Duke of Kent. His voice had just reached the adolescent stage when it changes into a falsetto at the most inopportune moments. His effort before the Duke sounded more like a yodeling performance than a speech. The headmaster of the academy, Dr. George Nichols, apologized to his distinguished guest, explaining,

"His voice is breaking."

"Quite so," replied the Duke, "but his ideas are sound."

He entered Oxford at fifteen, and distinguished himself in music as well as in literature. This double distinction gave him a feeling for words that fall upon the ear like a song. Few English writers have equaled the "subtle, sweet and mournful melody"—we are quoting Matthew Arnold —of Cardinal Newman's prose.

Shortly after his graduation from college, Newman lost his father and his sister. These successive tragedies, followed by a breakdown in his own health, deepened his mystical sense of "the world behind the veil." His doctor advised him to take a cruise in the Mediterranean for his health. It was on this cruise that he wrote "Lead, Kindly Light"—the poem that has sustained many thousands of people, just as it sustained Newman himself throughout the rest of his life.

> Keep Thou my feet; I do not ask to see
> The distant scene,—one step enough for me.

One step at a time, in the trembling hope that there is safety at the end. Even now he could sense, vaguely but instinctively, the outline of the road that he was to travel to the end of his days. A series of uncertain turns, with many dangers on the way, but ever forward to a certain goal.

III

ORDAINED as a minister of the Church of England, he served for a number of years as vicar of St. Mary's, at Oxford. Yet he felt that his soul, though dedicated to God, was as yet untouched by the divine spark. "I look on myself," he said, "very much as a pane of glass, which transmits heat, being cold itself. I have a vivid perception of the consequences of admitted principles, have a considerable intellectual capacity of drawing them out, have the refinement to admire them, and a rhetorical or histrionic power to represent them; [yet] loving the truth, but not possessing it, for I believe myself at heart to be nearly hollow . . . I believe I have some faith, that is all."

What he wanted to find was a deeper faith, a greater warmth, a clearer perception of the truth. For several years he felt that he could find them *within*, or at least bring them *into*, the Church of England. And so he joined a group of young men—members of the Oxford Movement—who tried to reintroduce "the traditional flower of Catholicism into the neglected gardens of the Protestant faith." Their movement came to be known as *Tractarianism*, because they wrote a number of *Tracts for the*

Times—diatribes against the "infidelity, the skepticism and the prosaic coldness" that had crept into the worship of the Anglican Church.

Several of these tracts were the work of Newman himself. The religion of England, he declared, had lost contact with the Infinite. And this was due to the fact that it had departed too completely from the traditions of early Christianity.

And then came his famous *Tract XC*—the work which, in the words of Gladstone, "shook the kingdom." Here was a Protestant clergyman, thundered the bishops of the Anglican Church, who wrote more like a Catholic than the Catholics themselves. Some of the bishops went so far as to accuse Newman of being a papal spy.

The storm that broke over his head resulted in his departure from the pulpit of St. Mary's. He had tried to interpret Christianity, as he understood it, in the spirit of Christ; and he had received nothing but hatred and abuse for his trouble. Yet, in his final sermon as an Anglican, he had nothing but kind words for his congregation: "O my brethren, should you know anyone whose lot it has been . . . in some degree to help you; if he has ever made you feel that there was a higher life than this daily one, and a brighter world than what you see . . . remember such a one in time to come, though you hear him not, and pray for him, that in all things he may know God's will, and at all times he may be ready to fulfill it."

His failure to rebuild Protestantism upon a broader Catholic—that is, a more universal—foundation was the first of his five great disappointments. But he met this disappointment, as he was to meet the other four, with a patient courage and a fervent desire to know God's will and to fulfill it to the best of his "frail human ability."

IV

HE had tried to remodel the Protestant Church after his own image—or, as he sincerely believed, after God's image—and he had failed. And so, like Jacob of old, he "parted with all that his heart loved," and set out "upon a dreary way over Jordan" into an alien land.

It was in the midst of a rainstorm that he made the crossing of the Jordan—figuratively speaking—from Protestantism to Catholicism. Having confessed his sins to Father Dominic, he remained prostrate for some time after the ordeal.

And it was many years before he completely regained his "Vision of Peace." From one of the greatest among the Protestants, he became one of the least among the Catholics. It was as if a general had been suddenly reduced to a private. The Protestants had rejected him, and the Catholics were slow to accept him. The conversion of a scholar meant little to them so far as the numerical growth of the Church was concerned. There were too few scholars to follow him. "But," observed a Catholic leader, "show me a grocer who has gone over, and I shall be very hopeful indeed."

Thus Newman found himself like an immigrant in a country whose manners and customs were unfamiliar to him, and whose inhabitants regarded him with an open hostility at worst and a constrained shyness at best. Even the Pope (Pius IX), when Newman came to see him after his conversion, was aloof and cold. For he feared that the conservative Protestant might turn out to be a radical Catholic.

But Newman bore his new cross with humble resignation. "Time," he wrote, "is short, eternity is long." Although he found himself lonely and misunderstood among men, he placed his reliance upon God. "What people can do here for me, and what they cannot, carries off my mind to Him who has fed me all my life long until this day, whom I find protecting me most wonderfully under such new circumstances, just as He has ever before, and who can give me that sympathy which men cannot give."

Newman might have remained resigned and obscure for the rest of his life, were it not for the disappointments that stirred him into greatness. The first of these disappointments, as we have seen, came when he tried unsuccessfully to restore the spirit of Catholicism to the Church of England. The second came when he attempted, again unsuccessfully, to establish a Catholic university in Ireland.

V

FROM the Catholic point of view, there was a crying need for an Irish university that would establish the faith upon a basis of reason. "For want of a university education," wrote Purcell, a biographer of the nineteenth century, many Irish Catholics "were placed at a disadvantage . . . Their intellectual inferiority was a reproach to the Church . . . and a danger to the Faith . . . In their controversial writings against unbelief and agnosticism, Catholics were apt to fall into blunders which exposed not only themselves, but their faith, to ridicule . . ."

This was the defect that Newman tried to remedy. He realized that a great many people in Ireland were opposed to a Catholic university as an impractical dream. Yet he depended upon Pope Pius to support him in his dream.

But the Pope felt otherwise about the matter. In the first place, there were no funds available for the support of such a university. The Irish people were too poor and hungry to bother about their education. After the famine of 1846, they had hardly enough money to feed their bodies, let alone their minds and their souls.

Moreover, there was a strong feeling in Ireland against the founding of an Irish university by an Englishman. The Irish were reluctant to trust even the Catholics among their English neighbors.

And, finally, the Catholic educators doubted the fitness of Newman for the founding and the management of a new university. He possessed the "tenacity of purpose," they admitted, but he lacked the "driving force" to create anything new.

And so Newman failed once again in his effort to do a constructive job. But out of the failure came one of the great books on higher education —*The Idea of a University*. In this book, Newman outlined his theory of education as a "preparation for the world." For the whole world is a university in which we are compelled to learn the intricate business of living with one another. A university training is "the education which gives a man a clear, conscious view of his own opinions and judgments, a truth in developing them, an eloquence in expressing them, and a force in urging them." Yet "it shows him how to accommodate himself to others, how to throw himself into their state of mind, how to bring before them his own, how to influence them, how to come to an understanding with them, how to bear with them." The ideal university, in other words, should teach us to defend our own ideas with conviction and to regard other people's ideas with tolerance.

And thus the ideal university should serve not as an ivory tower of academic aloofness, but as a laboratory in the science of daily living. The investigation of a political, moral, or practical truth must be "unshackled, independent, and free." For the student must be encouraged to feel that, "however his line of investigation may swerve now and then, it will be sure to come home, because truth can never be contrary to truth."

It was no wonder that his Catholic superiors distrusted his influence as a teacher of the faith. Freedom of investigation, as outlined in his *The Idea of a University*, was out of step with the cautious dogmatism of Pope Pius IX. Newman was an "ideal" Catholic, as he had been an "ideal" Protestant. His conception of religion, like his conception of education, was too lofty to meet the "practical" demands of the day.

And so his new faith, like his old, brought him at first nothing but loneliness and neglect. His way to greatness still lay ahead of him over the obstacles of defeat. He was to undergo three more disappointments before he reached the heights.

VI

His third great disappointment came when, at the invitation of Cardinal Wiseman, he undertook a new English version of the Bible. Here again he was ahead of his times. He selected a number of collaborators, spent a considerable sum of his own money, and devoted an entire year to the venture, when he received a sudden bolt from the blue. Cardinal Wiseman ordered him to stop the work, since another translation was being prepared by the Archbishop of Baltimore. Once more the authorities had decided that Newman was too unorthodox to represent the position of the Church.

Newman had now reached the disillusionment of old age. So many things that needed to be done, so invariably stopped when he wanted to do them! A failure when he had tried to stabilize the Church of England, an equal failure when he endeavored to liberalize the Church of Rome. "To myself," he wrote at this time, "I feel as full of life and thought as ever I was—but a certain invisible chain impedes me when I attempt to do anything."

This same invisible chain impeded him on two other occasions—when he undertook the editorship of the liberal Catholic magazine, *The Rambler,* and when he planned a Catholic intellectual center at Oxford. On both of these occasions, the bishops informed him that his Catholicism contained more doubt than dogma, and that he could better serve the Church with his silence than with his speech.

Five attempts at greatness, and five dismal failures. He found himself trapped, as he expressed it, like a strange animal—paraded in a cage for the admiration of the multitude, but kept constantly out of touch with the spectators for fear that he might do them some irreparable harm.

And then, when all seemed lost, he was rescued from oblivion by a strange quirk of fate. It took the vigorous attack of a Protestant to dramatize his greatness as a Catholic.

VII

THE ATTACK came in a book review written by the famous novelist, Charles Kingsley. In this review, Kingsley referred to Newman as a defender of the Catholic "disregard of the truth." Truth for its own sake, wrote Kingsley, "had never been a virtue of the Roman clergy. Father Newman informs us that it need not, and on the whole ought not to be; that cunning is the weapon which Heaven has given to the saints wherewith to withstand the brute force of the wicked world . . ."

Newman denied this accusation against him as a "distorter of the truth in behalf of the Faith"; and he entered into a bitter controversy with Kingsley. The outcome of this controversy was one of the masterpieces of English Literature—the *Apologia*. This book is a story of the spiritual pilgrimage of a human soul.

The apology of Newman's faith is free from all bitterness and personal spite. "I am now in a train of thought higher and more serene than any which slanders can disturb." His conversion to the Roman Church, he goes on to declare, was the result not of "lying and quibbling and double-tongued practice and cunning and cant and pretence," but of a growing and finally overwhelming conviction of what he came to see as the Truth. With the dramatic intensity of a Greek drama, Newman describes his adventure from hope to doubt, from doubt to despair, and then back again from despair to certainty and reconciliation and peace.

The writing of the *Apologia* was an emotional as well as a physical strain on Newman. He wrote the entire book in longhand—for he could not afford a secretary—and he often kept at it for twenty-two hours at a stretch. At one time, writes his friend, Father Ryder, "I found him with his head in his hands crying like a child over the, to him, well nigh impossibly painful task of public confession."

But, as a result of this confession, Newman had at last become a front-page celebrity. Both Catholics and Protestants acclaimed him as one of the great writers of the world. The *Apologia*, observed his English biographer, Richard Holt Hutton, "has done more to break down the English distrust of Roman Catholics, and to bring about a hearty good fellowship between them and the members of other Churches, than all the rest of the religious literature of our time put together." The world had now seen four great confessions—Saint Augustine's, Rousseau's, Amiel's, and Newman's. And of the four, declared Algernon Cecil, "Newman's book, like his character, is by far the noblest. Neither the sensuality of Augustine, nor the egotism of Rousseau, nor the weakness of Amiel soils its pages. From first to last his candle burnt with a clear, steady flame—*and Kingsley had taken away the bushel that covered it.*"

Newman was now famous, and happy. "I am (at 66) my own master," he wrote. "I have my time my own—I am surrounded with comforts and conveniences—I have no cares, I am in good health—I have no pain of mind or body. I enjoy life only too well. The weight of years falls on me as snow, gently though surely, but I do not feel it yet . . . My reputation has been cleared by the *Apologia* . . . I am as covered with blessings, and as full of God's gifts, as is conceivable. And I have nothing to ask but for pardon and grace, and a happy death."

Yet there was still one cross that he had to bear—the continued distrust of Pope Pius IX. The downfall of the papacy as a political power was now imminent; and, as a defense against the blows that were being inflicted upon the Church, the cardinals pronounced the doctrine of papal infallibility. According to this doctrine, the Pope, as the leader of the Roman Church, could make no mistake. But Newman refused to accept the idea of absolute infallibility. While the Pope's mission was divine, believed Newman, his judgments were subject to human frailty. And, in his attitude toward his new convert, Pope Pius was all too human. He resented Newman's spirit of moderation and restraint, and he stubbornly refused to give him his well-deserved promotion in the hierarchy of the Church.

But Newman bore this cross with a light-hearted resignation. He was content, even now, to cast his lot with the least of the flock. Whatever his station in the Church, he knew that he was within the range of the Shepherd's eye. There is a story that on one occasion an usher at Saint Paul's noticed a threadbare individual examining the alterations that were being made in the Cathedral. "Now then," said the usher, "move on. We don't want any of your sort here!" The man he was speaking to was Dr. Newman.

But Dr. Newman—so goes the story—only smiled at the thought of being "morally turned out" from the place where he so eminently belonged.

VIII

As HE approached his eightieth year, he continued to live contentedly within the sanctuary of his own heart. He remained undisturbed at the coldness that his liberal views encountered in high places. He revered the Pope even though he sometimes disagreed with him. Life, he felt, was too short to be wasted in acrimonious bickering. The duty of a true Christian was to reconcile rather than to quarrel, to unite rather than to divide. And so he spent his time writing his constructive books, corresponding with his friends, and consoling the sick and the bereaved. "God's angel," he wrote to a dying nurse, "will be with you every step you take—and I will try to help you with my best remembrances and sacred wishes as you descend into the valley. But you are to be envied, not lamented over, because you are going to your own Lord and God . . . Only pray for me in your place of peace and rest, for I at most can be but a little time behind you."

One after another his closest friends descended into the shadows; and he parted from them all with a heartening caress and a tender *au revoir*. His unassuming sweetness was like a rose casting its fragrance in the setting sun. One of his visitors at this time, Canon Scott Holland, describes the unforgettable occasion. "I recall," writes the Canon, "the swift, sudden way in which I found him beside me . . . I turned at the sound of the soft, quick speech, and there he was, white, frail, and wistful, for all the ruggedness of the features . . ." They discoursed, without a hint of bitterness on Newman's part, about the foibles of men as compared with the mercies of God.

He was ill now, and believed he was close to the end. He expected no further preferments or honors this side of the grave. Yet one day he was amazed to receive a letter from the new Pope, Leo XIII. In recognition of Newman's "signal services to the Catholic Church," Pope Leo had conferred upon him the cardinal's hat.

It was a belated but none the less welcome recognition. "He felt," observed one of his biographers, "as though the Heavens had opened and the Divine Voice had spoken its approval of him before the whole world." When Newman received the news, he exclaimed: "The cloud is lifted from me forever!" And thus, as some one has expressed it, "his life went down in a blaze of scarlet."

He lived for another decade—led by the kindly light, and attuning his last like his first days to the music of one of his own exquisite prayers: "May He support us all day long, till the shades lengthen, and the evening comes, and the busy world is hushed, and the fever of life is over, and our work is done. Then in His mercy may He give us a safe lodging, and a holy rest, and peace at the last."

IMPORTANT DATES IN THE LIFE OF JOHN HENRY NEWMAN

1801—February 21, born in London.

1816—Entered Oxford.

1820—Took his degree at Oxford.

1822—Elected fellow of Oriel College.

1827—Appointed Vicar of St. Mary's, Oxford.

1833-41—Editor of the *British Critic*.

1841—Wrote famous *Tract XC*. Resigned editorship of *British Critic*.

1845—Became converted to Roman Catholicism.

1847—Ordained as priest.

1854—Tried, unsuccessfully, to establish a Catholic university in Dublin. Wrote *The Idea of a University*.

1864—Had famous controversy with Charles Kingsley. Wrote *Apologia*.

1870—Wrote *Grammar of Assent*.

1878—Elected honorary fellow of Oxford.

1879—Made a cardinal by Pope Leo XIII.

1890—August 11, died, near Birmingham.

Abraham Lincoln

1809–1865

ON THE night of November 13, 1861, President Lincoln paid a visit to the home of George B. McClellan, general in chief of the Union Army. The servant at the door said the general was out but would soon return. "Very well," nodded Lincoln, "I will wait."

An hour later McClellan came in at the front door. "General," said the servant, "the President is waiting for you in the parlor."

"Is that so?" And without stopping to greet the President, McClellan walked upstairs.

Another half hour of waiting, and Lincoln became somewhat impatient. "Will you please inform the general," he said to the servant, "that I am still here?"

The servant went up to McClellan's room—and returned without his master. "Sorry, Mr. President, but the general asked me to tell you he's gone to bed."

McClellan was a strutting little cockerel of an officer whose bluster was far in excess of his ability. "What this fellow needs," observed Lincoln's friends, "is a good spanking with the flat of his own sword." But Lincoln only smiled. "I am ready to hold McClellan's stirrup for him, if he will only win us victories."

Such was Abe Lincoln—a rare combination of humor and humility that made him the beloved of men.

II

No PLAYWRIGHT has ever created a more dramatic plot than the life of Lincoln. Like the hero in an ancient Greek tragedy, he failed in almost everything he undertook; and when he did succeed, he found success more bitter than failure. He lost the only woman he loved; and the woman he married was more anxious to see him famous than to see him happy. He entered business, and failed. He ran for the United States Senate, and was defeated. He applied for an appointment to the United States Land Office, and was rejected. He ran for the vice-presidency, and lost. When finally he was elected to the presidency, it was in sorrow rather than in triumph that he rode into the White House. For, though passionately devoted to peace, he found himself compelled to plunge into war. Tenderest of fathers, he twice had to bow his head in mourning over the untimely graves of his children. Gentle toward every living thing, he was again and again called upon to sign the death warrants of runaway soldiers who were afraid to die. He was a soul attuned to the daylight yet forced to live in the night. And at last, when the dawn of victory arrived after the night of despair, Lincoln did not survive to see the day. His assassination came less than a week after the surrender of General Lee.

In the life of Lincoln the Great Dramatist of Heaven showed the little dramatists of the earth how to write a perfect tragedy.

III

THE DAY after Lincoln was born his nine-year-old cousin, Dennis Hanks, looked at him. "His skin makes me think of cherry pulp squeezed dry." The baby began to wail. "Aw, take him away!" exclaimed Dennis Hanks in disgust. "I guess he'll never come to much."

And indeed there was no reason for anyone to think otherwise. Lincoln's parents and three of his grandparents were uneducated and unambitious. But his fourth grandparent, the father of Nancy Hanks, was a "mysterious stranger from the South." Lincoln's mother, in other words, was a "natural" child. Lincoln thought that his poetical and political genius came from this unknown Southern grandfather. But his never-say-die spirit in the face of failure came to him from a whole line of pioneering ancestors. It took supreme courage to survive in the adventures of the American frontier. There was a concise and picturesque proverb that summarized the epic of America's migration to the Middle West: "The cowards never started and the weak ones died by the way."

Lincoln was descended from those who had the courage to start and the hardihood to survive. A poet born out of a race of pioneers. Lincoln's entire political career was a great epic poem in action.

As a young man he wanted to be a writer. He had drunk deep of the sap of the earth and the sweetness of the air. He had caught the rhythm of the swinging ax and the music of the growing grass. And he reproduced this rhythm and this music in a number of juvenile poems. He could work hard when he had to. But he preferred to *think* hard. "Abe Lincoln worked for me," remarked a neighbor, John Romine, "but he was always reading and thinking instead of attending to his job . . . He said to me one day that his father taught him to work, but he never taught him to love it."

When the day's work was over, he sat around swapping stories and "just learning to be friendly with people." One evening a farmer's wife upbraided him for his laziness. "What's going to become of you, Abe?"

"Me?" drawled Lincoln. "I'm going to be President of the United States."

Lincoln, of course, was spoofing when he said this. At the time he had not the slightest idea that he would attain to political distinction. But he had decided to go into politics. For he was not only a poetical pioneer but a practical Yankee as well. At an early age he had dedicated himself to a life of concrete usefulness. Instead of combining words into a great poem, he would help unite men into a great nation.

And so he announced himself as a candidate for public service. He canvassed his neighbors with humorous anecdotes and homely parables. These speeches were honest and unassuming prose poems. And his neighbors understood them just as readily as they understood the solid earth under their feet and the simple stars overhead. They trusted his uncouth ruggedness, his open smile, and his generous heart. He was so much like them and yet so very much above them. Like an oak tree in a forest of saplings. "There's suthin' peculiarsome about Abe," they said, "yes, an' suthin' kindlike an' strong." He could split a rail and pull a boat faster than any other man in Sangamon County; he could floor the strongest "rassler" in the state of Illinois; he could lift an ax by the tip of the handle between the forefinger and the thumb; and he could talk like an apostle out of the Bible. He was quite the homeliest man in the state, and just as lovable as he was homely, was this awkward Honest Abe, with his big gnarled hands, and his ill-fitting clothes, and his furrowed face and sensitive mouth and gentle eyes. A first-rate man to look after their interests. "If elected, I shall consider the whole people of Sangamon my constituents, as well those that oppose as those that support me." They elected him to the state assembly.

He was a young man of little learning and much wisdom. For he had touched life at many points. He had been field hand and ferryman, wood chopper and butcher boy, tanner and storekeeper and surveyor. And letter writer for all the inarticulate folk of the neighborhood. He had learned to understand and to reproduce in his own simple honest phrases the innermost yearnings of his fellows—men who toiled and suffered and lost their loved ones and kept toiling on. He, too, had loved and suffered. He had lost his only sister, his mother, and the girl he was about to marry. For several weeks following the death of Ann Rutledge he was almost out of his mind with grief. One night in a thunderstorm he rushed to the door of his house and cried: "I can't bear to think of her lying out there alone, with the rain and the storm beating on her grave!"

But he pulled himself together and carried on.

IV

As a child he had written in his notebook: "Abraham Lincoln his hand and pen he will be good but god knows when." And now he had made good much sooner than he, or anybody else, had expected. At a dinner given by his constituents in his honor the toastmaster referred to him as a young man "who has fulfilled the expectations of his friends and disappointed the hopes of his enemies."

Such was the verdict of the common people. But not of the expert politicians. When Lincoln took his seat in the assembly, one of the other members gave him a quick and appraising glance. It was his custom to do this whenever a new member arrived. He wanted to size up the men who might become his possible rivals in the future. For, though short in stature, this young assemblyman had a tall ambition. His brilliant mind was occupied with nothing less than senatorial and presidential dreams. His name was Stephen A. Douglas.

His quick appraisal of Lincoln apparently satisfied him that there was nothing to be feared from that quarter. Great statesmen, he concluded, were not hewn out of such unpromising timber. For a time he did not even take the trouble to make Lincoln's acquaintance. And Lincoln, on his part, paid no attention to Douglas. Neither of them suspected how closely their lives were to be intertwined and how vital a role their own destiny was to play in the destiny of America. The clash in their characters, in their ambitions, in their very appearance was but another manifestation of the perfect drama woven around the life of Lincoln.

And now there appeared upon the scene a person who was to bring about the first complication in the plot. One evening the two assemblymen met an aristocratic young lady from the South—a Becky Sharp type of character who was visiting her married sister in Springfield. Mary Todd was a buxom and beautiful and superficial little creature, whose mind was as bright as a bubble—and as empty. Puffed up with a superabundance of vanity, she was determined to become "the empress of all she surveyed." An exquisite dancer, she meant to dance her way into the heart of the most promising young man in America. When she met the suave Douglas and the uncouth Lincoln, she sized them up immediately. Crude power was nearer to the heart of America than cultivated splendor. Though Mary Todd's mind was shallow, her instinct was sound. She chose Lincoln as the more likely candidate for supreme honors. And so, much to the chagrin of Douglas—a feeling that was to play no little part in his future antagonism to the "homely interloper from the backwoods"—the elegant young lady gave her hand to Lincoln. Or, to be more exact, she took Lincoln's reluctant hand into her own and led him to the altar.

After his marriage Lincoln settled down to the business of making a living. He entered into a law partnership with William A. Herndon, bought a rickety, leather-covered sofa on which he could stretch out his full length of six feet four and dream away his time, allowing the papers to pile up on the desk and the dust to accumulate on the floor until the grass began to sprout in the cracks. He was set down as the untidiest and most eccentric young man in Illinois. He steadfastly refused to represent unethical clients. "I shall not take your case," he said to a man who had pointed out how, by a legal technicality, he could win six hundred dollars. "You may be legally right, but you are morally wrong . . . And by the way," he added as the disgruntled client turned to leave, "you look like a pretty energetic fellow. Why not try an *honest* way of making six hundred dollars?"

As for Lincoln himself, he made a fairly satisfactory living in spite of his scruples. Perhaps *because* of his scruples. For his clients appreciated his candor, and the judges admired his common sense. What he lacked in good manners he made up in goodness. And *that*, to the simple folk of Illinois, was the yardstick by which they measured a man's character.

He was popular with everybody—except his own wife. Theirs was not a happy marriage. Lincoln's unrefined manners clashed all too frequently with Mary's ungovernable temper. She treated him like a precocious but ill-behaved schoolboy. She nagged him because he sat down to dinner in his shirt sleeves, and went out to milk the cow in his shuffling slippers, and held up his trousers with one suspender, and ran ahead of the maid to open the door when guests arrived, and spoke to his fashionable visitors about pigs and chickens and turnips and horses, "just like the vulgar yokels from whom he had sprung." She was ashamed of his kind, she reminded him, and she never invited any of his kinsfolk to her house. He was fit to associate only with workingmen and plowmen, she told him contemptuously. In short, he was merely one of the "common people."

Lincoln listened to these accusations and smiled—drat that irritating smile of his! she stormed—and he pleaded guilty. He loved the common people, he confessed. "God too must love them, I guess, or He wouldn't have made so many of them."

For Lincoln was not ashamed of his lowly origin. On the contrary, he wore it like a badge of pride. His heart went out to the underprivileged because he was one of them. Intent upon their investigation of Lincoln's attitude toward the black slaves, many students of history have overlooked his attitude toward the white toilers. Lincoln abhorred wage slavery as intensely as he abhorred black slavery. "Inasmuch as most good things are produced by labor," he said in one of his early campaign speeches, "it follows that all such things of right belong to those whose labor has produced them . . . To secure to each laborer the whole product of his labor . . . is a worthy object of any government."

Lincoln was a friend of labor and an apostle of liberty. But he took care to distinguish between two kinds of liberty—liberty from exploitation, and liberty to exploit. In one of his speeches he pointed out this distinction by means of a parable. "A shepherd drives the wolf from the throat of his sheep . . . and the sheep of course thanks the shepherd . . . but the wolf denounces him." To the sheep the shepherd has given liberty from exploitation; but from the wolf he has taken away the liberty to exploit. "Let not the wolves cry *liberty*, when the word that they really mean is *tyranny*."

In every controversy between the so-called upper and lower classes, Lincoln was on the side of the underdog. He was not only the champion of the laborer but the friend of the immigrant as well. He laughed at the pretensions of those who referred to themselves as *Americans* and to their immigrant neighbors as *foreigners*. All of us, he said, are foreigners. The only native Americans are those who "wear the breechclout and carry the tomahawk." Our forefathers were immigrants when "they drove these Indians from their homes." How stupid, therefore, of us to look down upon "those not fortunate enough to come over so early as we or our forefathers."

Such was the ugly duckling with the strange figure and the unconventional ideas who walked through the streets of Springfield in the 1850s. So absorbed was he in his "peculiarsome" thoughts that he frequently passed by his friends without noticing them. One day he strolled along the sidewalk near his house, trundling behind him a cart in which his little son Willie was riding. The child fell out and lay crying on the street; but his father, unaware of what had happened, kept calmly pulling at the empty cart.

Yet he loved his children with the tenderness of a man whose own childhood had had more than its share of suffering. He allowed them to make his office their playground. "The boys," writes Herndon, "were absolutely unrestrained . . . They pulled down the books from the shelves, bent the points of the pens, overturned the spittoon—but it never disturbed the serenity of their father's good nature." To all of Herndon's suggestions that Lincoln "wring their little necks" the father had but a single reply: "Let them play. Time enough for trouble when they grow up."

We see Lincoln in one of his most revealing moments on a midsummer afternoon when Willie is about four years old. His mother has been trying to give the child a bath. Willie has wriggled out of the tub and scampered naked into the street. His father, sitting on the porch, is holding his sides with laughter at the sight of his pink-and-white little "monkey" who has slipped under a fence and is scurrying across a field. His wife stalks angrily up to Lincoln. "Stop that stupid hilarity and go fetch your son!" Still laughing, Lincoln starts after Willie. He catches him halfway across the field, gathers him up in his long gentle arms, covers his wet little body with kisses, and then mounts him on his shoulders to bring him back to his outraged mother.

Lincoln's tenderness toward his children extended to the entire human race. His was one of those rarely attuned organisms that rejoiced with the joys and suffered with the sufferings of his fellows. His universal sympathy included not only the whites but the blacks. From the very beginning he was interested in the emancipation of the slaves. As a young man he had taken a trip to New Orleans. There he saw the slave market where the Negroes were being auctioned off to the highest bidders. He saw a young girl driven like an animal up and down the platform in order that the prospective purchasers might look her over. "If ever I get a chance to hit that thing," he exclaimed, "I'll hit it hard!" To this end he dedicated his entire life. When he was elected to Congress he drafted a Bill to Abolish Slavery in the District of Columbia. The bill was defeated, but Lincoln refused to bow to his defeat. He returned to the fight again and again. During the Kansas controversy on slavery he raised his voice in behalf of the black men. When the Republican party was formed (1854) on the Jeffersonian principle of democratic equality, Lincoln was one of its most active organizers. And when Douglas, in his ambition for the presidency, was ready to encourage the extension of slavery in the South, Lincoln challenged him to a series of debates on the subject.

These debates between Lincoln and Douglas were something new in American politics. They were mental duels fought before a tribunal of the American people. And the weapons that the fighters used were the two sharpest tongues in the United States.

But in Lincoln's speeches there was something more than brilliance. To paraphrase his own words, it was out of the abundance of his heart that his mouth continued to speak.

It was during his debates with Douglas that his eyes began to fail him —the result of the continuous reading of historical and legal documents. To strengthen his physical vision he went into a jewelry store and bought a pair of eyeglasses—for thirty-eight cents. He fitted the glasses to his eyes by the then common method of trying on all kinds until he found the kind that enabled him to see well. And to strengthen his *mental* vision he used the selfsame method. He examined all kinds of human relationships until he found the kind that enabled men to get along well. And this relationship he summarized in the following words: "Stand with anybody that stands right."

As a result of this application of ethics to politics, Lincoln became a national figure. There had been talk of secession in the South, but Lincoln declared that America must remain united. "United and right." A house divided against itself cannot stand. And America must become not partially but completely free. "This government cannot endure permanently half slave and half free."

Douglas tried to belittle the significance of these words and the importance of Lincoln. "Mr. Lincoln," he said, "is a kind, amiable, intelligent gentleman, but not a national leader." But the common folk felt otherwise. He was just exactly the sort of leader they wanted in the national crisis of 1860. And so they rejected Douglas and elected Lincoln to the presidency.

Between his election and his inauguration his friends came by the hundreds to wish him Godspeed. And in spite of his busy hours he found the time to exchange a kind word with every one of them. Among his visitors was an old lady he had known when he kept store in New Salem. Lincoln was talking to a group of distinguished politicians when she arrived. But as soon as he saw her he left the group and walked over to her with a cordial greeting. Timidly she opened a package wrapped in brown paper and handed him a pair of coarse woolen socks. "Take them socks to the White House, Abe. I spun the yarn an' did the knittin' all by myself." Lincoln thanked her warmly, took the socks and held them by the toes, one in each hand. "Gentlemen," he said to the astonished bigwigs, "the lady seems to have got my latitude and longitude just about right, don't you think?"

Yes, his friends had got his latitude and longitude—moral as well as physical—just about right.

V

LINCOLN'S ELECTION to the presidency meant the fulfillment of Mary's ambition. But it also meant the end of Lincoln's peace of mind. The planters of the South had clamored for the election of Douglas. They had threatened to revolt in the event of a Republican victory. While still a candidate Lincoln had clearly understood the issue. His own election would result in a personal triumph and probably a national disaster. The election of Douglas, on the other hand, would bring obscurity to Lincoln, but it might possibly avert the tragedy of a war. But would it? Could any power on earth at this stage divert the sweeping tide of hatred that had descended upon the country? And if war must come, would Douglas be the man to steer his nation safely through the storm? Was he not too self-centered, too devoid of moral backbone, to take a positive stand for freedom and unity? Was not his heart, as a matter of fact, on the side of the rebels, the seceders, the slaveholders? Would Lincoln be morally justified, therefore, in stepping out of the contest? Did not the presidency need Lincoln more than Lincoln needed the presidency?

Such were the thoughts that tormented him during his campaign and immediately after his election. Rarely in history did a man experience a more bitter triumph. He hated strife. When war had been declared against Mexico (1846), he had raised his voice in protest. It had sickened him to see his country embarked upon a course of military conquest—"that attractive rainbow that rises in showers of blood." And now here he was, the most peaceful of men, compelled to lead his people into another deluge of blood.

Yet even at this late date the war might have been avoided or at least postponed if Buchanan, the outgoing President, had possessed a character of greater firmness. Buchanan saw the gathering storm immediately after the election of Lincoln. But he did nothing to stop it. Let his successor worry about it—if indeed there would be any successor. Again and again he remarked lugubriously, "I am the last President of the United States."

And so he sat irresolutely in the White House while South Carolina seceded two and a half months before the inauguration of Lincoln. Had Buchanan taken a prompt and decided stand against the secession of this state in 1860, just as Jackson had done in 1833, the Civil War might have been nipped in the bud. But instead of discouraging South Carolina, Buchanan actually encouraged it. He not only retained in his cabinet such men as Jacob Thompson, who had helped South Carolina to secede, but he permitted the transfer of arms from the North to the South. And he sat impassively by when six other states—Mississippi, Florida, Alabama, Georgia, Louisiana, and Texas—seceded between the election and the inauguration of Lincoln. When Lincoln was sworn into office on March 4, 1861, Buchanan gave him the Civil War as an inauguration present.

VI

THROUGHOUT THE WAR, Abraham Lincoln had a double danger to fight against—invasion from without, disloyalty from within. The Copperheads —a copperhead is a "venomous snake that strikes without warning"— were beclouding the issues of the war with the propaganda of racial hatred. But Lincoln faced the rebellion of the South and the obstructionism of the North with a single courageous purpose—to keep the states united. "My paramount object in this struggle," he said, "is to save the Union . . . If I could save the Union without freeing any slave, I would do it; and if I could do it by freeing all the slaves, I would do it; and if I could do it by freeing some and leaving others alone, I would do that. What I do about slavery and the colored race, I do because I believe it helps to save the Union."

Here we see Lincoln thinking aloud. And, as a result of his clear and logical thinking, he came to the conclusion that the only way in which he could save the Union was to free the slaves. The Emancipation Proclamation was the inevitable final paragraph in the thesis of Lincoln's philosophy.

Lincoln's entire philosophy may be summarized in a few simple words —impartial love for the united family of America. His attitude even toward the South was one of tenderness and pity. He always spoke of the rebels as "these Southern gentlemen." He had an intense hatred against slavery but no hatred against those who believed in it. "They are just what we would be in their situation." He regarded the slaveowners, no less than the slaves, as the victims of a diseased institution that must be purged out of society if the nation was to be healed. He wanted to bring about a twofold freedom—to free the black man from the slavery of his body and the white man from the slavery of his soul.

He was a man of infinite patience. He bore not only with the insults of McClellan but with those of his official family as well. When Seward and Chase reviled him, and Stanton referred to him as "that damned, gawky, long-armed gorilla," he neither rebuked them nor dismissed them from the cabinet. "It is a dangerous thing to swap horses in the middle of the stream." And when the swivel-chair patriots—the men who did all the inciting and none of the fighting—accused him of incompetence, he let them talk and went quietly on with his work.

The vituperations against Lincoln continued throughout his life. Everything he did, insisted his obstreperous opponents, was wrong. Even his Gettysburg Address was denounced in the hostile papers as "silly and sentimental and unworthy of the occasion." It was not until after his assassination that America awoke to his greatness. Destiny, it seemed, had deliberately injected a melodramatic climax in order to emphasize the beautiful drama of his life. For now, at last, Lincoln stood forth as a man among a nation of children. Father Abraham . . . with malice toward none, with charity for all.

IMPORTANT DATES IN THE LIFE OF
ABRAHAM LINCOLN

1809—February 12, born, Harding, Kentucky.

1831—Employed as clerk in general store at New Salem, Illinois.

1834—Elected to the Illinois state legislature.

1835—Death of his betrothed, Ann Rutledge.

1837—Began practice of law.

1842—Married Mary Todd.

1847-49—Served in the House of Representatives.

1854—Delivered (in Peoria) speech against the extension of slavery.

1856—Joined the new Republican party.

1858—Debated with Stephen A. Douglas on the question of slavery.

1860—Delivered address at Cooper Union.
Elected the sixteenth President of the United States.

1861—As commander in chief of the Union Army, assumed burden of Civil War.

1863—Issued Emancipation Proclamation.
Delivered Gettysburg Address.

1864—Re-elected President.

1865—April 15, assassinated, Ford's Theater, Washington, D. C.

Charles Robert Darwin

1809–1882

PASCAL ONCE REMARKED that the entire face of the world was changed by the shape of Cleopatra's nose. Almost two thousand years later the entire face of history was nearly changed by the shape of another nose. In the fall of 1831 the twenty-two-year-old divinity student, Charles Darwin, was about to sail as an unpaid naturalist on His Majesty's ship, the *Beagle*. But Captain Fitzroy, who commanded the *Beagle*, hesitated to take Darwin along because he judged, from the shape of Darwin's nose, that the young man had "neither the mentality nor the energy" to become a good scientist.

Had Darwin never sailed on the *Beagle*, he would most likely have taken Holy Orders and science would have lost one of its epoch-making works—the story of the evolution of the human race. Fortunately for the advancement of learning, however, Captain Fitzroy changed his mind about the shape of Darwin's nose and Darwin was allowed to sail on the *Beagle*. And thus the young theological student was launched upon a religious adventure of a new kind. He set out to explore and to interpret the word of God as inscribed in the Bible of Living Things. From the classroom of theology, the study of God, he graduated into the priesthood of anthropology, the study of Man. And it was the lifelong devotion of his priesthood to acquaint his fellow men with the story of their epic though as yet far from completed journey from the lowly to the sublime.

II

DARWIN was born at Shrewsbury, on the same day as Abraham Lincoln (February 12, 1809)—a coincidence which led one of his biographers to see him as "the emancipator of the human mind from the shackles of ignorance, just as Lincoln was the emancipator of the human body from the shackles of slavery." The year 1809 was lavish with its meteoric shower of geniuses. In that one year an entire basketful of them was dropped into the lap of humanity—Darwin, Lincoln, Gladstone, Chopin, Mendelssohn, Poe, Tennyson, Oliver Wendell Holmes and Elizabeth Barrett Browning, to mention only a few. Every one of these "superior children of the human race" contributed something toward the permanent beauty and nobility of the world—and the contribution of Darwin was not the least among them.

He came of excellent stock on both sides. His paternal grandfather, Erasmus Darwin, was a famous naturalist who wrote a poem on the *Loves of the Plants* and a prose work on the *Laws of Organic Life*. His great-grandfather on his mother's side was Josiah Wedgwood, the celebrated founder of the Wedgwood potteries. A healthy interest in the arts and sciences, therefore, was only to be expected in the Darwin household.

As a child Darwin was gentle, meditative, and acutely observant of his surroundings. Even when he was confronted with danger he was able to pursue his observations in the midst of his fear. One day, absorbed as usual in his thoughts, he was walking through the fortifications of Shrewsbury and stepped absent-mindedly over a parapet. Suddenly he found himself falling through the air—to his death, as he believed. Yet his wits were alert. This was but another interesting experiment for a scientifically-minded little fellow. "The number of thoughts which passed through my head during this very short but sudden and wholly unexpected fall was astonishing . . . all of which seemed hardly compatible with what physiologists have . . . stated about each thought requiring an appreciable amount of time."

From his earliest childhood he formed the habit of noticing things for himself. He loved to collect and to study all sorts of pebbles, shells, coins, birds' eggs, flowers, and insects. He rarely captured his insects alive, preferring to pick them up when he found them dead. For he did not think it right to kill them with his own hands. Yet with the naïve logic of childhood he felt no compunction about killing birds with a gun—at a distance. He enjoyed hunting for a number of years, until one day he saw the struggles of a wounded bird and made up his mind never again to bring suffering or death to any living creature for the mere sake of sport. "A gentle heart," said an ancient philosopher, "is but another name for a vivid imagination."

Darwin inherited his gentleness from his mother. But he had little opportunity to know her well, for she died when he was eight years old. His father, Doctor Robert Waring Darwin, was a huge mountain of joviality and efficiency—he weighed something like three hundred and fifty pounds—and, in the words of his son, "one of the wisest of men." Yet he was not sufficiently wise to understand his son's character. He considered Charles a good-for-nothing loafer whose only mission in life was to

"mess up the house with his everlasting rubbish." In order to knock
some "old-fashioned common sense" into his head, Doctor Darwin sent
Charles to a classical school. But the youngster paid no attention to his
Latin and his Greek. Instead, he fixed up a secret laboratory in his father's garden and began to dabble in chemistry and in physics. This, in
the opinion both of his schoolmates and of his teachers, was "the activity
of a deranged mind." The boys nicknamed him "Gas"; the head master
gave him up as a *poco curante*—a rather careless creature; and his father,
disgusted with his experimenting and his "rat-catching," removed him
from the classical school and sent him up to Edinburgh University to
study medicine.

At first Darwin was not disinclined to follow in his father's footsteps.
But the lectures on anatomy soon began to bore him. And as for the
lectures on materia medica, he found them "something fearful to listen
to." Moreover, his sympathetic temperament could not bear the sight of
the surgical demonstrations. One day, as an operation was being performed on a child, he rushed out of the amphitheater. At that period
they were still operating without anaesthesia, and the screams of the agonized child kept haunting him for years.

It was quite evident to Darwin's father that his son was not cut out
to be a doctor. And so he tried to turn him into a clergyman. As a youngster Charles had shown distinct religious tendencies. As he ran to school
each morning after breakfast he prayed to the Lord to aid him in arriving
before it was too late. But—and this was a point which his father had
overlooked—Darwin started so late for school that it was *necessary* to pray.
The youngster was not the type to adapt himself to the conventional life
of the student. For three years he drifted lazily along the curricular
requirements of Christ's College, Cambridge—years that were "sadly
wasted," as he tells us, "in praying, drinking, singing, flirting and card-
playing."

Yet it was here that he met the eminent scientist, Professor Henslow,
through whose recommendation he was allowed to sail as a naturalist on
the *Beagle*. Fortunately Doctor Darwin was wealthy enough to indulge his
son in his "impractical whims." The hurdle of financial worry, at least,
would be removed from his "unprofitable" quest for scientific truth.

III

FOR FIVE YEARS (1831–1836) the *Beagle* sailed over the seas and Darwin
was privileged to behold with his own eyes "the rondure of the world and
the mysteries of its teeming life." With the precision of a scientist and
the imagination of a poet—for every great scientist *is* a poet—he collected,
observed and classified the scattered fragments of the Chinese puzzle of
existence and tried to piece them together into a comprehensive and com-
prehensible design.

CHARLES ROBERT DARWIN   163

Thus far, however, he had formed no definite idea as to the direction in which his investigations were leading him. Like every true observer, he started not with a theory but with facts. It was to take him twenty years of laborious research before he could determine that his vast accumulation of facts, when examined impartially, pointed to but a single theory—the theory of evolution.

The whole world to Darwin was a big question mark—a problem in mathematics with many unknown quantities, a geometric theorem which must be solved rather than a work of art which must be admired. He confessed that at a very early age he had lost his taste for literature, art, and music. But he had found the other side of the golden coins of literature and art and music in his science.

And he possessed one precious thing that was greater even than his passion for science—and that was, a love for his fellow men. Once, when the *Beagle* had anchored off the coast of Brazil, he saw an old Negro woman, in a party of runaway slaves, dash herself to death over a precipice in order to escape from her pursuers. "In a Roman matron," he observed, "this would have been called the noble love of freedom. In a poor Negress it is regarded as mere brutal obstinacy."

The barbarism of slavery disgusted and repelled him beyond measure. "Near Rio de Janeiro," he records in his *Beagle Journal,* "I lived opposite to an old lady who kept screws to crush the fingers of her female slaves. I have stayed in a house where a young mulatto, daily and hourly, was reviled, beaten and persecuted enough to break the spirit of the lowest animal." Twenty years before the Civil War he expressed his detestation of slavery in words as passionate as ever came from the lips of an American abolitionist. "Those who look tenderly at the slave owner and with a cold heart at the slave, never seem to put themselves into the position of the latter . . . What a cheerless prospect, with not even a hope of change! Picture to yourself the chance, ever hanging over you, of your wife and your little children—those objects which nature urges even the slave to call his own—being torn from you and sold like beasts to the first bidder! And these deeds"—here speaks the spirit of William Lloyd Garrison himself—"these deeds are done and palliated by men who profess to love their neighbors as themselves, who believe in God, and pray that His Will be done on earth!"

Throughout his life Darwin kept his heart open to the sufferings of men just as he kept his eye open to the secret of their descent.

And his sensitive heart and observant eye were lodged in a feeble frame. Darwin inherited his father's stature, but he did not inherit his father's strength. His trip on the *Beagle* was an unmitigated torture of protracted sea-sickness. Added to the sufferings of ill health were the discomforts of a voyage that were enough to undermine the constitution of a more powerful man than Darwin. The food was insufficient and indigestible—to the end of his days Darwin suffered from repeated attacks of vomiting as a result of the "poisons he had absorbed on the *Beagle*." There were frequent spells of unendurable cold and unendurable heat. Again and again, in the swampy regions that he visited in his search for scientific data, he suffered from the bites of venomous insects. On some of his explorations into the jungle he was obliged to go for days at a time without water. Undermined by the accumulation of these hardships he returned from his voyage a broken man.

But a man eager for the adventure of science—and for the no less exacting adventure of marriage. Shortly after his return from his voyage he married his cousin, Emma Wedgwood, bought a large country house with a spacious garden, and settled down to raise a family of ten children and to discover if possible "the secret of their true ancestry."

As a first step in his search for the ancestry of the human race he compiled the story of his discoveries during his voyage on the *Beagle*— a scientific treatise that reads like a fascinating romance. For in everything that he wrote he had but a single aim—to make clear to others the truth as it appeared to him. "Honest simplicity" was his lifelong motto. "It is a golden rule," he said, "always to use, if possible, a short old Saxon word. Such a sentence as 'so purely dependent is the incipient plant on the specific morphological tendency' does not sound to my ears like good mother English—it wants translating . . . I think too much pains cannot be taken in making the style transparently clear and throwing eloquence to the dogs."

And he did have to take great pains in order to make his style transparently clear. He found good composition extremely difficult, and it was only by dogged determination that he was able to hammer out a free and easy and interesting style. "It's dogged as does it," he wrote upon a card which he pinned up over his desk.

He regretted that he had no taste for poetry, and yet his *Voyage of the Beagle* is full of poetical passages. Note, for example, his description of Brazil: "The land is one great, wild, untidy, luxuriant hothouse, made by Nature for herself, but taken possession of by man, who has studded it with gay houses and formal gardens." The first sight of this country threw him into "a perfect hurricane of delight and astonishment . . . The form of the orange-tree, the cocoanut, the palm, the mango, the tree-fern, the banana, will remain clear and separate; but the thousand beauties which united these into one perfect scene must fade away. Yet they will leave, like a tale heard in childhood, a picture full of indistinct but most beautiful figures."

The *Voyage of the Beagle*, after a hundred years, is still as romantic as a tale of adventure out of the Arabian Nights. Darwin's next book, however, was more purely scientific. It dealt with the nature and the habits of the barnacle, that curious little sea-animal which "stands on its head in the bottom of its shell-cup and kicks its food into its mouth with its feet." It took Darwin eight years to write this book. And they were perhaps the busiest eight years of his life. In sticking to this one subject for so long a period, Darwin seemed to have absorbed into his own character something of the tenacity of the barnacle. A good many of his friends ridiculed him for wasting so much good effort on so unprofitable a task. But he was winning a reputation as an outstanding naturalist and he was training the sinews of his intellect for the great work of his life.

For throughout these years he was gradually gathering his material, sifting it carefully through his critical mind, and building up his theory about the Origin of Species and the Ascent (misnamed the Descent) of Man.

IV

The theory of evolution was not original with Darwin. Thousands of years before the Christian era the writers of the Chinese sagas had expressed a vague idea of the development of man from the lower animals. This idea had received further elaboration at the hands of the Greek philosopher, Epicurus (342–270 B.C.), and of the Roman poet, Lucretius (96–55 B.C.). With the coming of Christianity, however, the story of Creation had superseded the theory of evolution, and it was not until Darwin's day that this theory was resurrected and placed upon a scientific basis.

When Darwin was ready to publish his theory of evolution he felt, as he put it, "like a prospective murderer." For he was about to kill the orthodox ideas about man and God. He expected everybody to treat him with contempt. In a letter to his friend, Professor Asa Gray of Harvard University, he wrote: "As an honest man, I must tell you that I have come to the heterodox conclusion that there are no such things as independently created species . . . I know this will make you despise me . . ."

But his genius had enabled him to come upon a great discovery, and his honesty would not let him rest until he made this discovery known to the world. And so he felt it his duty to kill an old dogma in order to reëstablish what he regarded as a still older truth.

But if he had to kill, he did so with a gentle thrust. At no point did he descend to bitter controversy. He simply stated his own side without attacking the other side. Indeed, he stated no side whatsoever—he merely presented facts. He did not want to hurt anybody or to disturb anybody's belief. "Let each man hope and believe as he can." As for himself, he found it not only reasonable but comforting to believe that man had risen from savagery to civilization rather than that he had fallen from civilization to savagery. His theory of evolution gave him the groundwork for a New Testament of his own—the Bible of the progress of man.

He had first formulated this theory of progress, in a tentative outline, as early as 1839—twenty years before the publication of the *Origin of*

Species. In 1842 he developed this outline into a sketch of 35 pages, and in 1844 he expanded it further into a manuscript of 230 pages. But instead of printing this manuscript he continued for another fifteen years to test his data, to pick flaws in his arguments, and to check and recheck his conclusions over and over again. For he was, throughout his career, his own most exacting critic, with the result that he was able to anticipate and to answer practically all the objections that were later to be raised by his opponents.

It was not until 1858 that Darwin was ready at last to publish the result of his investigations. And then, just as he was putting the finishing touches to his manuscript, he awoke one day to find that another scientist had unwittingly stolen all his thunder. On June the 18th of that year he received from his friend, Alfred Russel Wallace, an original paper on evolution with a request for his frank criticism as to the validity of the theory. Wallace was at that time living on the other side of the globe (in Malaya). He was altogether unaware of the fact that Darwin, too, had hit upon the idea of the origin of species through natural selection and that he had been quietly working on this idea for the past twenty years. And so it was with the utmost innocence that he was now asking Darwin to introduce *him* to the world as the originator of the evolutionary theory.

What was Darwin to do in this predicament? Wallace's article was an exact transcript of his own findings on the subject. "I never saw a more striking coincidence!" exclaimed Darwin in a letter to the famous geologist, Doctor Lyell. "If Wallace had had my manuscript sketch written out in 1842, he could not have made a better short abstract."

Darwin's first impulse was to step aside and to give Wallace the entire credit for the discovery. "I would far rather burn my whole book," he said, "than that he or any other man should think that I had behaved in a paltry spirit." Charles Lyell, however, insisted that in all fairness to himself Darwin ought to publish his own views at once. He expressed his conviction that Wallace would gladly accept the situation as soon as he learned that Darwin had anticipated him in the discovery by about twenty years.

Finally Darwin agreed to have the theory presented to the Linnaean Society as the *joint* work of Wallace and himself. And Wallace, not to be outdone in generosity, declared it to be "a singular piece of good luck" that gave him any share in "a discovery for which Darwin alone was responsible."

And thus ended one of the most remarkable controversies in history— a controversy in which each of the opponents tried to advance the interests of the other at the expense of his own glory.

Now that the theory had been presented to the scientific world, Darwin went rapidly ahead with the preparation of his manuscript for the general public. The first edition of the book was issued on November 24, 1859, under the cumbersome title—*The Origin of Species by Means of Natural Selection or the Preservation of Favored Races in the Struggle for Life*.

This book, which "swept away the story of Adam and Eve and the Garden of Eden in a deluge of scientific data," may be briefly summarized as follows: In this world of ours there is constantly being produced an un-limited multiplication of living creatures. The food supply, however, is limited. So, too, is the available living-space in the world. The result is a life-and-death competition between all living things, an everlasting strug-gle for existence. Those that are best fitted to their environment are able to live, and the rest are doomed to die. The evolutionists call this process the "survival of the fittest." But in the course of time the environment keeps changing—from sea to land, from valleys to mountains, from glacial periods to periods of warmer climate, and so on. During these changes it becomes necessary for the living creatures also to change, or to *evolve* from one species to another, in order that they may survive under the new conditions. The process by which this *evolution* takes place is called *natural selection*—that is, nature's selection of those characteristics which enable the species to survive, and her elimination of those characteristics which are no longer necessary for survival in the new environment.

This, in a nutshell, is the whole story of evolution. The unlimited multiplication of life leads to a struggle for existence and to the survival of the fittest through the process of natural selection and the consequent development from one species to another. In accordance with this theory, man is but a step removed from the so-called lower animals. Darwin ex-plains this step in his next book—*The Descent of Man*.

Darwin is generally credited (or discredited) with the theory that men are descended from monkeys. As a matter of fact, he never said anything of the sort. He believed that men and apes are both evolved from a com-mon prehistoric ancestor that is now extinct. The ape, in other words, is not our forefather but our distant cousin.

Man, according to Darwin, is the highest form of animal life on earth. He has gained the mastery over the other animals through the law of the survival of the fittest. By the word *fittest* Darwin means not necessarily the strongest or the most ruthless but the *most adaptable*. Among the lower animals, to be sure, natural selection assumes the form of elimina-tion through physical strife. Within the human sphere, however, the proc-ess of individual strife is being gradually superseded by the progress of social coöperation. Selfish aggressiveness is giving way to mutual aid. In spite of our occasional lapses—such as the ephemeral triumphs of a Napoleon or a Hitler—the law of civilization is slowly but surely emerging out of the lawlessness of the jungle. Step by step we are absorbing the lesson that the best way to insure the survival of the individual human being is to work for the friendly collaboration of the entire human race.

Man, believes Darwin, is a social animal. He is not a fallen angel, but a risen savage. His path is not downward, but upward. Yet, on the other hand, he is not a creature set apart from all other living creatures. On the contrary, he is intimately related to everything that moves and breathes and struggles to live. In the scale of evolving life he is still to be classed as an animal. But he is an animal with an infinite capacity for love.

V

THE LIFE OF DARWIN was perhaps the best proof of his theory of evolution. His capacity for love seemed to grow from year to year. He was drawn to people, and people in turn were drawn to him. In his bluish-gray eyes there was a perpetual twinkle of sympathetic understanding. Such was the kindly serenity of his face that strangers would come away from their first visit with tears of joy in their eyes. As for his intimate friends —and he had many of them—they found in his gentle personality a "perpetual benediction." For friendship to Darwin was the greatest of all the blessings bestowed upon the human race. "Talk of fame, honor, pleasure, wealth," he wrote in one of his letters, "all these are dirt compared with the affection of friendship."

But the friendliness of his character was most apparent in his attitude toward his enemies. In spite of all their vituperations, he never uttered a harsh word against any of them. On the contrary, he always thanked them for their criticism. For the primary object of his life, he said, was to ascertain the truth. And in the search of the hidden byways of truth, "two minds are better than one." He was at all times ready to acknowledge the weak links in the chain of his arguments—to concede his defeat whenever the arguments of his opponents were more convincing than his own. "If I am wrong, the sooner I am knocked on the head and annihilated so much the better."

He never assumed a superior attitude either toward his antagonists or toward his collaborators. Throughout his life he acted the part of the humble assistant rather than that of the imposing master. He was especially grateful to the unrecognized workers in the laboratory, the uninspired gatherers of data, the "hodmen of science," for the invaluable help they were able to give him. He looked down upon no creature, however lowly. His servants, like the members of his family, were in his eyes invested with the selfsame dignity—the dignity of their common membership in the society of the human race.

He possessed that true stamp of the superior mind—a modest honesty. One day Gladstone paid him a visit. When the Prime Minister left him, Darwin remarked: "Mr. Gladstone seemed to be quite unaware that he was a great man, and talked to me as if he were an ordinary person like myself." To which remark Gladstone, when it was reported to him, replied: "My feeling toward Mr. Darwin was exactly the same as Mr. Darwin's feeling toward me."

Darwin had something of Buddha's fellow feeling toward all mankind —indeed, toward all nature. He talked about trees and grass as if they were living things. He would scold a plant-leaf for its "ingenuity" in screwing itself out of a basin of water in which he had tried to immerse it. Vexed with the behavior of certain seedlings with which he was experimenting, he said: "The little beggars are doing just what I don't want them to." He looked upon every plant as upon a living personality. He enjoyed the beauty of his flowers, and he was thankful to them for the "graciousness" of their beauty. He would touch their petals gently, with the infinite love of a sage and the simple admiration of a child.

His character was Christlike, yet he refused to call himself a Christian. "For myself," he said, "I do not believe that there ever has been any revelation." He was not, however, an atheist, but regarded himself rather as an agnostic. He was not very certain, he said, of his belief in God. But he was quite certain of his belief in man. "I believe that in the distant future man will be a far more perfect creature than he is today." As for the immortal destiny of the individual soul, on this question too he was an agnostic. "The whole subject (of immortality)," he said, "is beyond the scope of man's intellect . . . But man can do his duty."

His own duty, as he saw it, was to toil unflinchingly throughout his life in order to bring a little more light to his fellow men. And he toiled, as we have seen, under two tremendous handicaps—his wealth, which made hard labor unnecessary, and his suffering, which made any kind of labor almost impossible. But he overcame his handicaps, thanks to his own firmness and to the gentleness of his wife. For Emma Darwin, whom he immortalized as "the best and kindest of wives," was the "one condition which enabled him to bear the strain and fight out the struggle to the end." Passionately devoted though she was to the doctrines of the English Church, she nevertheless stood side by side with her agnostic husband. She attuned her life to the slower tempo of his own semi-invalid existence, she encouraged him without ever driving him, she kept in touch with his experiments, she corrected his proofs and she fortified his arguments with effective words and phrases. Above all, whenever he was in pain she cared for him with such uncomplaining tenderness that he often said to her: "It is almost worth while to be sick to be nursed by you."

But Darwin repaid his wife's devotion with an equally tender devotion of his own. And the beautiful harmony of their life was reflected in the characters of their children. The Darwins were a family of *thoroughbreds* —all of them were thoroughly bred in the best British tradition of joyousness, generosity, and mutual respect.

The sense of respect—that is, the habit of sympathetic thoughtfulness for the feelings of others—was the keynote of the Darwin character. On his last visit to London, at the age of 73, Darwin was seized with a fainting spell just as he was about to enter the house of a friend. The friend was out; but the butler, noticing Darwin's condition, urged him to come inside.

"Please don't trouble yourself. I shall find a cab to take me home." And the considerate old naturalist staggered away from the door.

For three months he waited patiently for the end. "I am not the least afraid to die," he said. "I am only sorry that I haven't the strength to go on with my research."

His death was the signal for a worldwide chorus of denunciation. His enemies consigned his "unrepentant soul" to hell. But one old lady in England thought otherwise. "To be sure Darwin has proved there is no God," she said. "But God is so kind He will forgive him."

IMPORTANT DATES IN THE LIFE OF CHARLES ROBERT DARWIN

1809—February 12, born at Shrewsbury.

1831—Received B.A. degree at Cambridge University.

1831–36—Joined scientific trip around the world on the *Beagle*.

1840–43—Edited account of the trip.

1859—Developed theory of evolution in *Origin of Species*.

1878—Elected a member of the French Academy.

1882—Died, April 19, at Down, Kent.

Pope Leo XIII

1810–1903

In 1878, the fortunes of the Catholic Church were at a low ebb. The troops of Victor Emanuel had conquered Pope Pius IX, and the Vatican had lost its temporal power in the Papal States. For the last eight years of his life, the Pope was virtually a prisoner of the king. And the so-called "Forces of Enlightenment," encouraged by the revolutionary spirit of the age, were exulting that the Church had reached the end of the road. "The nineteenth century," wrote Gustave Flaubert, "will see the death of all religions. Amen! I shall not weep for any of them."

It was in this turbulent period that Pius IX died (February 1878), and that the College of Cardinals assembled in Rome for the election of a new Pope. Their choice fell upon Monsignor Joachim Pecci—a most unfortunate selection, in the opinion of many ardent Christians. For Pecci was in his late sixties, and far from well. When his name was announced to the populace as Pope Leo XIII, he burst into tears and almost fell into a faint. "I am a feeble old man," he said, "and I cannot assume so immense a burden. I shall collapse under it in a few days. It is a death sentence, and not the papal dignity, that they have just bestowed upon me."

Even among his supporters, there were many who feared that he would hardly survive his coronation. As for the enemies of religion, they were elated to see "a dying man appointed to preside over a dying Church." For, as they believed, both the Pope and the Church were "medieval survivals," out of touch with modern life.

Yet Pope Leo XIII not only survived for a quarter of a century, but brought the Church back to a fresh life attuned to the political and social spirit of the day. The last two popes who had preceded Leo had venerated the old and condemned the new. But Leo took upon himself the task of reconciling the old with the new. Tradition and progress, he declared, are equally vital in declaring the glory of God.

II

JOACHIM VINCENT PECCI, the sixth of seven children, was born (1810) at Carpineto—a village situated like an eagle's nest between two precipitous crags. It was a place suited for the exercise of the body and the soaring of the soul. His father, Count Lodovico, though a soldier in the Napoleonic wars, was at heart a man of peace. And his mother, Anna, was a worshiper of the gentle Saint Francis of Assisi. And thus the parents brought up their children in an atmosphere of tranquillity and love.

As a child, Joachim was studious rather than sociable. His favorite courses in school were poetry and science—the vision of heaven and the knowledge of the earth. At twelve, he wrote Latin verses of superior merit. At fourteen, chosen to deliver a Latin oration to his classmates, he took for his subject "Pagan Rome as compared with Christian Rome." The burden of his speech, as he expressed it, was to prove the superiority of the spirit over the sword.

At the Collegio Romano, he won prizes in physics, chemistry, and philosophy. But his excessive ardor for learning brought about a physical collapse. He suffered an attack of gastric fever which was to plague him, intermittently, for the rest of his life.

But he generally conquered his spells of sickness within a few days. The world's work was too important to wait for sick men. He finished his college course at twenty, his theological studies at twenty-two, and his legal training at twenty-five. For he had chosen, as his life's work, a career of civil service under the guidance of the Church. And, in order to prepare himself adequately for this work, he had undertaken to receive a Doctorate in philosophy, theology, and jurisprudence. And in all these fields he was so successful that the university register singled him out as "the young gentleman (who) has given such proof of his talent as to enable one to foresee that he will attain great distinction."

His main objective in life was to see a world at peace, under the divine guidance of God and the human wisdom of St. Thomas Aquinas. For this great philosopher of the Middle Ages, it seemed to him, had found a perfect harmony between the doubtings of science and the certainties of faith. The province of science, declared Thomas, deals with the changeable objects of the world. But the province of religion deals with the unchangeable truth. Hence science is *logical*, since it is dependent upon the laws of reason; and religion is *theological*, for it is founded upon the revelation of God. And between the logical and the theological there is no conflict. The two provinces of thought and faith are but the two aspects of the selfsame truth—the eternal reality of God.

Later on, we shall see how Pope Leo XIII applied the philosophy of St. Thomas Aquinas to the problems of his own day. But for the present let us return to the young theological doctor as he plunges from the tranquillity of his studies into the turmoil of the world.

III

Appointed as the papal governor of Benevento—a stronghold of smuggling, banditry, and murder—he promptly put an end to the violence by arresting the leaders. Some of them tried to regain their freedom through blackmail; others, through bribes; still others, through influence in high places. But the young governor was adamant against them. He had them clapped into jail, and the people were able to breathe freely again.

But Monsignor Pecci's work was not merely destructive of evil—it was constructive for good. He built roads for agriculture and commerce, lowered the taxes of the poor, and turned the eyes of many apostates back to the Church.

From Benevento he went successively to Spoleto, Brussels, and Perugia. And in all these places he encountered the lawlessness resulting from the Napoleonic wars and the disregard of human life. The blind were leading the blind. Unprincipled men had tried "to become the masters of those who no longer had any masters; they declared themselves the gods of those who had denied their God."

And, in every one of these provinces, it was the business of Monsignor Pecci to transform chaos into order, atheism into religion, poverty into prosperity, and desperation into hope. It was in Perugia that he found his hardest job, and it was here that he stayed for the longest time. He did his work so quietly that, in spite of its excellence, he thought that nobody took any notice of him. Yet he was content to remain an obscure bishop in a secluded spot—directing the province, writing his Latin poems, and bringing the peace of God into the hearts of the humble folk.

His most difficult task came in 1848, when the spirit of revolution had swept all over Europe. Under the banner of political freedom, the forces of the revolution were trying to wean the people away from the Church. For the Church, they insisted, was everywhere out of step with the times. It took all of Monsignor Pecci's diplomacy and energy to point out that there was no clash between religious worship and social aspiration—that, on the contrary, the Church was the best friend of the government—and of the common man.

As a concrete proof of his assertion, he opened night schools for workers, homes and educational centers for orphans, and popular banks where the poor could obtain loans without interest.

But, above all, he rebuilt a number of churches upon a foundation of faith and hope and good will among men. And, to supply the priesthood for these churches, he personally trained a number of young students in "the beauty of holiness and the holiness of beauty." It was no wonder, as an eyewitness of his episcopal labors observed, "that both Perugians and

foreigners . . . were wont to express their admiration not only at the rare
architecture and precious materials [of his churches], but at the concourse
of worshippers and the impressive order of the services." He allied himself, as another eyewitness declared, "not with the mightful masters but
with the rightful servants of the people."

In these quiet but vigorous labors he continued for over thirty years.
And, thanks to his wise leadership, Perugia remained for some time an
island of tranquillity in a stormy sea. But Monsignor Pecci was quite aware
of the storm. He knew which way the wind was blowing, and why. Owing
to the stubbornness of the less progressive elements among the clergy, the
dogmas of the Church were gradually being swept away by the doctrines
of Karl Marx. A great many people had come to believe that, in a real
sense, religion was "the opiate of the people." Concerned as they were
with the promises of the *next* world, some of the Church leaders had
forgotten the problems of the *present* world.

But, as Monsignor Pecci insisted again and again, the blemish of an
occasional sunspot is no true picture of the glory of the sun. And so he
tried to emphasize the positive aspect of the Catholic Church—its historical concern for the welfare of the masses; and at the same time he made
every effort to bring the priesthood into step with the progress of the
nineteenth century. And thus he had a two-fold struggle—to protect the
Church against the ultraradicalism of its enemies and the ultraconserva-
tism of some of its friends. It was his deepest desire to save the Church
from within as well as from without—to rebuild the old Christendom of
the Middle Ages into the new Christendom of the modern day.

But the revolutionists were determined to do away with the Church altogether. And at last they carried their fight into Perugia itself. Their
forces invaded the province; and after a vicious battle known as "the
Massacre of Perugia," they proclaimed "the dawning of a new day of
freedom." Monsignor Pecci, saddened by the struggle, talked to the
leaders of the resurrection as a father would talk to his wayward children.
As a result of his wise diplomacy, he obtained the release of several of the
Catholic leaders, as well as adequate compensation for the Church property that had been damaged in the fight.

Throughout the storm, it was his voice alone that both sides were
equally ready to heed. And he sent out a veritable flood of letters to the
insurgents and the faithful alike—imploring them to listen to reason and
to God. One year, when there was a famine in the land, he opened in his
episcopal residence a soup kitchen for the poor, revolutionists and
Catholics alike. And, throughout that period, he lived himself like an
ascetic. "Whatever I can spare from my own food will help to feed my
hungry brother."

And thus, when the cardinals assembled to select the successor to Pius
IX, they felt that Monsignor Pecci was the one man who could lead them
out of the storm. "The ship of the Church," he had said, "must direct

us toward our supernatural destiny, while providing in the course of our natural existence the necessities of peace, plenty, and security." And the frail old captain succeeded because he steered clear of socialism on the one hand and of fanaticism on the other. *In medio tutissimus ibis*. The middle course is the safest.

IV

WITH HIS RISE to new power came an accession of renewed energy. The tired old cardinal became a vigorous young Pope. When he had first heard his name mentioned as the possible successor to Pius IX, "his hand shook so violently"—we are quoting Cardinal Donnay, one of the electors present at the time—"that the pen it held fell to the ground." But, once enthroned in the Vatican, he wielded his pen with a hand so firm that it electrified the world.

On the night of the coronation, a mob had broken the windows in all the Roman houses where tapers had been lighted in honor of the new Pope. But within a few days, the mob that had come to stone remained to cheer. For one of the first official acts of Leo XIII was to issue a plan for the founding of societies to look after the material as well as the spiritual interests of the workingmen.

The liberal press was rejoiced to see in the Vatican "a new understanding of modern society and its exigencies." And the Catholic press was equally gratified to observe that Leo's understanding of the modern world was based upon a thorough insight into the duties and benefits of traditional Christianity. But everybody realized that the new Pope would stand for no philosophical quibbling or skeptical doubts. There can be no justice without Christianity, he insisted, just as there can be no Christianity without justice.

This was the keynote of all his encyclicals—his public messages of social justice and religious faith. "From the very beginning of our Pontificate," he wrote in the first of these encyclicals, "we have before our eyes the sad spectacle of the evils which assail mankind from every side . . . There is a contempt of the laws of morality, an insatiable yearning for the transitory goods of the earth, and a forgetfulness of the eternal, carried to an insane pitch . . . There is a wicked disposition of men's minds which is impatient of all lawful power . . . There is a perpetual ferment of dissension, begetting internal strife, and cruel and bloody wars . . ."

And what is the remedy for all this? A return to the Church. For "who will deny that it was the Church which did away with the miseries of slavery and lifted men once more up to their sublime dignity? that she it was who . . . took under her protection the sciences and the arts, founded and fostered the institutions of charity, and delivered the populations from squalid want?"

In short, "the Church claims that to her belongs the glory [and the duty] of preserving and developing the true civilization of the world."

Most of the other encyclicals of Leo XIII are concerned with the same idea, examined from different points of view. It is the *glory* of the Church, he declared, to have envisioned among the nations a brotherhood of men under the fatherhood of God. And it is the *duty* of the Church to translate this vision into a concrete fact.

To foster progress based upon truth—this, in a nutshell, was the purpose of Leo XIII. He had an ardent enthusiasm for the advance of modern science. He regarded the latest inventions as the fulfillment of God's promise at the creation of man. "How noble and majestic does man appear," he wrote, "when he awaits the lightning-flash and causes it to fall harmless at his feet, when he summons the electric spark and sends it as a messenger of his will through the depths of the ocean, over steep mountains, across boundless plains! How glorious does he show himself, when he forces the steam to lend him wings and bear him with the swiftness of the wind over land and sea!"

The inventions of men are but the revelations of the design of God. "Tell me, dear Brethren, does not something like a spark of the Creator manifest itself in man, when he summons the light and orders it to illuminate the darkness of the night in the streets of our cities and the rooms of our homes?"

And it is the business of the Church to recognize these inventions as the human flashes of the divine. "The Church, that most loving of mothers, who beholds all these things, has no thought of putting obstacles in their way; on the contrary, she rejoices at the sight and exults over it."

The old, in other words, is not the enemy but the friend of the new. Tradition is the platform that supports the construction of the tower of progress.

Yet, fundamentally, Leo XIII was as unbending as his predecessors. The established dogmas of the Church were as sacred to him as they had been to the earlier Popes. "We follow in the footsteps of our predecessors and confirm and repeat all those things (regarding the errors of the age) from this Apostolic Seat of truth." The fixed truth is the eternal wisdom of God, and the inventions of the world are the changing thoughts of men. It was this harmony between truth and thought, devotion and reason, divine certainty and human groping, that Leo XIII tried to impress upon the modern age.

In this effort, as we have already noted, he was but a "humble follower" of St. Thomas Aquinas. This man—the greatest of philosophers, in the opinion of Leo—had declared that there exists in the world "a fundamental element of invariable truth" which is unaffected by the material changes from day to day, "and which cannot lose anything of its validity in the passage of centuries." If we are to find our way at any moment in this continual "flux of time," declared St. Thomas, "we must use, as our guiding star, the illumination of the Catholic faith."

This was the fixed principle which Leo XIII applied to every religious, political, and social problem that confronted him. All the changes of the turbulent nineteenth century, or of any century, declared the "first of the modern popes," can be properly appraised and adequately adjusted if you approach them in the light of the Catholic faith. That is, if you examine "the shifting picture of history in the framework of eternal truth."

For there is an orderly design in the universe. In this design, everything has its proper place and meaning and motion. And every part contributes, in its own way, to the perfection of the whole.

And science, too, has its place in this design. For the knowledge of *human* things leads to the knowledge of *divine* things.

The aim of science, in short, is like the aim of religion. Both of them— the one by reason and the other by revelation—prove the existence, the wisdom, and the mercy of God. And thus, an idea is sound if it emanates from the contemplation of God's existence and wisdom and mercy. For such an idea corresponds to the harmonious pattern of the universe. But every idea that is godless is unsound, because it is outside of the pattern.

And thus liberty, democracy, and social justice can be effective only when they are integrated into the pattern of the universe under the guidance of God. Left to themselves without such guidance, they are bound to fail.

This was the yardstick by which Leo XIII measured the social upheavals of the day. In some quarters he has been acclaimed as an enthusiastic exponent of Marxism; in other quarters, as a bitter opponent. Both views are only partially correct. His various encyclicals, especially those dealing with the economic problems of the day, contain passages that might have been paraphrased from *The Communist Manifesto*. Note for example, the following words of *Rerum Novarum*, his encyclical on labor: "A small number of rich men have been able to lay upon the teeming masses of the laboring poor a yoke little better than that of slavery itself . . . Yet it is only by the labor of workers that States grow rich."

Yet there is a vast difference between the philosophy of Karl Marx and that of Leo XIII. Both of them had an ardent sympathy for the underprivileged, and a keen desire to alleviate their sufferings. But they were worlds apart in their approach to the problem. The proffered remedy of Karl Marx lay in a *materialistic* conception of history, while that of Leo XIII lay in a *spiritualistic* conception. Marx proposed to work *without* God, but Leo insisted upon working *with* God.

And thus Karl Marx preached class hatred and class war. Cutting across national, religious, and racial boundaries, he arrayed the world into two opposing battle-fronts—the exploiting capitalists on the one side, and the exploited laborers on the other side. But Leo XIII preached the order of peace as against the disorder of war. He looked upon the aggressiveness of capitalism, with its corruptions and exploitations, as a departure from the divine plan of Creation. The only way to restore the original plan, he

declared, was through a change of heart, a transformation of the spirit
from personal greed to social need, a reverential opening of the eyes to the
guidance of God. Let everybody, rich and poor, employer and employee,
master and servant, humbly accept the position into which God has placed
him. Let the wealthy employ their riches as a trust fund for the poor; and
let the mighty wield their power as a protection for the weak.

For every human creature, whether of high or low estate, "is stamped
with the seal of God"—a distinction which "no man may outrage with
impunity." And this distinction imposes upon us the common duty of coöperating with God in preserving the order of the universe. Class conflict would only add confusion to disorder, violence to exploitation,
bloodshed to hatred.

Let us therefore, declared Leo, have understanding and peace instead
of misunderstanding and war. Let us, with St. Thomas, realize that even
though we are equal in dignity before God, we are unequal in capacity,
fortune, and authority among men. In this life we must endure our in-
equality and fit ourselves into a harmonious and helpful collaboration
with one another and with God. For this temporal life is but a school
in which the unequally endowed students are destined to graduate into
an equal share of God's love.

As for Marx's insistence upon revolution—there will always, declared
Leo, be vast differences between the rulers and the ruled. A revolution
may reduce kings to beggars, and raise beggars to kings. But this will only
change the personnel, and not the nature of our human society. For the
principle of this society is based upon "inequalities of condition and
rank." Hence the aim of the socialists "to reduce all classes to one dead
level," maintained Leo, "is a vain striving against nature."

But all the classes [and nations] must learn to "groove into one another," instead of fighting one against the other. In this way only can we
attain individual happiness and universal peace.

The Pope's encyclical on labor—his *declaration of interdependence*—
was hailed as a new note not only in religious thinking but in social
planning as well. It gave a new impetus to those who had been trying
for some time to organize the workers upon a basis of "divine" justice.
"Who can describe," wrote one of the Catholic organizers, the Count de
Mun, "the astonishment, the general enthusiasm, the fervent prayers of
thanksgiving that this encyclical aroused in the hearts of all? Ideas that
until yesterday had been stigmatized as subversive and pernicious are today sanctioned by the highest [spiritual] authority in the world!"

V

Ninety-three years young, and as progressive as ever. Physically, he
looked like a reincarnation of Voltaire—slender, graceful, aristocratic, his
face wrinkled with wisdom and eager to break into a smile. Yet the smile

of Voltaire was cynical; that of Leo XIII, benign. Voltaire had said, *Ecrasez l'infâme!* Crush the Church as the greatest enemy of man. But Leo labored to defend it as man's greatest friend.

And it was as a gentle friend of all men, especially of those who labor and are in want, that he wrote to his bishops shortly before his death: "More than ever it is the people upon whom the welfare of the State depends . . . Go among the people! Go to the workers! Go to the poor!"

IMPORTANT DATES IN THE LIFE OF
POPE LEO XIII

1810—March 2, born at Carpineto, Italy.

1837—Ordained priest.

1841—Appointed papal delegate to Perugia.

1843—Sent as papal nuncio to Brussels.
Consecrated as bishop.

1846—Appointed archbishop of Perugia.

1853—Made a cardinal.

1878—Elected Pope.

1888—Wrote *Encyclical on Human Liberty.*

1891—Wrote *Encyclical on the Condition of the Working Classes.* This work has been called "the social Magna Carta of Catholicism."

1903—March 3, celebrated his jubilee as Pope.
July 20, died at Rome.

Wilhelm Richard Wagner

1813–1883

THE PORTRAIT of Richard Wagner, if depicted with a realistic and unbiased brush, presents a study in violent contrasts. It tells the story of an ugly personality that produced beautiful music. From earliest childhood he displayed an unbounded belief in himself, an utter disregard for others, and an amazing talent for poetry and music. At thirteen he translated, in his spare moments, the first twelve books of the *Odyssey*. He read Shakespeare in German translations, and he knew Weber's opera, *Der Freischütz*, by heart. The youngest of seven children, he lorded it over his brothers and his sisters whose sole reason for existence, he thought, was to dance attendance upon him. His mother and his stepfather—his father had died seven months after Richard's birth and his mother had married the actor, Ludwig Geyer—were scarcely less indulgent toward their beloved little tyrant. But when his stepfather died (in 1821) and the last restraining hand was removed from his undisciplined shoulders he became a source of real anxiety to his relatives. While still in his teens he began to associate with strolling players and musicians, and he became a not infrequent visitor to the smaller gambling dens of Leipzig. Once he staked his mother's entire pension on a single bet. Fortunately for his mother, he won the bet.

He borrowed money recklessly and as recklessly squandered it. "I must have money," he wrote again and again to his friends, "or else I shall go mad." And his friends were generally ready with their purses. For his supreme confidence in his own ability had become contagious. Though self-taught in his music, he felt certain of his ability to astonish and to conquer the world. He would write a German opera—he said—then another, and then still another. And after that he would go to Italy, where he would write Italian operas. And from Italy he would go to France, and there he would write French operas. And everywhere, he assured his friends, an enthusiastic public would shower him with honors and with cash. But in the meantime, "I must have more money or I shall go mad."

He had his moments of depression, to be sure, especially when his friends were a little slow in pouring their funds into the perpetual sieve of his extravagances. But he had a surprising knack for quick recovery. "His temperament," writes Pecht, one of the companions of his youth, "was like a watch spring, easily compressed, but always flying back with redoubled energy."

At twenty this energetic, reckless, yet extremely likable young braggadocio secured, through the theatrical connections of the Geyer family, his first important job on the stage. He became the chorus master of the small operatic company at Würzburg. Here (in 1833) he wrote his earliest opera, *The Fairies*, an exuberant and effervescent outpouring of his untamed youth. The next year he wrote another opera, *The Ban upon Love*, and then promptly disregarded his own ban by falling in love with the actress, Minna Planer. They were married on November 24, 1836— a day that Minna was to remember as the anniversary of her misfortune. Unhappy are they whose destiny ties them to the fiery wheel of genius.

II

THE FIRST YEARS of their married life were years of privations and disappointments and—on the part of Wagner, at least—undying faith in the ultimate triumph of his genius. In order to bring this genius to the attention of the public he wrote four more operas—*Rienzi, The Flying Dutchman, Tannhäuser* and *Lohengrin*. But the public paid little respect to them. For here was a wild and exotic and new kind of music language. And old ears are slow to catch new cadences. Wagner offered beauty to the world, and the world repaid him with contempt. He traveled everywhere seeking for recognition, and everywhere he met with the same rebuffs. And when his wife complained he silenced her with the words, "Your suffering will ultimately be rewarded by my fame."

"Your suffering . . . my fame." This was the keynote of his life. Let others wear the crown of thorns so that he might receive the reward of glory. Again and again he reduced her to shameful appeals for charity in order that he might be released from the inconvenience of making a living. "I am now fulfilling an unpleasant but, I believe, holy duty," she writes to Wagner's friend, Theodor Apel. "You say in your letter to Richard that it is impossible for you to do more for him than you have already done. . . . Let me, however, without any desire to boast, tell you what I did as a girl for my brother. . . . I undertook to pay for his studies at

Leipzig at a time when I had not even four groschen for my dinner. I pawned my earrings and such things, sent the money to my brother and kept only three pfennigs for a piece of bread. . . . I appeal to you, can you make no possible further sacrifice for Richard? In him there is a fine talent to be rescued. If we fail him, this talent will be brought nigh to ruin."

And Richard accepted his charities and nursed his talent and tortured his wife. Minna, he complained, could give him only *material* assistance, but she was incapable of giving him *spiritual* assistance. A man of his inner excitability, he said, needed "mental tending"—soul mates who understood his music and who could inspire him to his "supremest efforts." Perhaps he was artistically justified in this cruel attitude. It is possible that he needed this nectar of passion to feed the fires of his creation. But if this sort of food was life to Wagner, it was gall and wormwood to Minna. Time and again he formed a liaison with another woman and flaunted it in the face of his wife. And always to the injury of his unfaithfulness he added the insult of his excuse that he preferred his new mistress because of her intellectual superiority to Minna. Once, when he attached himself to Frau Mathilde Wesendonck, he assured both his own wife and Frau Wesendonck's husband that his heart bled for their misery but that the fates had decreed the sacrifice of their happiness to his genius. Glorious music for the world; cold consolation for the victims of this glorious music.

His unconventional views about music and love extended also to his politics. As soon as he finished *Lohengrin*, in 1848, he threw himself into the revolutionary agitation which at that time was sweeping over Germany. A warrant having been issued for his arrest, he fled to Switzerland —and took along with him into his exile the heart of another young woman, Madame Jessie Laussot.

Jessie Laussot was the English wife of the French wine merchant, Eugène Laussot. Wagner had met her in Dresden, and this rather fascinating young woman had expressed her admiration for him "in a way," he tells us, "that brought quite a new experience into my life." They began a regular correspondence, and in the early spring of 1850 Wagner received an invitation to the Laussot home. He accepted the invitation with alacrity, excusing himself to Minna on the ground that Monsieur Laussot had promised him an annuity that would free him "from the vulgar necessity of business to the noble cultivation of my art."

When Wagner arrived at the Laussots' he paid his respects to Eugène and then promptly deceived him behind his back. "I soon discovered," he writes in *Mein Leben*, "what a great gulf separated me as well as Jessie from her mother and her husband. While that handsome young man was attending to his business . . . and the mother's deafness excluded her from our conversation, Jessie and I exchanged our ideas upon many important subjects . . . And this soon led to a great bond of sympathy between us."

Together they planned to "flee from the ugly world," somewhere to Greece or to Asia Minor. To his wife he wrote that for *her* sake he thought it best to leave her. "For how can I otherwise ever make you happy? . . . I presume and hope that you are, if perhaps surprised, at any rate not alarmed by my decision."

In the meantime, however, Jessie's husband had got wind of the matter. He threatened to put a bullet through Wagner, and Wagner's enthusiasm for the "spiritual elopement" cooled off. He wrote a letter to Jessie, expressing his "contempt for the conduct of her husband"; and to his friend Karl Ritter, to whom he had confided his plans for the elopement, he wrote another letter, informing him that "nothing can be done with that mad Englishwoman (Jessie Laussot)."

Out of this whole sordid affair only one person—according to Wagner— came out unimpeachable, noble and pure. And that person was Richard Wagner himself. Laussot, said Wagner, had proved himself an arrant scoundrel; Jessie, a fickle jade; and Minna, a jealous fool. "Whoever has observed me closely," he wrote, "must have been surprised at my patience and kindness. . . . If those superficial judges have condemned me, I have fortunately become insensitive to their opinion. . . . As for Minna, she doesn't even understand what true love is, and her rage runs away with her. . . . She really is unfortunate—she would have been happier with a lesser man."

III

FOR TWELVE YEARS Wagner remained in exile, wandering from city to city and from love to love, always insistent upon his own comforts, always forgetful of the comforts of others—"a pocket edition of a man, a folio of vanity, heartlessness and egoism." His attachments for women were not always, as he would have us believe (and probably believed himself), motivated by purely spiritual factors. In the midst of a passionate affair with a young girl he found time for a brief interlude with an old lady. This old lady, a widow with a substantial fortune, had offered to give him "the not inconsiderable sum necessary to maintain me in independence for some time to come." Meeting with the objections of her relatives, however, she withdrew her offer; and Wagner, with a sarcastic fling at "the weakness of her not very independent character," returned to his young love.

And all this time he kept sponging on his friends. It was their duty, he said, to provide him with a living. How else, he asked, could he be free to give his best music to the world? Work like other people? Not he! "The director of the Zurich Theater," wrote Minna to a friend, "has offered Wagner two hundred francs a month if he will accept the post of

Kapellmeister. But he thinks it beneath his dignity to earn money and prefers to live on charity." To Wagner, however, this was not charity but tribute—a tribute to his art. "I am different from other men," he said. "The world ought to give me what I need."

He not only *petitioned* his friends for charity, he *demanded* it of them in a tone of arrogance—as if he were the benefactor and they the recipients. And indeed this was exactly the idea he conveyed to them. He gave them, he said, much more than they gave him—the golden coin of his brain for the baser metal of their pockets. He demanded not only money but hospitality. "Dear Hornstein," he writes to one of his "contributing" friends. "I hear that you have become rich. . . . In order to lift myself above the most distressing obligations that rob me of all freedom of mind, I want an immediate loan of ten thousand francs. . . . Now let me see whether you are the right sort of man! If you prove to be this right sort of man . . . the assistance will bring you into very close touch with me— and next summer you must be pleased to let me come to you for three months at one of your estates, preferably to the Rhine district. I will say no more just now."

Though he had helped him repeatedly in the past, the Baron von Hornstein was for once staggered by the sheer audacity of Wagner's letter. "Yet I must confess," he said, "that the very tone of the letter and the size of the sum made a refusal easier to me. What made it still easier was the knowledge that I was dealing with a bottomless cask. . . . My ten thousand francs would be simply a drop of water falling on a hot stone." His reply to Wagner was polite but sharp. "Dear Herr Wagner," he wrote, "you seem to have a false idea of my riches. I have just a fair income which enables my wife, my child and myself to live in a simple and decent manner. You must therefore turn to your really rich patrons, of whom you have so many all over Europe. . . . As for your offer to pay a long visit to 'one of my estates,' I am sorry that just now I can make no arrangements for such a visit. . . . If I can do so later, I will let you know. . . . Greetings to you and to your wife."

Wagner's reaction to this letter is an interesting study in the impudence of genius. "Dear Herr von Hornstein," he writes, "it would be wrong of me to let your answer pass without the censure that it deserves. It is quite probable that a man of my caliber will not again appeal to a person like you; yet I must point out to you, for your own good, the utter impropriety of your letter. . . . It is not for you to advise me as to who are my 'really rich' patrons—it is for me to decide. . . . If you refuse to have me at one of your estates now, it is offensive of you to tell me that you will have me at some future time. In this case, too, it is for me and not for you to choose. . . . Let this end the matter."

In all his quarrels—and he had many of them—Wagner felt convinced that he was absolutely in the right and that everybody else was absolutely in the wrong. He regarded himself, to quote the apt phrase of Ernest

Newman, as "the central sun of his universe." The sun must blaze, and all the world must bow down in worshipful service. Wagner believed—and he had the right to believe—that he had been born into the world for the sake of producing sublime music. To that end he was ready to sacrifice everybody, including himself if need be. Suffering, poverty, sickness—nothing could ever swerve him from his self-appointed task. If his ethical vision was somewhat blurred, his artistic ideal was steadfast and clear. And this ideal was, to give always of his best. Perhaps it would not be an exaggeration to say that he was anxious to secure a congenial background for the creation of his music rather than to provide a comfortable life for the recreation of his person. His egoism, if we may so express it, was probably more objective than subjective. Objective beauty through subjective suffering. If others had to suffer along with him, or even without him and because of him—why, it was their bad luck. At whatever cost, the fire must be kept burning on the altar of his art.

IV

WAGNER'S ART, for which he was willing to sacrifice his friends, was something new under the sun. Beethoven, he maintained, had said the last word in instrumental music. The next step would be "music fertilized by poetry." This is the sort of music poetry, or music drama, that Wagner set out to give to the world. "Words alone," said Wagner, "cannot express the highest kind of poetry. The words are the roots, and the music is the flower." To enjoy the perfect plant at the moment of its greatest beauty, you must get the harmonious combination of the two—roots filled with life sap, flowers bursting into color.

Yet the flower to Wagner was more important than the root. For he was primarily, like Beethoven, an instrumental composer. He carried over the idea of Beethoven's *Ninth Symphony* into the opera. He produced, especially in his later works, an orchestral stream of melody with vocal accompaniments and poetical word fantasies to round out the whole. Beethoven's *Ninth*, with its triumphant choral in the fourth movement, is a dramatic symphony. Wagner's operas, if we may coin the expression, are symphonic dramas.

All the elements in the symphonic dramas of Wagner—the orchestration, the vocal accompaniment, the words, the scenery, the plot—are woven into an integral and definite pattern. And the design in this pattern, the thread unit which binds the various parts into a compact whole, is what Wagner calls the *leitmotif*. These leitmotifs, varicolored little strands of melody, run throughout his operas like the repeated figures in a tapestry. They identify the characters in the operas, they feature the landscapes and they endow the music with a concrete and recognizable personality.

The leitmotif was not an invention of Wagner's. Other composers before him had made use of this musical label. But in the work of most of the earlier composers it had remained a lifeless identification tag—a mere repetition of the selfsame notes in the selfsame mood. Wagner took this rigid and lifeless formula and transformed it into the plastic features of a living organism. Like the face of a human being, the leitmotif of a Wagnerian opera reflects not only the changing emotions of the character but the sunlight and shadows cast upon the character by the development of the plot.

The leitmotif became more and more a prominent feature of Wagner's music as his art advanced. In his earlier operas he adopted the traditional form of the motif as a melodic symbol. It was not until the operas of The Nibelungen Ring—The Rhinegold, The Valkyrie, Siegfried and The Twilight of the Gods—that he turned this abstract symbol into a concrete form of musical portraiture. With the perfection of the leitmotif it may be said that Wagner introduced a new instrument into orchestral music.

For his genius, let us repeat, was primarily orchestral. The voice in a Wagnerian opera is but a part of the orchestra. This is true not only of the Ring but of the other operas of his later period—Tristan and Isolde, The Meistersingers, and Parsifal. As in the paintings of Leonardo, the human characters of Wagner form but a part of the intricate web of nature which he puts upon the canvas of his theater. And in this respect both Leonardo and Wagner followed the technique of the Great Artist Musician. In the music drama of the universe the life of man forms but a single note.

V

IT WAS A NEW CONCEPT of music and a new philosophy of life that Wagner tried to create in his operas. And the world was slow to recognize this fact. At the age of fifty-one he was still comparatively obscure and desperately poor. Fortunately, at that time he found a patron who stood by him for the rest of his life. This patron was the eighteen-year-old King Ludwig II who had just inherited the crown of Bavaria. Ludwig invited Wagner to Munich, where his operas began to be regularly produced and his fame became firmly established. But the spirit of Wagner remained as restless as ever. He had met and fallen in love with Cosima, the daughter of Liszt and the wife of his friend and musical colleague, Hans von Bülow. While still married to Bülow, Cosima had borne Wagner two children. Finally, when the story of their love had become a public scandal, Wagner and Cosima decided to flaunt the conventions in the face of their friends and to elope. For some years they lived openly together; and then, Minna having died and Cosima having been divorced from Bülow, the two lovers were at last able to legalize their union. They were married on August 25, 1870. Wagner was fifty-seven years old and Cosima thirty-three.

Their marriage was happy. For they had a common interest—both of them adored Richard Wagner.

The Indian summer of his life was pleasant but not always serene. Occasionally he marred the sunlight of his last days with the scowl of his Jovian anger and the thunder of his controversy. He despised everybody, and he insisted that everybody must love him. Toward the end of his life he became a vegetarian, and from that day on all the world must become vegetarian. If a flesh diet was necessary for the people of Northern Europe, then let the people of Northern Europe migrate to the South.

He was an amazing character—a man who was possessed of much genius and not a little madness. Like the ideal philosopher of Emerson, he was a bundle of contradictions—a Christian and a pagan, a patriot and an internationalist, an ascetic and a voluptuary. He praised the virtues of the poor and surrounded himself with every sort of luxury. He dressed himself in silk trousers and a silk jacket—heavily padded, for he was susceptible to drafts. His living room at Munich was decorated with "white tulle . . . rose-colored silks . . . yellow satins. . . . The ceiling was entirely covered with richly festooned white satin. . . . The ground was spread with a soft Smyrna carpet. . . . The couches were upholstered in a white flowered mohair. . . . The windows, the mirrors and the pictures were draped in silks and satins of various hues." And in the midst of all this sat the frowning little god in his crimson trousers and sang about the virtues of renunciation. For this doctrine of renunciation was the central theme of his music dramas.

Thoughtless as a rule toward others, he was astonished that anyone should ever be thoughtless toward him. On occasion, to be sure, he could display a great deal of charm; but it was the charm of a despot who gloried in his power over his slaves. He patronized people, he tyrannized over them, at times he even smiled upon them—but he never befriended them. The world, as he saw it, consisted of millions of ciphers that followed a single unit—himself. "He treats us all," writes Cornelius, who adored Wagner, "like so many pieces of spiritual furniture. . . . Wagner never for a moment thinks of anyone but himself."

VI

SUCH was the musical dictator of Germany when, in 1872, he laid the cornerstone for the dream theater of his life—the *Festspielhaus* (Festival Playhouse) at Bayreuth. This was to be the lasting monument to his genius—the temple in which the two arts, poetry and music, were to be joined in holy wedlock. Four years after the laying of the foundation stone the *Festspielhaus* was ready for the first production of *The Nibelungen Ring*. The opening night of the performance, August 13, 1876, marked an epoch in the history of music.

He lived five and a half years longer—a flaming little Vesuvius of a man, always extolling his own work, always condemning the work of others, a "protean nature" who would "leap like a tiger"—we are quoting his friend, Edouard Schuré—"pace the room like a caged lion, roar like a stag. When he was excited his words came out like screams; his speech lashed about at random. He seemed at these times like some elemental force unchained. . . . The least little contradiction provoked him to incredible fury." In his moments of joy he was no less demonstrative than in his periods of rage. "When I came to visit him," writes Liszt, "he wept, laughed and ranted out of sheer rapture for at least a quarter of an hour." And when some visitor rendered one of his own pieces with exceptional skill, "he would spring up"—Sebastian Röckl is our authority for this quotation—"embrace or kiss the singer warmly, or out of pure joy stand on his head on the sofa, creep under the piano, jump up onto it or run into the garden and scramble joyously up a tree."

None of his friends could escape the magnetism of this man. Yet none could remain for any length of time in the highly charged field of this magnetism. One by one they came to him, laid their hearts at the shrine of his genius, and then fell silently away. During the last days of his life he was practically alone.

But when he dropped dead (of a heart attack) on February 13, 1883, a unique personality had passed out of the world—a mischief-making child who had learned to converse with the gods.

IMPORTANT DATES IN THE LIFE OF
WILHELM RICHARD WAGNER

1813—Born, May 22, in Leipzig.

1833—Appointed chorus master of Würzburg Opera Company. Wrote his first opera, *The Fairies*.

1836—Married Minna Planer.

1839—Wrote *Rienzi*.

1843—Appointed Kapellmeister at Dresden.

1844—Wrote *The Flying Dutchman*.

1845—Wrote *Tannhäuser*.

1848—Wrote *Lohengrin*.

1852–56—Wrote *The Nibelungen Ring*.

1857—Wrote *Tristan and Isolde*.

1864—King Ludwig II, of Bavaria, called him to Munich.

1868—Wrote *The Meistersingers*.

1870—Married Cosima von Bülow.

1882—Wrote *Parsifal*.

1883—Died, February 13, at Venice.

Giuseppe Verdi

1813–1901

As a result of the Napoleonic conquests the Italian village of Le Roncole, in the province of Piacenza, was French territory. And it was in the French language that the young storekeeper, Carlo Verdi, recorded the birth of his son Giuseppe on October 10, 1813.

A few months later the Russian and the Austrian soldiers invaded the territory of Piacenza and, to vent their spite against Napoleon, massacred many of the inhabitants of that province—women and children as well as men. In Le Roncole a number of the women fled for refuge to the village church. But the soldiers pursued them and slaughtered them in the midst of their prayers. One of the women, however, was lucky enough to hide herself, together with her infant son, in the belfry. And this is how Giuseppe Verdi was saved from the sword that he might enrich the world with his song.

II

Though his parents neither sang nor played, their strange and silent child was passionately fond of music. His happiest hours were on Sunday, when he heard the organ at the parish church. At the age of seven he became an acolyte in the church. One day he was so enraptured with the playing of the organist that he forgot to hand the water to the priest. Whereupon the saintly man lost his temper and kicked him down the altar steps. When the child reached home, bruised and bleeding, his parents asked him what was the matter. His only reply was, "Please, I want to learn music."

Some years later the priest was struck by lightning, and the superstitious villagers saw in this tragedy a judgment from heaven for his ill-treatment of young Giuseppe.

But if heaven had seen fit to punish the poor fellow's outburst of temper, Giuseppe had long forgotten it. For his parents had bought him an old spinet, and this was more than a sufficient reward for his suffering. The village organist, Baistrocci, became his first instructor; but he was not nearly so hard a taskmaster to the young pupil as was Giuseppe himself. One day, when he was unable to strike a desired chord on the spinet, he became so enraged that he hit the instrument with a hammer. A piano tuner from the neighboring town of Busseto was called in to repair the instrument. He refused to take payment for his work. Instead he pasted inside the spinet a piece of paper with the following words: "I, Stephen Cavalletti, have repaired these jacks and put on the pedals, of all of which I make him a present, seeing how eager the young Giuseppe Verdi is to learn to play this instrument. His devotion to music is payment enough for my labor."

Within a short period Giuseppe's devotion to music had carried him beyond the capacity of his teacher. And so his parents sent him to Busseto for his further training. Compared to Le Roncole, the town of Busseto with its two thousand inhabitants was a very metropolis of art and culture. For it boasted a Philharmonic Society and a brass band. Thither the young musician of twelve repaired to seek his inspiration and his fortune. He took lodgings with a shoemaker, at five cents a day, and walked back to Le Roncole every Sunday for the church services. For he was now the assistant organist at the parish church—a job for which he received the munificent salary of forty lire (about eight dollars) a year.

The Sunday pilgrimages between Busseto and Le Roncole were not always pleasant. For he had to make them every week, rain or shine, winter as well as summer. One stormy Christmas Eve he fell into a ditch and was unable to get out until he was rescued by a passer-by. This life of all work and no play made Giuseppe a melancholy though by no means a dull boy. From earliest childhood he had never known what it meant to be carefree. Often he went hungry. If life was a beautiful song, it was also a tragic song. The future composer of the music of pity was receiving a thorough education in the school of suffering.

Fortunately, however, he soon found a patron in the person of Antonio Barezzi, a kindhearted and prosperous wholesale merchant from whom Carlo Verdi purchased the supplies for his store. Giuseppe had frequently visited Barezzi's warehouse on errands from his father. Barezzi took a fancy to the youngster; for he too, like Giuseppe, was an ardent lover of music. He played the flute and the clarinet, and he was the president of the Philharmonic Society.

It was with great joy, therefore, that young Verdi accepted an offer of apprenticeship in the warehouse of "Signor Antonio." He was to help Barezzi not only in his business but also in transcribing and arranging new music for the Society. In return for these services his patron gave him his board and his lodging and supplied him with teachers in Latin and in music. In short, young "Beppino" became an intimate member of the Barezzi household.

And the lover of Barezzi's daughter Margherita. The two youngsters played duets on the new piano which Barezzi had bought especially for them. Together they lived in their music and dreamed about their future marriage—a marriage which was to bring Verdi his greatest happiness and his greatest sorrow.

For the present, however, it was too early to plan for their marriage. For Verdi was still but a boy, and his musical education had just begun. A charitable society at Busseto made him a grant of three hundred lire a year, to which sum Barezzi added an allowance of his own, and Verdi went to Milan for the entrance examination to the Conservatorio.

He failed in the examination. But let us not blame the examiners for his failure. There were two definite and legitimate reasons for their rejection of Verdi—his excessive age and his insufficient knowledge. It was a rule of the institution that entering pupils must be under fourteen years of age and that they must show an adequate mastery of the piano. That the eighteen-year-old candidate showed a mediocre skill at the piano was a reflection not on the talent of Verdi but on the ability of his teachers. Indeed, the examiners praised his talent and recommended him to a private teacher, the composer Lavigna.

This, in spite of Verdi's bitter disappointment, turned out to be a lucky thing for him. For Lavigna was the cembalist in the orchestra of the Scala Theater, and it was through him that Verdi was able to become familiar with operatic music. Thus the failure of Verdi was but a step to success, a detour from the highways of academic erudition to the byways of independent creation. Verdi was born to be a writer of opera, and it was into this channel that a wise Providence had guided his steps.

For two years he studied under Lavigna, and then he began to make a name for himself. The conductor of the Milan Philharmonic Society had been planning to produce Haydn's *Creation*. At the last moment, however, he took fright. He complained that his chorus had been insufficiently rehearsed, and he suggested that Verdi take his place as the conductor. Verdi agreed to do this and turned an expected fiasco into a brilliant success.

As a result of this success the conductor of the Philharmonic urged him to write an opera and sent him a libretto. The title of this libretto was *Oberto, Conte di San Bonifacio*. The young musician of Le Roncole was now launched upon an operatic career that was to extend over a period of sixty years.

But before he wrote his first opera he returned to Busseto and married his boyhood sweetheart, Margherita Barezzi. Two years later, when he came once more to Milan, he was rich in the possession of a beautiful wife, a completed opera, and two little bambini, a boy and a girl.

III

Oberto was produced at the Scala Theater in the fall of 1839. Its success, to quote Verdi himself, was "not very great, but good enough." Good enough to secure for him a commission to write two more operas.

The first of these operas was to be on a serious subject. But no sooner had Verdi started on it than Merelli, the director of the Scala Theater, changed his mind. The financial condition of the theater, he said, necessitated the production of a comic opera. Accordingly he sent Verdi a new libretto, *Un Giorno di Regno* (A Day of Dominion), and told him to set it to music at his "funniest best."

But at this time Verdi was in no mood for "funny" music. For misfortune had begun to accumulate upon his head. He had become a prey to a series of heart attacks—due possibly to a constitution weakened by frequent hunger in his childhood days. Unable to work and overwhelmed by an accumulation of debts, he asked Merelli for an advance on his contract, only to be met with a refusal. In order to pay the overdue rent his wife was obliged to pawn her jewelry.

"This," wrote Verdi in later years, "was only the beginning of my troubles. In April (1840) my little boy fell ill; and before the doctors were able to diagnose the sickness, the poor little fellow died in the arms of his distracted mother. As if this were not enough, a few days afterwards my little girl fell ill in her turn, and she too died. And, as if even this were not full measure, my poor wife was seized with a violent inflammation of the brain, and on the 3rd of June a third coffin left my house. . . . And in the midst of these terrible griefs I had to write a comic opera!"

The opera, as might have been expected, was a complete failure. He took this failure all the more keenly to heart because he looked upon it as insult added to injury. The public, he complained, had no business "thus to maltreat the work of a poor sick young man, worried by the shortness of time, and with his heart bruised by his awful misfortunes." Apparently the audience had not been silent in its disapproval, and this especially had cut him to the quick. "Had the audience, I will not say applauded, but just received the opera in silence, I could not have found words enough to express my thanks."

As a result of "the punishment of the gods and the pitilessness of his fellow men," Verdi was tempted for a time to yield to his despair. "I was alone, alone, alone! . . . With my soul tortured by my domestic misfortunes, and chagrined by the callousness of the public, I felt certain that it was hopeless to look to art for consolation, and I decided I would compose no more."

But one night he met Merelli, and his resolution to compose no more was broken down. Merelli had handed him a libretto on the subject of Nebuchadnezzar. "Take it home," he said, "and read it. Not that I expect you to set it to music. I merely want you to tell me what you think of it."

Verdi took the manuscript home, read it and decided to write the opera. For it breathed a spirit of rebellion akin to his own. It told the story of a suffering, oppressed race. His own race, too, was suffering under the oppressive heel of Austria. Verdi was a rebel. His heart was aflame with Italy's battle for freedom. He would write music that would be a bugle call to this battle—harmonies that would give "sustenance and strength" to his fallen people, that would enable them to raise their heads, to square their shoulders and to throw off the fetters of their slavery.

It was in this mood that he wrote *Nabucco* (Nebuchadnezzar). And the people, sensing the mood and catching the rebellious spirit of the music, hailed Verdi as their national prophet composer, the Mazzini of the Italian opera. So deeply stirred was the audience on the opening night that at the end of each act the entire house rose in a united shout of acclamation. The most successful number in the opera was a chorus of the captive Hebrews—"Fly, my hope, on golden wings." This chorus was taken up by the Italian people and was flung like a hymn of defiance into the faces of the Austrian soldiers.

Verdi had returned from his solitude and had once more taken his place in the world. And this regeneration of his drooping spirits was due not only to the devotion of the public but to the affection of Giuseppina Strepponi. This talented young actress had sung the soprano part in *Nabucco*. Indeed, it was her ardent admiration for the music of this opera that had fired the entire cast into a supreme effort. Her admiration for the music was soon translated into admiration for the musician. Admiration ripened into love, and love opened the way to an intimate relationship between the two. For some years, however, this relationship remained unsanctioned by the legality of marriage, and people began to wag their tongues. Verdi, who was conventional neither in his music nor in his character, paid no attention to the idle gossip of the public. But when his former patron, Antonio Barezzi, added his own voice to the chorus of disapproval Verdi felt constrained to write him a letter of remonstrance. "After so long a silence," complained Verdi, "I did not expect to receive from you so formal a letter containing expressions which, if I interpret them correctly, have caused me great pain. If it were not signed by my benefactor, I should answer it very curtly, or not at all. But since it bears a name which it is my duty ever to respect, I must try to convince you that I do not deserve your censure. . . .

"I do not believe you would have written the letter if you had been following the dictates of your own heart. But you live among people who suffer from the habit of prying into the affairs of their neighbors and of condemning any action which does not conform to their own standards.

It is my custom not to interfere with others, and I expect others not to interfere with me. . . .

". . . I have not the slightest objection to raising the curtain which hides the mystery of four walls . . . I have nothing to hide. In my house there lives a lady, free, independent, like myself a lover of the country, the possessor of a private income which raises her beyond the need of patronage. Neither of us is obliged to account for our actions to anybody. Our relationship is our own affair. What justification has the public to ferret out the claims that either of us may have upon the other? Whose business is it whether she is my wife or not? . . . Who has a right to ostracize us? . . . And let me say this: in my house she is entitled to the respect due to myself—nay, more; and on no consideration whatever must this be forgotten. Her conduct and her character give her a special claim to the consideration which she, on her part, has never failed to show to others."

It was not until 1859—seventeen years after their first meeting—that they were married. Their union, both before and after the marriage, was happy, though their characters were in some respects incompatible. They differed especially in their views about religion. Giuseppina was a pious Catholic, and Verdi was an agnostic. But both of them, whether believer or not, possessed the divine grace of tolerance. Giuseppina felt sorry for Verdi's skepticism, but she respected it. "My *brigand*," she writes playfully in one of her letters to her physician Cesare Vigna, "professes, with a calm obstinacy which makes me furious, to be, I will not say an atheist, but a very doubtful believer." But even a "doubtful believer" or a downright unbeliever, she admits in another of her letters (written to her friend Clarina Maffei), may be blessed with the grace of a good character. "Verdi is a noble soul, and may God give him many years of happiness! . . . There are some virtuous natures for whom a belief in God is a necessity; others, equally perfect, are happier believing nothing. Manzoni the believer, and Verdi the unbeliever—these two great men give me food for thought."

As for Verdi's attitude toward Giuseppina, he looked upon her piety as a necessary prop for those who are not strong enough to stand alone; but he loved her for what he regarded as her weakness as well as for what he recognized as her strength. She was the conformist, and he the revolutionist. And Verdi as well as Giuseppina realized that the perfect union consisted in the harmonious blending of the two opposite characters. No, not opposite, but supplementary. In the dangerous voyage of life there are two things of equal importance—a steady hand to guide the tiller, and a fearless mind to chart the course.

Yet Giuseppina and Verdi, though different in their attitude toward the Church, were alike in three essential respects—their devotion to charity, their love for the solitude of the country and their passion for music.

Charity was the one subject that was never discussed between the two.

Each of them took the other's generosity for granted, and neither of them ever asked the other for an accounting of that generosity. "When we come to figure up our expenses," writes Giuseppina, "a conspicuous sum is always missing. And Verdi never offers an explanation—he doesn't have to. Every cent of that missing money has gone to help some poor devil in distress." Verdi, on his part, was equally tactful about the sums missing from Giuseppina's accounts owing to her own generosity. At times they collaborated in their charity—especially on those occasions when their fellow musicians were in need of help. Their spacious country home was always a haven for their less fortunate friends.

This country home of the Verdis, on the lake of Sant' Agata, had started with a small cottage and had gradually developed into a magnificent estate. For Verdi was a practical businessman and natural farmer. "I am and always will be a Roncole peasant," he said. He spent perhaps as much time on the cultivation of his land as he did on the writing of his music. He even assisted in the building of the various houses on the estate. "Verdi," confides Giuseppina to her friend Clarina Maffei, "has turned architect. . . . He is directing a legion of workmen at Sant' Agata. . . . I cannot tell you how often during the building operations beds, wardrobes and furniture danced from room to room. . . ." Once, when distinguished visitors came to the Verdis in the midst of their seemingly interminable process of building, "they had the honor of dining in a sort of anteroom, or rather corridor adorned with birds' nests where swallows flew in and out carrying food for their young." And Verdi was obliged to throw off his working clothes and to dress himself "respectably" in order to receive his guests. For Verdi was "always at work around the estate; and I assure you"—observes Giuseppina—"that he does his part as well as, and perhaps better than, a real architect."

Verdi was interested not only in the building but in the management of the estate. "My 'brigand' earns his daily bread as foreman at Sant' Agata." On market days he attended personally to the selling of his livestock. On his trips away from home he kept fully informed about the management of his estate and the movements of his hired help. "You say nothing of the servants," he writes during one of his absences to his caretaker. "Are they all dead? . . . How is the groom? What is he doing? . . . I understand that you do not give Milord (one of his horses) enough exercise and that you haven't as yet broken in the foal. This will not do. Horses will not keep fit and are likely to get fat and lazy if they are not exercised. And, I insist, the horses must be fed on our own hay." The gentleman farmer of Sant' Agata was a meticulous and exacting manager.

And in between the thousand and one duties pertaining to the management of his estate he wrote those "operatic experiments" which were gradually to bring him into the front rank of European composers. Thirteen operas in eight years: *I Lombardi*, *Ernani* (based on the poetic drama by Victor Hugo), *I due Foscari*, *Giovanna d'Arco* (Joan of Arc),

Alzira, Attila, Macbeth, I Masnadieri, Jerusalem, Il Corsaro, La Battaglia di Legnano, Luisa Miller and *Stiffelio.*

Verdi was not a dreamer whose spirit floated above the realities of life. His feet were planted firmly upon the ground. He had acquired, especially under the tuition of Giuseppina, the very practical art of translating his genius into hard cash. When he was invited to write *I Lombardi* he asked Giuseppina what price he ought to demand for it. She advised him to get as much as he could but not to go too far. Taking her advice he asked, and received, fifteen hundred dollars for this opera. From that time on his prices kept going up all the way from twenty-five hundred dollars for *Luisa Miller* to thirty thousand dollars for *Aïda.*

Verdi was that rarest of human beings—a supreme genius who lived to become a supremely rich man.

IV

VERDI'S PATH was paved with gold, but occasionally a sharp rock was injected into the pavement with the object of tripping him up. The Austrian censors, who found in his music a dangerous note of aspiration for Italian freedom, tried everything within their power to throw obstacles in his way. To be sure, they could not imprison him as they imprisoned the insurgent journalists and politicians and poets of Italy, since it was impossible to produce a legal proof of a concrete revolutionary thought expressed in the abstract language of music. But they employed every possible legal method either to forbid the production of his plays or to emasculate the plots in such a way that the plays appeared meaningless when produced. For example, they insisted on cutting the conspiracy scene—the very crux of the story—out of the revolutionary opera *Ernani.* In thus diluting the lifeblood of the plot they also compelled Verdi to water the strong wine of his music. In similar manner the censors tampered both with the words and with the music of *Joan of Arc, Macbeth, The Lombards* and *The Battle of Legnano.*

He encountered his greatest difficulty, however, when he tried to produce *La Maledizione.* This was in 1850, shortly after the unsuccessful Revolution of 1848. Verdi had taken a courageous part in that Revolution. He had set to music a patriotic poem commencing with the words, "Sound the trumpet, wave the black-and-yellow flag," and had sent it to his friend Manzoni (author of the famous novel *The Betrothed*) with the words, "May this hymn soon be sung, to the accompaniment of cannon, on the plains of Lombardy." That same year he had signed his name to a manifesto in which the Italian revolutionists had asked the help of France against Austria.

The Austrian censors were bent upon punishing Verdi for his insubordination. And their opportunity came when he submitted *La Maledizione* for their approval. They examined the opera and issued the following report to the director of the Fenice Theater in Venice, where the play was scheduled for production:

"His Excellency, the Military Governor of Italy, directs us to express his profound regret that the poet Piave and the celebrated Maestro Verdi should have found no better field for their talents than the revolting immorality and obscene triviality which form the argument of the libretto entitled *La Maledizione*.

"His Excellency has decided that the performance must be absolutely forbidden, and he instructs us at the same time to request you to abstain from making further inquiries in this matter."

Fortunately, however, there were among the music lovers of Italy a number of influential politicians, including the secretary of the military governor himself. Thanks to the intervention of these political supporters the ban was finally removed and *La Maledizione*, "corrected and expunged of its offensive revolutionary sting," received the official *nihil obstat*. It was produced at the Fenice Theater (March 11, 1851) under a new title—*Rigoletto*.

V

WITH *Rigoletto* Verdi had entered upon a new period in the development of his genius—a period of sixteen years in which he wrote nine operas: *Rigoletto, Il Trovatore, La Traviata, I Vespri Siciliani, Simone Boccanegra, Aroldo, Un Ballo in Maschera, La Forza del Destino,* and *Don Carlos*. He now worked less rapidly but more carefully than he had worked in the past. His voice had become mature, and he was anxious to expend it only upon his best efforts. A new note had come into his music—a note of pity for the sufferings of his fellow men. Rebellion had been mellowed into regret; hope had given way to grief. Life at its best was pathetic—a striving for the stars and a groveling in the dust. Every human drama, whatever the course of its action, must come to a tragic end. From aspiration to frustration—that, in a phrase, was the keynote of mortal existence. His nation had longed for freedom, had failed; the individual longs for happiness and fails. The story of the human race is a somber epic of broken ambitions. Let us set this epic to music. Let us sing a sorrowful hymn to human failure.

This is the dominant note in the operas of Verdi's second period. And this is largely the reason for the popularity of such operas as *Rigoletto, La Traviata,* and *Il Trovatore*. They strike within us a responsive chord of *self-pity* and *fellow pity*. As we listen to these operas in the theater we feel drawn together into a universal brotherhood—a family of equal shareholders in the common heritage of sorrow. We forget the melodrama of the plots in the genuine drama of the music. And the music of these operas, in a thousand different modulations, repeats the selfsame dirge—*we live, we suffer, we die.*

In spite of Verdi's material success during this second period of his production, his music was predominantly melancholy. It was a music that came out of the reflection of a mature mind.

VI

AND THEN CAME HIS OLD AGE and the third period of his production. He had taken a fling in politics, had allowed himself to be elected a deputy of the Italian Parliament and had found it not to his liking. And so he returned to his old love and wrote the three operas which have been justly acclaimed as the sunrise songs of the Italian musical renaissance.

He produced the first of these three operas, Aïda, in his fifty-eighth year. It was something new in Italian opera. For the first time the music flowed on continuously, like a living stream, instead of being divided into the stagnant pools of the old-fashioned arias, duets, choruses, trios and the like. The music and the drama of this opera are so closely intertwined as to form a perfect pattern of rhythmic beauty. Aïda is the practical demonstration of Verdi's credo that music must not only keep close to the words but must penetrate *through* the words to the subtlety of the thought that lies behind them. The spirit made flesh, the soul of music breathed into the body of poetry—this, in short, is the substance of Aïda.

Having given Aïda to the world, Verdi retired into silence. This opera, said his admirers, was his swan song. But they were mistaken. At the end of sixteen years he broke his silence with Otello, the supreme grand opera of Italy. And then, after another silence of six years, the old maestro of eighty astonished the world with Falstaff, his real swan song and Italy's supreme musical comedy.

For the composition of Otello and Falstaff Verdi was fortunate enough to secure the librettos of Arrigo Boïto. This poet, who as a librettist ranks with William S. Gilbert, succeeded in condensing the very essence of the Shakespearean dramas upon which these two operas are based. He transfused into his poetry not only the thought but the imagination of Shakespeare. Never before had Verdi's musical genius been challenged with librettos of such masterly technique and such living inspiration. And he was equal to the challenge. With the help of Boïto he succeeded in capturing both the tragic and the comic spirit of Shakespeare. In Otello and in Falstaff he translated immortal poetry into immortal music.

VII

BUT HE WAS TIRED OF LIFE, this sad old man who in his last hours had learned to laugh. He had always stayed away from people—afraid of their cruelties and indifferent to their applause. As often as he could he had refrained from attending the performances of his operas. For he preferred the solitude of Sant' Agata to the plaudits of the crowd.

And now he felt no longer at home even in his solitude. For Giuseppina was dead. All his old friends were dead. And his young friends? They were too absorbed in the flood tide of their own ambitions to bother about anyone who was floating away on the receding current of life.

The world was leaving him behind and rushing forward without him. Rushing to what? New wars, new oppressions, new cruelties, new hates. Yes, and *new songs*. A strange satire of the gods, this world of ours—a world governed by brute force, a world inspired by divine music. In the final scene of *Falstaff* the actors advance to the footlights and inform the audience that "everything in life is a huge jest."

Such was Verdi's farewell to the world. When he died (at the age of eighty-eight), Boïto expressed his indignation at the jest of the Fates who had removed this maestro from life. "I have lost many of those whom I have loved, and sorrow has outlived resignation. But never before have I felt such hatred against death and such contempt for its mysterious, blind, stupid, triumphant, infamous power."

And Boïto had reason for his violent denunciation of death. For rarely had it taken away so great a genius and so modest a man. "In character," writes Verdi's biographer Bonavia, "he was surpassed by none." When the king offered him a title he refused to accept it. His talent, he thought, was an authentic enough stamp of his nobility. Yet even his talent he regarded as but a secondary reason for his claim to distinction. A friend once asked him which of his works he considered the best. To this question Verdi replied: "My best work is a home for destitute musicians that I have endowed at Milan."

IMPORTANT DATES IN THE LIFE OF GIUSEPPE VERDI

1813—Born, October 10, in Roncole.
1829—Became conductor of an orchestra at Busseto.
1836—Married Margherita Barezzi.
1839—Produced his first opera, *Oberto*.
1840—Lost his wife and two children.
1849—Wrote *Luisa Miller*. Married Giuseppina Strepponi.

1851—Wrote *Rigoletto*.
1852—Wrote *Il Trovatore*.
1853—Wrote *La Traviata*.
1859—Wrote *Un Ballo in Maschera*.
1860—Member of Italian Parliament.
1871—Wrote *Aïda*.
1875—Made Senator.
1887—Wrote *Otello*.
1893—Wrote *Falstaff*.
1901—Died, January 27, at Milan.

Queen Victoria

1819–1901

I<small>T</small> IS five o'clock in the morning. King William IV has just died at Windsor Palace. The archbishop and the lord chamberlain have driven posthaste from Windsor to Kensington to report the king's death to Alexandrina Victoria, the king's eighteen-year-old niece and heir to the throne.

The new arrivals knock at the gate of Kensington Palace. But at first there is no answer. For it is too early for anybody to be up. After considerable knocking, however, they gain admittance. At six o'clock the Duchess of Kent, Victoria's mother, wakes up her daughter and tells her that the Archbishop of Canterbury and Lord Conyngham have come to speak to her.

She gets out of bed, puts on her dressing gown and steps into the room where the messengers are waiting.

They fall on their knees, and Lord Conyngham announces the news. "The king is dead. Long live the queen!"

That day—June 20, 1837—Victoria made the following entry in her journal: "Since it has pleased Providence to place me in this station, I shall do my utmost to fulfill my duty toward my country; I am very young, and perhaps in many, though not in all things, inexperienced, but I am sure that very few have more real good will and more real desire to do what is fit and right than I have."

A good sentiment, but a poor style. Victoria never felt quite at home in the English language. For English was not her mother tongue. Her father, the English Duke of Kent, had died when she was a small child, and her mother, the daughter of the German Duke of Saxe-Coburg, had trained her from infancy to speak the German language and to develop a German cast of thought. To the end of her days Victoria was unable to speak English perfectly.

II

ALEXANDRINA VICTORIA—they called her Drina in the family circle—was a spoiled child. She frequently flew into a passion, stamped her foot and disobeyed the instructions of her elders. Even before her coronation she displayed the temper of a little empress, and an *absolute* little empress at that. She would not do her lessons; no matter what anybody said, she *just wouldn't*. Bribes, threats, arguments, nothing would help. Her lessons remained undone.

From the very outset she was encouraged to regard herself as a creature of supreme importance. Occasionally she was allowed to play with the child of some marquise or duchess who came to visit her mother. But she was taught to regard such children as *playthings* rather than *playfellows*. One day little Jane Ellice was taken by her grandmother, Lady Ellice, to Kensington Palace. The two children were told to entertain each other in Victoria's nursery. When Jane Ellice, unfamiliar with the palace etiquette, began to handle Victoria's toys, the little princess stopped her. "You must not play with these," she said. "They are mine." Then she added: "And you must not call me Victoria, though I may call you Jane."

In the entire Kensington household there was but one person who was able to exercise any influence on Victoria. And that was her governess, Fräulein Lehzen. This lady, the daughter of a German clergyman, had observed the one vulnerable spot in the child's armor of stubborn self-sufficiency. Victoria had an affectionate little heart. Win your way into that child's heart and you can get her to do anything for you. Under the gentle, yet strictly efficient guidance of Fräulein Lehzen, Victoria began to enjoy her lessons and to look at least with indulgence, if not with respect, upon the other members of the household. Fräulein Lehzen, in short, succeeded in turning a rather insufferable little princess into a rather likable little human being. As she grew older Victoria became gradually impressed with the fact that there would be duties as well as privileges in that exalted office of queenship for which she was being trained. When she first definitely learned that she was destined for the crown, she spoke just a few words: "I will be good." These words, in which there was a curious mingling of egotism and humility, she repeated once more on that early June morning when Lord Conyngham knelt before her and announced: "The king is dead. Long live the queen!"

III

SHORTLY before her accession to the throne Victoria had met her two German cousins, Prince Ernest and Prince Albert. These two personable young fellows were the sons of her mother's oldest brother, the Duke of Saxe-Coburg. Victoria was very much impressed with them both—especially with Prince Albert. "Ernest," she wrote in her journal, "has dark hair, and fine dark eyes and eyebrows, but the nose and mouth are not good. . . . Albert is extremely handsome; his hair is about the same color as mine; his eyes are large and blue, and he has a beautiful nose and a very sweet mouth with fine teeth. . . . Both my cousins are so kind and good. . . . Ernest will be eighteen years old on the 21st of June, and Albert seventeen on the 26th of August. . . . They have both learnt a good deal and are very clever, naturally clever, *particularly* Albert."

When, after a visit of three weeks, her two cousins prepared to leave for their home in Germany, she felt desolate. "It was our last *happy, happy* breakfast," she confided to her journal, "with those *dearest* beloved cousins, whom I *do* love so *very, very* dearly. . . . Albert was playing on the piano when I came down. . . . I embraced both my dearest cousins most warmly. . . . I cried bitterly, very bitterly. . . ."

But, with the coming of the crown, she forgot her two cousins temporarily. With all her impetuous energy she threw herself into the business and pleasure of ruling her nation. Very small, very slender, and very vivacious, she danced her way immediately into the hearts of her people. "Little Vic," as they affectionately called her, stepped with a charming grace and a carefree laugh from her nursery to her throne. "A more delightful little being you never beheld," wrote Mr. Creevey, the professional gossip of Buckingham Palace. "She laughs in real earnest . . . and she eats quite as heartily as she laughs. I think I may say she gobbles. . . . She blushes and laughs every instant in so natural a way as to disarm anybody."

Her days were a succession of gilded hours. Eating, dancing, riding, social conversation in the drawing room of Buckingham Palace—such were the amusements that occupied most of her spare time. Occasionally she went to the opera, which she enjoyed, or to the drama, which she liked little and understood less. One evening she saw Macready in Shakespeare's *King Lear*. Throughout the beginning of the play she chatted and laughed with the lord chamberlain. Toward the end she began to pay more attention to the play. "What does Her Majesty think of this drama?" ventured the lord chamberlain. "A strange, horrible business," replied the queen, "but, I suppose, good enough for Shakespeare's day."

The serious business of the stage and the serious business of life were a little beyond her depth at this period. The guidance of her personal affairs she put into the capable hands of Dr. Stockmar, a German native of Coburg who had been her father's friend and family physician. As for the guidance of the state, she left this in the equally capable hands of the prime minister, Viscount Melbourne.

Lord Melbourne was the conservative leader of the Liberal Party. Fifty-eight years of age, but still full of life and gusto and ambition, brilliant, charming, wealthy, an aristocrat of the aristocrats, he had philandered and intrigued and studied his way through the world until he thoroughly understood every phase of English life and letters. Having married a woman who proved faithless, and having repaid her with a like faithlessness of his own, he was now a confirmed cynic about human character and human destiny. Leave well enough—or rather ill enough—alone, was his motto. "You'd better try to do no good," he said, "and then you'll get into no scrapes." Democracy appeared to him a dream and a delusion. He adored the young queen with her naïve and childlike egotism and her undemocratic belief in her own unquestioned perfection. And Victoria, in her turn, was enchanted with Melbourne. She bullied him, she petted him, she confided in him, she quarreled with him, and in the end she always obeyed him. Yet—so tactful was his policy with this little schoolgirl of a queen—he always succeeded in making her believe that she was expressing *her own* will when she was merely echoing *his* will.

And so, for a while, guided by the steady hand of Lord Melbourne, Victoria steered her ship through a smiling sea of public adulation. But suddenly a storm arose. England's respectability was rocked with a scandal about a lady and a gentleman of the court—Lady Flora Hastings and Sir John Conroy. These two members of the nobility had been seen returning from Scotland in the same carriage. Shortly after that the tongues of England began to wag. Lady Flora, it was whispered, was about to become a mother. And the young queen, instead of putting an end to these unseemly rumors, actually helped to spread them. Even Lord Melbourne had forgotten his discretion. He allowed the sharp little tongue of the queen to spin its merry tale of tittle-tattle. Things came to a head when Lady Flora was found to be innocent—an unfortunate victim of cancer of which she died within a few months.

The storm now broke. The adulation of the public had turned to resentment against Victoria. "Nobody cares for the queen," wrote Greville, the clerk of the Privy Council. "Her popularity has sunk to zero."

IV

THE queen was in disgrace and Lord Melbourne was sincerely repentant. His cynical old heart was for once touched to the quick. Like a father he began to watch over her, to lead her by the hand, to protect her against the ill will of her subjects, against the rashness of her own impetuous character. A husband must be found for her, a young man of her own age, to steady her, to bring her companionship, to produce an heir for the English throne.

And who better suited for that role than her young cousin, Prince Albert of Saxe-Coburg? Lord Melbourne urged this marriage upon her, and so did Dr. Stockmar. At first she objected. She liked her *dearest* cousin Albert, yes. But why marry him? Why marry anyone at all? Let her remain single. At least for a few years. Why all this hurry?

But royal marriages are made in heaven and in the council chambers of the prime ministers. And against the decrees of heaven and the prime ministers not even a queen of England could say nay. And so she finally agreed to see Albert if he cared to visit her again. "But," insisted the headstrong Victoria, "I will make *no final promise this year.*"

Albert arrived in England. Once more her journal became the confidant of her rapture. She admired his "exquisite nose," his "delicate moustachios," his "slight but very slight whiskers," and his "beautiful figure" with its "broad shoulders and fine waist." He arrived on a Thursday. The following Tuesday she received him alone and told him that it would make her "*too happy*" if he would consent" to marry her. Whereupon the prince murmured that he, too, would be very happy "*das Leben mit dir zuzubringen.*"

And so, once more, Victoria "made up her mind" to do what Lord Melbourne had decided as the best course for her.

They were married on February 10, 1840.

Chronologically, Albert was three months older than Victoria. Mentally, he was her senior by many years. He loved music, he had a healthy taste for painting and he was genuinely fond of literature. And, above all, he knew how to size up a man or a situation. But he showed not the slightest interest in politics. He was, in short, a spectator rather than an actor in the intricate game of life.

Perhaps, as Dr. Stockmar reported to Lord Melbourne, Prince Albert's inactivity in political matters was due to an inherent weakness in his constitution. Nothing serious, said Dr. Stockmar, but merely an indication for a quiet life.

At first there was little in common between this silent and scholarly prince and the ebullient and laughter-loving queen. He would have liked to surround himself with scientists and artists and writers, but Victoria "had no fancy to encourage such people." And so the adjustment period of their married life was a period of storms and quarrels. Both of them had strong wills, and if there was to be any harmony in the family circle one of these wills was bound to yield to the other.

And, surprisingly enough, it was the impetuous Victoria who yielded to the taciturn Albert. For she was madly in love with him. One day—so the story goes—Albert locked himself into his room after one of their wrangles. Victoria knocked furiously upon the door.

"Who is there?"

"The queen of England, and she demands to be admitted!"

The door remained closed against her. Another avalanche of knocks.

"Who is there?"

"The queen of England!"

Still the door remained closed. Again and again, the same repetition of knocks, the same question, the same answer.

Finally, the tapping on the door became more gentle.

"Who is there?"

"Your wife, Albert."

Whereupon Albert opened the door and admitted Victoria into his room.

V

DR. STOCKMAR took Albert in hand and gradually transformed him into a politician. For Stockmar, like Albert, was Teutonic, and both of them at bottom had a strong taste for absolute monarchy as against constitutional government. Lord Melbourne had passed out of the ministry, and Sir Robert Peel had taken his place. Victoria detested her new prime minister, and little by little she got into the habit of consulting her husband about important political decisions. And in all such decisions Prince Albert, guided by the ever-watchful Stockmar, molded Victoria's mind into a Teutonic form of political thought. At last there was absolute harmony between the royal couple. Albert had become the virtual king of England, and Victoria was content in her secondary role of obedient *hausfrau.* She looked after his health, she adored his cleverness, she followed his wishes and she presented him—after the good old German fashion—with a plentiful crop of royal children. "Thank God!" she wrote in her journal. "I now *know what real happiness* is."

But the English public resented her subservience to Albert. England, it was whispered, was being ruled, and ruled dictatorially, by a foreigner. And Albert, on his part, insisted upon his royal and marital rights to rule his queen, and through her, the entire populace of England. It was his privilege, he asserted to the Duke of Wellington, nay, it was his *duty* to "make his position entirely a part of Victoria's"—to fill up every gap which, as a woman, she would naturally leave in the exercise of her regal functions. Since he was "the natural head of the family," he continued, he regarded himself as the "superintendent of her household, the manager of her private affairs, her sole confidential adviser in politics, the tutor of the royal children, the private secretary of the sovereign and her permanent minister." In short, her lord and master, as well as the lord and master of England.

Prince Albert was supreme. Yet he was unhappy. For, after his own lights, he was a sincere and honest and benevolent and gentle ruler. He did only what, in his opinion, was best for his wife's people. And he, far better than they, he was convinced, knew just exactly what was good for them. For was he not a scholar? And a German? A member of that superior race of scientists and soldiers and philosophers? So why did the English people distrust him? Why did they not obey and respect and *love* him as he deserved?

By heaven, he would *make* them obey and respect and love him! He would show them how a German prince could work! From early morning till late at night he sat at his desk, reading dispatches, studying figures, and devising plans—plans that would make England a better, wiser, safer, and healthier place to live in. A place, for instance, like Germany. Ah, *that* was an ideal to live and to die for! "To turn England into a real monarchy instead of a sham democracy!"

Such was the foolish and impossible dream for which Albert toiled day and night and for which he finally laid down his life. The strain of his overwork proved too much for his none too vigorous constitution. He was stricken with an attack of typhoid fever. For a time it looked as if he might recover. His mind, as Victoria bent over him, would come out of its feverish wanderings and he would smile and murmur, *"liebes Weibchen."* But then there was a turn for the worse, and on December 14, 1861, the man who had dreamed of the absolute monarchy of England was summoned into the absolute democracy of death.

VI

THE rest of Victoria's life is a study in black and white—the long black night of her grief over the death of Prince Albert and the final white splendor of her glorious old age.

The death of Prince Albert was a terrific blow to Victoria. It was no ordinary anguish that she suffered at the loss of so beloved a husband. It was a *royal* anguish, a resentment against a destiny that had no respect for the feelings of a queen. How dared heaven to treat her like an ordinary mortal! No, she would *not* be treated like an ordinary mortal. She would act as though Albert were still alive, as though he were still there to guide her and plan for her and advise her. In a letter that she wrote to her uncle, King Leopold of Belgium, she expressed her "firm resolve . . . that *his* (Albert's) wishes—*his* plans . . . *his* views . . . are to be *my* law! And *no human power* will make me swerve from what *he* decided and wished." Victoria was determined to be ruled by the dead hand of an absolute king. "She became," writes Lytton Strachey, "an ardent champion of the Prussian point of view."

Her English subjects resented this attitude on her part. They liked neither her excessive Prussianism nor her excessive lamentation. She wanted to be regarded as a "dreary sad pinnacle of solitary grandeur." But her people merely regarded her as a selfish and stubborn little lady who forgot the interests of a hundred million *living* persons in her unreasonable adoration for one *dead* person.

And selfish and stubborn she remained, year after year. She had, she told her intimates, a sacred duty to perform. She must devote her life to the perpetuation of her husband's greatness. The English people had misunderstood him. That must not be. They must learn to understand him, to admire him, to *worship* him, even as she did. And so she ordered one of the leading biographers of England, Mr. Theodore Martin, to write a complete biography of Prince Albert. This biography, she insisted, must be written with *her* assistance, and under *her* supervision. The style was to be the style of Mr. Martin, but the thoughts were to be the thoughts of Queen Victoria. Mr. Martin undertook the job and finished it after fourteen years. It was a monumental work of four volumes—well documented, well planned, well written and, like the subject that it tried to immortalize, absolutely dead. Prince Albert stands forth in those pages as the gilded statue of a benevolent hero in a dime novel, too, too lovely to be interesting and too, too good to be true.

But the queen, unaware of the public snickerings behind her back, went on with the apotheosis of her prince consort. She built, at the cost of two hundred thousand pounds, a splendid mausoleum for Albert, and she set up, at the expense of several hundred thousand additional pounds, a commemorative shrine with a ten-ton statue of Albert, executed in bronze, as a centerpiece.

And then she rested from her immortalization of Albert and returned to live among the mortals of England.

The one man who brought her down from her unpopular pinnacle of "sad solitary grandeur," and who founded for her a shrine in the hearts of her people, was Benjamin Disraeli. And he succeeded in doing this by a very simple method. All the other Englishmen had criticized her excessive devotion to Albert. Disraeli praised it. He killed her vanity by feeding it. "The prince," he said (speaking of himself in the third person), "is the only man whom Mr. Disraeli has ever known who realized the ideal." As for Victoria herself, Disraeli frequently in addressing her used the phrase, "we authors, ma'am." Was there ever so delightful a minister as Dizzy? thought the queen, as she gave him her royal hand to kiss. And Disraeli took her hand and gracefully led her back to her estranged people.

When the people saw her they took pity upon her. A sad, stout, grayhaired, foolish, pathetic little woman. Nothing so very haughty about her, after all. Rather human, like themselves. A widowed mother. And she was having her sorrows, poor little thing. Her daughter, the Princess Alice, had died recently. And some of her dearest friends, too, had died.

And then there came an attempted assassination that almost cost Victoria her own life. The people were horrified at the attempt, and jubilant over its failure. Their pity for the little old lady was rapidly turning into affection. And Victoria, rejoicing in the changed attitude of her subjects, began to take an active and genuine interest in their public functions. She attended concerts, the theater, lectures. She was present at the laying of cornerstones and the launching of battleships. Once, at the opening of an international exposition in Liverpool, she drove through the streets in her open carriage amidst a pelting rain. She had guts, that gray-haired little queen of theirs!

At last she was happy—the beloved queen of a prosperous nation. The queen, but not the tyrant. The shadow of Albert's domination had now

passed out of her life. She was no longer interested in absolute dictatorship—except in her own family circle. Here she insisted upon her undivided sway as the royal matriarch. Children, grand-children, great-grand-
children, all of them trembled at the sound of her voice. On one occasion
the Prince of Wales, who was fifty years old at the time, was a little late
for dinner. The delay in his arrival was due to no fault on his part, but
he did not dare to face the displeasure of his mother. The attendants,
when they went to look for him, found him standing behind a pillar
and nervously mopping his forehead.

For Victoria was a martinet for promptness and a stickler for the etiquette of the royal court. The niceties of the conventions and the re-
spectfulness due to all those of superior rank must be followed to the last
letter. And yet she took a motherly interest not only in the welfare of her
own family, but in the joys and the sorrows of the palace attendants
down to the last laundress and scullery maid. In her later years she even
unbent her royal dignity to the extent of allowing her older courtiers,
especially those who had suffered from a recent illness, to sit in her
presence.

The older she grew the more human she became. And the less queenly.
For along with the growth of her personal prestige came the decay in
the prestige of the British crown. At the end of her life she was the most
popular ruler in English history. And, at that very moment, the idea of
royalty had reached its most unpopular stage in English history.

And thus she entered upon the twilight of her long life, receiving the
love of her people but not their obedience. When, in 1897, she rode
through the London streets on the sixtieth Jubilee of her reign, the adoration of her subjects knew no bounds. Her eyes were filled with tears
as she whispered over and over again: "How kind they are to me! How
kind they are to me!"

She lived another four years after the Jubilee. And they were not altogether happy years. For the imperial ambitions of England had plunged
the country into the Boer War. She suffered with the sufferings of her
people. She sympathized with their losses. She, too, had known the pangs
of a mother who lost her children. In spite of her old age she worked
steadily at her desk, doing everything in her power to serve the cause of
her country.

At last the strain and the worry began to tell. In the summer of 1900
her memory began to fail, and by the end of that year her strength was
well-nigh gone.

She lived long enough, however, to see the beginning of the new century. On January 14, 1901, she had a long interview with Lord Roberts,
the victorious British commander in the Boer War. This was the last
public act of her long life. A few days later (January 22, 1901) she
slipped quietly out of the drama in which she had played so prominent
a part.

VII

"I FEEL listless and sad," remarks Jane Marryot in Noel Coward's *Cavalcade*, "just as though Victoria's death were a personal grief. Strange, isn't it?"

"Yes," replies her friend, Margaret Harris, "I think everyone feels that."

IMPORTANT DATES IN THE LIFE OF QUEEN VICTORIA

1819—May 24, born at Kensington Palace.
1837—Succeeded to throne of England.
1838—June 28, Coronation.
1840—Married Albert, Prince of Saxe-Coburg-Gotha.

1861—Death of Albert.
1887—Jubilee of her reign celebrated.
1897—Diamond Jubilee celebrated.
1901—January 22, died, after longest reign in British history, on the Isle of Wight.

Florence Nightingale

1820–1910

"Forward, the Light Brigade!
Charge for the guns," he said:
Into the valley of Death
Rode the six hundred.

Theirs not to reason why,
Theirs but to do and die:
Into the valley of Death
Rode the six hundred.

When can their glory fade?
O the wild charge they made!
All the world wonder'd.
Honor the charge they made!
Honor the Light Brigade,
Noble six hundred!

THIS IS Tennyson's romantic picture of the battle of Balaclava, in the Crimean War. But here is Florence Nightingale's realistic picture of the scene that *followed* the battle:

"At the hospital (in Scutari) there are no clean shirts . . . The men have only rags saturated with blood . . . The hospital has been transformed from a barrack . . . and underneath its imposing mass are sewers loaded with filth, through which the wind blows fetid air up the pipes into the wards where the sick men are lying. Wounds and sickness, overcrowding and want of proper ventilation contribute to the foulness of the atmosphere . . . The wards are infested with rats, mice and vermin. Flooring is defective; furniture and even the commonest utensils for cleanliness, decency and comfort are lacking . . . The vermin might, if they had but unity of purpose, carry off the four miles of bedding on their backs and march with them into the War Office in London."

Tennyson speaks of the heroism of the men in the field. Florence Nightingale speaks of the stupidity of the men in the War Office. "The iron beds from England have arrived at Scutari, but the legs for the beds were put into another ship and sent on to Balaclava. The sick and the wounded at Scutari lie on mattresses on the stone floors." In another letter—"The officials in London have sent us plenty of rations, but they have forgotten to send us kettles to cook them in." And when finally the kettles arrived—"The meat was ordered to be cut into uniform pieces of the same size . . . Sometimes a patient got a lump entirely gristle, the next might be entirely fat or entirely bone; the fortunes of war."

The trouble with the (noncombatant) officials, said Miss Nightingale, was that they regarded the soldiers as military machines. "Suppose you break them and throw them into the dump heap; what then? We've got plenty of others to take their place."

Even the soldiers had come to look upon themselves as mere machines unworthy of the consideration of their superiors. "In going round the hospital with me," writes Miss Nightingale, "the Duke of Cambridge recognized a sergeant of the guard who had had at least one third of his body shot away, and said (the Duke) to him with a great oath, calling him by his Christian name and surname, 'Aren't you dead yet?' The man said to me afterward, with tears in his eyes: 'So feelin' of 'Is Royal 'Ighness, wasn't it, m'm? Bless 'is 'eart, 'e wondered why I ain't dead yet.'"

Into this cauldron of incompetence and pitilessness and suffering stepped Florence Nightingale with her heroic band of thirty-eight nurses, and created order out of chaos. Within a few months after her arrival at Scutari, the death rate in the hospital had been reduced from 40 per cent to less than 3 per cent.

II

WHEN Florence first announced to her parents that she wanted to become a nurse, they looked upon her with open-mouthed astonishment. What? The daughter of one of the richest families in England to enter into one of the lowest of professions? Why, nursing was not even a profession in those days. "Most of the nursing"—we are quoting a contemporary physician—"is done by drunken prostitutes who, when brought into the police court, are given the option of going to prison or to hospital service . . . They are often found in sleep under the beds of their dead patients whose liquor they have stolen."

When, therefore, she announced her decision to her parents, "it was as if I had wanted to be a kitchen maid." It was not for *such* a career that they had raised their daughter. Mr. William Shore Nightingale, the master of Embley Park in Hampshire, had meant Florence to be a lady, like her elegant mother. Why, this girl was the prettiest and the most accomplished of all the Nightingale children. They had given her an education fit for a princess—higher mathematics, music, art, science, literature. Italian, German, and French—and she spoke these languages as fluently as she spoke English. And the ancient languages, too,—"a capital young lady," once remarked the geographer, Sir Henry de la Beche, to the archaeologist, Warrenton Smythe, "a capital young lady, indeed, if only she hadn't floored me with her Latin and Greek."

A brilliant young lady, and as charming as she was brilliant. She had traveled all over Europe, and had gone up the Nile. She could converse with all sorts of people on all sorts of subjects. She had even attended the receptions of the queen. And all the eligible young men of England were at her feet. What in the world did she want?

"I want to get away from the boredom of it all." She had an independent way about her. And a temper. And a biting tongue in that pretty little mouth of hers. "Piling up miscellaneous instruction," she said, "is the most disgusting of all pursuits." And almost as disgusting was the piling up of miscellaneous acquaintances among the smart set. Watching Lord Melbourne snore after dinner in the royal presence. Applauding Prince Albert for his "imaginary" skill at billiards. "Dowagering out with Papa" to "pay her respects" to people for whom she hadn't the slightest respect. Complimenting Lady So-and-so on her "oh, so becoming" diamond brooch—which, in reality, became her like a "raspberry tart on a pumpkin."

Florence Nightingale wanted to get away from all this painted and powdered artificiality. She wanted to come to grips with life. To know real people in their real moments. Their moments of suffering. Her father frequently made her read aloud to him. A Victorian book of good manners entitled *Passages in the Life of a Daughter at Home.* She preferred to read by herself, and a book of a quite different tenor. *The Annual Report of the Fliedner Institute.*

This Institute was a German training school for nurses. Flo Nightingale had been born with a passion to nurse the wounded and the sick. Even as a child she had frequently left her games to mend her dolls and to bandage the wounds of the cottagers' animal pets in Embley. At the age of six, she tells us, she was already conscious of a "call" to a mission of mercy. As she grew older, she became more and more conscious of the star that she was bidden to follow. One afternoon—she was about eighteen at the time—Florence was walking with a friend on the lawn in front of the drawing room at Embley. "Do you know what I always think when I look at that row of windows?" she said. "I think how I should turn it into a hospital and just how I should place the beds." For a time, during her twenties, she thought of marrying and settling down. She even had a love affair or two. But she put out of her mind the thought of a married life. This sort of thing was not for her. In marriage, she noted, she might find satisfaction for her "intellectual nature" and her "passional nature," but not for her "moral nature." And it was her moral nature that won out. In 1850 she wrote in her diary: "I am thirty now—the age at which Christ began His mission . . . No more childish things, no more vain things, no more love, no more marriage."

She was ready now to follow in His footsteps and to enter upon her own mission.

"Father, mother, I am going to be a nurse."

"Why, you're insane!"

"Maybe I am. All I can say is, thank God for my insanity."

III

FLORENCE NIGHTINGALE had stolen many an hour from her social activities to study anatomy and to visit the county hospital. Once, on a trip to Germany, she spent two weeks at the Fliedner Nursing School. At first Herr Fliedner was afraid of her "frail aristocratic hands." But he did not know her sturdy democratic heart. "You won't want to scrub that corridor floor," he said. "Just try me," she replied. And when he tried her, he knew that she was made for nursing.

Before long she proved to the English skeptics, too, that she was made for nursing. Appointed manager of the Harley Street Sanitarium—an "Establishment for Gentlewomen during Illness"—she showed that she could not only scrub floors but bind wounds and, what was even more important, revive hopes. And, figuratively speaking, slap faces. How she did love to slap the faces of the bigots! "Clarkey, dear," she writes to one of her friends. "My committee refused me to take in Catholic patients, whereupon I wished them good morning, unless I might take in Catholics as well as Jews and their rabbis. So now it is settled and in print that we are to take in all denominations whatever . . . provided I make myself responsible for their visitors, receive the obnoxious animals at the door . . . and bring them downstairs again in a noose, and out into the street. Amen . . . From bigotry and all deceits, Good Lord deliver us!"

It was a herculean job that she undertook as the first female manager of a hospital. Chaperoning the "obnoxious animals" who came to visit the non-Protestant patients; supervising the untrained and ill-disciplined nurses; spraining her back as she lifted a patient to the operating table; catching a hot stovepipe in her arms to keep it from falling upon a sick child; holding down a blind woman who was threatened with insanity when an operation to restore her vision had failed; and defending herself against the petty jealousies and the continual bickerings of her male—and therefore her "superior"—colleagues.

Yet, with all her inexperience, she stood the ordeal and came out triumphant. "She seems as completely led by God as Joan of Arc," said the novelist, Mrs. Gaskell.

Led by God into a definite road. Reports were reaching England about the terrible conditions in the Crimean hospitals. "The old pensioners sent out to nurse the sick and wounded are not of the slightest use; the soldiers have to attend upon each other." "No sufficient preparations have been made for the care of the wounded . . . No bandages, no dressers, no nurses." The public began to clamor for a remedy to this evil state of affairs. And finally the clamor became crystallized into a single name—Florence Nightingale. "Why will not Florence Nightingale give herself to this work?" wrote Cardinal Manning to the London *Times*.

And Florence Nightingale heard the cry, and answered it. She sent a letter to Sir Sidney Herbert, an intimate friend of hers who was then serving as the British Secretary at War. "A small private expedition of nurses has been organized for Scutari, and I have been asked to command it . . . We shall feed and lodge ourselves there, and are to be no expense whatever to the country . . ." And then, realizing the stodgy skepticism of Victorian officialdom, she added a postscript: "Would you or some one else reassure the War Office about my qualifications? Please tell them that 'this is not a lady but a real hospital nurse.'"

Reluctantly the War Office consented to let the lady play the nurse. The whole thing would be a failure—no doubt of it! But let the madcap have her way.

And so, on October 21, 1854, Florence Nightingale set sail for the Crimea. The excitement of the trip, the tossing of the boat—there was a hurricane in the Mediterranean—and the management of the thirty-eight none-too-obedient nurses whom she had taken along with her—all these proved too much for her strength. She was ill when she arrived in Scutari. The soldiers carried her stretcher in relays, fighting for the honor, from the pier to the chaplain's house.

But she rapidly recovered from her illness. Who had time to be sick when there were so many wounded to be cared for? And so many mistakes to be corrected? And so much stubbornness to be overcome? The officials in charge of the hospital insisted that "everything is just as it ought to be." And they wanted no woman "to interfere with the efficiency of our organization."

Their "efficiency" had resulted in a welter of misery and disorganization and filth. It was the fault of no one man, but of an entire stumbling system which tried to advance toward the future with eyes turned toward the past. Of the Scutari hospital, as of Dante's Inferno, it was said: "All hope abandon ye who enter here."

But there was one who entered and who did not abandon hope. Florence Nightingale created sanity out of confusion through the simple process of cutting red tape. Shortly after her arrival, a consignment of 27,000 shirts was landed at Scutari and only waited to be unpacked. But the official "Purveyor" refused to allow the unpacking "without the permission of the Board." For three weeks the sick and the wounded "lay shivering in their nakedness" while Miss Nightingale kept vainly begging to have them clothed. Finally the Board got around to the matter "in the regular routine of business" and issued the necessary permission. On the very next occasion when a consignment of shirts arrived at the hospital, Miss Nightingale took matters into her own hands. She ordered the nurses to open the bundles and to distribute the shirts, while the "Purveyor" stood by wringing his hands and muttering that the world was going to "the women and the dogs."

But the women, under the leadership of Florence Nightingale, had their way. They scrubbed the floors and the walls of the hospital, they reorganized the wards and the kitchens and the laundries, they rearranged the distribution of the food so that nobody was obliged to go hungry, and they added to the menu a number of strengthening "appetizers," such as soups and wines and jellies—"preposterous luxuries!" growled Dr. Hall, the officer in charge. And they were able to do all this because they spent none of the government's money upon their "innovations," but depended upon Florence Nightingale's own funds, supplemented by generous contributions from a number of forward-looking men and women. "What a needless waste of money upon useless rubbish!" wailed Lord Stratford de Redcliffe, the British ambassador to Turkey. "I do wish they would spend this money upon a *worthy* object, the building of an Anglican Church in Constantinople!"

When one of the wounded soldiers heard of this, he said, "This 'ospital is our church, and Miss Nightingale is our ministerin' angel."

The grateful patients at Scutari came to regard her as "the lady with the lamp." Her mere presence restored to life many a man whom the surgeons had given up as beyond hope. The soldiers idolized her. They kissed her shadow as she passed through the wards. These battle-scarred men, who knew the meaning of fatigue, were amazed at the indefatigable energy of this angel of mercy. There were days when she would spend eight hours on her knees, dressing wounds and smoothing blankets over aching limbs. Sometimes she would assist the relays of surgeons at their operations for twenty hours at a stretch. How she found time for all her work was a mystery. For, in addition to her nursing, she attended to all the administrative and to many of the menial duties of the hospital. "I am really cook, housekeeper and scavenger, washerwoman, general dealer, storekeeper." And writer of letters extraordinary. Hundreds and hundreds of them. Letters with a *sting* to them, to awaken her sleeping countrymen out of their complacent dreams. "When I write civilly I have a civil answer —*and nothing is done*. When I write furiously I have a rude answer—*and something is done*."

Throughout her stay at Scutari, it was a continual struggle between an iron will and a granite wall of opposition. And the granite gave way.

Amazed at her treatment of the soldiers as if they were human beings, the conservative officials kept grumbling, "You'll only spoil the brutes." And Miss Nightingale replied, "That's precisely what I want to do. I want to spoil them as brutes and transform them into men."

IV

SHE RETURNED HOME an invalid for life. But her work, far from being over, was only just begun. Scutari was not the only hospital. The entire world was a sick room that needed nursing.

But again that intolerable opposition of the complacent and the blind. People praised her, and came in throngs to catch a glimpse of her, and did nothing to help her in her work. The government had offered her a man-of-war to bring her home to England. But she had refused it, preferring to slip into her country quietly and unannounced. "I don't want adulation, I want understanding."

And understanding was the last thing she was able to get. She tried to open a training school for nurses—a place where it would be possible "for a woman to be a person." And she was anxious to bring about a drastic reform in all the military hospitals and barracks of England. She interviewed every important personage in the government; she even secured an audience and a "God bless you" from Queen Victoria. But always, when the road seemed open, some obstinate official would get in the way.

One of the most obstinate of them all was Lord Panmure, Sir Sidney Herbert's successor as Secretary at War. Lord Panmure—because of his immovable stubbornness Miss Nightingale called him "the Bison"—had nothing personally against her. He merely disliked what he called "her busybodiness." The Crimean War was over, the country was at peace, and he, Lord Panmure, might be pleasantly engaged in his grouse shooting but for Miss Nightingale's silly notions about schools for nurses and military hospitals and sanitary reforms. What troublesome piffle! He would put a stop to all this—not by refusing his help, but by offering it and then giving as little of it as was humanly possible.

And so he began his campaign of benevolent negligence. And behind him stood a whole battalion of reactionaries—dear, devoted friends of Miss Nightingale's, every one of them. "You are so tired, and ill. Why don't you rest for a while, and then we can discuss the whole matter."

She replied to the Bison and his "lords of the out-of-date" in one of her trenchant letters: "I am lying without my head, without my claws, and you all peck at me." And then, to convince the *public* when she had failed to convince the *peers*, she wrote a long and provocative book on the subject—*Notes on Nursing*—and personally attended to its publicity until it was translated into several languages and reached into hundreds of thousands of homes.

The public listened and came to her assistance with petitions and contributions. And finally even the Bison allowed himself reluctantly to be
led by her steady hand. The training school for nurses was opened, the
military hospital was built, and the sanitary reforms were instituted.

But the Bison, even in his captivity, tried to make one last show of
his masculine prerogative. What would a woman know about the building
of hospitals? It was he, Lord Panmure, who would order the plans for
the building. The plans were duly drawn up and the construction was
already underway before Miss Nightingale had an opportunity to visit the
project. And then to her consternation she saw that the new hospital
was designed to reproduce all the worst faults of the outdated hospitals
of the past. She urged the Bison to stop the work, but without avail. *He*
knew what was best. "Look at the spot I have selected, and the front
view!"

There was but one thing to do—make an appeal to Lord Palmerston,
the Prime Minister. Point out to him, with appropriate charts, the evils
of the old and the advantages of the new. And so, armed with her documents and her wrath, she visited the Prime Minister, spent several hours
in his office, and left him convinced that she was in the right. "It seems
to me," he wrote to Lord Panmure, "that (in the new hospital) all
consideration of what would best tend to the comfort and recovery of the
patients has been sacrificed to the vanity of the architect, whose sole
object has been to make a building which should cut a dash when looked
at from the Southampton River . . . Pray, therefore, stop all further
progress in the work until the matter can be duly considered."

The work was stopped; and after the matter had been duly considered,
the hospital was rebuilt in accordance with the plans of Florence Nightingale.

V

FOR THE MOST PART NOW she was unable to be on her feet. But she went
on with her work. An extraordinary invalid. She lay in the upper room
of a little house she had bought on South Street, received the visits of
statesmen and generals and artists and poets and peers, and manipulated
with her capable pale hands the strings of a hundred reforms. On very
rare occasions she went out for a drive in the Park. And then the eager
crowds pressed around her carriage. "Let me touch your shawl, Miss
Nightingale."—"Let me stroke your arm."—"Let me just glance at those
radiant eyes." The people adored her. For she had opened the windows
of their old stuffy world to let in the air of a new physical strength. And
religious faith. One of the most interesting of the manifold activities of her
old age was the writing of a three-volume interpretation of the old Christian truths in the light of modern needs. *Femina sum.* "I am a woman,
and therefore I am interested in everything that appertains to the chil-

dren of the human family." She was eighty-two now, but not ready as yet to lay down her work. When her nurse tucked her in at night, she got out of bed to tuck in her nurse. And throughout the day, thinking and planning and dictating letters for the building of better hospitals, better churches, a better world.

And now she was ninety, and no longer able to work. "The black camel that kneels at every house" was slowly approaching her door. One by one her mortal faculties left her—"the excess baggage for the immortal journey of the soul." First it was her hands that died, and then her eyes, and then her mind. Fitful, fragmentary visions of the past kept flying over the broken screen of her memory. One night she woke with a start. "Am I the one who stood on that Crimean height?"

Yet before the end, one final flash of light. "Do you know where you are?" a friend asked her one day.

"Yes," she replied. "I am watching at the altar of murdered men." Then, with that old-time determination in her voice, "And as long as I live, I shall be fighting their cause!"

IMPORTANT DATES IN THE LIFE OF
FLORENCE NIGHTINGALE

1820—May 15, born at Florence, Italy; named after that city.
1844—Began to visit hospitals.
1849–50—Made trip to Egypt.
1850–51—Trained as a nurse.
1853—Studied nursing organization in Paris. Established a "Hospital for Invalid Gentlewomen" in London.
1854—Organized group of trained nurses to serve in Crimean War.
1856—Returned home at the end of the war.

1857—Founded the "Nightingale Home" for the training of nurses.
1858—Published book on the health problems of the British Army.
1862–90—Assisted in the establishment of several schools for nurses.
1907—Received the Order of Merit (at the age of 87).
1910—August 13, died in London.

Gregor Johann Mendel

1822–1884

IN THE SPRING OF 1850 Gregor Johann Mendel presented himself for examination as a high school teacher at Altbrünn. He had already taught for some time as a substitute teacher, but he was anxious to secure a permanent appointment. "The respectful undersigned," he wrote in his application, "would deem himself happy if he should be able to satisfy the highly respected examiners, and thus to fulfil his desire."

But Mendel was not able to satisfy "the highly respected examiners." They "ploughed" him in natural science. "The candidate," wrote the examiners, "has not mastered this subject sufficiently to qualify him as a teacher in the higher schools."

Disappointed in his first attempt, Mendel went back to his textbooks and several months later presented himself for a second examination. Again the examiners "flunked" him. "This (second) examination paper would hardly allow us to regard the candidate as competent to become an instructor even in the lower schools."

Such was the verdict of the contemporary "experts" on the scientific ability of one of history's outstanding scientists.

II

MENDEL'S FAILURE in his examinations was due to his originality. He wrote above the heads of his examiners. "This candidate," they complained, "pays no attention to technical terminology. He uses his own words and expresses his own ideas instead of relying upon traditional knowledge."

But Mendel continued to use his own words and to express his own ideas. For he came of a stubborn and tenacious stock. For generations the Mendels had stuck to their guns and insisted upon their rights. On more than one occasion they had defied the authorities who had tried to impose their arbitrary will upon them. It was in the Mendel blood to select a course of action, or to enter upon a train of thought, and to pursue it to the end in spite of all opposition or failure.

And the course of action that Gregor had selected was to discover and to demonstrate some of the hidden secrets of nature. To discover these secrets not out of the textbooks but out of the heart of nature herself.

Mendel's love for nature, like his tenacity of purpose, came to him from several generations of peasants and gardeners. Born in the Moravian village of Heinzendorf, "the flower of the Danube," he was brought up with a passion for growing things. His father, a peasant by profession, was a horticulturist by inclination. Mendel spent many an hour of his childhood tending the plants in his father's garden.

Tending the plants, and observing them. He developed an early love for study. "Just what is it that gives the colors and the shapes to the different trees and fruits and flowers?" Fortunately he was able to learn something about these secrets in his elementary schooling. For the Countess of Waldburg, the lady of the Heinzendorf manor, had insisted upon the introduction of the study of nature as part of the curriculum in the schools of the district. The school inspector, Pater Friedl, referred to this scientific study of nature in the elementary schools as a "scandal." But, luckily for Mendel's future development as a natural scientist, the Countess of Waldburg refused to eliminate this "scandal" from the Heinzendorf schools.

Following his elementary training at Heinzendorf, Mendel entered the high school at the neighboring town of Troppau. He worked his way through the six classes of the high school on "half rations." For his parents were unable to finance him to three square meals a day. As a result of his privations, he fell seriously ill (in 1839) and was compelled to interrupt his studies for several months.

His poverty and his illness threatened to put an end to his studies altogether, when a piece of good luck came to him in the shape of ill luck to his father. One winter day, as his father was chopping down a tree, the trunk fell upon his chest and partially crushed it. Unable to go on with his work on the farm, he sold it to the husband of his eldest daughter, Veronika, and gave a substantial part of the proceeds to his other two children, Johann and Theresia. The sum given to Theresia was meant as her dowry, but the young girl generously turned every penny of it over to Johann. Encouraged by this gift, Johann took up the study of philosophy at the Olmütz Institute and after four years of hard study, occasional illness, and perpetual hunger he was ready to enter upon his life's career.

But here was a perplexing question. Just what was Mendel's career to be? "It is incumbent upon me," he wrote, "to enter a profession in which

I may be spared perpetual anxiety about a means of livelihood." He went to one of his teachers, Professor Michael Franz, and asked his advice about this matter. Professor Franz recommended a monastic life as best suited to meet his pupil's requirements. And so, on October 9, 1843, Mendel entered the Augustinian Monastery at Altbrünn, assumed the name of Gregor, and settled down to a life of prayerful devotion and practical toil.

III

SHORTLY before Mendel's arrival at Altbrünn a botanical garden had been planted on the monastery grounds under the supervision of one of the monks, Father Aurelius Thaler, a botanist noted for his profound learning, spiritual fervor, and capacious thirst. Father Thaler was in the habit of following up a hard day in the garden with a merry evening at the tavern. Displeased with this friar's excessive love for the winecup the abbot of the monastery, Father Cyril Napp, decided one night to teach him a lesson. Decking himself out with all the insignia of his office, he sat down to wait for the erring member of his fold in the porter's lodge. It was not until late in the night when the wayward friar knocked for admission. His imagination, like his tongue, had been highly stimulated by "the cup that gladdens the heart." At the sight of his chief all dressed in his "heavenly regalia" he was for a moment flabbergasted. But he quickly pulled himself together. With a deep and reverential bow he addressed himself to the abbot: "Lord, I am not worthy to come under thy roof." Then he turned on his heel—and went back to the tavern.

This merry "godson of Friar Tuck" died just before Mendel came to the monastery. But he left behind him not only the memory of a pleasant personality but also the legacy of a well stocked and scientifically tended garden. This garden was to Mendel like a gift from above. Here he spent all his spare moments, "watching and nursing the plants from their infancy to their old age." And in this botanical interest Mendel was not alone. Several of his fellow monks, sons of peasants like himself, shared his love for scientific gardening. It was a congenial group in which he now found himself—congenial not only temperamentally but intellectually as well. In their evenings they discussed theology, literature, philosophy, science, and occasionally even politics. For those were the revolutionary days of the eighteen-forties. Men were opening their minds to new thoughts and their hearts to new visions. Even in the sheltered retreats of the monasteries these new thoughts and new visions had begun to take root. Some of Mendel's associates left the monastery for the larger world, since they preferred to fight rather than to pray for their fellow men.

As for Mendel, the revolutionary current swept him along for a while and then left him behind. He was a student rather than a fighter. In spite of his peasant tenacity—a tenacity which we shall see most vigorously displayed in his later years—he was too sensitive a soul for the blows and the bloodlettings of the everyday world. He could not bear to see suffering. He tried for a time to serve as a parish priest, but his superiors found him unfitted for this work, "the reason being that he is seized by an unconquerable anguish when he is obliged to visit the bed of a sick or a dying person . . . Indeed, this infirmity of his has made him dangerously ill, and that is why we have found it necessary to relieve him from service as a parish priest."

And so Mendel returned to his monastery and his garden. But he was dissatisfied with the passive life of the monastic order. His temperament was too energetic for mere contemplation. It craved for action as well. Mendel's was not only the receptive but also the instructive type of mind. He wanted to teach as well as to study. He applied for a position as substitute teacher in the local high school and got the job at a substitute's salary—that is, 60 per cent of the amount paid to the regular teachers.

His work at the school was satisfactory, his demeanor kindly, and his conduct "reputable—except for the fact that he has on six occasions been to the theater." However, the school authorities were inclined to wink at this "aberration" on his part. After all, they admitted, "he has never gone to the theater alone, but always in the society of one of his colleagues." In spite of his "fondness for mummery," they concluded, "he is competent enough to serve as a substitute teacher."

As a substitute, but not as a permanent teacher. For the examiners, as we have already seen, had decided that he was too ignorant a scholar to be entrusted professionally with the instruction of the young. He remained an "amateur" teacher to the end of his days.

IV

MENDEL'S TEACHING did not interfere with his monastic duties at Altbrünn. He continued to live at the cloister and to cultivate the plants in its garden. He was a jovial, short and stocky little fellow, with a high forehead, a wide and generous mouth, a healthy appetite, and a hearty laugh. His gray-blue eyes looked out through their glasses with a perpetual twinkle of cordial good will. He was a contented spirit in a beautiful world. Yet there were times when his contentment gave way to indignation. The world was beautiful, but man was doing his best to make it ugly. The dreams of the creators were all too frequently crushed by the ambitions of the destroyers. The Prussians had invaded Austria (1866) and their yoke lay heavy upon the inhabitants of the conquered land. "The Prussians entered Brünn on July 12," wrote Mendel to his brother-in-law, Leopold Schindler, "and their billeting was extremely oppressive . . . Horses, cows, sheep and fowls were carried off in great numbers; so were fodder and grain—with the result that even well-to-do landowners have been reduced almost to beggary . . . The (invading) soldiers occupy the beds, while the regular inhabitants are compelled to lie on the floor or to sleep in the stable."

But the evil of the Prussian invasion passed, and Mendel was able to go on undisturbed with his work. He had become interested in the cross fertilization of the common pea. "Out of the simplest things shall ye know the truth." Mendel hoped, through his study of the heredity of plants, to learn something about the secret of the heredity of man. "How can we explain the manifold shapes and colors of living things?" In order to find a possible answer to this question, he asked for a little plot of land in the monastery garden and proceeded to transform this plot into a living textbook. He selected twenty-two varieties of the edible pea—varieties differing in shape, size, and color—and for seven years he mated, remated, and transmated them and carefully noted the characteristics of their "children."

And this, in brief, is the summary of the characteristics he discovered in the successive generations of the "children of the garden":

1. When two different types of plants (or of animals) are mated, all the offspring of the next generation will be alike. This he called *the law of uniformity*.

For example, if you cross a red flower with a white flower, all the offspring will be gray.

2. When the uniform offspring of the different plants are mated, the resulting offspring will *not* be uniform, but will segregate themselves into different forms according to a definite numerical ratio. This he called *the law of segregation*.

For example, if you cross the gray flowers that have sprung from the crossing of the red flower and the white flower, you will get the following results:

Out of every eight offspring, two will be red, two will be white, and four will be gray. The crossing of the red flowers of this generation will always produce *red flowers*. The crossing of the white flowers of this generation will always produce *white flowers*. But the crossing of the gray flowers of this generation like the crossing of the previous generation of gray flowers, will out of every eight offspring produce *two red flowers, two white flowers, and four gray flowers*. And all these flowers in turn will act in accordance with the Mendelian law of segregation. The reds will produce only reds, the whites will produce only whites, and the grays will produce reds and whites and grays in the proportion of two reds to two whites to four grays. This law of proportional segregation will hold true of every successive generation of the "inter-marriage" of plants or of animals or of human beings.

The above is a somewhat loose and simplified explanation of the Mendelian laws of heredity. The crossing of two different breeds does not always produce an intermediate breed. If, for example, you mate a black dog with a tawny dog, you will most likely get a litter not of brown dogs but of black dogs. But all the dogs in this first litter will be *uniformly* black, and all the dogs in the interbreeding of this litter will be *segregated* into black, tawny, and brown in the ratio of two to two to four. Thus the Mendelian laws of absolute uniformity as a result of the breeding of two different types, and of proportional segregation as a result of the interbreeding of hybrid (or mixed breed) types, will still hold true.

V

SUCH was the mathematical design of nature that Mendel discovered in the laws of the physical inheritance of living and growing things. It took him seven years of patient research to make this discovery. And it took the world thirty years to realize that a great new discovery had been made. When he first read his paper on *Plant Hybridization* before the Altbrünn Society for the Study of Natural Science, his audience listened politely, applauded faintly, and promptly forgot the whole thing. He published the paper, and it lay neglected on the dusty shelves of a few libraries. Disheartened at this universal apathy toward his scientific efforts, he went back to his monastic duties and his teaching. In the cloister and the classroom at least he received a measure of recognition for his labors. Indeed he was rather popular with his fellow friars and his pupils.

Especially with his pupils. They liked their rotund and jolly little teacher—his figure had filled out substantially as a result of the plentiful rich food at the monastery—and they came eagerly to his classes, not so much to imbibe his knowledge as to chuckle over his anecdotes. He told them about the funny antics of his "children"—the plants and the insects and the animals which he kept in his garden and his cloister for his experiments. He related to them how one night, when he was asleep, his pet hedgehog had crept into one of his top boots. "Imagine my surprise in the morning when I tried to put on my boot and my big toe stepped upon a thousand needles!" He frequently invited his pupils into the monastery where he acquainted them at first hand with the habits of his bees and his birds and his mice. Whenever the circus came to town, he took his entire class along with him to have a little "chat" with the animals. One of these "chats" came near to proving rather serious to Mendel. In his effort to attract the attention of the monkeys in one of the cages, he got too close to the bars. Whereupon the largest of the monkeys snatched off his spectacles. It was only with difficulty, and at the expense of a number of painful scratches, that Mendel succeeded in persuading the animal to give up his glasses. In spite of his pain, he had a good laugh together with his pupils over his comical "wrestling" match with the monkey.

His pupils admired this good-natured sort of humor that could laugh at its own discomfiture. But most of all they admired his gentleness. His impartial smile served alike to compliment the brilliant and to encourage

the stupid among his pupils. Remembering his own grief at his failure
to pass his examinations, he rarely allowed any of his pupils to suffer a
setback. Toward the end of the term he asked whether any of them
wanted better marks. Then he would allow them to question one another.
Naturally each of them would be as lenient as possible toward his neighbor
in the hope of an equal lenience in return. To those of his pupils who still
fell behind after this friendly cross questioning he extended an invitation
to come to the monastery garden for special tuition without pay.

Finally, however, he was obliged to give up his teaching. For he received a new honor which required new duties. He was elected abbot of
the monastery at Altbrünn.

VI

ONE OF MENDEL'S FIRST ACTS as the new prelate of Altbrünn was to return
the kindness of his sister, Theresia, who had given up her dowry in order
that he might go on with his education. He now repaid her with the
education of her three sons, assuming the entire expense of their high
school and college training. And even to strangers he was lavish with his
purse. His gifts for the most part were anonymous. "There is no sense in
humiliating the beneficiary by advertising yourself as his benefactor."
Though he enjoyed a substantial salary as head of the cloister, he proved
to his own satisfaction the adage that "it is more blessed to give than
to receive."

Prelate Mendel loved to give and he loved to live. He always entertained his friends—out of his own pocket—at the monastery. On festival
occasions, such as the Corpus Christi day and the day of St. Thomas, he
kept open house and larder to the entire village. As for his Christmas
celebrations, they were like "a succession of enchantments out of the
Arabian Nights."

And yet he lived to taste the bitter fruits of unpopularity. For he
entered upon a course of action which, though it seemed to him justified,
was nevertheless stubborn and in the opinion of many of his acquaintances
ill advised. The Reichsrat had passed a bill (1874) for the taxation of
church property "in order to supply the financial needs of religious worship, and especially in order to increase the salaries of parish priests."
Mendel regarded this bill as unconstitutional and refused to pay the tax
on the monastery at Altbrünn. Instead he offered to send a "voluntary
contribution" to the state treasury, "since I do not close my eyes to the
fact that an increase in the Moravian religious fund is necessary."

The state refused to accept the contribution and Mendel refused to
pay the tax. For several years the obstinate struggle went on. In turn the
government tried to persuade him with promises of promotion and to
intimidate him with threats of punishment. But Mendel refused to be
either cajoled or frightened. His intimate friends advised him to give in.

Mendel's only reply was to accuse these friends of having turned against him. He regarded himself as a "lonely crusader struggling for the right." The state, on the other hand, looked upon him as a "foolish old man who refuses to obey the law."

As the years advanced and the struggle remained undecided, Mendel began to suffer from a pathological irritability. He complained before his nephews that he was persecuted. "There is a plan being concocted to send me to a lunatic asylum."

Such was the clouded and embittered atmosphere in which he spent the remaining years of his life. His one desire was to live to see the day when the "obnoxious law" against his monastery would be revoked. This desire was not destined to be fulfilled. In the spring of 1883 he suffered a heart attack. He recovered partially from this attack, and spent the last few months of his life "among his flowers and his birds and his bees." He had attached a wire cage to the monastery beehives and he had placed a number of bees in that cage. When one of his visitors asked him the reason for this "segregation" of the bees he explained jestingly: "I have put a queen there, together with a number of drones. The queen is choosing a proper husband, for it is just as unfortunate among bees as it is among human beings when a good woman is mated to a bad man." He was still experimenting with the laws of life though he knew that his own life was at an end.

The end came on January 6, 1884. A great concourse of people mourned the passing of a lovable though rather obstinate old priest. But not a single one of the mourners realized that a supreme scientist had just passed away.

IMPORTANT DATES IN THE LIFE OF GREGOR JOHANN MENDEL

1822—July 22, born at Heinzendorf in Austrian Silesia.

1843—Entered Augustinian Monastery at Altbrünn as a novice.

1847—Ordained priest.

1851—Entered University of Vienna.

1854—Began plant experiments that brought him posthumous fame.

1865—Published *Hybridization of Plants*.

1865–69—Formulated famous laws of heredity.

1869—Became abbot of Altbrünn.

1884—January 6, died at Brünn.

Louis Pasteur

1822–1895

H<small>E IS THE</small> <small>MEEKEST</small>, smallest and least promising pupil in my class," wrote the schoolteacher of Louis Pasteur. But the youngster had an insatiable curiosity. "Let me remind you," observed his teacher one day, "that it's the pupil's business not to *ask* questions but to *answer* them."

And he possessed another rare quality—a patient tenacity for work. "The three most important words in the dictionary," he wrote while still in his early teens, "are—*will, work, wait*. These are the three cornerstones upon which I shall build the pyramid of my success."

II

T<small>HE</small> son of a tanner, he got the smell of the leather in his blood. Once, when he was ill and homesick while studying at the *École Normale* in Paris, he wrote to his father: "If I could only catch a whiff of the tannery once more, I'm sure I'd get well."

From the smell of the tannery to the "odors of the laboratory" was but a step. From earliest childhood he had made up his mind to be a chemist. "Too bad he's wasting his time on this useless science," said the villagers of Arbois to his father. But Pasteur *père* had faith in his son. "I know I can depend upon Louis to do the right thing."

Yet even his father had begun to have his doubts when Pasteur received his Bachelor of Science degree with nothing better than a "mediocre" in chemistry. "Just be patient and trust me," wrote the unsuccessful student to his father. "I shall do better as I go on."

And he went on to study for his doctorate in chemistry. In order to earn his expenses he accepted a number of private pupils, teaching them from five to seven in the morning. And in order to stretch his earnings as far as possible he rationed his food, his recreation, and his firewood down to the bare level of subsistence. He frequently suffered from hunger pangs. "But fortunately I was also subject to frequent headaches, so that the one pain tended to cancel out the other."

During this period he received further fuel to his ambition in the lectures of the great chemist, J. B. Dumas. "You cannot imagine the popularity of these lectures," he wrote to his father. "M. Dumas is not only a scientist but a poet as well. He arouses the curiosity and kindles the imagination."

Spurred on by this man of superior understanding, Pasteur wrote two theses, instead of one, for his doctor's degree. When the news of this degree arrived at Arbois there was great rejoicing in the Pasteur home. "We cannot judge your essays," wrote his father, "but we certainly can judge your character. You have given us nothing but satisfaction."

Indeed a satisfactory if not a brilliant career was now open to Pasteur. He received an appointment as laboratory assistant to Professor Laurent at the *École Normale*. He entered upon a series of experiments in crystallography—the study of the forms and the structures of chemical crystals—and he began to attract notice as a young man who was likely, "through sheer doggedness, to attain a fair measure of distinction."

And then suddenly he threw all his chances to the winds. The Revolution of 1848 had broken out. Pasteur's imagination took flame "at the altar of freedom." He sacrificed his savings of a hundred and fifty francs to the cause and offered, "should the occasion arise," to sacrifice his life. He left his position at the college and enlisted in the National Guard at the city of Orleans.

Fortunately the occasion for his supreme sacrifice did not arise. When the Revolution was over he returned to his laboratory and to his interrupted study of "crystalline formations in chemical substances." As a result of his painstaking researches in this field, he laid the foundation for the discovery of several new chemical compounds. "It is merely a matter of constructing new kinds of buildings," explained Pasteur, "through the chance discovery of bricks and stones cut into new shapes and sizes."

His modest "chance discovery"—actually the result of many months of assiduous research—came to the attention of M. Pouillet, professor of physics at the Sorbonne. This eminent scientist provided Pasteur with a letter of recommendation that served as an open sesame to the doors of the University of Strasbourg. "M. Pasteur," wrote Professor Pouillet, "is a most distinguished young chemist. He has just completed a remarkable series of experiments. Given the opportunity at a first class university, he should go very far . . ."

In January, 1849, Pasteur entered upon his duties as professor of chemistry at Strasbourg. And at once he set to work upon a new research—the way to a woman's heart. The young woman in question was Mlle Marie Laurent, the daughter of the rector of Strasbourg University.

Shortly after his arrival at the university he wrote to the rector announcing his intention to propose to his daughter. "My father is a tanner at Arbois. My (three) sisters help him in his business and in the house, taking the place of my mother whom we have had the misfortune to lose last May. My family is comfortably off but not rich . . . As for myself, I have long ago resolved to surrender to my sisters the whole share of the inheritance which would eventually be mine. I have therefore no fortune. All that I possess is good health, good courage and my position in the University . . . I plan to devote my life to chemical research with—I hope—some degree of success . . . With these humble assets I beg to submit my suit for your daughter's hand."

The rector, like a sensible father, turned the letter over to his daughter and told her to make her own decision. The decision was unfavorable. But Pasteur was too well trained a scientist to give up a problem after a negative first result. "I am afraid," he wrote to the young lady's mother, "that Mlle Marie attaches too much importance to first impressions, which can only be unfavorable to me. There is nothing in me to attract a young girl. But memory tells me that when people have known me well, they have liked me." And like a good scientist who neglects no avenue of approach to the possible solution of his problem, he wrote a letter to Mlle Marie herself. "All that I ask of you, Mademoiselle, is not to judge me too quickly. You might be mistaken, you know. Time will show you that under this cold and shy exterior there is a heart full of affection for you."

His precise and persistent method won out. The marriage was announced for May 29, 1849. But at the last moment there was a hitch. The guests had arrived, the bride and her parents were waiting, the priest was ready for the ceremony—but there was no groom. "Where in the world is that young chemist?"

Where, but in his laboratory? His best friend, Chappuis, hurried down to the laboratory and found him there leaning over his test tubes.

"Did you forget about your wedding?"

"No."

"Then what are you doing here?"

"Finishing my work, you idiot. Surely you wouldn't expect me to quit in the middle of an experiment!"

III

His wife never regretted her decision to marry him. At times, to be sure, she scolded him for his "excessive absorption" in his work. "But I comfort her by saying that I shall lead her to fame."

And he did lead her to fame. And to sorrow. For it was not easy to be the wife of a scientist whose very brilliance aroused the jealousy and the hatred of his less gifted fellow scientists.

This jealousy and this hatred began to crop out at the very beginning of his career. His investigations had led him from chemistry to biology. "I am pursuing as best I can," he wrote to Chappuis, "the impenetrable mystery of Life and Death. I am hoping to mark a decisive step very soon by solving . . . the celebrated question of spontaneous generation." His closest friends urged him to refrain from this study. "I would advise no one," wrote Dumas, "to dwell too long on so controversial a subject."

For the origin of life was too "touchy" a question to be examined scientifically. Tradition was firmly and aggressively on the side of those who believed that life can originate spontaneously out of dead matter. Aristotle, for example, had declared that "life can be engendered by the drying of a moist body or by the moistening of a dry body." Virgil had stated that "bees can spring into life out of the carcass of a dead bull." Van Helmont had advanced the even more fantastic "method for the creation of mice" in the full-grown state: "Press a quantity of soiled linen into a vessel containing some grains of wheat or a piece of cheese for about three weeks, and at the end of this period the adult mice, both male and female, will spring up spontaneously in the vessel."

It was against this sort of traditional superstition that Pasteur dared to undertake his series of experiments. And immediately the older scientists began to aim their poisoned shafts against him. Especially virulent were Professor Pouchet, director of the Natural History Museum of Rouen, and Nicolas Joly, professor of physiology at the University of Toulouse. These two men, in order to "prove" their point against Pasteur, undertook a series of "experiments" which were neither adequately prepared nor accurately executed. "M. Pouchet and M. Joly," wrote Pasteur to his father, "may say what they like, but truth is on my side. They do not know how to experiment. It is not an easy art; it demands, besides certain natural qualities, a long practice which naturalists have not generally acquired nowadays." But his opponents went vigorously ahead with their denunciation of Pasteur. Proclaiming to the world that they had "definitely established the fact of spontaneous generation," they called Pasteur a "circus performer, a charlatan and a clown." Pasteur bore all this contumely with a patient smile. "A man of science," he explained to his wife, "should think of what will be said of him in the coming centuries, not of the insults or the compliments of the present day."

Finally the controversy as to the probable origin of life was referred to a commission of eminent scientists, including Professor Dumas. After a thorough examination of the findings submitted by Pouchet and Joly on the one hand and by Pasteur on the other, they handed down a decision in favor of Pasteur. "Life alone can produce life."

IV

HAVING established the evidence as to the *origin* of life, Pasteur next became interested in the problem of the *preservation* of life. A mysterious disease had attacked the silkworms in the province of Alais and the entire silk business of France was threatened with ruin. Pasteur, whose achievements had now won him a seat in the Academy, was invited to investigate and if possible to check the disease. Again a tempest of abuse descended upon his head. This tempest increased in volume as month after month went by and Pasteur was able to make no headway against the epidemic. "What does a chemist know about matters of healing?" complained the mulberry cultivators whose silkworms were dying by the thousands every day. And the public took up the cry. "A chemist? Not even that. He's nothing but a parasite living on the fat of the land while the business of France is heading for a crash." To all of which outcries and complaints Pasteur had but a single reply—"Patience."

And he needed patience. While he was investigating the silkworm epidemic one of his children died. Then another, and a third. "To go on persistently with your work under such conditions," remarked a friend, "must require a great deal of courage." "I don't know about my courage," replied Pasteur. "But I do know about my duty."

He stuck to his duty eighteen hours a day, from five in the morning to eleven at night. He suffered a paralytic stroke, and for a time the doctors despaired of his life. Yet his mind was active while his body lay paralyzed. It was in the "restful hours of his illness" that he discovered the solution to the problem upon which he had spent so much of his labor and strength. "The disease of the silkworms is inherited through diseased eggs from one generation to another. Eliminate the diseased eggs and you will produce a healthy crop of silkworms."

A simple solution after a heartbreak of toil. Yet the abuse against Pasteur did not stop even then. The silkworm seed merchants, who saw in Pasteur's formula an end to their indiscriminate selling of "bad seed for good money," began to spread malicious stories about him. As a result of these stories, the word passed around that Pasteur had utterly failed in his effort to stop the disease and that he had been driven out of Alais under a shower of stones.

When Pasteur heard this report—he was recovering from his paralysis at the time—he merely shrugged his shoulders once more. "Patience."

And his patience had its reward. The silkworm cultivators tried his remedy—and in every instance produced healthy crops. The grateful countryfolk of Alais set up a statue in his honor. But he found greater pride in "the honor of having alleviated, at my personal sacrifice, a misfortune that threatened my country."

V

His personal sacrifices had traced their story on his pale furrowed face and in his stern sad eyes. For his efforts in behalf of his fellows he received inadequate pay. Nor did he require more than he received. Once, when he

visited Napoleon III and the Empress Eugénie, the imperial couple expressed their surprise at his failure to derive financial benefit from his
scientific work. "In France," replied Pasteur, "a scientist would be lower-
ing himself if he worked for personal profit." At no personal profit he
undertook a series of experiments on the diseases of wine. Within a single
year the French wine industry had lost several million dollars as a result
of the mysterious "souring" of the produce. After a careful investigation
of the matter, Pasteur discovered that this souring was due to the action of
bacteria in the fermenting liquid. His problem now was to destroy the
bacteria without at the same time injuring the quality of the wine. He
tried several antiseptic substances, but with no result. And then he tried
heating the wine to various temperatures—and came upon a tremendous
discovery. If he raised the wine to a temperature of 55 degrees centi-
grade (about 131 degrees fahrenheit), he found that he could thus preserve the quality of the wine and at the same time destroy the poison of
the bacteria.

Such was the origin of the now universally accepted process known as
pasteurization—a process applied not only to wine but also to many other
varieties of perishable foods and drinks—especially to cream and milk. If
the world today enjoys a greater degree of health than was known in earlier
generations, no small part of the credit is due to the patience of Pasteur
in his study of the fermentation of wine.

VI

"To HELP mankind" was the primary object of his life. He entertained
the hope for a day of better health, higher aspirations, and a greater understanding between man and man. "To moral coöperation through international science." But in 1870 Kaiser Wilhelm I and his chancellor of the
crimson fist proclaimed a different kind of doctrine—"the glorification of
force and the extinction of moral justice." And their army proceeded to
put this doctrine into practice.

When the German army invaded France, Pasteur offered his services to
his country, but his partial paralysis disqualified him for fighting. He
showed his contempt for the German military madness, however, by returning an honorary diploma of Doctor of Medicine which he had received
from the University of Bonn. "I am led by my conscience," he wrote to
the Principal of the Faculty of Medicine, "to request that you efface my
name from the archives of your university, and to take back that diploma,
as a sign of the indignation inspired in a French scientist by the barbarity
and hypocrisy of him (Kaiser Wilhelm) who, for the satisfaction of his
criminal pride, persists in the massacre of two great nations." And the
answer from Bonn was couched in the characteristic arrogance of the
aggressor: "M. Pasteur—The undersigned, now Principal of the Faculty of
Medicine of Bonn, is requested to reply to the affront which you have

dared to offer to the German nation in the sacred person of its august
Emperor, King Wilhelm of Prussia, by conveying to you the expression
of its utter contempt . . . P.S. Wishing to keep its files free from taint,
the Faculty returns your letter herewith."

With a heavy heart Pasteur noted the depredations of the invading army
whose rule for conquest, as formulated by Bismarck, was "to leave the
inhabitants of occupied territory nothing but their eyes to weep from."

Added to Pasteur's general distress was his personal anxiety about his
son who had enlisted in the French army and who was now fighting under
General Bourbaki. The news reached Pasteur that Bourbaki had sustained a disastrous defeat and that his army was fleeing before the onslaught of the Germans. The stricken old chemist and his wife started off
in search of their son—hoping against hope that he might still be numbered among the living. In a dilapidated old carriage—the only vehicle
available at the moment—they set out from Arbois and followed the snow-
covered route of the retreating army. Everywhere the highways were littered with the bodies of the dead. Everywhere the sick and the wounded
stragglers, their uniforms hanging in tatters from their frozen bodies, were
begging for food and for the comfort of a blanket to wrap around their
shoulders. And everywhere a desolate old man kept repeating the selfsame question: "Have you seen Sergeant Pasteur?" The invariable answer
was a negative shake of the head. Nobody knew whether Sergeant Pasteur
was dead or alive. "All I can tell you," said one of the stragglers, "is that
out of twelve hundred men in his battalion of *Chasseurs*, only three hundred are left."

Slim chance of ever meeting their son again. . . .

At last, however, there was a ray of hope. Their all but dismantled
carriage had just limped into Pontarlier. A group of shivering soldiers
were huddled over a fire. "Sergeant Pasteur? Yes, we saw him yesterday
. . . He is still alive, but very low . . . Perhaps you can meet him on the
road to Chaffois . . ."

Out of Pontarlier toward Chaffois. A cart was rumbling over the frozen
road. Within it, on a bundle of straw, lay a soldier covered with a ragged
coat. It was too dark to make out his features. The questing old chemist
turned to the driver of the cart. "Have you seen Sergeant Pasteur?"

The soldier raised his head. "Father! Mother!" . . .

He recovered from his wounds, rejoined his regiment, and survived the
war. A grain of comfort in the sorrowful life of Pasteur.

VII

AFTER the war Pasteur continued with his self-imposed task of arresting
disease. In his researches on the silkworm epidemics and on the fermenta-
tions of wine he had discovered a single vital principle—that the malady
in each of these cases was due to the presence of poisonous micro-organ-

isms, or germs. Why not apply this principle in the treatment of human disease?

Pasteur was especially interested in trying out his ideas in surgery. The death rate that followed surgical operations was appalling. In the great majority of cases the decision to operate upon a patient was tantamount to a death sentence. "The opened wound," as Pasteur pointed out to a gathering at the Academy of Medicine, "is exposed to millions of germs—in the air, on the hands of the surgeon who performs the operation, in the sponges that bathe the wound, in the instruments that pry into it, and on the bandages that cover it."

When the members of the French Academy heard these words, they smiled into their beards and shook their heads and went on killing their patients with their "good old-fashioned" methods. In Scotland, however, there was one man who paid heed to Pasteur's warning. This man was Joseph Lister, professor of surgery at the University of Edinburgh. Following Pasteur's advice he submitted every object involved in the operation—his hands, his instruments, the sponges, the bandages, and even the area surrounding the incision—to a thorough disinfection of carbolic acid. And with splendid results. Within two years he reduced the fatalities of his surgical cases from 90 per cent to 15 per cent.

Yet the surgeons of the French Academy remained stubbornly opposed to Pasteur's theory of disinfection, even in the face of Lister's successful application of this theory. It was a new idea and therefore—they argued—it was a *bad* idea.

As for Pasteur, he was ready to accept and to fight for any idea—especially in the field of medicine—as soon as it was definitely supported by adequate facts. "The facts with regard to surgery have demonstrated, beyond the shadow of a doubt, that many a patient has died through the poisonous action of the Infinitesimally Small." And so he entered upon a crusade to stamp out a double source of infection—the physical microbe that attacked the human body, and the "mental microbe" that retarded the human mind. "I will force them to see in spite of themselves," he said again and again of his opponents. "They *must* see!" One day a member of the Academy of Medicine was lecturing to his colleagues on puerperal (childbirth) fever—a disease which in 1864 had killed over three hundred women in the Paris Maternity Hospital alone. The lecturer was explaining his ideas as to the cause of this fever, when a voice interrupted him: "Nonsense and fiddlesticks! It isn't any of the things you mention, but the doctors and the nurses that are responsible for puerperal fever. They murder the mothers by carrying the microbe from an infected patient to a healthy one!"

"And can you tell me," asked the lecturer sarcastically, "what this microbe of yours looks like?"

Whereupon Pasteur walked to the blackboard, took a piece of chalk and rapidly sketched the outline of a chain-like organism. "There, that is what it looks like."

The meeting was thrown into an uproar. The older doctors insisted that Pasteur was an interloper, an amateur, a man who knew nothing whatsoever about medicine and who had better stick to his chemicals and his crucibles. The younger men, however, paid heed to his words. Little by little they introduced his methods of sterilization until, as one of Pasteur's biographers (L. Descours) remarks, "the maternity hospitals ceased to be the antechambers of death."

VIII

PASTEUR continued to befuddle the reactionaries, to bring down their denunciations upon his head, and to fight his scientific battles for the preservation of life. Through his methodical process of repeated experimentation he discovered the principle of immunizing a person against the *violent* form of a disease by inoculating him with a *mild* form of that disease. This simple method of transforming a virus into a vaccine has saved an incalculable number of lives.

He first employed this discovery in the stamping out of an epidemic of anthrax—a deadly fever of the spleen—that threatened to exterminate the sheep and cattle industry of France. In the course of his researches in this field he was obliged, as usual, to fight not only against the virulence of the plague but against the equally stubborn virulence of human prejudice. At one of the meetings of the Academy of Medicine, Pasteur accused his adversaries of malignity as well as of stupidity. Whereupon one of the physicians, Dr. Jules Guérin, started up from his chair and made a rush at Pasteur. The pugnacious doctor was held back by a fellow member of the Academy, but the meeting ended in a general uproar.

The next day Guérin challenged Pasteur to a duel. But Pasteur returned the challenge. "My business," he said, "is to heal, not to kill."

And then came the most dramatic episode in his lifelong business of healing—his famous battle against hydrophobia. For some years he had been experimenting with the inoculation of the saliva of mad dogs into healthy rabbits. At times he varied his experiments by subjecting the rabbits directly to the bites of the mad dogs. On one occasion a large bulldog, though furious with pain and foaming at the mouth, persistently refused to bite the rabbit that had been thrust into his cage. It would be necessary, concluded Pasteur, to *suck* the saliva out of the dog's jaws and then inject it into the rabbit.

The dog was tied securely upon a table and Pasteur, with a glass tube in his mouth, bent down to the mouth of the enraged animal. "This," wrote a bystander, "was the supreme moment of Pasteur's life." Calmly, as if unaware of the fact that he was courting death, he sucked the venomous saliva drop by drop into the tube. And then, when he had gathered a sufficient quantity of the poison into the tube, he turned to his assistants. "Well, gentlemen, we can now proceed with the experiment."

Within a few months after this experiment an Alsatian boy, Joseph Meister, was bitten by a mad dog. His mother, on the advice of the local physician, took him to Pasteur. Here was an opportunity to test out on a human being the antirabic inoculation that had proved so successful in the case of animals.

Yet Pasteur hesitated. How certain could he feel that his remedy would succeed? Was it not within the realm of possibility that the inoculation, instead of preserving the victim's life, would only introduce a more aggravated type of the disease? Was he therefore justified in taking the risk, especially when it concerned another person's life?

He took the risk. And he won. The night following the final inoculation was one of sleepless terror for Pasteur but of peaceful sleep for the stricken child. Thirty-one days passed, and there were no recurring symptoms of the disease. The boy was completely cured. Pasteur had conquered hydrophobia.

IX

A NUMBER of belated distinctions—election to the Academy, the Cross of the Legion of Honor, medals, ribbons, diplomas, banquets, ovations, parades—and Pasteur remained through it all a modest seeker for truth. His present popularity was as amazing to him as his earlier disgrace. "I can't understand why people make such a fuss over me." Elected by the Government to represent his country at the International Medical Congress in London, he entered St. James's Hall amid a thunder of cheers. Unaware that he was the cause of the acclamation, he turned to his escort. "It must be the Prince of Wales arriving. I'm sorry I didn't come earlier."

He returned to Paris and to his work at the Pasteur Institute—a hospital built in his honor for the combating of infectious disease. And here he spent the rest of his days in his "humble effort," as he expressed it, "to extend the frontiers of life."

His seventieth birthday was the occasion of a national holiday. Pasteur attended a celebration in his honor at the Sorbonne. He was too feeble, however, to express in person his thanks to the delegates who had come from various countries to join in the celebration. He asked his son to read his speech for him. "Gentlemen . . . you bring me the greatest happiness that can be experienced by a man whose invincible belief is that science and peace will triumph over ignorance and war . . . Never permit the sadness of certain hours which pass over nations to discourage you . . . Have faith that in the long run the nations will learn to unite not for destruction but for coöperation, and that the future will belong not to the conquerors but the saviors of mankind . . ."

This was Pasteur's farewell message to the world.

IMPORTANT DATES IN THE LIFE OF
LOUIS PASTEUR

1822—December 27, born at Dôle, France.

1847—Graduated from the *École Normale,* Paris.

1848—Appointed professor in the lycée at Dijon.

1849—Appointed professor of chemistry at Strasbourg University.
Married.

1854—Made dean of the scientific faculty at Lille.

1857—Appointed director of scientific studies at the *École Normale Supérieure.*

1868—Became director of the chemophysiological laboratory at the *École des Hautes Etudes.*
Suffered paralytic stroke.

1873—Became life member of the French Academy of Medicine.

1887—Elected permanent secretary of the Academy of Sciences.

1889—Withdrew from all other posts to give entire attention to management of Pasteur Institute.

1895—September 28, died at Villeneuve l'Etang.

Leo Tolstoy

1828–1910

Tolstoy was one of those rare individuals who, instead of *rising* from the ranks because of his superior *ambition*, voluntarily *descended* to the ranks because of his superior *compassion*. Like Buddha, that other great man who had stooped to conquer, Tolstoy came of an ancient family of princes. One of his ancestors had been a close companion of Peter the Great. Born at Yasnaya Poliana (Sunny Glen) in 1828, he lost his mother at the age of two and his father at the age of nine. Together with his two brothers and his two sisters he was put into the care of a distant relative, "Aunt" Tatiana. This woman had two outstanding virtues, "serenity and love"; and she suffered from one great vice, a weakness for associating with feeble-minded pilgrims whom she regarded as mystics and saints.

Listening to the stories of these pilgrims, Tolstoy acquired an early taste for metaphysics which he was never quite able to shake off. To the end of his life he was given to day-dreaming and mystical speculation which often clouded the vigor of one of the supreme intellects of the nineteenth century.

In school he was a very dull pupil. His teachers used to say of the three Tolstoy brothers: "Sergei is willing and able; Dmitri is willing but unable; Leo is both unwilling and unable."

But he had an unusually serious outlook upon life. At the early age of five he had come to the conclusion that "life is not an amusement but a very heavy task." At sixteen he lost faith in the Orthodox (Greek) Church. Then followed a period of philosophical wanderings through "the desert of adolescence," as he termed it. Passing from religion to agnosticism and from agnosticism to nihilism (belief in nothing), he finally came to the verge of despair. He was nineteen years old at the time.

His unhappiness was due largely to his physical unattractiveness. He had a great hunger for admiration. "I wanted to be known by all, loved by all," he wrote in his diary. Yet he believed there could be no happiness on earth for anyone who looked as unprepossessing as himself. His face was "as ugly as a gorilla's"—small sunken eyes, low forehead, heavy lips, large bulbous nose, and enormous ears. He had the mind of an Ariel in the body of a Caliban. So sensitive indeed was he of his repulsiveness that he decided to put an end to his life.

Fortunately, however, he changed his mind and sought temporary forgetfulness in dissipation instead of permanent oblivion in death.

And then, one day, he discovered Rousseau.

This discovery was just the tonic he needed at the time. It reconciled him to his own ugliness and it opened his eyes to the beauty of Nature. He had rejected the religion of the Church. He now adopted the religion of Rousseau. He worshiped him like a god. He wore a medallion portrait of him hung around his neck as though it were a holy image.

Inspired by the philosophy of Rousseau, he wrote his first novel, *A Russian Landlord*. It dealt with the problem that was to occupy Tolstoy throughout his life—the eternal conflict between the ideal of the prophet and the indifference of the public. The hero of the novel, Prince Nekhludov, has left the university in order to help his peasants. But, like most other human derelicts, Nekhludov's peasants prefer to remain in the rut of their helplessness. They can understand a tyrant who beats them, but they hardly know what to make of a master who is kind to them. They shrink from him, they ridicule him, they look upon his proffered help with suspicion, they regard him as a spy, a scoundrel, a fool—anything but a man who is simply trying to be their friend.

Nekhludov is defeated. He sits down at the piano and strikes the keys. He has no talent for music. But his imagination weaves the song that his fingers are too clumsy to play. He hears a choir, an orchestra . . . The past and the future are blended together into a triumphant fulfillment of his dream.

In his mind's eye he sees the peasants, the moujiks, not only in all their ugliness, but in all their *lovableness* as well. He forgives them for their ignorance, their idleness, their obstinacy, their hypocrisy, their distrust. For now he looks not only *at* them, but *into* them. He sees their suffering, their patience, their cheerfulness, their quiet acceptance of life, and their courageous resignation in the face of death.

"It is beautiful," he murmurs. Even though they reject his advances, he now understands them and sympathizes with them. For they are all brothers, he and his peasants, flesh of one flesh and blood of one blood—a host of helpless moujiks living and toiling and dying under the lash of the pitiless landlord, Fate.

II

In 1851 TOLSTOY had gambled away his money and escaped to the Caucasus in order to get rid of his creditors. He joined the army in which his brother was already an officer.

At nineteen Tolstoy had courted death. Now, at twenty-three, he was a firm believer in life. He left behind him his philosophical doubts and his overwhelming sense of sin. He became once more interested in mysticism —and in beautiful women. Like the young Faust, he accepted the world and found it a diverting toy to play with. Every experience was good if only it added to the sum of his pleasure. "Nothing is wrong," he writes in *The Cossacks.* "To amuse yourself with a pretty girl is not a sin. It is only a sign of good health."

He steeped himself in the beauty of the mountains, he fought, he gambled, he loved, and he created masterpieces of poetic realism. Tales of childhood, stories of war, novels about the Cossacks, essays, letters—a whole torrent of them came from his pen in rapid succession.

Absorbed in his literary work, he paid little attention to his military duties. He was too fond of creation to take much interest in destruction. Though still proud of his uniform, with its pretty medals and its brass buttons, he was already beginning to see war in its true colors. In *The Invasion,* written at the age of twenty-four, he uttered his first cry of protest against militarism:

"Is it impossible, then, for men to live in peace, in this world so full of beauty, under this immeasurable starry sky? How can they, in a place like this, retain their feelings of hatred and vengeance, and the lust of destroying their fellows? All there is of evil in the human heart ought to disappear at the touch of Nature, that most immediate expression of the beautiful and the good."

Thus far, in his military maneuvers, he had seen only the *image* of war. In 1853, however, he came face to face with war itself. Russia had declared hostilities against Turkey, and Tolstoy was called upon to "do his bit" for the greater glory of the Czar.

At first he was carried away by the fervor of his patriotism. Like the other young men of his nation, he became suddenly ferocious. A wave of mystical frenzy had swept over him. He slew the Turks and thanked God for His assistance in the slaughter.

Before long, however, he got over the intoxication of killing. During the Crimean War he wrote three books. The first is all a-bristle with chauvinism. In the second he speaks sadly of the mutual slaughter of human beings. In the preface to the third he condemns the rulers of the world for turning their subjects into mere pieces of "cannon-fodder."

The longer he looked at war, the more clearly he saw it in all its hideousness. From now on, he would dedicate himself to a worldwide war against war. On March 5, 1855, he wrote in his diary:

"I have been led to conceive a great idea, to whose realization I feel capable of devoting my whole life. This idea is the foundation of a new religion . . ."

The religion of nonresistance, of international brotherhood, of universal peace.

III

In 1856 Tolstoy resigned from the army and returned to St. Petersburg (Leningrad). His reputation as a soldier and a writer had preceded him. He became at once a literary lion. The leading authors and artists of the city welcomed him into their inner circle. But he found them to be an uncongenial lot of snobs. They regarded themselves as the elect, the intellectual supermen of their time, the glory and crown of creation. They wrote for the *intelligentsia*, and looked upon the rest of mankind as unworthy to share in their exalted ideas. But Tolstoy's attitude was just the opposite of this. Literature to him was a religion—a holy gospel of beauty and wisdom that must become the common possession of all. Instead, therefore, of writing to entertain the few, he wrote to educate the many.

In working for the common people, he had no illusions about their intelligence. He was quite aware of their "bestial and contemptible side." But, like Prince Nekhludov, he felt that they were instinctively groping toward the light. They were merely waiting for a leader, a teacher, a man who would show them the way. "Go to the people to learn what they want . . . Try to understand their needs, and help them to satisfy these needs."

He opened a school for the peasants at Yasnaya Poliana. In this school he tried to be not a master, but a fellow disciple. For he maintained that all of them were nothing more than children trying to spell out the first syllables in the mysterious book of life.

The school was closed by the police, and Tolstoy was advised to leave the peasants alone in their ignorance. Then came months of sickness and despondency. Two of his brothers died of tuberculosis, and Tolstoy suspected that he himself was suffering from the same disease. He lost his "faith in goodness, in everything." Once more he began to think of suicide.

This time he was saved by his art, and by his love for the seventeen-year-old Sophia Andreyevna Behrs.

He married this child—he was exactly twice her age—and then entered upon a period of unclouded happiness that lasted almost fifty years. Gifted in her own right, Countess Tolstoy became, to use her expression, a "true author's wife." She took his dictation, she stimulated his fancy, she encouraged him, she made painstaking copies of his manuscripts, and she served as the model for some of his most charming characters.

Under the influence of his happiness, he wrote two of his greatest masterpieces—the tragedy of individual passion (*Anna Karenina*) and the epic of universal suffering (*War and Peace*).

In the story of Anna, the wife of Karenin, Tolstoy develops the theme of Goethe's poem: "The heavenly powers bring us into life; they compel us to sin; and then they abandon us to our sin and our pain." For the first eight years of her married life, Anna is faithful to her husband and happy in the love of her little son, Serozha. The child adores his mother like a goddess. All would have been well but for an unfortunate visit that Anna Karenina pays to her brother Stepan in Moscow. Here, in the gay and heartless society of the Russian nobility, she meets Count Vronsky, a suave and handsome and wealthy young man who loves a good horse, a good fight, and a pretty woman. Anna Karenina and Count Vronsky fall an easy prey to a mutual attraction.

Anna is not the first of Vronsky's conquests. Indeed, at the very moment of his meeting with Anna he is involved in a love affair with Stepan's sister-in-law Kitty, a charming and popular young debutante of Moscow. Kitty has many admirers. But she prefers two above all—Vronsky, whom she loves, and Konstantin Levin, whom she admires.

Konstantin, a Moscow nobleman, is a well-to-do and serious young fellow with a skeptical turn of mind. "He is unable to believe; he is equally unable to disbelieve." With a quizzical helplessness he looks on, while the tragedy unfolds before his eyes. Anna and Vronsky, he observes, are drifting helplessly toward each other. The two victims are aware of this fact, yet they can do nothing to stop it.

Anna is desperately hungry for Vronsky's love—and desperately afraid of it. She longs for the adoration of her son and for the protection of her husband. She decides to cut short her visit to Moscow and to escape from her infatuation. She buys a return ticket to St. Petersburg. On the train she finds Vronsky.

He is determined to follow her.

They meet often in the social circles of St. Petersburg. Society looks upon their affair with a snickering approbation. It is an interesting diversion for them—and a good subject for gossip.

As for Anna's husband, he calmly points out to her the folly of her course, and then prudently shuts his eyes. He will not run the risk of a divorce scandal, and he will not endanger his life in a duel.

But things are coming to a head. There is an accident at a horse race. Count Vronsky is seriously hurt. Anna makes a public display of her anxiety. And, when Karenin upbraids her, she confesses her love for Vronsky.

Anna implores her husband to set her free. But he is determined to have his revenge. He compels her to remain under his roof.

Tortured and humiliated and crushed, Anna continues her secret relations with Vronsky. She is torn between three emotions: her love for her little Serozha, her loyalty toward Kitty from whom she has taken Vronsky, and her passion for Vronsky. Kitty finally manages to forget Vronsky and marries Konstantin Levin. And this removes one of the difficulties of

Anna's position. But the other two difficulties, her love for Serozha and her passion for Vronsky, are still present in all their bitter intensity.

And now there arises a new complication. Anna gives birth to a daughter. Karenin is magnanimous toward Vronsky's child; but Vronsky, in his humiliation, attempts suicide.

Anna's position has become intolerable. She must make a choice between Serozha and Vronsky. She decides in Vronsky's favor.

But the story is not yet ended. The author has another somber thread to weave into his plot. Anna and Vronsky go abroad. For a time they enjoy a measure of happiness in their illicit passion. Then they return to Russia and once again implore Karenin to grant Anna a divorce. But Karenin refuses.

Anna grows meditative, then morose. And finally a flaming jealousy begins to consume her. She suspects Vronsky of unfaithfulness. Her only relief is in oblivion—the death-in-life that comes through morphine.

And then—the end. Suicide under the wheels of a train.

In *Anna Karenina* Tolstoy depicts the soul-struggle of an individual. In *War and Peace,* a story about the Napoleonic invasion of Russia, he pictures the soul-struggle of the human race. The struggle from savagery to civilization, from bloodshed to harmony, from hatred to love. The solution to the individual problem is not enough. The problem must be solved for all mankind. When Prince Andrei, the hero of *War and Peace,* lay wounded at Austerlitz, he suddenly caught a glimpse of the inner peacefulness of the world. He saw "the illimitable sky which broods above the outrage and abjectness of the earth," and the sight of it filled him with an indescribable joy. This inner peacefulness, this light which now and then breaks through the darkness of life, was something which Tolstoy was anxious to transmit to his fellow men. Yet he felt that he could not do this through the medium of his art.

He began to think of a new kind of art—the art of establishing a bond of sympathy between man and man. He wanted to lead the people to the light. He had lost faith in the Orthodox Church and—outside of his temporary interest in Rousseau—he had found no faith to take its place.

In his quest for the true faith Tolstoy went back to the Church. He reexamined its dogmas and its practices. For three years he submitted to all its ceremonies. But it was useless. "I fear I am too ardent a follower of Christ to be a conventional Christian." The Russian Church, he declared, had become a business institution. The clergy were too much intent upon enforcing the commandments of the Czar and too little intent upon advancing the teachings of Jesus. "In the Russian Church," he said, "the meaning of the Christian doctrine has absolutely disappeared."

And so he "broke away from the Church and went back to God." He became the prophet of a new religion—or rather, he interpreted anew the "well-nigh forgotten" religion of Buddha, of Isaiah, of Confucius, and of Christ. This religion, of which he hoped to become the self-effacing leader, was to dispense with all rituals and churches and priests. It was to be based upon a few simple commandments: Be no man's enemy; never give way to your wrath; and never resort to violence. This was to be the negative phase of his doctrine. On its positive side, his religion was a religion of protest. He protested against the extravagance of the nobles, the bigotry of the priests, and the tyranny of the Czar. He became "a communist, a dissenter and a rebel—in short, a true disciple of Christ." He was ready to give up his fame, his position, his wealth, his very life if necessary, for the service of mankind. He dressed in a peasant's smock and associated with the lowliest on equal terms. He stooped to conquer. He descended from his aristocratic aloofness to the common level of humanity; and in so doing, he raised humanity to new heights of moral grandeur.

The world hailed Tolstoy as a prophet. But his family regarded him as a fool. His wife began to fear that he was losing his reason. His children yawned and turned away whenever he spoke about the brotherhood of man. To live a life of utter unselfishness seemed to them a sure sign of insanity. It was all very well for him to sacrifice himself, they said, but what right had he to sacrifice *his family* to his peculiar ideals? He became a stranger in his own house. "Perhaps you will not believe me," he wrote in a letter to a friend, "but you cannot imagine how isolated I am, nor in what degree my veritable *I* is despised and disregarded by all those about me."

Yet in spite of his mental torture he went right ahead with the work of interpreting Christ in the language of the nineteenth century. Christ had tried to establish the kingdom of God. Tolstoy believed in establishing the democracy of Man. He wrote a number of essays and stories to illustrate the principles of human compassion and nonresistance to evil. As a reward for this, he was excommunicated from the Orthodox Church (1901).

As Tolstoy grew old, a fantastic new note crept into his teaching. Estranged from his fellow men, from his children, and from his wife, he began to look upon all human intercourse in a peculiar, mystical, unearthly light. He became an ascetic. Earlier in life he had condemned adultery. Now—at the age of 70—he advocated complete sexual abstinence. "He who regards a woman—even his own wife—with sensuality, already commits adultery with her." There is something pathetic in the spectacle of an old man who tries to rebuild the world in the image of his own impotent desires. He even went so far as to recommend the extinction of mankind through the establishment of absolute celibacy! But his mind was already slipping at the time. His mysticism was gaining complete mastery over his intellect. In his last novel, *Resurrection*, he puts the soul of an old saint into the body of a young sinner. Nekhludov—note that the hero of Tolstoy's last novel bears the same name as the hero of his first novel— is a study in paradox. He begins as a scoundrel and ends as a martyr. Within a few years this ordinary man goes through a moral transformation that it took the very extraordinary Tolstoy a whole lifetime to achieve.

Resurrection is one of the most beautiful poems of pity in the world. But it is the work of an old man.

IV

IT WAS the tragedy of Tolstoy to outlive his own greatness. During the last ten years of his life he advocated a social, political, and ethical ideal which could be possible only in a world of supermen—or of old men. As time went on, he became more and more the profound philosopher and the simple child. The very last act of his life, like almost everything that he did throughout his career, was a strange admixture of the stupid and the sublime. On October 28, 1910, at five o'clock in the morning, Tolstoy fled from the shelter of his home and went to seek peace in the wilderness. He was eighty-two years old at the time of his flight. Dressed in his peasant's blouse, his face beautified by age and furrowed by suffering, he wandered off, like Buddha, over the highways of the world. Buddha had left his home in search of life, but Tolstoy was going forth in search of death.

He wanted to die alone. Having dedicated his own life to pity, he now fled from the pity of his family. For several days he wandered from village to village, and at last fell by the wayside, never to rise again. To the physician who attended him, he said: "There are millions of human beings on earth who are suffering. Why do you think only of me?"

On Sunday, November 10, 1910, he found the peace which he had been seeking throughout his life. It was a little after six in the morning when his pain-racked body relaxed in that "final great deliverance" as he named it—"Death, blessed Brother Death."

IMPORTANT DATES IN THE LIFE OF
LEO TOLSTOY

1828—September 9, born at Yasnaya Poliana, Russia.

1847—Gave up university studies to settle down to farming.

1855—Served in storming of Sebastopol during Crimean War. Issued earliest literary works about Crimean campaign. Traveled in Germany and Italy.

1862—Married daughter of Moscow physician.

1865–68—Wrote *War and Peace*.

1875–77—Wrote *Anna Karenina*.

1894—Wrote *Master and Man*.

1896—Wrote *What Is Art*.

1899—Wrote *Resurrection*.

1901—Formally excommunicated by Russian Orthodox Church.

1910—Left home as wanderer. November 20, died at Astapova.

Paul Cézanne

1839–1906

A young couple walked along Rue Lafitte in December 1895. They were in the midst of a heated argument. As they were passing the window of a shop where a group of Impressionist paintings were on exhibition the man caught the arm of the girl. The girl struggled for a moment and screamed. "How *could* you upset me like this?" The man forced her to look at the picture in the window for a few seconds and then released his hold.

"*That*," he replied, "will teach you to be respectful to me from now on." By way of punishment for the quarrel the husband had compelled his wife to look at a painting of Paul Cézanne, *The Nude Bathers*.

Cézanne was only one of a school of artists who had lately sprung up to plague the art lovers in France. This school of Impressionists made a very poor impression. "People don't buy the Impressionists yet," remarked an old collector in 1895. "For they find them ugly. But you'll see—they'll come around to buying them, no matter how ugly they are. Perhaps they'll even hunt them down just *because* they are ugly, on the theory that that very quality will guarantee big prices in the future."

It took a long time, however, for the public to "come around" to Cézanne's work. At the age of twenty-seven he had sent his first painting to the Salon at Paris. He did not even receive a reply. He wrote the board a letter in haste and in anger. "I shall content myself with saying . . . that I cannot accept the ill-considered judgment of people whom I myself have not appointed to appraise me." He suggested that the board revive the former custom of exhibiting in the Salon des Refusées the paintings that had been rejected by the official Salon. In this way the public would become the judge. Cézanne got a reply to this suggestion. The board wrote him that it was beneath the dignity of art to re-establish such an institution.

Was it for such rebuffs that Paul Cézanne gave up his study of law and adopted the career of an artist, to his father's deep chagrin?

The Cézannes were solid countryfolk of Aix-en-Provence. The elder Cézanne, by dint of shrewd saving and hard work, had bought a small savings bank. When Paul was very young the father had given him a box of paints that he had purchased from a peddler. But he had no serious intention of making his boy an artist. It was all in fun. When Paul set about to paint in earnest and captured a second prize in school, Louis Auguste Cézanne was horrified. "Young man, young man, think of the future!" he cried. "With genius you die, with money you live!"

"But his name is Paul, isn't it?" persisted Mother Cézanne. She had dreams for her young son. Paul! Were not Veronese and Rubens named Paul?

The father, however, was obdurate. His son must be a lawyer, or at least a businessman. He entered him in the law school—but to no avail. Paul spent his leisure time putting the French legal code into verse. He shared his poetic dreams with another young man at the gymnasium in Paris. "Poetry is a great thing; there is no salvation but in poetry," said that young man. His name was Émile Zola. The future great novelist and the future great painter were close friends. Together they discussed politics, literature, and art—Socialism, De Musset, Hugo, Lamartine, Veronese, Rubens, Greuze. When, after a brief separation, the two met again Zola was beside himself with joy. "I've seen Paul!" he wrote to a mutual friend. "I've seen Paul! Do you realize all the melody that is contained in these three words?"

But Paul's father saw no melody in idle friendships and dreams. He called him to the bank at Aix-en-Provence. Paul stood at the counter and added figures. He passed money and stamped checks. A solid life! The father, however, was troubled with doubt.

> The banker, Cézanne, with fear in his eyes,
> Sees a painter-to-be from his counter arise.

The "painter-to-be" had too prodigal a temperament to be a lawyer or a banker. Hoarding money was not for him. At Paris he had scattered his coins to the winds. "Pardieu!" he had told the thrifty Zola, who had looked at him in amazement. "If I should die tonight, would you want my family to inherit the money?" Cézanne left the bank, threw away his lawbooks, and rejoined Zola in Paris.

II

HE WAS PRODIGAL in his art. Dogmatically he divided all art into "husky" and "emasculated" painting. He was "husky." He was young, reckless,

effervescent, unrestrained. He seized upon the husband of a woman who
kept a soup kitchen. The husband was a night watchman who slept in the
daytime. Cézanne induced him to pose in bed for him, painted him nude
and sent the work to the Salon—with the ill success which we have already
noted. Friends saw in his canvases nothing but a "dumping ground for
paint." He was fond of spilling buckets of color upon canvas, they said.
And Cézanne heartily agreed with them. What else could you expect from
a fellow who was famous for wearing a red vest and for having enough
money in his pocket to buy his friends a good dinner? He squandered
cash and color. Confident? He had no use for the art critics, "the professors
of daubery." A friend said, "Now that your painting has been refused at
the Salon, what are you going to send them next?" "A pot of—" replied
Cézanne. He had no use for the fashionable artists. When he was introduced to a group of them at the Café Guerbois he said to their leader:
"You primp yourselves up like a pack of lawyers. You're not worth a cent!"

But he loved the masters. He visited the Louvre daily and copied their
works. It was the Venetians he especially revered. The great Venetians,
with their spendthrift colors. Unnatural? Of course! Better than Nature!
He recalled a conversation he had had with his father. "My dear Paul," his
father had said, "what good can painting do you? How can you hope to
improve on what Nature has already done so divinely? You must be very,
very stupid!" Very stupid indeed! "If I were you," Paul had replied, "I
wouldn't worry about Nature, so long as Nature isn't worrying about your
bank."

To paint Nature, to *improve* upon Nature, *that* was the business of Cézanne. His eyes were dazzled by the flesh colors of Rubens and the Baroque
school. To him their world was the world of a giant dream. And—as he soon
came to realize—a dream beyond his grasp. Great visions were for people
who had eyes to see. But he had not those eyes. The truth, this fatal defect
of his, struck him with a sudden force as he sat in the Louvre copying the
epics of Tintoretto, the pastorals of Rubens. He had the feeling for color,
but he lacked the instinct for form. His eyes were unable to recognize a
three-dimensional space. It was as if he were invited to a banquet and all
his hunger for the lavishly displayed dishes were nullified by his constitutional inability to sense their taste. At art school his teacher had said of
him, "Cézanne has the proper temperament for a colorist; unfortunately
he has no ability for composition." He must set up a new style of his own;
he must write a new language; he must turn all the old theories of
aesthetics topsy-turvy and formulate an entirely new art on an entirely
new basis to fit the idiosyncrasies of his genius. Or else he must go back to
the bank and spend his life stamping checks.

III

THE WAR OF 1870 between France and Germany struck like a bolt out of the blue. France lost. The Socialists rose in rebellion, and Émile Zola wrote: "Cézanne, a new Paris is about to be born. It is our turn now!" Cézanne thought Zola was too sanguine. He joked about his friend's naïve optimism. Yet Émile Zola was right, at least so far as he himself was concerned. It *was* his turn now. He was to become a rich and famous writer, idolized by the smart set of his "new Paris." Cézanne, however, was destined to live a life of retirement and to endure many years of abuse from the critics of this selfsame Paris. For the one it was to be a new era of happiness and hope. For the other, the old era of despair. "When I behold that my house has not budged an inch, that my garden is just the same as it ever was," Zola wrote after the siege of Paris, "I am at last able to persuade myself that the two sieges are nothing but 'bogyman's stories.'" Not a chair in his house had been moved; not a plant in his garden had suffered! This was Zola's Paris, and he built cunningly upon its revolutionary tradition. But for Cézanne, postwar France was a nightmare. He had not gone back to his father's bank. Instead he had begun to develop a style of painting all his own, built around the strength and the weakness of his peculiar genius. He adopted a proud and independent credo: "Here is my work; I know you don't like it. If you come into my studio to buy it, so much the worse for you; no money refunded." He became interested in the work of those *enfants terribles*, Pissarro and Manet, and in Dr. Gachet, an eccentric old art collector who had the audacity to mother them. And he became the most abused painter of the day.

Very few men in the history of art have attained the notoriety of disrepute that was Paul Cézanne's. His bad fame grew by leaps and bounds in the years that followed the Franco-Prussian War. Paris for him had developed into an unholy nightmare, though it sounded with a salvo of hosannahs for his old friend Zola. Cézanne sat at the café and talked shop with a few people who tolerated him. The "new Paris" found him a man in his early thirties, married, with a little son. Was it disconcerting to him that he had spent three decades of his life doing nothing that might bring him fame? A friend once entered his studio and was assailed "by huge canvases hung everywhere, so frightfully colored" that he stood "petrified." A parrot in the room screamed out, "*Cézanne is a great painter! Cézanne is a great painter!*" "My art critic," said Cézanne, pointing to the bird with a smile.

At last an acquaintance of Cézanne's, a man who professed to admire the badly drawn, brilliantly colored artistic curiosities of Cézanne's new art, bought one of his canvases—a study of nude bathers in which every rule and proportion of the female body had been violated. This purchaser, Choquet by name, did not dare bring the painting home to his wife.

Finally he suggested that a third person, a friend of the family, should pay a visit to him with the canvas, under the pretense of showing it to him, and that he should then, "absent-mindedly," leave it with him. The ruse worked, and the nudes entered Choquet's house for permanent residence.

As time went on Choquet became a genuine disciple of Cézanne's work and urged all his friends to buy his canvases. He never succeeded in making a single sale, however. One day, to be sure, he managed to force a small painting as a gift upon one of his acquaintances, but he prefaced his offer with the timid remark, "I am not asking you to bring it into your house, of course."

"I should hope not!" replied the recipient of the unwelcome gift.

Cézanne was a man with an imperfect vision. There was something always lurking behind the landscapes he tried to paint—something he never was to grasp. The initiated whispered that he did not have the simple powers of an ordinary draughtsman—and they whispered something like the truth. Yet he possessed the undying fire that made him carry on with his strange lack of gifts and his strange hidden powers. He worked obstinately. Once in a while he caught a glimpse of the Promised Land. Would he be like the great Leader of the Hebrews—forced by the Lord to retire from his pilgrimage just when he was about to arrive at the fulfillment of his dream?

IV

His FRIENDSHIP with Zola had progressed badly. Zola had become an artistic success; Cézanne was an artistic failure. Zola's books sold in the hundred thousands; Cézanne could not give away his pictures. Zola sat in his luxurious parlor and pondered occasionally, with an exaggerated theatrical sadness, upon the companionship of their younger days. Now they had drifted apart. It was not that any harsh words had ever passed between them. One fine day Cézanne stopped coming to see Zola, that was all. He was no longer at ease in Zola's house, with the fine servants, the splendid rugs and the self-satisfied complaisant Émile sitting at his luxurious desk. Émile had become a bourgeois. The maid had looked daggers every time Paul had failed to wipe his shoes on the mat before entering the drawing room. And then one day the great man of letters passed through Paul's native town of Aix on a lecture tour. When Cézanne heard of Zola's arrival he was painting in the fields. He threw down his palette and forgot about his painting, forgot about his troubles, his bitterness, his defeats. Zola was in Aix! His old friend! He hastened to Émile's hotel, overjoyed. The coolness he had felt for him was a thing of the past. But on the way he met a friend who told him, "No use—do not go to the hotel." On the previous day someone had asked Zola, now that he was in Aix, whether he would not take a meal with Cézanne before he left. And Zola had answered that he had no desire to see that "dead one again."

Cézanne's eyes filled with tears. "The money-bloated idiot!" he raged, shaking his fist. He went back to his friendless paintings.

Then, suddenly, Cézanne's paintings began to sell. The younger set of artists in Paris, always on the lookout for something novel and something sensational, had acquired a new insight into Cézanne's master puzzles. They began to see "genius" where they had seen nothing before. A new religion was founded, and Cézanne was hailed as its prophet. Cézanne himself was slightly deaf, and he had to cup his hand behind his ear to catch the shouting of his newborn disciples. "Well, well," he remarked with a smile. "So they are putting my pictures into frames at last."

His neighbors in the province of Aix were amazed that his paintings were beginning to sell in Paris. Here in Aix Cézanne had for years offered his canvases to anybody who would come and get them. Unable to dispose of them in this way, he had abandoned a good many of them in the fields. Once Renoir had picked up a water-color sketch of *Bathers* that Cézanne had thrown away on the rocks. In the storeroom at Aix lay a rubbish heap of Cézanne's paintings, together with a broken bird cage, a cracked chamber pot, an old syringe. Friends, not wishing to insult the artist, had taken a few of the paintings for gifts and hidden them away in attics for the rats to eat. There now began an unholy scramble to recover these half-consumed "masterpieces." One old codger sold a small study which Cézanne had once given him as a token of friendship and retired from business on the price he got for it.

Cézanne was amused at the sudden stir he was making among the intelligentsia. A pack of idiots, he thought. Painting meant far more to him than fame. A pox upon those who praised him. A pox upon those who vituperated him. It was enough; he was Paul Cézanne, and he could tell this to any rude fellow he bumped on the street. What did the opinion of others matter to him?

As for his own estimate of his work, he was still painfully dissatisfied. Somehow he felt unable to express the intensity which beat upon his senses. Look at all the clouds, all the magnificent shapes and colors of Nature that he wanted to paint. Monet could; he had muscle. "Monet has not only muscle, but vision," he would murmur to himself. "And I?—I don't seem to possess the power to see."

V

CÉZANNE lived an almost celibate existence. Apart from his wife, women were to him "damn cats." Men he generally distrusted also. He suffered from a persecution mania. He felt that people were "trying to get their hooks into him." He hated the conventional professions. Teachers were stupid old women; scholars were asses. He even began to hate the old conventional painters—the men he had once so ardently admired. Rembrandt and Rubens, he said, should be "spat upon." When crowds stood before a masterpiece in the Louvre he felt like "blowing his nose and leaving the room." As the years wore on he became more and more of a misanthrope. The robust little peasant with the broad-brimmed hat, the heavy black beard, the solid step became, if you took his table talk seriously, the archhater of mankind and especially of the Salon that still refused to recognize his work. He was a curious mixture of self-depreciation and vulgar swagger. When Whistler, after looking at some of his landscapes, remarked, "If a six-year-old had drawn that on his slate his mother, if she were a good mother, would have given him a thorough spanking," Cézanne was enraged and hurt. His faith in himself was sadly shattered. And yet he blustered his way through the little streets of Aix, elbowing the sleepy villagers and shouting in proud defiance, "I am Cézanne!"

VI

On october 22, 1906, very few would have hazarded the statement that a great artist had just died. One painter, Henry Hamm, summed up the attitude of the majority when he wrote of Cézanne's work: "Its evident sincerity intrigues me; its clumsiness astonishes me." A decade before his death the *Revue d'Art* had published a searching though not altogether unfriendly analysis of Cézanne's work by George Leonte. "Because Cézanne has no other guide but his instincts," wrote Leonte, "he gropes, he hesitates . . . Can he really paint landscapes? He grasps their character, their color, their light . . . but he runs aground in the art of separating his planes and in giving the illusion of distance." Another contemporary critic spoke of the "awkwardness" of his design, the "heaviness" of his color. Still another critic summed up the general impression by calling Cézanne a workman of "remarkable gifts, but of troubled vision; not unskillful but made to appear unskillful by some manual infirmity." He had ideas, but he was incapable of expressing them, for "he seems not to know even the first principles of his craft." Two years before his death the air had not cleared. Some writers threw up their hands and confessed that Monsieur Cézanne was a painter whom the world would never be able to understand. Others, however, retorted: "Cézanne is not misunderstood; he is just incomplete." The man had a "fatal lack of facility." Most people criticized in whispers, for Cézanne had a "gang" of fanatical admirers, rough and ready to "beat up" anybody who was insolent enough to express his contempt for Cézanne's Chamber of Horrors. Cézanne, insisted these enthusiastic disciples, was a great, inspired, admirable painter. And the intimidated public agreed, but with the mental reservation—"The most admirable thing in his life was his perseverance in painting badly."

For a number of years a battle of bitter words has raged around the interpretation of Cézanne's art. His admirers have won out in the long run. Today Cézanne is an acknowledged master. The revolutionary qualities of his art, which repelled his contemporaries, are now generally regarded as the "auroral flushes" of a new era in painting.

What are these revolutionary qualities of Cézanne's art?

For one thing, there is an impersonal objectivity to his paintings—a complete detachment of the artist from his work, a characteristic which is at first sight disconcerting. All his landscapes seem to be represented in a strange absence of wind, of rustling foliage, of the play of light and shadow which make a scene alive, moving, real. The organic life is motionless. The atmosphere is rigid. It is as if the Creator had stopped breathing on the world He had made. Indeed, the "breath of life" is entirely absent from his scenes. Cézanne particularly shone in his painting of still life. The very characteristics which give the still-life objects of food and tableware firmness and grandeur appear, when applied to landscapes and people, rather confusing. Cézanne, when he painted a portrait, would tell the subject "to sit like an apple." "You wretch," he told Vollard one day, while he was doing his portrait, "you've spoiled the pose. Do I have to tell you again that you must sit like an apple? Does an apple move?"

Then, too, there is a neutral, timeless lighting, just as there is a neutral, motionless rigidity, to the paintings of Cézanne. The atmosphere that we see in a canvas by Corot, or by any of the other great interpreters of Nature, is surcharged with light and shadow; it glows with the green of foliage or with the blue of mountains in perspective. But a Cézanne landscape is completely devoid of atmospheric color in this sense. It is as if he did all his painting under a leaden gray sky.

But, most important of all, the illusion of space and perspective, which is the A B C of any elementary course in art, is completely disregarded in Cézanne. Small wonder that the critics grew red in the face when they first saw his pictures! There is no feeling of distance, no proper foreshortening of objects, no tension of planes, none of those conventional tricks which give an illustration its essential verisimilitude. In other words, there is no illusion of a three-dimensional reality in Cézanne's pictures. Cézanne revolutionized the entire intellectual conception of art, which had regarded distance and perspective as the primary values in the composition of painting. According to Cézanne, the primary quality in a painting is not perspective, but *structural form*. He does not see objects in relation to one another. "Everything in Nature," he said, "is an isolated cylinder or an isolated cube." The spectator finds it difficult to enter into Cézanne's dimension, for the simple reason that there is no such space dimension in his paintings. His "space" is completely independent of the body of his objects. All his objects, whether near or far, are massed together into an unrelated heap of sharply contrasted tints. The eye, according to Cézanne, cannot really see space. All it can see is structural form. And structural form, maintains Cézanne, depends not upon linear design but upon a solidity of color. The shapes of objects are obtained by a balancing of the adjacent areas of color. Cézanne created volumes of color with an authority that gives a monumental solidity to his work. He strips design to its primitive essentials. For him, design forms merely a line of demarcation between two patches of color. Cézanne aimed for an architectural logic beneath the ripple of atmospheric light. He sought for essential structural ideas that had existed in eternity long before the artists had come to earth. All artists, he thought, made the mistake of painting what they saw and calling it reality. He wanted to catch the true reality beneath the appearance, the true order of form that only the intellect but not the eye can comprehend. His still-life subjects gave him an ideal opportunity for his experiments. The most famous of his still-life paintings is the *Compotier*. A group of apples, a knife, a napkin, a fruit bowl and a glass half filled with water are placed on a tablecloth. These objects are so solidly drawn that each seems to rest infallibly in its position, as if ordained to stay there by the Creator. The painted apples are much clumsier and denser than any real apples. The napkin and the knife are drawn in a rectangular sweep. The fruit bowl and the glass of water are heavy oblongs. If one does not appreciate the hand writing of the artist, the picture seems awkward and ill drawn. Never theless there is a simple, logical relationship between the *colors* of the several objects. These colors are applied in a series of small, solid parallel strokes of the brush. They lie across the surface of the canvas without any regard for the contour of the forms. This painting, remarked one of Cézanne's admirers, may lack the illusion of life, but it contains the truth of eternity. To which a skeptic may reply, with Pontius Pilate, "But what is the truth?" Is the elemental solidity of Cézanne's studies in still life a glimpse of eternity or is it merely the result of a constitutional defect in Cézanne's vision? To answer this question categorically one must be more than an art critic; one must be a seer.

The same approach to the elemental, the same qualities of solidity that one finds in Cézanne's pictures of still life may be found also in his portraits. He approaches his subjects in a remarkably primitive manner. In his portrait of Madame Cézanne, for example, the model faces us squarely. She sits directly in the center of the canvas, rigidly upright. As if to set all the laws of composition at defiance, the chair she sits on is stiff and rectangular, giving a severe vertical sweep to the picture. The entire canvas possesses the symmetry of an Egyptian obelisk, a painted metaphor of monumental stability.

We find the same monumental stability—or, as his detractors would say, the same graceless incoherency—in his landscapes and his group paintings. His houses, his rivers, his mountains, his trees, his grass, his people—all his objects seem to defy not only the accepted physical but even the chemical and the mental and the moral laws of creation. But this, said Cézanne, is the sort of world we live in.

Whether Cézanne saw better than his fellow artists or was merely the victim of an eye disease that distorted the world in his sight will remain a moot question. But whatever the critics may say about the design of Cézanne's paintings, they are pretty unanimously agreed about his color effects. In the world of color Cézanne stands among the very great. As a young man he had set himself the task to excel Nature in the magic of her tints. In this task, most of his critics admit, he succeeded.

IMPORTANT DATES IN THE LIFE OF PAUL CÉZANNE

1839—January 19, born at Aix-en-Provence, France.
1863—Followed his friend, Émile Zola, to Paris.
1872-73—Came under the influence of the Impressionists.
1874—Exhibited with Renoir and Pissarro.
1877—Entered 17 paintings in one exhibition.

1879—Retired to Aix for remainder of life.
1880—Started on road to new style, resulting in his being called "the Father of Modernism."
1886—Married Hortense Fiquet. Inherited father's fortune.
1906—October 22, died at Aix-en-Provence.

William James

1842–1910

HIS GRANDFATHER, an Irish immigrant, was a practical man of the world. His father, an intimate of Emerson, was a freethinking mystic. Take the practicality of the grandfather and the mysticism of the father, add to them a pinch of Irish humor and a generous dose of American forthrightness, and you have the combination that was the personality of William James.

He was born (January 9, 1842) at the Astor House in New York City, and he lived in or near big cities for the greater part of his life. His attitude toward the world, therefore, was colored by his conception of the earth as a "parcel of nature crowded with company."

He loved company from his earliest childhood. And in spite of the easy circumstances of his family he was not snobbish in his attitude toward his companions. To a youngster who boasted about the exclusiveness of his playmates he declared, "I play with boys who curse and swear!"

He was an active youngster—in sharp contrast with his brother Henry, who was a quiet and contemplative little fellow. Since both of them showed an early aptitude for literature the friends of the family predicted that William would take up fiction as his field and that Henry would choose philosophy. It turned out just the other way around. To some extent, however, the prophets were correct. William James developed into a philosopher who wrote like a novelist, and Henry James developed into a novelist who wrote like a philosopher.

As to their early preparation for their respective careers, both William and Henry regarded it as a waste of time. In their effort to provide their children with the best education available their parents took them to Europe and enrolled them in one school after another—in London, Paris, Boulogne-sur-Mer, Geneva, Bonn. Always they sought for "the one perfect channel of truth" in which to bathe the precocious minds of the two youngsters. The result of this eclectic education was that the boys learned "a little of everything and not much of anything."

They did, however, acquire a facility in language which enabled them to devour all sorts of books on every conceivable subject. Thus their minds were trained to resemble long-distance swimmers rather than skillful divers. They were able to cover wide horizons of experience though they were incapable of plunging into the depths of the world's mysteries.

The mind of William James especially was ever restless, ever eager for adventure, ever curious for the new landscape before it had become thoroughly familiar with the old. His interests were so manifold that he found it difficult to make a final choice among them. And so he sampled every intellectual and artistic dish that was offered to his healthy appetite, dabbling in biology, anatomy, philosophy, chemistry, physics, natural history, and even painting. And in spite of his intellectual pursuits—or rather because of his intellectual curiosity—he managed always to find plenty of time for his social activities. In 1860 he joined the Swiss students' club, Société de Zoffingue, where he showed an active interest in its debates and a somewhat more passive though no less fascinated interest in its debaucheries. In the social parlance of the day, William James was "a hail-fellow-well-met" young specimen of the dynamic nineteenth century.

His dynamic versatility, however, must somehow be co-ordinated into a unified profession. It was not in his nature to drift aimlessly through life. He must now choose definitely between art and science. He chose science, entering the Lawrence Scientific School (Harvard University) in 1861.

But he had given up his brush only to become a painter with the pen. For few writers in the history of philosophy have been blessed with a more colorful style.

II

THOUGH he had decided upon a scientific career, William James was still uncertain as to the particular branch of science that he wanted to adopt as his life's work. For a time he thought of chemistry. But then his interest shifted to medicine. He entered the Harvard Medical School, took his degree, and then quit medicine for natural history. He joined the Brazilian expedition of Professor Louis Agassiz, a man whom he admired more than any other of his teachers. "Since Benjamin Franklin," he wrote many years later, "we had never had among us a person of more popularly impressive type."

Together with Agassiz he studied the fishes of the Amazon. And under the influence of Agassiz he learned to regard the objects of natural history as the "translation into human language of the thoughts of the Creator."

The philosophic scientist of Harvard had transformed the young naturalist into a scientific philosopher.

When he returned to the United States William James had a pretty clear idea as to the future course of his life. He would write and, if possible, teach philosophy. He attended a philosophical lecture by Charles S. Peirce, a man who was trying to introduce a new system of thought called *pragmatism*. "I couldn't understand a word of the lecture," said James, "but I felt that it had a definite message for me." He was to spend the rest of his life in the effort to understand and to interpret this "definite message" of pragmatism.

Before he entered upon this work, however, he underwent a physical breakdown and a siege of mental depression. For a time he thought of committing suicide. "No man," he said in later life, "is psychologically complete unless he has at least once in his life meditated on self-destruction." He took a trip to Europe for his physical and his mental health and within a few months was so completely recovered that he was able to "flirt in Bohemian" with his landlady's daughter. He had brought along with him his American democracy—or was it his Irish sense of humor? —for he accepted a "social" invitation to dine with an innkeeper's family. The talk, he said, was salty enough, but the soup tasted like the "perspiration of pigs."

On his return to America he was appointed instructor of physiology at Harvard College. From physiology he moved to psychology and from psychology to philosophy. These successive steps from one academic department to another were quite in keeping with the steps of his own mental development. For his intellectual progress was not "from the sky down, but from the ground up." Like Socrates, he was more interested in the problems of men than he was in the Providence of God. Not that he was skeptical about God. On the contrary, he found himself "less and less able," as he wrote to his friend Thomas Davidson, "to get along without Him." His main preoccupation, however, was with the Here rather than with the Hereafter. His philosophy grew out of his own needs. He had suffered a serious illness and he had "pulled himself back" into health. Man's salvation depended upon his own will. In the course of his reading during his sickness he had come upon the *Essais* of Renouvier, and he had been struck with the French thinker's definition of Free Will —"the sustaining of a thought because one *actively chooses* to sustain it when he might have other thoughts." William James had chosen to sustain the thought of becoming well. He had *willed* himself out of sickness. "From now on I will abstain from speculation and depend upon action." For action is the human will transformed into life.

This was but a continuation of Emerson's philosophy of optimism. But James added something to it. Or rather he modified it. He transformed the somewhat impractical idea of optimism, the theory that all's well with the world, into the more practical idea of *meliorism*, the theory that all's *not* well with the world but that we can make things better *if we will*. It was an excellent philosophy for America at that period (1872), for the country had just entered upon its golden era of expansion. It was the industrial age of Rockefeller, Carnegie, Gould, Harriman, Drew, Cook and J. P. Morgan. William James was one of those fortunate children of destiny—the right man born into the right time. He came as the prophet of the Free Will to a free nation.

Thus far, however, his philosophy was still in its seedling stage. He had no opportunity to develop it further at this time because he was asked to write a textbook on psychology for Henry Holt's American Science Series. He expected to produce the book within two years. It was twelve years before the manuscript was finished.

In the meantime he met, wooed, and married Miss Alice Gibbens. Legend has it that his father, Henry James the elder, had first seen her at the Radical Club in Boston and had exclaimed upon his return home, "William, I have just met the woman you're going to marry!" Whereupon the young philosopher, resenting his father's interference in his private affairs, replied, "I shall refuse to see that woman." "I don't care whether or not you *see* her," retorted his father. "All I want you to do is to *marry* her."

In spite of his rebellious rejoinder to his father's suggestion James did manage to see Miss Gibbens. And he fell a willing prey to "the great dark luminous eyes, soft brown hair, wild-rose complexion . . . and especially the smile which lit up her face and seemed to light up the world."

His marriage worked a miracle in his health—and in his habits. "She saved me from my *Zerrissenheit* (torn-to-pieces-ness) and gave me back to myself all in one piece." He had now found his mate and his métier. He settled down in Cambridge and devoted himself for the rest of his life to the cultivation of his philosophy.

III

HIS FIRST BOOK, *The Principles of Psychology*, marks the formal transition from William James the scientist to William James the philosopher. For this book is more valuable as a masterpiece of literary abstractions than as a repository of concrete facts. James cared very little for the objective phenomena of the mind, but he cared very much for the subjective personality to whom the mind belonged. His psychology, therefore, is a study of persons and not of data. Human thought, to William James, was not a mechanically connected series of separate ideas—a doctrine of the European psychologists—but a continuously flowing stream of consciousness analogous to the blood stream that flows continuously through the body.

Furthermore, said James, the study of human consciousness must be subordinated to the study of human conduct. Psychology is a preface to

Morality. "The physiological study of mental conditions is . . . the most powerful ally of hortatory ethics."

The mind, in brief, is not a material but a spiritual instrument. It is not a recorder but a prompter of our ideas. It is our teacher and guide toward a freer, juster, and better world.

And this brings James back to his philosophy of *betterment* or *meliorism*. Let us at the outset, he said, admit the fact that the world is full of evil. But precisely because of this fact we find our life worth while. For the presence of evil has given us our most precious possession—hope. Hope is that moral activity which prompts us to challenge and to conquer evil. It gives us the courage "to take life strivingly." The philosophers who declare that the world is growing better *regardless* of our will are equally wrong with those who maintain that the world will remain bad *in spite* of our will. We alone can improve the world, and we can do it *because* of our will.

For this world is not a finished unit but "an aggregation of separate and contradictory elements." And here we come to the second point in James's philosophy—his *pluralism*. The world is not a *uni-verse* but a *multi-verse*—a conflict of currents, some good, some evil. We must all of us try to conquer the evil and to establish the good. Is success certain? No. Is it possible? Decidedly yes. But if success is only possible at best, what is the good of striving? To this question James gives an answer which is not unlike that of the ancient Stoics. The mere chance of succeeding ennobles the struggle and makes it worth while. "Suppose," writes James, "that the world's author put the case to you before creation, saying: 'I am going to make a world not certain to be saved, a world the perfection of which shall be conditioned merely, the condition being that each several agent does its own *level best*. I offer you the chance of taking part in such a world. Its safety, you see, is unwarranted. It is a real adventure, with real danger, yet it may win through. . . . Will you join the procession? Will you trust yourself and trust the other agents enough to face the risk?'

"Should you in all seriousness . . . feel bound to reject the offer as not safe enough? . . . If you are normally constituted, you would do nothing of the sort. There is a healthy-minded buoyancy in most of us which such a universe would exactly fit. . . . It would be just like the world we practically live in, and loyalty to our old nurse Nature would forbid us to say no."

This is the old Stoic doctrine plus the modern American spirit. It is joy to fight the good fight even though the outcome may be in doubt. And after all, though the issue may be uncertain for the individual, it is pretty certain to be victorious for the race. For we have an efficient ally on our side—God. In the pluralistic philosophy of James, God is not supreme. He is merely one among many divine forces, "one helper . . . in the midst of all the shapers of the great world's fate." But he is "*primus inter pares*," first among equals. He is our teacher, our leader, our friend in the glorious struggle for a better world.

Let us then, with God's help, struggle gallantly on. Let us shape the world to our needs. Let us, in other words, live a *practical* life. And this is the third and cardinal point in James's philosophy—his *pragmatism*. The world we live in is not a theory but a fact. Indeed, it is a conglomeration of many facts. There is no such thing as *the* truth. What we call a truth is merely a working hypothesis, a temporary tool that enables us to transform a bit of chaos into a bit of order. What was true yesterday—that is, what was *helpful* yesterday—may not be true today. Old truths, like old weapons, tend to grow rusty and to become useless.

It is therefore impractical to try to reduce the universe to an "absolutely single fact." Truth is relative. Everything depends upon our individual point of view, and none of us has the right to say that *his* point of view is the only correct one. "Neither the whole of truth nor the whole of good is revealed to any single observer, although each observer gains a partial superiority of insight from the peculiar position in which he stands." And that superiority of insight which every individual has gained for himself is his own best tool in the struggle for the betterment of the world. Each man's faith, each man's church, each man's God is for him true if it enables him to cope with his legitimate daily problems.

That alone, therefore, is true which is expedient in practice. An idea is good only if it has a "cash value." Let us not, however, confuse the "cash value" pragmatism of William James with the crass materialism of our modern business life. The coinage of James's philosophical capital was not financial but moral. He looked down upon the mad scramble of his contemporaries for the accumulation of mere wealth. He scolded his fellow Americans for their worship of "that bitch goddess, success." His pragmatism was an ethical and therefore a practical urge to coöperation among the free members of a democratic society. The meaning of life, he believed, lies not in an isolated struggle as between man and man but in a united struggle of mankind against the forces of evil.

Pragmatism, said James, has no use for abstractions. It deals only with "concrete realities." It is not, strictly speaking, a system of philosophy. It is rather a "method for getting at the practical consequences" of all the philosophical systems. To quote the Italian philosopher Papini, James's pragmatism is "a collection of attitudes, and its chief characteristic is its armed neutrality in the midst of doctrines. It is like a corridor in a hotel, from which a hundred doors open into a hundred chambers. In one you may see a man on his knees praying to regain his faith; in another, a desk at which sits someone eager to destroy all metaphysics; in a third, a laboratory with an investigator looking for new footholds by which to advance toward wider horizons. But the corridor belongs to all."

IV

The corridor belongs to all. This is the very heart of James's philosophy. It was not his purpose to set himself up as the founder of a new school but as a guide for the practical interpretation of the old schools. He did not want to be a master, and he asked for no disciples. Again and again he quoted to his students the passage from Ezekiel: "Son of Man, stand upon thy feet and I will speak to thee." Let each man live upon his own spiritual capital. Let each one abide by his own truth. All that James was interested in doing was to stimulate man's mind, to release man's will, and to encourage man's action. Above all, he wanted to widen man's interests. For he himself was a man of wide interests. His own stream of consciousness embraced a large part of the general stream of life. He raised his voice against the unjust oppression of Dreyfus; he advocated a more equitable distribution of wealth; he threw himself actively into every sort of movement for human welfare; and he was foremost in urging a moral equivalent for war—that is, a concerted effort to abolish disease, to drain marshes, to build canals, and to reclaim wastelands instead of an organized fight to kill men. In short, he wanted to open to others, as he had opened to himself, "the entire universe as an adventure." And he made the universe a familiar landscape, illuminating it to his students with the sudden flash of understanding, the happy phrase, the Socratic jest. "This universe," he said in one of his lectures, "will never be completely good as long as one being is unhappy, as long as one poor cockroach suffers the pangs of unrequited love."

He always tried to make his ideas picturesque, concrete, alive. He classified them in such a manner that his hearers might tuck them away in their minds like the neatly folded articles of clothing in a wardrobe, to be taken out for use at a moment's notice without any confusion or fumbling. For example, in describing the attitude of various types of people toward the world he divided them into the *tough-minded* and the *tender-minded*. The tough-minded, he said, are the hardheaded businessmen, the builders, the political leaders, the realists, the men who act. The tender-minded, on the other hand, are the softhearted visionaries, the dreamers, the poets, the artists, the idealists, the men who think. James himself was an example of neither one of these extreme types. Instead he was an admirable synthesis of the two. He was *healthy-minded*.

He had a healthy mind but not in a healthy body. Throughout his adult life he suffered from a weak heart. During one of his summer vacations he lost his way in the Adirondacks. He overexerted himself in his effort to find the road, and when he finally arrived home he collapsed.

Although he recovered from this illness, he was never himself again. In 1907 he resigned from the Harvard faculty owing to his poor health. He lived just long enough to make a tour of Europe. He meant this to be a quiet and undisturbed health trip, but it turned out to be an exciting procession of triumph. Everywhere they followed the "great Professor Weelyam Yams" with acclamation, and everywhere they insisted upon his public appearance.

The ordeal proved too much for his weakened heart. When he boarded the boat to return to America (in the summer of 1910) everybody knew that his days were numbered.

As he neared the end of his journey he sank back into his steamer chair and whispered, "It is so good to get home!"

IMPORTANT DATES IN THE LIFE OF WILLIAM JAMES

1842—January 11, born in New York City.

1860—Studied art under William M. Hunt.

1861—Entered Lawrence Scientific Harvard University.

1861–68—Studied medicine, psychology and philosophy.

1869—Received M.D. degree at Harvard Medical School.

1869–72—Unable to practice owing to illness.

1872—Appointed instructor of physiology, anatomy and hygiene at Harvard University.

1876—Established first laboratory of psychological research.

1877—Appointed assistant professor of philosophy.

1878—Married Alice H. Gibbens.

1880–91—Wrote *The Principles of Psychology*.

1884—Helped found the American Society for Psychical Research.

1889—Named professor of psychology.

1897—Named professor of philosophy.

1897—Wrote *The Will to Believe*.

1898—Wrote *Human Immortality*.

1899—Suffered heart attack.

1902—Wrote *The Varieties of Religious Experience*.

1906—Published his famous *Pragmatism*.

1907—Gave his final course in philosophy at Harvard.

1910—Sailed in the spring, with wife, for a health cure at Nauheim.

Returned, uncured, in the summer.

August 26, died at Chocorua, New Hampshire.

Thomas Alva Edison

1847–1931

Genius is the ability to do the hardest things the easiest way. One day, when Edison was working on a practical lamp for his newly discovered electric light, he found it necessary to get the cubical content of an irregular glass bulb. Too busy himself to attend to the job, he called in his most brilliant mathematician to help him. Arming himself with many sheets of foolscap, the great savant sat down to work. A week later Edison asked him how he was getting along.

"Very nicely, Mr. Edison, but I am not finished yet."

Edison looked at the formidable array of charts and figures submitted by the mathematician. "How much longer will it take you to solve the problem?"

"Oh, another week, I expect."

"Let me show you how to do it in a minute," said Edison.

He filled the bulb with water.

"Now measure the water, and you've got the answer."

II

Edison possessed not only a knack for hitting upon the obvious, but an infinite capacity for taking pains. In his effort to perfect the storage battery, he had made ten thousand unsuccessful tests on various chemical combinations. "Isn't it a shame," said a friend, "that with all this tremendous labor you haven't been able to get any results?"

"Why, man," said Edison, "I've got lots of results. I've discovered several thousand things that won't work."

Edison came by his energy from a stock of sturdy pioneers who were forever seeking for the things that worked through the discarding of things that would not work. His great-grandfather, John Edison, fled from Staten Island to Nova Scotia in order to escape hanging as a Tory in the Revolutionary War. His grandfather, Samuel Edison, migrated from Nova Scotia in search of a better home and found it on the banks of the Otter River, in Upper Canada. His father, Samuel Edison—"a giant of a man" —became involved in a plot to overthrow the Tory regime in Canada and to replace it with a representative government like that of the United States. The plot was discovered, and "Sammy" Edison made his escape across trackless forests and icebound rivers—"it was my long legs that saved me"—until he found safety in the village of Milan, Ohio. Here he set up a mill and sent for his family through the kindly offices of a barge captain by the name of Alva Bradley. And here, in the midst of a blizzard on the morning of February 11, 1847, he greeted the arrival of his seventh child, a son. They christened the baby Thomas Alva—the second name in honor of Mr. Bradley.

From his very infancy Alva was preoccupied, ingenious, and ready to "learn something about everything." At six he set his father's barn on fire "just to see what it would do." It burned down to the ground, and almost burned Alva along with it. For this, the first of his experiments, his father punished him with a public spanking in the village square.

On another occasion he tried sitting on a nest of goose eggs to see if he could hatch them. All that he hatched was an omelet on the seat of his pants. Another spanking, another discovery of the things that would not work.

His entire childhood was a succession of experiments. When he was seven years old his parents moved to Port Huron, Michigan. The new Edison home had a lofty tower overlooking Lake Huron and the St. Clair River. Young Alva—Al for short—spent a great part of his time scanning the horizon through an old telescope perched on top of the tower.

Watching the heavens above, and studying the elements below. In the cellar of his house he had set up a chemical laboratory with "Poison Don't Touch" labels on all the bottles, in order to keep them away from inquisitive fingers.

"An addled youngster," said the neighbors. One day he fed an enormous quantity of seidlitz powders to his little Dutch playmate, Michael Oates. "Why did you do it, son?" asked his father. "Well, Pop," said Alva, "I wanted to see if the seidlitz powders would form enough gas in his stomach to make him fly."

The children left him alone to his "crazy" games. The elders shook their heads. Even his father thought there was something queer about him. The only one who believed in him was his mother. She encouraged him in his experiments, and on his ninth birthday she bought him a copy of Parker's *School of Natural Philosophy*. "The greatest present I ever received," said Edison of this book many years later.

He used this book not only as a basis for his experiments but as a stimulant to his imagination. And he fed his healthy imagination on many another volume. By his tenth birthday he had familiarized himself with such works as Hume's *History of England*, Sears' *History of the World*, Burton's *Anatomy of Melancholy*, Gibbon's *Decline and Fall of the Roman Empire*, and the *Dictionary of Sciences*.

Yet Al Edison was no bookworm. On the contrary, he was a very practical youngster. When the railroad was built between Port Huron and Detroit, he applied for a job as "news-butcher" on the train. A "merchant on his own" at twelve, he was not content with only one occupation. In his spare moments, when he had finished peddling his newspapers, he busied himself in the baggage car, writing and printing a newspaper of his own, or in a chemical laboratory which he had set up in another car. This laboratory, incidentally, cost him his job on the train and thus indirectly led to his study of telegraphy and to his first invention. One day, as the train was bumping over a rough road, a stick of phosphorus from Edison's pile of chemicals fell to the floor and set fire to the baggage car. The conductor extinguished the flames and kicked Edison out of his railroad laboratory into the bigger laboratory of the world.

Al Edison—at that time he pronounced his name *Eadison*—was not sorry to lose his job as a news peddler. In his daily trips from city to city he had become acquainted with the telegraph operators at the railroad stations. Their work fascinated him. He decided to become one of them. Devoting as many as eighteen hours a day to practice, he soon mastered the job, stretched a wire between the drugstore and the depot at Port Huron, and set himself up as a "private merchant of local messages." But the businessmen of the town preferred to receive and to deliver their local messages in person. His earnings averaged less than fifty cents a month.

Yet his knowledge of telegraphy, combined with his mental resourcefulness, enabled him to come to the rescue of his townsmen on one occasion when an ice jam had severed the wires between Port Huron and Canada. Due to the floating ice, it was impossible to make the repairs. But this did not phase Tom—he had now changed from his second to his first name. He promised to deliver the messages across the lake to Canada if they would supply him with a locomotive and an engineer. Smiling skeptically, the railroad authorities granted his request. But their skepticism changed to admiration when they saw the simplicity of his plan. All he did was to toot out a telegraph message on the engine in whistles of dots and dashes. At first there was no answer; but when Edison had repeated the message several times, a Canadian operator caught on and tooted back a message in reply. It was perhaps the first instance of "wireless telegraphy" on record.

A remarkably clever young fellow. And remarkably untidy. He spent his money on books and left practically nothing for his clothes. One winter he went without an overcoat and nearly froze to death. An experimenting vagabond. From city to city he drifted, and from job to job. Easily hired, easily fired. His ideas were too "crazy" for his superiors. Talked about sending two messages over a wire. "Why, any damn fool knows that a wire can't be worked both ways at the same time." This "lunatic" was a bad influence upon the other fellows in the office. "Out you go!"

And out he kept going, until finally he found his way to Boston. It was on a midwinter day in 1868 when he walked into the Boston office of the Western Union and asked for a job as a telegraph operator. The superintendent, George F. Milliken, looked up from his desk. What a disreputable-looking hobo! Pants too short and too tight and all but waterproof with smudge. Shoes torn and twisted out of shape. Hat so ragged that one of his ears protruded through a hole. Shirt a patchwork of tatters that had not been washed for weeks. And hair a matted jumble that seemingly had never known the touch of a comb.

Tom Edison had written from Canada to a Boston friend about this job, and the friend had shown the letter to Milliken. "If he can take it off the wire in such a script," said Milliken as he looked at the printlike handwriting of the letter, "tell him he can have the job."

But when Milliken looked at Edison, with his unkempt hair and his unwashed shirt and his rickety shoes, he was not quite so sure of the young fellow's ability. "Come back at five-thirty," he said reluctantly, "and perhaps I'll give you a trial."

Edison came back at the appointed hour and found the clerks grinning at their desks. They had prepared a practical joke against their country bumpkin who dared to ask for a job as a city telegrapher. They had wired to one of the fastest New York operators to send a special news report of eight hundred words, and now they sat back to see the fun.

Picking up a bundle of blanks, Edison placed himself at the table assigned to him. "Ready!" he signaled, and the message began to pour in. Faster and faster came the words, but Edison was equal to the job. As his fingers flew over the sheets, he glanced up; and then for the first time he understood the grin on the other fellows' faces. So they wanted to show him up, did they? Very well, he would teach them a lesson! Opening the key of his instrument, he tapped to the galloping operator at the other end: "Come on, boy, don't go to sleep. Shake yourself and get busy with the other foot."

The New York operator surrendered, and the clerks in the Boston office rushed up to Edison and showered him with their congratulations. Right then and there they acknowledged him as the fastest telegraph operator in the Western Union.

III

"ANY DAMN FOOL knows that a wire can't be worked both ways." Again and again the skeptics kept reminding Edison of this natural "fact." But

Edison persisted in his experiments and proved the "fact" to be a fiction. In the May issue of 1868 the *Journal of the Telegraph* made the announcement that Edison had "achieved the impossible." A few months later the following note appeared in the same journal:

"T. A. Edison has resigned his situation in the Western Union office, Boston, and will devote his time to bringing out his inventions."

A daring step for a penniless young man. It meant foodless days and sleepless nights. Offers to sell his inventions, delays, refusals, disappointments, but never despair. "You wait, they will come to me yet."

And they came to him sooner even than he had dreamed. A shrewd businessman for whom Edison had once worked, General Marshal Lefferts, was watching his inventions. He saw their financial possibilities. One day he summoned the hungry young wizard to his office. "How much will you take for all your contraptions?"

Edison thought quickly. Should he ask for three thousand? He could manage with that sum for the present. Five thousand? Oh no, that was preposterous! Lefferts would most likely kick him out of the office if he dared to mention that sum.

"Make me an offer, General."

"Very well, would you accept forty thousand?"

Until he received his check, Edison was not sure whether Lefferts had said *four* thousand or *forty* thousand. When he looked at the check he almost fainted. What would he do with all this fabulous amount of money?

Yet the fabulous amount melted away in a fabulously short time. His experiments always ran ahead of his cash. Opening a workshop in Newark, he paid the highest possible wages for the best possible workmen. "I have one shop which employs eighteen men," he wrote to his parents, "and I am fitting up another shop which will employ one hundred and fifty men." He had no accountant and kept no books. On one hook he hung all the bills he owed; on another, all the bills owed him. "This is the simplest sort of bookkeeping. Why ball myself up with all kinds of complicated figures?"

And thus, pouring his money and his mind into the secret crucibles of nature, he went on with his experiments. Multiple telegraphy—two, four, eight messages over a single wire at the same time. An electric stockticker instrument. An instrument that reproduced the human voice—"I'll bet you a barrel of apples against three dollars," he challenged the skeptics, "that this instrument will talk." An Aladdin's lamp that would light up the world with a new electric force. Crude discoveries thus far, mere foreshadowings of the miracles that he was to perform in these fields later on.

All work and work, save for a brief vacation to the "Wild West"—and time off to get married. Hardly a prepossessing bridegroom. Refused to wear white gloves at his wedding. "I've married a bear of a man," said his wife—the former Mary Stillwell—"but what an adorable bear!"

Though gruff and absent-minded toward the rest of the world, he was all tenderness toward Mary.

And, later on, toward the children—Marion and Tommy. He nicknamed them *Dot* and *Dash*. It was his greatest pleasure to play the clown for them in his spare moments. "He would don Mary's dresses"—we are quoting his sister-in-law Alice, who lived with the Edisons—"and romp and play around the house with the youngsters. They had a stereopticon and he would sometimes go behind the screen and stand on his head, and go through various antics to amuse them."

And there were times when to amuse his children meant the greatest physical torture. "He was a great sufferer from earache"—again we are quoting Alice—"and I have seen him sit on the edge of a bed and fairly grind holes in the carpet with the heels of his shoes, he would be suffering such pain."

A little play, much work, incessant pain, and an infinite patience—these were the ingredients which, combined with a flaming imagination, enabled Edison to transmute matter into motion and light. But most important of all, perhaps, was his extraordinary memory for details—his ability to co-ordinate apparently isolated facts into a coherent unit. Edison's memory was the amazement of psychologists. It was almost photographic in its scope. One day, as he was working over the plans for a new mechanical device in a cement plant, he examined the old machine, went home without having jotted down a single note, and compiled a list of six hundred items in the old machine that required modification or improvement. Hardly a bolt or a screw had failed to impress itself upon the retina of his mental eye.

His retentive memory was like a well-stocked and well-organized mechanic's toolbox. Everything was in its logical place; and whenever he wanted to put several facts together, he could get at them without any waste of time or unnecessary fumbling. As a result of this faculty of orderly analysis, he was able to do more constructive thinking in a day than the average man is able to do in a lifetime.

But his inclusive memory and his ability to mold individual facts into related units would never have got him very far were it not for his endurance. As a general rule, he slept only four hours a day. "Life," he said, "is too important to waste in excessive snoring. There are too many things to be done. There are so many experiments waiting, and it takes so long to bring even a single experiment to a definite conclusion." It took him many years to perfect some of his inventions—years of incessant toil, fifteen hours, sixteen hours, seventeen hours, sometimes even eighteen hours a day. "I have no time for loafing as yet," he said on his sixty-seventh birthday. "I shall begin to loaf when I am eighty."

A sublime endurance, an equally sublime courage. In 1915 his laboratory at West Orange, consisting of six buildings, burned down to the ground. The buildings were not insured, and the loss amounted to five million dollars. "That's all right," he said, "I'll make a fresh start tomorrow morning. No one's ever too old to make a fresh start."

IV

WHILE he was in the midst of his experiments with the electric bulb there was a sudden blackout in his own household. His wife Mary died of a heart attack. Eighteen months of mourning, and then he married again. In his personal habits he was still very much of a baby and needed someone to mother him. And fortunately his second wife, Mina Miller, proved like his first wife to be a good mother and congenial companion. It takes great patience to live with a genius. But it gives great satisfaction. Mina was able not only to appreciate his inventions but to share his thoughts. He often discussed his philosophy with her at the dinner table. He was profoundly interested in the mystery of life. He believed that every atom within the body, like the entire body itself, possesses an individual intelligence. "Look at the thousand ways in which atoms of hydrogen combine with other atoms to form the most diverse substances. Do you mean to tell me that they do this without intelligence?"

And then he went on to clarify his thought. "Atoms in harmonious and useful combinations assume beautiful shapes and colors, or give forth a pleasant perfume. In sickness, death, decomposition, or filth, the disagreement of the component atoms immediately makes itself felt by bad odors."

And the upshot of it all? The final union of the most intelligent atoms into the most intelligent substance. "Gathered together in certain forms, the atoms constitute animals of the lower orders. At last they combine in man, who represents the total intelligence of all the atoms."

"But where," asked Mina, "does all this gradual combination come from?"

"From some power greater than ourselves."

"Then you believe in an intelligent Creator?"

"I certainly do. The existence of a personal God can to my mind almost be demonstrated by chemistry."

Edison was not only a great inventor but a constructive idealist. He was interested primarily in the things that further the plans of God. In his own experiments he aimed at the inventions that serve life, and not at those that produce death. "Making things which kill men," he once said, "is against my fiber. I would rather make people laugh."

This was the principal objective of his life—to bring laughter into the hearts of the people. More laughter and greater light. "The world has been steeped in darkness long enough."

V

THE INVENTION of the electric light was the direct outgrowth of Edison's philosophy. And it was as simple in its conception as it was eventful in its result. It was one of those surprising discoveries of the obvious. If electricity can produce power and heat, argued Edison, there is no reason why it should not produce light—provided we can find something that will burn properly under the stimulus of heat and power. And so he began to seek a substance, which, like the bush of Moses, would burn without being consumed. In this quest Edison was not alone. Many others, on both sides of the Atlantic, had thought of electric lighting. An American inventor, J. W. Starr, had worked on incandescent lamps even before Edison was born. Another American, Moses G. Farmer, had provided his sitting room with a number of crude electric lamps twenty years before Edison's invention of incandescent light. In England, in France, and in Russia a number of scientists were producing equally crude lamps that would flare up for a short time and then flicker out. But Edison's chief rival in the search for the secret of practical and permanent electrical illumination was W. E. Sawyer. This American inventor had much of the brilliance but little of the patience of Edison. It was Edison who sat tirelessly in his laboratory, trying out one filament after another in his vacuum bulbs, ransacking every nook and cranny of the earth for the fiber that would give a brilliant and steady and, so far as possible, indestructible glow. And it was Edison who, refusing to admit defeat in the face of financial failure and the jeers of the scientific and journalistic world, finally discovered the magic fiber. On New Year's Eve, 1879, a throng of people from the surrounding cities had come to Edison's laboratory at Menlo Park, New Jersey. The ground of the little village was covered with snow. Suddenly, the switch of a button, and the darkness bloomed into a silver radiance under the flood of a dozen street lamps. On that New Year's Eve the genius of Edison had for the first time in history transformed night into day.

Just before the miracle had happened, a leading New York editor had exclaimed: "It has been absolutely proved that this sort of light is impossible—it is against the laws of Nature!"

VI

EDISON HAS BEEN ACCUSED of being a second-rate inventor and a first-rate businessman. He capitalized, it has been said, on the inventions of others. This accusation is, we believe, unfounded. It is true that others worked simultaneously with Edison on many of the inventions for which he is credited. But Edison worked harder and faster than the rest of them. And he worked under the handicap of his chronic earaches and his deafness. Indeed, he turned his handicap into an advantage. "It takes a deaf man to hear music," he remarked when he was experimenting on the phonograph. And when he was asked to explain this paradox, he said: "Most people hear only through their ears. I hear through my teeth and through my skull. Ordinarily I place my head against the phonograph. If there is some faint sound that I don't quite catch this way, I bite into the wood and I get it good and strong."

It was this faculty of hearing through his teeth and skull that enabled him to improve upon Alexander Graham Bell's invention of the telephone. Bell's instrument had been "hardly more than a mechanical curiosity," owing to the fact that it had been designed to serve both as a transmitter and a receiver. But Edison transformed it into an object of practical utility by giving it a separate mouthpiece and earpiece, instead of allowing the same tube to be used clumsily for both purposes. It sounds simple today. But it took Edison to think of it.

And many of the "simple" things that today make life worth living have had their origin in the magical laboratory of Edison's thought. Almost to the last day of his eighty-four years he worked on his experiments—an inspired, whimsical, untidy, modest, gentle, shrewd, and indefatigable Merlin. Out of his sorcerer's brain came an endless stream of electrical and mechanical servants to bring new amusements and new comforts to the human race. His inventions of the phonograph, the electric light, the motion picture, and the first crude "talkie" are merely the most popular of his hundreds of vital contributions to the applied science of the present day. His was perhaps the most universal mind in America during the nineteenth century. Once, when he visited Luther Burbank in his garden at Santa Rosa, the "plant wizard" asked him to register in his guest book. The pages of the guest book were divided into four columns, as follows:

> *Name   Address   Occupation   Interested In*

Under the caption *Interested In*, Edison wrote: "Everything." He was satisfied with nothing short of the sum of practical human knowledge.

In his endless quest for the practical, he was never satisfied with his past achievement. Always he looked toward the future. His prophetic vision saw many years ahead of the contemporary needs of his country. It is interesting to note that one of his very last experiments when death overtook him (1931) was concerned with the production of synthetic rubber.

And death itself, he was convinced, is but the transition into a new laboratory for greater experiments. "I've lived my life. I've done my work. Now I am ready for the next job."

IMPORTANT DATES IN THE LIFE OF
THOMAS ALVA EDISON

1847—February 11, born, Milan, Ohio.

1854—Family moved to Port Huron, Michigan.

1859—Became trainboy.

1862—Began to publish, for trainmen, the *Grand Trunk Herald*.

1863—Became telegraph operator.

1864—Invented automatic telegraph repeater.

1869—Came to New York. Invented improvements for stock tickers.

1872—Invented the kinetoscope (moving-picture machine).

1876—Moved to Menlo Park, New Jersey.

1877—Invented phonograph.

1878—Made chevalier of the French Legion of Honor.

1879—Demonstrated invention of electric light at Menlo Park.

1879-1931—Engaged in numerous inventions. Took out more than one thousand patents.

1931—October 18, died at Menlo Park, New Jersey.

Mother Cabrini

1850–1917

Though she could hardly speak a word of English, she was one of the great American pioneers. For her exploits widened the spiritual borders not only of America but of the entire world.

Yet she was so small and fragile that the doctors hardly expected her to live beyond her teens. The thirteenth child of a peasant family in the village of Sant' Angelo—about twenty miles from Milan—she was born prematurely in the midsummer of 1850. Legend has it that at the moment of her birth a flock of white pigeons circled above the house in the form of a dazzling crown.

They named her Maria Francesca, after the mother of Jesus and St. Francis of Assisi. And later on, because of her gentle disposition and her short stature, they nicknamed her Santina—*Little Saint*.

But this undersized little saint had a towering courage. Even as a child, she preferred the more difficult to the easier chores. "Anybody," she said, "can do the possible. The real fun is to do the impossible."

As she grew a little older, she heard stories about priests and nuns who had traveled as missionaries to distant countries. And one day, when the children were having a picnic on the riverbank, she made several little boats out of the waxed paper in which their lunch had been packed. And then, filling the boats with violets and forget-me-nots, she sent the fleet sailing down the stream.

"What are you doing, child?" asked her older sister, Rosa.

"They're missionaries, and they're going to China."

"But they'll never reach China. The paper will get wet, and the flowers will sink."

"Oh no, they won't. God will take care of them. God can do everything. And anyhow," when her sister kept shaking her head, "if they drown, they will become martyrs for the Faith."

On one occasion she almost became a little martyr herself. As she was launching her "missionary" fleet after a rainstorm, she slipped on the slithery ground and fell into the river.

She managed to splash her way to the bank; and there they found her, chilled and shivering on her knees, thanking the Good Lord for her deliverance from death.

From that day on, she had a horror of great waters; and the very thought of the ocean brought a pallor to her face. Yet she was to cross the ocean, which she dreaded so much, no less than thirty-seven times. Again and again she would say to her nuns, when they hesitated before a difficult or dangerous task: "It is not enough to do the possible. The thing for us is to attempt the impossible."

II

"Rosa, I am going to found a convent."

Her sister smiled at the eight-year-old Francesca. Such a frail little body, with such stupendous ideas. "Aren't you a bit young for this sort of thing?"

"I mean a convent for dolls. I'll dress them up in black, like real nuns, and I'll teach them the catechism."

But shortly after the "convent" had been established, the little "Mother Superior" decided that she had better close its doors. She had learned, from the parish priest, the spirit of self-mortification. She must dispossess the convent of its nuns. "I shall give my dolls away to the children who haven't got any. For the sake of the Bambino Jesus."

Self-mortification, and a passion for study—especially geography. She spent hour after hour tracing upon the map the distant places where the Apostles had brought Jesus to the heathens. "When I grow up I'm going to follow in the footsteps of the Apostles."

But she was so tiny, even upon her graduation from the School of the Sacred Heart, that the principal advised her to abandon the idea of ever becoming a foreign missionary. "There is ever so much work to be done at home, you know."

"There are plenty of people to do the work here. I must go to other countries, where the harvest is plentiful, and the laborers are few."

"You'll never survive the hardships, Francesca. You're so fragile and small."

"But don't forget that the Apostle Paul, too, was handicapped by a small body. He was less than five feet tall, you know."

And so there was no stopping this energetic little Santina who was determined to carry the Gospel across the sea. At twenty-four she felt that her family ties no longer kept her at Sant' Angelo. Sister Death had taken away her father and, a few months later, her mother. For a couple of years she had taught school and nursed the sick through a serious smallpox epidemic. Contracting the disease herself, she had come out of it more fragile than ever. An effort to become a nun had resulted in failure. Her own priest, Father Serrati, had advised the Superior to reject her, "for the sake of her own health." But, as usual, she persisted—"if God is with me, who can be against me?"—until at last she got her start as a missionary.

But even now it took her several years to convince the authorities that the strength of her spirit would overcome the weakness of her body. At first, they tried her mettle in various parts of Italy—Lodi, Vidardo, Codogno, Castel Giovanni, Grumello, Milan, Rome—organizing sisterhoods, teaching children, caring for the sick, begging from door to door, against her own refinement and pride, in order to build schools and orphanages and churches, and finally attracting the attention of Pope Leo XIII.

December, 1888. An audience with the Pope. "Mother Cabrini," he said, "have you ever thought of doing missionary work abroad?"

"Yes, Your Holiness. I have always longed to go to China."

"I have in mind not China, but America. Our Italian people there, as you know, are in need of spiritual help. They are bewildered by a new language, new customs, a new outlook on life. Moreover, a great many of them are exploited by unscrupulous businessmen. We must give them a guiding hand."

"But, Your Holiness, are there not Italians there who can help?"

"Not enough. The task is ours, yours. And so, Mother Cabrini, it seems that your destiny is not in the East, but in the West."

III

Per aspera ad astra. Through difficulties to the stars. Together with six nuns as her assistants, she set sail for New York on a cold March day in 1889. And her work for her Italian compatriots began right then and there, on the ship. Fifteen hundred immigrants, crowded together like cattle in the steerage. Like most of them, Mother Cabrini herself was terribly seasick. Yet she dragged herself from her bed, and looked after their physical comfort and spiritual hunger. One of the immigrants, an Italian boy, looked at her gratefully as she ministered to him. "Thank you, Mother Cabrini," he said. "I thought I left God in Italy. But I see you are bringing Him with you to New York."

When she and her nuns arrived in New York, there was no one at the dock to welcome them. Somehow they managed to stumble through the icy winds until they found lodging in a shabby Chinatown hotel. And so, in a way, Mother Cabrini had realized her dream: her first missionary service in America was among the Chinese.

Within a few days, however, she found a tenement in the Italian district. A cold, neglected, dark and dirty place that had been vacant for some time. But she and her nuns went down on their knees—first to offer thanks, and then to give the tenement a thorough scrubbing. This was to be the foundation for their first orphanage and school in America.

And then, an unexpected blow. The archbishop of New York objected to their idea of an orphanage. He had neither the funds available for the purpose, nor the confidence in the ability of Mother Cabrini. "I would advise you," he said, "to take the next ship back to Italy. You have undertaken a job that is impossible."

"Impossible?" she bristled. "This is precisely the word that I need. Here I shall stay, and here I shall do my work."

And she proceeded, along with her devoted nuns, to starve, beg, and pray until her dream for an orphanage began to take shape. Her persistence and her courage finally convinced even the archbishop that here was a woman of no ordinary stamp. He agreed to say Mass at the official opening of the orphanage; and a few days later, he helped her to welcome the first children who arrived at their new home.

Her work, however, was not confined to the children. In her search for orphans and funds, she had discovered among the adults much despondency and poverty and religious doubt. One of the chief difficulties of the Italian immigrants was the dishonesty of the "padrones"—the contractors who, taking advantage of the newcomers' ignorance of English, hired them out at hard labor, and then defrauded them of their earnings. These victims had been lured away from their homes in Italy by the promises of the padrones that in America they would find "a land of milk and honey, where a man can pick up gold in the streets." But the conditions they actually found in the slums of New York were such as to sap them of their faith in the honesty of men and the goodness of God.

And it was no little part of Mother Cabrini's labor to rehabilitate these countrymen of hers—to ease their financial burdens, and to help them recover their lost faith and hope.

Yet she herself remained humble in all her work. She never succumbed to the vulgarity of the publicity-hunters. The press had noticed the achievements of this "little saint," and a number of articles had appeared praising her to the skies. But she merely said: "Praise the Lord, not me. I am merely watching Him perform His miracles through us." Always in the forefront of the drudgery behind the scenes, never at the head in the public eye. "Whenever we walked in the street," remarked an assistant at the orphanage, "Mother Cabrini would say: 'If anyone speaks to us, let him believe I am one of the sisters. No one need know who I am.'" The only thing that might have distinguished her from the others was her stature. She was by far the smallest of the nuns.

IV

AND NOW there began a succession of journeys between the New World and the Old—a devoted shuttle-service for the Lord. First, a convent and

orphanage at West Park, across the Hudson. Fresh air for the little children who had been cooped up in the slums of New York. And then a trip
to Italy—at the request of the Pope who wanted her to establish a normal
school in Rome. Then, a series of voyages to Nicaragua, Panama, Chile—
a storm in the Pacific that threatened to capsize the ship, insects, reptiles,
earthquakes, tropical diseases and mountain frosts, struggles against the
despondency of the poor and the indifference of the rich—and everywhere
planting the gardens of her mission for God's kingdom on earth.

From South America, back to the United States. A visit to the Indians
at the Mosquitia Reservation; and orphanages for Italian and for Negro
children in New Orleans. Only a year before her arrival at that city, there
had been a lynching of eleven Italians on the charge that they had assassinated the chief of police. The air was still poisoned with hostility against
her compatriots when she and her nuns started to establish the first orphanage. Now and then she heard the ominous snarl, "Kill the Italians!"
when she made her way through the city streets. But she braved the hatred
of the bigots and the threats of the politicians. "I challenge your strength,"
she said, "for *my* strength is God."

And she won. In the house she rented for the Negro orphanage, the sisters had to cook their meals on an improvised stove in the courtyard. Their
drinking water came from the muddy Mississippi. And the entire table
service for the nuns—there were three of them at the start—consisted of a
spoon, a knife, and a fork which they shared in turn. They called it "our
community silver."

Shortly after their arrival in New Orleans there was an epidemic of
yellow fever. Mother Cabrini and her sisters promptly filled the gap in
the shortage of nurses, visiting hundreds of homes, cooking, cleaning, caring for the sick, allaying the fears of the dying, and bringing comfort to
the bereaved. Having no conveyance of their own, they went always on
foot, in the heat, rain, or slime. One of the sisters died; and her companions blessed her for her martyrdom, and redoubled their own efforts to
make up for her loss.

And yet Mother Cabrini was to look back upon her work in New Orleans as a vacation from her more strenuous labors. "In this warmhearted
world of Louisiana nothing is needed but to plant, and then to reap." It
was only after her experience in New Orleans that the real testing of her
endurance began.

V

From New Orleans she returned to New York. The Italians of that city,
she felt, needed a hospital of their own, where the nurses and the doctors
could speak their language and sympathize with their needs. And so, without financial help from the city authorities, and indeed against their

vigorous opposition, she established the first Italian hospital in the United States.

And now, another trip to Italy, for further orders from the Pope. This time, once again to the western coast of South America—Lima, Callao, Valparaiso, Tombe de Mora, and over a dozen other ports. And everywhere she brought "the light of the Lord" to those who had almost lost their way in the extended narrow corridor between the mountains and the sea. Along with the other hardships of the past, Mother Cabrini was now confronted with a new danger—the incessant threat of revolutions in the South American countries. "One trembles for the future that awaits the world," she wrote, "if God does not show an efficacious way out."

At this point, an order for a new adventure, more hazardous even than the old. A trip across the Andes to the eastern coast of South America. And this trip came near to costing her life.

Together with her nuns, she traveled over the precipitous mountains by train, coach, mule, and on foot. They started in the early spring, when the snows had not as yet completely melted. "Wait till the weather is warmer," their friends cautioned them. "The roads are too dangerous just now."

But, for Mother Cabrini, the Lord's work could not wait. "I shall take my chances, with God at my side."

And God must have been at her side to bring her safely across the yawning ravines and the rickety bridges overloaded with the winter snows. The first danger spot was "the Soldier's Jump"—a narrow crossing over a precipice. Mother Cabrini grew dizzy as she looked down from her precarious perch upon a mule. But her guide reassured her. "These animals can be trusted; they know their way." Mother Cabrini got safely across; and the other nuns, following her lead, were also able to reach the other side without mishap.

And then—a slow, winding ascent into the clouds. The wind grew colder, the fog heavier, and the oxygen more and more rare until the skin began to bleed and it became almost impossible to breathe. After a five-hour climb, they stopped at a cluster of cabins where they were joined by a number of other intrepid travelers. A supper of hard black bread, cheese, and coffee, a restless but prayerful night, and they were ready to start again at four in the morning.

For a while, the road was smooth and the scenery, bathed in the early sun, magnificent. But this was only the prelude to the most terrifying stage of the journey. There were now about forty-five people in the cortège. Mother Cabrini took the rosary in her hands and was about to invite the others—they were all Catholics—to do the same. But suddenly, around a bend in the road, the scene changed. They had come to a narrow, twisting ribbon of a road almost obliterated by the snow, with a precipice on either side. Mother Cabrini frantically tried to pull her mount now to one side and now to the other. But the mule knew better. He was familiar with the road, and he was determined to guide his passenger in spite of her in-experience and fright.

But the road became more and more precipitous, and the footing less and less safe. Mother Cabrini felt suspended in midair between heaven and earth. A single misstep, and it would be all over.

And then, a shout of dismay. The scouts had discovered that the road was blocked off. An avalanche of snow had opened a chasm just a few yards ahead. Several of the women began to cry. Two or three of them became hysterical. But Mother Cabrini, now that the danger was real, showed her true mettle. "I shall make the jump," she said, "to show the rest of you how easy it is." She had often leaped over even wider spaces, she told them. But she forgot that those leaps had been made in the supple years of her youth. Moreover, she failed to take account of the long climb and the rarefied air that had sapped her strength.

"Are you sure you can do it?" asked the anxious guide.

Mother Cabrini smiled. "With God, everything is possible."

She made her way to the edge of the chasm; and, as the guide stood ready, with staff in hand to help her if necessary, she leaped into space.

A shriek of terror from the onlookers. For the leap was too short. But the guide was on the alert. Throwing himself on the ground, he reached out his arms and caught her just as she was hurtling into the ravine. It was with a superhuman effort, and "with the help of God," that he managed to pull her back into safety.

But Mother Cabrini, for the first time in her life, had fallen into a dead faint.

It was some time before they revived her. By now, the chasm had been bridged with a number of fallen trees, and the company got safely across.

Further climbing, higher and higher into the teeth of the wind. At times, the guides had to hew their way through walls of snow and ice several feet deep. But at last they reached the topmost height—the *Cumbre*—which is the boundary line between Chile and Argentina. "It was a point from which it seemed we could behold the entire world," wrote Mother Cabrini. And, indeed, it was the entire world she had envisioned as the theater for her devoted work.

VI

BUT HER VISION was not completely fulfilled. Her fever-wracked little body was not quite equal to the strain. She never was able to include Asia and Africa in her missions. Yet she continued, for several years longer, to found orphanages, hospitals, convents, colleges, and schools throughout the countries of Europe and of North and South America. Again and again her labor was interrupted by an enforced vacation in bed. But always she recovered to go on, and on. "How can you endure such fatigue?" the

Pope asked her one day. Whereupon Mother Cabrini smiled, and said: "The heavy cross I bear, Your Holiness, lightens my task."

Her labors were so vast, and her foundations so numerous, that it would take volumes to give a complete account of them all. They called her "the Apostle to mankind." And, like the early Apostles, she went everywhere without funds, and only "with her staff and scrip under the blessing of the Lord." And, with her magic personality and her organizing genius, she served as a concrete example of her own lifelong credo. She made the impossible possible.

Incessant labor, repeated spells of illness, and relaxation only in her dreams. Not only in her day-dreams about the extension of her work, but in her visions when she was asleep at night. She frequently dreamed about God. "I spend my nights in heaven," she said.

VII

AGE AND SICKNESS were now beginning to take their toll. Yet no slackening in her work. "I have been condemned to hard labor for life," she said—and she accepted it as a blessed sentence. Among the last of her ministrations was her work in the mining fields of Colorado. Buried deep in their tomb from sunrise to sunset, the miners rarely saw the light. On Sundays, no church, no Mass, only a vague recollection of the families they had left behind and a heavyhearted resignation to the darkness that lay ahead.

But Mother Cabrini visited the families of the miners, and then descended into the earth to cheer the workers with the latest news about their loved ones—how they looked, played, and dressed, what they ate, and what ambitions and plans they had for their future. And her only compensation was the sparkle she saw in the workers' eyes under the artificial light of the mines. "Mother Cabrini," they said, "is not a human being but an angel in disguise."

To Seattle, Los Angeles, New Orleans, Chicago, back to New York and Italy—planning new homes and hospitals, and a sanatorium for tubercular children in California. Francesca Cabrini, mother to all the sick children of the world.

But now at last she was herself incurably sick. The World War of 1914. Much of her work was destroyed. Several of her homes were turned into Red Cross hospitals for wounded soldiers. Her great champion, Pope Leo XIII, was dead. The new Pope, Benedict XV, was also, like his predecessor, a lover of mankind. Upon his election to the Vatican, he issued a note calling the nations of the world to peace. Mother Cabrini cabled him her congratulations on his peace note; but the military authorities, intercepting the cable as a dangerous message, returned it to her.

A lung infection. The doctors advised her against any further travel. But, on one of her trips across the prairie, she had seen a beautiful spot for a convent. And now, while her life was ebbing away, she collected the funds, bought the land, and started the building.

The building was not yet completed when she died, just a few days before Christmas, in 1917. Her last words were a prayer—not for personal salvation, but for greater love. "Dear God," she said, "give me a heart that can embrace the universe."

IMPORTANT DATES IN THE LIFE OF MOTHER CABRINI

1850—July 15, born in Sant' Angelo Lodigiano, Italy.

1874—Founded the Institute of the Missionary Sisters of the Sacred Heart at Codogno.

1889—Arrived in New York. Took charge of a school in St. Joachim's parish.

1892—Established Columbus Hospital in New York.

1905—Established Columbus Hospital in Chicago.

1909—Became American citizen.

1917—December 22, died in Chicago.

1946—Canonized, July 7.

1950—Pope Pius XII named her the patron saint of emigrants.

Woodrow Wilson

1856–1924

ELECTION NIGHT, November 7, 1916. The tide had turned against Wilson, who was running for a second term. The East and the Middle West were rapidly drifting toward Charles Evans Hughes, the presidential candidate on the Republican ticket. At nine-thirty the *New York World*, Wilson's strongest newspaper supporter, conceded the election of Hughes. Wilson was resting in his New Jersey retreat at Shadow Lawn. At midnight his secretary, Joseph P. Tumulty, called him on the phone. "I'm sorry, Mr. President. It seems we're licked."

"Thank God!" was Wilson's reply.

The next morning, as he was shaving himself, his daughter Margaret tapped on the door of the bathroom. "Father, there's an extra edition of the *New York Times*. The West has swung in your favor. You've won the election!"

"Go tell it to the marines," retorted Wilson as he went on with his shaving.

Wilson dreaded the prospect of a second term in the White House. For it meant that he must lead his country into war. And he hated war with a hatred as intense as ever burned in the hearts of the ancient prophets. Both by training and temperament he was attuned to a life of constructive peace. He was a Celt, a visionary, a poet, a weaver of words, a dreamer of dreams. And a lover of his kind. He believed tenaciously in the might of right as against the right of might. As a child he had seen the devastation of the Civil War, and as a young man he had witnessed the degradation of its aftermath. He knew that when a country plunges into war it endangers the life not only of its body but of its soul. "Once lead the American people into war," he had remarked to Frank I. Cobb, editorial writer of the *New York World*, "and they will forget there was ever such a thing as tolerance. To fight, you must be brutal and ruthless. The spirit of ruthless brutality will enter into the very fiber of our national life . . ."

And so it was with a heavy heart that he allowed himself to be drafted into the campaign for the second term. "He kept us out of war" was the motto of his campaign managers. And, God willing, he *would* keep his country out of war. But he knew that he hoped against hope. In the avalanche of destruction let loose by the German military machine it was beyond the power of any man to keep America out of the war.

II

THOMAS WOODROW WILSON—he called himself "Tommy" until his senior year at Princeton—was a quiet child who preferred fairy tales to fights. When the soldiers paraded through the streets, he sat alone and aloof. He had a frail body and a strong mind. And a temper. He bossed his parents, and they in turn babied him. "Poor little Tommy is so delicate, we mustn't hurt his feelings." Flaxen-haired, freckled, with a rebellious stomach and bespectacled eyes, he was "predestined"—as his father jestingly remarked—to mental rather than to physical gymnastics. In his barn loft he organized a juvenile baseball nine, "the Lightfoots." He was not, however, their captain or their manager, but their "parliamentary leader." He taught them how to conduct their meetings in accordance with Roberts's *Rules of Order.* "Every one of the little chaps," Wilson recalled many years later, "knew perfectly well just what the previous question was, and that only two amendments to a resolution could be offered, which should be voted upon in the reverse order."

From earliest childhood he was a parliamentarian—and a disciplinarian. He was descended on both sides from a Scotch-Irish ancestry of printers and preachers. The love of, and the respect for, the Word was in his blood. It was not until his ninth year that he learned to read and to write —his parents wanted to shield him as long as possible from the hardships of a routine education. But he learned rapidly and he read voraciously. Night after night the light in his bedroom was on until long after nine, the prescribed bedtime hour for Tommy. But his parents never punished him. "Reading is the only dissipation I'm willing to allow him," said his father, the Reverend Doctor Joseph Wilson.

His father encouraged him in his reading—and in his writing. Both of them had a passion for the precise word. They delighted in verbal fencing. "You must wield the English language," Dr. Wilson advised him again and again, "into a flaming sword." Once, writes Newton D. Baker, Wilson took into his father's study an essay upon which he had spent much time and labor. "Dr. Wilson read the essay very slowly and then turned to his son. 'Exactly what did you intend to say in this?' The boy explained. 'Then why not say it?' And without further words, Dr. Wilson tore up the manuscript and let it flutter into the wastebasket."

But if the father was critical of the son, the son was equally critical of the father. He listened to Dr. Wilson's sermons with a severe—though proud—attention. And often after the sermon was over he pointed out how his father might have improved a passage by the insertion of a different phrase, a more picturesque figure, a word with a more resonant sound.

Like his father, Tommy was eager to become an eloquent speaker. Often on weekdays he would go into the church and "deliver a sermon" to the empty walls. On a midsummer afternoon, as he walked home from one of these "sermons," he was surprised to see the Negroes on the streets bowing to him obsequiously as he passed by them. Finally, his curiosity getting the better of his shyness, he asked one of the Negroes to explain the reason for their sudden outburst of reverence toward him. "We bow to you, Marse Wilson," replied the awed Negro, " 'cause you'se a great sup'r-natural preacher. We peeked in t'rough de window an' we seen you admonishin' de sperrits!"

III

BORN (December 28, 1856) in Virginia, Wilson was brought up in Georgia, whither his father had moved when Wilson was a year old. His training, therefore, was Southern. He was able at first hand to witness the bitterness of a defeat in war. He saw the trail of ashes left by Sherman's march to the sea. He spoke to rebel veterans, sullen, defiant men who, to use their own expression, were "conquered but unrepentant." He grew up with an overwhelming ambition—to help create a world without conquest or mastery or slavery or hate. And he trained his tongue and his pen to that end. His one hero was Lincoln. "When I remembered Lincoln and thought of all my greater material advantages . . . I believed I would be a poor creature indeed if, even without genius, I was not able to do some constructive work for the land that bore me and that I so loved."

"Even without genius." These words bothered him. Would he have the intellect necessary for the constructive work his country so desperately needed? In school he was mediocre—"neither good enough for distinction nor bad enough for censure." In September 1873 he entered Davidson College, and the following spring he returned home—a victim of physical and mental indigestion.

He retired to his room—his father was now pastor of the Presbyterian Church in Wilmington, North Carolina—and buried himself in his books. Especially books on history, philosophy, religion, and the science of government. He was in search of the Golden Grail of intellectual conviction. And one morning he discovered it. He had been sitting up until the small hours, "his elbows on his knees and his nose in a book on Gladstone," when the certainty he had been seeking flashed suddenly upon him. "Father," he cried as he burst into Dr. Wilson's study, "I have found it!"

"Found what?"

"The fact that I have a mind. A mind that can think and create."

His father blew a cloud of smoke from his pipe. "In that case, son, you had better go to Princeton." His own alma mater, Princeton was to Dr. Wilson the one institution that could transform his son's intellectual yearning into practical achievement. His boy, he felt even at that time, was destined for something great.

And Wilson, too, shared this feeling. "Tommy," recalls a classmate, "seemed to have an uncanny sense that he was a man of destiny . . . He was always preparing himself, always looking forward to the time when he might be called to high service. When he walked alone it was, as he explained, to have opportunity for calm reflection." In the words of another classmate, "Tommy Wilson in his undergraduate days displayed a passion for three things—Gladstone, Government, and God."

He loved society—especially the society of those who preferred mental to physical games. "The play of the mind was as exhilarating to him as the play of the body is to athletes." He joined the college debating club, where he amazed the other students with the facile dexterity of his phrases. "He tossed them about like colored balls—and he never missed the mark."

True to his Calvinistic training, however, Wilson debated not to dazzle but to convince. On one occasion he was selected by lot to speak in favor of the protective tariff. He flatly refused to do this. "It is my principle to uphold only that which I believe."

His classmates derided and at the same time admired his stubborn honesty. "Tommy is different, but he is a jolly good mixer for all that." He took part in many of the leading college activities. He sang in the Glee Club, he edited the *Princetonian*, he joined the Athletic Association (as an adviser, not as a competitor), and he managed the varsity baseball team. And above all he "practiced forever" at the most zestful game of them all—the exciting game of making friends. Princeton, as his father had anticipated, played no little part in completing Tommy Wilson's education.

IV

WOODROW WILSON—he had now dropped the "Tommy" from his name— was determined to be "someone" in the public life of the nation. At Princeton, whenever he met a tough opponent in an argument, he jestingly remarked: "I'll thresh it out with you when I meet you in the United States Senate." And now, as a preliminary step toward the Senate, he decided upon a legal career. A year's study at the University of Virginia Law School—and once more, as at Davidson College, he was obliged to leave his course uncompleted. An attack of the same old trouble, indigestion.

He returned home—and went on with his legal studies in private. Failure never bothered Wilson. He merely cast it off like an old garment.

Within two years he passed the bar and opened a law office in Atlanta.

Business was slack, and one day Wilson went on a picnic. When the company arrived at the grounds, Wilson got lost—and with him, Ellie Lou, the pretty and piquant young daughter of the Reverend Samuel Edward Axson. Lunch time, and everybody "hungry as a bear." Where in the world is Woodrow?

"I know," piped one of the children. "He's over there cutting a heart on a beech tree."

Shortly after the picnic their engagement was announced. "Woodrow Wilson," confided Ellie Lou to her brother, "is the greatest man in the world—and the best."

But the "greatest man and the best" could not make a go of the law. He had a disconcerting way of preferring justice to legality—a fatal error for a lawyer whose business it was to win cases and not to reform the world. "Your talents," Ellie Lou advised him, "are meant for the classroom and not for the courts."

And so he decided to prepare himself for an academic life. "There are more roads than one to a career of public service." He entered the Graduate School at Johns Hopkins and won his doctorate with a thesis on congressional government.

He married Ellie Lou and accepted an offer to teach at Bryn Mawr—a newly opened college for "masculine women." Wilson was unhappy at Bryn Mawr. He preferred to associate with feminine women. And his students preferred to associate with masculine men. They showed little respect for their young professor who instead of an athletic body had developed an athletic mind. Wilson was glad to be relieved of his duties at Bryn Mawr when he received an offer to teach at Wesleyan University (in Middletown, Connecticut).

Wilson understood men, and men understood Wilson. They disregarded his awkwardness, his short body stilted upon his long legs, his big ears, his northern Irish "horse face," his jutting jaw, and his large and sensuous mouth. They were interested mainly in the golden nuggets of wisdom that came tumbling out of that brave and homely mouth. And they forgave him for his inability to play football. For he had such an uncanny ability to devise winning formations for the players. Though never a member of a varsity team, he was appointed assistant football coach—and directed the Wesleyan team to a championship.

He acquired a national reputation as a teacher. In the spring of 1890, Princeton invited him to return as professor of political science. Wilson was elated. "If I cannot *lead* men, I can at least *teach* them to lead."

V

HIS CAREER AT PRINCETON is the story of an initial success and of a subsequent failure—a failure, however, which led to a greater success. Such was the destiny of Wilson. He was a man who never submitted to defeat. Even at the end of his life, as we shall see, it was not Wilson that failed. It was the world that failed Wilson.

But to return to Princeton. When Professor Wilson arrived at this "delightfully aristocratic" institution he set out to transform it into a *devotedly democratic* institution. And the students, with the exception of a handful of silver-plated snobs, responded with the enthusiasm of youngsters invited to new intellectual adventures. For several years in succession the senior class voted him the most popular member of the faculty. They listened to him with something akin to adoration when, in October 1896, Princeton College was formally reborn into Princeton University and "Godfather Wilson" was called upon to deliver the christening address. "The business of the world," he declared on that occasion, "is not individual success, but its own betterment, strengthening, and growth in spiritual insight." A new note in American education. A saner and humaner interpretation of the American credo.

And this note he repeated six years later when he was elected president of Princeton. "We must deal with the spirits of men, not with their fortunes." No longer would Princeton be an adolescent "country club." From now on it would become an experimental laboratory in the fine art of democratic living. He raised and stiffened the academic requirements, with the result that over a hundred "gentlemen loafers" were expelled for failure in their studies.

And then, while the fathers of these discredited youngsters were sharpening their axes, Wilson threw another bombshell into the academic sluggishness of the college campus. He proposed to abolish the aristocratic collegiate societies, with their exclusive eating halls and their luxurious clubhouses. In their place he outlined a group of democratic living quarters within a Gothic quadrangle—to be known as the "quad" system—eating commons and sleeping commons in which all the students were to be leveled up from social distinctions to simple devotions.

Wilson's bombshell exploded. The college world was in an uproar. "What—must a gentleman eat with a mucker?"

Wilson took up the fight for the muckers—and lost. The faculty refused to adopt his plan for the democratization of Princeton. But the loss of this battle led him to the winning of a far greater battle—the democratization of America. A number of political idealists had been following his fight. And as they watched this Scotch-Irish professor with the fearless heart and the peerless tongue, they saw in him the makings of a superior statesman. They offered him the candidacy for the governorship of New Jersey. He accepted the offer (1910) and won the election.

VI

THE POLITICAL IDEALISTS of New Jersey had brought about his election.

And now the political bosses of New Jersey hoped to bring about his submission. "Sure, he promised to fight political graft. But we know them teacher birds. Lots of gab and no go." What was their surprise to find that the academic Dr. Wilson possessed not only "go" but a vigorous boot! One of his first acts as governor-elect was to denounce Boss Jim Smith of New Jersey, who was running for the United States Senate. "You can't do this to *me*, Mr. Wilson!" But Mr. Wilson went right ahead and kicked Jim Smith out of his senatorial dreams. The professional ward heelers throughout the country rubbed their eyes in amazement. Here was a new phenomenon under the sun—a politician who kept his word! But the political idealists saw themselves a step nearer to the fulfillment of their vision. Here was a man to whom the word Democracy was not merely a campaign slogan but a religious creed. Presidential timber this—a leader who was upright, clean, and unafraid.

And ambitious. Fortunately for the progress of America, Woodrow Wilson was selfish enough to crave for the glory as well as for the responsibility of leadership. His was not the humility of the saints, but the pride of the prophets. In order to be a great statesman, he knew that he must be a clever politician.

It was this double quality of adroit politics and solid statesmanship that won him the election to the presidency in 1912. And it was this double quality that enabled him to sway the sentiment of the Congress into the enactment of several laws designed to help the weak against the strong. He carried on from where Jackson and Lincoln and Theodore Roosevelt had left off. He reduced the tariff, enacted a graduated income-tax law based upon the principle "from each according to his ability to pay," dispersed the concentrated power of the banking interests into twelve federal units, imposed a legal curb upon the expansion of selfish corporations and unlawful monopolies, and strengthened the position of labor by legalizing trade unions and boycotts and picketing and by declaring that injunctions could not be issued against strikers except to prevent deliberate injury to property. Wilson was not a radical but a liberal. "We shall restore, not destroy," he had proclaimed in his inaugural. He was willing to leave the upperdog with his reasonable hunk of meat provided the underdog got his juicy bone. But it *must* be juicy, he insisted, and nourishing enough to sustain life and hope and the energy to emerge from the bottom of the heap. "Such is our national way of life."

His international, like his national, policy was based upon the principle of competitive fair play. In this principle of fair play he saw merely the modern application of the Golden Rule. He looked with approval upon every honest government that respected the rights and the opinions of the governed. He recognized the republic of Sun Yat-sen in China and he refused to recognize the dictatorship of Huerta in Mexico. The happiness of the people, he maintained, is of greater importance than the avarice of its rulers. Or of its investors. He put a drastic check upon the tendency to protect the foreign investments of American capitalists with the lives of American soldiers. It was his desire to abolish two false doctrines that stood in the way of human progress—the divine right of capital to rule the land, and the divine right of gunpowder to rule the world.

He was the happy leader of a peaceful nation. And then, in 1914, there came a double blow to him. His wife died, and Europe exploded into war. From that time on there was no happiness or peace for Wilson.

From the firing of the first gun he knew that unless the war came to a speedy end America would be dragged into it. The earth had grown too small for isolationism. The needs of humanity had become too complex, the exchange of world commerce too interdependent, the activity of every individual too closely related to the activity of every other individual, for any one country to remain unscathed when the other countries had been caught in a conflagration. When he accepted the burden of a second term, he did it as an unwilling soldier drafted into a hateful war. But the job had to be done. Perhaps, if he remained at the helm, he might make this a war to end war. A holy cause to die in—a noble vision for a man of peace.

When, on April 2, 1917, Wilson asked Congress to declare war, it was not Wilson nor the American Government nor the American people that made the decision. It was the ruthlessness of the German military machine. Or, if you will, the inexorable course of human destiny.

Wilson was a tragic figure on that gray spring morning in Washington. A prophet turned warrior. Like the prophets of old, he had prayed to God that the burden of the fatal message might never be his to proclaim. For a time he thought of resigning from the presidency. But a soldier must never desert.

As he rode back to the White House on that tragic day, Pennsylvania Avenue was lined with cheering crowds. But there was no cheer in the President's heart. "How strange to applaud a message of war," he remarked. "A message of death for our young men."

VII

The allies won the war and Wilson launched his Fourteen Points—a brave argosy of peace in a tempest of vindictive and selfish hatreds. Open covenants openly arrived at . . . an end to secret diplomacy . . . absolute freedom of the seas . . . free trade among equal races . . . reduction of armaments . . . the right of all countries to govern themselves . . . a league of nations to make war forever a thing of the past. And the blind leaders of men, both here and abroad, took these Fourteen Points and tore them up and turned them into the confetti of a rancorous victory parade. They cheered Wilson to the echo and rejected his dream. They corrupted his peace without victory into victory without peace. The cynical politicians of the day made two fatal mistakes. They were too harsh and too lenient—too harsh to the German people, too lenient to their military machine. They shut Germany off from the means of making an honest living, and they allowed her to develop the means of subsisting through dishonest force. The Treaty of Versailles was one of the most tragic paradoxes in history. It left the enemy both with the food for its venom and with the instrument for its sting.

Wilson foresaw this, and he knew that the scrapping of the Fourteen Points was but the prelude to another war. The world had failed him. The masters of the nations had betrayed his hopes—the hopes of their own people. His New Testament of international good will was too splendid for the spiritual astigmatism of 1919. "We are ruled," gibed Clemenceau with cynical candor, "by our dead."

But Wilson knew that his great vision would be judged by the living. And Wilson was right. At the end of another devastating war, humanity had learned its lesson. The historic year 1945 saw the laying of the cornerstone for the building of his utopian dream—the United Nations of the World.

IMPORTANT DATES IN THE LIFE OF WOODROW WILSON

1856—December 28, born, Staunton, Virginia.

1879—Graduated from Princeton.

1886—Received degree of Doctor of Philosophy from Johns Hopkins University.

1888—Appointed professor of history and politics at Wesleyan University.

1890–1910—Served first as professor of political jurisprudence and then as president of Princeton University.

1910—Elected governor of New Jersey.

1912—Elected the twenty-eighth President of the United States.

1912–16—Engineered the Federal Reserve Act, the Federal Trade Commission, and the Clayton Act (against the abuses of large monopolies).

1916—Re-elected to the presidency.

1917—Delivered message to Congress for declaration of war against Germany.

1918—Drew up the Fourteen Points and went to the Paris Peace Conference.

1919—Returned and laid before Congress the Versailles Treaty. Toured the country in behalf of the "League of Nations Covenant." Brokenhearted at the failure of his country to accept this covenant.

1924—February 3, died, Washington, D.C.

Sigmund Freud

1856–1939

The family into which Freud was born was a laboratory for the study of mental conflicts. As a child he found himself with a young mother who was the second wife of his elderly father. His stepbrother by the first marriage had a child of his own, and thus Sigmund was the uncle of a little boy older than himself.

All this was very confusing to Sigmund. His mother, it seemed to him, should have been married to his stepbrother, for both of them were young; and his father should have been married to his nanny, for both of them were old. As for his nephew and himself, they found in the same man the personalities of two different people. For Jacob Freud was a father to Sigmund and a grandfather to Sigmund's nephew.

It was in this labyrinth of family relationships, with their loves and hatreds, their obligations and quarrels and jealousies and fears, that Sigmund Freud's mind was first pointed in the direction of his future career. From the very first, he seemed to have been destined for the exploration of the individual's reactions to his perplexities as a member of the human family. "My present annoyance," he wrote many years later in his *Interpretation of Dreams*, "draws reinforcement from springs that flow far beneath the surface, and so swells to a stream of hostile impulses toward persons who are in reality dear to me." It is in the experiences of our early childhood, as Freud went on to explain, that we develop our ambivalent character—that is, our propensity to love and to hate the same people at the same time.

II

When Sigmund—the family called him "Sigi"—was four years old, his parents moved from Freiberg to Vienna; and it was in this city of brilliance, bigotry, and burlesque that the young Jew grew up and remained for the greater part of his life. He learned to admire and to despise the life of the Viennese who "waltzed around in a circle and never marched ahead."

As for himself, he preferred to be a spectator rather than an actor in the musical comedy of Viennese life. He refused to join either the Christians who tormented the Jews, or the Jews who tried to imitate the Christians. He stayed largely by himself, devoted to his studies, and demanding only a quiet place where he could work undisturbed. During his adolescent years, he rarely joined his family at meals, but ate alone in his room among his favorite books.

Yet he was gentle and generous whenever his friendship was put to the test—especially in the struggle of right against might. His college classmates, though they often baited him for his Jewishness, nevertheless selected him as the spokesman of their grievances against the injustice of their teachers.

And thus he came to regard himself as a sort of modern Messiah who would eliminate the iniquities and the dissensions of the world. Just how he would do it, he could not as yet tell. Perhaps, as a famous lawyer, he would reorganize society and undo the injury inflicted upon his people. He owed it to himself, as an individual and a Jew, to do something great. Lost as a child in the mishmash of his family, he had been told repeatedly that he would never amount to anything. And now, reviled as a Jew in the blindness of a hostile world, he was reminded again and again that the cards in the game of life were stacked against him.

Well, he would show his family and the rest of the world! He became obsessed with a will to power—not by the sword, but by the spirit. He gave up the idea of becoming a lawyer—eloquence was not among his greatest gifts—and decided to study medicine. Especially the disorders of the mind—the mystery of human nature, the hidden springs of mental action, the origins of its errors, the reasons for its sickness, the possible ways to the cure.

Throughout his medical course, he was fascinated with the work of Dr. Ernst Bruecke, a professor of physiology at the University of Vienna. For several years he worked under Bruecke at the physiological laboratory of the university, and absorbed his teacher's painstaking technique in the investigation of nature. It was Freud's hope—encouraged by Bruecke's interest in him—that he would become an assistant at the laboratory upon his graduation from the medical school. But his hope was frustrated. "There is no place here for a Jew."

And so he entered the Vienna Public Hospital as an interne, and studied the anatomy of the brain under Dr. Theodor Meynert. But here again Freud was frustrated. He found it impossible for a man "of his origin" to secure a paying job either as a teacher or as a research fellow in cerebral anatomy. In order to settle down to a married life—he had fallen in love

by this time—he found it necessary to become a medical practitioner. He
would specialize in nervous diseases. In this field there was one man—
Professor Jean Martin Charcot—who stood head and shoulders above the
rest. With the help of a traveling scholarship, Freud went to Paris to
study under Charcot.

He became deeply impressed with Charcot's experiments in hypnotism.
The hypnotic state, declared the French professor, can be induced only
in those people who suffer from hysteria. And since the word *hysteria* is
derived from the Greek *hysteron*, which means *uterus*, Charcot regarded
hypnotism as a treatment for disturbances in the womb—or, more broadly
speaking, in the physical relationships between the sexes.

And thus it was through his study of hypnotism that Freud became interested in psychiatry as a possible cure for sexual maladjustments.

But for the moment he was more concerned with his own problems.
Paris in the spring, and thoughts of home and his fiancée. One day, as he
was strolling along the Boulevard St. Michel, he saw a group of young men
and women ahead of him. Every now and then they stopped in their
walk and broke into a spontaneous dance. It was so good to be young and
alive and in love! Time to return and marry and enter upon a medical
career of his own.

He married Martha Bernays in the autumn of 1886, opened an office in
psychiatry, and raised a family of six children within ten years.

Yet his wife, though prolific, was rather frigid. And this was but another cross current that determined the direction of his thought. It was, to
a great extent, the frustration of his intimate life with Martha that motivated his researches into the desires and the repressions of the subconscious mind.

III

FOR A TIME, he could find neither profit in his practice nor a laboratory
for his experiments. And so he worked alone, using his own mind as a
laboratory, and reporting the results of his self-analysis to his former professors at the university. But these pundits met his views with contempt.
He had departed from the hypnotic methods of Charcot, and had begun
to chart a new course. In his scanty practice, he had been surprised to discover hysteria among men as well as among women; and when he mentioned this fact to a prominent surgeon, the man laughed in his face.
"My dear fellow," he said, "how can you talk such nonsense? Since
hysteron means the *uterus*, how can a man be hysterical?"

"Perhaps, sir," ventured Freud, "it might be a good idea to abandon old
words when they fail to denote new discoveries."

But the surgeon shrugged his shoulders and turned scornfully away.

New discoveries, and new terms. Freud found himself alone in a strange
and terrifying field. The subcellar of the human mind. Nobody before him

had delved into this unknown region. There were no textbooks to guide him, and no teacher to stretch out a helping hand. Some of his professors, to be sure, had hinted at a possible explanation for many nervous disorders. "Doctor Josef Breuer, for example, had once made a veiled reference to a patient of his, a married woman who had suffered a mental breakdown. 'Those cases,' remarked the doctor, 'are always secrets of the alcove.' And when I asked him what he meant, he explained to me that by the word *alcove* he meant *conjugal bed*. Yet the doctor refused to talk any further about the subject. 'These matters, you know, are taboo.' "

And now Freud discovered that the taboo applied not only to his studies but to his person. The general public, and even some of his colleagues, pointed to him as "that nasty little Jew who pries into the secrets of the bed-chamber." All sorts of ugly rumors began to circulate about him as a demon of unbridled license. Yet, in his personal life, he was one of the most abstinent of men. One day he told a friend that on the previous night he had been disturbed by a dream about a woman of the streets.

"Well," suggested the friend, "why don't you do something about it?"

"But," retorted Freud, amazed at the suggestion, "I'm a married man!"

Abstemious in his own appetites, he delved more and more deeply into the appetites of others—studying their expressions and repressions, and the resultant mental and physical disturbances of his patients. And little by little he came to the conclusion that many, if not all, cases of neurotic illness are the result of some conflict that takes place in the subconscious mind of the patient.

This discovery of the subconscious mind, the struggle of the secret desires to assert themselves, and the effort of the psychic censor to keep them down, marked the beginning of the new medical science now known as psychoanalysis. And the basic purpose of this new science was to bring the secret desires into the open, to face them in all frankness, and to conquer them by leading the patient into a state of self-confidence through a greater degree of self-knowledge.

The strongest of all these suppressed secret desires—to Freud it seemed the *only one* that caused neurotic disturbance—was the *libido,* or the craving of the sexual instinct. In every case that he treated, he thought he found at the bottom a problem of sex. This result of his investigations, Freud declared, not only surprised but disturbed him. He apologized for his findings, as if he were the author who had created these sex problems rather than the scientist who was trying to solve them. But the masses kept on accusing him as a "dispenser of pornography under the guise of medicine."

Yet Freud went ahead with his research, enduring the storms of abuse, and learning more and more about the new strange science of soul analysis. Studying his patients and digging into the recesses of his own thoughts, he discovered that the unfulfilled desires of our subconscious minds are frequently paraded as fulfilled actualities in our dreams.

He wrote a book about this—the *Interpretation of Dreams*—and shocked the world into an orgy of renewed vilification. But a handful of scientists acclaimed this book as a new formula for human relationships. "When I had finished the book," wrote Hanns Sachs, "I had found the one thing worth while for me to live for; many years later I discovered that it was the only thing I could live by." For this book, as Freud expressed it, was the *via regia*, the royal road to the understanding of one's own thoughts and desires and of their conflicting attitudes toward the thoughts and desires of other people. Our dreams, observed Freud, open the door to the innermost ambitions and frustrations which we have thrust aside in our waking hours. And thus, in our dreams, we commit murders and perversions and adulteries and thefts which, in our waking hours, we subconsciously desire but are ashamed to bring into our consciousness.

A dream, in other words, is the lifting of the lid over the seething kettle of our emotions. Were it not for this release of the pent-up passions within our hearts, we should all go insane. Insanity, indeed, is the explosion of a mind that has been clamped down beyond the point of endurance. And it was only the insane or unhealthy mind that concerned Freud at the beginning of his career.

What then, according to Freud, is the remedy for an unhealthy—or, as he termed it, a neurotic—mind? Dig into the patient's memory about his dreams, he said; get at the *trauma*, or wound, that has resulted from the repressions which have caused these dreams; help the patient to go back if necessary—according to Freud, it always *is* necessary—to his earliest childhood in order to arrive at the original cause of the trauma; and then, when you have discovered this hidden cause, bring it into the open and help the patient to express his suppressed desires—not, however, in their crude and perhaps cruel form, but by a process of sublimation.

It was this process of sublimation that Freud regarded as the keynote in the treatment of his patients. By *sublimation* he meant the *conversion of the power of a lower or destructive impulse into a higher or constructive action.*

In discussing his psychoanalytic method for the treatment of neuroses, Freud often used a picture post-card as an illustration. The picture showed a country bumpkin trying to blow out an electric light in a hotel room. "If you attack the symptom directly," he said, "you act like this ignorant yokel. To turn off the disease, you must look for the switch."

IV

As a result of his *Interpretation of Dreams* and his successful treatment of neurotic diseases, Freud attracted a small circle of followers. They came to hear his lectures at the university, where he had been appointed as an instructor—he never received the honor of a full professorship—and where he was permitted to teach only on Saturday nights when not too many students would care to attend. There were rarely more than fifteen people present at these lectures.

But what they lacked in quantity, they made up in enthusiasm. It is this small group of "disciples" to whom we owe the present popularity of psychoanalysis. Finding the Saturday lectures insufficient to give them all they wanted to know about the new science, they met Freud informally once a week at his home. He lived in the "refined" section of the Viennese ghetto, on a hilly street half way between the "Junk Market" at the bottom and a Gothic cathedral at the top. His office and living quarters were on the second floor of the tenement house. The first floor was occupied by a butcher shop. The study in which his "disciples" met was a room with but a single window that faced a dark courtyard. But the walls were covered with bookshelves that reached from floor to ceiling; and the inexpensive but attractive furniture was set off by a number of antiques in glass cases.

The occupant of this study, like the room itself, was rather plain on the outside but precious within. Of medium height, slender and quiet and unpretentious, he had a trimmed black beard, rather heavy mustache, and the white face of a student who had seen too little of the outdoors. But his deep-set eyes were black and penetrating. They looked right through you—not, however, with the accusing gaze of an inquisitor, but with the smiling inquiry of a friend. "Come now, tell me everything if you will; and then perhaps I can help you to help yourself."

As his little group of disciples sat at the feet of this unassuming Messiah, they came to regard *all neuroses as disturbances of the sexual function*. Later, as we shall see, some of his followers departed from this radical point of view. For the moment, however, they were more interested in the extension of psychoanalysis from the treatment of *sick* minds to the study of *all* minds. Under the painstaking guidance of their teacher, they discovered in the analysis of dreams "a new-found land, which has been reclaimed from the regions of folklore and mysticism." And the signposts of this new land, as set up by Freud, pointed to the following features in the understanding of the human psyche:

1. The structure of the mind has a subconscious cellar of hidden memories, motives, and conflicts, as well as a conscious upper compartment of purposes, emotions, and thoughts.

2. The subconscious exerts a powerful influence upon our character. It is as definitely a part of the mind as the beating of the heart is a part of the body; and the subconscious is just as little subservient to our rational control as the beating of the heart or the breathing of the lungs.

3. In order that we may thoroughly understand and intelligently direct our *conscious lives*, we must learn to analyze the mainsprings of our *un-*

conscious minds. In other words, we must know what it is that makes our minds tick if we want to keep them in good running condition.

4. The surest way to the understanding of the unconscious mind is to analyze our dreams. For dreams are always meaningful and never accidental; they serve as the accurate indicators of our secret thoughts.

5. And thus, with the recognition of the unconscious and the analysis of our dreams, we can learn to weigh, measure, classify and to some extent regulate the psychological functioning of the human mind.

V

THE SUBCONSCIOUS REGION of the mind, declared Freud, is "a part of our biological inheritance." It is the repository of all the fundamental instincts of the human race. "Especially the sex instinct, or *libido.*" (The Latin word *libido* means *lust.*) The impulse toward sexual fulfillment, said Freud, is the one important motivation in all human activity. Every emotional distress, whether or not it results in a neurosis, is caused by the stifling of a sex desire. The conventions of our puritanical society, he declared, have developed a censor within our consciousness. This censor is generally on the watch against the emergence of our subconscious libido, and the subconscious is always on the alert to outwit the censor and to give the libido full sway.

At times when the consciousness is weak—when we are asleep, for example—"the libido rises to the top" in the form of a dream. But even then the censor will not allow our lustful thoughts to pass undisguised beyond the gate. And hence, declared Freud, the subconscious is compelled to clothe these thoughts in conventional symbols. This explains the nature of our dreams. A dream, according to Freud, is a distorted masquerade of our desires. Thus a dream may reveal the object of a subconscious lust and disguise the act, or it may reveal the act and disguise the person. And very frequently the dream will disguise both the person and the act.

And thus there is an incessant struggle between the urging of the unconscious and the censorship of the conscious. And this struggle results in the various disturbances of the human mind. These disturbances, observed Freud, exist not only in diseased minds but in all mental behavior. Psychoanalysis, therefore, offers a new approach to the entire field of psychology.

And, as some of his followers began to complain, a too pessimistic approach. For it reveals us to ourselves as creatures of subterranean lusts, hypocritical suppressions, and neurotic complexes. Thus every boy, according to the Freudian view, is at some time or other disturbed by a physical desire for his mother and a consequent jealousy of his father. Freud called this disturbance the *Oedipus complex.* (Oedipus was an ancient Greek king who—unintentionally—killed his own father and mar-

SIGMUND FREUD   299

ried his own mother.) And every girl, according to this same Freudian view, is subjected to a similar complex—a physical longing for her father and a consequent rivalry against her mother.

These childhood complexes, maintained Freud, become the motive power behind all our human activities. Sex is not only the *source* of life, but the one factor that determines our *way* of life.

This extreme point of view is wrong, declared Alfred Adler and Carl Jung, two of Freud's leading disciples. The underlying impulse of our behavior, maintained Adler, is not the lust for sex but the will to power. "The basic cause of neuroses," he said, "is not a sexual disorder but a sense of weakness, a feeling of inferiority." The child wants to be a man; the failure, a conqueror; the vagabond, a king. And Jung advanced still another decisive motive for our conduct—the human urge toward the divine. "The subconscious," he said, "is not a cesspool but a well-spring" —a source not only of evil passion but of sublime aspiration. Man, declared Jung, possesses not only a body and a mind, but a soul.

Yet, however much the three leading psychoanalysts might have differed, they all agreed on one point. Our subconscious, they said, is a repository of antisocial impulses, libidinous dreams, and frustrated desires. And these impulses, dreams, and desires may take one of three directions: unhindered *expression*, resulting in beastliness, sensuality, and crime; excessive *repression*, leading to perversions, compulsions, and mental disease; or *sublimation*—that is, disciplined redirection into religious devotion, social service, scientific discovery, cultural achievement, and creative art.

And thus the psychoanalyst, as envisioned by Freud and developed by his followers, has come to regard himself not only as a doctor of mental disease but as a teacher with an expert understanding of the human mind.

VI

LIKE WORDSWORTH, Freud believed that "the child is father of the man." All the mental disturbances of our adult life, he said, can be traced to the emotional conflicts of our childhood. Perhaps Freud was so intent upon the psychology of children because he was so deeply attached to them. He always went out of his way to do them favors. One day he brought a rocking horse as a birthday present to the three-year-old son of Max Graf, a former adherent who was currently among his bitterest critics. And—although Freud was nearing fifty and none too strong—he carried the unwieldy bundle up four flights of stairs. "His father may be my enemy, but his child is still one of my best friends." From his adult disciples, Freud exacted the utmost reverence toward his psychoanalytical creed. But from their children he expected nothing but the reciprocity of love.

As time went on, the "pied Piper of Vienna" found more and more opposition among the parents whose growing children, as they complained, he was trying to divert into new and dangerous thoughts. But, in spite of this opposition, his fame gradually spread—especially in foreign countries. In 1909, he was invited to deliver a series of lectures in the United States. He was amazed at his favorable reception in this country, where the educators looked without prejudice upon the ideas which so many Europeans had dismissed as offensive.

When he returned to Europe, he was again attacked as the purveyor of offensive thoughts. Little by little, the circle of his intimate disciples kept melting away. As he watched their defection, he became disillusioned but never embittered. Not even when Jung, the most favored among them all, became a Nazi and attacked his former master as a "perverted psychologist" because he was a Jew. "The Jewish psychology," wrote Jung, "is negative rather than positive. It fails to recognize the creative germs in the Aryan subconscious . . . Freud and his followers cannot understand the German psyche."

And then, as a prod to the aggressive "creativeness" of the German psyche, Jung asked a provocative question: "Will Freud and his followers be taught a better lesson by the powerful National Socialism at which the whole world looks with astonishment?"

The Nazis took the hint and administered the indicated lesson. They began to hound Freud, together with the millions of other Jews in Germany. And Freud retaliated with a book in which he identified himself with Moses—the religious leader who was thwarted by the rebellion of the masses who worshiped the fleshpots of Egypt and the Golden Calf. For, like Moses, Freud regarded himself also as the founder of a new religion—the faith of the individual in his own power to reorganize his character upon a basis of sanity.

But, under the proddings of their paranoiac dictator, the Germans had gone mad. They ordered the burning of his books and the destruction of the publishing company that printed them.

It was an unfair fight between an inhuman colossus and a sick man. For Freud had undergone several operations on a cancerous growth in his mouth. In one of these operations, part of his tongue had been cut away, so that he found it difficult to speak distinctly. And one day, as he returned home after a visit to the hospital to have his jaw scraped, he found the Gestapo—Hitler's secret police—at his home. They had confiscated his property; and it was only a miracle that saved his life.

The miracle took the form of an intercession, on the part of President Franklin D. Roosevelt, to have him set free. After considerable controversy, the Nazis agreed to let Freud depart from Austria for a ransom. One of Freud's former patients, Princess George of Greece, raised the required ransom—250,000 shillings. And, on June 4, 1938, the eighty-two-year-old exile was driven out of the home which he had occupied for over forty years. "Like the rescued officer of the *Titanic*," he drily remarked as he left Vienna, "I didn't abandon the ship. The ship abandoned me."

Freud had to be carried to the train in a wheel chair—"a fragile death's head dressed jauntily in a green hat and green topcoat." His destination was England, the haven of many a noble refugee in the past.

Together with his family, he settled at Hampstead, near London. Here, in spite of his illness and his recent ordeal, he tried to resume his old routine—rising at eight, seeing patients in the morning, and working on his correspondence and his manuscripts in the afternoon. It was in England that he wrote the final chapters of *Moses and Monotheism*.

And, with the ending of the book, came the end of his life. The cancer which had afflicted him for sixteen years was now beyond the reach of medical skill. He died three weeks after England had declared war on Germany.

In death he was as simple as he had been in life. At his request, his body was cremated without any funeral ceremony, and his ashes were placed in an old Etruscan vase which he had bought in London. A slender marble column upon which the vase is mounted bears the following unadorned inscription:

Sigmund Freud, 1856–1939.

One day, when an English admirer had asked him how he felt about his belated popularity, he replied with an anecdote about Oliver Cromwell's victorious entry into London. "Are you not proud," said one of Cromwell's soldiers, "that so many came to see the chosen of the Lord enter in triumph?" And Cromwell answered: "Three times as many would have come to see me hanged."

IMPORTANT DATES IN THE LIFE OF SIGMUND FREUD

1856—May 6, born Freiberg, Moravia.

1876–82—Did research work in physiological laboratories.

1884—Began to practice medicine in Vienna.

1885—Lecturer in neuropathology at the University of Vienna.

1885–86—Studied hypnotism under Dr. J. M. Charcot.

1895—Published *Studies in Hysteria*.

1906—Gathered a group of "disciples" and associates, including Eugene Bleuler, C. G. Jung and Alfred Adler.

1908—Presided over first International Congress of Psychoanalysis.

1909—Lectured in the United States.

1936—Elected to the British Royal Society.

1938—Exiled to London.

1939—Published *Moses and Monotheism*.
September 9, died in London.

George Bernard Shaw

1856–1950

I HAVE GOT the tragedian and I have got the buffoon in me, and the buffoon trips me up in the most dreadful way." This confession of G.B.S. is a perfect miniature portrait of his character. Bernard Shaw—he disliked to be known by his first name—was an idealist with too playful a pen. When he wanted to sting people into indignation, he merely tickled them into laughter. He was an angel of vengeance armed with a quiverful of lollipops, a preacher who turned handsprings on the pulpit while delivering the most sacred of his sermons. One day he watched the tomfoolery of Whimsical Walker at the Olympia Circus. After the performance he begged to be introduced to the famous mountebank. "It is very nice of you," said Whimsical, "to shake hands with an old clown." "Not at all," replied Shaw. "It's just one old clown shaking hands with another." Never taking himself seriously, he was yet amazed that nobody else ever took him seriously. He wanted most of all to hear the world say to him, "What a supreme teacher!" All that he ever heard, however, was "What a clever guy!"

II

HIS FATHER was a drunkard with a sense of humor. His mother was a humorist with a sense of art. Both of them were interesting characters. "We as children," wrote Shaw of himself and of his two sisters, "were obliged to find our way in a household where there was neither hate nor love, fear nor reverence, but always personality."

And he found plenty of personality outside as well as inside of his home. Every day he was taken out by a servant "who was supposed to air me on the banks of the (Dublin) canal." Actually, however, she took him to visit her friends either in the taverns or in the city slums. The "curious child" absorbed the smelly drinks and the soggy food and the sordid misery of the poor, and he grew up with an instinctive hatred of it all.

Every Sunday he was compelled to go to church. He found this experience so distasteful that he never cared to go to church after he grew up. "If you want to commune with God, look for Him out-of-doors. You'll never find him inside on Sundays listening to those insufferable sermons."

At night he recited a prayer of his own composition—not, however, at his *bedside* but *inside* his bed. "God doesn't like cold prayers uttered while kneeling on the floor; he prefers to have them come warm from under the blankets."

Shaw's secular, like his religious, education fell upon a rebellious soil. He learned Latin irregularly from an educated uncle, and forgot it—he tells us—when he began to study it regularly at school. As for arithmetic, he "managed laboriously" to master addition, subtraction, and multiplication; but he never could conquer division—"because my teacher kept saying two into four, three into six and so forth." As for doing a problem in four figures—"give me a slate and half an hour's time, and I can produce a wrong answer."

His parents, in the effort to make an educated fool out of him, sent him to one school after another. Finally they gave it up. He left school, and remained for the rest of his life an uneducated wise man.

He detested prescribed study, but he loved impromptu reading. And his reading skirted the entire horizon of the world's literature.

Above all, however, he loved music. His mother was an accomplished musician, and the children grew up to whistle from memory the sonatas of Beethoven and the oratorios of Handel. In his early teens, Shaw learned to play the piano—without a teacher. His mother had now left her erratic husband; and Bernard, as the "head" of the family, felt that maybe he ought to do something about supporting them. He tried clerking in Dublin for a while, made a fairly good living at it, and gave it up in disgust. He then went to London, tried musical criticism, practically starved at it, and loved it. He took an unholy pride—he tells us—in being a burden to his impoverished mother. "I did not throw myself into the struggle for life: I threw my mother into it."

For he had discovered a direction for himself. He had a genius for writing; he was a consecrated artist. "The true artist will let his wife starve, his children go barefoot, his mother drudge for his living at seventy, sooner than work at anything but his art." He allowed his mother to teach music to unmusical pupils until she was ready to drop from exhaustion. He tramped the sidewalks in gaping boots and in trousers with holes— not always mended—in the seat. He shrugged his shoulders when the friends of the family called him a good-for-nothing vagabond. He smiled into his untrimmed gingerbread beard when people pointed to his shambling skeleton of a figure and then pointed to their heads. He knew that everybody regarded him as queer. He *was* queer, different from the general pattern of mankind. He was an artist. Daily he wrote his stint of a thousand words, finished five novels and hundreds of articles, earned a total of £6 (about $30) for the entire labor of ten years, and gradually —at his mother's expense—"made a man of myself instead of a slave."

III

AT 26, HE BECAME a vegetarian—partly for humanitarian reasons, partly for reasons of health. Those who eat flesh, he said, are not only cannibals but walking cemeteries. A diet of vegetables and a glass of water, he maintained, kept him "ten times as well as an ordinary carcass eater." At about the time of his dietary reform, he also became interested in political reform. He had read Karl Marx's *Das Kapital*—a book which he regarded as a revelation. "The reading of that work . . . provided me with a purpose and a mission in life." He became a soap-box orator, preaching the "gospel according to St. Marx" about three times a week for a period of twelve years.

And then he gave up persuading the workers and tried to convert the intellectuals. He joined the Fabian Society—so named after the Roman general, Fabius, whose motto was: "Don't fight until the right moment arrives; but when the right moment arrives, fight like hell." The Fabians believed in socialism as a constructive evolution rather than as a destructive revolution. Their tendency was to emphasize the delay rather than the fight. Bernard Shaw, however, had come to the society fresh from the soap-box. He believed that even in the delay there is a weapon with which you can conquer the enemy. The weapon of the tongue. In his first public address at the Fabian Society (1885), he lashed out at capitalism in a new English style—irony with a Shavian flourish: "It is the desire of the President (of this society) that nothing shall be said that might give pain to particular classes. I am about to refer to a modern class, burglars, and if there is a burglar present I beg him to believe that I cast no reflection upon his profession." And then, continuing this vein of irony, Shaw embarked upon a subtle comparison between the capitalist and the burglar: "I am not unmindful of his (the burglar's) great skill and enterprise, his risks . . . or his abstinence; nor do I overlook his value to the community as an employer on a large scale, in view of the criminal lawyers, policemen, turnkeys, gaolbuilders and sometimes hangmen that owe their livelihoods to his daring undertakings." And then, having established the "respectability" of the burglars, he goes on to assure the capitalists that he regards them as equally respectable: "I hope any shareholders and landlords who may be present will accept my assurance that I have no more desire to hurt their feelings than to give pain to burglars; I merely wish to point out that all three inflict on the community an injury of precisely the same nature."

In this speech Bernard Shaw had discovered both his mission and his livelihood. He would save humanity by appointing himself as its prophet; and he would enrich his purse by delivering his prophecy as a jest. From now on his life, like one of his most serious plays, *Androcles and the Lion*, was to be "a great religious drama—with leonine relief."

A new sort of play—a new sort of clown. And the world was shocked and tickled at the spectacle of Gabriel disguised in the motley of Punch. "The only reproach with which I became familiar was the everlasting 'Why can you not be serious?' Soon my privileges were enormous and my wealth immense."

His first pulpit was a magazine in which he wrote musical criticisms under the pseudonym of Corno di Bassetto—"an instrument that gives forth melancholy sounds suitable for a funeral." And then, having laid to rest all the bad music and all the bad musicians in London, he turned his criticism to the stage. For three years he worked as a dramatic critic under the tutelage of Frank Harris, editor of *The Saturday Review*. It was a superb intellectual extravaganza, this spectacle of London's foremost libertine and England's leading ascetic thumbing their noses together at the public, while the public went into paroxysms of laughter. One thing the two men had in common—a dramatic genius for self-praise. Frank Harris pictured the world as a capital "I" surrounded by an ocean of dead fish that stank in his nostrils. As for Bernard Shaw, "I yield to no man" —he wrote—"in the ingenuity and persistence with which I seize every opportunity of puffing myself and my affairs." In both cases, however, this egotistical bunkum was merely the assumption of a false front. Under the mask of their effrontery, both Shaw and Harris were sad and solitary thinkers who saw much to be done in the world but who did not know how to do it.

The dramatic flair in Harris led him into all sorts of adventures in which Harris was either the hero or the villain. The dramatic flair in Shaw impelled him to write plays in which all the heroes and the villains are mortals created after the image of Bernard Shaw.

His attitude toward his plays, like his attitude toward life, was that of an apostle who tries to save the world with a decalogue of paradoxes. He poked fun at the motheaten respectabilities of his age, yet he accepted every one of them. He was not an iconoclast—a breaker of images. Instead of *breaking* them, he merely shook them, to the horror of all the bystanders who expected them to crash at any moment—and then, when they were teetering on end, he carefully replaced them upon their pedestals.

Like a mischievous child, he played at being naughty because, by doing so, he could attract everybody's attention. He built nearly all of his dramas upon this paradox of pretending to be naughty while really meaning to be nice. He led his characters—especially his women—into all sorts of compromising situations, and then he led them safely out again before they were compromised. "How glorious it would be to yield, but how prudent it is to refrain!"

This formula—of rushing close to the fire and then jumping away just in the nick of time—becomes rather monotonous when you find it repeated over and over again in his dramas. Only a few of them are free from the Shavian cliché. And these few plays are—in our opinion—among his best. This is especially true of *Saint Joan*. In this drama about the consecrated Maid of Orleans we penetrate beyond the grinning mask to the tender heart. Here at last Shaw speaks without cap and bells—"the prophet at his best without his silly jest." Here we get the quintessence of Shaw's philosophy—his indignation at man's cruelty, his impatience at his stupidity, his sadness at his suffering. The human animal is a strange admixture of passion and pity—passion when he is powerful to hurt, pity when he is powerless to help. God sends us his prophets, and in our moments of anger we slay them. And then, in our hours of repentance, we sanctify their ashes. Their *ashes*, but not their *persons*. Twenty-five years after the Church had burned the body of Joan of Arc, the selfsame Church rehabilitated her name. "But I will tell you this," observes King Charles to Ladvenu in the epilogue to the play. "If you could bring her back to life, they would burn her again within six months, for all their present adoration of her." And why all this cruelty? Because our human vision is out of focus. "You do not see aright. That is the great thing: you must see." Until that day arrives, "a Christ must perish in torment in every age."

And then comes the final cry from the spirit of Saint Joan, from the innermost heart of Bernard Shaw: "O God that madest this beautiful earth, when will it be ready to receive Thy saints? How long, O Lord, how long?"

IV

MANY THOUGHTFUL PEOPLE, while admiring the prophet in Bernard Shaw, have learned to despise the clown. And foremost among these thoughtful people was Bernard Shaw himself. One evening, at the final curtain of *Arms and the Man*, Shaw took his call as author. There was an outburst of tremendous applause, punctuated suddenly by a solitary *boo*. Shaw held up his hand for silence. And then, turning in the direction of the *boo*, he said: "I quite agree with you, my friend. But what can you and I do against a houseful of the opposite opinion?"

Before the houseful of society, Shaw played the mummer. In his private life, however, where he did not have to put on a show, he was a quiet, friendly, modest gentleman—the word here should be divided into its components, *gentle man*—with an English headful of ideas and an Irish heartful of love. Simply, unobtrusively—many of his closest friends even were unaware of it—he launched all sorts of plans for the betterment of conditions among the poor, and labored for countless hours as a committeeman in an effort to bring these plans to fruition. His chief objective was to see Christianity applied to everyday life. Christian reciprocity through economic socialism—this, in a phrase, embraced the innermost kernel of his philosophy. He has often been called—and at times called himself—an atheist. Yet the Bible was to him the greatest of books. "You cannot begin to appreciate it until you are sick of the novels and plays and other trash that our grown-up babies feed on." As for his attitude toward Jesus, "I see no way out of the world's misery but the way of Christ"—provided the teachings of Christ are taken out of the cloister and put into practical use. "This man (Jesus) has not been a failure yet; for nobody has ever been sane enough to try his way."

V

IN SPITE OF his mannerisms and his mummeries, Shaw was a Christian Puritan. He was abstemious in his appetites—including even the sexual appetite. In all his long life he yielded only two or three times to the "illicit intimacies of the flesh." In addition to these few diversions, he enjoyed two lasting devotions—a passionate love-affair (on paper) with Ellen Terry, and a dispassionate cordiality (in person) with his wife. In his letters to Ellen Terry, "the most enchanting actress who ever graced the stage," he made himself "more fatuous even than Beethoven." Yet in his conduct toward his wife he was the soul of tenderness and fidelity and tact. His "very well-regulated house," wrote Mrs. Patrick Campbell, "came before everything. Whatever might betide, Mrs. Shaw must not be kept waiting ten minutes."

His love-letters, like his dramas, were part of his mummery. They were literary exercises—efforts to show his admirers how clever he was. He loved to pin down an emotion with an epigram—even though the emotion might be lacerated in the process. Often, in his attempt to be witty, he failed to be wise. In his anxiety to make the telling retort, he would hurt even those who tried to be friendly to him. Once a beautiful actress—the story has been wrongly attributed to Isadora Duncan—made him a proposal. "With your brain and my body," she said, "we would produce the perfect child." "But suppose," rejoined Shaw, "the child were to inherit *my* body and *your* brain."

VI

JESTERS, as G. K. Chesterton once observed, are among the most serious people in the world. They clown in order to attract attention. They flavor the wormwood of truth with the teaser of molasses. Otherwise the ill-behaved children of the world will refuse to take the medicine for their spiritual sickness. "If people didn't laugh at me," wrote Shaw, "they couldn't endure me."

And so, with tongue in his cheek but with sadness in his heart, he uttered the most serious truths with a grin on the face. An ardent lover of democracy, he selected its vices for ridicule rather than its virtues for praise. A hater of all tyranny, he was ready to shoot his epigram at the antityrants if by so doing he could raise a laugh. "All these anti-Mussolinians," he wrote in 1933, "are idiots." Horrified at all forms of destruction, he would not forego his merry quip in favor of the destroyer. "It is unfair," he jested, "to call Napoleon a wholesale butcher. Any sharpshooter in his army killed more men than Napoleon." In 1925, when he refused the Nobel Prize for Literature, he gave a very sensible reason for his refusal: he did not need the money. This money (about $35,000), he said, "is a lifebelt thrown to a swimmer who has already reached the shore in safety." But, having made this wise observation, he could not resist the temptation of spoiling it with a wisecrack: "I can forgive Alfred Nobel for having invented dynamite. But only a fiend in human form could have invented the Nobel Prize." No wonder that a disciple once exclaimed in his perplexity, "Do you mean what you say, Mr. Shaw, or are you saying it just to be mean?"

In his late years, however, Bernard Shaw spoke clearly and unmistakably on two subjects—the Russian Revolution, and the Second World War.

In 1931 he visited revolutionary Russia, in company with Lady Astor. He not only found *kasha* (a thick Russian gruel) "the best porridge in the world," but he discovered on the faces of the Russian workers and peasants a buoyancy, a freedom from apprehension, a reflected sense of security such as he had not been able to see anywhere under "capitalist civilization."

Shaw admired Stalin. But he had no sympathy for Trotsky. He was opposed to Trotsky's agitation for the immediate spread of communism to every other country. Nevertheless, he looked upon the Russian experiment with the greatest admiration and the greatest hope. Russia, he believed, need not *force* the rest of the world into socialism. The rest of the world, having seen its success in Russia, would *adopt* it of its own free will.

Shaw admired not only the political but the military organization of Russia. When Germany attacked her in June, 1941, he stood almost alone in predicting a Russian victory. "The news," he said, "is too good to be true . . . It is beyond anything we could have hoped for . . . Germany has not a dog's chance."

As for his attitude toward the war in general, Shaw had never before the outbreak believed in its possibility. Nobody, he declared, would be mad enough to start it. "Any statesman who is not desperately afraid of starting a cannonade should be sent to a mental hospital." But when Hitler proved himself to be that mad statesman, Bernard Shaw abandoned his pacifism of eighty-three years. "There are now no war aims, and no peace aims, except the aim of winning the fight."

When at the age of ninety-four he slipped in his garden, broke his thigh, and was rushed to the hospital for an operation, he refused to let the doctors shave his beard to administer the anesthetic more easily. He warned his physicians that their professional reputations would suffer unless they killed him, "for a doctor's fame is based upon the number of eminent patients he has lost." Shaw survived the operation; in fact, his tough old bones knitted together cleanly; however his fall had aggravated an old kidney ailment and it was of kidney poisoning that he died on November 2, 1950. In accordance with his wishes, he was cremated and his ashes were mingled with his wife's. Always the prince of laughter, he was working on a light comedy at the end. But nature, the even greater playwright, stepped in and abruptly ended the larger drama of Shaw's life, freeing him to write God knows what rollicking epilogues in heaven.

IMPORTANT DATES IN THE LIFE OF GEORGE BERNARD SHAW

1856—July 26, born at Dublin.

1871—Got job as clerk.

1876—Came to London.

1876–84—Tried, unsuccessfully, to succeed as a writer.

1884—Joined Fabian (socialist) Society.

1892—Finished, in collaboration with Willian Archer, his first play (Rhinegold).

1893—Wrote his first play without collaboration (The Philanderer).

1898—Published Plays Pleasant and Unpleasant.

1923—Wrote his last important play, Saint Joan.

1926—Awarded Nobel Prize for Literature.

1931—Visited Russia.

1933—Delivered his only lecture in the United States.

1950—November 2, died in Ayot St. Lawrence.

Henry Ford

1863–1947

A NEW monster had appeared on Main Street. A horseless carriage. "It shoots as it travels!" exclaimed the people as they heard it backfire. In Galveston, Texas, a prominent citizen was so terrified by the backfire that he drew a gun. "If that happens again," he yelled to the driver, "I'll kill you!"

In another state the new monster passed by a farmer and his wife in a wagon. The horses reared in alarm, and the woman leaped from the wagon and took to the woods. The driver stopped the car, walked over to the farmer, and asked whether he could help him tame the horses. "Hell, no," said the farmer. "But you can help me tame my wife!"

II

THE CREATOR of one of the world's most amazing miracles began life simply enough. His father was a Michigan farmer of intermingled Scotch, English, and Irish blood. A good basis for sobriety, imagination, and grit. "The young fellow," said his neighbors of William Ford, "has a clever hand and a kind heart." Always ready to help a fellow with the repairing of his tools and the plowing of his fields. A year after his marriage to Mary Litogot, when the papers were filled with the news of the Battle of Gettysburg, his first child Henry was born. "I want to see my son dedicated to the work of peace."

It was a peaceful home in which Henry grew up. One of the earliest incidents he could remember was watching his father at work in the fields. Long, straight furrows, so pretty to the sight. But here was a furrow that was not so straight. The plow had been turned aside at one point. "Why did you do it, Dad?" For answer, his father took his hand and led him to the spot. There, on the ground, was a song sparrow's nest. "I didn't want to disturb it, son."

A peaceful home, and a busy one. Plenty of chores to do in the fields, in the barn, in the house. And, for a family living so far away from the supply stores, all sorts of gadgets to invent. Screw drivers out of shingle nails. Gimlets out of knitting needles. Tweezers out of corset stays. And, always, their own and their neighbors' watches and clocks to repair. "Has your timepiece stopped going? Leave it to Henry. *He'll* fix it!"

As often as not Henry would take a clock apart even when it needed no fixing. He wanted to see how well he could put it together again. "Every clock in the Ford home," remarked a friend jokingly, "shudders when it sees Henry coming."

In school Henry paid more attention to his gadgets than to his books. Indeed, his books served merely as a screen behind which he kept tinkering with his watches. The bigger the book, the better the shield between Henry's fingers and the teacher's eye. "Henry," said the teacher one day, "you seem to be more interested in your geography than in any other book."

But sometimes his teacher caught him at his "idle play." And then Henry had to sit in the corner with a girl—the regular punishment for misbehavior in school.

He found the punishment almost as pleasant as the crime.

But the pleasures of his childhood were arrested by an abrupt shock. He was only twelve when his mother died. "From that day on the house was like a watch without a mainspring."

Four more years of schooling and tinkering around with all sorts of machinery, and then he left home for a job in Detroit. Or, rather, two jobs. In the daytime he was an apprenticed mechanic; at night, a cleaner of clocks. His total pay for the two jobs was three dollars a week.

But he was ambitious. He wanted to become a mass producer of watches. Two thousand a day at a manufacturing cost of thirty cents and at a selling price of one dollar. A great boon to humanity, and a tidy profit for himself.

He went ahead with the idea, designed the machinery, cut the dies, and secured a partner. And then he had to give up the idea. "I could easily make two thousand watches a day. But how in the world could I sell them?"

A disappointed dream. But disappointments are only the seeds of future dreams. The idea of mass production had taken root in his mind. "Patience. It will come to flower in due time."

For the present Henry Ford yielded to his father's call for help on the farm. Nineteen years old. The golden age of courtship. It was on New Year's Eve that he met Clara Bryant, a dark-haired girl with a sun-bright smile. "Such a lovely young lady." "Such a sensible young man."

Apprenticeship for marriage. Six years of working and saving and planning; and then, on Clara's birthday (April 11) in 1888, she became his bride.

A new home, a new piano, and the reawakening of an old dream. Something to be produced on a large scale. An inexpensive, serviceable, pleasure-giving gadget for his fellow men.

But what? Ah, he had it! A new kind of carriage. A sort of privately owned railway coach. Self-propelled, like a steam engine. He began to tinker with the idea on his farm. He took the cast-iron wheels of an old mowing machine, attached them to a crude locomotive with homemade cylinders, built a fire in the boiler, and tried it out. A spasmodic start, a splutter of steam, and the carriage came to a stop.

Another attempt, another, and still another—water tubes, fire tubes, flash designs. Same results. The thing would not go. "The steam engine will never do for a common-road passenger car."

And then, an inspiration. One day in Detroit he saw a new kind of engine. It was operated by gasoline. That evening he explained the idea to his wife. He had read about it in the *World of Science*. "I've been on the wrong track, Clara. What I'd like to do is make an engine that'd sort of pump pop into pop bottles. A gasoline engine that'd take the place of a horse."

He drew a diagram on the back of a music sheet. "You see, if I could harness such an engine to four wheels——"

"Yes, Henry."

"But to do that, we'd have to give up the farm and move to Detroit. I'd need tools, and money, and all that sort of thing."

"I understand, Henry. I'll be ready when you say the word."

And so, on a late September day in 1891, they spread out the racks of their hay wagon, heaped all their belongings upon it, and started off in the direction of their dream.

III

DATE, August 12, 1896. Scene, the banquet room of the Oriental Hotel, Manhattan Beach, Long Island. Occasion, the convention of the officers of the Edison Electric Company. At the head sat Thomas Alva Edison himself.

Conversation about the presidential race between Bryan and McKinley, the plight of Cuba under the oppression of Spain, the expansion of American industry both at home and abroad. And then the talk drifted on to some of the latest industrial developments in the United States. One of the dinner guests touched Edison on the arm. "Do you see that young fellow across the table?"

"Yes. What about him?"

"Well, he's invented a gasoline car."

"Really? Sounds very interesting." And turning to Henry Ford, he said, "Young man, do you mind telling me about that new car of yours?"

The man who sat next to Edison vacated his chair and invited Ford to take his place. The young inventor began to explain his idea to the old inventor. Edison nodded approval. "Looks as if you've really got something." And then, "Tell me how you explode the gasoline in the cylinder."

"By electricity, sir." And taking a menu card from the table, Ford roughly sketched the principle of his make-and-break mechanism.

Edison's fist came down upon the table with a bang. "That's the thing, young man! Your car carries its own power plant—it's self-contained—no fire, no boiler. You've got it. Keep it up!"

Henry Ford kept it up. He was now the chief engineer at the Edison plant in Michigan. A very efficient young fellow, said the neighbors, but a little queer in the head. Spent all his evenings in a little alley shop behind the house, hammering away at some crazy contraption while everybody else was having a good time.

Wasting his time, and wasting his money. Didn't save up for a rainy day. Spent it all on useless tools. "Wonder what his wife must think? Doesn't she want to buy a new dress once in a while?"

But Clara Ford had the utmost faith in her husband. "Don't worry about me, Henry. My new dress can wait. Go right ahead."

At last his car was ready. "Like a strange, living creature from another world. You get into the seat, move a handle, and off it goes!"

Yet people were skeptical. A pretty enough toy, to be sure, but it would never do for practical purposes. Henry Ford, they said, was on the wrong track. Nobody but a fool would piddle around with a gasoline engine when everybody knew that the coming motive power was electricity.

And nobody but a fool—or a genius—would give up the security of an engineer's job for the insecurity of an inventor's dream. A "crank" with no future, a wife and a child to support, and a sputtering motor as the only collateral against want. Yet he managed to get the co-operation of a few other "cranks" like himself. They formed a little company with a capital of ten thousand dollars. The formation of this company was announced (August 19, 1899) in the *Detroit Free Press*. The item was sandwiched in between two advertisements—cucumbers at four cents a dozen, and cabbages at two cents a head.

The life of the company was short. One by one, Ford's backers lost heart and backed out.

But not Henry Ford. Slowly, patiently, fanatically, he went on with his dream. Another group of backers, another company dissolved. Two failures within three years. "Why don't you give up this crazy idea and go back to your job?" But Henry Ford "dug in with his toenails" and hung on. He built a racing car to enter in a meet against five other cars. A bicycle rider by the name of Barney Oldfield became interested in the car. "How do you run it?"

"Step in and find out."

Barney Oldfield stepped in. It took him but a few minutes to get the hang of the thing. "Let me race this car for you, Mr. Ford."

Henry Ford shook his head. "You've never driven a car before. It would be risking your life, you know."

Barney Oldfield insisted. "I might as well be dead as dead broke," he laughed.

Reluctantly Ford consented. Barney Oldfield drove the car and won the race.

From that day on financial backing was no longer a problem to Henry Ford.

IV

A NEW FORD COMPANY was organized with a cash investment of twenty-eight thousand dollars. The investors hoped for some profit, but had no idea to what a fantastic degree their hopes would be realized. One of them, the sister of James C. Couzens, put one hundred dollars into the company. In due time her one-hundred-dollar investment was worth three hundred and fifty-five thousand dollars.

These fabulous profits were due not only to the inventive skill but to the business genius of Henry Ford. His aim was mass production to reduce the cost of every car; his motto, a better product at a lower price. With this objective in mind, he kept on increasing his capacity and improving his cars—Model A, Model B, Model C, and so on until he got just what he and the public wanted—Model T. The famous "Tin Lizzie"—the toast and the jest of America. "No show," wrote Roger Burlingame in *Engines of Democracy*, "was a complete success without a Ford joke. For six years, this is said to have taken the place of all paid advertising." The publishers issued anthologies of "uncanny stories about a canny car." The Ford cars were said to have overrun not only the entire world but the underworld. A magazine writer quoted His Satanic Majesty as saying to a visiting motorist, "Help yourself to one of these cars and take a spin around Hades."

"But, Your Majesty," replied the motorist, "these are all Fords."

"Sure," said the Devil. "That's the Hell of it."

The more they joked about the Ford, the more popular it became. "Two flies," wrote Luke McLuke in his *Phord Philosophy*, "can manufacture 48,876,552,154 new flies in six months, but they haven't anything on two Ford factories." In this joke, with all its exaggeration, there was almost more truth than travesty. In the summer of 1927 the output of the Ford Model T had reached the almost astronomical figure of fifteen million cars.

V

HENRY FORD was now the butt of every humorist in the country. Every paper must have its quota of witticisms about the Ford "flivver." Some of these witticisms were rather derogatory in tone. They got on the nerves of Ford's associate, James C. Couzens. One day he sent the following letter to the editor of the *Detroit News*:

Sir—*I hereby forbid you ever again to mention the name of the Ford Motor Company in your publication.*

JAMES COUZENS, *General Manager*

At the same time he canceled all the Ford advertisements in that paper.

The editor sent out a representative to see Ford. "Jim has no sense of humor," laughed Ford. "I'll cancel his cancellation, and you can go right ahead with your jokes. I think they're funny. All good publicity."

Henry Ford had a strong sense of humor, and a heart full of compassion. When the first World War broke out he was horrified at the spectacle of man's inhumanity to man. At the suggestion of a number of idealists, he fitted out a ship to carry to Europe a delegation that might arrange for an armistice between the belligerent countries. "If I can be of any service whatever in helping end this war, I shall do it if it costs me every dollar and every friend I have."

The idea of the Peace Ship became a standing joke among the newspapers. "This Vessel of Mercy," wrote Walter Millis, "was launched, to the undying shame of American journalism, upon one vast sea of ridicule."

The mission was from the first doomed to failure. But Ford gave to it all his strength and energy and faith—"one of the few really rational and generous impulses of those insane years"—until February 1917, when the aggressiveness of the Prussians compelled the United States to sever diplomatic relations with Germany.

And then Ford threw himself heart and soul into the task of helping America prepare for the war. He converted his automobile plants into factories for the building of sea, air, and land weapons—Liberty motors, anti-submarine Eagles, caissons, helmets, ambulances, gas masks, battle tanks, and trucks. "I am a pacifist," he declared. "But if we can't have peace without fighting for it, by all means let us fight . . . And let us fight . . . with all our hearts and souls, until the end."

VI

HENRY FORD was a man with his head in the clouds but with his feet planted firmly upon the ground. Little by little he bought out his associates, until finally he alone controlled the Ford Motor Company. His organization had become an empire within a republic. It was a benevolent empire, to be sure. Like the more charitable of the Russian czars, he regarded himself as the Little Father of the men and the women who worked under his protection. He gave them good wages—too good, in fact, complained some of the professional economists. "Henry Ford," declared the *Wall Street Journal*, "has [in the establishing of a minimum wage] committed economic blunders if not crimes." He opened commissary stores

where his workmen got the necessities of life at prices substantially lower
than those prevailing in the rest of the country. He kept his workers employed even during the depression, when such employment meant a considerable financial loss to himself. His friends predicted his early
bankruptcy. But Ford only smiled.

For he was a perfect mechanic. He knew that a machine is at its best
when it is well oiled. His workers were human machines. Keep them in
trim, and the wheels will turn around without any friction or delay.

The workers, therefore, must accept Mr. Ford's kindness and Mr. Ford's
commands. They must have no minds, no desires, no complaints. It was
for him, and not for them, to decide whether their work was too hard or
too speedy or too long. When his workers tried to organize themselves
into a union and to join the CIO, he dismissed the eight "ringleaders."
And when the workers, in retaliation, went on strike, he did everything
within his power to put down the strike. He resented the interference
of the workers, of the courts, even of the government, with his own "benevolent" way of doing things. Yet when the CIO was granted the legal
right to organize his men, Henry Ford was big enough, in spite of his
resentment, to accept the inevitable. "It's the law, and we're living up
to it. If it's wrong, we'll find out. If it's right, we haven't anything to
lose."

Henry Ford had his errors of judgment. Some of these errors resulted
in inconvenience, and at times even in injustice, to others. But in every
case, when convinced of his error, he made the necessary amends. In 1927,
for example, a paper which he had founded—the *Dearborn Independent*
—published a series of articles prejudicial to the Jews. These articles resulted in a libel suit against him. Believing in the accuracy of the statements as published in the articles, he spent more than a million dollars
in preparation for his defense. In the course of the trial, however, he
became convinced that the articles in question were unfair. Whereupon
he made a public apology for the malignment of the Jewish race. "It has
since been found," wrote the editor of the *Independent*, "that inaccura-
cies were present in the articles . . . Such statements . . . are withdrawn."
In addition to this general retraction, Henry Ford issued a personal apology. "I deem it to be my duty as an honorable man to make amends
for the wrong done to the Jews as fellow men and brothers, by asking
their forgiveness for the harm I have unintentionally committed, by re-
tracting so far as lies within my power the offensive charges laid at their
door, and by giving them the unqualified assurance that henceforth they
may look to me for friendship and good will."

The pettiness of error, the bigness of retraction, and the leavening grace
of good will—these were among the fundamentals in the character of
Henry Ford. In spite of his faults, he was intrinsically just and gentle and
good. His goodness extended not only to his workers—among them there
are fifty deaf-mutes, two hundred with crippled arms, and twelve hundred

with only one eye—but to all helpless living things. Once, while he was having a new house built, he moved with his family into an old cottage. The cottage had been vacant for some time, and a couple of birds had made their nests just above the front door. When Ford noticed this he put up the following sign on the front porch:

"Please use the back door. There is a nest of young phoebes in one corner of the porch, and a robin's nest in the other corner. Mr. Ford does not want anyone to use the front door until the little birds have left their nests."

He built hospitals, established schools, and rehabilitated worn-out acreage for farming. "It is my aim to develop young men and to restore old men." One day he visited the distinguished Negro scientist, Dr. George Washington Carver. He found him in poor health. "Pretty hard job to climb the stairs to your bedroom, isn't it, Doctor?"

"Oh, I manage it somehow," replied the old man.

Henry Ford turned the conversation to other matters. The next day, however, a number of workmen arrived at the home of Dr. Carver.

"What's the meaning of this?"

"We're going to install an automatic elevator, sir. Mr. Ford ordered it for you."

VII

HENRY FORD wanted to see a country happy at work, happy at play. As for himself, he enjoyed his play as much as his work. He loved to go off "gypsying" into the forest with his three cronies—Harvey Firestone, John Burroughs, and Thomas Edison. One day the four "vagabonds" were riding through the countryside in a Model T. A mazda lamp had burned out, and Ford stopped at a gas station to buy a new bulb. "By the way," he said to the owner of the station, "the man who invented the bulb is sitting out there in the car."

"You don't mean Thomas Edison?"

"Yes, I do." Ford's eyes roved to the rack behind the counter where he noticed a number of Firestone tires. "And it might interest you to know that one of the other men in the car is Harvey Firestone."

"Do tell!"

"And *my* name," with a twinkle in the eye, "is Henry Ford."

"Glad to meet you, Mr. —— Hey, hold on a minute. If you tell me that guy with the whiskers out there is Santa Claus, I'll call the sheriff!"

VIII

HENRY FORD in his seventies. Thin white hair, high forehead, blue-gray eyes, thin face furrowed with thought, firm lips that readily relax into a smile, long sensitive fingers, plain inexpensive clothes, plain inexpensive tastes. His greatest pleasures were the pleasures of the home. The one red-letter day of his old age was his fiftieth wedding anniversary. Bridegroom of half a century of golden honeymoons. "It is probable," observed the *New York Herald Tribune* on this occasion, "that the Fords are the richest couple on earth. Whether that fact is more astonishing than their record of having remained married fifty years is a matter for debate. And they remain essentially simple people . . . they still dance with each other. It may be that, in more matters than one, they are the richest people in the world."

In the course of the celebration Henry Ford submitted to a newspaper interview. "What," asked one of the reporters, "is your formula for a successful marriage?"

"The same as for a successful car," replied Ford. "Stick to one model."

A successful marriage, a fabulous portion of riches, and the common human cup of sorrow. A few years after the red-letter day came the black-letter day of his life. His only son, Edsel Ford, died.

But Henry Ford carried on. As in the first World War, he now turned all his resources and all his energy to helping his country win the second World War. His hatred of war had now matured into a hatred of aggression. Henry Ford was still true to his lifelong dream of peace. "What," he was asked, "do you think will come out of this war?"

"Out of this war," he replied, "will come the Great Awakening—the establishment of the Brotherhood of Man and the Federation of the World."

It was with this dream in his heart that he died—peacefully and simply as he had lived—on April 7, 1947.

IMPORTANT DATES IN THE LIFE OF HENRY FORD

1863—July 30, born, Greenfield, Michigan.

1876—Became interested in repairing watches.
Became mechanic in Detroit.

1888—Married Clara Bryant.
Employed by Detroit Edison Company.

1892—Completed his first gasoline motorcar.

1899—Organized Detroit Automobile Company.

1902—Went into business for himself.

1903—Formed the Ford Motor Company.

1909—Began to specialize in Model T car.

1915—Chartered Peace Ship in effort to end World War I.

1918—Ran unsuccessfully for United States Senate.

1927—Completed car number 15,-000,000.

1939-45—Devoted self to government war work.

1947—April 7, died, Dearborn, Michigan.

George Washington Carver

1864–1943

O NE of the foremost agricultural scientists of the century, George
Washington Carver, was born into slavery on a plantation near Diamond
Grove, Missouri, during the Civil War. No human being had a less aus-
picious beginning to a distinguished career. His birthday was no more
recorded by his owner than that of a chipmunk.

The years of the War between the States were among the most hectic
in American history. Thieves rode high and handsome, plundering plantations and carrying off all movable property. One turbulent night a band
of these pirates on horseback swooped down upon the stock of Moses
Carver, an industrious German farmer of Newton County, Missouri. They
made off with a slave mother and her son. Moses Carver, understanding
the tricks of the trade, dispatched a neighbor to follow the thieves and
offer them other goods in exchange for his blacks. His emissary tracked
down the robbers and discovered that the mother had already been sold.
But he bartered Moses Carver's race horse, valued at three hundred dollars, for the baby.

Cynical friends were amazed that Carver should yield a fine-blooded
horse for an undernourished black baby, racked by whooping cough
through long exposure to the cold. This sickly infant would never grow
into a man fit for heavy manual duty on the plantation. In the business
of slavery the only heart most men knew was the suit of red in a poker
hand. But a miracle had taken place in the House of Carver—the miracle
of love. Carver's wife had grown exceedingly fond of the child of her Negro
servant. She gathered him in her arms and nursed him back to health.
When the war was over and slavery was put to rest in the graves of the

blue and the gray, the little Negro was adopted by his former owners. He was given their family name and, in addition, the Christian surname George Washington "because of his truthfulness."

The whooping cough signaled a long siege of illness for the little lad. He grew frail as a plant. Since he was unable to labor in the fields, Mrs. Carver kept him in the kitchen and taught him to prepare meals, to bake and brew and iron and sew. After the day's work, however, the lad roamed in the forest around the farm. He loved to whittle the wood of the trees. With one of Moses Carver's hunting knives he fashioned crutches for a crippled boy in order that he might play with the other children.

No human being was ever more sensitive to the growth of life. Born an outcast from the society of men, he sought the society of plants. He perceived that flowers received an equal blessing from the rain and sunshine whether they were white or black or yellow. And he knew instinctively, before he was old enough to formulate his knowledge, that it was from this variety that the community of nature drew her beauty and her strength. He brought armfuls of flowers and shrubs to play with in his room. He went to sleep gripping these playmates in his hands. And whenever his little friends were sick, he transplanted them and healed them with uncanny skill.

With the men and women around him he was incurably shy. As a result of frequent attacks of the croup, he had developed a stammer in his speech, and much of the time no one could understand what he said. But the plants knew. He spoke to them in the touch of his fingers. And seeking additional ways of speaking the joy within him, he painted and sketched them. With all his being he felt that he had been appointed to make things grow. But his brain was enchained. One day he chanced across a blue-backed Webster speller. It was a formidable tool for self-expression. He plunged into a welter of words, much like Abraham Lincoln years before him, mastering countless cryptic spellings whose meanings he had not the slightest notion of.

But homespun learning was not sufficient. A school had been established for colored children in Neosho, eight miles from the Carver farm. To Neosho the ten-year-old George now turned his steps, with the blessings of his foster parents who had been impressed with his talents. When he reached his destination he found a stable for his first night's lodging. He lay down exhausted in the company of the horses.

He took his place by the other children on the bench of learning. After school hours he trekked from family to family, seeking work. A Negro family provided him with food and a bed in return for his services in the kitchen. Within a year he had absorbed all that the honest but limited teacher could offer. Folk spoke highly of the schools in the state of Kansas that were open to Negro and white pupils alike. George took the road to Fort Scott, Kansas. He hopped into a mule wagon on the way and arrived in the community faced, as usual, with the problem of food and lodging and without a cent in his pockets.

Then commenced the pathetic routine. He knocked on doors to barter his services. He washed clothes, scrubbed floors, milked cows, snatching hungrily at an education. For seven years he remained at Fort Scott, going to school at odd hours. And then one night he came face to face with the stark tragedy of man's inhumanity to man. While performing an errand, he came to the town jail. An insane mob dragged a Negro prisoner from his cell and vented its vengeance upon him in the streets. George ran shuddering to his lodgings. In the thick of the night he slipped out of the town and picked his way along the road, searching for the dawn.

II

HE CONTINUED HIS QUEST for schooling and for work to keep his bones together while he learned to converse with savants and saints. Most of his time was consumed in scheming for his next loaf of bread or for a lesson book he required. But while he struggled with his bleak surroundings, God's gifts were maturing within him. Hounded and neglected and famished, he was yet one of fortune's princelings to whom destiny had bequeathed a priceless inner life that someday all men would envy. With his hands he wove intricate and dazzling crochet patterns, earning a few cents and satisfying his compulsion to create. Who could have acknowledged the bright world that was locked within the unprepossessing body of this Negro lad? When he received his high-school diploma at seventeen and took a train to Missouri to visit the Carvers, whom he had not seen in eight years, the ticket agent sold him a ticket at half fare, judging by his height that he was under the full-fare age.

Casting about for money to enter college and crown his long struggle for an education, he secured a room in Minneapolis, Kansas, for five dollars a month and opened a laundry service. His industriousness made many friends for him. The business venture proved profitable. Better food stimulated his growth, and he shot up almost as quickly as the beanstalk in the fable, until by the time he was twenty-one he reached nearly six feet.

He applied to Highland College in Kansas and was accepted by mail. Overjoyed, he sold his laundry, severed all business and social ties with Minneapolis, and set out for the school. But when he presented himself in person, the president found that he had made a serious error. It had never occurred to him that the candidate was not a white student. "Sorry, but we don't take Negroes here," he announced. And he shut the door on George.

It was a rude jolt for the Negro lad who had already suffered so many jolts. But he refused to lie down and play dead. Self-pity was a term he had not learned to spell in his Webster. The United States Government had opened lands in western Kansas for settlers, and many pioneer folk had grasped eagerly at the opportunity. Realizing that college was out of the question for the present, George migrated westward. He filed a claim for one hundred and sixty acres, built a sod house, and planted his crops. For two years he tended his farm and thought things out in the wind and sun and blizzards. But even in the Kansas desert he refused to relinquish his dream. Eastward lay the fulfillment of his destiny, a life of culture and learning. He had not survived a kidnaping on a plantation and lived through twenty-one years of misery merely to build upon the sand. Two years after the filing he proved upon his claim. He was too restless to remain the required five years on the property and obtain it free. He took out a mortgage for three hundred dollars and turned his steps toward Iowa.

And now fortune presented him with her first genuine smile. She gave him the key with which to unlock the final recesses of his intellectual self. An acquaintance informed him of a college at Indianola, Iowa, which had been established in accordance with the wishes of Bishop Matthew Simpson, an abolitionist and a lifelong friend of Abraham Lincoln. It was inconceivable that a college with such an origin would discriminate against a Negro. George hiked the twenty-five miles to Indianola and applied for admittance to Simpson. And he was accepted. Years later, when he had joined the ranks of the most renowned scientists of the age, sought after by governments and academic institutions everywhere, he remarked in a voice charged with feeling, "It was at Simpson that I first realized I was a human being."

Upon paying his entrance fees on his first day at Simpson, he discovered that he had ten cents left in his pocket. A woman offered him her woodshed to live in. Once again he turned his skill at needling and ironing clothes to financial account. He bought a washtub and went into the laundry business, servicing the college students and successfully meeting his bills. But his battle to earn a living was of minor importance now. The long struggle with a hostile world had ended in a victory for him.

The years at Simpson were the first genuinely happy years of his life. He began a systematic study of botany and the allied sciences. His fellow students, admiring his mental abilities, had accepted him as a companion in full. He assumed a leading musical role in student concerts, participated in the literary societies, and took piano lessons and paid for them with his paintings. His love for art competed with his enthusiasm for botany. He rapidly rose to the top position in his art class, and he permitted himself to dream that perhaps he would make a profession of his painting. He talked it over with his teacher, who declared that a career in art was not practical for him. Painting pictures would bring him personal satisfaction. But a colored man of his talents had no right to think in terms of private achievement. And George agreed. To enlist in the service of his fellow Negro, he needed more than the skill to paint canvases. "I

can be of more service to my race in agriculture." With this decision
firmly taken, he rounded out two years at Simpson and matriculated at
Iowa State College of Agriculture and Mechanic Arts to broaden his training as an agricultural chemist.

Upon receiving his bachelor's degree in science, he was offered a job by
a florist. He refused. "I did not earn my education in order to arrange
flowers for the dead." A much more vital position was tendered him. So
impressed were his professors by his wizardry in botany that they selected
their first Negro graduate for an appointment on the faculty! It was a
fascinating assignment. He was appointed assistant botanist and placed in
charge of the greenhouse. Here he experimented in bacterial research and
painted his beloved plants to his heart's content. He was like a young colt
let loose in a pasture. His knowledge of plants astounded both his students and the professors alike. Stories of his achievements spread beyond
the campus, and he accepted invitations to speak before horticultural societies throughout the state. By the time he obtained his master's degree
in 1896, and his formal training at Iowa was finished, talk about his
brilliance had reached the official ears of numerous university circles. He
was sought after by some of the most important faculties in the country.
Characteristically enough, he chose the one position most suited to his
temperament and to his ideals.

In 1881, Booker T. Washington, born like Carver into slavery, had assumed direction of an educational institution whose aims were far more
shining than its material assets. Several million Negroes, suddenly freed
from the shackles of physical slavery, had been plunged into economic
serfdom, mired helplessly on mortgaged farms, ignorant of the first principles of feeding and supporting themselves. Tuskegee was established to
train teachers to impart to their people the elements of an education. Reports reached Washington, as he was organizing his faculty, of the brilliant young Negro botanist in Iowa. He immediately wrote to Carver
requesting his services to direct the Department of Agriculture at Tuskegee. "If you are willing to come here," he wrote, "we can pay you fifteen
hundred dollars a year and board, board to include all expenses except
traveling. This perhaps may not seem a large salary, but from the first we
have made a policy of trying to get teachers who come not . . . for the
money but . . . for their deep interest in the race." And Carver answered
the summons. "I will go to my people."

III

WHEN HE ARRIVED at Booker T. Washington's educational center, Carver
discovered that Tuskegee had none of the facilities of Iowa State College.
He could not find enough space even for the valuable mycological specimens he had collected. "My room is full of mice and they are damaging
my boxes," he complained to Washington. There was no sewerage system

at the institute, let alone an adequate laboratory for him to work in. Washington calmly answered his complaints. "The equipment must be in the head of the man and not in the laboratory." The young professor was not slow to take the hint. He set to work fashioning his materials by hand. He turned an old bottle of ink into a bunsen burner, stored his chemicals in teacups, collected the discarded zinc tops of fruit jars, and used a horseshoe for a bell with which to summon his classes. One day Washington, indicating the barren ground around the buildings of the institute, declared to the young botanist: "Our people have always been challenged with signs telling them to 'Keep off the grass.' Do you think you can grow grass out there for them?" And Carver, with the skill that was in his fingers and the knowledge of soils in his mind, covered the grounds with a rug of grass.

Cotton, the cash crop of the South, had pretty well exhausted the farm land of its fertility for food crops. Carver made a thorough analysis of the Alabama soil and discovered just what elements had to be added to transform it into a productive land. And when he had devised methods for turning the desert into Canaan, he visited the farmer and brought him the results of his laboratory research. For Tuskegee was not only a university for students, it was an experimental center for the benefit of the whole community.

He originated an "experiment wagon," from which he gave portable demonstrations of the results of his research. He remained for several days at a farm settlement, frequently setting up headquarters in the county courthouse. A field was plowed for demonstrations in planting, a garden selected for vegetable displays; wives were instructed in model housekeeping. He examined blighted crops and, with the uncanny instinct of a doctor diagnosing ailments in human beings, he invariably tracked down the disease and saved them. His success at plant doctoring became legendary.

Devotedly he continued his dual role, teaching students and performing public service for the community. To free him from the minor jobs that plagued a teacher at Tuskegee, Washington created a Department of Agricultural Research. Now that Carver was at liberty to indulge in limitless research, he produced results that rivaled the fabled alchemists. He investigated the clays of the countryside and extracted from them tints and stains which the Negro farmers were able to employ with startling success on the walls of their houses. Shoveling up red clay and processing it through successive stages of oxidization, he rediscovered the royal blue with which the Egyptians had painted the tombs of their kings and which had been lost to man for centuries. He developed from the clay also a powder to scour silver and a dust to kill the Colorado beetle on white potatoes. In addition he devised fifty-three different products from the feathers of domestic fowls. "And I have only begun to show their wonderful possibilities."

He found new methods for curing and pickling meats, provided a hundred ways to serve the tomato, and discovered more than two hundred and fifty medicinal properties of plants. When war came to the United States in 1917, and American markets were cut off from the aniline dyes of Germany, he perfected an amazing series of vegetable dyes as a substitute, processing more than five hundred varieties from the roots and stems and fruits of twenty-eight plants. The country suffered from a wheat shortage. And this Negro Paracelsus demonstrated the possibilities of using the sweet potato as a bread maker. For years he had been making eggs from the Puerto Rican sweet potato.

But the results of one investigation in particular were so startlingly picturesque that they won for him instant recognition in the hearts of millions of his fellow men. Since 1912 the boll weevil had swept from Mexico into Dixie Land and had systematically destroyed the cotton. This struck a vital blow at Southern prosperity. And it became evident that salvation lay only in the discovery of another crop that could be used as a business substitute. Carver, convinced that the "Creator had deposited somewhere in the ground something that could take cotton's place," began a long, arduous research, hunting for a clue to the plant. He tore apart the sweet potato and put its chemical elements together into different syntheses. He extracted starch and sugar and more than one hundred other products before he was finished. But none of these were as marketable as cotton. Then he examined the pecan but decided it would not do. Finally he turned to the peanut, whose properties had intrigued him for years. But was it worth while to try to break the peanut? It seemed a pretty worthless plant, used chiefly to feed hogs.

Years later he was fond of relating to his students how he began his successful experiments with the peanut. "I went into my laboratory and said, 'Dear Creator, please tell me what the universe was made for.' And the Creator declared, 'You want to know too much for such a little mind. Ask for something your size.' Then I asked, 'Dear Creator, tell me what man was made for.' Again the great Creator answered, 'Little one, you are still asking too much. Make your request a more proportionate one.' 'Tell me then, Creator, what the peanut was made for.' Then the great Creator taught me how to take the peanut apart and put it together again. And out of this came all these products which the Creator taught me to make."

In 1921 an association of peanut growers in the South, witnessing what the Tuskegee professor had done with the "lowly" peanut, requested that he appear on their behalf before a Senate committee for a tariff to protect their product. Carver arrived at the Capitol carrying a box crammed with the fantastic products he had extracted in his laboratory. He entered the committee room and sat down quietly in the rear while a score of speakers argued for and against the legislation. By the time his name was called, the senators were weary with statistics and anxious to go home. Some regarded the Negro listlessly, some with amused tolerance.

What did this old fellow know about the tariff? they asked themselves.

The chairman of the committee warned Carver that he had only ten minutes of speaking time. The professor nodded and plunged into his story of the peanut. When his ten minutes were over, the senators shouted for him to continue. He did, for an hour and a half. Never before had they witnessed such a demonstration! He drew from his box milk, cereal, coffee, Worcestershire sauce, face cream, printer's ink, mock oysters, soaps, salads, vinegar, butter, oil dyes, wood stains, paints, flavors, axle grease, shampoos. And as he presented each item he told the politicos that he had extracted each one from the peanut!

At the conclusion of the amazing performance John Nance Garner rose and declared in behalf of his colleagues: "You have made the most wonderful exhibition ever presented to this committee." And all the senators rose to their feet and applauded. Although Carver declared that he had not appeared in behalf of the tariff but in the interests of science, the Senate wrote into the Smoot-Hawley Bill the steepest rate ever accorded the peanut growers, and a new high-powered Southern industry was born.

Indeed, "Mr. Creator" had played a smart trick on men. Through the genius of a scientist who had been born a slave, a quarter-of-a-billion-dollar industry sprang up in the South, bringing it great wealth. But Carver refused to take a cent of the profits. "Mr. Creator did not charge anything to grow a peanut, and I cannot accept money for my work with it." Before he died Carver had wrested more than three hundred products from the peanut. He had shown mankind how it was possible to live almost entirely on it alone.

A certain Mr. Tom Huston, who had established a business on Dr. Carver's investigations, once asked the scientist what gift he would most like to receive. "A diamond," instantly replied Carver. Huston purchased a diamond set in a platinum ring. He sent it to Carver. Then he dispatched a friend to find out if the professor was pleased with the present. When the visitor asked Carver where his diamond was, the scientist opened a case of geological specimens—and there it lay among his minerals!

IV

AT THE TIME when George Washington Carver's demonstrations with the peanut first brought him to the attention of men everywhere, he was nearing sixty. His hair had silvered. He walked with a slight stoop. His sense of humor was as fertile as the soils he nourished. Once a reporter for a national magazine described him as being toothless. "Fiddlesticks!" exploded Carver. "What a pity he didn't ask! Then he would not have made such a shameful error. If he had taken the trouble to inquire, I could have proved I am not toothless. I had my teeth right in my pocket all the time."

His colleagues were often shocked at his "lack of dignity." He was incorrigible in his dress. He donned scarves and ties dyed in his own plant juices to determine their wearing characteristics. Daily he picked for his lapel a native flower, and it refused to wilt even in the hottest weather. In 1937, when he attended the unveiling of a bronze bust of himself, he wore the suit in which he had graduated from Iowa State College more than forty years before. At Tuskegee commencements he yielded to custom and appeared in an academic gown—with the tassel of his cap dangling on the wrong side.

He was not interested in making money. At the crest of his fame he continued to draw his fifteen hundred dollars a year from Tuskegee. The treasurer had to follow him and plead with him to cash his salary checks, some of which had gathered dust for months, so that the books could be cleared. Edison offered him one hundred and seventy-five thousand dollars a year if he would join his research staff. But he was unwilling to leave Tuskegee. Henry Ford, who became an intimate friend and enthusiastic admirer, tried time and again to wean him from the institute. But the Detroit industrialist failed to win his services. "Mr. Washington is not with us any more in person, and I wouldn't be true to this great cause if I should leave here."

Lavish honors were tendered him. He received a Doctor of Science degree from Simpson College, his alma mater. He was elected a fellow of the Royal Society of London, one of the most exalted of scientific bodies. Governments wooed him. Before the first World War, Germany requested his advice on the best means of growing cotton in her African colonies. In 1931 Joseph Stalin invited Carver to visit the Soviet Union and assist in the cotton industry. But Carver declined to go because of his age. In 1935 the United States Government appointed him consultant to the Division of Mycology and Disease Survey in the Department of Agriculture, but he was permitted to carry out his duties from Tuskegee Institute.

For the greater bulk of his life Carver had worked without any assistants, carrying on his tremendous researches down to the last detail with his own hands. But when he passed his seventieth year he at last became anxious to train someone in his philosophy and methods so that his work would not die with him. And he selected as the inheritor of his professional knowledge Austin W. Curtis, Jr., a Negro graduate of Cornell University. The indoctrination of Curtis was a leading incentive that kept Carver alive during the remaining seven and a half years of his life. The professor and assistant worked side by side in the laboratory, traveled together, and gave lectures on the same platform. Inevitably the scientific mind of Curtis was fashioned in the image of his teacher.

As a further preparation to extend the life of his labors, the professor contributed his savings, over thirty thousand dollars, to the endowment of the George Washington Carver Foundation, a research center for promising Negro scientists. Meanwhile he continued his own experiments to make happier the fortune of man.

His lean body was bent and his steps dragged. But he entered his laboratory daily, as long as he was able, and watered his flowers. When an attack of pernicious anemia laid him low, his greatest sorrow was his inability to inspect the new greenhouse which the institute had recently built. When he gained sufficient strength to leave the hospital, he resumed his walks in the woods at dawn and he painted with his fingers in the pigments of the Alabama clay.

Finally Tuskegee, to whom he had remained loyal, was ready to receive him in her warm friendly earth. Booker T. Washington had already been put to rest, and there was a bed beside him waiting. In January 1943 the aged scientist took leave of the plants in this life.

IMPORTANT DATES IN THE LIFE OF GEORGE WASHINGTON CARVER

1864–Born near Diamond Grove, Missouri.

1890–Entered Simpson College, Iowa.

1894–Received his B.S. from Iowa State College of Agriculture and Mechanic Arts.

1896–Received master's degree in science from Iowa State College of Agriculture and Mechanic Arts.

Appointed to faculty at Tuskegee Institute in Alabama.

1916–Named a fellow in the Royal Society of Arts, London.

1921–Displayed more than one hundred extracts from the peanut before United States Senate committee.

1923–Awarded the Spingarn Medal for most distinguished contribution by a Negro to science.

1935–Appointed to United States Department of Agriculture, Bureau of Plant Research.

1940–Established the George Washington Carver Foundation.

1943–January 5, died, Tuskegee, Alabama.

Marie Curie

1867–1934

I N 1903 MADAME CURIE was the most celebrated woman in the world. She had just shared the Nobel Prize in Physics together with Pierre Curie and with Henri Becquerel. Screaming headlines in the newspapers, thousands of letters from autograph seekers, innumerable requests for lectures, messages from "departed spirits" forwarded through the "collaboration" of trance mediums, banquets, honors, titles, reporters, photographers, curiosity-hunters—all these had descended upon her in an avalanche of unwelcome hosannas. Manufacturers of popular articles solicited her endorsement. A horse breeder asked for her permission to name his favorite horse after her. For many years the spotlight of public adulation kept singling her out as the foremost of public characters—save one. As she got out of a train to deliver a lecture in Berlin one day, she was pleasantly surprised to find herself alone. The mob had stormed to another part of the platform where Jack Dempsey was getting out of the same train. The world's champion physicist was not quite so important a personage as the world's champion pugilist.

Madame Curie thoroughly despised the distinctions and the distractions of glory. She regarded herself as a captive chained and led unwillingly in a triumphal procession. She threw away her caps and her gowns and her titles and her medals as soon as she got them. The only things she kept were the menus from the banquets at which she sat as a martyred guest. "These menus, made of thick, hard cardboard, are so convenient for scribbling down my mathematical calculations."

Speaking of this most modest of celebrated women, the most modest of celebrated men—Albert Einstein—once remarked: "Marie Curie is, among all distinguished people, the only one whom fame has not corrupted."

II

Manya sklodovska, known today as Marie Curie, came of a Polish stock of noble and honest peasants. Her parents had risen above the soil into the rarefied atmosphere of higher education. Her father was a professor of physics at the Warsaw High School, and her mother was an accomplished pianist. Manya—a pet name for Marya—inherited her father's brains and her mother's hands. She showed an early aptitude for experimental science. But her parents did not allow any of their five children to do much studying. There was a taint of consumption in the family. Whenever Manya became absorbed in her books, Madame Sklodovska would put her hand gently on the child's head. "Go and play in the garden, Manyusha. It's so beautiful outside."

Every evening at their prayers the children added a final sentence: "And please, God, restore our mother's health."

But it pleased God to take Madame Sklodovska from her children— there were four now; one of them had died of typhus. Manya was only ten when she was left motherless.

It was a sad and impoverished family that gathered around the table after Madame Sklodovska's departure. Manya's father had lost his position in the high school because of his aspiration for the freedom of Poland from the tyranny of the Russian czar. He had opened a boarding school, but with indifferent success. The maintenance of his family seemed a task beyond his feeble powers. Four healthy mouths to be fed, four growing bodies to be clothed, and four active minds to be educated. Desperately he invested his inadequate savings in the hope that the numerator of his possessions might grow equal to the denominator of his needs. But he lost his entire investment. He had nothing to look forward to.

Nothing but four children with superior brains and superior grit. All these children were destined to rise from poverty to achievement. For the strength of the Polish soil was within them.

And the aspiration of the Polish heart. The aspiration of a free soul in a chained body. The Sklodovski children, like their father, were rebels. They fought against adversity and they fought against tyranny. Every morning when Manya walked to school, she passed by a statue dedicated "to the Poles faithful to their Sovereign"—that is, to the Poles who were faithless to their country. Manya always made it a point to spit upon this statue. If, by inadvertence, she failed to perform this act of disrespect, she turned back to make good her failure—even at the risk of coming late to school.

This gallant little rebel expressed her contempt for oppression not only in the absence but also in the presence of her oppressors. Among her teachers who represented the alien governing power over Poland was Mademoiselle Mayer, the German superintendent of studies. This "slithering spy with her muffled slippers" was a little bit of a woman with a prodigious capacity for hate. She made life unbearable for her Polish pupils—especially for "that Sklodovska girl" who dared to answer her lashing tongue with a scornful smile. But Manya was not always content with a mere smile of silent scorn. One day "the spy" attempted, with a none too gentle hand, to straighten Manya's unruly Polish curls into a conventional Gretchen braid. In vain. Manya's hair, like her spirit, refused to yield to the tyrant's touch. Exasperated at "the capricious head and the contemptuous eyes" of her Polish pupil, Mayer finally shouted:

"Stop staring at me like that! I forbid you to look down upon me!"

Whereupon Manya, who was a head taller than Mayer, replied sweetly: "I can't very well do anything else, Mademoiselle."

Yet in spite of her rebellion Manya carried off the gold medal at the completion of her high school course (in 1883). It had become a habit with the Sklodovskis to win this highest award for scholarship. There were by this time three gold medals in the family.

And now, said her father, enough of study for the present. Let her go to the country for a year and build up her body. "This pretty child must not, like her mother, fall a victim to consumption."

Manya gladly consented to her father's suggestion. For she loved her play as she loved her work. She yielded herself "body and soul" to the luxury of idleness. "My dear little devil," she wrote to her school friend, Kazia, "I can hardly believe there is any such thing in existence as geometry or algebra." She spent her summer days roaming in the woods, swinging, swimming, fishing, playing battledore and shuttlecock, or just lying on the grass and reading—"no serious books, I assure you, but only absurd and harmless little novels." And she spent her winter nights and days—dancing. Those Polish dances! Starting at sunset and continuing in relays as the revelers, with the fiddlers at their head, journeyed from farmhouse to farmhouse, dancing away the night, beyond the dawn, beyond the sunset of the following day and into the sunrise of the next. And the most tireless as well as the most graceful dancer of them all was Manya Sklodovska. "All the young men from Cracow asked me to dance with them . . . very handsome boys . . . you can't imagine how delightful it was . . . It was eight o'clock of the (second) morning when we danced the last dance—a white mazurka." And then she had to throw away her slippers of russet leather, for "their soles had ceased to exist . . ."

III

AFTER HER YEAR'S VACATION she returned to Warsaw and to an uncertain future. Her older sister, Bronya, wanted to study at the Sorbonne, in Paris. So too did Manya. But there were not enough funds in the family to finance even one of them, let alone both, through the university. An insoluble problem, it seemed, yet Manya found the solution. "I will get a job as governess and help you through college. Then you will get a doctor's degree and help me in return."

It seemed an audacious plan, but it worked. Manya became a "teaching servant" in the family of Madame B——, a stupid, vulgar, and intolerant woman who economized on oil for the lamps and who gambled away her money on cards. "My existence," wrote the young governess, "has become unbearable . . . I shouldn't like my worst enemy to live in such a hell." Fortunately she was able to exchange this for a better position in a somewhat more intelligent home. Her new "mistress," Madame Z——, was fully as intolerant though not quite so vulgar as her former employer. "Madame Z—— has a bad temper, but she is not at all a bad woman . . . Some of her children—she has a whole collection of them—are really delightful."

Especially Casimir, the eldest son. A university student at Warsaw, he had come home for vacation and had promptly fallen in love with the pretty little Sklodovska who not only could talk like a scholar but who could dance like a goddess. And Manya, affectionate and sensitive and lonely, returned his love.

But there was to be no marriage between them. Casimir's mother refused to accept a governess into her family—forgetting that she herself had been a governess before her marriage. For a time Manya played with the idea of suicide. "I have buried all my plans, sealed and forgotten them," she wrote to one of her cousins. "The walls are too strong for the heads that try to break them down . . . I mean to say farewell to this contemptible world. The loss will be small, and regret for me will be short . . ."

She got over her despondency, however. The Sklodovskis were not the suicide type. She returned to her teaching and her scrimping and continued to support Bronya at the Sorbonne. The latter, thanks to Manya's assistance and to an inborn talent for enduring the pangs of hunger, succeeded in starving and studying her way through to a medical degree. She married Casimir Dluski, a fellow student in medicine, and was now ready to conclude her half of the bargain with Manya. The young governess was able at last to see the fulfillment of her most ardent dream. The Sorbonne!

IV

MARIE SKLODOVSKA—she had registered her first name in the French manner—student in the Faculty of Science—age, 23—hair, ashen-blonde—personality, taciturn—ability, exceptional. She always sat in the front row at the lectures; but the moment the lectures were over, she glided out like a shadow. Her sad experience with the social conventions had planted within her an aversion for all sorts of society. "Fine hair, fine eyes, fine figure of a girl," remarked the boys at the university. "But the trouble is, she won't talk to anybody."

For four years "she led the life of a monk." Refusing to be a burden to her sister, she lived alone. She had hired, at fifteen francs (about $3) a month, a sixth-floor attic in the Latin Quarter. The only light came in through a loophole in the slanted ceiling. The room had no heat and no water. In this prison of a room she lived upon a general diet of bread and butter and tea—with the luxury of an egg or a fruit thrown in on the rarest of occasions. In the winter she put a handful of coal into a toy stove and sat doing her equations with numb fingers long after the fire had gone out. Then, at about two in the morning, she crept into an iron bed with insufficient covers.

One day a classmate reported to the Dluskis that Manya had fainted in front of her. Casimir hurried to her attic where he found her at work on her next day's lessons.

"What did you eat today?"

Manya looked up with an evasive smile. "Today? I don't remember."

"Come, come, Manya. No evasions. What did you eat today?"

"Oh, cherries . . . and everything."

Finally he got the confession out of her. For the past twenty-four hours she had lived on a handful of radishes and half a pound of cherries. Much against her will he carried her off to his house where Bronya fed her and rested her up for a few days. And then, in spite of all the protestations of the Dluskis, she returned to her attic and her hunger and her books.

She lived in the world of her books. And of her lectures. In spite of her poverty and her hunger, she felt like an intrepid explorer adventuring over an unfamiliar sea. And she meant to make every mile of it familiar as she kept journeying from day to day to an ever expanding horizon. Physics, chemistry, mathematics, poetry, music, astronomy—the entire circle of the earth and the heavens had come within the range of her intellectual domain. But above all she was interested in her experiments. She regarded the laboratory as a delicate musical instrument upon the keys of which, with the skillful fingers inherited from her mother, she kept constantly seeking to combine old notes into new tunes.

Her professors, delighted with her imagination and her enthusiasm and her skill, kept encouraging her to undertake new researches. And one day, emboldened by her success, she declared that she would carry her special researches not into one but into two fields. She would try for a double master's degree—in physics and in mathematics.

And she succeeded. She passed first in the master's examination in physics (1893), and second in the master's examination in mathematics (1894).

A brief vacation in Poland, and then back to Paris—and to her second love affair. After her first unfortunate plunge into the whirlpool of romantic passion, she had vowed to dedicate the rest of her life to a single passion for science. She had no use for men.

And at that time there lived in Paris a young man, Pierre Curie, who had no use for women. He, too, had devoted his life to the exclusive pursuit of science.

One day they met at the apartment of M. Kovalski, a Polish professor of physics who was visiting Paris. "When I came in," wrote Marie, "Pierre Curie was standing in the window recess near a door leading to the balcony. He seemed very young to me, although he was then aged thirty-five. I was struck by the frank expression of his eyes and by a slight appearance of carelessness in his tall figure. I liked his slow, reflective words, his simplicity and his smile, at once grave and youthful. We started to converse on matters of science . . . and before we knew it we were friends."

Pierre Curie, the son of a French physician, had become a bachelor of science at sixteen and a master of physics at eighteen. When he met Marie, he was head of the laboratory at the Parisian School of Chemistry and Physics. His achievements had already placed him in the front rank of French scientists. He had formulated the principle of symmetry in the structure of crystals. Together with his brother Jacques he had discovered the important phenomenon of piezoelectricity—that is, the generation of electricity by means of pressure. He had invented a new apparatus for the precise measurement of minute quantities of electricity. And he had constructed an ultra-sensitive instrument—known as the *Curie Scale*— for checking the results of scientific experiments.

For all these achievements he was receiving from the French State the miserable salary of three hundred francs (about $60) a month.

On this inadequate salary he timidly proposed marriage to Mademoiselle Sklodovska; and Mademoiselle Sklodovska—with equal timidity, it must be confessed—accepted.

Yet the marriage turned out to be not only a partnership of genius but also a comradeship of love. After an unconventional wedding without a lawyer or a priest—both of them were freethinkers—they enjoyed an equally unconventional honeymoon bicycling over the country roads of the Ile-de-France. Then they returned to Paris and settled down to the work which was to bring glory to the name of Curie and healing to an afflicted world.

V

MARIE TOOK CARE of the house, gave birth to a baby girl, then to another, studied for her doctorate in physics, won a fellowship with a monograph on the magnetization of tempered steel, and spent all the rest of her time collaborating with her husband in his experiments. The doctors warned her of a tubercular lesion in the left lung—the Sklodovski family taint. They advised her to go to a sanatorium. But Marie would not think of it. She was too deeply absorbed in her laboratory work. She and Pierre had become interested in the experiments of Henri Becquerel. This eminent French physicist, while examining the salts of a "rare metal," uranium, had discovered that these salts emitted a ray which apparently could penetrate opaque objects. A compound of uranium, which he had placed on a photographic plate surrounded by black paper, had made an impression on the plate *through* the paper. This, so far as we know, was the first human observation of the penetrating quality of certain strange types of rays.

What was the nature of this mysterious property of penetration through opaque objects? And whence came this peculiar energy? These questions exercised a strong fascination upon the minds of Marie and Pierre Curie. Here was a subject for original study, a thesis worthy of a doctor's degree at the Sorbonne!

Such was the enthusiastic yet humble beginning of the research that led to the discovery of radium. Marie had started out on the road to an ordinary doctorate. She found at the end of the road—the Nobel Prize in Physics.

But the traveling of the road was long and arduous and heartbreaking. It took a man and a woman of supreme imagination and of supreme courage to go on unfalteringly to the end.

Almost from the first they encountered insurmountable difficulties—and they surmounted them. The laboratory that the director of the School of Physics gave them for their experiments was an old and dilapidated woodshed. In this damp and cold shanty of a workroom—in the winter the temperature of the laboratory averaged about 44°—the consumptive little pioneer and her husband plunged resolutely into the unknown. With their pitiably inadequate apparatus they examined the nature of uranium and found that the mysterious radiation of this metal was an *atomic* property—a scientific discovery which years later (in 1945) was to lead to the invention of the atomic bomb. And then the light of a great thought fell upon Marie. Perhaps uranium was not the only chemical element that possessed the power of irradiation. Perhaps there were other substances with even greater powers of "penetrating the impenetrable." She must try and see . . .

And so another and even more daring venture into uncharted seas. Madame Curie took up all the known chemical bodies and submitted them to a rigorous test. And before long she discovered what she was after. Uranium was *not* the only element with that mysterious power of irradiation. Another element, thorium, possessed the same power in about the same degree. To this power Madame Curie now gave the name of *radioactivity*—the active and *penetrating* property of certain types of rays.

But this was only the beginning of her research. In her examination of some of the compounds of uranium and of thorium she had found a *far more powerful* radioactivity than could have been expected from the quantity of uranium or of thorium contained in the compounds. Whence came this extra power of radiation? To this question there was but a single answer—the compounds must have contained a chemical element whose radioactivity was far greater than that of uranium or of thorium. But Madame Curie had already examined all the *known* chemical elements and found no such powerful radioactivity in any of them. Therefore, she concluded, there must be a hitherto unknown element that possessed this power. *A new element.*

With beating heart she went to see her sister one day. "You know, Bronya, the radiation that I couldn't explain comes from a new chemical element. The element is there and I've got to find it!"

And now she set about the business of finding this new substance. It was in the pitchblende ore—an oxid of uranium—that she had noticed the tremendous power of radiation. Somewhere in this ore lurked the mysterious source of this power. The radioactive part of pitchblende, thought Madame Curie, must represent an exceedingly small fraction of the ore in its crude state, since no scientist before her had ever been able to discover it. Perhaps this new element would be found to consist of not more than one per cent of the pitchblende, concluded the cautious young Polish scientist. How great would have been her astonishment had she then realized that the new element she was trying to isolate consisted of only *one ten-thousandth of one per cent,* or *a millionth part,* of the pitchblende ore!

Marie and Pierre—they had always worked together on these researches—were now certain that they were on the threshold of a new discovery. But how to get beyond the threshold? Pitchblende, out of which they hoped to isolate their new element, was an expensive ore. It was mined in Bohemia for the extraction of the uranium salts that were used in the manufacture of glass. A ton of pitchblende, with the uranium that it contained, was far beyond the Curie pocketbook. It was a problem that seemed beyond solution.

But they solved it. If the new element, they reasoned, existed in the pitchblende and was yet different from uranium, then it could be isolated from the *residue* of the pitchblende *after* the uranium had been extracted. This residue was regarded as almost worthless. The Curies could have considerable quantities of it for little more than the cost of transportation.

And so these "queer" scientists, to everybody's amusement, began to order tons upon tons of "rubbish" to be shipped to their woodshed. And when this "rubbish" arrived they began to throw it, shovel by shovel, into an old cast-iron stove with a rusty pipe. For four years they kept at it like a couple of stokers in the hold of a ship—shoveling, gasping, coughing at the noxious fumes, forgetful of their discomfort and intent upon a single thought—to lure the secret of the new element out of the blazing metal.

And finally they lured out the secret—two secrets. For instead of one they found two new elements—a substance which they named *polonium* after Marie's native country, and another substance which they called *radium*.

The nature of polonium was amazing enough. Its radioactivity was ever so much more powerful than that of uranium. But the nature of radium was the eighth great wonder of the world. For its power of radiation was found to exceed that of uranium by *one and a half million per cent*.

VI

IT WAS CUSTOMARY for the recipients of the Nobel Prize to call for it in person at Stockholm. But the Curies were unable to make the journey. They were too ill. Quietly, modestly, humbly they went on with their work—and with their privations. They spent all their money on their further experiments and remained gloriously forgetful of their personal interests. When the therapeutic value of radium was established—it had been found effective, among other things, in the treatment of cancer—their friends urged upon them the necessity of patenting the process of extracting radium. To do so would have meant considerable wealth to the Curies, since radium was valued at $150,000 a gram. But they refused to derive any income from their discovery. "Radium is an instrument of mercy and it belongs to the world."

They refused not only profits but honors as well. All they asked of the world was to give them a good workroom for their experiments. When the dean of the Sorbonne wrote to Pierre that the Minister had proposed his name for the Legion of Honor, Pierre—seconded by Marie—replied as follows: "Please be so kind as to thank the Minister and to inform him that I do not feel the slightest need of being decorated, but that I am in the greatest need of a laboratory."

On one occasion, however, Pierre did allow his name to be presented for distinction. His scientific colleagues had insisted that he become a candidate for the Academy of Science—not so much for the sake of the honor itself as for the opportunity it would bring him to secure a professorship at the Sorbonne. *And a laboratory*.

Reluctantly he started out upon his round of visits to the members of the Academy. It was the regular custom for every candidate to make these calls and to "drum up" his own qualifications for the honor. Here is how one of the Parisian journalists describes Pierre Curie's "campaign" for the Academy: "To climb stairs, ring, have himself announced, explain why he had come—all this sordidness filled him with shame in spite of himself. But what was even worse, he had to set forth his distinctions, declare the good opinion he had of himself and boast of his knowledge and of his achievements—ordeals which seemed to him beyond human endurance. Consequently he extolled his opponent sincerely and at length, saying that M. Amagat was much better qualified than he, Curie, to enter the Academy . . ."

The Academy elected M. Amagat.

Pierre Curie was highly successful in his efforts to escape from fame. So, too, was Marie. Her simple disguise for avoiding recognition was to remain undisguised. Nobody at first sight would have suspected that the young peasant woman in her unassuming black dress was the celebrated winner of the Nobel Prize. One day an American reporter, hot on the trail of the Curies, had heard that they were spending their vacation in Le Pouldu, a fishing village of Brittany. Arriving at the village, he inquired his way to the Curie cottage. He found a rather unassuming young woman sitting barefoot on the doorstep.

"Are you the housekeeper in this place?"

"Yes."

"Is the lady inside?"

"No, she is out."

"Do you expect her in soon?"

"I don't think so."

"Could you tell me something intimate about her?" asked the reporter as he sat down on the doorstep.

"Nothing," replied Marie, "except one message that Madame Curie told me to convey to reporters: *Be less inquisitive about people, and more inquisitive about ideas.*"

VII

FINALLY Pierre Curie was accepted into the society of his inferior— and therefore envious—fellow scientists. "I find myself in the Academy without having desired to be there and without the Academy's desire to have me."

After several meetings with his colleagues he wrote to a friend: "I have not yet discovered what is the purpose of the Academy."

Yet it served one good purpose—it enabled Pierre to get an appointment to the Sorbonne. Together with the appointment came the offer of a well-equipped laboratory. The lifelong dream of the Curies was about to be fulfilled.

And then, one rainy morning in April, 1906, Pierre left his home to visit his publisher. A few hours later they brought his lifeless body to Marie. He had slipped on the wet pavement, and a heavy truck had run over him.

Marie's happiness was at an end. But not her work. She accepted an offer to assume her husband's professorship at the Sorbonne—it was the first time in French history that a position in higher education had been granted to a woman. She went on with her experiments in Pierre's new laboratory, of which she had now become the director. She took care of her children. She prepared papers on her researches. And every night, before going to bed, she wrote an intimate account of her thoughts to her dear departed. It was as if she were writing a letter to someone still alive.

"I am offered the post of successor to you, my Pierre; your course and the direction of your laboratory. I have accepted. I don't know whether this is good or bad . . ."

"My Pierre, I think of you without end. My head is bursting with it and my reason is troubled. I can not understand that I am to live hence-forth without you . . ."

"My little Pierre, I want to tell you that the laburnum is in flower, the wistaria, the hawthorn and the iris are beginning—you would have loved all that . . ."

"I no longer love the sun or the flowers. The sight of them makes me suffer. I feel better on dark days like the day of your death, and if I have not learned to hate fine weather it is because my children have need of it . . ."

It was for her children's sake that she went on—and for humanity's sake. A little more work to lessen the sufferings of her fellows. In 1911, when she received the Nobel Prize for the second time, she accepted it merely as another opportunity to widen the scope of her researches. The healing power of radium—this now was the paramount quest of her life. When the World War of 1914 broke out, she organized and personally supervised a number of X-ray outfits for the treatment of wounded sol-diers. Throughout the length and breadth of the country she journeyed —an angel of mercy with a beautiful white face and with pained and acid-bitten fingers.

In spite of her fatigue and her pain and her sorrow she was always ready with her encouraging smile and her gentle word. "Will it hurt?" asked the frightened soldiers when they saw the formidable X-ray appa-ratus. "Not at all," was her invariable reply. "It's just like taking a photo-graph."

The war was over. Travels, distinctions, interviews, medals, lectures, banquets—and labor and sorrow. And, to the very end, an "incurable inaptitude" for material success. "Dreamers," she said, "do not deserve wealth, because they do not desire it."

She was now approaching the end of her dream. "Ah, how tired I am!" she murmured as she came home from her laboratory one day. The next morning she could not rise from her bed. The doctors who came to ex-amine her were unable to diagnose her disease. It resembled influenza, tuberculosis, pernicious anemia—yet it was none of these. Not until after her death did they discover the real nature of her illness. It was "radium poisoning"—the gradual decay of the vital organs through a lifetime of excessive radiation.

Madame Curie had died a martyr to her work.

IMPORTANT DATES IN THE LIFE OF
MARIE SKLODOWSKA CURIE

1867—November 7, born in Warsaw.

1883—Graduated from Warsaw Lycée at 16.

1891—Entered the Sorbonne, in Paris.

1895—Married Pierre Curie in Paris.

1898—Together with husband, extracted radium from pitchblende.

1903—Received Davy Medal from Royal Society.
Awarded Nobel Prize in Physics.

1906—Her husband was run over by a dray and killed.
Succeeded him as professor at University of Paris.

1911—Awarded Nobel Prize in Chemistry.

1921—Honored by President Harding.

1929—Received from President Hoover a gift of $50,000 for the purchase of radium for therapeutic uses.

1934—July 4, died, Haute-Savoie.

The Wright Brothers

Wilbur Wright, 1867–1912

Orville Wright, 1871–1948

ON DECEMBER 17, 1903, Orville Wright made the first historic flight in a heavier-than-air machine. Five years later, after many successful flights witnessed by hundreds of spectators, there were a number of scientists and editors who were still unconvinced. "Human flight," wrote Professor Simon Newcomb, "is not only impossible, it is illogical." And the editor of one of America's leading magazines returned a report on an authentic flight with the following comment:

"While your manuscript has been read with much interest, it does not seem to qualify either as fact or fiction."

II

IN SPITE of its terrible destructiveness in war, the airplane, we believe, will prove to be the instrument that marks the shortest distance between human hearts. For this instrument will have succeeded more than any other in drawing the earth into a unit, in combining widely separated communities into a friendly next-door neighborliness. The airplane is the final conqueror of time and space and isolation. In 1852 it took Ezra Meeker six months to travel by ox team over the Oregon Trail to Washington. In 1924 this ninety-three-year-old pioneer sped over the same distance, by airplane, in one day.

III

FOR THOUSANDS OF YEARS the secret of air travel had eluded the ingenuity of the world's greatest scholars. Yet the magicians who finally discovered it were two uneducated bicycle mechanics. Wilbur and Orville Wright were the sons of a clergyman. Their two older brothers and their sister were college graduates. But they themselves had only a few years of schooling. Like Benjamin Franklin, Walt Whitman, Mark Twain, Thomas Edison, and Henry Ford, the Wright brothers proved that a college degree is no passport to immortal achievement.

But if Wilbur and Orville Wright were no scholars, they were, in the true sense of the word, poets. A *poet*, by its Greek definition, is a *maker*, a *creator*, a man who transforms dreams into actualities—in short, an *inventor*. There is very little difference between the creative genius of a Shakespeare and inventive faculty of an Edison. The one forges dead syllables into a living poem, and the other combines lifeless materials into a throbbing machine. The process is the same—the fusing of odd old bits of memory into some hitherto-undiscovered aspect of the sublime.

The Wright brothers shared in this faculty of fusing old memories into new discoveries. Like Edison, they developed at an early age an almost uncanny ability for remembering details. Added to this, they both displayed a passion for mental and physical gymnastics. It was his excessive fondness for "idle" reading and for athletics that prevented Wilbur's graduation from high school. But their reading helped them to spread the wings of their imagination. And their athletic training enabled them to come safely down to earth when they took their first ride on the bucking bronco of the air.

The two boys became interested in flight when their father one day brought them a mechanical toy called a *helicopter*. This "flying top" had two propellers that caused it to whizz into the air when it was wound up. The two boys took the helicopter apart, put it together, and then took it apart again, in order to discover the secret of its flight. They noticed that the propellers of this toy pushed against the air just as the paddles of a boat push against the water. Throwing the dismantled toy into a rubbish heap, they stored up in their memory the lesson that they had learned from it.

Later they watched the flight of a box kite, and then they turned to the birds. For hours they would lie on their backs, their eyes intent upon the lifting and the drifting of the wings against the sky. They noticed that some of the birds, especially the sea gulls, had a slight warp, or dip, to their wings. It was this warp, they observed, that enabled the birds to maintain their balance and to make their turns in the air. This fact, too, the boys carefully stored away in their memory for future use.

A couple of restless youngsters, with observant eyes and active minds. And fingers always on the itch to be puttering with tools. They built and sold kites for pocket money, constructed a wooden lathe with a foot treadle and with marbles for ball bearings, invented an improvement on a hay-baling machine, and designed an original device for folding newspapers. All this before they were out of their teens. "The boys," said their teachers, "are bright, but they are unable to concentrate on their school textbooks." True enough. Their minds were centered upon the far more important mechanical textbook of the universe.

Their thinking was almost entirely extracurricular. They delved into the mysteries of nature. They pondered upon one of the most baffling of these mysteries—the sustaining power of the air. They began to read up on the history of man's attempts at flight. They learned about the mythical wings of Icarus, the crude experiments of Leonardo da Vinci, the enthusiastic but fruitless efforts of Chanute, Mouillard, Ader, and Lilienthal, and the scientific researches of Maxim and Langley. They noted that there were two schools of thought with regard to the possible conquest of the air— those who believed in the kitelike gliders, and those who experimented with the birdlike motor machines. They decided to begin their own experiments with the motorless gliders.

From the very start they found themselves handicapped. Men like Ader and Maxim and Langley had the advantage of a large working capital for their experiments. But the only capital in the possession of these two young mechanics—they had opened a bicycle shop at Dayton, Ohio—was an inexhaustible supply of enthusiasm and a daredevil willingness to take risks.

With these two assets, Orville and Wilbur set to work in the back yard of their bicycle shop, laying their "crazy" plans and collecting homespun and rubbish for the building of their first glider. "And with this contraption," laughed their father, "you expect to conquer the kingdom of the birds!"

The neighbors shared the good-natured ridicule of the father. So the Wright boys were planning to fly, were they? Well, it couldn't be done! Men were meant to stay down on the earth. Otherwise they'd have been given wings. And that was that!

But the Wright boys believed they could do it. They had made an intensive study of Lilienthal's papers on *The Problem of Flying and Practical Experiments in Soaring*. True enough, Lilienthal had been killed in a crash of his gliding machine. But before his fatal accident he had made several successful hops through the air in his glider. "What Lilienthal has done with a glider, we can do with a motor machine."

First, however, they would begin where Lilienthal had left off—with a gliding machine. They had studied the causes of Lilienthal's failures— and these failures had been far more numerous than his successes; they had calculated the lifting and the balancing power of flat and of curved wings; they had measured, by means of a funnel which they had invented for the purpose, the pressure of the air on moving bodies; and they had reached the conclusion that the secret of aerial navigation lay in the proper equilibrium between the airship and the air. And thus they completed their first scientific glider—at a cost of fifteen dollars. It was a peculiar-looking object—a box kite of cloth and wooden ribs that resembled an enormous chicken coop.

In order to try out this glider, they asked the Weather Bureau at Washington to recommend a spot where they could find steady winds, low hills for take-off, and soft sand dunes for landing. Willis L. Moore, chief of the bureau, informed them that Kitty Hawk, North Carolina, was such a spot.

Here the two brothers took their aircraft on September 25, 1900. And here, without any fuss or witness, they began their practical experiments. At first they tried to send their glider up like a kite. It took to the air without any trouble. Their calculations had been correct. There was plenty of *lift* to the creature. Then they proceeded to the next step. Pulling their wood-and-canvas Pegasus down to earth, they prepared it for its first aerial ride with a human being upon its back. Wilbur stretched himself out on the lower wing, face down, took the controlling reins in his hands, and the next minute found himself flying through the air.

It was one of the strangest experiences within the memory of man. Wilbur Wright had set himself adrift in the Nowhere, without any roads to guide him and without any anchor under his feet. It was a terrifying moment. He grew panicky. "Let me down," he cried, *"let me down!"*

In later years, when Wilbur had become an expert pilot, he recalled this episode with a smile. The "appalling" altitude to which he had been lifted from the ground in his first flight was eight feet.

IV

THE WRIGHT BROTHERS had now proved that man could *glide* through the air. But the more important question still remained unanswered. Could man *fly* through the air? For three years they experimented with motors and propellers in an effort to supply the answer. Years of hard work and continual disappointment. At one time Wilbur was so discouraged that he was ready to give up. "Not in a thousand years will man ever learn to fly."

But Orville, the younger and the more daring of the two, kept urging his brother to go on. New wind tunnels, new airplane models with wings of various edges and curvatures, and tables upon tables of calculations and resultant figures for their subsequent tests. "Will you boys ever stop working?" asked their father, with a skeptical smile.

"Not until we have built a machine that can fly," replied Wilbur.

"And *that*," rejoined Orville, "will be only the *beginning* of our work."

See them now at their work in the back yard of their bicycle shop. Wilbur, thirty-six years old, tall and rangy, face closely shaved, firm thin lips, muscles of steel, and a steel-like glint of determination in his gray-blue eyes. Orville, thirty-two, shorter and more compact, with a heavy dark mustache that conceals the firmness of the upper lip, but with the same determined gray-blue glint in his eyes. Two dynamic machine men, their feet planted upon the ground, their hearts uplifted toward the skies.

And at last their heart's desire seemed about to be fulfilled. Toward the end of 1903 they had finished their first motorplane—the result of several years of theoretical calculation. They took it to Kitty Hawk for its practical test in the air.

But just then they received bad news. The scientific world had come to the "final conclusion" that flight in heavier-than-air machines was impossible. Professor Langley of the Smithsonian Institution had built, with the aid of government funds, an intricate and costly airplane. An imposing group of scientists had gathered on the banks of the Potomac to watch its initial flight. But it refused to fly. The dream of the ages, agreed the scientists, must remain an unattainable dream.

It was under these discouraging conditions that Wilbur and Orville prepared to make their first attempt with their modest little "air toy." Like the Langley machine, it was equipped with propellers and a motor. But unlike the Langley machine—and this was a secret which the Wright brothers were keeping to themselves—it was built upon an entirely new principle. As a result of their persistent experimentation, the two unschooled but observant young mechanics had at last discovered the true principles of air pressure—a discovery which had eluded the mathematical calculations of all the trained scientists. Their airplane, crude and inexpensive as it was, had been designed in accordance with these newly discovered principles. Theoretically, it ought to work. But *would* it? What business had they, a couple of bungling tinkers who had not even had a college education, to set themselves up against the scientific verdict of the greatest contemporary scholars? And so it was with a mingled feeling of hope and misgiving that they got ready for their take-off.

Monday, December 14, 1903. The two brothers toss a coin for the opportunity to make the first test. Wilbur wins the toss.

The test results in complete failure. The plane, after staying in the air for three and a half seconds, topples sideways to the ground.

Two days of repairing the broken parts, and the Wrights are ready for the next attempt. It is now Orville's turn.

December 17. The day is overcast. A raw northeaster blows in from the Atlantic half a mile away. The two pioneer airmen, their blood thinned from too much confinement in the bicycle shop, are stamping their feet and flapping their arms to keep themselves warm. They wear no overcoats, for an overcoat would hamper their movements in this dangerous experiment. As they prepare their clumsy mechanical bird for its tentative flight, they observe a flock of sea gulls soaring gracefully overhead. A raucous shriek from the gulls, as if in mocking challenge to the men below. The brothers are practically alone on the dunes. Only five spectators have taken the trouble to come from the near-by village. One of them looks from the birds to the plane and remarks with a sneer. "So *that* rigamajig is a-goin' to fly?" "Sure it is," rejoins another of the spectators, "in a hundred-mile tornado!"

The brothers, paying no attention to the jeering remarks, tune up the motor. With a roar that drowns out the beating of the surf, the engine begins to spit fire and smoke from the open exhaust. Orville climbs into the wings. "Let her go!"

A moment of breathless expectation—the moment for which a hundred million years had been waiting. Orville grasped the controls—and then the miracle happened. The first mechanical airship began its historic flight.

V

A YOUNG REPORTER, H. P. Moore of the Norfolk *Virginian-Pilot*, heard about the flight and set his imagination to work. He prepared a wholly fictitious story about a "long journey" through the air, at the end of which the operator of the machine ran over the ground yelling "Eureka." He sent the story to twenty-one newspapers, only three of which took the trouble to print it. When Orville learned of this incredulity on the part of the editors, he merely shrugged his shoulders and laughed. "No wonder they disbelieved the story. It was an amazing piece of work. And yet, though 99 per cent wrong, it did contain one correct fact. There *had* been a flight."

But neither the editors nor the public would recognize this fact. "A couple of silly boys bucking against the eternal laws of nature." Some of their Dayton acquaintances were even sarcastic about it. "Flying and perpetual motion will come at the same time," sneered one of them. And another, "There is only one thing that could lift a machine off the ground —spirit power. And the Wright boys are not even spiritualists."

No, the Wright boys were just a couple of mischievous youngsters. Especially Orville. He had a habit of storming up the steps to his bedroom on all fours, like a child. It did not bother him or Wilbur that the world looked skeptically upon their work. Their invention was a fascinating game, nothing more. Even in after years, when the world had come to recognize their work, they refused to be puffed up. They had merely "pulled off" a good play in their game. They retained their good-natured modesty when colleges showered them with honorary degrees and kings favored them with their smiles. They came both to the college presidents and to the kings dressed in their ordinary street clothes and their caps.

They felt no pompous awe in the presence of royalty and they expected the public to feel no pompous adulation in their own presence. Again and again they refused to make public speeches. "I know of only one bird, the parrot, that talks," said Wilbur, "and the parrot can't fly very high." They were careless about the medals and the ribbons which they received from scientific societies. They carried them around, together with other commonplace doodads like screws and bolts and scraps of paper, in their pockets. And they felt more chagrined when they mislaid a bolt than when they lost a medal. They possessed, in other words, the simplicity of greatness.

They never married. Their sister Katharine, who taught at the local high school, provided them with all the feminine companionship that they needed. Together with their old clergyman-father, they enjoyed that most perfect of human relationships—a harmonious family.

But suddenly the harmony was shattered. On May 30, 1912, Wilbur died of typhoid fever. He was only forty-five at the time, and his death meant the ending of one of the greatest inventive partnerships in history. Throughout their work the two Wright brothers supplemented each other. Together, they formed one supreme intellect. But apart, neither of them could accomplish much. In spite of his genius, Orville felt physically and mentally lost without his brother. And he never found himself. The invention of the airplane had come out of the interplay of their ideas. It was like a spark generated by the clashing of two swords. And when one of the two swords lay broken, the other remained inactive in its sheath. For a little while after his brother's death Orville tried to go on. He experimented and made improvements on the stability of the airplane. But his heart was no longer in the work. With the passing of Wilbur, Orville had grown from a boy into a man. Aviation had ceased to be a game for him. It was now a business. And Orville hated business. After three years as president of the Wright Company, he resigned.

VI

On DECEMBER 17, 1928, the United States celebrated the twenty-fifth anniversary of human flight. A monument had been erected at Kitty Hawk in honor of the Wright brothers. Orville had been invited as the principal guest. He stood beside the monument and smiled sadly at the cheering crowd. "Mighty eagle of the air!" they called him. But it was a broken eagle that stood there, with his frail gray head uncovered to the sky. His eyes roamed over the sand dunes. Drifting sands—drifting years. Past landmarks obliterated—past friendships buried. He felt suddenly cold and alone in the great crowd. His mind went back to the Ohio graveyard, where his brother lay cold and alone. Two brave eagles, equally indifferent to the jeers and the cheers of the world.

IMPORTANT DATES IN THE LIVES OF
THE WRIGHT BROTHERS

WILBUR WRIGHT

1867—April 16, born, Millville, Indiana.

1903—Constructed first successful airplane.

1904–08—Continued successful airplane experiments.

1908—Won Michelin Prize in France.

1909—Flew from Governors Island to Grant's Tomb and back. Received gold medal from French Academy of Science.

1912—May 30, died, Dayton, Ohio.

ORVILLE WRIGHT

1871—August 19, born, Dayton, Ohio.

1888—Finished high-school education.

1903—Finished, with Wilbur, first successful airplane.

1905—Made first long-distance flight near Dayton, Ohio.

1909—Received gold medal from French Academy.

1915—Sold his interest in Wright Aeroplane Company.

1917—Awarded Albert Medal from Royal Society.

1920—Won John Fritz Medal.

1925—Received John Scott Medal.

1948—January 30, died, Dayton, Ohio.

Mohandas K. Gandhi

1869–1948

GANDHI was one of history's most amazing paradoxes—a soldier who fought with the weapons of a saint. Whether his mission or his methods were correct, only the future generations will be able to tell. For us of the present generation, however, it is interesting to note the career of this strangest of mystics who tried to impress "the image of God upon the faces of brutes."

II

MOHANDAS KARAMCHAND GANDHI—the name *Mahatma, the Great-Souled,* was given him by his followers—was descended from a race of "fighters and forgivers." His father and his grandfather were leaders of the people who gloried in suffering for their independent spirit. His mother, on the other hand, was an ardent devotee of the religious principle of *Ahimsa,* noninjury to all living things. From earliest childhood, therefore, Gandhi was brought up in a paradoxical atmosphere. His character became a battleground between rebellion and religion. And he achieved intellectual peace only then when he reconciled these two contradictory ideas into a new moral doctrine—rebellion *through* religion.

But before this reconciliation which was to distinguish him as a man apart, he tried to live like the other "Hindu gentlemen" of the day. He became engaged at eight, married at twelve, went through the public schools of Porbandar, the "White City" of India, entered the College of Ahmedabad at seventeen, and at nineteen went to England to complete his studies at the University of London.

While at the university he was interested in watching those "quaint Britishers" and at times he even tried to imitate them. He ate meat at one of their "barbarian" dinners—and nearly perished with disgust. "For nights I was unable to sleep; I felt like a murderer."

After three years of study in London—a period in which, as he informs us, he "wasted a lot of time and money trying to become an Englishman" —he returned to India (1891) and settled down to the practice of law at the Supreme Court of Bombay. Though he refused all cases which he regarded as unjust, he soon built up a lucrative clientele. His average income, his friend Gokhale tells us, was about $25,000 a year. He was well on his way to respectability and wealth—the envy of all the ambitious young men in India.

But suddenly he gave it all up. He had found a new case to try—the case of the oppressed against the injustice of the oppressors. It was no longer a legal but a moral service to which his life was dedicated. And the only pay he received for this service was in the currency of abuse. Here is how it happened:

Gandhi had been called to Pretoria, South Africa, to represent a client in an important trial. At that period there were about 150,000 Hindus living in that "civilized white" colony. These countrymen of Gandhi's were being subjected to every sort of persecution, ranging all the way from looting to lynching. And then, as a final indignity, the government decided to pass the Asiatic Exclusion Act—a bill designed not only to stop the immigration of Hindus into South Africa, but to disfranchise all the Hindus who were already living there.

It was then that Gandhi voluntarily undertook the cause of justice against force. His first step was to prove that the Asiatic Exclusion Act was illegal. And he won his point. His next move was to abandon his legal practice—"at best an immoral profession"—and to become "one of the dispossessed." Whereupon the white people in South Africa accepted him at his own valuation. They spat upon him, kicked him out of their trains, refused him admission to their hotels.

But Gandhi fought back. He had discovered his new secret weapon— "a religious strike against all violence." A folding of the hands and a refusal to participate in the enemy's business. Even at the point of the sword. "The soldier must never be afraid of death."

To those who objected that passive resistance leads only to defeat, Gandhi declared that, on the contrary, passive resistance leads only to victory. The sword can kill but it cannot compel. "The aggressor may destroy some of us, but he can never enslave the rest of us." For this new weapon of nonviolent nonco-operation, maintained Gandhi, was the one weapon in the world which would enable the weak to overcome the strong. "It was this weapon which brought about the victory of the early Christians against their Roman oppressors." Faith conquers force.

Relying upon this weapon of faith as against force, Gandhi wielded it even beyond the point of *forgiving* his enemies. He *helped* them when they were in distress. His new kind of warfare was designed to kill not the man but his meanness. Gandhi's aim was to liquidate his enemy by turning him into a friend.

And, strangely enough, it worked. Whenever the government in South Africa was in distress, Gandhi suspended his plan of nonco-operation and offered his active assistance. During the Boer War, he organized an Indian Red Cross and was twice cited for bravery under fire. In 1904, when a virulent plague broke out in Johannesburg, he personally attended to the sick regardless of whether they were Indians or whites. At first neither the whites nor the Indians could make out this peculiar man with his peculiar methods. Time and again he was beaten by both sides for his trouble. Once he was so brutally manhandled by the mob that he was taken for dead and cast into a ditch.

But gradually the little world in South Africa began to realize the "power of his weapon that healed as against the powerless weapons that killed." Gandhi had triumphed in his bloodless battle. In 1914 the Hindus in South Africa were given their independence. "What else am I to do with you?" wrote General Smuts, the commander of the army which had been fighting against Gandhi. "You help us in our day of need. How can we lay hands upon you? . . . You refuse to injure the enemy . . . You desire victory by self-suffering, and never transgress your self-imposed limits of courtesy and chivalry. And that is what reduced us to sheer helplessness."

III

GANDHI had proved one thing in South Africa. You may imprison or destroy thousands of individuals, but you cannot imprison or destroy an entire people. So long as the soul of a nation insists upon freedom, there is no army in the world that can take this freedom away. You cannot enslave a nation that refuses to do your work. "This is the secret of my new weapon."

And now, having tested this weapon upon the little battlefield of South Africa, Gandhi proceeded to try it out on a much larger scale in India. The Hindus were smarting under the yoke of the British imperialists. They had tried sporadic revolts, but with no success. "And so I have come to teach my countrymen a new kind of revolt. A hatred not against our rulers, but against our rulers' hatred. I will minister to you as my brothers, but I will not submit to you as my overlords." Once again he would meet violence with nonviolence. Indeed, he started his "war" against England with a friendly campaign. He went to London (1914) to organize an Indian ambulance corps as a help in England's struggle against Germany. And England responded with an equally friendly gesture of her own. She promised India her independence after the war. Gandhi believed the promise and risked his life again and again for his "British brothers."

But when peace was declared in 1918, the British imperialists went back on their promise. Some of them were motivated by a spirit of selfish greed. India was too rich a prize to let go. Others, however, sincerely believed that if India were set adrift, she would fall a prey to civil war. In any case, the disillusion of the Hindus was terrible. The fire of revolt blazed across the land. And Gandhi led this revolt and tried to hold it confined within nonviolent bounds.

Many of the Hindus, however, took violent exception to Gandhi. His good will, they pointed out, had been repaid with derision. "Where is your vaunted weapon now?" they mocked.

But Gandhi had learned the supreme patience of the East. "Wait and see. Permanent victories are not won in a day."

And so he went on with his peculiar warfare. Now that England had emerged from distress, he resorted once more to his policy of nonco-operation. This refusal to take orders was not merely a passive form of resistance. It was an active crusade of "disobedience to injustice." For Gandhi, in his own strange way, was a fighter. He had no use for pacifists. He trained his armies as rigorously as any general. "I cultivate in my soldiers," he said, "the courage of dying without killing . . . I believe that nonviolence is infinitely superior to violence, forgiveness more manly than punishment," dignity more precious than indignation, silent defiance more powerful than blustering force.

In these words of Gandhi there was nothing original. They had been spoken time and again before him. But he went a step beyond his predecessors by putting these words into practice.

And with the stubbornness of a fanatic he believed in the ultimate triumph of his method. "I know that many people of the West—and even here in the East—consider a nonviolent victory impossible to achieve. I admit that it may be far off; I admit that it may not be realized in my lifetime. It may even take generations. But it is bound to come in the end."

And when nonviolence is achieved—declared Gandhi—"not only will the causes of civil war have been rooted out, but aggression from foreign nations will be a thing of the past." Force can not exist where faith is supreme.

The faith of Gandhi was in the brotherhood of man. Your enemy is your foolish brother. Minister to him when he is hurt; disobey him when he tries to hurt you. No enemy can ever be strong enough or savage enough —maintained Gandhi—to withstand the fire of love.

IV

It was on April 6, 1919, that Gandhi first launched his campaign of "loving disobedience" against his "English brothers" who were bent upon oppressing his people. On that day he declared a *hartal*—a public cessation of work—for all India. The people took this up as an occasion for religious solemnity. "Order reigned everywhere"—save in the city of Delhi. Here a few disturbances broke out. Gandhi went to this city to quell the rioters. The government had him arrested, whereupon several Hindu communities broke into revolt. The unrest was unusually keen at the city of Amritsar. On April 11, General Dyer occupied the city and easily put down the revolt. "Order has been restored everywhere." On the fifteenth there was a national holiday. A throng of people—men, women and children—gathered in a public square of Amritsar. At this point General Dyer lost his head. He fired upon the unarmed crowd with machine guns and then strafed it with bombs from airplanes. Five hundred people were killed in the massacre.

Here was a tragedy that put Gandhi's doctrine to the test. "Of what avail is your faith now against the bullets and the bombs of the enemy?"

But unlike General Dyer, Gandhi did *not* lose his head. "It was no white road along which I promised to lead you to victory . . . This is war." He warned his people that they must "contemplate with equanimity not a thousand murders of innocent men and women, but many thousands before we attain a status in the world that shall not be surpassed by any nation." What though they lost their lives in their nonviolent resistance? "In violent resistance, too, many thousands of soldiers lose their lives." Indeed, *all* of us ultimately lose our lives in the universal battle of existence. But *their* battle—he told the Hindus—would be won not by the number of the enemies they could kill, but by the number of the enemies in whom they could kill the *desire* to kill.

As for General Dyer, Gandhi felt no hatred against him. "How can you hate a man whose mind is sick?" He merely requested the British government that the general be recalled. The British government acceded to this request.

But the strange war between faith and force went on. For Gandhi wanted nothing less than the freedom of India. "The foreigners are welcome here as guests; they are not wanted here as usurpers." He wrote a letter to this effect and posted it to the British viceroy of India. First of all, he surrenders his decorations and his honorary titles: "It is not without a pang that I return the Gold Medal granted to me by your predecessor for my humanitarian work in South Africa, the Zulu War Medal granted in South Africa for my services as officer in charge of the Indian Volunteer Ambulance Corps in 1906, and the Boer War Medal for my services as assistant superintendent of the Indian Volunteer Stretcher-bearer Corps during the Boer War of 1899." And then, after a brief reference to the Amritsar massacre, he concludes: "I can retain neither respect nor affection for a government which has been moving from wrong to wrong . . . The government must be moved to repentance. I have therefore ventured to suggest nonco-operation . . . which, if unattended by violence, must compel the government to retrace its steps and undo its wrongs."

The government took back his medals and presented Gandhi with another gift—a prison term. Together with Gandhi, twenty-five thousand other Hindus were arrested. They sang joyously as they were marched off to jail.

At his trial, Gandhi admitted his guilt. Having rebelled against the government, he confessed, he had deliberately broken the law. "I do not ask for mercy," he said to Judge Broomsfield, who presided at the trial. "I do not plead any extenuating act. I am here, therefore, to invite and cheerfully submit to the highest penalty that can be inflicted upon me for what in law is a deliberate crime and what appears to me to be the highest duty of a citizen. The only course open to you, sir, is either to resign your post or to inflict on me the severest penalty."

Judge Broomsfield, not to be outdone in chivalry, replied: "It would be impossible to ignore the fact that in the eyes of millions of your countrymen you are a great patriot and a great leader. Even those who differ from you in politics look upon you as a man of high ideals and of noble and even saintly life."

And then the judge, having praised Gandhi for the justice of his cause, sentenced him to prison for the illegality of his conduct. The story is told that a professor of law at Harvard was once trying to explain to his students the decision in a famous court trial. "This may be legal, sir," objected one of the boys, "but it isn't just." Whereupon the professor replied with a cynical smile, "If you want justice, young man, go across the street to the Divinity School. This is the Law School."

Gandhi, having himself been trained in a law school, knew what to expect at his trial. And he accepted his imprisonment in the same spirit in which Jesus had accepted his crucifixion. Forgive them, Father, they know not what they do. "By my suffering," said Gandhi, "I propose to conquer the world."

V

GANDHI was a religious leader upon whose unwilling shoulders Destiny has imposed the burden of politics. His concern with his country's independence was only secondary. His primary interest was universal Truth. "I am wedded to India," he said, "because I believe that she has a mission for the world." But his religious quest for the Truth, he went on, "has no geographical limits. I have a living faith in it which will transcend even my love for India herself." His political activities were but an avocation to his religious mission.

Though many people doubted the wisdom of his politics, very few people questioned the nobility of his religion.

This religion, Hinduism, is in its essential elements little different from the other great religions of the world. All of them try to point to the fatherhood of God through the brotherhood of man. Gandhi's religion was somewhat more inclusive than most of the others. It united all living creatures into one related family. The individual, whether man or beast or bird, is not a separate chunk of animated matter but an integrated member of a single living organism. *All life is one.* To eat any *living* creature was to Gandhi as abhorrent as to eat any *human* creature. One of the most stringent commandments of the Hindu religion as interpreted by Gandhi is this—"Thou shalt not destroy life in any form." Every living thing was to Gandhi "a poem of pity," and he understood with equal tenderness the language of human distress and the inarticulate cry of the beast. The centermost point of Gandhi's religious philosophy was the inviolable sacredness of life and the consequent sinfulness of bloodshed. "Since we have no power to create, we have no right to destroy."

Gandhi's sympathy for all living things stemmed from his belief in reincarnation. The individual soul, he maintained, is embarked upon a pilgrimage of many lives. It travels from body to body along the ocean of existence, sometimes in the form of a man and at other times in the form of an animal. Every deed in every one of our incarnations impresses its stamp upon our soul and determines the form it will assume in the next reincarnation. This is the doctrine of *Karma,* the law of human conduct. If a man does justice and loves mercy, he will be reborn into a higher and happier man. But if he gives himself up to evil, he will be degraded into "an outcast or a weasel or a rat." Heaven and Hell, therefore, are not *beyond* the life of the earth, but *within* it. And reward and punishment for every human deed and thought are not merely ethical abstractions but practical facts. The history of every soul is a complete story of many chapters—not, like the single life of the individual, a meaningless jumble, but a rounded and rational and purposeful design. If a man is *treated* unjustly in *this* life, it is because he has *acted* unjustly in a *previous* life. Everything is evened up in the end. "Every virtue and every crime will receive its due pay when the sum of life is complete."

Every man, therefore, is the architect of his own fate. He can *will* his own future—not only in this life but in the lives to come. And the greatest consummation of life—declared Gandhi—is final *release* from life. The existence of the individual at best is hell; and heaven will come to each man at last when his self is dead and his personal soul is absorbed into the selfless, universal soul of God. And then there will be for him no further rebirth into the bitterness of life.

Since all our individual souls are finally absorbed into the universal soul of God, it follows—maintained Gandhi—that all men are equal. "The insignificant is as big to me as any." No man is despicable. The pariah is no less worthy of consideration than the priest. "It is against the genius of Hinduism to arrogate to oneself a higher status or to assign others to a lower. All are born to serve God's creation." Gandhi fought a lifelong crusade against the attitude of his own countrymen toward his "suppressed brothers," the "untouchable" outcasts. "I would rather be torn to pieces than disown my brothers of the suppressed classes . . . I do not wish to be reborn; but if I have to be reborn, I should want to be of the *untouchables* so that I may share their sorrows . . . and that I may endeavor to free them from their miserable condition." As an earnest of his sincerity, Gandhi adopted an "untouchable" child into his family.

It is the supreme duty of man—asserted this modern Apostle of Hinduism—to lighten the sufferings of his fellowmen. And when the tide of fellowship is at a low ebb, when man has forgotten his duty to man, Krishna the God of Love comes down to earth in human form. "For the protection of all that is good, and the destruction of all that is evil, for the establishment of *Dharma*—the Law of Truth—Krishna must be born and reborn, for ever and ever." And suffer and die, that mankind may be redeemed.

Jesus, believed Gandhi, was one of these revelations of God in human form. As for himself, Gandhi was far too modest to claim any divine or even saintly attributes. "I am called *Mahatma*, but I am an ordinary man. I have blundered and committed mistakes." He is a soldier accidentally promoted to high rank. "I am perhaps the poorest general any army ever had." But he had discovered, he was convinced, a new way of war. India's independence, he declared, will come "not through *body-force* but through *soul force*." For such is the verdict of all the great religions of the world.

VI

GANDHI regarded himself as the humblest of men. And he lived accordingly. His dress was a simple loin-cloth; his dwelling, a hovel amost devoid of furniture; his food, a handful of dates, a sip of orange juice, and a cup of goat's milk. Again and again he begged his people to look upon him as in no way different from the rest of them. But the lowly folk insisted upon regarding him with a love that bordered on adoration. "Not since Buddha has any man in India been so universally revered." They flocked to him by the thousands to hear his voice, to touch his emaciated body, to be "sanctified and saved" by the blessing of his tender homely lips.

And Gandhi took this adoration with a good-humored smile. "Foolish, lovable children." And it is with a smile of equal good humor that he regarded those other compatriot children—the foolish and arrogant maharajahs of India. One day he delivered a lecture before a gathering of these maharajahs. He urged them to give up their money and their jewels. As he kept on speaking, his distinguished audience melted away one by one, until there was nobody left—as Gandhi afterward expressed it—"but God, the chairman and myself." A few minutes later the chairman, too, left. "Poor fellow," said Gandhi, "he must have felt very uncomfortable in that strange company."

Gandhi never lost his good nature in the face of discourtesy. In 1931— the year of the depression—he paid a visit to London. One of the reporters, who believed that the badge of civilization is a necktie and a pair of pants, began to make fun of the visitor's loin-cloth. "The only difference in our dress," laughed Gandhi, "is that you wear plus fours and I wear minus fours." And then he added: "If this depression keeps up much longer, I shall be the best dressed man in England."

Gandhi despised the so-called "civilization" of the present day. "It is only a veneer that conceals a savage heart . . . It takes note neither of morality nor of religion." His own definition of civilization, the *true* civilization, is summarized in two words—"good conduct."

It is with *good conduct*, or with *soul force* as he generally preferred to call it, that he proposed to fight his battle for freedom against "all enemies, whether yellow or brown or white." Gandhi, his disciples believe, was the greatest teacher in the world. But he was a teacher for the future and not for the present. Passive resistance, as even Gandhi himself admitted, requires an army not of men but of supermen. "What do you think?" he asks in his *Sermon on the Sea*. "Wherein is supreme courage required—in blowing others to pieces from behind a cannon or with a smiling face to approach a cannon and to be blown to pieces?"

What Gandhi called for is a race of soldiers with a concrete courage and an abstract sword. This "sword of passive resistance," he wrote, "is twice blessed. It blesses him who uses it, and him against whom it is used. Without drawing a drop of blood, it brings nothing less than victory."

The impossible dream of a religious visionary? Perhaps. But what if they, the religious leaders, are the only practical philosophers and we, the men of the world, are the impractical fools? Our methods of violence have led us from bloodshed to bloodshed. How do we know where their method of nonviolence will lead us until we have given it a trial?

VII

LIKE Abraham Lincoln who was struck down by an assassin shortly after the supreme goal of his life had been achieved—the preservation of the Union—so Gandhi's career was terminated by an assassin's bullet only months after India won her independence. On August 15, 1947, the culmination of Gandhi's political life was reached when India was formally recognized by the British as a nation. Five months afterwards while staying in the home of a friend in New Delhi, Gandhi made his way through the garden to hold a prayer meeting dedicated to ending the religious strife between the newly freed Hindu and Moslem races, when a young Hindu, a member of Gandhi's political opposition, rushed up and fired three bullets into him. He was carried into the house and died within thirty minutes.

The life of "the greatest Indian since Buddha," the supreme apostle of peace, was ended by violence; but Gandhi lives on in the hearts of his people as a saint—a saint who practiced more Christianity in an hour of living than many self-professed Christians achieve in a lifetime.

IMPORTANT DATES IN THE LIFE OF
MOHANDAS K. GANDHI

1869—October 2, born at Porbandar.

1893—Went as lawyer to South Africa.
Abandoned legal profession. Adopted principle of noncooperation as weapon against violence.

1899—Served in hospital corps during Boer War.

1914—Secured passage of Indians' Relief Act in South Africa.

1914–18—Served in ambulance corps during World War I.

1919—Launched campaign of nonviolent nonco-operation against English rule in India.

1921—Acclaimed as Mahatma.

1922—Arrested by British government in India.

1924—Released.

1930—Again arrested, together with 27,000 followers.

1931—Released, sailed for Round Table Conference in England.

1932—Returned to India, and to prison.

1933—Undertook humanitarian work on behalf of "untouchables."

1942—Committed India to nonviolence in every war.

1947—Won national independence for India.

1948—January 30, died, New Delhi.

Guglielmo Marconi

1874–1937

"CHE orecchi grandi ha"—"What large ears he has!" exclaimed a relative as she saw the newborn babe.

"With these ears," said his music-loving mother, "he'll be able to intercept the still small voices of the air."

And from infancy Guglielmo grew up to be a studious, introspective, and dreamy child. From his Irish mother he inherited his imaginative mind; and from his Italian father, his restless hands. And with these restless hands he was able to transmute his dreams into realities.

He was born (April 25, 1874) at Bologna. "This city," said an ancient oracle, "will enrich the world with two great gifts—one for the palate, and one for the mind." His prophecy turned out to be true. For it was a Bolognese butcher who invented the sausage—named *bologna* after the city of its origin; and it was a Bolognese scientist whom Destiny was now educating for the invention of the wireless.

Marconi received his entire education from private tutors. His father, an expert and wealthy agriculturist, was unwilling to entrust his delicate child to the public schools. Curled up in the library of his father's estate at Pontecchio, near Bologna, Guglielmo devoured hundreds of books upon all sorts of subjects. He was especially fond of reading about steam engines and electricity and chemistry. And always he tried to put his reading to the test. "Yes, that's what they say. But how will I know until I try it for myself?" In one of the attics he fixed up a little laboratory—"a magician's workroom." And one day he became attracted to the larger laboratory of the outdoors. He tried to extract nitrate from the atmosphere. This experiment resulted in failure, but it turned his attention to the treasure-house of the air. There were so many sounds that rippled over the air-waves—his large ears were unusually sensitive—such a labyrinth of syllables that waited to be captured and disentangled and rearranged into a definite sense. What happened to all the words that people were uttering, casting them into the air like so many pebbles into a lake? Were these words forever lost, or did they keep floating over the earth, just waiting for some instrument to recapture them?

And once, as he turned these thoughts over in his mind, he read an article about the experiments of the German physicist, Heinrich Hertz. His heart leaped up within him. Here at last was a clue to the mystery! Professor Hertz had invented an electric oscillator which could throw a spark from one end of a room to another without any visible connecting link. How did this spark travel across the room? Over an air-wave apparently, like a piece of wood floating over a water-wave in a lake. If this should prove to be true, would it not be possible to direct a sound from one spot to another, just as a boy might direct a piece of wood over the surface of the water? And if an electric spark or a sound could be made to leap across a room, could it not also be made to leap across a field, a city, a country, a continent, perhaps even an ocean? The distance that a sound could travel over the air would depend upon the power of the electrical push, just as the distance that a piece of wood could travel over a lake would depend upon the power of the boy's hand-push.

The thought was terrifying in its simplicity. "It was so elementary, so obvious in logic," remarked Marconi years later, "that it seemed difficult to believe no one else had thought of putting it into practice. I argued, there must be more mature scientists who had followed the same line of thought and arrived at almost similar conclusions. From the first the idea was so real to me, I did not realize that to others the theory might appear quite fantastic."

A vivid dream. And the boy inventor—he was only twenty at the time— proceeded to see whether he could not make it real. Impulsively he rushed in where the graybeard professors feared to tread. Together with his brother, Alfonso, he built a crude apparatus with which he tried to ensnare the elusive Hertzian spark. But in vain. Again and again he rebuilt his instruments, and rearranged them, but always with the same negative results. "The graybeards must be right, after all."

He had grown pale and drawn in his efforts. His father begged him to desist from his "crazy" dreams and to settle down to a "practical" job. Even his mother warned him that he was headed for a nervous breakdown. As for the friends of the family, they looked upon him and shook their heads. "Most likely he will land in the insane asylum."

"Ma non mi persi di coraggio"—"But I did not lose my courage." He went right ahead with his "insane and useless experimentations"—and one day he announced that he had a surprise for his parents. Inviting them into his attic workroom, he pressed a button whereupon a bell buzzed in the living room two stories below.

"But how did you do it?" asked his mother. "There are no connecting wires."

"That's just it. I have invented the wireless transmission of sound."

"God bless you!" exclaimed his mother as she embraced him with tears in her eyes. But his father merely turned away with a contemptuous shrug. "So you've invented wireless," he said. "So what?"

II

SIGNOR MARCONI was skeptical about his son's work. Yet his generosity got the better of his skepticism. He contributed a sum of 5,000 lire (about $1,000) for his son's further experimentations with that "crazy contraption of his." Guglielmo was elated. "With this sort of encouragement, I shall encircle the world with my voice."

"See that it enables you to encircle your body with your rags," smiled Signor Marconi. "Your invention seems to me of no practical value whatsoever."

"Maybe so. But we shall see." And Guglielmo went resolutely ahead with his experiments.

It was a time (1892–1895) of great scientific expectation. The leading physicists felt that they had arrived at the borderland of revolutionary discoveries. Especially in the medium of electricity. The opaque was becoming transparent. An electric ray could be made to pierce through a granite rock or a solid wall. "Here," wrote the eminent English scientist, Sir William Crookes, "is unfolded to us a new and astonishing world . . . Here is revealed the bewildering possibility of telegraphy without wires . . . This is no mere dream of a visionary philosopher. All the requisites needed to bring it within grasp of daily life are well within the possibilities of discovery, and are so reasonable and so clearly in the path of researches . . . that we may any day expect to hear that they have emerged from the realms of speculation to those of sober fact."

This prophecy, made by an Englishman, was first fulfilled in England. The Italian government had refused to encourage Marconi in his experiments; and so the twenty-two-year-old inventor, accompanied by his mother, set out for London. Here he found a sympathetic ear, and a public amazed at his wizardry. "What," asked a reporter, pointing to Marconi's instruments, "do you propose to do with them?"

"I propose to send signals over the air."

"Even through a fog?"

"Yes."

"Do you mean to tell us that your signals will penetrate anything and everything?"

"I am forced, as a result of my experiments, to believe so."

And he went on to prove the validity of his belief. At first he sent his messages over a distance of 100 yards; then, by "pumping" more and more power into the transmitter, he extended the distance to three miles, eight miles, eighteen miles. And then, on March 27, 1899, Marconi pressed the sending-key of a wireless which he had set up at Wimereux, a village on the west coast of France. Across the channel, at Dover, an assistant was "listening in." A few moments of tense silence, and then a return signal over the wireless from Dover to Wimereux: "Your message received. Perfect."

The bystanders overwhelmed Marconi with their congratulations. But the young inventor brushed them aside. He was too busy for all these superficialities. "Now that we have conquered the channel," he said simply, "our next job is to tackle the sea."

III

THE ENGLISH GOVERNMENT issued patents to Marconi; and a group of English businessmen organized for him a Wireless Telegraph and Signal Company, with a capitalization of 100,000 pounds. Thus encouraged, Marconi went on with his experiments. He established a series of stations along the coastline of England, and he equipped a number of vessels with broadcasting instruments. In this way he made it possible for the vessels to report their positions from time to time and to call, whenever necessary, for help. Even the skeptics were now becoming slowly convinced. "There's something in this wireless after all."

And one foggy night in April, 1899, came the first real test as to the value of wireless telegraphy. In the heavy darkness the steamer *R. F. Matthews* collided with the *East Goodwin Lightship*. A frantic signal into the air, and the miracle happened. The signal was intercepted, lifeboats were sent to the stricken vessel, and the entire crew was saved.

Thus far, however, Marconi had succeeded only in short-range communications. To be sure, he had dreamed of spanning the Atlantic with his wireless. But such dreams, believed the sober-minded academicians, were preposterous. When S. S. McClure printed in his magazine an article about the achievements and the expectations of Marconi, a professor at Clark University called the publisher to task for "foisting such absurdities upon the public." It was impossible, insisted the professor, for wireless telegraphy to travel over long stretches of the earth's surface. "The laws of physics are against it." The earth is round; but the Hertzian waves, maintained the professor, lead straight up into the air, or at most travel off at a tangent away from the curvature of the earth. Thus a wireless message, broadcast—let us say—from New York, might travel to Jersey City, or even to Newark; but beyond that point, it would trail away from the earth on a tangent into infinity.

Such were the cocksure theories of the academicians. But the experiments of Marconi knocked these theories into a cocked hat. They demonstrated a very strange and very important property of the Hertzian waves.

These waves flow over the ocean of the atmosphere in a curve that is parallel to the curvature of the earth. "The Hertzian waves, therefore," insisted Marconi, "will eventually carry a message, just as the ocean waves can carry a ship, all the way around the earth."

And he proceeded with his experiments to transmute *that* dream into a reality. Little by little he extended the range of his wireless to twenty-five miles, fifty miles, seventy-five miles. He was invited to America to report by wireless the international boat race between the *Columbia* and the *Shamrock*. The report was a sensational success; but to Marconi, it was merely a relaxation that fitted him for further efforts. His fixed purpose now was to span the Atlantic with his wireless. "Do you really think this is possible?" asked a reporter.

"I cannot think otherwise," replied Marconi. "All we have to do is to build a transmitter powerful enough to hurl the waves across the sea."

IV

THURSDAY, December 12, 1901. Marconi, frail, sad, keen-eyed, thin-lipped, is sitting at a desk in the John Cabot Memorial Building—a bleak tower upon a bleak hill on the Newfoundland coast. He holds a telephone receiver close to his ear and gazes through the window over the thundering Atlantic. The waves are too blustery today. Will he be able to intercept the wireless that is about to be flashed across for the first time from England to America? For a moment he takes his eyes off the horizon and looks up into the air. A kite, driven by a heavy wind, is tugging violently at a copper antenna that holds it fastened to a pole. Will the slender wire stand up against the fury of the storm? On several previous experiments the kite had been torn away from its mooring. But this must not happen today. Two continents are awaiting the outcome of *this* experiment—and almost universally with an attitude of cynical disbelief. *"Of course it can't be done!"*

Marconi waited and wondered. *He* knew that it *could* be done. And yet . . .

The signals in England were to begin at 3 o'clock English time—that is, at 11:30 Newfoundland time.

Half-past eleven. Twelve. Twelve-fifteen. Marconi sits glued to the earphone. No sound other than the lashing of the wind. Perhaps he was wrong after all? Perhaps the skeptical public was right?

Twelve-twenty. Twelve-twenty-five. Twelve-twenty-nine. How slowly the minutes dragged! It looked as if the whole thing would be a fiasco after all. Wouldn't the public have a good laugh over it? Another pseudoscientist with his crazy dreams . . . Oh, well . . .

Twelve-thirty. Marconi grew suddenly tense. Were his senses deceiving him? No, there they were. Three clicks, faint but unmistakable. The signal agreed upon—the Morse code for the letter S.

Marconi went back to his hotel, but spoke to no one about the amazing news. He first wanted to verify the experiment on the next day, and on the day after that—he had arranged with his assistant in England to repeat the signal on three successive days. On every one of these occasions the experiment was crowned with equal success.

He was now ready to make his statement to the press. On December 15 the *New York Times* featured the historic words: "Guglielmo Marconi announces . . . the most wonderful scientific development of recent times. He states that he has received electric signals across the Atlantic Ocean . . ."

And while the world thundered its praise, Marconi went quietly on with his work.

V

IN MARCH, 1905, Marconi took a vacation from his work. He married an Irish noblewoman, Beatrice O'Brien, daughter of Lord Inchiquin. A brief enchanted honeymoon, followed by nineteen years of disenchantment. Marconi was not the domestic type. He belonged too much to the world to cultivate the patient intimacies of a happy marriage. Though the union resulted in three children, it was finally dissolved (1924). A second marriage (1927), this time to a beautiful Italian, the Countess Maria Cristina Bezzi-Scali, proved to be more successful. Marconi had learned to play as he grew older—he bought a yacht, the *Elettra*, which served him both as a laboratory and as a pleasure palace—and his newly acquired ability to relax resulted in quieter nerves and a less irritable temper.

The rest of his life was a continual process of growing young. "Science," he said, "keeps one forever youthful. I cannot understand the savant who grows bowed and yellowed in a workroom. I like to be out in the open looking at the universe, asking it questions, letting the mystery of it soak right into the mind, admiring the wonderful beauty of it all, and then think my way to the truth of things." He lost his right eye in an automobile accident, and remained unbowed. He won the Nobel Prize—the highest of awards—in physics, and remained unspoiled. And it was in this courageous and unassuming pursuit of his experiments, the perfection of the wireless and the conception of its even greater offspring, the radio—dreams to encircle the globe, to reach the ear of someone listening in upon another planet ("even *this* may some day be possible, who knows?") —that death overtook him on the *Elettra* (July 20, 1937). "And he embarked upon another ship to continue his explorations in another sea."

IMPORTANT DATES IN THE LIFE OF
GUGLIELMO MARCONI

1874–April 25, born at Bologna.

1895–Began experiments with electromagnetic waves.

1896–Took out, in England, first patent for wireless telegraphy.

1897–Established wireless communication from land to sea.

Organized Wireless Telegraph company.

1898–Established wireless communication across the English Channel.

1899–First sea rescue (of *East Goodwin Lightship*) through wireless.

1901–Established wireless communication across the Atlantic.

1902–Patented the magnetic detector.

1905–Patented the horizontal aerial.

1909–Received Nobel Prize for physics.

1912–Introduced the "timed spark system."

1918–Sent first message from England to Australia.

1937–July 20, died, Rome.

Winston Churchill

1874–

IN 1900 WINSTON CHURCHILL came to New York for his first American lecture tour. Mark Twain introduced him to the audience in his characteristic fashion: "Ladies and gentlemen, I give you the son of an American mother and an English father—the perfect man!"

What Mark Twain uttered as a jest turned out to be a prophecy. In this world of human imperfection, Winston Churchill comes pretty close to the universal ideal of the perfect man.

Born prematurely (November 30, 1874), he was dubbed, from the hour of his birth, "Young Man in a Hurry." As a child he hated the severity of mathematics but he loved the magic of words. He abhorred the lessons assigned to him by his governesses and his teachers. Never would he truckle to the demands of these tyrants who kept on nagging him, "Do this," and "Don't do that." Good Lord, hadn't he a mind of his own? He tried to appeal from their dictatorship to his mother; but she, thoroughbred sportswoman, was too fond of her hunting to pay much attention to him. "She shone for me like the Evening Star. I loved her dearly—but at a distance."

At seven he was trundled off to (St. James) School—with fourteen pairs of socks, three half crowns, and two clenched fists. The headmaster handed him a Latin grammar. "You must learn to decline *mensa*."

Winnie looked in perplexity at the various cases until he came to the vocative—*mensa, O table*. "What does this mean, sir?"

"This is the expression you must use when you address a table."

"But, sir, I never address a table."

For answer, the headmaster administered a caning. The boys in his school must be taught their discipline early. But Winnie did not take lightly to his master's idea of discipline. Snatching the man's hat, he kicked it to pieces. Another beating, another outburst of temper. "The little rascal is going to be hard to handle."

An intractable child. To this day, writes H. G. Wells, "I can think of him as . . . a mischievous little boy, a knee-worthy little boy. Only by thinking of him in that way can I go on liking him."

But his masters at St. James found nothing likable in this tempestuous little roughneck. They requested his removal from their midst. His father transferred him to a school conducted by two elderly ladies at Brighton. "A small red-headed pupil," one of his teachers observed of him, "the naughtiest boy in the class. I used to think him the naughtiest boy in the world."

Still a very poor scholar in Latin and in mathematics. But a good student in French—there are no silly vocatives, O *table*, in this language —and a veritable magician in the use of English words. And a memory in which a poem stuck like a fly alighting on fly-paper. He read a stanza once or twice—and there it was, forever fixed.

His assigned lessons were as distasteful as ever. He was almost grateful for the interruption to these lessons when he came down with an attack of double pneumonia. In those days, double pneumonia was almost always fatal. But Winnie pulled through. "The child," remarked the doctor, "has a charmed life."

Throughout his days, Winston Churchill was to lead a charmed life. Fire cannot burn, nor bullets pierce, the man whom the gods have elected to do their work.

Recovered from his illness, Winston took the examinations for Harrow. He had hoped to be examined in French, poetry and essay-writing—subjects in which he could shine. Instead, he was examined in Latin and mathematics. He just barely managed to squeeze through.

And just barely squeezed through his entire career at Harrow. True, the headmaster admired his "literary powers" and expressed his belief that young Winston might possibly distinguish himself later in life. But when the final marks were computed for the entire school, Winston Churchill's name stood out—last.

His father, a better than average scholar and a man prominent in public life, was sadly disappointed. "What, my son, do you intend to do with yourself?"

"I shall be a soldier so long as there is any fighting to be done. After that I shall have a shot at politics."

"But first of all, there's Oxford to think of."

"If you don't mind, sir, I had rather go to Sandhurst."

Lord Randolph Churchill did mind. At heart a pacifist, he did not relish the idea of his son's going to a military school. Winston insisted, however, and Lord Randolph finally consented.

Winston took the examinations for Sandhurst and failed. He took them again, and again failed. He tried a third time—and succeeded through a lucky chance. He knew that one of the assignments at the examination would be the drawing, from memory, of a map of some part of the British Empire. But the British Empire, unlike ancient Gaul, was divided into very many parts. Gambling on a long shot, he threw into his hat several slips of paper, each bearing the name of a British colony or dominion. Then, closing his eyes, he drew one of the paper slips from the hat. New Zealand. This was the map he studied.

At the examination the instructor said, "Gentlemen, you will kindly draw a map of New Zealand."

II

FOR THE FIRST TIME, Churchill finds himself in his element. He tries for a cadetship in the cavalry—and succeeds. You do not have to solve an algebraic equation in order to become a daredevil in the saddle. And Churchill loves the saddle, loves the whistling of the wind through his hair, as he gallops over the drillground. "No hour of life is lost that is spent on horseback," he writes exultantly. "Young men have often been ruined through *owning* horses, or through *backing* horses, but never through *riding* them. Unless, of course, they break their necks, which, taken at a gallop, is a very good death to die."

A steady seat, an old Oriental proverb has it, will often rescue an unsteady head. In spite of his academic deficiencies, young Churchill finished eighth in a class of a hundred and fifty at Sandhurst.

A great triumph, a commission in the Fourth—the Queen's own—Hussars. And a great tragedy, the death of his father. Lord Randolph, Chancellor of the Exchequer, had succumbed to a weak constitution and to the calumnies of his political enemies. Winston stood at his bedside. "The dunce of the family," he vowed, "will take revenge on the whole pack of curs and traitors!" His work, he felt, was mapped out before him. His life was to be a constant campaign—against the enemies of England from without, against the enemies of his father from within.

His campaigning began under his regimental leader, Colonel Brabazon. Rarely were commander and subaltern more closely in accord. Both of them lisped. "The gwass is veddy gween." "Yeth, thir, veddy gween indeed." Both of them were less concerned with authority than with common sense. And both of them concealed, under a formal military gruffness, a very informal love for literature. Their daily duties performed, they could sit together for hours quoting English poetry to one another.

Partly through the influence of Brabazon but largely because of an inner urge, young Churchill began to look for another outlet to his restless energy. He wrote a number of short stories and a novel, *Savrola— The Tale of a Revolution in Laurania*. Not a literary masterpiece, but a penetrating attempt at self-revelation. The hero of the story, Savrola, is a prototype of Winston Churchill—a young man eager to be the honest and intelligent leader of a revolution. "All the other revolutionists throughout the course of history have been either scoundrels or fools." Hiring himself out as a war correspondent to the *Daily Graphic*, Churchill had taken a trip to Cuba, to report a political upheaval in that colony. He had seen, at first hand, enough of the intrigues of the so-called "liberators" to disgust him with that tribe for the rest of his days. "While the members of the old régime are masters of the art of suppressing the truth," he wrote in one of his articles, "the leaders of the new are adepts in inventing falsehoods." And in another article—"I sympathize with the revolution—not with the revolutionaries."

But enough of articles and of stories—for the present. There is fighting to be done. Threats of rebellion in India. Churchill's regiment is ordered to Bombay. A battle against the Mamunds, "a tribe utterly pestilential in their cruelty." In the midst of the battle, Churchill leaps down from his horse and clambers up a hill together with a detachment of infantry. Always where the fighting is thickest! They reach the top of the slope. The forest comes alive. A blaze of bullets from behind every rock and from the branches of every tree. Impossible to stand this fire. The detachment retreats. But not Winnie Churchill. A comrade has been wounded —right eye slashed out by a Hindu dagger. Can't leave him behind to the mercy of the enemy. Churchill tries to carry him down the slope. He finds himself surrounded. Laying down the wounded man, he takes out his revolver. It balks. He snatches up an abandoned rifle. By the Devil, it works! Twenty, thirty, forty rounds. The enemy gives way. Churchill brings his man safely down to camp!

"Nobody but Winnie could have come out of that with a whole skin. A charmed life—what else can it be?"

And a charmed life he carried into his other campaigns—in India, in the Soudan, in South Africa, wherever he served in the line—never behind the line—either as soldier or as war correspondent. Generally he served as both, finding equal activity for his pistol and his pen. Always he sought the center of the fight, and always he came out unscathed. Once he was captured by the Boers, and made use of his captivity to catch up with his reading. Gibbon, Lecky, Carlyle, Stuart Mill, Plato's *Republic*, Aristotle's *Politics*, Winwood Reade's *Martyrdom of Man*. Great men, great thoughts. But enough of them now. There were great deeds to be done. This imprisonment was getting on his nerves. He made his escape, hid himself in a coal mine, found himself packed amidst a shipment of coal bags in a freight car, and finally reached his own lines.

Not only a man with a charmed life, but a daredevil to boot. In his spare time he had trained himself to become a champion polo player. Once, when he was stationed at Hyderabad, the Golcondas, champion polo team of India, challenged his team to a match. "A slaughter," predicted everybody, feeling sorry for poor Churchill and his mates. The match did indeed turn out to be a slaughter—for the other side. Final score: Hussars 9, Golcondas 3. But Churchill, who had led the onslaught at center, almost collapsed at the end. He had played the entire game with a broken shoulder.

A fighting-cock who knew his worth. Nothing of the shrinking violet about him. In one of the articles which he sent as a war correspondent to the *Allahabad Pioneer*, he wrote glowingly about "the courage and the resolution of Lieutenant Winston Churchill, of the Fourth Hussars."

III

HE HAD SERVED as a soldier while there was fighting to be done. And now that the fighting was (temporarily) over, he had his shot at politics. He ran for Parliament (1899) on the same ticket with a labor leader—"the Scion and the Socialist," they were dubbed—and lost. He had received, however, a great deal of publicity during the campaign. "The Youngest Man in Europe," an enthusiast had written of him in the *Daily Mail*, "possesses qualities which make him, almost at will, a great popular leader, a great journalist, or the founder of a great advertising business. What he will become, who can say?"

Least of all, Winston Churchill himself. But he was eager to find out. Another try for Parliament—and this time he was successful. Smiles, handshakes, huzzahs wherever he turned. What a colorful event for England! A Rough Rider in the House of Commons—so gallantly reminiscent of that other Rough Rider across the sea who had just been elected Vice-President of the United States.

But politics is a costly game. To rise in power, he must keep open his purse. A rather lean purse, unfortunately. He decides to fatten it through a lecture tour over England, in Canada, in the United States. Everywhere he electrifies his audiences with the story of his battles, his capture, his breathless escape. He returns with sufficient capital to carry him on to the top.

Back to Parliament and his maiden speech. Here the public sees revealed a new Winston Churchill—a man with a heart. Like Lincoln, he speaks words of charity for his erstwhile enemies, the Boers. "If I were a Boer fighting in the field—and if I were a Boer I *should* be fighting in the field . . ." Liberal words, these. The Conservatives in Parliament shook their heads in disapproval. "He's going to be a hard man to handle . . . Stands against his own light."

But Churchill did nothing of the kind. He knew precisely where he was facing—forward and upward, in order to keep his *country* facing forward and upward. To preserve the Empire—united, righteous, and strong.

He advocated a powerful navy. The heart of the British Empire, he pointed out, is an island; for the very flowing of its lifeblood it depends upon the channels of the sea. "The Admiralty is the only office strong enough to insure the British Empire."

Strange words for a soldier, this advocacy of a strong navy against a strong army. But what matters the branch of service so long as a man is anxious to serve?

And what matters the party through which a man can attain to service? Parties always meant less than principles to Winston Churchill. Liberal, Conservative, Whig, Tory, Labor—these were but slogans for the rallying of political support. The essential thing was to insure "a Government that will think a little more about the toiler at the bottom of the mine and a little less about the fluctuations of the share market in London . . . a Government and a policy which will think the condition of a slum in an English city is not less worthy of attention of statesmen . . . than the jungle of Somaliland." Political observers often smiled cynically and called him a turncoat. What he actually did was merely to turn his eyes always in the direction of the light.

IV

IN 1905, UNDER the first liberal Prime Minister in a decade, Churchill was appointed Under-Secretary for the Colonies. In this office the "men of all colors and creeds" had a friend who understood them and meant them well. Especially the Boers had reason to be grateful to him. In his effort to solve the Boer problem, he pointed out to Parliament again and again that "we must insure not only British wishes but Boer assent." When the Liberals—the party to which he now belonged—had voted to grant a constitution to Transvaal, he implored the Conservatives to make the vote unanimous: "With all our majority we can only make the constitution the gift of a party. You can make it the gift of England."

From liberalism he turned to radicalism. "Why have I always been kept safe within a hair's breadth of death except to do something for the poor?" But he stopped short of socialism, because of its avowed purpose to put an end to competition. "The existing organization of society is driven by one mainspring—competitive selection. It may be a very imperfect organization of society, but it is all we have got between us and barbarism."

A crusader for justice within the bounds of private enterprise. And in his vigorous fight for justice he felt "as if I could lift the whole world on my shoulders."

And thus, carrying lightly the burden of humanity, he reached his thirty-fourth year (September, 1908) when, to quote his own words, he "married and lived happily ever afterwards."

With the accession of a loving and understanding wife, his ambitions and his achievements grew more rapidly than ever. A little too rapidly, perhaps, for his success tended to make him precipitate. "He is too apt to act first and think afterwards," observed Lord Haldane. Yet "of his courage," Haldane confessed, "one cannot speak too highly."

A man of courage was needed in the Admiralty. For there were too many deadweights who kept the British navy down. And once appointed to that office, Churchill proved to everybody's surprise that he was also endowed with a great measure of wisdom. He was himself impressed, and he tried to impress the Government, with "a sense of ever-present danger." Germany, he was convinced, was constantly on the jump to start a war against England; and it was his habit suddenly to ask the question, "What happens if war with Germany begins today?"

The British navy must be prepared for any eventuality. Battleships, cruisers, destroyers, even seaplanes—this as early as 1913—sprang up under the magic touch of Winston Churchill. His insistence upon a strong navy occasioned a break with the radicals; for most of them were pacifists and believed in reducing, rather than in expanding, the instruments of war. Churchill alone saw the war clouds gathering just above the horizon.

And then the storm broke. Winston Churchill, still under forty, was now First Lord of the Admiralty. Upon his shoulders alone rested the success or the failure of the British navy. And of the British army, too; for it was the navy that must transport the men and the arms to the battlefield on the continent. In the presence of his associates he wore—to quote one of them—"a happy face." But when alone, he had his moments of misgiving. In spite of all his efforts prior to the war—time and again he had worked on a twenty-four hour basis—the pacifists had had their way. England had been caught in 1914 unprepared.

That is, the army had been caught unprepared, but not the navy. When, as a result of the Dardanelles fiasco Churchill was asked to resign from the Admiralty, Lord Kitchener paid him a visit. After he had chatted with him about the latest news, he turned to go. And then, with a sudden impulse, "Well, there is one thing at any rate they cannot take from you. The Fleet was ready."

V

RESIGNATION, but no respite. From the navy he transferred his services to the army. Major Winston Churchill, of the Oxfordshire Yeomanry—a man who, in spite of his setbacks, still appeared to his colleagues to exhibit "great form and tearing spirits."

All quiet on the battlefront. Churchill whiled away his time learning a new art—painting. He enjoyed bright colors, bold strokes—mirror of his own bright and bold personality.

His headquarters were close to the front—too close, thought his superiors who were fond of him, for his safety. His brains were too precious for his body to take too many chances. "Do you realize," said the Commander-in-Chief, "that this is a very dangerous place?" "Yes, sir," replied Churchill, "but after all, this is a very dangerous war."

A brave spirit, and a perfect *confrère* to that other brave spirit,

Clemenceau. One day the two stormy petrels met on the battlefield, where Clemenceau was paying a visit to the British troops. There was active fighting going on at the time. "You really ought not to risk your life under fire," said Churchill. Whereupon Clemenceau retorted, "*Mon ami, c'est mon grand plaisir.*" ("My friend, it's my great pleasure.")

November, 1918. The end of the war; and the end, it seemed, of Churchill's career. "To keep him out of mischief," they relegated him to the post of Minister of Munitions. A meaningless job, now that peace had arrived. Politically he was almost friendless. Due to his honest habit of sacrificing the expedient for the just, he had become anathema to all the parties. Neither the Conservatives nor the Liberals nor the Laborites could "trust" him as a tool to do their bidding. He had a "peculiar" philosophy of his own—the permanent interest of the entire British Commonwealth. So foreign to the interests of a *party*—that is, a *part*—of England. No significant role for *him* now to play in the politics of the time.

Obscure tasks. Yet he entered upon them, as usual, "in good form, very energetic and very cheerful."

And then, an attack of appendicitis. While he lay convalescing in the hospital, an election for Parliament came up. His wife fought his campaign for him. Two days before the voting he got out of his invalid's chair and addressed his constituents at Dundee. Angry faces, shaken fists, muttered threats. At the polls he was overwhelmingly defeated.

VI

TWENTY YEARS of comparative obscurity—writing, lecturing, painting. And always dreaming of the day when he would come back. His critics looked unkindly upon his dream. "Mr. Churchill," wrote H. G. Wells, "believes quite naïvely that he belongs to a peculiarly gifted and privileged class of beings . . . His imagination is obsessed by dreams of exploits and a career . . . Before all things he desires a dramatic world with villains —and one hero."

This caricature was unfair to Churchill. He had his human share of egotism, to be sure, but his chief interest was the welfare of England. It was of England that he thought when he warned the world (1932) against the advent of Hitler. He was almost alone to see, in the stirring of the Nazi uprising, a threat to all Europe. A prophet in the wilderness. "It is good to live in the wilderness; it gives you time to think." He thought about England's danger, and her weakness in face of it, and he was terrified at the thought. Terrified, and determined to transform England's weakness into England's strength. He spoke of the new menace in modern warfare—the menace of air attack. "This cursed, hellish invention and development of war from the air"—he insisted as far back as 1933 —"has revolutionized our position. We are not the same kind of country we used to be when we were an island . . ." He called again and again for "an airforce at least as strong as that of any power that can get at us."

But England only half-listened, and slept. "A fire-eater, doesn't know what he is talking about." Hitler went on with his preparations for the most stupendous adventure of gangsterism in history—and England slept. Slept under Baldwin, slept under Chamberlain—while Hitler collected his tools, and Mussolini launched upon that prelude to international burglary in Ethiopia, and Hitler and Mussolini aided and abetted Franco in the murder of a legally constituted democratic government in Spain. Slept while Hitler robbed nation after nation, and slaughtered their people, and kept gathering and sharpening his tools against England herself. And Churchill looked on with a great rising anger in his heart against a British government "decided only to be undecided, resolved only to be irresolute, adamant for drift, solid for fluidity, all-powerful to be impotent."

Munich and Chamberlain's disgraceful flight in an airplane to lick the dust off Hitler's boots—"Chamberlain crawled to Hitler on all fours," a clever journalist remarked, "at two hundred miles an hour." And still England slept. "No need for alarm," Chamberlain reported. "Herr Hitler is a gentleman. He has promised us peace."

But Churchill knew better. "We have sustained a defeat," he declared, "without a war."

And then, the avalanche. The air attack on England. The threatened defeat of civilization. Almost too late, they called Churchill to the rescue. The Young Man in a Hurry. Great need for hurry now if civilization was to be saved.

Churchill's mood as he undertook the job was realistic, but unafraid. "I have nothing to offer but blood, toil, tears and sweat." Yet out of this blood and toil and tears and sweat, he emphatically declared, would come triumph in the end.

Electric words. Overnight they transformed England into a nation of heroes. Throughout the country, but a single resolve—to *bear* arms, to *make* arms, to *win the victory!* "Victory at all costs, victory in spite of all terror, victory, however long and hard the road may be."

A long and hard road, indeed. But with Churchill leading the way, what other end could there be but victory?

Dark days and nights. The blackout of the world. The drone of Germany's planes over London. "The capital of humanity" in flames. The imminent invasion of England. But Churchill kept on presenting to the world a countenance undismayed. "We shall defend out island, whatever the cost may be, we shall fight on the beaches, we shall fight on the landing grounds, we shall fight in the fields and in the streets, we shall fight in the hills; we shall never surrender."

The old Churchill determination. The old Churchill courage. And the old Churchill defiance. Hitler at last had met his master—the man who could outguess him step by step. June, 1940. Hitler was in possession of the entire coastline of the Continent from the North Cape to the Pyrenees. In his evil hands he wielded two irresistible instruments—an undefeated army and an unlimited air fleet. He was poised for the invasion of England. But there was one man who stood in the way. Churchill, armed with a weapon greater than all the accumulated might of Hitler. A spirit that refused to go down in defeat. He braced his countrymen for their "finest hour," and he hurtled the challenge into Hitler's face: "Come on, we shall easily devour your entire hostile horde!"

Hitler hesitates, and is lost. The invasion of England is "indefinitely postponed." The fighting heart of Churchill—"I shall be a soldier as long as there is fighting to be done"—has saved the day for the human race.

When the fighting was over and the United Nations had won the war, he was "honorably discharged" from his post. His countrymen felt that the new day required a new guide. And so, in the elections of 1945, they replaced the tried warrior with an untried man of peace. Yet in looking forward with their new social leader, Clement Attlee, the voters of England cast a reverent glance upon the fighter who had preserved for them the right to vote him down.

During these years following the war, Churchill devoted himself to his literary endeavors. He had formerly published *Life of Lord Randolph Churchill*, *My African Journey*, *Liberalism and the Social Problem*, and a four-volume history of World War I, *The World Crisis*. Following the publication in the 1930s of two books, *My Early Life* and *Marlborough, His Life and Times*, he took time away from his writing. During these years, however, he collected material for his most famous historical publications, the series on World War II, including *The Gathering Storm, Their Finest Hour, The Grand Alliance*, and *The Hinge of Fate*.

Britain was to call him back from his writings, however, for in 1951, a Conservative Party victory at the polls returned Churchill to power as Prime Minister and he devoted the ensuing years to preventing his country and the world from being blasted into annihilation by an atomic war. Age has crept up on Churchill; he suffered a stroke in 1953 that reduced his physical efficiency. In 1955 he relinquished the office of Prime Minister to Sir Anthony Eden, his protégé, and he officially retired from political life. However, the man who fought in the armies of Queen Victoria, who directed the British navy against the Kaiser and saved England from Hitler will never cease battling for causes as long as there is life in his body. In his eighties, Churchill believes steadfastly in man's ability to stave off a nuclear destruction that would plunge human society into the dark ages. And if he has any additional request to make of the fates that have been so kind to him, it is to be permitted to live long enough to witness a durable accommodation between the Western democracies and the communist world to this end.

IMPORTANT DATES IN THE LIFE OF
WINSTON CHURCHILL

1874—November 30, born at Dublin.

1895—Joined the Fourth Hussars.

1897–98—Served in India.

1898—Served in Egypt.

1899—Served in Boer War.

1900—Elected to House of Commons.

1903—Appointed Under-Secretary of State.

1910—Became Home Secretary.

1911—Became First Lord of the Admiralty.

1915—Relieved of Admiralty post.

1916—Appointed Minister of Munitions.

1919—Appointed Secretary of State.

1924—Elected to Parliament from Epping.

1924–29—Served as Chancellor of the Exchequer.

1939—Reappointed First Lord of the Admiralty.

1940—Became Prime Minister and leader of England's war efforts.

1941—With Roosevelt, issued the Atlantic Charter.

1945—Churchill government ousted by Labor Party victory.

1951—Returned to power as Prime Minister.

1955—Resigned and designated Eden as his successor.

Albert Schweitzer

1875–

I<small>T WAS</small> E<small>MERSON</small>, we believe, who observed that every now and then nature gets tired of its half-men and quarter-men, and produces a complete man. One of the best modern examples of this extraordinary achievement of nature is Albert Schweitzer. At thirty he was acclaimed as a genius in philosophy, literature, theology, and music. In each of these fields, had he so desired, he could have risen to fame and fortune. For he possessed the energy as well as the brilliance of those who climb to the top. And yet, at the very threshold of his promise, he turned away from success to devote himself to service. In a true Christian sense, he was ready to lose his life in order to find it.

The story of his pilgrimage from the intellectuals of Europe to the savages of the jungle is one of the great epics of the human spirit. So let us meet this master of humility who, at the age of thirty, decided to become a doctor of medicine that he might mend the broken bodies of his less fortunate brothers in Africa.

II

A<small>S A</small> C<small>HILD</small>, he was blessed with many endowments—loving parents, a vigorous body, a keen mind, manual dexterity, and a love for music, people, nature, and God. His father was a pastor at Günsbach, a little town in Alsatia. In this connecting province between France and Germany, little Albert came under the influence of two civilizations. And in his father's church, he learned a lesson in tolerance between two religions. For, owing to the poverty of the townspeople, both the Catholics and the Protestants were obliged to worship in the same House of God. Thus, from his very infancy, Albert got to know the essential unity in the external diversity of individuals and nations and creeds.

His sympathy toward other people extended to all living creatures.

In addition to the bedtime prayer his mother had taught him, he improvised a little prayer of his own: "O, heavenly Father, protect and bless all things that have breath. Guard them from all evil, and let them sleep in peace." When he was about seven, he went into the woods one day, together with some other boys, to hunt birds with a bean shooter. But just as they were aiming at a flock of robins, he heard "the voice of God" warning him: "Thou shalt not kill!" He waved his little arms and drove the birds away—to the disgust of his companions who gave him a drubbing for his interference with their sport.

At eight, under his father's tuition, he began to study the organ. And at eighteen, he was an expert not only in the playing but in the building of organs.

In his studies, he was as proficient as in his music. He found himself in perfect harmony with himself, his family, and the world.

But, again and again, he heard the prompting of the Voice. Like Socrates and Swedenborg and other great mystics before him, Schweitzer experienced this Voice not merely as a figment of the imagination, but as a concrete guiding spirit in his life. "You are unusually gifted," the Voice kept telling him, "and you must pay an unusual price for your gifts."

"Pay for my gifts? But how?"

"In the form of service for those who are less richly endowed."

III

HE ENTERED the University of Strasbourg as a student of theology and philosophy. Tall, wiry, flashing eyes, unruly black hair, a captivating smile, and a heart filled with music and devotion and love. When he came into the classroom for the first time, the students and even the professor smiled at his ungainly figure. For the long and lean freshman was dressed in a suit borrowed from a short and stocky uncle. But people forgot his clothes when he began to talk.

And especially when he sat down at the organ or the piano. Though he still took lessons in music, he was now able to outplay most of his teachers. One of them, to show off his skill to his young pupil, struggled through a difficult fugue of Bach; and then, handing the music sheet to Schweitzer, he said patronizingly, "Now, my boy, play *that* if you can." Schweitzer took his place at the instrument, put the music aside, and played the fugue from memory, omitting not a single note.

But music, he felt, was not his vocation. His great passion, at the time, was theology. He was anxious to get at the very heart of the Christian ideal through an intimate study of the life of Christ.

At the height of his allegiance to the Prince of Peace, he was drafted for compulsory service in the German army. Throughout his training, he carried a Bible along with his gun. By day he followed the commands of his officers; and by night he pondered over the commandments of the Lord. After a year of service in the army, he was released from the study of mass slaughter and returned to the nobler study of mass salvation.

Several years of further training in the arts of peace, a thesis on the Last Supper, and a doctorate in theology. And the leisure hours filled with music. Studies in Plato, Goethe, Spinoza, a thesis on the religion of Kant, and a doctorate in philosophy. And again music, and more music. A traveling fellowship in Paris, articles, lectures, plans for a book on the ethics of civilization, an instructorship in the university, a pastorate at the Church of St. Nicholas—and still the Voice kept prompting him. "Not this, my son, not this!"

"What, then, am I required to do?"

"When the time comes, you will know."

IV

HE WAS THIRTY NOW, and the toast of the intelligentsia in France and Germany. He had written a biography of Bach which the critics hailed as a masterpiece of musical appreciation. His lectures and his concerts were so popular that there were not enough tickets to go around. The Alsatian wizard, the favorite of fortune, the beloved of God.

And yet, he was very unhappy. In spite of his personal success, he found the world "inexplicably mysterious and full of suffering." He had been introduced to Romain Rolland, and he had listened to this intellectual rebel's indictment against man's inhumanity to man. One day he met an Alsatian missionary to Africa who was home on furlough. He learned from him about the miseries of the black men brought on, to a great extent, by the white men's lust for power and traffic in alcohol. Jungles of poverty, ignorance, and disease—and so few devoted people to help them. What they needed most was friendly guidance and medical aid.

Doctors of Medicine. But Schweitzer was only a Doctor of Music, Theology, and Philosophy. He longed to help them, but he had taken the wrong course. The road he had chosen was directed toward progress, and not regression into the wilds of Africa.

Progress? What, he asked himself, was the meaning of this word? Personal success? Artistic achievement? Literary fame? But what about his relationship to his fellow men? Was not *this* the purpose for which he had been born—to bind together the members of the human family into a fellowship of hope? Was not the gift of a strong body and superior mind bestowed upon him as a trust to be shared with others? Again the Voice came to prompt him in his perplexity: "Whatever you have received more than others, in health, in ability, in success, in a pleasant childhood, in harmonious conditions of home life, all this you must not take to yourself as a matter of course. You must pay for it. You must render in return an unusually great sacrifice of your life for other lives."

And now the time came for the Voice to speak no longer in riddles, but clearly at last. "Give up your other ambitions and achievements and hopes. Start all over again. Study medicine; and, when you have received your diploma, go as a medical missionary to Africa."

When Schweitzer told his friends about his decision, they thought he had lost his mind. "Don't waste your precious talents," said one of them, "like a general going into the firing line with a rifle."

But Schweitzer knew what he was about. He had discovered the one job for which he was most eminently fitted. And so, in the fall of 1905, he started upon his new career as a medical student. The dean of the faculty gently hinted that Schweitzer ought to go to the psychiatric ward instead of the classroom. But Schweitzer smiled. For he felt that he was merely repaying his debt when he enrolled himself in "the fellowship of those who bear the mark of pain."

V

It TOOK HIM six years to complete his medical studies. Then, a year of internship, and marriage to a young nurse who, like himself, had decided upon a career of missionary service.

And then he applied to the Paris missionary Society for a place where he might build a hospital in the African jungle. They selected Lambaréné, a district in the French colony of Gabon near the equator. "But you may go," they declared, "on only one condition. You must agree to practice medicine, but not to preach theology." For they were afraid that he might "infect" the natives with too radical a picture of Jesus. He promised to keep his theological views to himself, whereupon they reluctantly allowed him to go.

His immediate step now was to raise money for the venture. When he came to see his friends, they greeted him warmly. But when he asked them for contributions, there was a sudden drop in the temperature of their affection. Whatever they gave, they gave with the feeling that it would go down the drain. For they regarded the project as too nebulous, and Dr. Schweitzer as too much of an idealist to turn so wild a dream into a reality. All in all, he collected but little as a result of his "begging" expedition.

To these slender funds he added his earnings from a number of organ recitals, and his royalties from his Bach book which now had been published in France, Germany, and England. Thus he scraped together enough money for the building of a modest hospital, and for its maintenance over a period of perhaps a year or two.

And so, together with his young bride, he set sail for Africa on Easter Sunday, 1913, as the church bells spelled out the Resurrection of Life and the beginning of a new career dedicated to the black brotherhood in the Family of Man.

VI

THEY ARRIVED at the mouth of the Ogoway River, close to the equator, and plunged into a wilderness of tropical forests with the strange beasts and birds shouting their angry disapproval of the white intruders into their jungle. At first they sailed up the river in a steamer; but after a time, when the windings became too numerous and the stream too narrow, they transferred into a canoe. They passed along the sites of village after village along the banks. But most of them were deserted. When Schweitzer asked the reason for this wholesale depopulation of the jungle, a French trader at his side replied significantly: "Sickness and alcohol."

At last they reached Lambaréné. Green slopes, tropical fruit trees, small white mission huts, smiling black faces, a stifling heat that enveloped them like a blanket—and just beyond the village, the huge, dark tangle of a primeval forest that seemed to enclose them as in a prison cell.

This, then, was the place selected for Dr. Schweitzer's experiment in healing. The missionary society in Paris had promised to have a building of corrugated iron ready for his use. But they had forgotten about the laziness of the natives. Schweitzer was obliged to start from scratch.

And to drive the natives for their own good. Under his strict but kindly supervision, they transformed a henhouse into a hospital. The hardest worker of them all was the "Magic-Man" Schweitzer himself. "He can carry the heaviest rocks and cut down the biggest trees of any man in Africa," said one admirer to another as they watched him at his work.

But most of all they admired his medical and surgical skill. They could not get over the miracle of anesthesia. "Since the Doctor came here," wrote a native girl to the Missionary Society, "the most wonderful things have happened. First of all, he puts the sick people to death; then he cures them; and after that, he brings them back to life again."

Having heard of his magic, the natives from all the surrounding territory came to him in droves. "Here among us," said one of the natives, "everybody suffers from that Devil Worm, pain. The jungle devours its own children."

And Schweitzer, aided only by his wife, treated scores of patients every day. They came to him with all sorts of diseases—malaria, sleeping sickness, strangulated hernia, heart trouble, dysentery, typhoid, elephantiasis, bone infections, and skin eruptions. The one disease from which they were absolutely free, strangely enough, was cancer.

Added to their suffering from sickness was the torture of fear. The "black children of the jungle" were obsessed with an overwhelming fear of wild beasts, the Devil, the trickery of the white men, and the wrath of the gods. Schweitzer soon learned that he must try not only to mend their bodies but to heal their souls. Fortunately, his missionary associates in Africa released him from his promise to refrain from preaching the

Gospel to the Black Folk. They felt that the story of Jesus, coming from the lips of their own doctor, would hearten the natives with added healing and hope.

And they were right. Schweitzer preached to them one day a week, and ministered to them seven days a week; and little by little he saw them emerge from the jungle of their despair.

But this was only the beginning of his work. In the building of the hospital and the reconstruction of the lives of the natives, Schweitzer assumed the duties not only of a doctor and preacher, but of an architect, carpenter, stone mason, plumber, house painter, and judge. His skill as a laborer was the admiration of the entire province. And his judicial decisions were worthy of Solomon himself. One day he heard a dispute between two of the natives. One of them had taken the other man's canoe without his knowledge and gone off fishing. And now both the owner of the canoe and the fisherman claimed a right to the entire catch.

Unable to come to a satisfactory agreement, the two men brought their quarrel to Schweitzer. He heard both sides, and then arrived at the following conclusion:

"Both of you are right, and both of you are wrong. You"—pointing to the owner of the canoe—"are right because your friend should have asked your permission for the use of your boat. But you are wrong because you were too lazy to fasten your boat with a padlock, or to go out fishing yourself on a moonlight night when the catch was likely to be good.

"And you"—pointing now to the other man—"are right because you didn't sleep off your laziness like your friend, but took advantage of the bright night to go fishing. But you are wrong because you took the boat without the owner's permission."

And then Schweitzer pronounced sentence: "The owner of the canoe is to get one-third of the catch; and the man who caught the fish is to get one-third."

"What about the remainder?" they both asked.

"The remainder," said Schweitzer, "belongs to me for taking the time to settle the argument." And when the two men looked at him in surprise, he added with a smile: "I shall give all of my share to the patients in the hospital. For this trial has taken place on the hospital grounds."

VII

UNDER THE RIGID but fatherly supervision of their "Magic-Man," the hospital was at last completed. Consultation room, operating theater, sterilization room, dispensary, and dormitory. He now had a few white assistants as well as a native interpreter whom he had named Joseph. This man, though unable to read and write, could speak eight African dialects in addition to French and English. He had a flare for gaudy shirts and neckties which were quite in contrast with the rough working-clothes worn by Schweitzer. "Him chief doctor," Joseph explained to the visitors. "But me chief dresser."

Schweitzer found neither the occasion nor the time for formal dress. There was too much work to be done. A constant stream of patients, many of them coming with their wives and families and friends. The sick must be cared for, their companions fed and lodged, and the thousand-and-one administrative duties attended to. Twelve hours, fifteen hours, eighteen hours a day—and still the work remained unfinished. His wife was as indefatigable as himself, and his handful of assistants did as much as was humanly possible. But the results never seemed to measure up to the task. Scorching heat in the dry season, stifling damp in the rainy season. Disappointment, weariness, an occasional flare of temper, impatience with the inadequacy of the hospital facilities, a spell of tropical sickness which kept him in bed for a time—but never a moment of regret. He was supremely happy in his work. He had given up his civilized life, and now he really *lived*.

For he had found the real meaning of civilization—the progress of turning back to help others along the way. Yet he did not altogether turn his back upon his former culture in Europe. He saved some of its best features—particularly his love for literature and his passion for music— to soften the hardships of his life at Lambaréné. He spent every spare moment in writing or in playing upon his organ-piano—a gift sent him by the members of the Paris Bach Society. "My craving for music," he said, "is like other men's craving for tobacco or wine." Hungrily he went to his favorite instrument, fingering the keys, improvising a tune, practicing a Bach fugue or even a single phrase over and over again until it became perfect under his magical skill. The lonely doctor in the jungle of the Ogoway River was still one of the greatest organists in the world!

VIII

1914. Dr. Schweitzer and his wife were planning a trip to Europe— partly to get a much-needed vacation, but more especially to raise money for the hospital through a personal lecture and concert tour. But, as they were completing their plans, the World War broke out. The governor of Equatorial Africa informed Schweitzer that, as a German subject living in a French colony, he must regard himself as a prisoner of war. "You and your wife are to remain in your own house," ordered the governor, "and you are to communicate neither with the natives nor with the Europeans at the mission."

"But what about my hospital work?" asked Schweitzer.

The governor shrugged his shoulders. "C'est la guerre," he said.

"But I assure you I can be trusted."

Again the governor shrugged. "One can never tell. The danger of espionage, you know. Something you may inadvertently say or do may lead to dangerous results."

And so, the "crazy squabble of the civilized people," as the natives called the war, put an end to Schweitzer's labor of mercy among the savages. For some time, at least.

Savagery, and civilization. News reached Lambaréné that ten of the white men who had gone home from the mission to join the French army had been killed. "Ten men already!" cried one of the natives. "Why don't the white tribes get together and stop the war? How are they going to pay for all those dead men?"

"What do you mean?" asked Schweitzer.

"Whenever we have a war here," said the native, "we pay for all the men we kill, whether we are the winners or the losers. So, you see, we can't afford to have big wars."

Which of the two races, Schweitzer asked himself, was the more civilized —the white or the black? One day he received a letter informing him that his mother had been trampled to death during a cavalry charge in the village street. The world had gone mad! The Prince of Peace was being crucified again and again by the very men who professed to be his devout disciples. A new Gospel was needed—a flaming message that would convert the Christian nations to the religion of Christ.

And so he plunged once more into the book he had been planning all these years. It must teach the world a reverence for life. "I am life which wills life, in the midst of life which wills to live." The old commandment, *Thou shalt not kill*, must be transformed from a negative into a positive ethic. *Thou shalt preserve life*, promote it, foster it not only in your fellowmen but in every creature that breathes and moves and longs to live. "My relation to the world is not passive but active." For all of us have a duty to perform—to live, let live, and *help live*. "The ethic of Reverence for Life is the ethic of Love widened into universality. It is the ethic of Jesus," translated into the language of the twentieth century.

But, in the midst of the writing of his Newer Testament, he was again interrupted. The authorities ordered the Schweitzers to be interned in France as prisoners of war.

The horrors of confinement in a concentration camp, sickness, starvation, bleak winds, stone floors, insufficient blankets, and brutal guards. And then, at long last, armistice and peace. Years later, when his friends asked him about that phase of his life, he said: "Let us forget that time of hatred and fear."

IX

AFTER THE WAR, he returned to Lambaréné. But this time he went alone. His wife was too ill to accompany him. Besides, they had a little daughter now—Rhena, three years old. He built a modest home for them at Königsfeld, in the Black Forest, and left them in the care of a colony of Quakers—"the simple, true followers of Christ."

When he arrived at Lambaréné, he found everything in ruins. But, instead of despair, he felt a surge of hope at the dismal spectacle. It was a challenge to build a bigger and better hospital.

The job proved almost, but not quite, beyond his endurance. The natives, as before, had to be driven and threatened and cajoled to do their work. And his own strength had been sapped by his hardships at the concentration camp. In the course of the building, he developed ulcers on his feet, so that he could not wear any shoes. But he went right ahead, an example to those who pleaded imaginary ailments as an excuse for their laziness. In one of his letters to his friends he wrote of "the terrible contest between the European worker who is always in a hurry, and the child of nature who has no conception of time." Why bother to work, they insisted, when they had their food from the trees, their shelter from a tangle of saplings, and their warmth from the sun?

But finally they did manage to finish the hospital. And when the job was done, Schweitzer was completely exhausted. "What a blockhead I was," he exclaimed, "to come out here to these savages!"

"Yes, Doctor," observed a native assistant. "You are a blockhead here in Africa, but not in heaven."

And, little by little, Schweitzer succeeded in transplanting a bit of heaven in the African jungle. Occasional trips to Europe, for visits with his family and lectures and concerts to raise funds for the hospital. Honorary degrees, literary prizes, adulation—but always his chief work was among his black brothers in the jungle—"to mend their broken bodies and to wake their sleeping souls."

And then, another nightmare—not for the blacks, but for the whites. A psycopath had run amuck in Germany, and the whole country had become infected with his criminal insanity. "Heil Hitler!" And before the madness was over, the whole world had been swept into a whirlpool of blood.

This time, fortunately, Schweitzer was not interned as a prisoner of war. And, in the midst of the deluge of death, he adhered to his faith in the ultimate Reverence for Life. "I do not believe that we shall tread the road of destruction to the very end . . . Because I have confidence in the spiritual power of truth, I believe in the future of mankind."

X

1945, and Schweitzer's seventieth birthday. While the world was singing his praises, he celebrated the occasion by working from dawn to twilight in the hospital. To a friend who had urged him to take a vacation, he wrote: "It can't be done. I must be in my place every day for many reasons . . . For there are too few of us. I have other jobs alongside the duties of a doctor . . . I am the one who starts the motors every morning, who does the marketing at half-past eight, who goes to the plantation every day to examine what the workers have done (or haven't done). I must see to it that the fruits are gathered and put on straw to keep them fresh.

"And I was forgetting. Who will look after the pharmacy, if I am away? Who will see that the medicines don't spoil (in the tropical heat), that the catgut for the operations is watched, and the disinfectant solutions are cared for? . . .

"So you see, my friend, I must just let my fellow workers take holidays and keep dreaming of the time when I, too, can take a rest, sleep and walk as much as I like, and spend the whole day and half the night at my historical and philosophical writing . . ."

1955. Eighty years old now, and still at his innumerable tasks. Operations at the hospital, occasional trips to Europe for lectures, a brief visit to America, and writing, writing, writing at every possible moment he could spare. Medical works, histories, religious biographies, philosophical essays, and a four-volume study of civilization—the diagnosis of its sickness, and the prescription for its possible cure. "If I live to be a hundred, I shall never find the time to complete my work." For his task was perhaps the greatest ever undertaken by a single man—to bring health to the sick, and sanity to all mankind.

As for his personal happiness, "I have been so busy," he remarked to a friend, "that I haven't had any time to give it a thought. As an individual, I have long ceased to exist . . ."

Once, in a talk that he gave to the boys at an English school, he had expressed the same idea in a somewhat different way. "I don't know what your destiny will be," he said. "But one thing I know: the only ones among you who will be truly happy are those who have sought and found how to serve."

IMPORTANT DATES IN THE LIFE OF ALBERT SCHWEITZER

1875—January 14, born at Kaysersberg, Alsace.

1899—Received Ph.D. degree from the University of Strasbourg.

1902—Appointed curate of the Church of St. Nicholas, in Strasbourg.

1903—Appointed head of Theological College, Strasbourg.

1905—Wrote biography of J. S. Bach.

1906—Wrote *The Quest of the Historical Jesus.*

1911—Received his medical degree.

1912—Wrote *Paul and His Interpreters.*

1913—Went as a medical missionary to Lambaréné.

1922—Wrote *On the Edge of the Primeval Forest.*

1926—Wrote *Self-Portrait.*

1933—Wrote *Out of My Life and Thought.*

1945—70th birthday. International radio broadcasts in his honor. Schweitzer hard at work in Lambaréné.

1952—Awarded Nobel Peace Prize.

Albert Einstein

1879–1955

ONE day his father brought him a compass. It was a small toy to amuse the child. Albert trembled with excitement as he gazed upon the "magic" needle turning toward the north. He saw before him not a plaything but a miracle. He was too young to understand the principle of magnetism, yet instinctively he felt that he was standing upon the threshold of an enchanted world.

It was the same way with the little fellow when he played the violin. His eyes glistened, and his hand shook far too passionately for a healthy youngster. It was the music that so agitated him. Very often he would stand as if in a trance while his mother played a Mozart or a Beethoven sonata on the piano. But when the talk turned to politics and people spoke of Bismarck and the rise of the German Empire, Albert would grow frightened and leave the room.

He was a queer child. Not much like the son of an electrical engineer. One day a regiment of the Kaiser's soldiers marched through the streets of Munich and "all the good Germans" flocked to the windows to cheer. The children especially were fascinated at the sight of the flashing helmets and the arrogant goose-step of the soldiers. But Albert Einstein shuddered. He despised and feared these "fighting monsters." He begged his mother to take him away to a land where he would never have to become one of them. And his mother, to quiet her son, promised that she would.

A queer child indeed. He had none of the enthusiasms, and little of the mentality, of other children. His father was pained at the reports from Albert's teachers. They told him that the boy was mentally slow, unsociable, "adrift forever in his foolish dreams." They nicknamed him *Pater Langweil—Father Bore*. But Albert was unaware of the anxiety of his elders. He felt very keenly alive in a world full of wonder. And he probed into this world all by himself. He needed no other company. He composed songs and set them to words in praise of God. He played in his garden or walked in the streets singing his songs aloud. He was incredibly happy.

But soon he was to learn bitter things. At home he had been brought up in the Jewish faith. At the state school he was instructed in the Catholic religion. And the heart of the child found nothing irreconcilable between the Old Testament and the New. They were both beautiful poems, sad and true, these stories about the sufferings of the Prophets and the martyrdom of the Saviour. He loved both stories with an equal fervor, just as he loved his compass and his songs. But one day the teacher brought into the classroom a large nail. And he told the students that this was the nail with which Jesus had been crucified. And suddenly all eyes were turned upon Albert, as if *he* had crucified Jesus. He saw the faces of his fellow students transfixed with a strange kind of hatred. And he could not understand it. His face blushing with shame—for the others, not for himself—he rose from his seat and rushed out of the room.

He was alone, save for the companionship of his books. He formed a friendship across the centuries with Euclid, Newton, Spinoza, Descartes —mathematicians and philosophers whose works he had mastered before he was fifteen. And he adored the poets and the musicians—Heine, Schiller, Goethe, Beethoven, Mozart and Bach. Here was a world of order, of harmony, of law—a logic that reacted as a balm upon a sensitive nature bewildered by the illogic of his teachers and his fellow pupils.

When Albert was in the secondary school he found it more necessary than ever to "drown his solitude in his books." For his father had lost his business and had moved his family to Milan in the hope that the change of scenery might bring back his financial health. Albert was left alone in Munich.

On his vacations, however, he visited Milan and found the Italian atmosphere congenial to his dreaming soul. He renounced his German citizenship. But he did not apply for Italian papers. He desired to remain unattached—a citizen of the world.

His father was annoyed at his eccentricities. The time had come for Albert to shoulder the responsibilities of a man. He was already sixteen. Herr Einstein urged him to forget his "philosophical nonsense" and to apply himself to the "sensible trade" of electrical engineering.

Albert was desolate. His very instincts rebelled at the idea of his becoming a tradesman. But how could he stand up against the whole world?

He got the answer to this problem one day when he read an essay of Emerson's. "If a man plant himself indomitably on his instincts, the world will come round to him."

II

ALBERT'S STUBBORNNESS won out. His father allowed him to specialize in mathematics. He took the entrance examinations for the Zurich Polytechnic Academy—and failed. He was deficient in his knowledge of foreign languages.

Back to the secondary school and his study of syntax. After a brief and intensive application to his prepositions and his participles he presented himself once more as a candidate for the Zurich Polytechnic Academy. This time he was successful.

His plans had now matured. He would prepare himself for a teaching position in mathematics and in physics. Voraciously he read every book he could find on these subjects. But his intellectual appetite had extended to several of the kindred fields in philosophy and in science. He yielded to the spell of Ernst Mach's positivism and of Darwin's evolution. He absorbed the utopian economics of socialism. He admired the methodical pessimism of Schopenhauer and the methodical optimism of Kant. And always, as in childhood, he developed his intellectual dreams within the framework of his passion for music. He visited the Music Hall and listened to the magic of Joachim's violin. And then he retired to his lodging and improvised on his own violin until late into the night.

And thus he finished his studies and received his teacher's certificate. But he received no teacher's appointment. He was a Jew. Wherever he applied for a position, he was met with the same evasive answer: "Personally I have no objection; but there are others, you see . . ."

For a while he resorted—unsuccessfully—to private tutoring, and then he got a clerical job at the Swiss patent office in Berne. Hour after hour he bent over his desk adding his figures and dreaming of the stars. In his spare moments he covered his note paper with complicated mathematical formulas. But when he heard the footsteps of his employer, he threw the paper into the basket. Dr. Halle, kindly as he was, had no sympathy for the "speculative nonsense" of his young employee.

But to Einstein these studies of his spare moments were anything but speculative. His abstract formulas—one of them held within it the secret of the atomic bomb—had taken on the texture of reality. He had found, he believed, a new key to the riddle of the universe. But he confided this belief to only a few of his intimates—and to Mileva Maric, his Serbian schoolmate whom he had made his wife. "I have been trying to solve the problem of space and time."

When he finished what he regarded as the correct solution to the problem, he brought it into the office of the *Annalen der Physik*. "I would be happy," he said timidly to the editor, "if you could find the room to publish this in your paper."

The editor found the room, and the obscure clerk of the Swiss patent office became one of the most famous scientists in the world.

III

EINSTEIN was twenty-six when he solved the problem of celestial harmony. It was the solution of the artist as well as of the scientist. He had tried to analyze the pattern of the stars just as the musician analyzes the pattern of the sonata. How are the parts interrelated in order to produce the concordance of the whole?

All the earlier attempts to solve the structure of the universe, observed Einstein, had been based upon a false assumption. The scientists had supposed that whatever seemed true to *them*, looking out upon the universe from their *own* point of view, from their *own* relative position in their *own* little corner of the world, must necessarily be true for *everybody else*, looking out upon the universe from *every other* point of view. But actually—asserted Einstein—there is no such absolute truth. The same landscape presents different faces to different people looking upon it from different vantage points. It is one thing to the pedestrian, quite another thing to the motorist, and still another thing to the aviator. Every experience is *relative* to the person who undergoes that particular experience. The only objective reality in the universe is that which constitutes *a combination of every possible point of experience*. Absolute truth can be ascertained only through the sum total of all relative observations. This is but a mathematical way of restating the Spinozist doctrine that the Mind of God is the combination of all human minds encompassed within the framework of eternity—*sub specie aeternitatis*. Einstein was a thoroughgoing disciple of Spinoza.

But not of Newton. Contrary to the doctrine of Newton that everything tends naturally to remain at rest, Einstein declared that everything is actually in a state of motion. But the velocities of the various moving bodies of the universe, he explained, are relative to one another. To this relativity of motion, however, there is one exception—the constant velocity of light. This velocity—about 186,000 miles a second—is the maximum speed that we know. It is the one unchanging factor in all our equations about the relative speed of moving bodies.

The law of relativity, declared Einstein, applies not only to the *speed* but also to the *direction* of a moving body. Suppose we drop a stone from a tower to the ground. To us the stone will appear to fall in a straight line. To a theoretical observer in space—to Einstein an "observer" meant either a person or a recording instrument—the stone would describe a curved line, inasmuch as this observer would record not only the motion of the stone upon our planet but also the motion of our planet around its axis. To still another observer, stationed not in empty space but on another planet, subject to a different motion from that of our own planet, the falling stone would describe still another path. All the paths, or directions, of a moving object are therefore relative to the various vantage points from which the movements of the object are observed.

And so we find that both the *speed* and the *direction* of a moving body are relative. But this, continues Einstein, is not yet the whole story. There is a third factor in relativity—the relative *size* of a moving body. All bodies contract in motion. To an observer sitting inside a rapidly moving train the train is longer than it is to another observer who watches it from the outside. The rate of the contraction of a moving object increases with its increasing speed. A stick measuring a yard in a state of so-called rest would shrink to zero if it were set in motion at the speed of light.

Space, then, is relative. So, too—declares Einstein—is time. The past, the present and the future are merely three points in time analogous to the three points in space occupied by—let us say—Washington, New York, and Boston. Scientifically speaking, it is just as logical to travel from to-morrow to yesterday as it is to travel from Boston to Washington. To an impartial observer of the universe all time, like all space, would be present in a single glance.

Time, like space, is a matter of relative motion. If a man could attain a speed greater than the speed of light—which of course is humanly impossible—he would overtake his past and leave the date of his birth in the future. He would see effects before their causes and he would see events before they actually occurred. Time is merely a planetary clock that measures motion. Each moving planet has its own system of local time which differs from all other time systems. The time system of the earth, far from being an absolute measurement for time everywhere, is nothing but a local schedule of the earth's rotation around the sun. A day is a measurement of motion through space. Our own point in time depends wholly upon our own position in space. The light which brings us the image of a distant star may have traveled through space for a million years before it reached the earth. Hence the star that we see today is the star of a million years ago. Similarly an event that took place upon the earth thousands of years ago—like the Battle of Marathon—may have just reached the eyes of an observer on another planet who consequently looks upon this event as an episode of today.

Today upon this planet, therefore, may be yesterday upon another planet and tomorrow upon a third planet. For time is a dimension of space—and space is a dimension of time. Actually—asserts Einstein—the universe consists of a space-time continuity; both space and time are dependent upon each other. Neither can be expressed independently. Both must be considered as co-ordinate aspects of motion in our mathematical approach to reality. The world is not three-dimensional. It consists of the three dimensions of space and of an additional fourth dimension—time.

IV

EINSTEIN was amused at the flurry of attention that he received for his "superior" wisdom. "Before God we are all equally wise, equally foolish," he said. He was not the least bit excited when he received the offer of a professorship at Zurich. Professors had always bored him. He was an artist. He had no use for the pedantic type of mind. "Pedants collect their facts as dogs collect their bones—only to hoard them in the dust." Few of the so-called scholars, he had noticed, understood the meaning of speculative thought. Hardly any of them were dreamers. They laughed when you told them that it is possible for the scientist to search for the secret of physical laws just as passionately as the composer searches for the secret of musical harmony. "The great scientist and the great composer are alike in one respect—both of them are great poets."

It was as a poet that Einstein greeted the arrival of his first child. He took far greater joy in wheeling the baby carriage than in delivering his lectures at the university. He trembled before the vacuous eyes and the gaping mouths of the audiences who had come to purchase a penny's worth of knowledge at the fountain of his wisdom. He was not a man to lead crowds or to teach crowds or to mingle in crowds. He was a solitary student, "a singular, taciturn, lonely seeker." It mattered little to him that he had built up a solid reputation amongst the learned societies of Europe, that the distinguished mathematician, Poincaré, had greeted him as the "conqueror of Newton" and that the eminent physicist, Lorentz, had acknowledged him as one of the foremost scientists of history. It was unessential that the famous universities of Utrecht and of Leyden had offered him professorships. He looked back regretfully upon the old days when he had served as a clerk under Dr. Halle—a position in which he had found the time and the quiet to carry on his researches without ceremony, without ostentation, without banquets.

He finally accepted the position of *professor ordinarius* at the University of Berlin. For his family must live somehow. During his walks through the streets of the Prussian capital he continued to build upon his theory of relativity. His early speculations had led to a great number of interesting conclusions. But they had given rise to an equally great number of further questions. A "demoniacal curiosity" had taken possession of him to seek out the final lair of truth—the underlying cadence in the movement of the stars through the symphony of time and space. More and more in his moments of relaxation he turned to his violin and improvised new themes that gave wing to his speculative thoughts.

But there was a sudden interruption to these thoughts. Europe had exploded into war (1914). The sensitive soul of Einstein recoiled in dismay. "This war is a vicious and savage crime. I would rather be hacked to pieces than take part in such an abominable business."

But few people now listened to him. Creative thought had no place in a world bent upon destruction. It was all a matter of relative values . . .

Throughout the conflict Einstein lived in a cosmos of his own creation. Shutting himself up in a shabby little attic away from the other rooms in a Berlin apartment house, he set to work verifying and elaborating upon the essential principles of his theory of relativity. The slightest domestic episode was enough to start him off on a significant train of thought. Once he climbed a ladder to change a picture on the wall. But absent-mindedly he forgot the business at hand, lost his footing and landed on the floor. When he got to his feet he commenced to speculate on the causes of the upset. The fall of the ladder in Einstein's attic was destined to play no less important a role in science than the fall of the apple in Newton's garden. For it led Einstein to undertake a critical analysis of the theory of gravitation.

Once more, as in the analysis of motion and space and time, he arrived at startling conclusions. The physicists, he declared, had been fundamentally wrong in their belief that objects *fell*, in the sense that they were *pulled down* to a center of gravitation. Scientifically speaking, no object is ever pulled down. Indeed, there is no such thing as "down"—or "up"—in the universe. "The motion of a body is due solely to the tendency of matter to follow the path of least resistance." Bodies in their travels through space select the easiest paths and avoid the most difficult. There is no more reason to assume an absolute gravitational force through space than to assume an absolute dimension of time. Just as there are local schedules of time, so too there are local fields of gravitation. But these fields have no mysterious force or pull. Every mass—like the sun, for example—creates at its center a curving or "warping" of the neighboring space into a "hill." And the masses in the vicinity of that hill—like the earth and the other planets of the solar system—move around the slopes of that hill for the simple reason that this is the easiest way for them to move. Einstein proved this "curvature" theory of space by means of a series of mathematical formulas. The significant point of the theory is this: The shortest distance between two points is not a *straight* line, but a *curved* line, since the universe consists of a series of curved hills and all objects in this universe travel around the curved slopes of these hills. Indeed, in this universe of ours there is no such thing as motion in a straight line. A ray of light traveling toward the earth from a distant star is deflected, or turned aside, when it passes the hill-slope of space around the sun. Einstein figured out mathematically the exact degree of this deflection.

And his figure proved to be correct. At the eclipse of 1919 the observatories of Cambridge and Greenwich, each acting independently of the other, sent out an expedition of astronomers to photograph the direction of the starlight during the eclipse. Both groups found that their photographs corroborated the prediction of Einstein almost to the exact decimal point which he had figured out in his mathematical formulas. The ray of light *did* curve in the manner and the degree as described in the calculations of Einstein. A new conception of the universe had been born in the human mind.

When Einstein received the photographs of the astronomers he looked at them with a cynical twinkle in his eye. "Now that my theory of relativity has been proved true," he chuckled, "Germany will claim me as a German and France will declare that I am a citizen of the world. Had my theory proved false, France would have said that I am a German and Germany would have declared that I am a Jew."

V

No ONE was more surprised at the sudden deluge of fame that descended upon Einstein than the scientist himself. Like Byron he awoke one day to find his name on everybody's lips. Not only learned men of science but millions of common people throughout the world had adopted him as a household idol. The results of the astronomers' expedition had been telegraphed to all the newspapers. He was kept busy posing for photographs, submitting to interviews, turning down offers from Hollywood—including one invitation to make a film at forty thousand dollars a week. In his bewilderment he turned to his wife. "This won't last. It *can't* last. People have gone temporarily crazy and tomorrow they will forget all about it." Fame was the last thing he desired. As his notoriety kept increasing from month to month he became frankly annoyed. He had hoped to spend his entire life in quiet research. And now he couldn't hear his own thoughts for the noisy acclamation. What did people want with him? Why would they not permit him to live like anyone else? What barbarous nonsense was all this? "Everybody talks about me, and nobody understands me."

Indeed, nobody even *cared* to understand this amazing juggler of mathematical ideas. One evening a young lady introduced her fiancé to the pastor of her church. The following day the pastor met the bride-to-be and took her aside. "I approve of your young man in every respect save one," he told her. "He lacks a sense of humor. I asked him to explain to me Einstein's theory of relativity and he actually tried to do it."

Einstein's popularity had risen to appalling heights. He could not take his daily walk in the streets without being surrounded by photographers, reporters, and autograph hunters. Every day baskets of mail arrived at the little Berlin apartment. Famous statesmen, obscure pacifists, unemployed workmen, lovelorn ladies—everybody wrote to him. The supreme irony had settled upon him. "I have become a demigod in spite of myself." A young devotee volunteered to be his disciple in "cosmic meditation." An inventor confided to him his plans for a new flying machine. A would-be explorer asked his advice on a trip to the Asiatic jungles. An actor begged him to become his manager. A cigar manufacturer announced that he had produced a new brand of cigars and named it *Relativity*.

"The public looks upon me as a strange new animal in the circus of the world." He smiled. And he tried to go on with his work in his quiet, modest way. When he was invited to speak to a distinguished group of scientists at Oslo, he pulled out a shabby dinner jacket and brushed it carefully. "If anyone thinks I am not dressed elegantly enough," he told his wife, "I'll put a tag on this coat with the notice that it has just been brushed." He arrived for another of his lectures—at the University of Berlin—in a homely pair of sport knickers and sandals. He walked about the streets of Berlin wrapped in an old sweater and in new dreams. Let the circus-minded public gossip and glare. He would be just simply himself.

His simplicity was no theatrical pose on his part. Once the queen of Belgium invited him to pay her a visit. Never suspecting that a reception committee of state dignitaries would await him at the station in their limousine, he alighted from the train with a suitcase in one hand and a violin in the other and started on foot for the palace.

In vain the dignitaries looked for him at the station. Finally they returned to the queen with the announcement that Einstein had apparently changed his mind about coming. And then they espied the dusty figure of a little gray-haired man tramping up the road.

"Why didn't you use the car I sent for you, Herr Doktor?" asked the queen.

Her guest looked at her with a naïve smile. "It was a very pleasant walk, Your Majesty."

He asked for no limousines in his journey through life. All he wanted was just "a very pleasant walk." He was disturbed when the crowds lined the way and cluttered up the landscape of his thoughts. They made such unreasonable demands upon him. When the editor of a successful American magazine offered him a staggering fee for an article on any subject that he might care to discuss, tears of rage sprang into his eyes. "Does the impudent fellow think I am a movie star?" he cried to his wife.

He hated wealth. He would have none of it. "I am absolutely convinced that no wealth in the world can help humanity forward." What the world wanted most, he said, could never be bought with money. "The world has been ravaged by war. The old hatreds are festering. The world needs permanent peace and lasting good will."

When the war was over, he tried to establish his dream of world peace upon a basis of reality. He undertook a series of "reconciliation lectures" in the "enemy" countries. At a time when it was dangerous to speak German in the streets of Paris the scientist in a gentle voice explained his cosmic philosophy and won the entire audience back to a sympathy for his German countrymen. When he stood on a London platform the quiet hostility with which the audience first greeted him as a German melted into tolerance and swelled finally to loud acclaim. The universality of his thinking made people ashamed of their puny provincialism. He showed them the design of an interstellar harmony. And he foretold that some day there would be a similar harmonious design among the nations on the earth.

He met Aristide Briand, the French premier, and discussed with him the necessity of a Franco-German pact to end hatred. He accepted a post as the German representative of the League of Nations committee for intellectual co-operation, and he discussed with Henri Bergson the architecture of the "New Republic of Decency" that the men of good will were bent upon raising throughout the world. "It is plain that we exist for our fellow men—in the first place for those upon whose smiles and welfare all our happiness depends, and next for all those unknown to us personally but to whose destinies we are bound by the tie of sympathy."

Others were not so convinced of his credo. He barely escaped assassination at the hands of a Russian noblewoman who harbored imperialistic ambitions. All over the world the gentle scientist who had desired nothing more than an opportunity for his private studies—unless it be public justice for his fellow men—became a target for political abuse. Cries were raised against him on the grounds of his racial origin. Antisemitism had caught postwar Germany in full tide. He was aghast at the savage intolerance of his German countrymen, but he felt convinced that under the right kind of leadership they might yet return to the sanity of their old time cultural and moral standards. When he found his name high on the black list of the German right-wing assassins he crossed over to the refuge of Holland.

But he encountered the ferment of unrest even in that tolerant country. Indeed everywhere in the world humanity seemed to be beating a hasty retreat to barbarism. People had lost their sense of proportion. The Mark Twain Society offered him the position of honorary vice-president. But when he learned that this society had offered a similar post to Benito Mussolini, Einstein flatly rejected the dishonor.

He went on a journey to the Orient. In India he was shocked to see millions of men living in slave labor and transporting their fellow men literally upon their backs. He refused to become a party to such human degradation. He never rode in a rickshaw throughout his entire trip. He went to China and saw men and women and children groaning aloud at their work in the cotton mills. He visited Japan and discounted the ceremonious treatment he received at the hands of the grownups. Instead, he turned to the Japanese children. He accepted from them scrapbooks of their drawings. And he listened with joy to their talk. "In the children lies the hope of the world." They must never be brought up to hate. They must never abuse the hard-won achievements of the human race. "Let us hope," he told his little friends, "that your generation will put mine to shame."

VI

THE wandering philosopher-minstrel, with his mathematical formulas and his violin, traveled on to Palestine and Spain and Latin America. Finally he arrived in the United States. And here at last he found a land where human beings of all classes lived together in tolerable friendship.

One day in November 1932, while Einstein was talking to a group of scientists on the Pacific Coast, a winter storm broke with fury in Berlin. Adolf Hitler took over the affairs of the German people.

The German Government, hoping to receive the indorsement of the "world-builder" for the Nazi regime, begged Einstein to return. Hitler would "overlook the fact that he was a Jew." But Einstein refused. And so Hitler put a price of twenty thousand marks upon his head. A band of storm troopers broke into his summer home at Caputh on the charge that he had concealed a quantity of arms and ammunition with which to overturn the government. They found in the "arsenal" nothing that resembled "arms" except an old bread knife grown rusty with disuse.

Hounded from his native land—the Nazis had received his resignation from the University of Berlin "without regret"—he was appointed (1933) a life member of the Institute for Advanced Study at Princeton, New Jersey. Here he hoped to go on, peacefully and quietly, with his old academic curriculum of human friendships and cosmic dreams. He served in his post of theoretical physics from 1933 to 1945, following which he resigned, retaining the title of professor emeritus.

During these years, however, Albert Einstein was again called from his quiet studies. In October of 1939, he signed a letter to President Roosevelt, at the instigation of his fellow scientists, explaining the potentialities of atomic energy as a military force. Following the destruction of Hiroshima in 1945, however, he became a militant advocate of world government as the only practical method for attaining international peace.

In 1955, at the age of seventy-six, Albert Einstein died, leaving behind him the memory of a modest man with a love for music and for his fellow men, the memory of one of the most comprehending of all human minds.

IMPORTANT DATES IN THE LIFE OF
ALBERT EINSTEIN

1879—March 14, born at Ulm, Germany.

1894–1900—Studied in Switzerland.

1901—Appointed examiner of patents at Berne.

1905—Published his *Theory of Relativity*.

1905–09—Developed quantum theory.

1909—Appointed professor of theoretical physics at University of Zurich.

1913—Became Director of the Kaiser-Wilhelm Physical Institute in Berlin. Elected a member of the Prussian Academy of Sciences.

1921—Elected to the British Royal Society.

1922—Received Nobel Prize in Physics.

1925—Received Copley Medal of Royal Society.

1933—Exiled from Germany, he became a life member of the Institute for Advanced Learning at Princeton, New Jersey.

1935—Received Franklin Institute medal.

1939—Wrote a letter to President Roosevelt explaining the potentialities of atomic energy as a military weapon.

1940—Became an American citizen.

1945—Became a pacifist and advocate of world government.

1955—April 18, died at Princeton.

Helen Keller

1880–

PETER FINLEY DUNNE and Mark Twain were discussing the blindness of Helen Keller. "God, how dull it must be for her," exclaimed the author of *Mr. Dooley*. "Every day the same, and every night the same as the day!"

"You're damned wrong there," retorted Mark Twain. "Blindness is an exciting business, I tell you. If you don't believe it, get up some dark night on the wrong side of your bed when the house is on fire and try to find the door."

Helen Keller, because of her handicap, has enjoyed the excitement of trying to find the door out of the darkness—not only for herself but for the rest of mankind. Hers is the cause of the blind leading the blind, and the seeing as well, to a new vision of life.

II

AT HER BIRTH she was normal, like other children. When she was twenty months old, however, she was stricken with an illness—the doctors called it "an acute congestion of the brain"—which deprived her of her sight and her hearing and consequently of her speech. Her parents looked pityingly upon her. Another of those human creatures condemned to the existence of an animal. How could she ever be expected to have *sense* if she was deprived of two fifths of her *senses*? People who were merely blind, or merely deaf-mute, could be taught somehow to communicate with the rest of the world. But this child who was blind and deaf and mute—what hope was there ever for *her*?

A pathetic little animal who could neither understand nor make herself understood. Instinctively she felt that she was different from the rest of the world, and this feeling made her furious. She kicked and she screamed and she scratched at the people who tried to approach her. Unable to play like other children, she amused herself by tearing their clothes and snipping their hair with a scissors. A pitiable nuisance. There was no way of teaching her to behave. One day she locked her mother in the pantry, and she laughed as she felt the vibration of her mother's pounding against the door.

A nuisance and a danger. She had a baby doll and a baby sister. She loved her doll, because she was allowed to play with it. But she did not love her baby sister, because she was not allowed to play with *it*. Once she found the baby sleeping in the cradle which belonged to the doll. In a fit of temper she overturned the cradle, but her mother fortunately caught the baby as it fell to the floor.

A danger not only to others but to herself. Accidentally spilling a glass of water on her apron, she spread it out to dry before the smoldering fireplace. When the apron failed to dry quickly enough, she drew nearer and threw it over the live coals. In an instant her clothes were ablaze. Her old nurse barely managed to save her life by throwing a blanket over her. "Poor thing," said her relatives, "it might have been more merciful if she had burned to death."

And then there dawned a miraculous day when a teacher came to her and made her a member of the living world.

III

IT WAS THANKS to Alexander Graham Bell, inventor of the telephone, that Helen's parents were able to get the "miracle teacher" for their child. Mr. Bell, who had a tender feeling for the "imperfect specimens of the potter's clay," had suggested that Mr. Keller write to the Perkins Institute for the Blind with reference to Helen's problem. As a result of Mr. Keller's letter, the director of the institute recommended Miss Anne Mansfield Sullivan as a suitable teacher for the six-year-old Helen.

Anne Sullivan, a graduate of the Perkins Institute, was one of those rare geniuses who flower out of the muck of poverty and disease. Her father was a ne'er-do-well drunkard, her brother had died of tuberculosis, and she herself had been threatened with total blindness up to the age of eighteen, when a successful operation had partially cured her. At twenty, when she became Helen's teacher, she had recovered enough of her vision to read for the child and to lead her into a new world.

But how to begin? How to transform thoughts into words when the child had no conception of human language? Anne Sullivan found a way. The morning after she arrived she gave Helen a doll—an object with which the stricken child was most familiar. And then, using the code for the blind, she slowly spelled out with her fingers into Helen's hand the word *d-o-l-l*. This finger play, to Helen, was a fascinating game. Flushed with excitement, she clumsily imitated the motions, *d-o-l-l*. Then she ran downstairs to her mother and traced those funny motions into *her* hand. "At that time," writes Miss Keller in *The Story of My Life*, "I did not know that I was spelling a word or even that words existed; I was simply making my fingers go in monkeylike imitation." Little by little, however, Miss Sullivan got her to realize that these motions had a meaning. *They pointed out a thing*. Something she played with. Something for which she had once thrown her baby sister out of her cradle. And there were other motions that pointed out other things. *D-o-g* meant something with a fuzzy snout that romped around you. *C-u-p* meant something out of which you drank. *H-a-t* meant something you put on your head when your mother took you out visiting. What a wonderful game! What a wonderful world! It was so full of so many things. *And everything had a name!*

One day she learned a new set of words—*mother, father, sister*. So that's what they were called. She had known them all her life without knowing it. And *teacher*. The name of that lovely new playmate of hers. Come, let's keep on playing the game. It's such fun! Give me more names, more, more. The child's hunger for knowledge was insatiable, and Miss Sullivan fed it with a resourcefulness that was amazing. In the springtime, when the daisies and the buttercups arrived and the birds and the squirrels awoke to new life, her teacher gave her blind little scholar an "insight" into the secrets of nature. And, "as my knowledge of things grew, I felt more and more the delight of the world I was in."

And then Miss Sullivan opened up for her a new delightful world—the world of books. She taught the child to read by supplying her with slips of cardboard on which various words had been printed in raised letters. New things, new names, new ideas. Stories. Poems. Pretty thoughts, pretty rhymes. She could not hear those rhymes, but she could feel with her fingers the same sorts of letters at the ends of the lines. Like the pattern of pretty trimmings on her Sunday dress. After all, you don't have to hear and you don't have to see the beautiful things of the world. You get to know them anyhow. You sort of *feel* your way to them.

Why, even those who can see and hear—Anne Sullivan had told her—must *feel* their way toward lots of things. *Hope*, for instance, or *joy*, or *love*.

"Now take love, Helen. Nobody can see it or hear it or taste it or smell it or touch it. Yet it's there just the same, strong and beautiful and real. How do you know? You can just *feel* it, that's how you know."

"Yes, Anne, *I* can feel it. I love *you*."

And thus the soul of Helen unfolded gradually, until one day—miracle of miracles!—she learned to speak. The process was long and laborious and at times seemingly hopeless. The method, briefly, was as follows: Her teacher pronounced certain sounds while Helen passed her fingers over her teacher's tongue and lips and throat as these sounds were being pronounced. Then, passing her fingers over her own organs of speech, Helen tried to imitate the sounds by imitating the positions of these organs.

After a seemingly endless succession of failures, the child—she was ten years old at the time—finally succeeded in articulating the letters of the alphabet. And then came the great moment of her life when she stammered out her first connected sentence—"It is warm."

The barrier between herself and the rest of the world had at last broken down. She was—almost—like other people! Her preliminary training had rescued her from the prison of her isolated helplessness. And now she was ready to enter with her peers into the competitive race of higher education.

IV

In 1896, accompanied by her teacher, she entered the Cambridge (Massachusetts) School for Young Ladies in preparation for Radcliffe College. Miss Sullivan attended the classes with her, took the necessary notes and then interpreted them to Helen in the code language for the blind. Her examinations Helen took at home under the supervision of the principal who had learned the "manual alphabet" and who spelled out the questions into her hand. She answered the questions on a typewriter by means of the touch system. "She'll never make it," said her teachers at the start. But she made it, and within a comparatively short time. Only a year after her admission to the Cambridge School she passed her preliminary examinations for Radcliffe—and received "honors" in English and in German. Two years later she passed the final examinations and entered Radcliffe College —still inseparable from her "beloved" Anne Sullivan.

And now she was no longer aware of her handicaps. Together with the rest of the students she was ready to plunge eagerly into the hidden world of knowledge. "In the wonderland of Mind I felt as free as the next." She studied Shakespeare under Professor Kittredge and English composition under Professor Copeland—"men who were able to give new sight to the blind." It was Charles Townsend Copeland—known affectionately to his students as "Copey"—who discovered her genius as a writer. "You have something of your own to say, Miss Keller, and you have a manner of your own in saying it." He suggested that she expand some of her classroom compositions into a story of her life. She followed the suggestion and gave to the world one of the rarest of human documents—the struggle of a soul, hedged in by excessive limitations, to penetrate an unlimited universe. And the universe, as she found it in her undergraduate days and throughout her later life, was a magical place of "large loves and heavenly charities." Blindness, she declares, is nothing; and deafness, nothing. We are all blind and deaf to the eternal things. But nature is kind to us all in her very unkindness. She has endowed all of us, possessors of five puny senses at most, with an infinite sixth sense—"a sense which sees, hears, feels, all in one."

The Story of My Life was published in the *Ladies' Home Journal,* and later in book form. In the meantime Helen Keller had been graduated from Radcliffe—*cum laude*. With the money she received from the sale of her manuscript she settled down with Anne Sullivan on a farm in Wrentham, Massachusetts, for a life of writing and contemplation. A silent, soothing, yet exciting world. Rambles into the woodland—Anne Sullivan had strung a wire from tree to tree, so that Helen could go walking all alone without being lost. Excursions with her friends in her rowboat on the lake—"It is fun to try to steer by the scent of water-grasses and lilies, and of bushes that grow on the shore." Canoeing in the moonlight—"I cannot, it is true, see the moon behind the pines, but I can fancy that I feel the shimmer of her garments as I trail my hand in the water." Imagining the world as it really is—"Has anyone ever known the *real* world?" Translating the sensations of sight into the sensations of touch—"Often I had felt petals showered upon me by a passing breeze, and so I could imagine the sunset as a vast rose garden from which the petals had been shaken and were drifting through the sky." And, most joyous experience of them all, reading books—"Literature is my Utopia." Anne supplied her with all the classics printed in Braille, and her sensitive fingers were kept constantly busy "looking" into the hearts of the masters. No need to pity Helen Keller on her Wrentham farm, with Anne Sullivan for her guardian and the entire world for her company.

And then a third person joined their rich and exciting world. John Macy, one of her English instructors at Radcliffe. He married Anne Sullivan and came to live with them at Wrentham. "I cannot enumerate the helpful kindnesses with which he smoothed my paths . . . Once, when I was tired with the manual labor of my copying, he sat up all night and typed forty pages of my manuscript, so that they might reach the press in time." A new variation in the old triangle of two women and a man. A triangle not of passion and jealousy and revenge, but of faith and charity and love.

V

FOR A BRIEF SPRINGTIME of ecstasy Helen Keller was herself to experience the love of a woman for a man. During a brief vacation of Anne Sullivan and John Macy a young man had come to her as her secretary. Love laughs at locksmiths—and at the makers of all other sorts of barriers. The young man proposed to Helen; and Helen, in a moment of yearning forgetfulness, accepted him. "For a brief space I danced in and out of the gates of Heaven, wrapped up in a web of bright imaginings." But she rapidly awoke to the reality. Physical love, marriage, the joys and the responsibilities of motherhood—these things were not for her. She must remain content in this world of her own, surrounded by her dreams and her books.

And her friends. It has been granted to few to enjoy so many and such abiding friendships as were Helen Keller's. Among those who gave her of their very hearts—to mention only a handful—were the philanthropists

H. H. Rogers and Andrew Carnegie and Otto Kahn, who tided her over many a dismal bog when her finances were low; Mark Twain, that sad man of laughter who always used to tell her that she saw better than most people—"The world, Helen, is full of unseeing eyes, vacant, staring, soulless eyes"; Frank Doubleday, her publisher, "whose kindness to me has been the kindness not only of a friend but of a father"; Eugene Debs, "that neglected St. Francis of the twentieth century"; and Alexander Graham Bell, of whom she wrote at the time of his death—"Although life has never seemed the same since we learned . . . that Dr. Bell was dead, yet the mist of tears is resplendent with the part of himself that lives on in me."

Her life was saddened by the departure of her friends. But she went on with her work of teaching both the seeing and the blind. She traveled across the country on a lecture tour—she had learned to speak with sufficient clearness to make herself understood on the platform—and she was hailed everywhere as a "miraculous freak of nature." She was amused at the picture that she got of herself through the newspapers. "I learned for the first time that I was *born* blind, deaf, and dumb, that I educated myself, that I could distinguish colors, hear telephone messages . . . that I was never sad, never discouraged, never pessimistic, that I applied myself with celestial energy to being happy . . . We supplied [the newspapers] with the facts when we were asked for them; but we never knew what became of these facts." What the stunt-seeking public failed to recognize about Helen Keller was merely this—that she was a human being with somewhat more than her share of mortal affliction and decidedly more than her share of immortal genius. The gods had given her less sight but more vision than the ordinary.

Her vision enabled her to see into the future of mankind. She believed that the salvation of humanity would come through an intelligent application of Socialism—food for the hungry, shelter for the homeless, education for the ignorant, peace among the nations, and justice for all. "There is in the world today too much thoughtlessness and too little joy." If the greedy were able to *think* better, the needy would be able to *live* better. In her contemplation of human progress, she said, she was neither too sanguine nor too despondent. "Like the poet Henry van Dyke"—she wrote—"I am not an optimist; there's too much evil in the world and in me. Nor am I a pessimist; there is too much good in the world and in God. So I am just a meliorist, believing that He wills to make the world better, and trying to do my bit to help and wishing that it were more."

And so, like a sundial—"I record only the serene hours of life"—she lived in her beautiful world and tried to do her bit to help make it more beautiful. And when the shadows fell across her path she brushed away her tears and waited patiently for the next bright day. One of the darkest shadows of her life fell when Anne Sullivan died (1936). It was as if a part of her own soul had died. "I suppose," observes Dr. Richard C.

Cabot, "that such an extraordinary partnership of two human souls has never existed before upon this earth." For a time Helen Keller was like a lost creature. But finally she shook off her despondency, and with the help of her new secretary, Miss Polly Thompson, she went on with her work. Went on interpreting through her sensitive mind the world which she "saw" through her sensitive fingers. And how vividly she could see with those fingers of hers! One day she visited the studio of the sculptress Malvina Hoffman. Among the statuary that she studied, she came upon the figure of a man. She felt the folds of the cloak, the rope girdle, the sandals on the feet. "A monk," she said. Then she went on and felt a wolf pressing its head to the man's side, a rabbit resting in his arms, a bird nestled in the fold of his cowl. She traced her fingers back to the man's face. It was raised toward the sky. "A lover of God and a friend of the animals . . ." And then, "I see! It is St. Francis!"

Like St. Francis of Assisi, Helen Keller is convinced that the end of the road toward which she is so patiently groping is but the beginning of a more beautiful road. "I cannot understand the poor faith that fears to look into the eyes of death." For beyond lies the city of the sun, where she knows that she will meet again her departed friends. A confirmed Swedenborgian, she declares that after her death she will for the first time be *truly* able to see. And so, "with steadfast thought I follow sight beyond all seeing, until my soul stands up in spiritual light and cries, 'Life and death are one!'"

Today she lives quietly in a house near Westport, Connecticut. In 1946 a fire destroyed her previous home, gutting many of her valuables including a manuscript she was working on. On the grounds of her present residence there is a Japanese lantern in which a light burns steadily. It will not be put out while she lives. In her middle seventies, she retains a youthful, eager face with bright blue eyes that, unlike those of most blind people, are keenly alive. Miss Polly Thompson, her present companion, reads her news headlines and important articles at breakfast. A number of news stories are brailled for her. In this way Helen Keller keeps up with the latest developments in the world. She will never grow too old to be indifferent to the trials of people around her.

IMPORTANT DATES IN THE LIFE OF
HELEN KELLER

1880—June 27, born, Tuscumbia,
　　Alabama.
1882—Deprived of sight and hear-
　　ing and speech through se-
　　vere illness.
1887—Got Anne Mansfield Sullivan
　　Macy as her teacher.
1890—First learned to speak.
1896—Entered Cambridge School
　　for Young Ladies.
1900—Entered Radcliffe College.
1902—Wrote *The Story of My Life.*

1904—Graduated with honors.
　　Entered upon a lifelong ca-
　　reer of writing and lecturing.
1936—Lost, through death, her
　　"dearest friend and teacher,"
　　Anne Sullivan.
1938—Published *Helen Keller's
　　Journal.*
1940—Published *Let Us Have
　　Faith.*
1955—Celebrated her 75th birth-
　　day amid nationwide hon-
　　ors.

Franklin Delano
Roosevelt
1882–1945

From too close a view it is difficult to see a forest because of the trees. Similarly, from too close a view it is difficult to see a man's character because of his characteristics. The perspective of time and space will be necessary for a final evaluation of Roosevelt's personality. Those of us among his contemporaries who try to appraise him are likely to slip into the dangerous pitfall of his too-ardent admirers, who call him a St. Francis in politics, or into the equally dangerous pitfall of his too-bitter opponents, who look upon him as a ravenous wolf in sheep's clothing. To an impartial observer—and at such a stormy period no observer can be altogether impartial—Roosevelt seems to have been a dynamo of energy dominated by an instinct for justice. His energy often drove him into error, but his justice generally brought him back to the right course. "Roosevelt is a man who loves to fight—and who fights to love."

II

He came by his love for fighting and his instinct for affection through the Roosevelt ancestral strain. The Roosevelts are a peculiar tribe—a family of strong, rich adventurers who possess a friendly sympathy for those that are not strong enough to adventure for riches. Born on the banks of the Hudson, he grew up to look upon humanity as a stream of travelers going up and down the river—an endless and living unit of interdependent motion. His father, like many of the other Roosevelts a combination of the successful businessman and the practical philosopher, explained and strengthened in his growing boy this American sense of active interdependence. Not only this, but the constitutional and the ethical right of every human creature to his life, his liberty, and his pursuit of happiness. On Sundays he pointed out the pleasure yachts that took the wealthy upon their cruises and the passenger boats that carried the workers upon their excursions. "God has made the same river and the same sky for us all. And he wants all of us alike to share in their bounty."

The only child of his father's second marriage—he had a grown-up half brother by his father's first marriage—young Franklin developed a great hunger for companionship. And his father encouraged, rather than hindered, this wholesome hunger. Although he educated him at home, he allowed him to make the acquaintance of the village youngsters—the children of the farmers and the butchers and the coachmen and the grocers and the gardeners of Hyde Park. These children, Franklin was surprised to learn, were—save for their clothes and other such unimportant externals— just as human and just as likeable as the wealthier children who came to visit them at their Hyde Park estate. This so-called *estate*, his father maintained, was in reality just a mere *farm*. There was nothing pretentious about James Roosevelt. A simple, companionable, democratic, human father who possessed a rare gift—he knew how to train a sensitive child into a sensible man.

From his father and from his companions young Roosevelt got his love for human beings. And from his mother he derived his love for the sea. She told him how her father had captained his own sailing ship and had brought his cargoes of tea from China. As a child she had sailed on her father's ship, and once in a storm she had come dangerously close to losing her life. But, added his mother, she was never afraid.

Excellent environment for the unfolding of an impressionable character. In his father he found a superior teacher, in his mother a superb playmate. She was so very much nearer to Franklin's own age—there was a difference of thirty years between his father and his mother. The Roosevelt family represented *three* rather than *two* generations—a long stretch of years and experiences for young Franklin to absorb.

Such was the heritage of Franklin Roosevelt: an eagerness to see humanity on the go, a passion for universal companionship, a longing for adventure, and a laughing fearlessness in the face of danger. He was growing up into fit timber either for the captain of a ship or the leader of a state. Whatever might be his future career, he was pretty certain to show the necessary spunk.

And the proper kind of education. His father saw to that. As a supplement to his book study, James Roosevelt enabled him to travel and to study places and men. For eight successive years, between the ages of seven and fourteen, young Roosevelt spent his vacations abroad in the company of his parents. And thus he learned to know the peoples of Europe and their languages and their ways. And, too, he got to know the difference between free nations and those that were led by the leash. In London he and his tutor were once stopped at the door of the Kensington Museum. "Sorry," said the attendant, "but you can't go in. The Prince of Wales is inside." Whereupon Roosevelt showed his membership card in a nature club to which his father had once in a playful moment elected him. "Oh well," remarked the attendant, "in that case you can go right in." And within a few moments Roosevelt found himself face to face with the future king of England.

Quite different, however, was his experience in Germany, where he once spent a cycling holiday with his tutor. As they were passing through the countryside near Strasbourg they were arrested four times within a single day—once for picking cherries, once for taking their bicycles into a railroad station, and twice for other inadvertent infringements of the universal German *Verboten*. "The German credo," laughed Roosevelt, "is— *Forbidden to live!*"

III

HIS FREQUENT VACATIONS on shipboard had aroused in him a desire to go to sea like his grandfather. But his parents advised him that he must first round out his education. They must send him to a good preparatory school and to a good college. Groton and Harvard.

He entered Groton, where his hearty voice and his handsome features stamped him at once as a "regular guy." He displayed not the slightest arrogance toward anybody—except the arrogant. For these "blustering cymbals of gilded brass" he had little sympathy. He criticized them for their boastfulness about their fathers' income. "How much does that income add to the value of your character?"

Yet Roosevelt was no prig. Even when he criticized he did so with a good-natured smile. If some of his classmates acted foolishly at times— "Well, we are all of us fools, most of the time." He held out the hand of unaffected friendship to all those who were unaffectedly willing to meet him halfway. "There goes a real thoroughbred!" said the boys at Groton.

And at Harvard. They elected him to their clubs, they took him into their confidence, and they appointed him to the editorial board of the *Crimson*. Here, too, as at Groton, he insisted upon taking a fellow for what he *was* rather than for what he *had*. In an editorial which he wrote just prior to the election of the class-day officers, he insisted that these officers be elected on the basis of fitness rather than on the basis of friendship. "There is a higher duty than to vote for one's personal friend, and that is to secure for the whole class leaders who really deserve the position." Let the class poet and the class orator, for example, be selected from among those who were most highly gifted rather than from among those who were most highly pedigreed.

Already he was feeling his way toward a new kind of politics—democracy based upon honest common sense.

And it was about this time that he became definitely interested in a political rather than in a naval career. His fifth cousin, Theodore Roosevelt, had just been elevated to the presidency of the United States. It was like a bugle call to Franklin. Cousin Theodore was a fighter for justice. Had been so all his life. A fine man to emulate. A fine career to follow—this setting to right the wrongs of his fellow men.

Yet the call at the start was none too insistent. He was a young man just out of college, with a personal income of five thousand dollars a year —his father had recently died and left him a substantial fortune—with a healthy appetite for living and a resplendent and congenial world in which to live. A carefree and pursefree Prince Charming, adored by the ladies, admired by the men. A favorite of fortune, destined for an early marriage and a life of contented ease.

He married. But he did not settle down to an easy life. For his young wife was, like himself, a Roosevelt. A fighter of the good fight and a righter of wrong. Eleanor Roosevelt, a niece of Theodore Roosevelt, was as sensitive as Franklin. But her sensitiveness was translated into thought rather than into action. She represented the poetry, as he represented the prose, of the human quest for justice. Like Franklin, she was an ardent observer of life; but, unlike him, she was an equally ardent reader of books. Franklin had noticed some of the ills of society. Eleanor had studied to discover their remedies. While a student at a fashionable school in London, she had taken excursions into the slums to see how the poor lived. She had noted their hardships and she had listened to their grievances. And she had studied the literature of labor, of Henry George, of Karl Marx. Once she had marched in a workers' parade. Her sense of obligation had been aroused. Something *must* be done to make the hard lot of the poor easier. "And you, Franklin, are the man to do it."

And thus it was through the road of social service that Roosevelt started upon his stony climb to political fame.

IV

In 1910 he entered upon his first political campaign—a Democrat running for the state senate in a Republican district. And he won. "The Roosevelt smile," said the voters, "is irresistible."

But, his colleagues in the senate soon discovered to their surprise, his independence was also irresistible. "That young Roosevelt has a mind of his own." "Yes, and a *dangerous* mind, too." He had set himself against the boss politicians of his own party—a bad precedent, they insisted, for a young upstart in public office. And the worst of it was that he could not be bribed. He was too well off. And he could not be ousted. He was too well liked. The bosses tried to fight him—in secret, in the open. But he could not be budged. "There is nothing," he laughed, "that I love as much as a good fight." What in the world were they going to do with this "fresh college kid"?

And the "fresh college kid" threw himself into another fight—for a reduction of the working week in New York State to fifty-four hours. And won.

It was in the same spirit of fighting independence that he went as an anti-Tammany Wilson delegate to the Democratic National Convention in 1912. At this convention, as one of the Tammany bosses put it, "the two educated guys"—Wilson and Roosevelt—"stole the show." Franklin Roosevelt played no unimportant part in bringing about the nomination and the election of Woodrow Wilson.

When Wilson was elected he offered Roosevelt his choice of three posts. He could become either Collector of the Port of New York, Assistant Secretary of the Treasury, or Assistant Secretary of the Navy. Without a moment's hesitation, Roosevelt decided to throw in his lot with the navy. For that was where his heart lay.

He immediately set to work advocating a larger and more effective American "patrol of the seas." For the world, as he had realized in his travels, is but a little cluster of trading posts, not *separated* but *connected* by the universal highway of the ocean. An easy road for the merchant, an equally easy road for the aggressor. A war in one continent, therefore, is a direct threat to the peace of the other continents. This elementary fact of modern geography Roosevelt recognized even before the first World War. America, he insisted, must have a navy big enough and strong enough to guard against any aggression from whatsoever source it might suddenly arise.

And he succeeded in strengthening the navy despite the opposition of those who could not see beyond the horizon. When America entered the war (in 1917), the young Assistant Secretary of the Navy had become, next to the President, perhaps the hardest-working man in the government. "At times," Mrs. Roosevelt tells us, "sleep was practically eliminated for days." He personally scrutinized the repairing, the fueling, and the arming of the ships, the building and the fortifying of adequate supply bases and arsenals and training stations, and the allocation of the necessary funds for the designated needs without any wasting of red tape or time. In his effort to generate action, and still more action, he broke enough laws, as he himself laughingly remarked, to send him to jail for nine hundred and ninety-nine years. Here, for example, is just one of his admirable though "illegal" transactions as related by the New York contractor, Elliot C. Brown, to Roosevelt's biographer, Ernest K. Lindley: On June 27, 1917, Roosevelt examined a site for a receiving-ship cantonment in New York City. On June 28 he gave the contractor an order to go ahead with the work. On June 29 the plans were on the way; on July 5 the ground was broken; on August 4 the work was completed; on August 11 breakfast was served at the new cantonment to sixty-eight hundred men. And then, two months later, Roosevelt received from the government an official authorization to build that cantonment!

But Roosevelt was not content with his activities as a government official. He wanted to see action on the battlefield. He was young and healthy and eager to risk his life when so many other young Americans were risking theirs. He pleaded with the President to release him from his post. Wilson refused his plea—Roosevelt was too valuable a man where he was. The President did, however, allow his young subordinate to sail on an inspection tour of the fifty-odd American naval stations in the war zone. A dangerous job, but Roosevelt loved danger. He traveled over the submarine-infested Atlantic, visited the Azores, Corfu, and the Orkney Islands, called on King George in London and on Clemenceau in Paris. On his return trip he contracted the flu and came home a very sick man.

But soon he recovered sufficiently to take another journey to France—this time in connection with the Peace Conference. Not as a member of the conference, but as a supervisor for the demobilizing of the naval stations abroad. Again he had an opportunity to meet Clemenceau. And a remark that Clemenceau made to him on this occasion must have given Roosevelt much deep thought. "You wonder why we want to end this war with such a hard peace? Don't forget this tragic fact—that for the last century and a half every Frenchman who ever reached the age of seventy has been compelled to take part in a struggle against an aggressive Germany."

Roosevelt's return from this second trip was on the *George Washington*, the same ship that was bringing Wilson back a victor in the war and a victim of the peace. Roosevelt saw a great deal of his sad but still hopeful old prophet-chieftain on this trip. Someone pointed out to him the chair and the table on which Wilson had written the first draft of the League of Nations Covenant. Roosevelt asked his President for this "memento of a great historic occasion," and the President graciously presented it to him.

And thus Franklin Roosevelt inherited the desk and the dream of Woodrow Wilson.

V

In 1920 Roosevelt resigned from his post in the navy to run for the vice-presidency on the Democratic ticket. He conducted the campaign with his usual strength and sincerity and fire. He went on a speaking tour that took him into every state in the Union and kept him busy with an average of eleven speeches a day. The theme of his campaign was the perpetuation of Wilson's League of Justice. It proved too noble a message for too selfish an age. Roosevelt was defeated.

And then suddenly there came another and greater defeat. It was in the summer of 1921. A plunge into the ice-cold water of his summer home at Campobello, an hour of careless lolling in a wet bathing suit, a slight chill —and then years of silent suffering in the grip of a paralysis that seemed determined to kill. But Roosevelt was even more determined to live. He came out of this tragedy with weakened limbs and a strengthened soul. Illness is the best teacher of philosophy. The world offers many a curious angle to a man who is compelled to study it from an invalid's pillow. The ancient Greek philosophers had an apt saying—"Wisdom comes through suffering." Before his illness, Roosevelt had been an honest politician. After it, he became a devoted statesman.

While Roosevelt was making his fight for life, Alfred E. Smith had risen to the top of the Democratic party. And now that Roosevelt had won his fight, he joined forces with Al Smith for the regeneration of the political life of America. It was a union between the poor little rich boy and the rich little poor boy—a combination of the Harvard and the Bowery accents into a new American dialect. A new though unnamed party arose as a result. This new party, which may be termed as the Aristodemocracy of 1928, cut deeply into both of the old parties. It united the progressive elements both in the Democratic and in the Republican camps. It fell short of electing Al Smith to the presidency, but it succeeded in sweeping Franklin Delano Roosevelt into the New York State House and, four years later, into the White House.

VI

ROOSEVELT came into the White House with a vision, and he summarized this vision in four words—*the more abundant life*. As a convalescent at Warm Springs, in Georgia, he had witnessed physical suffering; and on his recovery he had devoted more than half of his fortune to the relief of such suffering. And now, in the midst of the depression, he witnessed economic suffering throughout the country and decided to devote all of his strength to the relief of *this* suffering.

When he took over the reins of the government he found himself at the head of a hopeless, spiritless, and strengthless nation. He revived its hope and its spirit and began slowly to restore its strength.

His program at the outset was chaotic. But, in a crisis, deliberate planning is impractical. While the rescuer is trying to make up his mind as to whether to take a boat or to swim out to a drowning person, the poor victim is likely to die. What is needed in such an emergency is—first, quick action for survival; and only then, leisurely planning for recovery.

This is what President Roosevelt tried to do. The entire banking system, the heart that was pumping the economic lifeblood into the nation, was on the verge of collapse. He promptly performed an emergency operation. Declaring a bank holiday, he closed all the banks in the country, subjected them to a thorough examination, and then removed the unsound institutions and reopened those that satisfied the Treasury Department as to their soundness.

His next step was to try to provide food for the hungry. There were fifteen million of them when he stepped into his executive office on March 4, 1933. The next morning, at breakfast, a friend asked him about his immediate plans. "I have seen," said Roosevelt, "the aged and the infirm, the poor and the helpless, standing for hours in breadlines waiting for their crust of bread and bowl of thin soup. The first thing I want to do is to take them out of those lines, rehabilitate them, feed them, make them happy once more. No nation can ever amount to anything while its people are in want."

This, throughout his first two terms in the White House, was his primary objective. To get the American people out of want. In order to accomplish this objective, he initiated his New Deal. This New Deal, to our contemporary and therefore limited point of view, resembles a labyrinth of wisdom and foolishness and compassion and justice and jumbles and contradictions and mistakes. Its general direction, however, appears to have been rightward and lightward—the conservation of the national resources for the common good; the harmonious balance of the various group interests in the United States; the reorganization of the spirit of the Supreme Court; the utilization of the federal subsidies for local needs; and the development of a policy of good neighborliness throughout the Western Hemisphere with a view to its ultimate fruition into a Pan-American League of Nations. Above all, the right of every American to enjoy the "four freedoms"—freedom of speech, freedom of worship, freedom from want, and freedom from fear.

But a brief summary—indeed, *any* summary—is altogether inadequate to encompass the rapid kaleidoscope of intermingled permanent laws and emergency measures known as the New Deal. In an effort to answer the question, "What is the New Deal?" the editors of the London *Economist* wrote a thoughtful and factful book of one hundred and fifty pages—and confessed at the end that "the answer is still incomplete." For the blueprint of the New Deal was no less than an attempt to break the ground for a new road to ethical, social, and economic fair play.

But hardly had the work begun when a horde of international brigands blocked the way. Roosevelt had to turn his attention from the establishment of national justice to the building of a national defense. Aware of his fitness as a pilot through dangerous waters, the country drafted him for a third term. And elected him, in spite of the unquestioned ability of his Republican opponent, Wendell Willkie.

And then, a year after his election, the storm broke. The treacherous attack on Pearl Harbor. Before the attack our country had been divided —our enemy thought, *irreconcilably* divided—both on the domestic and on the foreign policy of President Roosevelt. The radicals complained that he was creeping too slowly on the road to salvation; the conservatives, that he was rushing too rapidly on the way to perdition. The employers insisted that he had allied himself with the labor agitators against honest enterprise; the workers, that he had united himself with the greedy exploiters against honest labor. The interventionists contended that he was giving aid and comfort to the aggressors with his policy of appeasement; the isolationists, that he was giving unnecessary provocation to one of the belligerents in a war that was none of our business.

But the attack on Pearl Harbor (December 7, 1941) produced a miracle. It united the country into a single passionate resolve for victory against the forces of evil. No more radicals or conservatives, employers or workers, interventionists or isolationists, Democrats or Republicans—but Americans all, eager and determined to follow the leadership of the Commander in Chief.

And from the beginning of the war to his untimely death (April 1945), Roosevelt stood forth as a commander whom his countrymen followed with the utmost faith. For he was a master of world politics and a fighter of unconquerable grit. For him the word *defeat* simply did not exist. He had already fought a war, more terrible than Hitler's, and he had come off victorious. His attack of infantile paralysis, his doctors had declared, would either kill him or leave him helpless for the rest of his days. But he had stubbornly refused to die or to submit to a life of invalid despair. For many years he had fought against destiny—and had come out smiling at the end. In the darkest days of his illness he had kept on encouraging his doctors, who held out not a single word of encouragement for him. Again and again he had told them: "Never fear, I'll beat this thing yet!"

This was the man, and this the motto, around whom America rallied to win the war. And is still rallying, some years after the war, to win the peace.

IMPORTANT DATES IN THE LIFE OF
FRANKLIN DELANO ROOSEVELT

1882–January 30, born, Hyde Park, New York.

1904–Graduated from Harvard University.

1907–Admitted to the bar.

1911–12–Served in the New York state legislature.

1912–Appointed Assistant Secretary of the Navy under President Wilson.

1920–Defeated as the Democratic candidate for the vice-presidency.

1921–Stricken with infantile paralysis.

1924–Conquered the disease.

1928–Elected governor of New York.

1930–Re-elected to the governorship of New York.

1932–Elected the thirty-second President of the United States.

1933–Unsuccessful attempt to assassinate him at Miami, Florida.

1933–36–Inaugurated the "New Deal" in the economic and social life of America.

1936–Elected to a second term in the White House.

1940–Elected to a third term in the White House–an act without precedent in American history.

1941–Drew up, with Winston Churchill, the "Atlantic Charter."
Assumed duties as Commander in Chief of a united nation in the war against Germany, Italy, and Japan.

1944–Elected to a fourth term in the White House.

1945–April 12, died, Warm Springs, Georgia.

Samuel Goldwyn

1884–

Undoubtedly the most colorful producer in Hollywood is a Polish Jew who fled from the Warsaw ghetto at eleven, arrived in America by steerage and became a millionaire at thirty-four. Entering the motion picture industry when it was in swaddling clothes, Sam Goldwyn produced the first feature film in America, and boosted a number of vaudeville hoofers and stock-company mummers into film idols known throughout the world. Goldwyn is the last of the pioneer producers still active in pictures and he has supplied a major share of the integrity that exists in the industry. His important pictures reflect the high-water mark of the motion picture art— *All Quiet on the Western Front, Arrowsmith, Dodsworth, Wuthering Heights, The Little Foxes, The Best Years of Our Lives.* It is an extraordinary and heartwarming fact that this immigrant from Poland, whose formal education ended with grammar school, has refused to insult the intelligence of the American people with the childish, meretricious films characteristic of so many of his competitors. Goldwyn has lured the finest authors to Hollywood to help him raise the general level of movie-making; yet, despite his fanatical devotion to the best, he has succeeded in making a fortune at the box office. Goldwyn's success has been the best testimonial to the good sense of the American public.

II

Goldwyn started life with everything against him. Born a Jew in a country saturated with anti-Semitism, he lost both his parents before he was eleven. As young as he was, he conceived the ambition of fleeing to America. He knew that an aunt of his lived in England and he believed that if he could reach her, she would finance his way across the ocean. To escape over the Polish border, he had to bribe a smuggler to row him across a river past the frontier guards. The smuggler took most of his money. Just before landing, the boy tumbled into the water, got soaked to the skin, and lost his remaining cash. He begged his way across Germany, managing to reach Hamburg. He stood on the dock watching ships depart for America and tears welled up in his eyes. He had no money for the passage. Tearfully he wandered through the streets of Hamburg until he came to a store bearing the name of the owner which was similar to one he had known in Warsaw. He rushed up to the man.

"I've run away from Poland. I will kill myself before I go back. Please help me get to America!" He stopped, choked with sobs.

The store owner took up a collection and put Sam on a boat for England. Upon arriving in Birmingham he looked up his aunt and found she was too poor to help him get to America. He went to work in a blacksmith's shop. His job was to pump the bellows with his feet, but he lacked the necessary strength to keep up a steady fire and he soon found himself without work. Friends of his aunt finally took up a collection to send him to the United States "where I had heard that a man could work with his brains instead of with his feet."

Sam arrived in New York at thirteen. He learned that other Polish immigrants had gathered in Gloversville, upstate, and were earning a living cutting gloves. Sam joined them and got a job in a glove factory. Although the place was a sweatshop by present-day standards, it was a revelation to this underprivileged boy to "find a place where work was rewarded and where the more a man worked, the more he was paid."

He was a hard worker. He struck up an acquaintance with the owner's son, Abe, who was serving an apprenticeship in the shop. Abe was lazy and Sam arranged a deal with him. He offered to work an hour longer than necessary, taking over part of Abe's job and permitting him to knock off an hour earlier. In return Abe used his influence to get Sam the best skins in the shop. One could cut gloves from good skins much faster than from poor ones and since the cutters were paid on a piece basis, the arrangement meant a good deal more money for Sam. Within two years he was earning twenty dollars a week.

This was the wage level at which many of the cutters rested on their laurels. "Some of my friends were well satisfied," Sam recalls, "they felt they had reached the top; . . . but there were also others who looked beyond the factory walls."

These were ambitious men who hoped to become salesmen. Sam listened to them and found out there was virtually no limit to the money salesmen could make. He saw them lounge on the verandah of the town's most lavish hotel, smoking expensive cigars; and he determined that he would become one of them.

He was fifteen when he went to the factory owner and asked to be sent out on the road selling gloves. The boss was hard to convince. He did not think much of a teen-ager's chances to succeed in a very tough field. To

prove his ability, Sam asked to be assigned to a territory where no salesman had succeeded in selling the firm's gloves.

"Okay," replied the boss. "I'll send you to Pittsfield, Mass. The number one store there has consistently refused to carry our gloves. If you can
sell it, I'll make you a regular salesman."

Sam went to Pittsfield and succeeded where his predecessors had failed.
He got the order; and the boss kept him on the road. Salesmanship was
the genii lamp that made Sam's dreams come true. He rose steadily until
at thirty-one he became the sales manager of a rival glove firm at a salary
of fifteen thousand dollars a year.

And then occurred one of those gambles in business that can turn a man
into a multimillionaire or drive him into bankruptcy. Sam's office was on
Fifth Avenue in New York and he used to walk to his home on Sixty-First
Street. On the way he would pass a nickelodeon where five-minute movies
were shown.

This was in 1913 and the movies were looked upon with contempt by
the impresarios of show business. They were two-reel "chasers", so-called
because they were used between vaudeville shows to chase the audience
out of the theater and empty the seats for the next performance. The
films were poorly made and were the despair of theater owners. Optome-
trists, declaring they could leave the viewer with a permanent squint,
warned their patients away from them.

Sam, however, was fascinated by these "chasers". Since it was not considered in the best of taste to be seen in a nickelodeon, he would first
make sure that none of his friends were watching before he slinked in;
and he would spend thrilling moments watching barroom slapstick and
cops-and-robbers films. The idea struck him that this gimmick, so ridiculed
by show people, could definitely be developed into a serious medium of
expression; why could not a far-sighted producer make full-length feature
films out of great novels and plays? The possibilities fired his imagination
and he became a one-man crusader for full-length films.

Three years previously he had married Blanche Lasky, a sister of Jesse
L. Lasky who was an impresario for vaudeville acts. Sam invited his
brother-in-law to go into the movie business with him. Jesse looked at
him in amusement. "Look, Sam, I'm a showman. I want to bring people
into the theater, not chase them out!"

Sam persisted in his campaign, however, and his salesmanship finally
wore down Lasky's resistance.

To direct their first film, Lasky got in touch with a struggling young
playwright named Cecil B. DeMille. DeMille was so fed up with poverty
that he was on the point of going to Mexico to take part in a revolution
when Lasky contacted him. There was one blemish to DeMille's qualifications. He had never directed a movie in his life, nor had he ever seen
one directed. But that did not phase the partners.

They decided to make a picture about Indians—a sure-fire theme. De-

Mille had once visited Flagstaff, Arizona, and he had seen a number of redskins standing about lazily at the railroad station. "If we shoot the picture in Flagstaff, we can get all the Indians we need free of charge," he reported. And so Sam and Jesse put DeMille on a train for Flagstaff. But it arrived there in the middle of a snowstorm. When DeMille got off, there was not an Indian in sight. He decided to continue on the train to the end of the line. Returning to his seat he rode all the way to Los Angeles.

Several days later, Sam and Jesse received a telegram from him. "Have proceeded to a place called Hollywood. Want authorization to rent barn for seventy-five dollars a month."

The partners were disconsolate. They had never heard of Hollywood. California was supposed to be a land swimming in sunshine. They could not understand why DeMille needed a barn when he could shoot the picture out of doors. Nevertheless they wired cautious approval. "Authorize you to rent barn on a month to month basis. Don't make long-term commitment."

And that's how Hollywood was born.

Sam engaged Dustin Farnum to play the lead role in the film. He offered him, in lieu of salary, five thousand dollars worth of stock in the company. But Farnum, like practically everybody else, had no faith in movies. "I'll take the five thousand in cash," he insisted. If he had accepted the stock, within three years he would have been worth more than a million dollars.

The chief problem confronting the partners was how to raise money for producing the picture. They estimated it would cost fifty thousand dollars. They had fifteen thousand dollars between them. Suddenly Sam had a brain-storm. Why couldn't he sell the distribution rights to the exhibitors before the film was completed? Such a thing had never been done, but Sam decided to give it a try. He went to the largest film exhibitor in California and told him about the wonderful new screen epic in preparation. Then he delivered his big sales punch. "Why, for this movie you'll be able to charge as much as twenty-five cents for admission!"

Impressed, the exhibitor paid Sam four thousand dollars for the rights in his territory. Sam traveled into every state in the union peddling the film and managing to raise forty thousand dollars, five thousand more than his original goal. There was a clause in the contract that The Squaw Man, as the film was to be called, had to be delivered to the exhibitors by a certain date or their money would be refunded. On the date agreed upon, Sam sent an assistant down to the Jersey freight yards to meet the train that was bringing in the prints of The Squaw Man from the coast. A violent blizzard had hit the area; telephone wires had been overthrown; the railroad tracks were buried in three feet of snow. There was no sign of the train. For forty-eight hours this "welcoming committee-of-one" huddled in the freight shed, grabbing snatches of sleep and sending out for meals. On the third day, a moving particle of ice emerged through billows of smoke and the Erie Special snorted into the station. Theater exhibitors from all over the country had assembled at the Loew's theater awaiting the film for forty-eight hours. Their tempers were definitely on edge when the cans arrived, but they were persuaded to stick with the venture.

Before presenting the film to the exhibitors, Sam and Jesse took a print into a projection room for their own private screening. When *The Squaw Man* began to unwind, Jesse's face grew white. "We're ruined!" The actors appeared sliced off at the waist, heads floating below their feet. Hives of players rose like clouds and whizzed crazily around the screen; buildings danced, jerked, turned somersaults.

A catastrophe had overtaken DeMille. Not having sufficient funds to buy his own photographic equipment, he had hired different photographers by the day. Each brought his own camera; one had a Pathé camera, another an Edison, a third a Lumière. Each used a different type of film. The perforations at the sides of the film were spaced unevenly and the picture jumped its sprockets as it unwound for projection.

Sam rushed with the film to Philadelphia and placed it before Sig Lubin, the owner of a film laboratory. "Can you do anything with this?" Faced with bankruptcy, he hardly dared hear the answer. But Lubin, after examining the print, said, "I can fix this up." He merely had to paste new, accurately spaced sprocket holes on the sides of the film; and he did the job in twenty-four hours. Lubin helped make movie history. For once the heads of the actors were implanted firmly on their shoulders again, *The Squaw Man* became a sensational hit.

The partners followed *The Squaw Man* with several other successes. The new movie industry grew at a dizzy pace that took all America by the ears. Within a matter of months, producers became wealthy beyond their wildest expectations. Hollywood turned from a cow town into a movie center as lavish as anything out of the Arabian Nights.

Sam was a restless fellow, and shortly after his company merged with a rival studio headed by Adolph Zukor he pulled out and went adventuring on his own. He became friendly with Edgar and Arch Selwyn, Broadway producers who held the copyrights to a library of plays; and he persuaded them to form a new company with him for the purpose of putting the best in drama on the screen.

Sam's last name at this time was Goldfish, a translation from his Polish one. The new company was named Goldwyn by merging the first syllable of Sam's name with the last syllable of Selwyn. Sam grew to like the name of the company—so much so that he had his own name changed legally to Goldwyn. And he has been known by this ever since. (The wits of Hollywood had been making life unbearable for him by cracking jokes about Goldfish; and this was his way of ending the torture.)

When the Goldwyn Company was formed movies had become popular; but they were still not fashionable. They were looked down upon by the intelligentsia and the carriage trade. To lure the ultrafastidious into movie theaters, Sam recruited opera stars, offering large financial inducements to sign with him. He signed Mary Garden and Geraldine Fararr to play in the screen versions of *Thais* and *Carmen*. Both films were stupendous flops. The intelligentsia still would not bite. When Geraldine Fararr, a proud woman, realized that Sam had lost his shirt on her, she tore up a contract obligating him to pay her an additional $250,000.

The Goldwyn Company, in the throes of these financial difficulties, was forced to merge with another firm to form the Metro-Goldwyn-Mayer Company. But Sam had had enough of partners and stockholders. He sold out his share and withdrew from films. For a spell he turned author and he dictated his memoirs. However, he could no more keep away from films than a fish could live out of water. With the hundred thousand dollars he received from the *Pictorial Review* and book royalties from his memoirs, he reinvested in the movies. But he had learned his lesson. This time he became an independent producer. "I find that it took too much time to explain my plans . . . to associates; now I can save all that time and energy and put it into making better pictures."

III

For THIRTY-TWO YEARS now Sam Goldwyn has been an independent producer—the leading one in the world. He has never taken in a partner or kowtowed to outside investors. Gambling solely with his own money, he has never hesitated to risk it in the interests of good taste. Once when a picture, *Nana*, failed to live up to his expectations, he shelved it in the middle of production. He wrote off the four hundred thousand dollars he had sunk into it rather than release an inferior film.

From the day he entered movies, Goldwyn has regarded the industry not as a factory for turning out western thrillers and Grade B shockers, but as a medium for creating films that do not insult the public's intelligence. Unlike the majority of producers, Goldwyn has respected writers above all other Hollywood personnel. He has believed that the screen should be utilized primarily as a vehicle for authors and that the actors should conform to the demands of writers, rather than vice versa as has generally been the case.

As soon as he became an independent producer, to offset the competition of the matinee idols his competitors had invested in, stars like Mary Pickford, Douglas Fairbanks, and Charlie Chaplin, Goldwyn organized a subsidiary, Eminent Authors Incorporated, and set out to recruit the cream of the nation's writing talent. This was a revolutionary approach. Hitherto the movies had been considered too undignified a medium for any worthwhile author to devote his talents to. But Goldwyn changed all this. He even tried to get Bernard Shaw to work for him, but the Irish wit de-murred. "The trouble, Mr. Goldwyn, is that you are interested only in art and I am interested only in money," Shaw said facetiously.

Sam did manage to lure Maurice Maeterlinck to Hollywood. This cele-brated dramatist, mystic, and philosopher, whose fantasy, "The Bluebird," had thrilled audiences in Europe and America, proved to be a little too much even for Sam, whose educational background was after all rather slim. When Maeterlinck arrived in Hollywood, Sam found that he could not speak a word of English and when it came to signing a contract he had extreme difficulty making himself understood.

"You'll be getting as much money as Rupert Hughes," he explained to Maeterlinck. When the interpreter translated this, the playwright looked at Sam blankly. To underscore the fact that Maeterlinck was receiving the same treatment as other authors, Sam showed him the contracts of several.

"Do you know Gertrude Atherton?"

"Non."

"Do you know Mary Roberts Rinehart?"

"Non."

"Louis Bromfield?"

"Non."

Sam turned to the interpreter. "What's the matter with this guy. Is he dumb?"

For his first film effort, Maeterlinck, who had no conception of what the movies required, tried his hand at preparing a scenario from a natural science book he had written—*Life Of A Bee*. He brought the manuscript to the unsuspecting Sam who read through the first few pages. A puzzled look came over his face. "Who's the hero of the story?"

"A bee," replied Maeterlinck, his face shining with enthusiasm.

"Good God!" muttered Goldwyn placing his hand on his head, "A bee!"

Shortly afterwards Sam saw Maeterlinck to the train and bade him farewell. "That's all right, Maurice." He put his arm around the world-famous author. "You'll make good yet."

Maurice Maeterlinck was Sam Goldwyn's outstanding failure in his campaign to adapt the works of major authors to the screen. With other writers he was successful to a gratifying degree. According to Hollywood standards, Goldwyn is a small producer. He has put out on the average three or four films a year compared to the thirty or forty features turned out by MGM. But what Goldwyn has lacked in quantity he has made up for in quality. His best pictures, tailored to his exacting standards, have had what has come to be known as "the Goldwyn touch." The characterizations are honest; the plots are sincere, true to life, and bereft of the usual Hollywood hokum.

Although Sam has deliberately kept the spotlight upon his authors, he has by no means neglected building up stars. This after all is an indispensable feature of the business. The list of Goldwyn "discoveries" is a virtual who's who of Hollywood celebrities. Sam signed Will Rogers when he was a cowboy in the Ziegfield Follies. He discovered Rudolph Valentino, Vilma Banky, Pola Negri, Robert Montgomery, and Merle Oberon among others.

Sam has used his make-up department and cameras with uncanny skill. When he first signed Robert Montgomery, his associates, reporting on the screen tests, said, "His neck is too long." "No," replied Sam after examining the tests. "His collars are too short." He had special collars sewn for Montgomery and developed him into a big box office attraction.

During the era of silent films, Goldwyn imported Vilma Banky, a blond Hungarian actress to Hollywood. For weeks the Goldwyn hair-dressers shampooed her hair, brushed it, arranged it this way and that. Finally they came up with what they considered a suitable hair-do to flatter her. Shortly afterwards, Miss Banky had dinner at the Goldwyn home. Sam stared at her through the meal. Finally he said, "No, Vilma, your hair *still* isn't right." He sent his wife upstairs for a brush, hairpins and comb, set Vilma down before a mirror, and worked on her himself. He arranged her hair the way she finally wore it when she appeared on the screen and created a sensation.

His uncanny aesthetic sense was dramatically demonstrated in the case of Danny Kaye. Goldwyn had heard about a young, dark-haired singer-comedian "wowing" them at the Copacabana in New York. He flew to New York, took in one performance, and signed Kaye to a starring contract without so much as having him take a screen test. Then he had a script prepared for the first Kaye vehicle, recruited a supporting cast and built sets. Only then did Kaye, having finished his New York engagements, come to Hollywood. When he was put through the routine of a screen test, the studio was plunged into consternation. Danny's features were angular; his nose exaggeratedly long and thin on the screen. Numerous tests were made; different make-ups tried, various types of lighting experimented with—to no avail. Although a fortune had been sunk into the picture, Sam's advisers told him to write off the investment. Terribly depressed, Sam walked into the projection room for one last look at the tests. Several of them were run off as he watched listlessly. Then suddenly he stiffened up. "I've got it!" He reached for the telephone and called up the hair-dressing department. "I'm sending Danny Kaye over to you immediately. *I want you to dye his hair blond!*"

The peroxide bottle softened Kaye's features and boosted him to stardom. But for Sam's extraordinary visual sense, Kaye might be an unknown today.

In one case, however, Goldwyn's plans for developing a star miscarried. He brought the Polish film actress, Anna Sten, to Hollywood hoping to make another Vilma Banky out of her. He paid her a large salary while she struggled to learn English under the tutelage of teachers. He felt that in addition to her acting ability, Anna could develop into a first class singer and dancer. Despite the report of experts that her voice was tinny and disagreeable, Sam continued with his plans. Her clumsiness as a dancer was so great that Goldwyn in a desperate effort to teach her the can-can was reduced to hopping around on one foot and winding his other leg around his neck. The morale of the company skidded during the efforts to put Anna across. During one scene, the actress herself became so nerve-wracked by the pressure that she collapsed. "Give her whisky!" shouted Sam grimly. The drink was forced through her lips. She revived, collapsed again and was again revived to struggle through the scene. During the shooting of a boudoir scene in which she lay on a bed amidst extravagant surroundings, a photographer, reduced to the point of exhaustion by retakes, kicked over a fuse box, received a shock, and fell to the floor unconscious. The studio doctor was summoned. Ignoring the photographer, he drenched the nostrils of the star, who had fainted dead away, with ammonia.

Anna Sten was Sam's greatest professional disappointment.

Sam made another bad guess about an actress. But the results were happier. Shortly after the Goldwyn Company had been formed, a young hopeful, Miss Frances Howard, was brought to the studio for a screen test. When the film was run off for Goldwyn he called in the head of the test department and scolded him. "Why do you waste the company's time and money taking a test of this woman? She's impossible!"

A year later, Miss Howard became a sensation on Broadway; she was signed by Paramount and developed into a star of the silent films. In April, 1925, Sam dramatically admitted his error in judgment—he married Miss Howard.

Through the years Sam and Frances have become known as Hollywood's ideal couple. Frances has been in the habit of spending mornings at the Goldwyn studio weeding out scripts, participating in story conferences, and giving Sam the benefit of her excellent business judgment. Afternoons she attends to her household chores and evenings she calls for Sam in the family car. The chauffeur usually drops them several miles from their home so that Sam can get exercise walking.

IV

TODAY, in his seventies, Goldwyn remains Hollywood's most authoritative spokesman. His genius for publicity has made him a household name. Shortly after he became an independent, realizing he had a hard row to hoe and determining to pull out all the stops in publicity, Goldwyn called in his chief press agent. "Belasco became known all over America by wearing his collar backwards. What can I do to make myself famous?"

The publicity department put its collective heads together and the celebrated Goldwynisms were born. There was a grain of truth in the picture built up of Goldwyn as a man who mixed metaphors and scrambled up ideas. But Goldwyn's weakness for occasional grammatical lapses has been grossly exaggerated by the abundance of manufactured gags his publicity men have ground out for exploitation by columnists and feature writers who have the attention of the public.

Some of the Goldwynisms that have made the rounds—which are genuine and which are phony, it would take a modern Solomon to determine —are as follows: "A verbal contract isn't worth the paper it's written on." "Our comedies are not to be laughed at." "I can answer you in two words, im-possible!"

It is claimed that once Sam wanted the services of a writer who was pledged to another producer. The rival producer suggested that the dispute be brought before a board of arbitration. "OK," said Sam, "I'm a fair fellow. I'll submit to arbitration. But remember, no matter what is decided, Mr. McG— comes to work for me!"

Despite the hogwash of manufactured Goldwynisms, there is little doubt that Sam is a flamboyant and eccentric character. He lives, eats, and sleeps movies; and when he is in the throes of developing a picture, he expects everybody around him to have a direct pipe line into his thoughts. One midnight he phoned an assistant, rousing him out of bed. "The woman must die in the end!"

"What woman?" muttered the assistant. It took some time before he awoke to the fact the boss was plotting a movie, and by then Goldwyn had hung up and was regaling another of his associates.

Although Sam has a remarkable memory for business details, he continually forgets his own phone number. Once while driving with Harpo Marx, he desired to stop and phone home. "What's my number?" Harpo told him. "Write it down; I'll never remember it." He took the pad with him into the telephone booth.

A fighter at the drop of a hat, Goldwyn is always putting pressure on people to obtain his ends. Once he called up a fellow producer, Daryl Zanuck. "Daryl, you're in trouble."

"What trouble, Sam?"

"You've got a certain actor—and I want him."

On one occasion when Sam attended the rushes of one of his films, he could not grasp the meaning of a certain scene. His director insisted that the scene was easy to understand. He turned to Sam's fifteen year old son, Sammy, Jr., and asked if he understood it.

"Sure," said Sammy, Jr.

Goldwyn exploded, "Since when are we making pictures for kids!"

Sam is superstitious. When things are going too well for him, he actually becomes depressed, keenly aware of the fickleness of fate. Only when he hits the skids does he breathe a sigh of relief.

Once when a competitor asked him how a picture was doing, his face lit up. "I'm losing my shirt on it." When he was asked about another film, he scowled, "Looks like it will make a million."

During the first World War he hit bottom. He had lost large sums of money in opera stars who turned out to be film duds. The war had reduced audiences. The government, to save fuel, had cut down the use of electricity for commercial consumption so that it was extremely costly to make pictures. As if this all were not enough, Goldwyn fractured his ankle playing handball and was laid up in a hospital. His business associates came to his bedside with long faces to report that the company was facing bankruptcy. Sam beamed at them. "If that's the worst you have to tell me, gentlemen, I see nothing but roses ahead!"

Goldwyn has always faced bad luck with courage and his wife has displayed equal bravery. Both of them are people with strong faith. Once Sam negotiated a deal for the film rights to the Broadway hit, *Dead End*. Shortly afterwards, he underwent a serious operation. While he was convalescing, his stitches burst and his wound became reinfected. The doctors summoned his wife and told her they did not expect him to live through the day. While Frances stood in the corridor of the hospital, a Goldwyn business associate rushed up to her. It seemed that when Sam had negotiated for *Dead End* he had made a down payment of $25,000. The remainder of the price—$140,000—had just become due. "It must be paid this afternoon, Frances, or we'll have to forfeit the property. It's up to you to decide what to do. If Sam doesn't recover—!"

"Pay the $140,000!" replied Frances. "Sam's going to get well. He's going to do that picture. And it will be a good one."

Sam did recover; he made *Dead End*—and *Dead End*, in turn, made Hollywood history.

Goldwyn is a deeply sensitive individual—and while it is true that words frequently fail him, or betray him, his sensitivity is felt by all who come in contact with him.

After Helen Hayes finished her magnificent performance in *Arrowsmith*, Sam tried to find words to tell her how profoundly he had been stirred by her. He was overwhelmed with emotion. The words would not come. "Let's go into my office," he finally said, "I want you to read a letter I wrote about it."

Not very long ago, Sam received a letter from his old boss in Gloversville asking him to address a local businessman's club. Sam accepted. He had not been to Gloversville since he was sixteen, and the associations of his early life, the memories of his struggle to free himself from poverty, now crowded in upon him with a strong impact. He and Frances put up at a local hotel and as the time approached for him to go to the club, he grew as nervous as a kitten.

When he arrived he was surrounded by Mr. Aaron, his old boss and fellow glove workers who pumped his hand and remarked how he had not changed in all these years. Then a man touched Sam's arm. "There's someone in the lobby who wants to know if you remember Hamburg."

Sam walked into the lobby and saw a very old man in a leather chair. He stared at the man. "Why, of course—!" Tears came into his eyes. It was Mr. Libglid, the Hamburg storekeeper to whom a little Polish refugee boy had come begging for fare to take him to his British aunt and who had collected the money to send him to England. Mr. Libglid had been driven out of Germany by Hitler and he was now working in Gloversville.

Sam asked if there was anything he needed, anything he could do for him.

"Not a thing," replied Mr. Libglid, "I'm a pretty good glovemaker."

"He's the best in my plant," chimed in Mr. Aaron.

Much has happened since Sam came to America by steerage. And much has taken place in the movie industry since Sam dispatched Cecil B. DeMille to photograph Indians for *The Squaw Man.* Hollywood has grown from a barn rented for seventy-five dollars a month to a city employing over thirty thousand artists and craftsmen who turn out four hundred feature films a year.

And Sam remains the industry's outstanding spokesman. Once when a reporter asked him to define the reasons for his success, he replied tersely, "Showmanship; whatever everyone else is doing—I do something else."

In 1947, *The Best Years of Our Lives,* Sam's film about veterans returning from the second World War and featuring Harold Russell, the soldier who had lost his arms and learned to get along with hooks, stirred the heart of America. The film received the Academy Award and eight other prizes—just about every one available. No other film in history has gained so many prizes as this one. And yet Sam was not content to rest on his laurels. He was anxious about the future. "Suppose next time I make a stinker. I'm worried about that."

The basis of Sam's achievement is this attitude toward things. As a kid, when he attended a fair in Gloversville the barker offered to pay ten dollars to anybody who could climb to the top of a greased pole. "I wrapped my arms around the pole and sneaked up with what seemed a superhuman effort . . . I won the ten dollars. In addition, I learned a very important lesson, namely, that while I could climb the pole, it was more difficult to stay on it once I had reached the top . . . I have found that life is much like that."

It is this drive to keep continually on his toes, to accept each new achievement as a challenge to do even better in the future, that has kept Sam triumphantly on top. Because of him the movies have not yielded entirely to the siren songs of the hucksters and the American people have been afforded rare experiences of cinematic art.

IMPORTANT DATES IN THE LIFE OF
SAMUEL GOLDWYN

1882—August 17, born Warsaw, Poland.

1897—Arrived in the United States.

1902—Became naturalized citizen of the United States.

1913—Produced *The Squaw Man*.

1919—Formed Eminent Authors Pictures, Inc. and Goldwyn Pictures Corporation.

1923—Published memoirs, *Behind the Screen*.

1925—Married Frances Howard.

1930—Produced first talking picture hit, *All Quiet on the Western Front*.

1931—Produced *Arrowsmith*.

1932—Produced *Dodsworth*.

1947—Won the Motion Picture Academy Award for *The Best Years of Our Lives*.

1953—Produced *Hans Christian Anderson*.

Sister Elizabeth Kenny

1886–1952

THE Kennys brought up their large family—six girls and five boys—
in the Australian bushland. The father, an Irish immigrant, was a veter-
inary; and the children, especially Elizabeth, inherited from him a fighting
courage and a love for living things.

At six, Elizabeth practically lived on horseback, riding through the bush
for the family mail, helping to round up the stock, and racing a young
cousin to her grandparents who lived ten miles away.

And at eight, she encountered her first mortal danger. While she was
playing in the bush, she came suddenly face to face with a poisonous
adder. Trained to speedy action, she snatched up a stick and brought it
down on the reptile's head. Then she picked it up and carried it proudly
to her mother—only to realize that she had been carrying a live snake.
For no sooner had she dropped it on the ground than it wriggled away
in terror of its human enemy.

It was a miracle, said her mother, that any of her children survived
the continuous risks they took. Throughout her life, Elizabeth Kenny was
to take all sorts of risks, and to fight against all kinds of obstacles—and
to win again and again as if by a miracle. Yet there was nothing supernatural about her victories. They were merely the result of fearless determination and common sense.

II

IT WAS at an early age that the future course of her life began to take
shape. One of her younger brothers, Bill, was puny and weak. As she
watched him at his exercise, she felt that something must be done to
build him up. When the children went out on hikes through the forest,
she recalled, he was the first to tire. And when they went to school,
the others had to carry him "piggy-back."

This wouldn't do at all, decided sister Elizabeth. And so she picked up a book of anatomy in her father's library and plunged into the study of muscles—their composition, development, relationship, and function. As an aid to her study, she rigged up a mechanical figure with strings and pulleys to demonstrate the actions of the muscles. Elizabeth was only fourteen at the time.

As a result of her study—in which her brother joined her with the utmost enthusiasm—Elizabeth became fairly familiar with the muscular interdependence of the human body. But more than that, she taught Bill how to isolate his muscles by voluntary contraction; and she enabled him to develop a physique that became the pride of the Kenny family.

This, she felt instinctively, was the sort of work to which she would like to devote her life. The rebuilding of the human body from weakness to strength. And in this ambition she found a helpful ally—Doctor Aeneas J. McDonnell, a surgeon who had once healed her broken wrist when she fell off a runaway horse. At his recommendation, she entered upon a nursing course in a private hospital.

She had the mentality and the energy for a successful nurse. "I was tall and strong and fresh-cheeked," she wrote. "I loved the wind and the rain, the sunshine and the earth-rocking thunder storms." These were indispensable qualities for a woman dedicated to the long and lonely rides in the bush, and to the hardships of nursing in homes that were many miles removed from doctors and drugs.

And she had a sense of humor which enabled her to make the best of any difficult situations. Once, she writes, she was caught in a downpour while on a long ride to a patient. Instinctively she found a way to enjoy a refreshing shower and at the same time to keep her clothes dry. "I got down from my horse," she writes, "disrobed, made a bundle of my clothes which I placed on a stump; then, unsaddling my horse, I set the saddle atop the bundle and over that threw a waterproof blanket I carried with me . . . I, myself . . . sat topping everything on the stump, enjoying a wonderful bath while my horse turned his back to the storm. I recommend this mode of ablution," she adds, "to anyone who is not too bashful in the presence of gum trees, birds, and the inquisitive koala bear."

III

AN ENGAGEMENT to a handsome young Australian, a quarrel with her fiancé because she was too much in love with her profession, and the beginning of a life-long devotion to a single cause—the lessening of pain.

She was only twenty-three when she made her great discovery. This discovery, which was to revolutionize the treatment of infantile paralysis, was the result of her inadequate facilities as a bush nurse. In her case, necessity was indeed the mother of invention.

It happened at a cottage in an isolated part of the bush. Elizabeth

Kenny had been called to attend to a child who had been taken ill. She had expected to find nothing more serious than a cold or an upset stomach. But the scene that met her eyes filled her with dismay. The little girl lay upon a cot, her helpless body twisted all out of shape. One leg was drawn up toward the face, with the foot turned downward, and the heel pointing outward. One arm lay with the elbow bent stiffly across the chest. Any effort to straighten the deformities resulted in excruciating pain.

This was the first case of its kind Elizabeth Kenny had ever seen. In order to treat it properly, she must wire for medical advice. The nearest telegraph station was several miles away. And so she mounted her horse, galloped to the station, and sent off her wire, explaining the symptoms and asking for the remedy.

Hours of suspense, and then the disheartening reply: "Infantile paralysis. No known treatment. Do the best you can." The telegram was signed by Dr. Aeneas McDonnell.

Anxiety, but no panic. For "panic plays no part in the training of a nurse." Filling a frying pan with salt, she heated it over a fire and then poured it into a bag and applied it to the diseased leg.

No relief.

Then she tried something else. She prepared a linseed poultice and put it in the place of the salt-bag.

Still no relief. The added pressure of the poultice served only to increase the pain.

And then, as a last resort, she tore a woolen blanket into strips, dipped them in boiling water, and wrung them out. And now, while the strips were still warm, she wrapped them gently around the tortured muscles. Within a very short time the child's whimpering ceased, and she fell asleep.

After a while she awoke, and whispered, "I want them rags that wells my legs!"

And thus, accidentally, Elizabeth Kenny had discovered a new method for "welling" the victims of infantile paralysis. The "Kenny Treatment," of which this incident was but a preliminary hint, was to become the subject of much heated controversy among the medical profession. And, in the end, it was to establish Sister Kenny as one of the world's medical pioneers.

IV

SHORTLY after her experience with the sick child, she opened a modest clinic for convalescents from infantile paralysis. And some of her "cures" amazed Dr. McDonnell who kept closely in touch with her work. But the rest of the medical profession remained highly skeptical. In any case, she had little opportunity at this time to prove the value of her treatment.

For World War I put an end to this chapter of her life. She enlisted as a nurse in the transport service; and for the next four years she shuttled between Australia and Europe, looking after the wounded troops. Sister Kenny was not, as many people believe, a nun. The term "sister" was applied to Australian nurses who served as officers in the navy during the war.

In the course of her journeys over several seas, she was in constant danger from storms and submarines. On one occasion her ship was reported lost off the coast of Africa. Upon her arrival in London, she went to headquarters and asked for her pay. But the paymaster refused her request. "Sister Kenny," he said, "is dead." It took her some time to persuade him that she was still very much alive. And then, having received her pay, she guided her ship-companions through the process of proving that they, too, were still in the flesh; and together they went out to celebrate their resurrection.

Flashes of humor to keep their spirits alive—occasional games and parties to relieve the tension of sickness and suffering and death—and back-breaking toil, with the constant threat of the enemy lurking in the depths. No shiplights at night whenever they sailed through a danger zone. "I spent more time in the darkness," she wrote, "than any other woman in the world."

And, when at last the war was ended, Sister Kenny came home with a leg shattered by a shrapnel wound and a heart diseased from overwork. As she lay in the hospital after a severe heart attack, she overheard one of the doctors saying to another: "She is close to the end now. Just a few months left—three, four, five at the most."

A couple of hours later, when the doctor came to examine her, he found her fully dressed. "What's the meaning of this?" he asked.

"I'm going home," she said. "This isn't the end of my journey; it's just the beginning."

And Sister Kenny, who had been pronounced dead at one time and dying at another, remained alive and in harness for more than a quarter of a century.

A trip to England—"I believe the sea air will restore my health"—a short visit to her father's family in Ireland—a pilgrimage to Lourdes— "I am willing to try anything once"—and a return trip to Australia, fresh and energetic and full of fight.

And, indeed, much fighting lay ahead! A few weeks after her return, she received a letter from a cousin who lived about four hundred miles away. In this letter, the cousin told her about a mutual friend whose seven-year-old daughter had become a hopeless cripple. At least, that was the prognosis of the doctors. Could Elizabeth Kenny be of any assistance in this case?

Elizabeth Kenny accepted the challenge. Upon her arrival at the patient's home, she saw that the child suffered from *cerebral diplegia*—

paralysis of both legs. After a series of unsuccessful consultations with the leading physicians of Brisbane, she took the child to Dr. McDonnell. But he, too, gave her a discouraging report. "These are the cases in which the medical world is helpless. There's nothing *we* can do, so go ahead with your own treatment. But don't say anything to raise the parents' hope. Frankly, I think the case is incurable."

With the responsibility thus placed upon her own shoulders, Sister Kenny began a course of "muscular manipulations" to restore the movements of the legs. The treatment took over three years—but the results were amazing even to Sister Kenny herself. Another forward step in helping the lame to walk!

But, for Sister Kenny, another storm of opposition along heartbreak road. "How dare a mere nurse rush in where doctors fear to tread?" She opened an infantile paralysis clinic at Townsville, an Australian seaport on the Pacific. And here, patient after patient came out either completely cured or vastly improved. Again and again she tried to explain her methods to the medical world. But she was generally met with outbursts of laughter, or at best with an icy silence.

Yet now and then she got an attentive ear. And her explanation was simple, logical, and straight to the point. What is known as "infantile paralysis," she said, is really not a *paralysis* but a *spasm* of the muscles. In the onset of this disease, therefore, the muscles are not permanently killed; they are just temporarily contracted. And so the proper treatment is the very opposite of the orthodox method. The doctors are wrong, she insisted, when they immobilize the patient—that is, when they put his body into casts or splints. This imprisonment, she maintained, only tends to kill the muscles that are already weakened by the spasm. The thing to do is to leave the body free; and to re-educate the weakened muscles, by proper exercise, until the spasm is relaxed and the strength is restored.

In other words, the *paralysis* of a muscle is accompanied by the destruction of its nerves; but the *spasm* of a muscle has no such condition —the nerves are still alive and able to send their impulses to the muscle. And the way to treat such impaired muscles, declared Sister Kenny, is not to *weaken* the nerves by immobilization, but to *strengthen* them by stimulation so that their impulses can be translated into useful motion.

But it took Sister Kenny more than two decades to prove to a hostile medical world that she was on the right track. Now and then she received a reluctant nod of approval; but for the most part, she was dismissed as a fanatic or a downright fake.

Yet, convinced of the soundness of her method through her many successful cures, she went ahead with her work, training nurses, opening clinics, lecturing on every possible occasion, and never receiving any pay for her treatments.

Another heart attack—a siege of two weeks when she had to fight for her breath—and then back again to her longer and harder fight. She wrote a textbook about her methods, and prepared a film to demonstrate her successful treatments. But the Australian medical authorities still persisted in their disbelief. "Eyes have they but they see not; ears, but they hear not." She was now receiving a great deal of publicity—but of an unfavorable sort. "Feeling against my work was running high," she wrote, "and an . . . endeavor was underway to crush the work at all costs." But she stuck to her job and held her temper. "'He who angers you,' my mother used to say, 'conquers you.'"

Her hair was now prematurely white. But her courage was still young, and her success was just around the bend of the road. One of the children she had cured was the English niece of an Australian physician who had noticed her work. As a result of this cure, she was invited to demonstrate her methods in England. Just before she left her Townsville Clinic, the parents of her patients, together with a number of other citizens, held a meeting in her honor. At least the people, if not the doctors, believed in her. As she rose to bid the assembly farewell, everybody stood up to sing an old Scotch refrain:

> Better loved ye canna be,
> Will ye na come back again?

V

THE ECHO of the Townsville ovation was soon to be heard around the world. Successful treatments in England and in Poland. The cure of a Parisian patient whose "paralysis" no less than eighteen doctors had pronounced incurable. A short visit to Australia, only to meet another wave of opposition. And a return to Europe and to further success. A committee of British physicians, appointed to study her methods, issued a favorable report. A similar committee in Australia had once stated: "Miss Kenny's abandonment of immobilization is a grievous error fraught with great danger." But the British committee now declared: "Her abandonment of immobilization has not caused any deformity . . . All recent cases treated have been totally and permanently cured."

Yet Sister Kenny herself disclaimed any total and permanent cure. Her method, she maintained, prevented unnecessary injury and in many cases restored muscular movement. But it produced no miracles. While she insisted upon her right—even her duty—to put a stop to the dangerous orthodox treatments, she held out no panacea against the disease in her own revolutionary treatment. "I can warn against the old, and help with the new," she said. "That is all."

And it was in England that she had been given her first official encouragement to prove the effectiveness of her work. Following the British report, the Australian doctors, too, began to relax their opposition. Their approval was reluctant and slow, to be sure; but little by little they came around to her point of view.

For the evidence as to the rightness of her method was piling up all the time. There was, for example, the case of little Marie. When admitted to a hospital in which Sister Kenny was allowed to do occasional work, Marie had suffered from infantile paralysis for three years. Her wasted little body was still imprisoned in a plaster cast. When Sister Kenny began to remove the bandages, the child broke into a perspiration of terror. "Don't be afraid, dear," said Miss Kenny. "You're not going to melt into thin air. And you don't have to be wrapped up like a mummy to be kept all in one piece."

When the cast had been completely removed, one of the other nurses looked in admiration at the stiff little body. "Isn't she beautifully straight?"

"Yes," replied Sister Kenny. "There are several thousands lying just as straight in the town cemetery. And," she added, "under the old treatment she'd have about as much chance to recover the use of her legs as those dead people."

When she began her own treatment of little Marie, the superintendent of the hospital looked on with a skeptical smile. But as the treatment progressed from day to day, his skepticism gradually disappeared and he became one of the ardent supporters of the "new way."

And then there was the case of little Donald. At the request of his parents, Sister Kenny took him over when all the doctors who had treated him had failed to give him relief. His legs were in splints when she first saw him. As soon as the splints were removed, the feet dropped and there seemed to be no life in the muscles. One of the hospital doctors, who was passing by at the time, asked sarcastically: "And how long will it take you to readjust these dropped feet?"

Sister Kenny looked at the clock. "It is now a quarter after twelve. Come back tomorrow at this time, and you'll see the feet in their proper place."

With a look of disdain, the doctor left the ward.

Sister Kenny then proceeded with her treatment. She relaxed the spasm, applied moist foments to ease the pain, and gently stimulated the muscles until they raised the feet to their normal position. "The whole operation," she writes, "took less than ten minutes."

The following day, to the astonishment of the doctors, Donald moved his feet in any direction suggested to him. Three weeks later, he went home a well and happy child.

VI

AN INVITATION to the United States—and then, world recognition at last. In Los Angeles, San Francisco, Denver, Chicago, and New York, she read papers to explain her methods, and conducted demonstrations to prove them.

But her most encouraging reception came at the Mayo Clinic in Rochester, Minnesota. Sister Kenny writes amusingly about her first impression of the City of the Great Surgeons: "I couldn't help remarking to my host—a professor of physical therapy—that the members of the Mayo family had contributed almost as much to the civic life of the place as they had to the medical. I said to the professor, 'Is there anything in Rochester that does not belong or did not originally belong to the Mayos?' The professor smiled and pointed to a cat that was crossing the road. 'To whom does the cat belong?' I asked. The feline obligingly stopped, looked me in the face, and said, 'May-o!'"

Yet, even in Rochester, Sister Kenny found a measure of opposition at first. The doctors at the Mayo Clinic, as in so many other places, were inclined to regard her as a bush nurse. "If your method is so good, why are the majority of the physicians against it?" Yet, in spite of their skepticism, they gave her a chance to demonstrate—not only at the Clinic, where there were few cases of infantile paralysis, but at the Children's Hospital at Saint Paul, where there were many.

And the results of the demonstrations were so convincing that the president of the University of Minnesota invited her to deliver a series of lectures to his medical staff.

From now on, Sister Kenny's honors began to multiply. The National Foundation for Infantile Paralysis publicly recognized the value of her treatment. Dr. Morris Fishbein, editor of the *Journal of the American Medical Association*, announced over the radio that the Kenny method had been proved to be sound. Dr. Wallace Cole, a physician at the Mayo Clinic, arranged to set aside several thousand dollars from the annual March of Dimes for the training of nurses in the Kenny treatment. The *Canadian Public Health Journal* reported: "We were astonished to see Miss Kenny restore what we had recorded as completely paralyzed and flaccid muscles to full function by restoring mental awareness." And the University of Minnesota opened a hospital, named the Elizabeth Kenny Institute, for the new treatment of infantile paralysis.

Yet her belated triumphs, like her earlier disappointments, left Sister Kenny unperturbed. She was not interested in her personal success. Recognition for herself meant merely more help for the helpless, more healing for the sick. And so she laid aside her medals, and forgot her honorary degrees, and merely shrugged her shoulders when she was hailed as "the outstanding figure in the medical world today." No time for banquets and acclaim, just as there had been no time for heart attacks and despair. There was work to be done! When the story of her life was prepared for the screen, she graciously thanked Mary McCarthy, the author of the script, and Rosalind Russell, the leading actress, and went back to her wards. It was here—in the smiling faces of her patients—that she found the real recompense for her toil. And it was in the clapping of little hands saved from the ravages of disease that she found her sweetest applause. She regarded as the greatest tribute of her life the words spoken by Dr. Baker, Chancellor of New York University, when he presented her with an honorary Doctorate of Humane Letters. "In many parts of the world," he said, "little children start their morning devotionals with a prayer for Sister Kenny."

For Sister Kenny had found a cure for 87 per cent of her patients, whereas the orthodox methods had cured only 13 per cent. And it remained only for Dr. Jonas Salk to discover a preventive that promised to make the cure of Elizabeth Kenny unneccessary. Two great medical pioneers—the healer of the sick, and the killer of the sickness.

IMPORTANT DATES IN THE LIFE OF
SISTER KENNY

1886—September 20, born, Wanalda, New South Wales, Australia.

1902—Graduated from St. Ursula College, Australia.

1910—Began to develop the "Kenny Treatment."

1914–18—Served as army transport nurse in World War I.

1927—Wrote *Infantile Paralysis and Cerebral Diplegia.*

1933—Opened clinic at Queensland, Australia.

1940—Began her work in the U.S.A.

1942—Wrote *Kenny Concept of Infantile Paralysis and Its Treatment.*

1943—Wrote *They Shall Walk.* Elizabeth Kenny Institute established in Minnesota.

1943–1950—Established clinics in California, Michigan, New Jersey, and New York.

1952—November 30, died, Toowoomba, Queensland, Australia.

Dwight David Eisenhower

1890–

In 1942, when the Allied invasion of Europe was being planned, a number of generals were prominently discussed in the press as the possible leaders of that invasion. One man was completely overlooked—Eisenhower. "Just another cipher" among the twenty million unknown soldiers who were fighting in the war.

And when Eisenhower was selected as the commander in chief of the invading forces, the news came crashing like a bombshell into an astonished world. "Never heard of the man. . . . Who is he? . . . How did they know about him? . . . What has he done to be singled out above all the rest?"

The answer to these questions constitutes the substance of our story. The invisible development of a seed until it suddenly springs into flower. The latent evolution of a genius until it suddenly flames into achievement. Success is frequently a combination of little incidents and a great soul. The incidents come from without; their transformation into an essence of greatness comes from within.

Such, in brief, is the structure of Eisenhower's life.

II

Born in Denison, Texas, he was christened David Dwight Eisenhower. Later he transposed the first two names. Still later he accepted the nickname "Ike" as the most suitable to his character. Homespun and friendly and unassuming and frank. Familiar as a blade of grass, congenial as the light of the sun.

His German ancestors, like the Puritans of England, had come to America in quest of religious freedom. They belonged to a group called Brethren in Christ—a Quakerlike sect of lovers of justice and haters of war. His grandfather was a lay preacher among the Brethren. His father, an engineer by profession, was a religious teacher by conviction. With the help of his wife, whose parents were also members of the Brethren in Christ, he tried to inspire his children with a hateless and spiteless courtesy toward the world. "For all of us belong to a single family—and the love of our Father extends to us all."

The selfsame spirit of tolerance toward the people of Europe, where Ike's ancestors had lived; of Texas, where he first saw the light of day; and of Kansas, where he grew to be a man. He was only two years old when his parents moved to the Kansas city of Abilene. Here his father got a job as engineer at the Belle Springs Creamery, and Ike—"barefoot boy with cheek of tan"—grew up in the give-and-take spirit of American democracy. Learn to get along with your brothers, to respect your parents, to demand justice for yourself, and to dispense justice to all. The American creed of mutual helpfulness. The Eisenhower boys took their turn building the kitchen fire at four-thirty in the morning. "A disagreeable job, but it has to be done." More pleasant, however, was the cooking of the family dinner on Sunday. In this job all the boys participated—to give their parents a rest. Great fun preparing the mush and puddin', and especially making the piecrust. For the dough could be rolled into a ball for a game of catch. And, also, you could play catch with the dishes. Big Ike—Edgar—would wash them and toss them to little Ike, who would dry them and then in turn toss them to Arthur, who would stack them on the shelves. "Work isn't half bad if only you can turn it into play."

And schooling, too, if you can season it with athletic games. Ike had developed into a good football player. Practice on the gridiron, home lessons, and firing the boiler at the creamery—his father had secured him this job. A good life, this—full of mental and physical excitement, interesting companions, and devoted friends. Friends with whom you could discuss things, play ball, and—in your rare spare moments—play poker. Ike Eisenhower had become the best poker player in town. For he had an amazing memory and an uncanny skill in outguessing his opponents. "The entire trick in poker," one of his older friends—"Joner" Callahan —had pointed out, "is to know the percentages, to calculate the chances, and to figure out what the other fellow has in mind."

The entire trick in poker and—as Eisenhower was to prove many years later—in war. For the present, however, his thoughts were far from the idea of war. This idea was not within the precinct of the Eisenhower way of life. At the time of the Spanish-American War the Eisenhower boys had tried to play "soldiers"—to their mother's displeasure and their own smarting backsides. After the thrashing she had explained her ideas on the subject. As a child in Virginia, she had seen her home ransacked first by the Confederate soldiers and then by the Yankee troops. "That's what the war did to them, turned them into savage animals . . . God forbid that you boys should ever go to war."

Yet the game of war had a fascination for Ike. Not as a struggle of beasts in the jungle, but as a conflict of human wits. He was fond of reading Clausewitz. "Of all the branches of human activity," this military expert had declared, "war is most like a game of cards."

A sporting fondness for the intricacies of poker, a scientific interest in the complexities of war. But, above all, a sincere effort to finish the day's work before he entered upon the evening's play.

III

AT HIS GRADUATION from the Abilene High School, the "class prophet" expressed the opinion that "Ike will wind up as a professor of history at Yale." Not so wild a prediction for a youngster who was to be appointed president of Columbia. But none of his classmates suspected the road over which he was to travel to that post.

A year after his graduation he entered upon the first milestone of that road. At the suggestion of his classmate, Everett Hazlett, he took the examinations both for Annapolis and for West Point. And to his surprise —"I never was much of a student"—he was top man in the navy test and runner-up in the army test. The power of concentration, and the determination to win.

He was appointed to Annapolis, but the appointment could not be confirmed. The maximum age limit for entrance to the naval academy was twenty; and Eisenhower, who had gone to work when he was through with his high-school course, was now twenty-one. The age limit for the military academy, however, was twenty-two. Eisenhower requested his senator, Joseph L. Bristow, to change his appointment to West Point; and when the ranking candidate failed in his physical test, Ike was chosen in his place.

At West Point he starred in football and was a little better than average in his studies. Owing to an injured knee, he failed to develop into an all-American athlete. But he succeeded in developing into an all-American character. Everybody loved his friendliness, his optimism, his ability to take orders with a smile, his fondness for practical jokes—even though the laughs were at his own expense—his enthusiasm for work, and especially his courage in the face of danger and his courtesy toward all men of whatever religion or race.

It was during one of his vacations from West Point that his townsmen were able to see something of this manhood and magnanimity that had become so integral a part of his character. Envious of his reputation as a West Pointer, some of the old "gang" inveigled him into challenging Dirk Tyler, a professional Negro prize fighter, to a boxing match. When Ike saw the gigantic Negro, his bulging muscles and impassive face, he felt literally sick. But he put on a bold face and threw down the challenge.

"When do you wanna fight?" asked Dirk.

"Right now."

They repaired to a public "gym," where they stripped for the fight. A large crowd had collected. They were anxious to see the "kill."

And they saw it. Not, however, as they had expected. It was Ike who knocked out the Negro. And in the very first round.

For a time after the fight it was a dismal world for Dirk Tyler. They taunted him as a "no-account bastard and a yellow-livered coon." The little boys took to throwing stones at him, and the older fellows "ganged up" on him in a sadistic reaction to their former fear.

But Ike did not like this. "Come on, fellows, lay off. He did the best he could. It's no fault of his that he lost. Or that his skin is black."

And when some of the fellows still persisted in their abuse, Ike took matters into his own hands. "Brave guys, hey? Well, if you're so brave, stop picking on Dirk and start picking on me!"

IV

WHEN he was graduated from West Point (June 12, 1915) he ranked 61 in a class of 168. He stood high, however, in engineering, military science, and drill.

Commissioned as a second lieutenant in the 19th Infantry, he looked upon the opening battles of the first World War with a professional but somewhat detached interest. A chess game played by foreign experts. Intriguing enough, but no American championship at stake. He studied the campaigns, applauded the good plays, criticized the bad ones—and executed one outstanding play for himself. He got married. To Mamie Geneva Doud, the daughter of a successful meat packer.

There was a great difference in their social rank, for the Douds were very wealthy. But there was no difference in their love. And so they took their unequal union in stride and soon learned to march in mutual adoration and harmonious step. Mamie's father offered no financial assistance —"Let the youngsters stand on their own pins." And Ike was quite willing and able to stand on his own feet.

But it meant a long and patient and at times disheartening stand before anything worth while turned up. Football coach at the Peacock Military Academy; instructor of the National Guard at Camp Travis; teacher in the Officers' Training Camp at Fort Oglethorpe, and afterward at Fort Leavenworth; commander of the Tank Training Center at Camp Colt. From second to first lieutenant, to captain, to major, to lieutenant colonel. But no orders for active duty. America had now entered the war. But no opportunity for Eisenhower to get into the line-up. He was too valuable as a teacher, a side-line director, a coach. The youngster had too rare a talent to be wasted in field duty. He knew how to turn civilians into soldiers. For he understood people, and could get them to understand him.

To trust him, to obey him, and, if necessary, to contradict him. He knew how to *give* and *take*. Above all, he disliked the rubber-stamp type of man, the "yes-man." If a subordinate disapproved of his ideas, and had a good reason for his disapproval, let him come out with it! One of his lieutenants at Camp Colt kept applauding him for his ability as a commander. "Nobody else could have done such a perfect job, sir."

"Do you really think so?"

"Yes, sir!"

"Find everything here just right?"

"Yes, *sir!*"

"Well," snapped Eisenhower, "get out and find something wrong with the place. No camp can be *that* good. Either you're a flatterer or you're as big a fool as you think *I* am."

Yet Eisenhower's work at Camp Colt, while not *that* good, was good enough to earn the Distinguished Service Medal. For his "unusual zeal, foresight, and marked administrative ability in the organization and preparation for overseas service of technical troops of the Tank Corps."

Superior ability in preparing other men for overseas service. But no luck in getting an overseas assignment for himself.

At last, however, the long-deferred hope was about to be realized. Early in November 1918 he rushed into his house waving a piece of paper and shouting triumphantly to his wife. "I've made it, darling! My orders for sailing to France!"

His wife, with a smiling face and a sinking heart, held out her hand for the paper. "It's wonderful, Ike. When do you go?"

"Here, read it."

She took the paper. "You will proceed to Camp Dix for embarkation on November 18."

But on November 11 the war was at an end. Ike Eisenhower seemed destined for a job behind the scenes.

V

NINETEEN TWENTY-ONE—a year that brought to Eisenhower a great tragedy and, though he was unaware of it at the time, the opportunity that was to culminate in his final success.

Three years earlier he had been blessed with a son—little Icky. A bright and playful and lovable little "rascal" of a child. Never after his most difficult days at the army post was Eisenhower too tired for a game of tag with Icky. The child played so eagerly, and so hard. Too hard, perhaps.

One day in December 1920 he caught cold. It developed into scarlet fever. On January 2, 1921, he died in his father's arms.

Every year thereafter, wherever he happened to be stationed, Eisenhower sent flowers to his wife on Icky's birthday.

His immediate grief at Icky's death, however, was somewhat assuaged by a new set of duties under a new command. Chief of staff to General Fox Connor, commander of the 20th Infantry in the Canal Zone. General Connor had met the young officer through George Patton. He had admired his enthusiasm, his geniality, his ability to get along with people, his quickness in sizing up a situation, and his thorough understanding of military technique. A good man to pacify the natives and to organize the defenses of the Panama Canal.

Eisenhower accepted the job with alacrity. Just what he needed to make him forget. The 20th consisted largely of Puerto Ricans—men of boiling tempers and sluggish limbs. Eisenhower did not blame them for either of these faults. They were merely the product of their tropical environment. And so, instead of bullying them into a discipline to which they had not been accustomed, he set them an example of efficiency and cheerfulness and self-restraint which many of them were only too anxious to emulate. "Look at the Headquarters—white-painted fences, pretty flower beds, spotless furniture, dusted floors. Better keep our own quarters like that." A spick-and-span commander, a spick-and-span outfit. No slovenliness in any camp with a man like *that* at the head.

And no fooling around, either. Ike Eisenhower was a combination of tactfulness and tenacity—when a friendly reminder failed, it was followed by a strict command. His soldiers loved his smile, but shriveled up before his frown. "The young man," observed General Connor, "is definitely headed for higher things."

But, for the present, his fortunes were definitely on the downgrade. In the peacetime contraction of the army, his rank had been reduced consecutively from lieutenant colonel to major and from major to captain. "No prospect of another war, and no chance for advancement in times of peace." General Connor tried repeatedly to get him into the School for the General Staff, at Leavenworth. But in vain. Instead he was appointed —once again—as a football coach. The Third Area Eleven at Camp Meade.

General Connor tried to console him. "Cheer up, son. This job, too, may have its use. Study your tactics on the football field. Try to outguess the other coach. All this knowledge will come in handy someday."

For Connor was certain that another war was coming. "And sooner than anyone thinks. Everything in Europe points to it—and in the Pacific, too." And the general was equally certain that Eisenhower possessed the necessary qualities for leadership in that war. He had observed him at his command, and he had talked to him again and again. A superb capacity for absorbing and remembering facts, for sizing up a situation and making a quick and logical decision, and for *getting things done.* "Men will follow you because they like you . . . When the time comes, I and my generation will be too old . . . It will be up to you youngsters . . . I mean you in particular . . . I want you to be ready to answer the call."

But the next call was for another "useless" job. Recruiting officer at Fort Logan. Again it was General Connor who kept up his spirits. "A good place to mark time . . . and to keep up with your studies . . . I still have faith in your star."

Perhaps, thought Ike with a grim smile. For the present his star was but an invisible flicker among the hundred million others in the American sky.

Yet life had its compensations. His presence at the recruiting office in Colorado brought his wife more closely to her parents. His wife, and their new son. All their affection was now centered in this child. It softened their pain at the loss of their other child and their disappointment at the comparative obscurity of Eisenhower's career. Happiness is not only in the glare of the sun. "Even the shadow can outline the image of God."

And thus Eisenhower, like a good soldier, was faithful to his little jobs and—at the same time—on the alert for something big. And the big opening came in the form of a telegram from General Connor. "Be ready—make no move—don't even breathe—Fox Connor."

Appointment to the General Staff School at Leavenworth.

VI

EISENHOWER had traveled a long way from West Point. Against the keenest competition of some of the army's "smartest" brains, he came out first in his class. "You are now [June 1926] marked for advancement on the Eligible List of the General Staff."

An overseas order, to prepare A Guide to American Battlefields in Europe. A golden opportunity to study at first hand the terrain and the tactics of World War I. When he returned from Europe he was an encyclopedia of information about the gigantic chessboard upon which any future war game might be played.

And then some further intensive training in the art of war. A student-officer at the War College in Washington. Major Eisenhower—he had been promoted now—had at last attracted the attention of the military leaders in the United States. An officer with a superior mind.

Nineteen hundred and thirty to 1938. The years of *depression* and *oppression*. Business failures, idle workers, closed banks. And the inevitable result of economic anarchy—political dictatorship. Madness in the saddle, savagery on the gallop without bridle or rein. Yet even now the world was asleep. Very few saw the approaching danger. Especially in the United States. "We are so far away . . . protected by two oceans . . . safe and snug in our isolated home."

But a few men with a keener vision could sense the coming storm. And one of these farsighted men was Major Eisenhower. Assigned to several important tasks—in the office of the Assistant Secretary of War, on a second mission to the battlefields of France, on the staff of General Mac-Arthur during a military inspection tour of the Philippines—he became more and more insistently aware of the military unpreparedness at home and the threatening catastrophe from abroad. Both in the East and in the West.

And yet he was descended from a long line of pacifists. He had an intense hatred against war. When Chamberlain came back from Hitler with a promise of "peace in our time," Eisenhower defended the English statesman. "Next to the loss of freedom," he explained to his son, who was now studying at a private school in the Philippines, "war is the ultimate calamity which can befall a nation . . . It is so horrible that imagination cannot grasp it in all its hideous aspects."

"But what are the chances against war," asked his son, "so long as Hitler is in power?"

"Well," smiled Ike, "there's always a chance that somebody might shoot the s.o.b."

Nineteen hundred and thirty-nine—and Eisenhower still hoped for peace. And prepared strenuously for war. He helped organize the defenses of the Philippines. The Filipinos adored him—his infectious good nature, his democratic camaraderie, his simple code of honor, his amazing capacity for work, and his utter relaxation in play.

He left the Philippines on December 13, 1939—and sailed immediately into troubled seas.

VII

WHEN HE RETURNED TO AMERICA he was amazed at its complacency. Everybody ridiculed the "phony" war in Europe and the "silly" fracas in China. "Don't you understand what the hell's going on?" he insisted. "The Germans and the Japs are aiming at the conquest of the world. *They're aiming at us!* They've been preparing for this for the past twenty years. And what have we done about it? What are we going to do when they strike?"

Nothing but jeers and boos for an answer. "Alarmist Ike!"

But Ike was not content with being an alarmist. He turned his sense of alarm into creative action. Defense against imminent attack. He was ordered to Fort Lewis as executive officer of the 15th Infantry. A wide-awake regiment which had just returned from China. The men had seen the Japanese invasion and they knew what it meant.

Knew, but remained unafraid. Their regimental crest bore the inscription, *Can Do*. "Fellows after my own heart!" said Ike.

A reciprocal feeling. The boys took their "Exec" immediately to *their* hearts. One day, as he inspected the kitchen, he saw a pile of raw meat freshly ground for hamburgers. With one hand he grabbed an onion and with the other a fistful of meat, and continued his inspection as he munched his spicy tidbit. "My God," muttered the cook, "raw meat! Tough guy!"

Tough guy, and *good* guy. Knew how to settle a soldier's quarrels without a fight. There had been a long-standing feud between two privates. There was bad blood between them, and they were always "itching for a scrap." Ike sent for them and ordered them to wash a window—one on the outside and one on the inside. For a time he watched them scowling at each other across the pane, and then he burst into laughter. The two men forgot their scowls and joined in the laugh. It was the end of their feud.

Always good-natured when his men behaved. But a whiplash of fury when they disobeyed. There was never any "monkey business" under Eisenhower's command.

And yet, fifty years old now, and only lieutenant colonel at a regimental post. But from now on the action grows faster, and more dramatic. The actors are attuned to a more accelerated peace, and those who are the most efficiently trained are hurried to the fore. Colonel Eisenhower, and then chief of staff of the Third Army, and now Brigadier General Ike. He has won his first star as official recognition for his defensive tactics in the maneuvers between the "Red" Army and the "Blue." As a result of these tactics, the battle has ended in the total "annihilation" of the "enemy's" tanks.

But it has meant terrific work. Relax for a while now and catch your breath. A December Sunday at Fort Houston. "I'm dead tired, boys. Guess I'll treat myself to a nap. Call me if anything happens."

A few minutes later it happened. The attack on Pearl Harbor.

VIII

THEY CALLED HIM TO WASHINGTON. Assistant to General Gerow, Chief of War Plans. A period of darkness and defeat. Yet here is a man who is preparing the strategy for an attack. A job for a football coach. The best *defense* is a good *offense*.

A most *efficient* coach. In March 1942 promoted to major general. Next month appointed head of operations for the United States Army. A month later ordered by General Marshall to England. On an inspection tour. To inspect and—though Eisenhower was unaware of it—to be inspected. "Let's see if he's the man."

On his return from England, General Marshall asked his British colleagues whether they would approve the assignment of Eisenhower to the chief command of the American forces in the European theater. The answer was a unanimous and enthusiastic *yes*.

General Marshall summoned Eisenhower to his office. They discussed the plans for the invasion of Africa. "In your opinion," asked the Chief of Staff, "are the plans as nearly complete as is humanly possible?"

"Yes, sir," replied Ike, "I think they are."

"And you are ready to OK them?"

"Most heartily, sir."

"I'm glad to hear this," said Marshall, "because you're the man to carry them out."

As he walked down the steps in the Munitions Building he met an old friend of his—General Francis B. Wilby. "What's the matter, Ike?" asked Wilby. "You look as if you had just swallowed a camel."

"Brother, I have!" And then, with a catch in his throat, "They're sending me over in charge of the whole shebang."

IX

GENERAL EISENHOWER'S ACHIEVEMENTS in the European theater are familiar history. Asked to deliver a message to America on the Fourth of July, he replied: "There is no time for messages until we can say them with bombs and shells."

And this is precisely how he spoke to the world until the job was completed. Dynamite for the enemy, dynamic inspiration for the allies. Here was a general who knew his *job*—a lifelong application to military science had prepared him for it—and who knew his *men*. An expert in the geography of the battlefield and in the terrain of the human soul. Cheerful—at least on the surface—when others were despondent, friendly when others were captious, daring when others were hesitant, and sincerely democratic at all times and to all men. His character was an amalgamation that cemented the soldiers of many countries into a single army. No separate Americans, or British, or Russians, or French, or Negroes, or Jews—just an undivided unit of coöperating "buddies" inspired with a single aim—Victory. Once he had occasion to praise an officer to General Hastings Ismay. "Was he British or American?" asked the general. "I honestly don't remember," grinned Eisenhower. On another occasion he dismissed an officer for calling a fellow officer a "British bastard." "I don't mind your calling him a bastard if he is one," said Ike, "but I'm damned if I'll let you call him a *British* bastard."

The selfsame unruffled courtesy in victory and defeat. Jealousy against him within the army, criticism at home—"Why did he do this, and why didn't he do that?"—accusations that he was playing politics—"What business had he to negotiate with Darlan?"—clamors for his removal during the Battle of the Bulge—"Why didn't he anticipate von Rundstedt's attack?"—and through it all he acknowledged his mistakes, accepted his defeats, and worked indefatigably toward the final day. "I *know* we shall win!"

And every last soldier in the ranks had caught fire from this dynamic leadership; and they, too, knew that they would win. When he visited a contingent in the field, they shouted themselves hoarse in their adoration for "Ike, Ike, Ike!"

And then, as the invasion was nearing the end, even his critics were convinced. His mistakes had meant but the human groping of genius instinctively bent upon the one right course. In the international rivalry of human affairs there can be no greater tribute to a man than the homage of a foreign press. "The charge entrusted to Supreme Commander Eisenhower," wrote the *London Times*, "meant nothing less than the liberation of the continent . . . No choice could have been more acceptable to all the Allied Services."

X

He came back from the war with the "same size hat." Throughout the ovations that greeted him across the land, he remained the selfsame man that he had always been. An American with a democratic vision, a brilliant mind, and a modest soul. More than ever now he hated war and longed for a world-wide coöperation in which the common man would be able to "preserve his freedom of worship, his equality before the law, his liberty to speak and act as he sees fit, subject only to provisions that he trespass not upon the similar rights of others."

Appointed to the presidency of Columbia University (1947), he accepted this latest honor—like all the others—with humility and a smile. Asked, in a press interview, whether he preferred to be called General Eisenhower or President Eisenhower, he replied: "Please call me by the name I like best of all. Just plain Ike."

And this was the name the people liked best of all when they elected him, in 1952, to the Presidency of the United States. "I like Ike" was the slogan that helped to sweep him into the White House by the biggest popular vote in American history.

Eisenhower has brought to the office of President the same dignity and fair-mindedness that distinguished his previous public roles. No American has ever functioned more successfully as President of all the people, despite their party labels and partisan prejudices. He has salvaged the Republican Party and raised it to a position of strong political influence once again and he has infused free private enterprise with a new vitality. Like most men who have been close to the horrors of the battlefield, he abhors war. One of his first achievements as President was to help terminate the Korean War and bring American soldiers home to their families and jobs. Instead of putting government into business as had been the practice of the New and Fair Dealers, Ike has put business back into government. He has gathered around him a team of able businessmen who have administered according to the highest standards of business efficiency. Ike's chief problem today, as it was when he was a commanding general, is to maintain the freedom not only of America, but of all peoples who are unwilling to be bullied into totalitarianism. He believes in a strong America because, as he puts it, "Only strength can coöperate . . . Weakness . . . can only beg." In a speech during a tour of New Hampshire, Eisenhower simply and eloquently expressed the goals of his foreign policy. They are an epitome of his social philosophy. "We merely want to live in peace with all the world, to trade with them, to commune with them, to learn from their culture as they may learn from ours . . . so that the products of our toil may be used for our schools and our roads and our churches and not for guns and planes and tanks and ships of war."

IMPORTANT DATES IN THE LIFE OF DWIGHT DAVID EISENHOWER

1890—October 14, born, Denison, Texas.

1892—Parents moved to Abilene, Kansas.

1915—Graduated from West Point.

1918–19—Served as instructor at tank training centers in United States.

1921—Appointed to staff of General Connor in Canal Zone.

1930–38—Instructor at various camps, two inspection trips to France and preparation of manual on *American Battlefields in Europe*.

1939—Served on staff of General MacArthur in the Philippines.

1942—Appointed commander of Allied forces in invasion of Africa.

1944—Appointed commander-in-chief of Allied forces in invasion of Europe.

1945—Represented United States in Allied Military Government of Germany. Appointed Chief of Staff of United States Army.

1947—Chosen president of Columbia University.

1952—Elected President of the United States.

1953—Helped terminate Korean War.

1955—Met leaders of Russia in Geneva to work out a program for avoiding atomic war.

1955—Stricken with coronary thrombosis. Recovered.

Helen Hayes

1900–

Mrs. charles macarthur of Nyack, New York, is a friendly, outgoing person. She is frequently seen on the streets airing her spaniel, Caesar; she appears at civic functions, gets as passionately stirred as her fellow townsmen over community issues. Mrs. MacArthur is like thousands of other Americans living in small towns, except for one thing: she has a second life as well; to millions of theater and movie goers she is Helen Hayes, first lady of the stage and screen.

Miss Hayes has none of the qualities usually associated with stage queens—stateliness, beautiful features, fiery sex appeal. She is barely five feet tall. When she first went to Hollywood to test for a movie, Louis B. Mayer shook his head; he wondered how his make-up men could infuse sex appeal into her. "Well, we'll just have to keep you acting every minute."

Like the pitcher who strikes out batters with only a dinky curve but plenty of head and heart, Helen Hayes has conquered the stage and screen with her brainy acting and her elfin charm. For twenty-five years she has ruled the roost in a variety of roles. She is the girl every soldier leaves behind when he goes to war; and the mother every farm boy keeps a hallowed memory of as he sows his oats in the big city. She is the wistful, unborn daughter in every daddy's heart—the enchanted child who might have been, who meets a prince charming during the peak of a fairy-tale professional career and is crowned queen to be happy forever.

But even this tiny woman who has shared with America her own bubbling happiness has not been spared the sting of sorrow.

II

Helen hayes brown was born in 1900 in Washington D. C., the daughter of a sales manager for a wholesale butcher. Her mother had always wanted to be an actress but never got further than a week's engagement in stock. As a baby Helen was not pretty. She had a tuft of heavy black hair that grew close over her nose and gave her an owl-like expression. But this incongruity was offset by her beautiful blue eyes.

From the time she walked she assumed the airs of an actress. Once her mother put her into a bathtub and left her to play while preparing supper. When she returned she found the child had draped a towel around her head in Egyptian fashion and was waving a palm leaf as she lay indolently in the tub. "I'm Cleopatra in her bath." Her mother stared at her in astonishment; then she recalled that she had recently taken the child to an art gallery where there had been a painting of Cleopatra in her *barge*. Helen had simply misunderstood one word.

When Helen was five, a friend of the Browns started a stock company. He told her father he had a role for a child who could remember her lines. "Why don't you let Helen try," suggested Mr. Brown. "I'll bet she can remember them!"

This was Helen's introduction to the stage. Since she was still too young to read, her mother taught her the part. This led to other stock engagements. The Browns had no idea Helen would make acting her career. Indeed there was some indication that she had leanings toward music.

When she was six she was taken to hear Mischa Elman give a violin recital. Throughout the concert, Helen fidgeted with excitement. On the way home she kept up a feverish run of chatter. Her mother, believing she had been overstimulated by the music, said to her husband that evening, "Look what the concert did to Helen. We can't deny her violin lessons any longer." Unfortunately, Helen's ecstasy had nothing to do with Mischa Elman. It was the prelude to an attack of the measles.

In those days child actresses were stereotyped. Their hair was bleached golden and curled like a French doll's. They wore dresses that barely covered their rumps. Helen, with her unbleached hair, her long plain dresses, stood out like a sore thumb. But one showman was sufficiently impressed to sign her up—Lew Fields, the comedian.

When Helen's father learned that Fields wanted her to make the stage her career, he objected. He had given her permission to play in stock with no serious purpose. He felt that acting was an undignified career and he refused to have the name of Brown associated with it. But Helen's mother supported Fields.

"OK," suggested the comedian. "We'll cut off the Brown and just call her Helen Hayes. It will take up less space in lights."

Helen opened with Fields in *Old Dutch*, a musical whose score was composed by Victor Herbert. Although she was too tiny to reach the mirror in her dressing room, she insisted upon putting on her make up herself. She was lifted onto a shelf and she sat with a box of grease paint daubing herself before each show.

This child with the grave manners entranced sophisticated New York audiences and captivated the heart of Fields himself. The hardened old trouper became passionately fond of Helen. When *Old Dutch*, after a successful Broadway run, went on tour, Fields was faced with a problem. Most cities allowed children under sixteen to play on the stage; but when the cast entrained for Chicago, Field's agent wired that the city law would prevent Helen from making an appearance there. Fields sent for an adult midget to take Helen's place; but after several rehearsals, he muttered, "I just can't play those scenes without Helen!" He contacted a high ranking city official and the provision was lifted temporarily for Helen.

After completing her tour in *Old Dutch*, Helen continued to delight audiences in other roles. One opening night Diamond Jim Brady occupied a box with Lillian Russell and the orchestra scintillated with a clientele that usually reserved their jewels for the opening of the Metropolitan Opera. Long before the days of Jackie Coogan, Shirley Temple, and other child stars of the movies, Helen Hayes had become the toast of America.

She was as indolent as she was talented. She made no effort to train for her roles. Like Topsy she just "growed" into them. During rehearsals she did not even bother to say her lines aloud. When her cue was announced she would tap her head and say her lines to herself. At first her managers were afraid she was not learning her part and would cause a fiasco on opening night. But soon they became aware of her fabulous memory. On opening nights she would suddenly become brilliantly vocal and score a new triumph. Lew Fields had a theory for her strange behavior. He was certain that she had Scotch blood. "She had to see $2 in every seat before she could act."

At eight Helen was already a veteran trouper who had played in one-night stands throughout America. She arrived in one town during a violent blizzard and was directed with her mother to quarters above a saloon. All night the fumes of alcohol were wafted up to them and roisterers ruined their sleep. The theater in which Helen played had no doors on the dressing room. Sheets had to be hung over the openings. There was no running water or lavatory plumbing. The cast washed with ice water.

This was the "golden age" of the show trouper, before the present era of fancy summer theaters and plush hotels, when stars like John Drew, William Gillette, and Maude Adams toured the hinterlands under extremely rugged conditions. Like her colleagues who cherish the theater for its heroic associations, Helen Hayes looks back on those days with nostalgia.

As she grew more and more skillful as an actress, she projected illusions that fooled experts. In her teens she took part in a school debate over a public issue of the times, the building of the Panama Canal. Present in the audience was Joseph Tumulty, secretary to President Wilson. He and the other judges were so impressed with Helen's grasp of politics that they suggested she go to law school and become an attorney. Helen said afterwards to her mother, "I don't know any more about the Panama Canal than you do. I merely studied the arguments like a part in a play and I gave a performance. The reference books I had stacked at my elbow were merely props. Please, Mother, let me stay in the theater."

Though Helen continued to mature in her technique, she remained physically small. At fourteen she could have passed for a child of ten. At sixteen she was anxious to quit child roles and play ingénues. But the managers were perplexed. She did not look a day over twelve. On one occasion when Helen learned there was a role open for an ingénue, she eagerly primed herself for it. She practiced crossing her legs and smoking cigarettes—but to no avail; the part was given another actress. Another time when she received a summons for a tryout, uncertain as to whether the manager was casting for a child or an ingénue role, she dressed to play it both ways. She wore her hair down like a child's but put on high heels. People stared at her as she walked to the manager's office. Again she was turned down as an ingénue. She began to fear she would have to play children for the rest of her life.

To grow taller became an obsession. She looked forward to each new birthday hoping it would increase her height. Each year, regardless of the current fashion, she dropped her skirts an inch or two to signify her increasing maturity. But people refused to be deceived.

After one performance, Mary Garden, the opera star, visited Helen in her dressing room. Instead of shaking hands with Helen she placed her hand on the actress's stomach and muttered, "Why she hasn't the diaphragm of a baby, but what extraordinary carrying powers her voice has! It's astonishing!"

At sixteen Helen played the lead in a road company version of *Pollyanna*. A puppy and kitten who were used in the first act and were known as "Sodom" and "Gomorrah" traveled with the cast and frolicked in the hotels and trains, causing commotion along the way.

In the haphazard scheduling of road shows at that time, the play did not always fit the audiences. *Pollyanna*, a sticky little piece with a schoolgirl theme, had trying times with the backwoods customers who stomped into the playhouses. One night when the cast arrived in a town in Montana, the theater manager said to Helen: "Your show better be good, young lady. The theater's been sold out to cowboys just in from a roundup. If they don't like the entertainment, they're liable to start shooting through the ceiling!"

Before the performance, Helen looked out of a peephole in the curtain and saw an audience consisting of hombres in ten gallon hats, spitting tobacco and fingering shooting irons. Her stomach was ready to turn over. However, as the play progressed, she noticed the men were blowing their noses to hide their tears. The cast left the theater as quickly as possible, passing rows of horses hitched to the posts of saloons. "We were anxious to get out of that town pronto," Helen reminisces. "We weren't kidding ourselves. The cowboys were sobbing at the play because they were drunk. If they ever found out when they sobered up that they had paid their money to see a Sunday-school play, they would have shot us on the spot!"

One of Helen's peculiarities was that she had a phobia for noise. Indeed, she trained herself to ignore applause and therefore was frequently unable to gauge the effect of her acting on an audience. One comedy role called for her to hide in a closet holding a revolver in her hand. Behind the closet door she was supposed to sneeze. As the revolver went off, another actor was supposed to rush to the door, open it and Helen would stagger out with a smoking revolver in her hand.

However, since Helen could not stand the noise, a property man would be stationed out of sight of the audience. When Helen entered the closet she would hand the revolver to the property man who would shoot it off while she stuffed fingers in her ears to deaden the report. Then he would put the smoking revolver into her hand as the closet door was opened. He also had a spare revolver in case the first failed to go off.

One night Helen sneezed as usual but the revolver did not go off. The trigger was stuck; a moment later, the property man pulled the trigger of the spare revolver; and although it was twice the size of the gun Helen was supposed to be holding, he handed it to her. Then, by accident, the property man released the trigger of the first gun which was no longer jammed and the loud bang almost ripped Helen's ears apart. She staggered out of the closet white as a ghost. The audience broke into gales of laughter. Helen went through the rest of the play with her knees quaking. When the curtain fell, she exclaimed, "What a blood-thirsty audience! Couldn't these people see I was scared to death!"

Even in playing juvenile roles, Helen was noted for her meticulous attention to details. When she began rehearsing for the part of the dream child in Barrie's *Dear Brutus*, she was horrified to hear how incongruous her Southern accent was as she spoke Barrie's lines. At first she thought of giving up the role but her manager insisted that she stick with it. "Quitting this part would be a tragedy; it is the coward's way out. You will simply have to sweat to overcome your accent."

Helen bought a copy of Shakespeare's *Sonnets* on the way home from rehearsal and she spent days reading them aloud to her mother. Morning, noon, and night they had sonnets for conversation. Her diction gradually improved and with it her interpretation of the role. She achieved a heart-warming triumph in *Dear Brutus*.

On a much earlier occasion she had been given a role which required her to deliver one line, "Good evening," in Polish. The head of the beauty parlor in the neighborhood where Helen and her mother lived was a Pole. "Look, Mother," she suggested, "why don't you have your hair done in the beauty parlor. I'll accompany you and while he is working on you he can repeat 'Good evening' several times. I can learn that way." It cost Mrs. Brown five dollars but it was worth it. For a role in another Barrie play

Helen hunted up a Scotch fortune teller to learn the exact nuances of the accent used by Scots.

At sixteen Helen got her first "crush" on a man, Alfred Lunt, who acted with her in *Clarence*, a play about a discharged soldier that opened on Broadway shortly after the Armistice. Lunt had just fallen in love with the glamorous Lynn Fontanne and, needless to say, he had no eyes for a sixteen-year-old miss who looked as if she were still attending grammar school. Helen carried her torch in secret. Today she is one of the most ardent supporters of the fabulous Lunts.

Alfred Lunt's part in *Clarence* called for him to play the saxophone. During rehearsals there was one high note he simply could not get right and he kept the cast in stitches with his jokes about it. "It's the spirit of Adelina Patti, the opera singer, coming back for another farewell performance!"

Clarence was a smash hit. When the curtain fell on opening night, the audience tore up their programs and showered the pieces around like confetti. Men tossed their hats into the air; many a customer went home bareheaded or with somebody else's topper. The cast was mobbed by crowds as it left the theater.

Despite her small stature, Helen's technical brilliance finally won her ingénue roles and her greatest performance during this period was as the all-American debutante in Booth Tarkington's *Babs*. Helen was nineteen. When the play opened in Boston, the Hollis theater was jammed with Beacon Hill debutantes and blue bloods from Harvard. After one matinee, a young Harvard man called at the stage door to see her. Helen's mother asked him what he wanted. He blushed to the roots of his hair. "I want Miss Hayes's corset. I've been dared to bring it home as a fraternity initiation."

On another occasion, as Helen left the theater, a Harvard student rushed over and fell on his knees before her. "I have the honor of asking your hand in marriage." Then, as bystanders cheered, he mumbled, "Look, Miss Hayes, I don't mean this; but I had to do it for my fraternity." Helen turned to her mother with a twinkle. "What audacity! He might at least have given me the opportunity to refuse him!"

During the Boston run of *Babs*, Helen continued to be the sweetheart of Harvard. The new jazz age described by F. Scott Fitzgerald, the Princetonian, had seized Harvard too. Helen was bombarded with proposals. One collegiate asked her to come with him to Peru. She strolled with him on the Boston Common as he painted a glowing picture of their future. Finally when "I got to know every blade of grass and my tongue was hanging out, I asked him to buy me a soda." But the suitor had only fifteen cents in his pockets, ten of which was for carfare back to Cambridge. He bought her a nickel Hershey bar and helped her eat it. So ended the Peruvian dream.

At one point tragedy marred the run of *Babs*. An actor who played

Helen's father had a lengthy scene with her in the third act. When he made his entrance one evening his face was ashen and he stumbled over to her. "I've forgotten my lines!" She gave him his cue. A minute later he whispered "What do I say?" Once more she gave him his cue; but his eyes had gone vacant. Suddenly he put his hand over his heart and slumped against her. They carried him to the wings; he died of a coronary thrombosis on the way to the hospital. But true to the traditions of the theater, the show went on. Helen's role called for her to remain on the stage until the end. Limp with shock she played scene after scene sitting in a chair. But her voice remained firm and she gave everything she had to the part.

With *Babs*, Helen's reputation as an ingénue was assured. And she received a final accolade. Her name went up in electric lights. This momentous occasion took place when *Babs* reached Springfield, Massachusetts, on its tour. The manager directed Helen to a bench in a park directly facing the theater and pointed to the blazing marquee. "Well, Helen, you've made it!"

"My job's only begun. I'll have to work mighty hard to keep it there." Whenever she had a spare moment she sneaked out to the park bench and gazed up at her name "in diamonds."

Now that she was an established star, her manager took pains to surround her with an atmosphere of glamor. In those days, the top actresses were discouraged by their managers from making public appearances outside of the theater. Charles Frohman even prohibited Maude Adams from riding with strangers in the elevator that took her to her hotel room. When Ethel Barrymore ate several meals in a restaurant, Frohman declared it took him a full year to restore the illusion about her. "Nobody will pay to see a star if they can see her any time for nothing!"

Helen Hayes, however, was too unpretentious a person to be impressed with these glamor-building stunts. She resisted every attempt of her manager to keep her wrapped in cellophane and she continued to remain as unaffected as the woman next door.

Nevertheless, she had to make one concession. She hired a maid to attend her in the dressing room. The candidate, who was sent by the Jeanne d'Arc Home for an interview, turned out to be a Tartar.

"I have never worked for anybody in the theater before," she said in broken English. "I have worked only for *ladies*."

When Helen asked her name, she replied, "Marthe Bastard."

Not certain she had heard correctly, Helen asked her to write the name out on paper. Sure enough—there was no mistake about it. After a pause the girl said, "I'd like to have my mail sent to the theater. How do I write the address?"

Helen fully appreciated what her fellow actors and the stage hands would do with the name "Bastard" when they observed it on an envelope. Tactfully she broached the subject of the maid's changing the last three letters of the name. "We don't want anyone making jokes about you,

Marthe. How about calling yourself Miss *Baston?* That's close enough to the original."

Marthe shrugged. "You can change my name if you desire, Madam, although I see nothing wrong with it. After all it *is* in the dictionary."

The theater, as actresses know from tragic experience, is the most precarious of professions. An actress sits on top of the world as long as her play draws packed houses. If her next vehicle turns out to be a turkey her debts begin to mount. Even after her name was in lights, there were financially lean years for Helen.

After one run of bad luck at the box office, she was invited by Dudley Digges to join a group of other actors on their uppers who were establishing a summer theater at Woodstock, New York. "Some of us will paint the scenery," Digges explained, "others will make the costumes and the props; we'll put on a grand season."

Helen joined the Digges company in Woodstock. Its first play opened in a ramshackle barn. The roof was leaky; no flooring had been laid and straw was spread under the seats. In the middle of the play a thunder storm broke and drenched the audience. People rushed for their cars without waiting for the curtain to fall.

Despite these hardships the experience was fun. Woodstock has become an affectionate memory for many artists.

During this period of financial insecurity, George Kaufman and Marc Connolly, fresh from their smash hit *Dulcy,* called on Helen to read a play they had written for her. "Do you play the piano?" Kaufman inquired. "Your playing has an important bearing on the play." Although Helen did not play the piano, she replied without batting an eyelash. "Of course." "Fine, Miss Hayes," chimed in Connolly. "You'll sing an old spiritual and accompany yourself on the piano."

When they left Helen turned to her mother. "We've got to rent a piano right away."

At that moment their bank balance was meager. But that was only part of the difficulty. "How are you going to learn to play and sing a spiritual in six weeks, Helen?"

"I'll do it."

When they entered Wurlitzer's, the clerk suggested, "Why don't you *buy* a piano? You pay out as though you were renting it."

"Well—we'll have to take the cheapest one."

Helen engaged a teacher who taught her the spiritual by ear. However when she tried singing and playing it she found that her fingers and her voice refused to work together. They had a colored cook who was greatly disturbed at the way Helen was singing the spiritual. Mrs. Brown relieved the colored girl of her cooking chores for a week and she became Helen's singing teacher. Then, after the girl went back to the kitchen, Helen stood for hours beside her at the sink humming the tune with her until she grasped all the nuances of the untutored Negro voice. Helen gave a successful performance in this play that turned out to be a hit.

One success led to another. The Kaufman play was followed by an offer from the Theatre Guild. The Guild was the aristocracy among theatrical producers and most actors would have grabbed at the chance to play for it practically for nothing because of the prestige involved. When Miss Teresa Helburn of the Guild called up and offered Helen the role of Cleopatra in Bernard Shaw's *Caesar and Cleopatra,* she was astounded. Known as "America's leading actress without sex appeal," she had never dreamed that she would be offered the chance to play the foremost siren in history. And precisely because she was nettled by her critics and anxious to prove that she could bring sex to this role, Helen would have snatched up the Guild's offer at any price. But by chance her mother who had a shrewd business head picked up the phone.

"What will Miss Hayes's salary be?" she asked coolly.

"Two hundred and fifty dollars a week and two per cent over eight thousand."

Mrs. Brown hung up.

The phone rang again. Once more Miss Helburn was speaking. "We were cut off."

"No we weren't," retorted Helen's mother. "I hung up. There was no answer to be made to your ridiculous proposal."

However, after further bargaining, the salary was set at three hundred and fifty a week and Helen signed.

When news passed along the grapevine that Helen Hayes had been cast for Cleopatra there was head shaking. George Jean Nathan, the critic, wrote: "In our opinion, while we think Miss Hayes a good actress, we do not think she is biologically suited to the part."

During rehearsals, Helen was seated in a restaurant booth when she overheard two men discussing show business. One of them remarked, "Helen Hayes playing Cleopatra is the most absurd piece of casting ever done in the theater. What does *she* know about life?"

Despite this discouraging attitude on the public's part Helen stuck doggedly to the job of portraying the voluptuous young queen of Egypt. And before one of the most dazzling first-night audiences in New York's theatrical history she scored a magnificent *tour de force.*

Following her success as one queen, Maxwell Anderson approached her to play another and she achieved a triumph in *Mary of Scotland.* Mary had been a tall woman and Helen added four inches of padding in her shoes. But the illusion she created on the stage was not due to physical causes primarily. After a performance, Dr. William Lyon Phelps came backstage and said, "You grow before our very eyes; you appear every inch of Mary Stuart's six feet!"

"Well, if you must know, I *think* myself tall," replied the actress.

III

JUST BEFORE her success in *Mary of Scotland*, Helen was invited to a
tea party at the studio of Miss Neysa McMain, an artist. Here she met
a whimsical young man, Charlie MacArthur, the dramatist whose play
Lulu Belle had captivated New York and who was shortly to collaborate
with Ben Hecht on an even more resounding success, *The Front Page*.
The son of a minister from Scranton, Pennsylvania, Charlie was a rolling
stone who gave off the blaze of a diamond. During the first World War
he walked out of the American army and joined the Canadian Black
Watch to get into the fighting sooner. After the Armistice he became one
of the ace reporters in Chicago, keeping the town on edge with his flamboyant antics and torrid news beats in the era of Al Capone and elegant
gangster funerals.

Migrating to New York, he became a leading wit of Broadway, be-
guiling even the highly discriminating George S. Kaufman, Dorothy
Parker, and Franklin Adams with his droll manners.

And now he laid siege to Mary of Scotland. Upon meeting Helen he
handed her a fistful of peanuts to munch on. "I regret that I cannot
offer you emeralds."

Helen was twenty-nine when she gave her heart to this young *boule-
vardier*. Charlie had already been married once, to a Miss Carlyle Frink.
He had impulsively popped the question during a tour of Coney Island.
But the first Mrs. MacArthur was unable to seal up Puck with a wedding
ring. Unable to match or understand his mercurial nature, she was relieved
to let him go. During the divorce proceedings she said, "I wouldn't take him
back if he came wrapped in a crackerjack box!"

But the lady who played queens was able to keep pace with Charlie.
Helen and Charlie were married in 1928 and their life together has been
one of the true fairy tales of Broadway.

MacArthur could not even become a father without creating a sensation.
The whole nation had to get in on the proceedings. While playing in
Coquette Helen became pregnant. When the play reached Los Angeles
on tour, Helen was compelled to leave the cast to have her baby. Since
Coquette could not draw audiences without her, it was decided to terminate the run. According to their Equity contract, actors were ordinarily entitled to two weeks' severance pay; this pay could only be waived by "an
act of God." The management decided that Helen's delivery was an act of
God and withheld the pay. The dispute went to the American Federation
of Labor; the press headlined the case and for several weeks the entire
country debated whether or not Helen's baby was an act of God. Finally
the AFL ruled that it was not an act of God, and under pressure from it
the management paid the cast its severance money. Henceforth, Helen's
little girl was known as the "Act of God" baby.

While Helen was in the hospital Charlie told her he was fixing up a nursery. When she saw it she was astounded. The chief article in the room was a pool table. Little Mary MacArthur learned to walk by holding on to the edge of the table, and when she grew tall enough to see over the top, she played for hours throwing the balls into the pockets.

For the child's first birthday Charlie told his wife he would fill the house with their friends. Helen was skeptical that sophisticated adults would come out in force to celebrate the birthday of a baby. But she had underestimated her husband. Charlie had sent invitations asking the recipients to meet Al Capone.

Despite his love of fun, Charlie continued to work hard at his profession and he achieved new professional heights. One year after his marriage, he teamed up with Ben Hecht to produce *The Front Page*. And after this came *Twentieth Century* and the memorable movies, *The Scoundrel* and *Crime Without Passion*.

Helen, too, was lured to Hollywood and she experienced some of her most satisfying triumphs—and bitterest disappointments—in her screen work. At first the movie nabobs, deploring her lack of "sexiness," were dubious about her prospects. "If only you had Norma Shearer's face," Louis B. Mayer sighed.

Helen was depressed with Hollywood. The very first day she returned from the set she told her mother, "On the first shot, half a dozen cameramen got into a huddle and discussed the best way of lighting my face, which from their pantomiming I gather must be the ugliest they had ever had to work on . . . I know I'm no beauty, but on the stage with simple make up I have been complimented on my looks."

When this picture, *The Sin of Madelon Claudet*, was given a preview, Helen and Charlie went to see it and were heartsick. The production, the direction, were wretched. They slunk out of the theater and got into their car where they sat without a word. Finally, a Metro executive came over and said consolingly, "You know brilliant acting on the stage is worthless here in Hollywood."

The picture was shelved by Metro and marked down as a failure. However, Irving Thalberg, one of the more imaginative producers in Hollywood, returned from Europe, viewed the film and decided it could be salvaged. The scenario was rewritten; Helen developed a new interpretation for her part. Scenes were retaken and the picture was previewed again. Neither Helen nor her husband attended this preview and when friends told them that the audience was enthusiastic they scoffed at the reports. Only when the picture was near the end of its run in New York did they summon up courage to see it. As the picture unfolded, Helen, recalling the hard work and heartbreak associated with the filming of it, began to groan to herself. A man sitting behind her and not recognizing who she was, leaned forward, tears pouring down his cheeks, "If you don't like the picture, other people do, so shut up or I'll call the usher!"

The Sin of Madelon Claudet had been snatched from the brink of disaster and turned into one of the most dramatic successes ever enjoyed by Hollywood, thanks to the persistency of Irving Thalberg.

Helen followed this by playing opposite Ronald Colman in *Arrowsmith* for Samuel Goldwyn and opposite Gary Cooper in *A Farewell to Arms*. And now she dominated Hollywood as absolutely as she ruled Broadway. But the movie Moguls were unable to find any more adequate roles for her. She made one picture based on a third-rate script that had been adapted from a second-rate novel. As bad as the script was, Hollywood censors insisted upon cuts for the sake of "morality" that would have made it even worse. Even the studio heads were shocked and they pleaded with Helen to see Mr. Breen, the censor, and talk him out of the cuts. Helen felt like telling Mr. Breen, "I can't agree with you on rejecting this script on moral grounds, but if you will only reject it on the grounds of art, I am with you heartily!" But she knew that this would break the hearts of the studio heads and so she suffered in silence until the film was completed; and then she returned to Broadway, fed up with Hollywood.

Now at the age of thirty-five, at the height of her technical brilliance, she was offered the role for which she will be remembered above all others. While she was spending the summer at Nyack in 1935, Gilbert Miller, her producer, who was visiting London, sent her a play about Queen Victoria written by Lawrence Housman, the English poet. Miller wanted her to examine *Victoria Regina* as a possible vehicle for the fall. Helen was worn out from work. She put the book away in her library and forgot about it. Several weeks later, looking for something to leaf through, she picked up *Victoria Regina* and took it with her to read down by her swimming pool. In no time, she was under its spell. She heard several of her house guests coming down to the pool and, unwilling to be interrupted by them, she disappeared into the shower room, locked the door and continued to read the play standing against the wall. As she finished the last scene, tears poured down her face. The thought occurred to her that Gilbert Miller, not hearing from her, had offered the role to someone else. She became so frantic that she could hardly unlock the door. She rushed by her guests at the pool without a word, sent a telegram to Gilbert Miller, "I must do *Victoria Regina*. Cable me immediately if OK."

The answer came back, "The play is yours."

In preparing for the role of Victoria, Helen undertook meticulous research. She traveled to London and toured the museums and galleries to collect data on the British queen. Charles Laughton brought her to Kensington Palace and showed her the bed the young Victoria had slept in before she ascended the throne. The play called for Helen to portray the queen at all ages. With Laughton, an expert in make up, she discussed how to make up her face to resemble the fat round countenance with baggy cheeks that had been characteristic of the queen at sixty. Laughton suggested that she put a slice of apple in each cheek. Helen visited the elderly Marchioness of Milford-Haven, who was Victoria's granddaughter, for side lights about the queen's behavior. At first Helen had some misgivings that her American accent would be inappropriate for the queen, but she learned that Victoria had spoken with a thick German accent. The Marchioness informed her, "My grandmutter spoke chust as gut Anglish as I do."

Helen practiced speaking with the same degree of accent as the Marchioness. She absorbed herself in the personality of Victoria to the extent of ordering authentic copies, even to the material, of the gowns the queen had worn.

Victoria Regina opened in New York on December 26, 1935. The first nine scenes were received with applause, but when the curtain went up on the final scene, showing the queen at sixty seated at a table in Balmoral Castle with a widow's bonnet over her puffy red face, the audience gasped. People whispered, "That can't be Helen Hayes!" Others exclaimed, "Good God, it's impossible for an actress to change like this!"

When Helen began to speak her lines the applause became deafening, and for several minutes she was unable to continue.

After the curtain fell, her dressing room was mobbed with well-wishers. But the greatest tribute of all came, unwittingly, from a Russian countess who had never before seen the star. "It is so extraordinary, Miss Hayes, how you managed to look *so youthful* in the opening scenes!" So vividly had she played the part of old age that the countess could not believe she was actually thirty-five. The only dissent to her portrayal came from Count Cavadonga, the great-grandson of Victoria. "I'm afraid you made Victoria a much sweeter woman than my mother told me she was. I understand she was an old shrew."

But if Helen erred at all, it was the fault of her heart, not her head.

During the two-year run of *Victoria Regina*, Helen took on other commitments which gave her a busy time of it. She signed to do a radio show on Monday nights from eight to eight-thirty. To meet the demands of a tight schedule, she would go to the theater at seven, apply make up and dress as Victoria. Then, putting on a coat with a zipper and a hood that covered her wig of long hair, she would go up to the radio station in a private elevator. When her broadcast was over, she would rush down to her car; the chauffeur had the engine running. A policeman stood on the running board and, while the chauffeur kept the siren going, the way was cleared from the studio to the theater. Upon her arrival at the stage door her maids would hand her her powder puff and mirror, give her zipper a pull, and the actress would step out of her coat and onto the set.

With the closing of *Victoria Regina*, the first lady of the stage undertook new portrayals with the humility that has characterized all her work. She appeared in *Ladies and Gentlemen*, a light comedy written by

her husband and Ben Hecht; she gave an incomparable portrayal in Mary
Chase's whimsical *Mrs. MacThing*; she played Harriet Beecher Stowe.
Curiously enough, she has always stood in awe of Shakespearean roles, but
when she finally undertook to play Portia in *The Merchant of Venice*,
she brought to it dimensions that had not been achieved by any other
actress. A celebrated lawyer who was present in the audience remarked
that this was the first time he had ever seen a Portia who looked intelligent
enough to pass a bar exam.

IV

IN HER MIDDLE FIFTIES, Helen Hayes is still the acknowledged queen of
the stage. She has received honors from all over the world. She has been
given the degree of Doctor of Letters and she received the first Academy
Award from Hollywood for her acting in *The Sin of Madelon Claudet*.
She lives with her husband in Nyack, New York, in a house packed
with antique furniture. Amid these relics is a plaster cast of Helen's
expressive hands. In vivid contrast to the past are the modern paintings
which the actress has collected with a passion commensurate with her
love for antiques.

Her neighbors relish her as a simple woman. She is too genuine a
person to permit them to be awed by her. Once when the Nyack police
department staged a benefit in the town hall she was asked to make a
brief speech. Just before she went on, the master of ceremonies, a local
boy, came over with an anxious look, "Gee, Mrs. MacArthur, I forgot to
ask you. You want a piano in your act?"

No two people will ever grow old more gracefully than Mr. and Mrs.
MacArthur. Throughout their married life, Charlie has supplied the
rollicking touch that has served to supplement her seriousness. Whenever
she is on tour, he calls her long distance, stretched out comfortably with
the telephone on his stomach, quipping for minutes on end regardless of
the cost.

Charlie's airy disregard for money was manifested early in their wedded
life. He once called her long distance during a tour and announced that
he had taken a five-year lease on an apartment back home. Since she had
not seen the rooms she was disturbed. The following night he phoned
again, "Don't worry, dear. You didn't seem very enthusiastic about the
apartment as I described it—so I cancelled it and I signed a five-year
lease on another one!"

Charlie loves to frequent the Stork and the 21 clubs; both are keen
competitors and he is not above playing a joke on their owners, close
friends of his. Once he brought his wife to the 21 and after looking over
the menu, muttered, "Same old food." He summoned the owner, asked for
a telephone to be plugged in at the table. Then he called up the Stork and
asked for the headwaiter. "What do you have for dinner tonight?" The

headwaiter read items from the menu. Charlie ordered a dinner for two and then, as the owner of the 21 stood by in a stew, he added: "And send it over right away, please—to Mr. and Mrs. Charles MacArthur at 21."

Yet even this couple, so zestful in their hold on life, have not been spared suffering. In 1949, Mary MacArthur, their daughter, died of poliomyelitis. At six Mary had appeared briefly with her mother in *Victoria Regina.* A beautiful girl at nineteen, she had already played a number of roles in summer stock and was looked upon as a gifted young actress by the critics. It was while preparing for her first appearance on Broadway that she succumbed to polio.

The sympathy which Helen's family and friends displayed in the weeks that followed moved her to declare afterwards: "For forty-one years I gorged myself with success and happiness . . . I never knew what it was to need people. But I have been made aware in the last year . . . I suppose you might say, this last year I fell in love with the human race."

Now for the first time the actress became dissatisfied with being isolated behind the footlights in fairy tales. She felt a need to take a more active part socially in the world. She accepted a role of leadership in the fight against infantile paralysis, rallying the nation's women to contribute money and encouragement to research. She became friendly with Dr. Jonas Salk and was among the first to wire congratulations when he developed his polio vaccine.

Though mellowed by suffering, Helen continues to approach the stage with zest. She is concerned over the shortage of young actresses who are being trained to replace her and her contemporaries. "The leading stars, Katherine Cornell, Ethel Barrymore, Lynn Fontanne, are all in their fifties or older. Who's going to play the Juliets?"

Continually now she dwells on this theme. "There are so many talents waiting to be nurtured now. I want to find a new talent and develop it. I planned to do it with my daughter. Now I shall do it for someone else."

Recently Helen Hayes participated in the drama, *The Skin of Our Teeth,* which was set up by the American National Theater and Academy for Salute to France. This production was one of three, including also *Medea* and *Oklahoma,* which were sent over to Paris as a good-will gesture.

IMPORTANT DATES IN THE LIFE OF
HELEN HAYES

1900—October 10, born in Washington D.C.

1908—Played first Broadway role, in *Old Dutch.*

1915—Graduated from Sacred Heart Convent.

1918—Scored stage triumph in *Dear Brutus.*

1928—Married Charles MacArthur.

1930—Daughter Mary born.

1931—Makes first Hollywood picture, *The Sin of Madelon Claudet.*

1932—Awarded as outstanding actress by Motion Picture Academy of Arts and Sciences for *The Sin of Madelon Claudet.*

1935—Signed to long-term radio contract; opens in *Victoria Regina.*

1940—Named radio's best actress of the year.

1949—Daughter Mary died of polio.

1955—Played in ANTA production of *Skin of Our Teeth.*

1955—Fulton Theater renamed Helen Hayes Theater.

William Samuel Paley

1901–

No AMERICAN industries have had more colorful histories than radio
and television. From the day Marconi sent his first wireless message over
the Atlantic to the present hour when American networks encircle the
country in a billion-dollar business that brings an Arabian Nights' entertainment into millions of homes, many gifted people have contributed
their talents to radio and television; but no one has brought to them a
greater sense of responsibility and intellectual maturity than an American
who was born before radio networks were even dreamed of and who, upon
graduating from college, had no more inkling that he would one day play a
major role in the entertainment world than that he would fly to the moon.
William Samuel Paley has come a long way since 1928 when he quit
manufacturing cigars and threw in his lot with radio. But the gamble paid
off. Paley has risen to the very top of industrial America and the country
has benefited from his career as much as he has personally.

II

WILLIAM PALEY was born in Chicago in 1901; he entered the Western
Military Academy in Alton, Illinois. He spent one year at the University
of Chicago and transferred to the University of Pennsylvania. He got a
bachelor's degree, specializing in economics.

Upon graduating, he went into his father's cigar business. As a matter
of fact he had been training for the job since he was eighteen. Summers
he would work in the factory rolling the Java wrappers and Havana fillers
into londres, panetellas, perfectos. He traveled to Cuba and to Holland
to observe tobacco growing at first hand. Upon entering the business full-
time he was made a vice-president in charge of sales.

A strapping six footer with a warm, ready smile and a perpetually suntanned face, Bill Paley exuded charm. When the cigar girls went on strike in one of the company's factories, he took the feminine ring leaders out to lunch and talked them into a quick settlement. A young man about town with plenty of money to burn, Bill Paley displayed a shrewd sense of long-range implications in business and an enlightened sense of what was best for himself.

One year there was a bumper crop in tobacco and the farmers were anxious to unload at virtually any price. The other buyers suggested to Paley, who was the biggest buyer, that he ought to peg the price which was normally thirty-two cents a pound at fifteen cents. When Paley refused to do this, the dealers thought he was crazy. Actually he was shrewder than they. By maintaining the price at thirty cents he kept the bottom from falling out of the tobacco market and he made it feasible for the farmers to plant seed for the next year's crop. This guaranteed a future tobacco supply for his firm.

However, despite the measures he took to protect his business, the cigar industry was in bad shape. During World War I, young men had developed the habit of smoking cigarettes, and the sales of cigars, which during the 1890s and 1900s had been the leading staple of smoking, had drastically fallen off. By 1927 the daily production of La Palinas had dropped from six hundred thousand to four hundred thousand. During this year, while Bill Paley took a business trip through Europe, his father and uncle were approached by the representatives of a small chain of radio stations, the Independent Broadcasters Inc., who talked them into advertising their La Palinas over the network. Commercial radio was only five years old. Big business in general had not yet been attracted to it as an advertising medium. No one knew how large an audience it actually had or whether advertising over it paid. However, clutching at any straw, they signed a contract to pay fifty thousand dollars for thirteen weeks of radio ads. "This may be the biggest blunder we've ever made!" declared Bill's uncle, as he put down his pen.

When Bill returned from Europe, he shared the elder Paleys' misgivings. At close to four thousand dollars a week the experiment was no laughing matter. Bill and other businessmen knew all about the advantages of advertising cigars in the newspapers and magazines and on billboards. But this new medium—what about it? How could one even check up on the returns of the ad? Assuming that millions listened to the music and jokes that went out over the airwaves, was that a guarantee that they would buy La Palina cigars, merely because of a few spot announcements? It all seemed ridiculous.

Paley listened, waited—and was astounded at the results. Not only did the sales of La Palinas rise—they *soared* upwards, 150 per cent! The contract was quickly renewed. Within six months the Paleys' production increased from four hundred thousand to a million cigars daily!

Here, undoubtedly, was a new medium of communication whose power had hardly been tapped, whose possibilities were unlimited. Paley not only took a long look at radio; he decided to enter the business. Independent Broadcasters, Inc., was owned by a friend of his father, a Mr. Jerome Loucheim. Loucheim was anxious to sell out because other interests were occupying his attention. Paley needed no urging. He obtained a twenty-four hour option to purchase control of the radio chain, and on September 25, 1928, three days before his twenty-seventh birthday, he bought it. Independent Broadcasters, Inc., was "more like a spider's web than a network." It consisted of a few small stations east of the Mississippi and south of the Mason-Dixon Line. Paley renamed the chain the Columbia Broadcasting System. He bought control of it for four hundred thousand dollars. Today it could not be purchased for a hundred times that price.

III

PALEY at first thought his new business would be subordinated to his cigar business. He planned to devote no more than two days a week to radio. He was dead wrong. One cannot enter the radio business casually. It becomes an obsession. The CBS stations even in those times were on the air sixteen hours a day. "I thought I was taking over CBS. It took me over," Paley reminisces. His chief problem was how to get some sleep.

It was love at first sight with Paley. His passion was to last throughout the years; it still flames within him. "My imagination went wild over the possibilities of radio, but wild as it went, it didn't keep up with the realities."

Long before Paley became president of CBS, radio had had a colorful history. In 1903 Lee De Forest had launched not only radio but the entire electronics industry with his invention of the three-electrode thermionic electron tube. Three years later he was able to transmit human speech across his laboratory and three years after that he broadcasted phonograph music to his friends several blocks away. They had arranged to wave signals to him reporting the success of their "reception", and passers-by on the street were frequently astonished to discover men leaning out of the windows of respectable office buildings waving towels feverishly in the air.

After World War I big business stepped into the picture to turn this fascinating plaything to commerical use. In 1921 telephone wires were used for the first time to bring a broadcast of the Chicago-Princeton football game from Chicago into the homes of a New York listening audience. People all over the nation began putting on earphones and tinkering with crystal sets. In those early days one was never certain what he would pick out of the air. Usually it was an event when you got anything.

When Paley purchased his network the industry was still in its pioneering phase. There was an opportunity for rapid expansion under skillful direction. Within a year, CBS under Paley extended its network from the Mississippi to the Pacific Coast. Paramount Pictures paid five million dollars for a substantial share of stock. Within three years Paley and his organization moved into ten floors of a building at 485 Madison Avenue in New York. They are still there, having more than doubled their space.

Curiously enough, radio in its infant days, when the ownership of sets was scattered, was a medium for high-brows. It was not until sets entered the homes of millions that the industry geared itself to provide mass entertainment. At this point advertisers stepped in and flooded radio with sponsored shows.

In 1924 one government official had declared, "The quickest way to kill broadcasting would be to use it for direct advertising . . . If a speech by the President is to be used as the meat in a sandwich of two patent medicine advertisements, there will be no radio left."

This prediction was made by Herbert Hoover, then the Secretary of Commerce. Congress had saddled him with the job of supervising the radio airwaves. Hoover summoned the leaders of the industry and urged them to declare against the use of radio for advertising purposes. However, even though Hoover's efforts were futile—for the sponsors saturated the airwaves with apostrophes to soap and laxatives—as late as 1929 when the National Association of Broadcasters drew up a code of ethics for the industry, it resolved to limit advertising only to daytime hours, declaring that advertising plugs should not be permitted to disturb the recreation and relaxation of evening audiences. This brave manifesto was subsequently discarded.

William Paley from the beginning approached radio with humility, and he revolutionized the values of the industry. In a business that was only too eager to play it safe, Paley refused to stand pat, to succumb to stereotypes. With the advent of mass audiences, other networks kept to a minimum programs designed to please discriminating listeners. Paley objected to this neglect of minority groups in the mad scramble to please advertisers.

"We all recognize the simple truth that you cannot have a healthy democracy without minorities. . . . As broadcasters we must never lapse into the position of conspiring, even unintentionally, against minorities."

And so, while other networks succumbed to the "soap box" psychology in their programming, Paley signed up the New York Philharmonic Symphony to broadcast the music of Mozart, Bach, Beethoven. The move was a gamble. His colleagues were convinced that Americans would stand only for jazz. Paley had to force the Philharmonic "down the throats" of the station managers. But his faith in the American people paid off. People who had never had the opportunity to go to a concert now became acquainted with the musical classics over his airwaves and they became a loyal and fanatical audience. This audience grew to millions and encouraged the subsequent experiment of putting grand opera on the air. Through the years Paley has broadcast the nation's leading symphony orchestras and has presented every opera singer of consequence over his microphones.

Furthermore, Paley initiated the practice of cutting the time of commercials, banning plugs for laxatives and depilatories and other commercials that were not in the best of taste. This policy cost him over a half a million dollars annually during the early days.

Paley was far ahead of the rest of the industry in other instances. Determining to exploit the educational possibilities of radio, he developed the *Columbia School of the Air* in coöperation with the United States Office of Education. His staff assembled some of the widely used textbooks of the primary and secondary schools and had them adapted by a few carefully selected writers and an imaginative program director. The results were a series of tri-weekly programs piped into classrooms and enthusiastically endorsed by school teachers from Maine to California.

Paley followed this up with another "first"—the *Church of the Air*, bringing the sermons of Catholic, Protestant, Jewish, Mormon, and Christian Scientist preachers over the microphone. He also introduced a program, in *Invitation to Learning*, that discussed the great books of the past. Today *Invitation to Learning* has a listening audience of several million people, many of whom, lacking formal education, would never have come in contact with the great treasures of literature if it had not been for Paley's gamble.

Although Paley has pioneered in public-service features, he has by no means neglected entertainment. He discovered for radio Bing Crosby, Kate Smith, Frank Sinatra, and the Boswell Sisters, and developed them into radio stars. He sponsored Orson Welles when the actor was feeling his oats with the Mercury Theatre. It was over Paley's network that Welles delivered his Martian broadcast that chilled America. To further the development of radio entertainers, Paley has created the Columbia Artist's Bureau and he also established the Columbia Concert Corporation which has handled a number of concert artists outside the radio field.

Paley's early success in using radio as a medium of education induced one sponsor to finance Admiral Byrd on an expedition to the South Pole. A radio station was set up in the Antarctic and Byrd sent a weekly report to the American people. This proved to be a liberal education in practical geography and science.

Just as Paley put a lifelong interest in music to practical use, he promoted an interest in journalism. Until he entered radio, news broadcasts consisted of dull, five-minute summaries sandwiched unobtrusively between entertainment programs. Paley realized that an informed America made for a strong nation. In Europe the dictators were on the march. There was a possibility that America might have to fight for her freedom. Paley built up a news staff that made journalistic history. He was the first broadcaster to sacrifice paid advertising programs to bring to the American people outstanding news events, sponsored by the network.

"Broadcasts of simple events in foreign nations, such as a Christian festival in an old market place, the music from a cafe or a boat race, are a great service to the cause of humanity," he felt.

He introduced the voice of Pope Pius XI, Mahatma Gandhi, Albert Einstein, and Bernard Shaw over the American airwaves. He carried the funeral of King Albert in Brussels, Hitler's historic address to the Reichstag just after he took power, the London Disarmament Conference in 1930, King Edward VIII's abdication speech. He established the practice of holding news roundups, transmitting reports from correspondents in Europe and Asia. Indeed he established the style for American news gathering in the years immediately preceding World War II and during the conflict. When Hitler seized Czechoslovakia, a Paley man, H. V. Kaltenborn, initiated his on-the-spot broadcasts that made radio history. When Hitler invaded Poland and began World War II, Paley-trained men were at their posts preparing the American people for the ordeal they were soon to share. When America was finally committed to battle, Paley men went in with the troops, flashed first-hand accounts of the fighting in Tunis and Algiers, the landing at Leyte in the Pacific. At three of the five major surrenders of enemy forces, a member of Paley's staff was the only American newsbroadcaster present to report the proceedings. Some of the foremost talents in radio journalism were developed under Paley's direction— Edward R. Murrow, William L. Shirer, Quentin Reynolds, Eric Sevareid, Elmer Davis, Quincy Howe.

Paley's network was the only one that assumed responsibility for the contents of its news programs. As one of his executives put it, "If a prospective sponsor wants to put on a news show he has to choose from the news analysts the network considers qualified. We don't allow a sponsor to put on some abrasive-voiced crackpot just because he's got the money to do so."

Paley overthrew one journalistic shibboleth. It had been the habit of the various branches of journalism—the press, magazines, news commentators —to refrain from criticizing one another. Paley initiated a program, *CBS Views the Press*, which threw this tradition out the window and let in some fresh clean air. Paley's staff analyzed the editorial and news coverage of leading newspapers with candor, exposing prejudices and oversights. The survey was carried out so honestly and so obviously in the public interest that the newspapers gave a grudging assent to it. Subsequently they did even more; they selected it for the Newspaper Guild's Page One Award!

When it looked just before World War II as though Hitler was making serious progress in his efforts to turn South America against the United States, Paley on his own initiative made plans for broadcasting the propaganda of American democracy to our southern neighbors. He established the first international network—providing for a two-way exchange of programs—ever developed by a broadcaster.

He flew to South America, arriving in Buenos Aires "after a harrowing trip over the Andes. The wind howled, snow-capped peaks zoomed past the windows and I found myself pressing full blast on the button of my oxygen tank, as if there were some security involved in blowing one's head off."

Paley found the Latin Americans excessively warm-hearted. In Santiago, he commented upon the wine served at dinner and the host sent twelve cases of it to his New York home. In Rio de Janeiro he admired a shirt worn by a Brazilian businessman. When the Brazilian came to see him off at the airport, he presented Paley with a shirt of the same material. Another business leader gave him a beautiful antique shawl for his wife. Paley observed with interest that radios in Latin America were frequently shared by families and installed in cantinas, grocery stores, and other public places. In Ecuador even the busses were equipped with receivers.

He understood the proud, sensitive Latin Americans "whose great cities were founded when Plymouth Rock was only a rock," whose universities of Mexico and San Marco in Lima "were approaching their hundredth anniversaries when Harvard was founded."

When America entered World War II, Paley's insight into the psychology of foreign peoples served him in good stead. He became a colonel in the department of psychological warfare, spreading Allied propaganda among the occupied peoples. When American troops invaded North Africa he helped organize information broadcasts over local radios; when Mussolini was overthrown he rebuilt the Italian radio network, and he continued this work as American soldiers advanced into France and Germany. Radio had been one of the Nazis' most effective weapons in their campaign to subjugate the Germans; and the devastated cities, the hordes of homeless people were tragic evidence to Paley of what happened when the power to broadcast was misused.

Paley emerged from the war with a new insight into the ability of radio to accomplish good or evil.

He rejoined CBS as a civilian at a time when the industry had reached a tremendous new stage in its development—commercial television.

IV

THE BASIC PRINCIPLE of television (the word is formed from the Latin *video*, "I see," and the Greek *tele*, "at a distance") occurred to scientists as far back as 1873 when a telegraph operator in Ireland reported that his instrument reacted differently in sunny and cloudy weather. Scientists were quick to deduce that light and shadow could be transmitted electrically. The problem was how to develop an instrument for transmission.

It remained for John Logie Baird, a Scotch businessman who was forced by ill health to quit amassing a fortune and devote himself to "tinkering" with electronics as a hobby, to find the answer. For years he labored in a workshop above a flower store in London to develop a photoelectric cell that would be capable of transforming light signals from a picture into equivalent variations of electric currents. He tried all sorts of light-sensitive cells; he even went so far as to borrow a human eye from an eyebank and construct a cell out of the visual purple—to no purpose.

But then on October 2, 1926, he turned the corner; the wonder of true television occurred. Baird had been using "Bill", a ventriloquist's doll, for his subject, and hitherto Bill's face had appeared on the screen as a blob of white with three black circles vaguely indicating the position of nose and eyes. On this date, however, Bill's face suddenly flashed as a recognizable image with complete shading and detail. Even the top of his head could be clearly distinguished. Flushed with pleasure, eager to try his "electric eye" on another human being, he rushed down the stairs and grabbed hold of an office boy who worked on the floor below, dragging him into his workshop. Then, seating him before the battery of blinding lights, he hurried over to the screen. Sure enough, the lifelike face of the office boy peered out at him! Baird changed places with the boy and invited him to cast an eye on the screen. And the office boy became the second person in the world to witness the miracle of television.

Three years after this date, the British Broadcasting Corporation cautiously initiated a half hour of experimental television broadcasts over a newly built transmitter. In the meantime the United States plunged into research on its own to make television a commercial reality. Two engineers, Farnsworth and Zworykin, developed the "image dissector" and kinescope which replaced with an electronic system Baird's clumsy mechanical method for scanning. In 1928 General Electric sponsored America's first televised news event—Al Smith's acceptance of the Democratic nomination for the presidency. The picture was transmitted to two receiving sets in a laboratory. However it was not until World War II brought an accelerated development in electronics that television became feasible for the millions.

When Bill Paley returned to CBS in 1946 only a few thousand television sets were in the hands of the public. The big advertisers had not yet been lured into sponsoring programs; the industry was operating on an exceedingly tight budget. "Actors who don't eat are popular in television," remarked one observer. Whenever feasible, the studios used puppets instead of flesh and blood actors who required salaries. Animals in the zoo became featured performers; snakes and ducks developed into stars.

A substantial portion of the programs were devoted to showing films that were on the point of disintegrating from old age. When one hoary film was unloaded by a movie company, the television studio staff had to run the eight reels three different ways at a private screening before they were certain which was the proper sequence for giving the story sense. Many radio actors were unnerved by the prospect of having to be seen by audiences to whom they had been merely a voice for years. The hero of one radio soap opera stood five feet one to the heroine's six feet. A televised showing of them would have brought guffaws from their following. The couple had to quit playing romantic roles and become a comedy team. Some of the radio news commentators, fearing that viewers would be bored looking at their faces for ten or fifteen minutes, grew fancy whiskers to "add interest" to their features.

The catastrophes caused by the intense heat of the cameras were legion. Candles employed to adorn sets melted before the eye. Dry ice, used to give the effect of fog, evaporated so quickly that not even a trace of mist was suggested. Silverware, employed in drawing-room scenes, became as red hot as steam irons, blistering the hands of the players. One sponser was horrified when an advertising display of his frozen deserts melted before they could be demonstrated.

The early cameras played embarrassing tricks. A group of men, televised at a fashionable dinner, appeared to be dressed in gray dinner jackets with black lapels. The wool of their jackets had reflected the infra-red rays of the camera while the satin of the lapels had absorbed them. Fair-complexioned actresses photographed with coffee-colored skin. The camera failed to pick up tears and milk had to be used for crying scenes. Once a dancer wearing a broad white sash pirouetted against a white background and the entertainer seemed to be sawed in two.

Once television cameras were assigned to pick up the bathers at Coney Island. The eyes of the camera penetrated the artificial fabrics worn by many of the women and the scene was turned into a nudist colony.

Neither audience nor sponsors knew for sure what would happen during those early telecasts. Once the advertisers for a dog food had trained a canine to be telecast devouring biscuits made by the sponsor and turning in disgust from all rival brands. However, when the show went on, the dog was seized with stage fright; he devoured the wrong brand, sniffed with disgust at the sponsor's food and slinked off the set. For his next appearance, the food of everyone but the sponsor was sprinkled with an insecticide.

From such humble beginnings, television has grown into a billion-dollar industry. Its gigantic programming problems can be recognized by comparing them with the demands made upon the movie industry. The entire finished production of new motion pictures turned out by the studios averages about two hours daily. This would be just enough to fill the hours from six to eight in the evening on a single television network. And the major TV networks provide a combined seventy hours of new entertainment each day.

Upon returning from the war, William Paley accepted the challenges of television with the enthusiasm and farsightedness he had displayed when radio was young. Indeed, as early as 1936 he had imported Peter Goldmark, a brilliant young engineer, from Hungary, to direct the network's research. In addition to developing a system of color television that was the first to be approved by the government, Goldmark also developed the long-playing phonograph record and a high-fidelity phonograph.

Upon rejoining CBS, Paley astounded the industry by doing what no competitor had dreamed of doing. He put a college professor into the top operating position in his business. Moving himself up to chairman of the board, Paley made Dr. Frank S. Stanton, a psychology professor, president of his network.

With a professional psychologist at the head, Paley went all out to raise the intellectual level of television programs. Realizing that advertising agencies, for all their good qualities, are not dedicated to raising the taste of television programs, Paley conceived a plan to keep important programs out of the control of the hucksters. He developed what has become known in the industry as the network package. The network itself creates programs, puts on its own shows, develops its own stars, instead of serving merely as a pipe-line for ad agencies. The network program has been a revolutionary step. It may well be the salvation of television. That Paley was justified in believing the network could invest money in its own programs and still make profits was dramatically proved by the success of the first of these packages—"I Love Lucy", starring Lucille Ball and Desi Arnez. It has gained the nation's largest audience of viewers; at times it has played to 70 per cent of all TV viewers. Another Paley package, "The Toast Of The Town", featuring Ed Sullivan, is a smash success. Today Paley's scheme has been adopted throughout the industry.

Continuing to give the public the best in news programs, Paley made Edward R. Murrow a vice-president in charge of documentary events. One program, *You Are There*, which permits the audience to be eye witnesses at historical events like the assassination of President Lincoln, the battle of Lexington, and the death of Socrates, has been a very skillful means of making history real and vivid for millions. Documentary presentations of juvenile delinquency, housing, and racial discrimination are featured by Paley as sustaining programs with the lavishness usually devoted to top sponsored programs. And for lighter fare, Paley gives the public Arthur Godfrey and Jackie Gleason.

Paley believes he has solved the problem of using television to provide people with a greater understanding of events. The answer is to present education as exciting entertainment. "To television's audiences, history must be made to seem not a recitation of facts and dates but rather a spy-glass into the past where characters live again. Science must be discussed not as a series of abstract phenomena but as an answer to the daily needs of man in his struggle with his environment . . . Geography can be no mere description, but rather an actual experience of the world. Every listener, in short, must be made so aware of the direct application of this material to his own life that he listens as avidly as to sheer entertainment."

V

TODAY, this six-footer, perpetually sun-tanned and smiling, is as vigorously young in spirit, as tenacious of principle, as ever. Disliking red tape and formal procedure, he has created an atmosphere of informality in the organization apparent even to the casual visitor.

Once while he was riding to his office, two Italian radio singers stepped into the elevator and began gossiping in their native tongue. One of them looked at Paley and muttered to his friend: "This tall guy in the corner is the president of CBS." "What the devil do I care!" retorted the other. Paley, who knows Italian well, chuckled, "I don't blame you at all!" to the consternation of the singers.

From the first, Paley surrounded himself with youthful executives. "We had to take young men," he explains. "No middle-aged executive secure in his field would have entered the fly-by-night business of radio in 1928." Over the years Paley has continued to replenish himself with young, bold men; his older associates, also, while they have aged around the temples, remain as young in mind as their boss.

Paley's personal life has prospered under as lucky a star as his business career. He married Barbara Cushing, the youngest daughter of Dr. Harvey Cushing, the brain surgeon. A beautiful woman with "the finely chiseled features of an old Italian miniature," Barbara was a fashion editor for Vogue before her marriage and she has frequently been listed among the ten best dressed women of the year. According to the astute television commentator, Jinx Falkenberg, "The difference between Barbara and other women who wear beautiful clothes is that Barbara *does* something to them . . . She even looks good in blue jeans."

Barbara's sisters, Minna and Betsey, are married to Vincent Astor and John Hay Whitney, multimillionaires. It was while relaxing on Whitney's estate in Long Island, Greentree, that Paley met Barbara and fell in love with her.

Despite his hectic business life, Paley spends every hour he can snatch at home with his family in Rye, New York. He is an avid collector of Matisse, Picasso, and other modern painters. He likes to paint in oil and water colors, and he frequently relaxes by driving a motor boat and playing golf.

In 1951, President Truman, recognizing Paley's farsightedness and hard-headed progressivism, appointed him to head a five-man committee to study the long-range aspects of the nation's material resources. Paley, after a thoroughgoing investigation, submitted to the President his recommendations for keeping the nation prosperous. His report was optimistic because he has complete faith in the American people.

Paley knows that as long as the workers in his own field are ready to translate the aspirations of the public into their own daily goals, television will develop into a serious and adult medium. Every hour of the day the nation's telecasters face a popular election; they are committed to stand or fall by the votes of John Q. Public. "The sovereign right of every television viewer in America to turn to another channel or to shut off his set entirely when he doesn't like a program has been the greatest single factor in television's onward march."

Paley, sportsman that he is, revels in this daily gamble; and he is unafraid of the future, for his sympathies are one with the people.

IMPORTANT DATES IN THE LIFE OF WILLIAM SAMUEL PALEY

1901—September 28, born, Chicago.

1922—Graduated University of Pennsylvania, B.A.

1928—Became President of the Columbia Broadcasting System.

1929—Organized Columbia Artists' Bureau.

1931—Inaugurated first commercial television broadcasts in U.S.

1943—Went overseas for the Office of War Information.

1945—Appointed colonel in Department of Psychological Warfare.

1946—Appointed Dr. Frank Stanton to be President of CBS. Became Chairman of the Board of CBS.

1951—Selected by President Truman to be Chairman of Materials Policy Commission.

Marian Anderson

1902–

In the summer of 1935, Salzburg swarmed with musical celebrities for the annual festival. For years Toscanini, Walter, and topflight opera singers had held the spotlight with their virtuosity. But on one particular afternoon, the cream of society assembled to hear a colored singer from the United States who was virtually unknown to her countrymen. The audience had gathered largely out of curiosity to hear the Negro singer interpret the spirituals made famous by her people—a form of music many of the Europeans had never listened to before. Everybody present in the audience had heard that the singer's voice was unusual, but few were prepared for what followed. When the tall, slim young woman from Philadelphia closed her eyes and commenced to sing, her face was transfigured by ecstasy; a thrill went through the hall. The air seemed saturated with an unworldly radiance that had never before been experienced by the living.

At the end of the performance Arturo Toscanini turned to a friend. "What I have heard today one is privileged to listen to once in a hundred years." He expressed to the manager of the young singer a desire to meet her. The manager, overwhelmed by this flattery from the usually reserved conductor, assured him that he would ask Miss Anderson to step down from the platform and come to him.

"Oh, no," retorted Toscanini, "I shall go up to see *her!*"

II

Marian Anderson was born in the Negro slums of Philadelphia. Her father was in the ice business. Her mother had been a schoolteacher before her marriage. As a young child, Marian displayed a passion for music. When she was six she set her heart on a violin displayed in the window of a pawnshop. But her parents could not afford to pay the $3.45 necessary to buy it. Marian went to work scrubbing doorsteps until she collected enough nickels and dimes to purchase the violin.

Entering a church choir at eight, she revealed an extraordinary range of voice. Although she was a contralto, she could reach high C and low D; her tones covered three octaves. She not only learned the contralto part of every song, but the parts of the soprano, alto, tenor, and even bass; and if any of these singers were absent, she would sing their roles effortlessly. The Negroes of the neighborhood, who knew genuine music when they heard it, booked the girl at various socials and community concerts, paying her from fifty cents to two dollars. Some of the more sanguine of them prophesied to her parents: "Someday that little miss is going to earn fifty dollars a concert!"

Her parents smiled at this "little joke." Such prophecies were "fantastic." Within fifteen years Marian was earning $2500 a concert; she was the highest-priced singer in the concert world!

Until she was sixteen Marian received no singing lessons. She could not afford them. But when she graduated from high school, her principal had her audition before Guiseppe Boghetti, a voice teacher in New York. To the day of his death Boghetti, who had developed a number of top operatic voices, never forgot the impression Marian first made on him. "When she had finished singing *Deep River*, I just couldn't move. She had none of the refinements. She simply sang it the way she felt it, with all her natural feeling for music. She has never sung it better since."

Marian's neighbors passed the hat, raising money to pay for her musical training. These souls who were poor in worldly goods but wealthy in their aesthetic appreciation, actually launched her on her career.

After several years of training, Boghetti entered Marian among three hundred contestants in auditions with the New York Philharmonic Orchestra. The winner of the first prize was to appear with the orchestra at a concert in Lewisohn Stadium. The judges, wearied by the parade of mediocrities who assailed their ears, were exceedingly short-tempered by the time Marian appeared. Boghetti had warned her, "Even if they sound the gong on you, keep on singing. I want them to hear the trill you do at the end."

This warning was unnecessary. The audience not only heard Marian through enthralled, but violated a rule by breaking into a spontaneous ovation.

Marian appeared with the Philharmonic and it seemed that her professional career was on its way. However, five frustrating years were ahead of her; years that would certainly have crushed a less dedicated spirit than hers. Because she was a Negro, opera was closed to her. And concert managers were not very eager to sign her. Others of her race had been accepted as comedians, or as musical-comedy singers; but never before had a colored girl sought admittance into the world of serious music which was supported by wealthy and socially prominent patrons of the arts. One New

York manager placed her under contract, but nothing developed. Music critics wrote glowingly about her voice and wondered, "but what can this poor colored girl do with it?"

Finally Boghetti came up with a solution. If she could not win a reputation in her own country, she could make the attempt in Europe where prejudice against Negroes was less in evidence. "If you remain here, Marian, it will only be a question of time before your early momentum will be completely forgotten and you will die in obscurity. Europe is your only chance."

And so the young Philadelphia Negress was forced to find her artistic freedom in the countries of the old world. Aided by a Julius Rosenwald scholarship, she went to Germany and steeped herself in the language and artistic atmosphere of a people who had nurtured Beethoven, Schumann, and Brahms; who had given humanity the incomparable *lieder*.

Marian held her first European recitals in Berlin. Gradually word of an important new artist spread through the musical grapevine. It reached Sweden where Helmer Ernswall, a concert manager, became interested. "A Negro girl with the name of Anderson would certainly be a hit in Sweden!" he told his associates. He sent one of them, Kosti Vehanen, a Finnish pianist, to Berlin to report on Miss Anderson's voice.

Marian had scored a *success d'estime* with musical sophisticates, not with the public at large. When Mr. Vehanen arrived in Berlin, he found her singing in a dilapidated old room for an audience of fifty or sixty, accompanied on an upright piano. Before she began her spirituals, she would explain their meaning to the audience. Vehanen was wonderstruck by the music. He had never heard its like before. It came from the sighing fields of cotton, the agony endured on old Southern plantations. It came from a world that was as ancient as the African jungle. Vehanen was at first baffled by the musical idiom, but he sensed it to be the utterance of authentic genius.

Marian was given a contract by Helmer, and Vehanen became her accompanist. Under his guidance she added to spirituals the songs of Schubert, Brahms, Sibelius. Her new associates groomed her in other ways. She had been accustomed to wearing the same rather dowdy hat for all occasions. Vehanen determined to get rid of it tactfully. Once while rehearsing, Marian took off her hat as usual and placed it on the piano. As soon as her back was turned, Vehanen grabbed it and shoved it quickly into a corner behind the piano. When the rehearsal was over, Marian asked him, "Didn't I have my hat with me when I came in?"

"I didn't see it," said Vehanen, suddenly becoming absorbed in packing his music.

Marian was forced to buy new and more becoming hats; and once the ice was broken she followed with a substantial wardrobe of attractive clothes. At first Marian had an idea that her hands were large and clumsy, and she tried to conceal them on the platform by draping her handkerchief over them. Vehanen persuaded her that they were impressive, artistic hands and their display became one of her chief graces.

Marian found a receptive public among the Scandinavians and soon she was selling out the hall wherever she appeared. The demand for seats was so lively in Finland that for one recital even the conductor of the Finnish National Opera could not get a ticket. He asked Marian if he could sit on the stage beside her and turn her music pages, so anxious was he to attend.

On one occasion, Vehanen brought Marian to Sibelius in his country villa. Sibelius asked her to sing for him and suggested that before she begin they have a cup of coffee. Marian, believing that coffee was not good for her before singing, requested they drink at the end of her recital. When she finished, Sibelius went to the door of the salon and called out to his maid; "Never mind the coffee. *Let's make it champagne!*"

In toasting Marian, the Finnish maestro added: "My ceiling is much too low for your voice. . . . My door shall always be unlatched for you!"

Marian's success in Sweden was as extraordinary as it had been in Finland. She once sang in a church where it was the habit of the audience to wave their handkerchiefs instead of clapping as a sign of their approval. When Marian finished her first number, not a handkerchief was waved. The audience sat in silence wiping away the tears.

Once while touring the hinterlands in Finland, Marian entered a church in an out-of-the-way little village to rehearse for a coming concert. While going through a song in the organ loft, she heard footsteps. A high ranking government official appeared and whispered to her accompanist. "The President of Finland is downstairs with his staff. Will you be disturbed if we listen for a while?"

When the rehearsal was over, the President thanked Marian for the pleasure she had given him. "We have been on an inspection tour of munition plants. As we passed this church we were astonished to hear such beautiful singing. We entered to find out who the owner of the voice could be. Imagine finding such magnificence in a little church buried deep in the snow!"

Upon finishing her Scandinavian concerts, Marian toured the continent, earning acclaim in every major city. She packed the Opera House in Paris. Only Kreisler and Rachmaninoff before had been able to sell out the Paris Opera House for a solo performance. She captivated audiences in Salzburg, enthralled the fastidious and highly critical Italians, thrilled music lovers in England and in Central Europe. And then she toured South America and received ovations in Rio de Janeiro and other cities.

She was a colorful traveler. Her suitcases, packed with the finest gowns, her phonograph, recording machine, radio, electric iron, and sewing machine, were familiar objects to the porters who cared for her on numerous railroads. Her accompanist, Vehanen, added a colorful touch of his own. He traveled with a little turtle, "Calle," who lived out of his coat pocket. During meals, "Calle" always squatted between Marian's and Kosti's plates and was given his serving of salad leaves first.

In the course of her bookings, Marian traveled to Russia where she received as much enthusiasm as elsewhere. On her initial trip, the train crossed the border between Finland and Russia on a one-track bridge, painted white on the Finnish side, red on the Soviet. Marian was halted by Red customs officials and questioned in great detail about her recordings. While she waited for clearance, they played several of her records, nodding their heads approvingly.

For a recital in Moscow, Marian had planned to sing Schubert's *Ave Maria,* but Soviet officials insisted that the song be referred to on the program simply as "an aria by Schubert." This was in keeping with the anti-religious spirit fostered by the government. While appearing in Leningrad, Marian visited a cathedral that had been turned by the Reds into a museum. Featured in it was a hideous mummy with the derisive inscription, "Can *this* body live after death?"

Marian was introduced to Shostakovich and other luminaries of Russian music. She had dinner at the home of the composer, Ippolitov, and was amused by the way he served. Whenever he saw that someone's plate was empty, he would unfold a specially designed trick fork, reach across the table, pick up the succulent meat cakes and drop them into his guest's plate.

Marian also met Stanislavsky, the famous dramatic teacher, and he sent her a basket of white lilacs upon her departure.

Marian and Kosti saw much suffering in Russia. Once while the singer went shopping, Kosti spent the afternoon in a Moscow park. From his bench he observed a crippled woman limping from person to person begging. Since begging was a crime, she had to hold out her palm surreptitiously, keeping an eye cocked for the police. She was an elderly woman with wispy gray hair and a panic-stricken look. Vehanen slipped a large bill into her hand. When she saw the denomination she shrieked with joy. She dropped down at Vehanen's feet and kissed his shoes. Vehanen could feel her trembling as she gripped him; she would not let go. People looked at them curiously; a policeman came into view.

"Here, let go of my feet," whispered Vehanen. "A policeman is coming!"

The crone stood up, stuffed the money into her pocket and disappeared into the shrubbery as noiselessly as a phantom. This experience lingered in Vehanen's memory for years.

Marian and Kosti gave recitals in all the major centers of Russia. They saturated themselves with the wild color of the Caucasus, visited the tempestuous peasants at their daily chores. They toured the sulphur baths at Tiflis where female attendants massaged customers with their feet, dancing a tattoo on their bellies; they came across a deaf and dumb boy of twelve who had a trained bear for a companion. This mute fed his pet wild cherries and hugged him passionately.

The recitalists underwent a variety of hardships in the primitive areas of Russia. Once during a concert in a sanatorium in Kislovodsk, the lights went out. After a hurried search, two candles were found, placed on either side of the piano music, and Marian resumed her singing in the semidusk.

While flying in a plane to Baku in the oil fields, they ran into a heavy storm. They could see the pilot working frantically to steady the plane. Suddenly the engine slowed and the plane commenced to dip; Marian and Kosti clenched their hands and prayed to God. Unable to pick up speed, the pilot prepared for an emergency landing, and as the plane dove toward the ground it narrowly escaped crashing into a cluster of trees. The pilot landed deep in mud and Marian and Kosti were smeared from head to foot as they struggled to the waiting room.

Such hair-raising adventures were not confined to Russia. Other tours provided their share of excitement. Once when they were visiting a snake farm outside Rio de Janeiro a huge cobra managed to escape from confinement. As he crawled toward them, Marian, displaying no fear, took several quick steps backwards and snapped pictures of him. Meanwhile Kosti rushed for the caretaker and told him of the cobra's escape. The caretaker smiled skeptically. Mr. Vehanen must surely be mistaken; such a thing had never happened before. Kosti grabbed his arm and hauled him over to see for himself. Astonished, he grasped the cobra by the neck and returned him to the pit. All the while Marian continued to take pictures of the incident.

III

AFTER Marian's recital in Salzburg during which Toscanini so unreservedly complimented her, she reached the zenith of her fame. She averaged eighty recitals a year and was usually booked up solidly two years in advance. She had come a long way from the years in Philadelphia when she sang for fifty cents and the neighbors had to raise a fund for her training. She was now acknowledged to have the greatest contralto voice of her generation. Music lovers marveled at the "fantastic colors and velvety texture" of her tones.

"If Marian were to sing the telephone book from beginning to end," observed one critic, "she would make it a memorable experience."

Audiences never ceased to wonder at her extraordinary vocal range. "She has what might best be described as a pair of voices," wrote one critic. "The upper half is brilliant and heady, a soprano for all purposes. The lower half is that hair-raising, deep voice the like of which I have never heard before." In singing Schubert's *Erl König* and others of his dramatic *lieder*, she achieved astonishing effects.

She expressed the religious grandeur of Handel in a way that had never been done before. In general her interpretations of songs were highly personal, frequently other-worldly. She found her own beauties in a melodic phrase that had been sung thousands of times by others, revealing to audiences treasures that had previously been overlooked. So severe were her aesthetic demands that the lyrics of a song had to be worthy of the music for her to sing it. No matter how splendid the melody, she would refuse to interpret it unless the words satisfied her sense of poetry. To save her voice she was in the habit of rehearsing her songs an octave lower than they were written and frequently she sounded like a man while she kept the wraps around her tones. Her highly personal interpretations nowhere found finer expression than in spirituals. Frequently during a moment of high emotion she would spontaneously change the melody and improvise notes of her own.

Her singing of the *Crucifixion* particularly stirred her audiences.

> They crucified my Lord,
> An' He never said a mumblin' word. . . .
> Not a word, not a word, not a word.

Invariably when she finished this song, her listeners were too stunned by the emotional impact to applaud. They would sit for some seconds in a trancelike mood before they could rouse themselves to attend to the next number. Once when the final notes of the *Crucifixion* died away, her accompanist himself was too overcome to continue. "No one moved. I hardly dared to close the music and open the next song and when I finally did so my hand was trembling."

Marian had a remarkable musical memory. On one occasion she undertook to sing the alto solo part in Brahms's *Alt Rhapsody* under the direction of Bruno Walter. She had signed for only one appearance and had not had the time to memorize the difficult music before the rehearsal. She sang it with the score in her hand. When the rehearsal was over, Walter, a taskmaster, said, "Miss Anderson, when one sings under my direction, she does not use a score."

"I will sing the part tomorrow from memory," Marian vowed to Kosti. All night she rehearsed with him. The following afternoon at the concert she took her place in front of the orchestra without a score and sang the part without a single error. At the conclusion, Bruno Walter stepped forward and shook her hand.

Once Marian had emerged as a supreme artist on the continent, it became inevitable that she would return to her own country. However, the same prejudiced people who had refused to give her a hearing during her early years of struggle now objected to her returning with a white accompanist. They felt that Negro singers should appear on the concert platform only with colored pianists; they suggested that Kosti Vehanen be left behind. But Marian replied to her New York manager in a wire from Paris:

"Mr. Vehanen and I will arrive in New York on December 17." That was that.

The first day at sea on the *Ile De France*, the ship rocked violently. While Marian was on her way to her cabin, she slipped, fell down a flight of stairs and fractured her foot. She spent the rest of the voyage in her cabin. However, she had promised to sing at a ship's benefit and, unwilling to disappoint the audience, she made an appearance. Carried to the stage, she stood on one foot, leaning against the piano as she went through with her recital.

With her first American concert only a week away, her manager was afraid it would have to be canceled. But Town Hall in New York had been sold out and Marian refused to let the ticket holders down. However, special arrangements had to be made. Before the concert began, the curtain was lowered so that she could be carried on the stage in a chair. Kosti and a nurse helped her over to the piano where she stood on her sound foot, resting on the instrument. Her fractured foot was concealed beneath her flowing gown and the audience had not been told beforehand that she was injured. Only after she had sung four numbers did Marian reveal that her foot was in a plaster cast and that she was standing up "to make things pleasanter for your eyes."

The touchy question of race prejudice came to a head when the headquarters of the Daughters of The American Revolution in Washington refused to allow Marian to give a recital in their Constitution Hall. This attitude by no means reflected the majority opinion of the DAR, but represented the views of several short-sighted people in temporary control. It resulted in a national uproar. Americans from every walk of life wired their protests. The United States Government offered to sponsor an out-of-doors concert for the singer, to be held in front of the Lincoln Memorial on Easter Sunday, 1939.

The symbolism of the event was not lost on the American people. Marian Anderson represented the finest flowering of the genius of those people Lincoln had dedicated his life to freeing. If the marble could have turned to flesh on that memorable Easter Sunday, it would have smiled at the scene before it.

Marian was escorted by motorcycle police to the Memorial. Seventy-five thousand people were gathered waiting for the concert to begin. It was the largest assembly for a concert in American history. Among those present were the Chief Justice of the United States, high-ranking cabinet members, and leading senators and representatives from both parties. "Marian was calm," reported Kosti afterwards. "She held her head high. I went to the piano first to fasten the music, for a soft wind was blowing. When I saw the immense crowd, I had a feeling it would be of little use to begin to play, for I was sure that no one could possibly hear us."

Marian's voice lived up to expectations that day and the news of the concert was headlined throughout the country. The rank and file members of the DAR asserted their true feelings about her and the organization was big enough to make a handsome apology. In 1943 the DAR invited Marian to sing in Constitution Hall and they went further than other organizations, permitting Negroes to sit next to white people in the audience.

IV

TODAY Marian is acknowledged by enlightened Southerners as enthusiastically as she is throughout the rest of America. She has been accepted, like Jackie Robinson, the Negro baseball player, without any reservations; the essential decency of America has always ultimately asserted itself despite preliminary fumblings.

For years Boghetti, her former teacher, had advised Miss Anderson to marry a man who would make her happy. "Neither man nor contralto was meant to live alone." Finally at forty-two, she married Orpheus Fisher, an architect. The couple live in a spacious, modern stone and glass house, designed by her husband, near Danbury, Connecticut. Marian frequently entertains her friends with informal jazz concerts, accompanying her own singing on the piano. She collects jazz recordings made by leading orchestras as a relaxation from her own serious music.

Like many artists living under tension she has her superstitions. She will never say good-by in a doorway or put a sharp instrument into anybody's hands on the day of a concert. She is generous with her earnings. When she received the Bok award for her musical achievements, she used the ten thousand dollars prize money to set up Marian Anderson scholarships for talented young singers, to be awarded regardless of race. Like most people in public life she receives letters from cranks looking for a handout. Once she received a letter from a woman: "Please send me $2,000 as I would like to open a flower shop in your honor. I shall call the place 'Marian'. It will be good publicity for you." Another panhandler let her know, "My winter coat is in awful condition and needs much fixing."

Today in her fifties, Marian remains in excellent control of her medium. In 1949 she underwent an operation for the removal of a cyst on her esophagus and for a while it was feared that her voice would be permanently impaired. However these fears were groundless; striking evidence of her comeback was given in the fall of 1954 when she received an invitation to join the Metropolitan Opera Company and to make her début in the role of the gypsy, Ulrica, in Verdi's *Masked Ball*. This was the first time a Negro singer had been invited to appear as a Met star. The world's greatest contralto had been rendered the final accolade.

She remains as extraordinarily humble toward her art as when she began to sing. She is convinced that her voice is a blessing from God and that all credit for its achievements should be given Him. She feels that the colored girl from the Philadelphia slums could never have risen to her present position in a universe ruled solely by blind atoms, by the laws of chance. She looks upon each of her recitals as a religious experience. And people who have seen her eyes close in ecstasy during the unfolding of a song are certain that she has been close to God during those moments. She believes that she has been purged spiritually in tempo with her development as an artist and that she is today closer to the Marian Anderson God wanted her to be than ever before. In discussing herself professionally she uses the pronoun "we" to strip herself of the least taint of egotism.

"There was a time when we were very much interested in applause and the lovely things they [the audience] said. But now we are interested only in singing so that the audience will depart feeling a little better than when it came."

IMPORTANT DATES IN THE LIFE OF
MARIAN ANDERSON

1902—Born in Philadelphia.

1925—Won appearance as singer with New York Philharmonic Orchestra.

1930—Went to Germany to continue musical training.

1935—Scored success at Salzburg Festival.

1935—Made successful début in Town Hall upon return to the U.S.

1939—Sang in White House for King George and Queen Elizabeth of Great Britain. Awarded Spingarn Medal for "highest achievement" for one of Negro race.

1943—Married Orpheus Fisher.

1949—Underwent operation for removal of cyst from esophagus.

1954—Joined Metropolitan Opera Company and made début in Verdi's *Masked Ball*.

Ralph Johnson Bunche

1904–

In the summer of 1948 the United Nations faced its first serious test. War had broken out between the Israeli and the Arabs in Palestine. The UN was called upon to stop the war. If it failed, the peoples of the world would conclude that it was merely a new edition of the impotent League of Nations and the hopes for an effective world organization that could command the respect of humanity would be buried.

The eyes of the world were focused upon the Hotel des Roses on the Greek island of Rhodes where the Arab and Israeli delegates had assembled to attempt to work out an armistice. Presiding over the negotiations was a heavy-framed American diplomat with a round, Buddha-like face. As chief representative of the United Nations on the spot, he had assumed entire responsibility for the talks, and the hopes of humanity hung upon his judgment.

For three months he sat with the negotiators twelve hours daily. As the days of bickering passed into weeks, the tempers of the delegates became ragged; their nerves were frazzled almost beyond endurance. Then, during one of the most critical sessions, an aide placed a message in front of the American chairman. As the delegates leaned forward expectantly, Ralph Bunche opened the envelope, glanced at a slip of paper. His face relaxed in a smile.

"What is it, Mr. Bunche? Have you received good news from your country?"

"Excellent news. The Detroit Tigers have just taken another double-header!"

Then Ralph Bunche, who as a kid had been a mascot of the Tigers and who had rooted for them ever since, lit up a cigarette. "OK, gentlemen, let's get down to business!"

This was an example of Bunche's ability to relax, to inject fun and humor into a situation saturated with anxiety—qualities which enabled him eventually to steer the negotiations to a successful peace in the Holy Land.

II

RALPH BUNCHE was born in the Negro section of Detroit. His father ran a barbershop in the first story of their dilapidated home that leaked rain and snow during the winter and let in the wind to nip the limbs of the shivering family. When he was eight Ralph became a newsboy, and though all the other colored newsies hawked their papers in the Negro section, Ralph boldly ventured into the white community where he could make more money—as much as thirty-five cents a day. Despite sickly parents and a wretched daily diet, Ralph had been granted a powerful physique. He was an excellent athlete. He played baseball on the swill-littered streets, using a broomstick and a tobacco sack filled with pebbles and grass. One day the newspaper gave its newsboys a free ticket to see the Detroit Tigers, and Ralph went into the park to watch Ty Cobb and company display their skills. He became fascinated with the team and climbed into the bleachers whenever he could scrape up the price. He got to associating with the players, handed each his favorite bat. Once he was invited to sit on the bench, and when the team went into a winning streak, the players made him their mascot and reserved him a permanent seat by their side.

However, when Ralph was ten, he had to part from the Tigers. His father's business had deteriorated and the family was faced with bankruptcy. They moved to Toledo, Ohio, where Fred Bunche hoped to find a new job. But the financial situation remained critical. Fred developed a serious cough; he had not the strength to hold on to any job for long. Ralph and his sisters went barefooted summers to save their shoes for school.

In addition to his father's constant coughing, Ralph's mother came down with rheumatic fever. Each parent seemed to get worse worrying over the health of the other. One day Fred suffered a severe hemorrhage and the doctors insisted that the family move to a hot dry climate. They entrained for Albuquerque, New Mexico, and moved into an adobe hut. Ralph was eleven. When trains came in, he would carry the luggage of travelers to the hotels for tips. Then he got a job in a bakery working until midnight stripped to the waist. He was not quite twelve at the time. Both he and his mother loved music and enjoyed going to the band concerts held in a park some distance from their house. However, since they could not afford carfare for both, Ralph would put his mother on the trolley car and run twenty blocks to the park.

The rheumatic fever burned away his mother's strength and she died within a year of their reaching Albuquerque. Three months later his father coughed out his lungs. Ralph and his sisters were left orphans. His grandmother took complete charge and ruled with a matriarchal will.

Lucy Bunche was a tiny, frail woman who weighed barely over a hundred pounds. She had been born a slave in Texas and had been a schoolteacher in Indian country. Widowed at thirty-five, she had come to live with Ralph's parents and it was she who now kept the little family from disintegrating under the hammer blows of poverty and death. She took the children away from Albuquerque with its tragic associations and moved to Los Angeles. She infused them with her own stubborn, unconquerable energy. She became the lodestone in young Ralph's life; she put the teeth into him, the steel into his spine, and kept his eyes looking upward toward the summit. "If white people ask why you are black," this ex-slave told Ralph, "you ask them why they are white." One must be courteous, thoughtful, but proud and keenly aware of his rights as an American citizen.

At fourteen, Ralph entered Jefferson High School in Los Angeles and amazed his teachers with his scholastic brilliance. The faculty adviser was astonished to have this Negro lad inform him he was trying out for the debating team. None of the Negroes who had previously attended the school had ever dared to compete on a team of white boys or face white audiences. But Ralph won a place on the team and excelled as a debater. Moreover, he made the football, baseball, and basketball teams and won his letter in all three sports. He graduated high school among the upper ten in his class, winning every scholastic honor available. But he was not a bookworm. He excited only the admiration of his fellow students. There were not any other fellows around who could hit a baseball or plough through tackle harder than he.

Between classes, Ralph had taken a variety of jobs. He worked as a "pig boy" in the composing room of the Los Angeles *Times*, carrying lead bricks to the linotype machines. One summer he took a job in a carpet-dyeing factory rolling huge vats filled with boiling chemicals. Nights he came home sweaty and exhausted, smeared with the steaming dyes. Still another summer, he worked as a house servant for Charles Ray, a star of the silent films. He swept his beach house, served drinks to Ray's movie friends, and kept his clothes pressed.

Upon graduating from Jefferson High, Ralph was granted a tuition scholarship by U.C.L.A. The scholarship did not cover his living expenses and he had to work hard outside the lecture room. He got a job as the janitor of a woman's gymnasium, sweeping floors from five until eight every morning. Then he would grab his books, rush across the street to a cafeteria and study his lessons over breakfast.

Suddenly he lost weight, tossed restlessly at night, refused to eat. The doctors diagnosed a mastoid and he underwent two operations. The trouble had been caused by a piece of straw which had lodged in his inner ear when he had slept in a hayloft during a summer outing. His operations left him with a phlebitis in his leg—an infection from which he suffers periodically even today.

Ralph was forced to stay out of college for a year. When he re-entered he refused to spare himself physically. He took another job as a janitor, scrubbed floors in neighborhood restaurants. Despite his setback he ran away with honor after honor, played varsity basketball and helped the team win the Conference championship for three straight years. He was chosen president of the debating society, made Phi Beta Kappa, and was graduated *summa cum laude*.

By the time he reached his senior year, Ralph had won the attention of the leaders of the Negro community and the question of what career he would follow became a matter of public interest. Several prominent Negro politicians suggested he become a lawyer; but Ralph shied away from this prospect. He knew that his legal activities would be confined to whatever criminal cases developed among his people and that if he eventually entered politics he would be forced into the status of a demagogue ward heeler bartering blocks of colored votes. He felt he would be happier as a teacher; and when Harvard University offered him a fellowship for graduate studies, he accepted eagerly.

After paying off his college expenses, he did not have the train fare to get from Los Angeles to Cambridge. But the community raised nickels and dimes and presented him with a thousand dollars. Arriving at Harvard he moved into a room in a Negro slum of Boston and tackled the problem of how to keep his "nest egg" from vanishing too quickly. He drew five dollars a week to live on and did his own laundry. He discovered that when he plastered a wet shirt on his wall before retiring, it would have a freshly-groomed look the next morning. He pressed his pants with a second-hand iron he heated over a gas flame. He was plagued with bed bugs and roaches and when he found they were too numerous to be exterminated, he made peace with them. He fed the roaches and nicknamed them after his Harvard professors.

He roamed through the bookstores and bought volumes second-hand, deducting from his expenditure for food. The price of textbooks was a serious item. A Los Angeles bookseller who was a friend had given him a letter to a Cambridge bookseller requesting that Ralph be granted a discount. One afternoon when he came into the Cambridge store with the letter, the owner, a Mr. Philips who was an elderly fellow with thick glasses, peered at Ralph and said, "OK, I'll hire you; you can begin working now."

Ralph was astonished. Apparently the fellow had advertised for a clerk and being unable to see very well had mistaken him for a job applicant. However, Ralph did not need a second invitation; he went to work with a will, exulting over his good fortune. He sold books after classes, earning twelve dollars a week.

One afternoon a woman walked into the store, looked him over and spoke in an undertone to the owner. Mr. Philips came over to Ralph.

"My boy, are you colored?"

"Of course," replied Ralph puzzled. "Don't you know?"

The old man cleared his throat. "I have very poor vision. But several of my customers have confided to me that you are a Negro. I asked my wife to come in this afternoon to check up. You look white enough to me."

"I—I'm quite light complexioned."

"Well, son, it really doesn't make a damn bit of difference to me or to my wife either." He shook Ralph's hand. "Come into the back and have a cup of coffee with us!"

He wasn't the only Negro taking graduate studies at Harvard who suffered from the barbs of discrimination. There were, for example, William H. Hastie, who was to become Governor of the Virgin Islands, and Charles R. Drew, preparing for a career as a distinguished surgeon. Ralph played poker with them into the wee hours, discussing the social problems they and other oppressed men and women were suffering the world over in this "enlightened" twentieth century. All three men were exceedingly brilliant and could have made a career among white people if they had chosen; yet all of them resolved to stay with their people and provide them with leadership. When, in 1928, Ralph received his master's degree in political science, he was offered a teaching post at several white universities; but he preferred to accept a position at Howard, the all-Negro university. He set up the political science department and did such a good job of it that Howard has since graduated a number of Negroes who have become internationally known political scientists.

Ralph let fresh air into the somewhat musty and formal policies of Howard. The administration, acutely sensitive to any criticism that might appear in the white press, established abnormally rigid standards of behavior. Negroes could not be merely as *good* as other people, declared the Howard authorities; they had to be *better*; they could never afford to relax, to let their hair down.

On one occasion, a female student was caught kissing a young instructor and the authorities prepared to expel her from the university. The girl was a senior, and the episode took place on the eve of her graduation.

Ralph defended the girl at a faculty meeting. "What in the world is a little kiss!" he exploded. "I give the girl credit for having warm blood in her. This girl has worked four years for her degree. She has already bought her dress for graduation. Her parents scrimped to send her here. Do you realize what an expulsion may do to her life?" He paused. "With all due respect to you gentlemen, I warn you if this young lady is expelled, I will give the story to the newspapers myself!"

Thanks to Ralph Bunche, the girl was graduated.

At the time he defended the girl, Ralph himself was involved in an affair of the heart, and this unquestionably increased his insight into such things. He had fallen in love with the prettiest pupil in his class, Ruth Ethel Harris. She was preparing for a teaching career and she was taking special courses in political science when she and Ralph met. Since Ralph planned to return to Harvard in the fall to prepare for his doctorate, the couple decided to wait before marrying.

Separation was hard. But Ralph, skillful at poker, played industriously to win money for weekend trips to Washington. He drew a map representing northeastern America up to Newfoundland and he divided the territory into squares. Whenever he lost at poker, he would place a red pin (representing himself) at Newfoundland. When he had a fairly successful night, he would move the pin into New Hampshire; and whenever he had substantial winnings, he would stick the pin in Washington D.C.; and he would arrive the following weekend.

Finally the couple set the wedding date for June 23, 1930; and Ralph placed himself on a rigid budget, cutting his food expenses down to twenty-five cents a day. By dint of yeoman scrimping, his bank balance rose to one hundred and fifty dollars, just barely enough for his honeymoon. A week before leaving Cambridge for the wedding, he decided to try his luck to increase his bank balance. He got into a poker game with several Harvard instructors and graduate students. The game began at eight in the evening. Within two hours he lost a hundred dollars of his savings. He tore off his tie, gulped down a glass of water and paced nervously around the room. To recoup his losses, if possible, he remained in the game and by two in the morning he had only twenty dollars left. The prospects for a honeymoon seemed ended. He thought of wiring Ruth to let her know the wedding would have to be postponed; but before taking this step, he mopped his brow, downed another glass of water and continued playing. The other players were completely exhausted and one suggested that a 6 a.m. time limit be set to the game. Belatedly, for his final hand, Ralph received excellent cards. His heart leaped—was there time to retrieve his losses? Since it was the last hand, the stakes were generous. With difficulty Ralph controlled his exultation. Not a muscle in his face moved as the future diplomat raised his hand and showed a full house to win the pot. He trembled as he counted the nickels and dimes. The winnings were a few pennies over a hundred and fifty dollars! Offering silent thanks to God he left the room vowing he would never play another hand of poker. He has kept this promise. When Ruth heard the story, she chuckled, "It wouldn't have really mattered; so we *wouldn't* have had a honeymoon!"

III

AFTER receiving his doctor's degree—the first Negro to earn a Ph.D. in political science—Ralph Bunche continued his intensive research into the social problems of supressed minorities. But this energetic, outgoing professor was not bookish by temperament. He obtained his knowledge chiefly through on-the-spot study of race problems. In 1936 he took a two years' leave of absence from Howard and traveled to Africa to study the status of non-European peoples. By chance he had made friends with a student who came from the Kikuyu tribe in Kenya and this African had written his people that Dr. Bunche would call on them. Ralph arrived on safari and found the tribal elders assembled to welcome him. Through an interpreter he told them about his own African background; how his ancestors had been carried across the water, enslaved in a strange country; how they had eventually been freed and had begun to prosper. When he finished, an elderly chieftain, clothed in a loin cloth, stepped forward, declaring that he was bestowing on the American the name of *Karioki*, which means, "He who has returned from the dead." Ralph was feted as an adopted son; and the name *Karioki* accompanied him to every African village he visited.

Upon his return to America, Ralph wrote a number of articles on his sociological findings for academic magazines. The subject of racial discrimination continued to absorb him. He regarded the problem objectively, with the eye of a political scientist. He was not angry at white people. He understood the economic and psychological reasons for their attitude. Only by helping them to a greater understanding of the Negro could the tension be alleviated.

When Dr. Gunnar Myrdal, a Swedish sociologist, announced that he was undertaking a comprehensive sociological study of the American Negro, Ralph was delighted with the news; and when Myrdal, upon arriving in America, asked Ralph to join his research staff, he acquiesced. Myrdal, Bunche, and several associates piled into an automobile to tour the South and collect material at first hand. They distributed questionnaires to Negroes and whites in each locality, asking for information of jobs, housing, financial relationships between the races.

When the research for the book was completed, Ralph helped Myrdal transform the masses of notes into text. For weeks he dictated day and night to stenographers. His wife brought him changes of clothing and food to his desk. The typewritten manuscript ran to 3300 pages. When the *American Dilemma* was published it created a sensation among scholars and intelligent laymen. It remains the definitive volume in the field.

When Ralph was thirty-seven, America entered World War II. He was regarded as the nation's foremost authority on colored peoples of the world. Colonel Donovan's Office of Strategic Service recruited him to direct research. The military were preparing to invade North Africa and it was essential to collect intelligence reports on how the colonial people felt about Hitler, and whether an American army would be received with friendship. Bunche brought his vast personal knowledge of Africa to the problem. His reports contributed to the success of General Clark's intelligence mission and to the invasion by American troops. Indeed, high-ranking officers sent back such enthusiastic reports about the intelligence work Bunche and his assistants had done that in 1944 State Department officials approached him to head the territorial desk.

Bunche was certainly the most qualified man for the job, but when his photo was attached to the file and it became known that he was a Negro, certain influential people in the State Department tried their best to block his appointment. For six months they managed to hold it up until word of their intrigues reached the Secretary, Cordell Hull. When he studied Ralph's qualifications the usually mild-mannered Tennesseean grew scarlet. He called in the intriguers and hit the ceiling with them. That night he personally phoned Bunche and offered him the job. It was the first time in American history that a Negro had been asked to take over a desk in the State Department.

Bunche was idolized by the young intellectuals in the State Department. Some of the highest-ranking officials in the government would visit his home socially to discuss political and economic problems over a sandwich and a glass of beer. It was a curious sight to see limousines, bearing top license numbers, draw into the all-Negro street and unload their distinguished occupants at his doorstep.

When the war ended in Europe, Bunche helped prepare the groundwork for the Dumbarton Oaks Conference which dealt with the economic rehabilitation of the postwar world. And when this task was completed, he helped draw up the charter for the new United Nations Organization. Bunche concentrated on the question of trusteeships and he formulated policies that were destined to influence the future well-being of millions of people in Asia, the East Indies, the Near and Middle East. His recommendations were substantially adopted as the official policy of the United Nations.

Despite its initial fumbling and bickering, the UN loomed as mankind's best hope for establishing a sane world order. When in 1948 a crisis developed that threatened to strangle this organization before it had gotten out of its swaddling clothes, Ralph Bunche was as much concerned as any man alive.

The trouble arose out of the creation of the Jewish state of Israel. For half a century Zionists had looked forward to establishing Palestine as their national homeland. In 1917, Balfour, the British foreign minister, had declared that after the war Palestine would be turned over to the Jews. However, the postwar British government, beset by international difficulties and anxious to placate the Arab world, refused to carry out the Balfour Declaration. The situation reached crisis proportions immediately after World War II, when Britain, exhausted in manpower and money, surrendered its mandate over Palestine and left it up to the UN to settle the dispute.

Thousands of Jews, driven out of Europe by Hitler, had moved into Palestine and swelled the Zionist chorus for a homeland. But the Arabs who had lived in Palestine for thirteen centuries were equally insistent that Palestine should not be turned into a Jewish nation. Both sides mobilized, and war broke out in the spring of 1948. The world looked to the UN to step in and stop the hostilities. People were convinced that if it was unable to deal with a local conflict it would certainly be powerless to prevent any new world wars.

The UN appointed Count Folke Bernadotte, a nephew of the Swedish King, to be the chief negotiator, and Ralph Bunche was asked by Trygve Lie, the UN secretary, to go along as Bernadotte's chief assistant. "You know that part of the world better than anybody else around here, Ralph."

Bunche met Count Bernadotte in Paris and escorted him to the Holy Land. On the plane, he briefed Bernadotte on the background of the dispute. The descendant of royalty and the grandson of a slave took an immediate liking to one another and became fast friends. It was a remarkable and unprecedented relationship. When they arrived in Palestine, Ralph took Bernadotte on a tour of the battlefields. One afternoon as they drove alongside the sand dunes, they were fired upon by snipers. The driver of the car slumped over dead. Ralph vaulted into his seat and slammed on the emergency brake just in time. Then he held a UN flag over his head and shouted at the top of his voice, first in Hebrew then in Arabic, "Who has dared to fire upon peacemakers?" He walked down the road to the car behind the leading one. Since he was unarmed, in full view of the snipers, UN personnel shouted for him to seek cover. But he continued on his way. There were several wounded men in the car he approached. He jumped into it, and supporting one of the wounded men with his arm, drove them back to Jerusalem.

Time and again, Bunche made the trip to the front, exposing himself to snipers' bullets. "The only safe credentials we had in no-man's-land," he recalls, "were the accelerators of our cars."

It was decided to invite the Arab-Jewish delegations for negotiations to a place removed from the tension of battle. The Greek island of Rhodes was selected as the site for the parleys. When headquarters had been set up, Bernadotte prepared to fly back to Palestine to make final arrangements for bringing the delegates to Rhodes.

"You'll come along with me, Ralph?"

Bunche decided he would remain behind for a day to prepare a report to the UN on the progress achieved to date. He saw Bernadotte off at the airport and returned to his study. Bernadotte arrived in Jerusalem and inspected a government building for temporary business quarters for his visit. Then he stepped into an automobile for the trip to his lodgings. Seated behind him was Colonel André P. Serot, a swarthy-complexioned officer of the French air force. As they rode along the dunes, a jeep carrying five Israelis swung into view; a Sten gun opened fire with twenty blasts. Colonel Serot slumped dead immediately; Count Bernadotte died

on arrival at a hospital. The assassination had been carried out by the
Stern Gang, a terrorist organization repudiated by the Israeli government.
Out to get "Number One and Number Two" of the UN negotiation
staff, they had killed the dark-complexioned Frenchman seated beside
Bernadotte in the belief he was Ralph Bunche!

When Bunche received news of the killings he was overwhelmed with
grief. He had been deeply attached to Bernadotte. The first press des-
patches to America had reported that he had been killed with the Count.
It took him five hours to put through a phone call to his wife, Ruth, to
let her know he was unharmed. Only a miracle had spared him.

Trygve Lie phoned Jerusalem and upon learning that Bunche was safe
he asked him to take over Bernadotte's position as acting mediator. A
military adviser recommended to Ralph that he ride in an armored car
with guards standing on the running board. But Ralph shook his head.
"No. That is not the way to begin negotiations. Peacemakers don't bear
guns. Anyhow, I'm not important enough to be assassinated."

News of Bunche's appointment made headlines in America. For the
first time Bunche's name, known previously to a few, was flashed to millions. At first the papers were unable to dig up photos of him and it was
not until forty-eight hours after the initial news that a picture was found.
Then the word swept around America that the United States' top negotiator at Rhodes was a Negro. The response was heartwarming. Americans were astonished and proud that the grandson of a slave should have
risen so high in international councils. Especially in the South, newspapers wrote editorials of tribute, and millions of progressive Southerners
were generous in their congratulations.

But Bunche's work was cut out for him; it was too early to talk of
triumph.

He had obtained the consent of the Arab and Israeli delegations to
meet and discuss terms for an armistice, but the guns were still roaring
at the front, the dead were mounting daily, and the bitterness of both
sides toward one another filled him with anxiety over the outcome of
talks.

Bunche prepared meticulously for the meeting. He informed the
guards at his headquarters that they must salute the members of both
delegations and show them equal respect. He even examined the dossiers
of the interpreters to make certain that none were partisans and likely to
distort what was said in translation.

The Arab delegation was the first to arrive. Bunche shook hands with
each member and seated them at one side of the table. A few minutes later
the Israeli delegation was announced. As they entered the conference
room the Arabs remained seated. Dr. Walter Eytan, the Jewish leader,
walked over to the Arab leader, Seif ed-Din, with his hand outstretched.
But the "Sword of God," as the Arab was known by his countrymen,
refused to shake it. He turned his back on Eytan and stared at the

wall. The Israelis strode out of the room; Bunche followed, pleading with them to return. "I'm flying back to Palestine immediately!" Dr. Eytan exploded. "I'll take no insults from an Arab!"

Bunche re-entered the conference room. "Why were you so childish?" he chided Seif. "You have insulted not only the Israeli but the United Nations!" The "Sword of God" grew red-faced. He muttered an apology and volunteered to meet Eytan personally to express his regrets.

Bunche arranged an informal meeting between the two in his own quarters that evening. The Arab appeared bringing Bunche a present of a jeweled scimitar. Dr. Eytan showed up with a dagger inscribed with the official Israeli seal. Seif ed-Din cleared his throat. "I am sorry for having insulted you, Dr. Eytan."

"Oh," replied the Israeli, "I was to blame for not holding my hand out long enough. You probably didn't see it."

Both laughed and settled down to converse in an Arabic dialect. Bunche did not understand it and he could not tell whether the men were hurling imprecations or chatting as friends; but his interpreter whispered that everything was going nicely; they were swapping war experiences.

However, the rocky road of negotiations still lay ahead. For three months Bunche sat at the head of the conference table chain-smoking and trying to effect a meeting of minds. Only his supreme patience kept the conference from breaking up on several occasions in an atmosphere of supercharged emotionalism. "Every time you blew your nose you offended someone," Bunche recalls. Mrs. Doreen Daughton, his English secretary, reported afterwards that Bunche was magnificent in his patience. "I never saw him lose his temper once."

He opened the daily conferences at ten in the morning. At midnight he was still going over his papers preparing memoranda for the next meeting. One by one his assistants would drop off to bed exhausted. At one in the morning Bunche would put aside his notes for an hour of billiards, or to take an airing through the streets of Rhodes. Then he returned to his study with renewed vigor. He slept an average of four hours a night.

Daily he hammered away at the delegates with one theme. "You cannot afford to fail!" And again, "While we are debating, Jews and Arabs are dying in battle. You gentlemen may be exploiting this or that advantage at the front, but the widows of the dead know no victory."

And as he sat among them, a monument of perseverance, the Arabs and Israeli learned to admire, indeed to worship him. "Why not take a day off, Mr. Bunche; you are driving yourself too hard," they suggested. And he replied, "Gentlemen, I will rest when you sign an armistice and permit me to."

As the bickerings of both sides dragged on interminably, and no solution seemed in sight, the world grew cynical. Editorials in the press spoke angrily of the impotence of the UN. Was it to become another League of Nations? Even members of Bunche's own staff sniped at him in messages home. But Bunche persevered despite the knife-stabbing. He was thoroughly exhausted, but he refused to admit this to the delegates. He was determined to wear them down to the point of even greater fatigue than he suffered; to outlast them until they were compelled to throw in the sponge and sign a final agreement. His phlebitis bothered him and he had to put bandages on his leg daily. But he kept calling sessions for longer and longer hours.

And gradually his tactics paid off; the conferees moved toward an agreement. As the climax approached, he kept them in session for twenty consecutive hours—from nine one morning until five the next. He even withheld breakfast from the famished conferees until they settled the final points. The last issue, in creating an armistice line, was whether the border town of Aujua should belong to the Jews or Arabs. Bunche persuaded the negotiators to place the town in neutral territory. At last pens were put to paper; the armistice was a reality. Upon signing, Seif ed-Din, the Arab leader stood up and said, "Dr. Bunche, you are one of the world's greatest men." Dr. Walter Eytan, the Israeli, not to be outdone, chimed in, "You have earned the thanks of the world for your superhuman labors."

Bunche cleared his throat. "One moment, gentlemen. I was sure you would come to an agreement and I wish to express my personal gratitude." He went to a closet and brought out a set of exquisite pottery he had purchased for the delegates. Each piece bore the inscription, *Rhodes Armistice Negotiations*. He had bought the pottery many weeks previously, had it engraved and put away for this occasion.

"But Dr. Bunche," several Arabians and Israelis asked curiously, "what would you have done with this pottery if no agreement had been reached?"

"I'd have smashed the damn things over your heads!" he smiled.

IV

PEACE had been brought to the Holy Land, the UN had survived its first critical test, eleven months after Bunche had flown out to Palestine on Trygve Lie's orders. Now when he stepped off the plane at La Guardia Field, his wife was waiting for him. He was directed to an open touring car; an escort of motorcycle officers swung in ahead. He was entirely unprepared for what followed. When the car turned up Fifth Avenue, the sidewalks were found to be jammed with people several lines deep. A blizzard of ticker tape and confetti poured down from office windows. Whenever the limousine stopped, throngs of cheering people broke lines and virtually mobbed Bunche. New York was giving him one of the biggest hero welcomes in her history.

When Bunche finally was settled in his hotel, he turned to his wife.

"Ruth, I'd like to break the neck of the one who planned this." There were tears in his eyes.

Letters of congratulations poured in to Bunche from kings, statesmen, and ordinary men and women all over the world. Leaders of the UN urged him to embark on a lecture tour from coast to coast. "You are a symbol of the United Nations. You must explain to the people in plain language the meaning of our organization."

And Ralph accepted the task. During the tour he received thirty-nine honorary university degrees. When he reached the West Coast, Los Angeles declared a "Ralph Bunche Day" and a million Angelenos cheered him in a ticker-tape parade. The tour wound up with a dinner at the Waldorf. To an audience of a thousand diners who were honoring him— leaders in politics, science, the arts—he declared: "I have a number of very strong biases. I have a deep-seated bias against hate and intolerance . . . I have a bias against war; a bias for peace. I have a bias which leads me to believe in the essential goodness of my fellow man . . ."

On September 22, 1950 Ralph received the crowning tribute to his career; he was awarded the Nobel Prize for Peace. "I had a cocktail to celebrate the news," he confessed before flying to Stockholm to receive the prize money which amounted to about thirty thousand dollars. "I never should have done it. I am a cautious fellow usually and I never spend money before I get it."

Today, as the top director of the Trusteeship Division of the UN, Dr. Ralph Bunche remains dedicated to the welfare of dependent peoples. In campaigning for human welfare he listens neither to the siren calls of the starry-eyed radical or the bleatings of the social reactionary. He keeps to the middle of the road. He realizes that in the United States, despite the few bigots who have tried to blur its dream, one Negro managed to rise to a position of eminence from which he has been able to influence the councils of the world and to associate professionally with the nephew of a Swedish King.

Today a photograph stands on Dr. Bunche's bookcase, inscribed, "To Ralph, with deepest gratitude for your devotion and loyalty—Folke Bernadotte." This is Bunche's most cherished souvenir.

Bunche is saddened by the fact that many of his fellow countrymen do not sufficiently comprehend the value of the United Nations or appreciate the unobtrusive, day-by-day work it is doing to promote better understanding and tolerance among the peoples of the world.

"It's just poor public relations," he insists, "which focuses the attention of the public upon matters the UN has failed to work out satisfactorily and soft pedals the really splendid things it is accomplishing daily in various areas."

Despite his devotion to the UN, Ralph's first love remains teaching. He hopes that one day soon he will be able to leave public office and retire to a classroom where he can help the young prepare to shoulder the problems of the future intelligently to make the world a better place to live in. But whether he returns to Harvard or Howard, or accepts another position in public service when his tour in the international forum is at an end—indeed he was invited by President Truman to become Assistant Secretary of State, but was unable to accept the position for personal reasons—it is a safe bet Ralph Bunche will continue to fight for decency and justice and peace with the warm-hearted smile and the hearty handshake that is his internationally recognized trademark and that has made him friends around the globe.

IMPORTANT DATES IN THE LIFE OF RALPH JOHNSON BUNCHE

1904—August 7, born in Detroit.

1922—Graduated Jefferson High School in Los Angeles.

1927—Graduated *summa cum laude* from U.C.L.A.

1930—Married Ruth Ethel Harris.

1931–32—Studied with a Rosenwald fellowship in Africa, Europe, and England.

1934—Received Ph.D. in political science.

1936–38—Studied with a post-doctoral fellowship from the Social Science Research Council.

1941—Joined Office of Strategic Services.

1944—Appointed to State Department as an advisor on African and colonial matters.

1946—Headed trusteeship section of United Nations secretariat.

1947—Appointed Bernadotte's assistant to mediate Palestine dispute.

1948—Became acting negotiator in Palestine dispute.

1950—Received Nobel Prize for Peace.